THE MUSIC OF MULTICULTURAL AMERICA

★ THE MUSIC OF MULTICULTURAL AMERICA ★

PERFORMANCE, IDENTITY, AND COMMUNITY IN THE UNITED STATES

Edited by
Kip Lornell and Anne K. Rasmussen

University Press of Mississippi • Jackson

www.upress.state.ms.us

The University Press of Mississippi is a member of the Association of American University Presses.

Manufactured in the United States of America

First printing 2016
∞
Library of Congress Cataloging-in-Publication Data

The music of multicultural America : performance, identity, and community in the United States / edited by Kip Lornell and Anne K. Rasmussen.
pages cm. — (American made music series)
Includes index.
ISBN 978-1-62846-220-3 (hardback) — ISBN 978-1-4968-0374-0 (paper) — ISBN 978-1-62674-609-1 (ebook) 1. Popular music—United States—History and criticism. 2. Music—Social aspects—United States. I. Lornell, Kip, 1953– editor. II. Rasmussen, Anne K., editor.
ML3477.M85 2016
780.973—dc23
2015020139

British Library Cataloging-in-Publication Data available

CONTENTS

THE MUSIC OF MULTICULTURAL AMERICA

1.1. "In Perfect Harmony": left to right, top: Joanna Meinl, Rachna Nivas, Anjali Nath. Bottom: Leah Brown, Farah Yasmeen Shaikh. From the *Hindustan Times*, January 24, 2004. Courtesy Chitresh Das.

Website and Acknowledgments

For media examples associated with this publication, visit www.atmuse.org and choose "Musics of Multicultural America" from the list of publications on the left side of the page.

The editors would like to acknowledge and thank Dr. Alan Burdette, director of the Archives of Traditional Music at Indiana University, who imagined and then developed a website to host the audio and visual contents that are linked to each chapter. The development of this website and the publication of photographs in the volume were subsidized by a publication subvention from the Dean's Office of Arts and Sciences at the College of William & Mary and we are grateful for their support. Our team of veteran authors is to be commended for updating their chapters so conscientiously and for responding to our many emails as well as for tolerating our long silences. We also welcome the authors of four new case studies in our collection and thank our new authors for their excellent contributions. Craig Gill, assistant director/editor-in-chief at the University Press of Mississippi, deserves our deepest gratitude for his enthusiastic support and for ushering our volume into a new, revised and expanded edition. Finally, we are indebted to the many students and colleagues, too numerous to mention here, who have contributed productively and enthusiastically to this collection and this field of study since the publication of the first edition of our book in 1997.

- 1 -

INTRODUCTION

Kip Lornell and Anne K. Rasmussen

The Music of Multicultural America is a collection of fifteen essays on music in the United States that, together, present a sample of music making in a variety of American communities. One of our goals is to introduce the diversity of musical styles, genres, and repertoires that constitute the contemporary American soundscape; another is to highlight the role of music making in community life. Using the methods of historical research, oral history, and ethnographic fieldwork with musicians and their audiences, all of the contributors to this volume investigate how people make and experience music on a local level. *E Pluribus Unum*, the Latin phrase meaning "Out of Many, One," is the motto that has both described a nation of immigrants and provided the country with a guiding methodology for governance. Although this maxim has served as the idealized expression of the nation's identity for more than two hundred years, the assertion that America is a diverse, multicultural nation of immigrants has always been a tenuous claim. Our policies regarding immigration, our continuous renegotiation of political, physical, and ideological borders—indeed our very notion of "American-ness"—are all issues that are subject to public debate and constant reinterpretation. The dialectic between "many" and "one" fundamentally informed the groundbreaking volume *Musics of Multicultural America*, which we edited and Schirmer published in 1997. Our new, updated, and expanded volume, with its more descriptive title *The Music of Multicultural America: Performance, Identity, and Community in the United States*, continues the conversation. The tension between the competing notions of American music either as a streamlined product of the American melting pot or as a diverse collective that is inclusive, eclectic, and dynamic continues to be at the heart of our work.

In many ways our collection, because it focuses on music making in America, critiques the hegemony of Western European art music in college and university curricula, by, as Deborah Wong put it in the first edition of our book, "Just Being There."[1] An alternative to the standard canons of music history, *The Music of Multicultural America* also moves beyond established histories of American popular music characterized by chronological studies of musical styles, offered in courses such as "Jazz History" or "The Development of Rock 'n' Roll." Our case studies invite readers to think about American music in ways that are inclusive, nuanced, and complex. Created by communities with a common history, social bond, or agenda, musical activity that falls outside of the generally recognized categories of mainstream American music is woven into the fabric of our culture and plays on, largely unnoticed by the general public. Throughout the United States, regional, grassroots, community-based musical cultures not only exist, they thrive!

WHO MAKES AMERICAN MUSIC?

The impact of the continuous influx of "new" Americans from all over the world remains just as important today as it was around 1900, a time when the phenomenon of immigration to America, at that time mostly from Europe, is widely recognized as the single most important aspect of the nation's formation. Whereas immigration was conceptualized as a one-way process in the past, many American immigrant communities today are thought to be part of larger diasporas with relatives, friends, and ancestors located in real and imaginary homelands and various locales throughout the world. The gradual settlement of American territory by a crazy quilt of immigrants, mostly from Europe but also from Asia, Africa, the Middle East, and Central and Latin America, was facilitated at first by the management, removal, and annihilation of a multicultural collective of First Nation peoples: American Indians, who thrived in North America prior to the arrival of Europeans. Based on Christian doctrines of manifest destiny and scientific principles of Darwinian determinism, the European exploration and settlement that gave rise to the nation's multicultural motto, *E Pluribus Unum*, was based on practices of both inclusion and exclusion. It is precisely this mix—who and what is "in" and "out"—that informs our constructions of individual, community, and national identity, and, as we show in this volume, music is central to this process.

Parallel to the ongoing process of European immigration and the near obliteration of Native American peoples and cultures, practices and ideas surrounding race loom large among the formative processes in this country's constitution. As Joseph King, who studies the work of African American authors, writes: "Racial hierarchy and American national identity grew up together" in a land where "whiteness was overtly assumed to be a defining characteristic of 'American'" (King 2001, 145). The end of the Civil War in 1865 marked the beginning of the nation's commitment to an egalitarian society and the birth of an ever-developing, although sometimes uneasy, recognition of the innumerable contributions that new-world Africans and their descendants have made to American culture. In this postwar period and throughout the twentieth and into the twenty-first centuries, African American expressive culture became one of the most distinguishing features of American life and especially of American music. Qualities of "African American-ness" helped differentiate America from its European ancestors in innumerable ways.

America's vernacular music has, in fact, been shaped by African American culture since enslaved Africans first arrived. Musical techniques and elements like call and response, improvisation, and bluesy intonation, which sound so familiar to us in the twenty-first century, were originally African American musical practices. Moreover, since the first decades of the twentieth century and the advent of recording and radio, formative African American musics like blues and jazz have influenced almost all types of American popular music. It is impossible to imagine what American music would sound like today had it not been affected so profoundly by the presence and contributions of African Americans.

An Anglo American/Afro American dichotomy has, thus far, shaped most histories of American music. In our volume, however, this model is diversified with a more finely nuanced and inclusive map of American musical terrain. In fact, a desire to move beyond the simple black-and-white picture of American music provides the strongest impetus for this book. Furthermore, we want our collection to transcend the folk/art, Anglo/Afro, secular/sacred dyads that informed the initial establishment of an American music canon, if a canon does indeed exist. We strive to look beyond labels created by the music industry, from race records to iTunes, categories such as jazz, rock, popular, gospel, folk, hip-hop, and blues, along with other twentieth-century genres, that have defined but also limited the taxonomy of America's music.

As co-editors, our interests in America's musical diversity grew naturally from our initial encounters with American music histories, our academic training, our personal engagement with mass media, and by way of our own ethnographic fieldwork and scholarship. Anne Rasmussen's work among Arab Americans led her to wonder about music making in any number of "unsung" communities, even that of her own Scandinavian grandparents in the Midwest (see Rasmussen 2004). Kip Lornell's work documenting an array of American vernacular musics convinced him that broad categories of American music were neither numerous nor subtle enough to describe the musical landscape he found within the United States (Lornell 1989 and 2002). Our long-standing interests in regional and community music, fueled by emergent trends in scholarship, inspired this project when it began in the mid-1990s and continue to motivate us today.

DIVERSITY AND AMERICAN MUSIC

Readers of this volume will surely have their own ideas about American music. It is well known that music in the United States is indebted to the European and African cultures that were originally imported and implanted in American soil from the early 1500s through the mid-1800s. African and European musical roots have become entangled at various points in history to produce such extraordinarily popular and influential twentieth-century hybrids as jazz, rock 'n' roll, and hip-hop, styles of music and musical subcultures that have not only become monumental features of our own landscape but that are also played and enjoyed worldwide. As artists, audiences, consumers, and students of American music, we recognize distinctions between classical music, folk or vernacular music, popular music, religious music, music for the stage, and so forth. We also realize that regional differences exist among the musics created in the United States: that music created by Acadians in southwestern Louisiana (or the San Francisco Bay area) is very different from the music created by Finnish Americans living in the Minnesota Iron Range near the Canadian border. Moreover, we are aware of the general differentiations that are made between "high" and "low" culture, between fine and popular arts, distinctions that are liberally applied to music, literature, dance, and other cultural manifestations in the United States (see Levine 1988).

Music Patronage

What makes all of these American musical scenes and subcultures tick? Universities, conservatories, concert halls, theaters, and large arts organizations like symphony orchestras and opera companies are among the elite institutions that teach students, employ faculty, and contract professionals in the "fine arts." In most countries, including the United States, institutions for the performing arts—for example, the Kennedy Center in Washington, the Metropolitan Opera in New York, the Hollywood Bowl in Los Angeles, Symphony Hall in Boston, along with places like museums and libraries—are not only venues for artistic production, they are also iconic national landmarks.

Arts institutions that support and stimulate musical production for public consumption involve large casts of players and producers, who themselves are products of extensive training. As such, "high" culture events such as opera, musical theater, or orchestral music are very expensive to produce. While large ensembles rely on ticket sales for revenue, they almost always need more financial support than they can generate from paying customers. Corporate support, along with subventions by cities or states, for such "high" culture is crucial for the mere existence of these ensembles and venues. Thus many arts institutions in the United States are funded privately, but often with major grants from state and local organizations, private philanthropy, and support from the federal agencies like the National Endowment for the Arts.

Ironically, although these institutions of "fine arts" symbolize American national culture, they have traditionally been dedicated largely to European artists and their works. When you attend a concert of symphonic music, an opera, or a ballet, or when you yourself study or participate in these kinds of productions, composers like Beethoven, Bizet, or Tchaikovsky, who are German, French, and Russian, respectively, are likely to be on the program. This stratum of musical activity, one that leans heavily toward the music of Europe, is most directly and openly endorsed by American institutions of higher education, by corporations, and by arts agencies. Without institutional support or patronage, few, if any, of these orchestras or opera companies would exist. While the great masterworks of Western art music play on in our music appreciation classes and our concert halls, music educators might ask, where is the rest of the music of the world? Where is music from the twentieth or twenty-first century? Where, in particular, is American music?

Occupying another side of the cultural spectrum from "high-brow," Western art music are folk, vernacular, traditional, and popular musics. Such grassroots, community-based, "low-brow" musics are likely to be experienced in private contexts, for example in family rituals like weddings and religious holidays. Community musics sometimes spill out into more public venues such as restaurants, bars, parks, places of worship, or neighborhood festivals, contexts that invite a range of participants. One of the ways that community musics have become more public and accessible is through civic neighborhood fairs and festivals, which, in the United States have become among the most common contexts to welcome diverse music making.

Depending on where you live, your local musical landscape might include Mexican mariachi, Scandinavian polka, Buddhist music from the Thai temple, church-based African American gospel music, Middle Eastern dance or concert music, an American Indian "drum," or old-time music from the Appalachian Mountains. Sometimes such music may be classified as folk or vernacular music by the people who play and appreciate it; but many kinds of ethnic and community-based music in the United States may be more accurately described as traditional, classical, sacred, or art music. Lumping America's musical diversity into one convenient category tempts misrepresentation of both the music and the people who make it. Furthermore, even though some of these kinds of music and dance have been in the United States for a century or more, they are still often thought of as "world music" or "ethnic music," something that is other than or outside of the mainstream. Although this attitude has changed considerably over the last few decades, the marginal status of many kinds of American music and of the people who play them is reflected in our cultural institutions, from the concert hall to the university to our public schools. This volume of essays suggests some different ways to think about American music and underscores the importance and pervasiveness of informal music making on local and regional levels.

Mass Media

Mass media are probably the most powerful force in music promotion and patronage in contemporary America. Radio since the 1920s, and major record companies beginning at the turn of the century, are two of the media that have promoted popular music in the United States. Beginning in the 1950s, evening and late-night television programs like *The Tonight Show* and *The Lawrence Welk Show* helped boost the careers of countless musicians. During the mid-1960s programs such as *Shindig, Hullabaloo*, and *American Bandstand* brought contemporary popular music to a "teen audience," followed by *Soul Train*, which began its thirty-five-year run in 1971. Beginning in the early 1980s, MTV and later VH1 became the dominant new media to broadcast popular music to cable-connected consumers twenty-four hours a day with the new format of the music video—a miniature film the length of a pop song, which usually combines live footage of a singer or a band with a dramatization of some sort of storyline set in a particular context.

Since the publication of the first edition of this book, YouTube.com has emerged as a primary vehicle for the dissemination of music. This innovative 2005 site (purchased by Google in 2006) democratized access so that virtually any video clip, whether a commercial and professionally produced music video, an excerpt from a film, a snippet of a bootlegged live concert performance, or an experiment in someone's living room, may be uploaded in a matter of minutes and made accessible to anyone in the world with an internet connection. The number of "hits" or viewings on most music available via Youtube.com is small (usually in the hundreds or low thousands) but some YouTube clips "go viral": it took less than six months from its initial posting on July 15, 2012, for Korean PSY's K-pop, hip-hop influenced "Gangnam Style" to eclipse the billion-hits mark.

It is difficult to overstate the impact of twenty-first-century digitally based media on the flow of music, because such technology enables not only the broadcasting of music but also communicating about music among musicians and their publics. YouTube.com helped revolutionize the ability to post all sorts of video material, from archival historic recordings to entire "channels" devoted to artists that range from Native American rock bands (like Redbone, for example) to the pop diva Beyoncé.[2] Social media such as Myspace, Facebook, Twitter, and the app Bandsintown also facilitate instant communication about musical projects and events between musician and audiences. Music you may never hear on mainstream terrestrial radio (or even the satellite behemoth SiriusXM) may have a vibrant media presence online through technology that is virtually free and accessible to an international culture of creators and consumers. The co-evolution of music and technology not only facilitates communication of music and about music, it facilitates new possibilities for the creative process itself, something Aram Sinnreich, in his book *Mashed Up* (2010), has called "configurable culture."

If, for example, you want to check out the Go-Go music scene in Washington, D.C., you will probably check in at www.tmottgogo.com (Take Me Out to the Go-Go) or try YouTube.com to see who has just uploaded a new old-school or bounce-beat selection. Should zydeco and Cajun music interest you, your Internet bookmarks might include cajunmusicnetwork.blogspot.com. For photographs, videos, and a very detailed calendar of powwows across the United States, you will almost certainly monitor www.powwows.com on a regular basis. Likewise http://fasola.org is for folks who enjoy singing sacred harp music. Arab Detroit (www.arabamerica.com) is a comprehensive website that keeps track of concerts, parties, exhibits, and events for people involved in that community; and anyone wanting to find an Irish-music session will surely check the internet for times and places where people meet to play (try http://www.cceboston.org). Social media and the ability to publicize the inner workings of a musical subculture are not only useful for the members of a particular subculture, they are also available to the curious student or adventurous musician ready to expand his or her soundscape. For example, in April 2011 students in Kip Lornell's class "Introduction to Ethnomusicology: Music as Culture," at George Washington University, investigated the uses of music during the "Arab Spring" for their group fieldwork project, by utilizing personal interviews, articles, blogs, videos, and music posted on social media. Surely the ongoing impact of technology and social media will only increase, both for enthusiasts and for those pursuing more in-depth research and scholarship.

UNIFYING THEMES AND ISSUES IN THIS COLLECTION

The literature on community music making, or what Mark Slobin calls "micromusics" (Slobin 1993), both within academia and in the popular press and mass media, has accelerated exponentially in the last thirty years, bringing heretofore-invisible musical scenes into the public eye and ear. The fifteen ethnographic case studies in this collection bring attention to just a sample of the myriad musical communities in the United States and suggest a number of units that fit well into a semester course syllabus. The essays presented here are based on the combined methods of historical research and ethnographic fieldwork and present just the right balance of depth and diversity. Our authors write from varied perspectives, yet a number of themes exist that unify our collection of vignettes of American musical life. Most of the themes, questions, and issues examined in these case studies are relevant for other studies of music and community. Any of these themes might be used as points of departure for a special unit or focus within a course or for students' independent research and fieldwork projects.

Thirteen Unifying Themes

1. The inherent, complex intersections among music, community, and identity
2. The role of core cultural institutions, including families, places of worship, and community celebrations that support musical activity
3. The actions of individual musicians (both professional and amateur) who lead and participate in music-making activities
4. The trends related to musical preservation, innovation, renewal, or atrophy that occur at different times or simultaneously within a musical subculture
5. The ways in which music is transmitted among generations, sometimes skipping a generation or more
6. The means by which musical performances articulate, challenge, and teach gender or age roles and other social constructs

7. The evaluation of a group's access to and use of mass and electronic media in the construction of community within and across geographical and political boundaries
8. The phenomenon of music as a commodity in the commercial marketplace, on local, regional, national, or even international levels
9. The role of regional and national sources of music patronage, for example, colleges and universities, museums and concert halls, festivals and fairs, and tourism management
10. The importance of the fieldwork experience in shaping our view of the music, the way we represent musicians and communities through our writing and other productions, and in opening doors to collaborative research and production
11. The porous, often flexible boundaries and eclectic constitution of American micro-musics that feature and depend on the participation of both "insiders" and "outsiders"
12. The impact of political, economic, and cultural events as well as of natural disasters on a community's music making
13. The multi-sited aspect of many of America's musical subcultures and the flow of music and musicians within diasporic communities that span the globe

CHAPTER OVERVIEW

Several of the case studies included in this book explore the ways in which musical traditions are initially brought to the United States from outside our geopolitical boundaries and then adapted to fit a new environment. In his chapter on polka music in Wisconsin, Jim Leary traces the history and development of the music of Czech Americans who immigrated, along with millions of other Europeans, to the United States during the waves of immigration that occurred from the middle of the 1800s to around 1920. Polka, in addition to surviving the test of time among Czech Americans, became the official state dance of Wisconsin in 1993. Similarly, Ann Spinney's contribution explores the range of musical performances that occur among Irish American musicians living in metropolitan Boston. In particular, Spinney focuses on the contexts for informal music making, from "kitchen rackets" to "sessions" that propelled Irish American music and dancing into the twenty-first century. Spinney's chapter highlights the perpetual transatlantic flow of musicians and dancers between the so-called "old country" and the "new world" in networks of diaspora that are now an intrinsic part of Irish music and dance in the present day.

Henry Sapoznik, in his contribution on klezmer music, describes a musical genre brought to America by Ashkenazi Jews of Eastern Europe, many of whom migrated to the United States beginning in the late nineteenth century. Although klezmer music was a well-established cultural phenomenon among Jews in Eastern Europe, by the 1920s it took on a life and sound of its own in the United States. As the Jewish community in America embraced mainstream values and practices of the 1950s and 1960s, klezmer music went into "hibernation." Since the mid-1970s, however, klezmer has experienced a revolution of renewal and has come to represent and express Jewish identity, not only in the United States but in Europe as well.

Mark DeWitt introduces us to Cajun music and culture, though not in its conventional hearth region of southwestern Louisiana and southeast Texas. Instead, Dewitt explores Cajun and zydeco music making in the Bay Area of California, from San Francisco to Oakland, where an expansive community resides with strong ties to Cajun culture that date to World War II. DeWitt's study raises important questions about the roles that migration, regionalism, and family play in the (re)formation and continuity of musical communities in a new geographic location. DeWitt also addresses the complex relationship between so-called "outsiders" and folk "revivalists" and those with strong, direct ties to Cajun or creolized culture, so-called "insiders." In many ways his study raises some of the same issues—for example, the emblematic nature of music—that Daniel Sheehy addresses in his essay about mariachi music.

Sheehy's essay reveals just one aspect of a cultural exchange across the fluid geographical and conceptual Mexican American border that has been ongoing since the eighteenth century. By tracing the history of mariachi music in Mexico, Sheehy reveals a cultural phenomenon that was constructed by and through mass media—particularly film and radio—and used to represent a new, urbanized Mexican identity. When adopted by Mexican-American musicians in the United States, mariachi became a flexible category of performance that works in almost every context from ritual to festival and across the spectrum of social and economic classes. Perhaps like polka music in Wisconsin or Cajun music in Louisiana, mariachi has become emblematic of the southern and western regions of the United States, even for mainstream America.

Anne Rasmussen describes a vibrant Arab American musical scene in and around Detroit and Dearborn, Michigan, that took root in America's industrial heartland in the mid-twentieth century and was later enriched by a post-1965 wave of immigration. Since the 1960s Dearborn's Arab American musical community has received a continuous influx of immigrants due to social and political events in the Middle East that have caused the urgent migration of tens of thousands. With the current Lebanese, Iraqi, Yemeni, Palestinian, Syrian, Egyptian, Saudi, and North African musical mix, Arab music in Detroit and Dearborn reflects an American musical microcosm of the contemporary Arab world. A transnational exchange of musicians and music media, from cassette tapes to cable television to social media, keeps musical trends circulating throughout the Arab diaspora; and the insistence of Arab families to keep their expressive culture alive in spite of social and political strife in that diaspora facilitates a bustling Middle Eastern musical subculture in midwestern America.

In his chapter on Americans from the West Indies, Gage Averill identifies the circulation of Trinidadian cultural expressions throughout the diaspora as essential to the creation of a pan-Caribbean ethnicity in the United States. The New York Carnival remains a well-established late summer event for Americans of

Caribbean heritage, who use the preparation in the panyards and steelband music on parade as a way to celebrate and create community. Averill helps us understand how the summer New York carnival is a creative adaptation of the spring carnival events that happen in Trinidad and all over the Caribbean by considering the annual flow of practitioners and the rhythms of the community. In addition to responding to the practical and economic factors of Caribbean New York, this event helps promote the values of ethnic pride, education, and responsibility among the youth of the community.

Two chapters discuss long-standing, ever-evolving musical traditions among Native American and Mexicano people in the Southwest. In her chapter on *matachines*, Brenda M. Romero discusses a ritual music and dance drama that is maintained through performance by both native Pueblo communities and Mejicano populations of Hispanic heritage. The matachines music and dance complex that developed from the confluence of Hispanic and Native American culture in southern Colorado and northern New Mexico also reveals roots from medieval Moorish Spain, a detail that adds to the history and, as Romero writes, the lineage and contemporary authenticity of this cultural performance.

Describing another aspect of Native American performance, Jim Griffith portrays the evolution and current practices of *waila* musicians who reside in southern Arizona. Like matachines, a product of Native American and Mejicano hybridity, waila draws from the ceremonial and entertainment music of numerous local groups including the Tohono and O'odham peoples (also known as Pima Indians), the Yaqui, Mexican Americans, and country and western musicians and audiences. These chapters by Griffith and Romero, as well as the chapter on mariachi music by Sheehy, provide a sampling of the border culture of the American South—an area of the country rich in an array of performing arts that are often totally unknown or at least largely underappreciated outside of the Southwest.

As illustrated in the chapters by Griffith and Romero, the efforts to subjugate and often eradicate Native American culture following the "discovery" of America by European explorers were not entirely successful. In their chapter describing the music and dance practices of contemporary northern powwows, Chris Scales and Gabe Desrosiers demonstrate how these events have become ubiquitous and powerful forms of modern Native American popular culture. Emerging in Oklahoma in the early years of the twentieth century as a creative response to US federal government policies that attempted to suppress indigenous cultural and religious practices, early powwows were a unique cultural fusion of the music and dancing featured at Wild West shows and the ceremonies to honor Oklahoma Indian warrior societies. By the end of the century, the singing and dancing styles from these two contexts spread across North America, transforming and being transformed by local tribal practices, and emerged as vibrant and vital wellsprings of intertribal Native American creativity. Scales and his co-author and fieldwork consultant Desrosiers introduce the singing groups and dancers that travel the country to perform at powwow celebrations hosted by Native American communities across the Northern plains and beyond.

During the nineteenth century and prior to the immigration of massive numbers of European immigrants that has occurred since the Civil War, African American and Anglo-American musical practices set the foundation for American music. Two distinctive forms of Christian sacred music—shape note singing, a tradition located primarily (but not entirely) among Anglo-Americans in the middle South; and gospel quartet singing, which originated in African American communities of the mid-Atlantic and Southern plantation states—are the subjects of two chapters of our book. Both traditions are rooted in four-part harmony singing, but yield startlingly different results.

Ron Pen explores the Anglo-American tradition of singing from shape-note hymnbooks in central Kentucky. Through a historical narrative that begins before American independence and brings us up to the present day, Pen explores not only the history of this strong American musical tradition, but the evolution of the unique social context and performance practice of the communities he calls "the fasola folk." Pen's chapter examines not only the longevity of the tradition maintained through the continuous oral transmission of one relatively homogenous Christian Anglo American community, but also the emergence of a more recently self-identified community of shape-note singers of ecumenical heritage, ethnicity, and religion. Affinity practitioners, both performers and audiences, who participate in a particular music scene due to their affinity (or attraction and commitment) rather than because of ethnic or family ties is a theme of other case studies in this volume, particularly the chapter by Sarah Morelli.

The community of black American gospel quartet singers that thrived in Memphis, Tennessee, from the 1920s through the 1970s is the focus of Kip Lornell's essay. Through his description of the social organization, the training, and the performance practices of quartets in Memphis, Lornell reveals a musical tradition that developed its own musical community. This community interacted not only with other types of gospel groups but also with singers performing in the realm of popular music. African American gospel quartet singing has been progressively overshadowed by the dynamic sounds of gospel choral music, and as a distinctive genre of a cappella, four-part harmony singing is all but extinct in the twenty-first century.

Immigration histories of Asian Americans reveal aspects of musical and cultural hybridity that capture American musical diversity in the contemporary moment. Susan Asai looks at the music making of Americans of Japanese heritage across three generations, but focuses on third-generation Japanese Americans, called *nisei*, and the ways in which they learn about, choose, perform, and experience music rooted in their culture heritage. Because of the eradication of much Japanese American cultural practice in the internment camps on the West Coast during World War II, young musicians of Japanese heritage do not always have the simple option of drawing from the traditions of their parents. Rather, as innovative individuals, every Japanese American musician must search for and define his or her own Japanese musical memory and expression. Asai introduces cutting-edge artists and their work in the jazz and avant-garde pop scenes of urban America.

Sarah Morelli introduces us to a music and dance scene in the San Francisco Bay Area located in the studio of North Indian kathak dance master Pandit Chitresh Das and his Chitresh Das Dance Company. Das began teaching this classical form of Indian dance, one that requires years of dedicated study, to members of the Indian immigrant community and interested American women in the 1970s. This was a time when India was beginning to make its mark on American popular culture, particularly in California, where there was both a large Indian immigrant community and a dynamic counterculture of young people, intellectuals, and artists interested in diverse forms of expression. Since the 1970s, Das has been teaching American women, some of whom have gone on to perform in national and international arenas, and to gradually fashion a unique fusion of North Indian and American modern dance. Morelli, herself a dancer and an ethnomusicologist, highlights the ways in which kathak dance empowers women but also interprets the ways in which issues of gender and authenticity intersect with expectations about race through this "ethnic" dance scene.

Finally, Riot Grrrls, a musical culture of and for women, is presented by Theo Cateforis and Elena Humphreys. Much like contemporary punk and straightedge, two other rock phenomena that emerged and flourished in the 1980s and 1990s, Riot Grrrl is also a movement that promotes independence, self-reliance, and takes a decidedly anti-corporate, staunchly feminist stance. While their essay narrates the origin and development of the New York scene, Riot Grrrl became a national musical and cultural movement with hubs across the country whose connections were facilitated by mass and social media that today are all but obsolete. The music spread by way of phonograph records or cassettes (usually self-produced), and the community connected through ephemeral magazines, called "fanzines," created by and for the community. Although Riot Grrrl reveled in live musical performances, this movement also explored the possibilities of the Internet, most notably early listservs like The Well, that seem primitive today but were on the technological edge in the late 1980s.

ABOUT THE CONTRIBUTORS

The contributors to *The Music of Multicultural America* are scattered across the United States and work in colleges, universities, and within in the public sector—places like libraries, archives, and arts institutions. Trained in the academic fields of ethnomusicology, folklore, American studies, anthropology, history, ethnic studies, and international studies and languages, we share a common interest in and commitment to music in the United States as it is most broadly defined. We have all been engaged in fieldwork among the communities we introduce. Some are players, singers, or dancers in the communities we describe. Although many do not share the same social and cultural background as the people we study and write about, a few of us qualify as insiders in these communities: Asai is a third-generation Japanese American; Romero grew up as a Mexicana in the Southwest; Sapoznik accidentally tripped over his own Jewish musical roots while playing American old-time music; and Spinney returned to her Irish American heritage though engaging in music and dance as an adult. Whether insiders or outsiders to the traditions we describe, all of us bring a valuable perspective to the cultures we have chosen to explore.

Whatever our status as researchers, we are all aware of the potential power of our positions as patrons and advocates for our consultants and their cultural practices. We inevitably became involved in the maintenance and development of a community's cultural performances through playing, singing, dancing, and teaching. We have also stimulated and extended exposure to these traditions through the production of such documentary endeavors as conference papers, books, articles, recordings, and films, and through the presentation of live performance. Through our involvement as educators in festivals and concerts, our sponsorship of educational and public projects, and the documentation of musicians and their communities, we have assumed active roles as publicists and advocates. Many of the authors for this volume have worked in festival contexts, conducting research, acting as interpreters, building stages, writing grant proposals, advising, producing, and performing, sometimes alongside the people about whom we write. And many of us perform and teach the music and dance traditions we document. Advocacy, through the public presentation of community arts, has naturally become an extension of our fieldwork and publication.

Since the 1970s, multicultural festivals have become the primary context for showcasing diversity through the arts. Virtually every city in America presents celebrations of culture that are orchestrated and executed by local organizations. Such efforts to galvanize community energy and present it publicly lead to the institutionalization of arts agencies committed to the celebration of diversity and to education by, about, and for local communities. For example, since the 1960s the organization Urban Gateways has conducted educational and cultural programs that highlight the contributions of various Hispanic, African American, Eastern European, and other communities in the Chicago metropolitan area. In addition to the dizzying array of neighborhood and holiday festivals in New York, arts agencies like City Lore, the World Music Institute, and the Center for Traditional Music and Dance devote their energies full-time to the documentation and promotion of the culturally diverse communities of New York's five boroughs. On the national level, the Smithsonian Folklife Festival, held annually on the Mall in Washington, D.C., is sponsored by the Smithsonian Institution's Center for Folklife and Cultural Heritage. This multicultural festival, which invites participation both from within the United States and from abroad, is mounted for ten days at the end of June and early July, and is supported by a triad of the Smithsonian Institution, corporate sponsorship, and money contributed by the states and countries that are featured each summer.

Sometimes festivals that showcase folk or ethnic music and musicians can be completely self-supporting, combining the efforts of grassroots organizers and planners with community and corporate sponsorship on a local level. For example, Milwaukee, with its large German American population, hosts an Oktoberfest complete with polka, bratwurst, and craft beer. This annual event draws tens of thousands of people to the city. Similarly, the German American community in New Ulm, Minnesota (hometown of the Bohemian American polka legend Whoopee John Wilfahrt), hosts an annual fair in October with local and regional polka bands that perform daily. Annual Arab festivals, in Detroit and Dearborn, are planned and presented every summer through a complex process of negotiation among the community leaders and artists in Michigan's multifaceted Arab American community. And in Brooklyn, New York, during the late summer, people from throughout the Caribbean participate in a uniquely American version of Carnival (usually associated with the beginning of Lent in early spring) when many blocks are taken up with food and soca, steelband, reggae, calypso, and dance.

We invite you, our readers, to think about your own experiences with community music, perhaps through your families, among friends, and in your neighborhoods and cities. We encourage you to extend your classwork or research and to actively participate in a local music scene by attending a festival, joining an ensemble, signing up for a workshop, or volunteering or even interning at an institution that promotes diverse arts and local artists. Most of the authors in this volume have helped their own students identify and apply for internships in cultural and arts agencies like the Smithsonian Institution. This kind of work, also known as "public sector" or "applied" ethnomusicology (or folklore or anthropology), is one of the most exciting, satisfying, and increasingly popular ways to build bridges between musicians, communities, and the broader public.

EARLY STUDIES OF AMERICAN MUSIC AND CONTEMPORARY DISCOURSE

The Music of Multicultural America speaks to an audience that is interested in both the sound of American music and in American music as a social and cultural phenomenon. We write with reference to a family of allied academic fields that includes American studies, ethnomusicology, folklore, and cultural studies. We build on a literature from American music, cultural geography, the study of world music, and scholarship on ethnicity and identity; a selection of important works from these fields is cited and suggested for further reading at the end of this introduction.

Until the 1950s, research by academic scholars about American music focused primarily on European-derived musical forms that were attributed to formally trained (usually male) composers and represented in staff notation. This is particularly true for historical musicologists who followed a Germanic model of scholarship that evolved in the late nineteenth century. These scholars often overlooked or deliberately ignored American vernacular and popular music, and most of them limited their research to the analysis of written or recorded musical works and the writing of biography. Although the paradigms of musicology have been under scrutiny for several decades by the scholars themselves, many musicologists continue to define the study and teaching of music history in terms of "Great (European) Men" and their "Great (European) Works."

There were, of course, a handful of pioneering scholars, almost none of them academically trained in historical musicology, who worked outside the established scholarly boundaries of European oriented musicology. Beginning in the middle 1920s, Sigmund Spaeth wrote elegantly about popular music (1927); Frederic Ramsey and Charles Edward Smith coauthored the first book devoted to jazz (1939); George Pullen Jackson published studies of white gospel music in the southeastern states (1933); John and Alan Lomax wrote a study of the life and lyrics of the Louisiana-born songster Lead Belly (1936), and Alan Lomax's collection of thousands of recordings from hundreds of practitioners has become an available archive and monument to American musical diversity. (See also the Lomax Collection online at www.research.culturalequity.org.) Ruth Crawford Seeger and her husband, Charles Seeger, were among the handful of activists who, during the 1930s, studied and taught courses at colleges and universities that included American vernacular music. They were especially interested in American folk music, and worked with traditions such as old-time fiddle tunes, children's play songs, and Appalachian folk music (Crawford Seeger 1953).

The first edition of Gilbert Chase's ambitious survey, *America's Music*, helped challenge Eurocentric hegemony in the mid-1950s (Chase 1992). Chase, who initially was trained in historical musicology and also worked as a music critic and teacher, broadened the scope of scholarly discourse by including information about jazz and Tin Pan Alley composers. Subsequent editions of Chase's book embraced even more styles of vernacular music as the author added facts and insights about black American and popular music. The trend toward inclusion has gradually escalated, and today we not only have much more balanced surveys of American music history that take race, gender, and ethnicity into account, but also specialized textbooks that are devoted to such vernacular forms of American music as jazz, rock, and folk.

Since the 1970s the number of scholarly books about American vernacular music (written by both academic and non-academic authors) has increased dramatically. Most of these books discuss a single topic, for example Bill Malone's panoramic *Country Music U.S.A.* (Malone and Neal 2010) or the even more geographically focused *Big Road Blues*, a study of Mississippi blues by David Evans (1982). In 1972 the University of Illinois Press launched Music in American Life, the first scholarly series devoted exclusively to this subject. The first book in the series, *Only a Miner: Studies in Recorded Coal-Mining Songs*, is Archie Green's classic study of mining lore, songs, and music (Green 1972). Since its inception this series has published books on topics as diverse as Chicago soul music, cowboy songs, African American gospel singing, the music of Jewish immigrants, bluegrass, music at the White House, Kansas City jazz, and the definitive biography of country music legend Jimmie Rodgers.

In 1995 the University Press of Mississippi launched its own American Made Music Series with a particular emphasis on the South and a mission to reach a wide audience and not merely academics. Among the scores of titles in this series are books about jazz pioneer Wilbur Sweatman, zydeco music, Starday Records, blues tourism, and southern gospel music. A decade later Duke University Press announced Refiguring American Music, to publish "bold, innovative works that pose new challenges to thinking about the nature and character of American Music." In 2012 Chris Scales (a contributor to this volume) published *Recording Culture: Powwow Music and the Aboriginal Recording Industry on the Northern Plains* in that series.

As the number of books and articles focused on music in the United States grows, many take a broad historical and developmental approach adapted from the field of musicology. These texts also tend to privilege musical products and producers (texts, recordings, repertoires, composers) over musical processes. For example, Richard Crawford's fine textbook *America's Musical Life* (Crawford 2001) provides students with a historical survey that looks back to the seventeenth century and considers primarily the music making of white European immigrants and Africans who came to the continent as slaves and their descendants. Other encyclopedia-style texts that have expanded the field of American music studies include the *Garland Encyclopedia of World Music* with its volume "United States and Canada," edited by Ellen Koskoff (2001), and the *Cambridge History of American Music*, edited by David Nichols (1998). With articles on region and genre as well as on processes and issues that shape American music and music scholarship, including ethnographic fieldwork, by top scholars with contemporary perspectives and methods, these are invaluable resources.

Since we conceived of and began to work on the first edition of this book in the mid-1990s, new publications have moved the scholarship about American music forward. *American Popular Music: A Multicultural History* takes a cue from our book, but instead of sharply focused case studies, Glenn Appell and David Hemphill (2005) provide a sweeping overview that relates the story of American popular music from African American, European American, Latino, Asian, and Native American perspectives. Similarly, Norm Cohen's edited volume *Ethnic and*

Border Music: A Regional Exploration (Cohen 2007) consists of six essays, including "Irish Music in America" and "Chicano/Latino Music, from the Southwest to the Northeast" that cover their topics with a similarly broad stroke. In 2013 Larry Starr and Chris Waterman published a new edition of *American Popular Music: From Minstrelsy to MP3* that displays an increasing awareness of the diversity of our popular music traditions, most notably the importance of Latino popular music emanating from Los Angeles, New York, and south Florida.

We believe that *Musics of Multicultural America*, the first edition of this book, helped move the study of American music into new territories, as it raised questions about the very nature of American music. Certainly only a minority of the people who picked up a copy of the book expected to read about the music culture of Pima Indians in Arizona, Brooklyn's steel pan orchestras, the Spanish-Indian musical mix found in New Mexico known as matachines, or Arab Americans in Dearborn, Michigan. Although *The Music of Multicultural America: Performance, Identity, and Community in the United States* expands the number of case studies, we still believe that many of the issues and concepts that we raised in 1997 remain underexplored, underappreciated, and largely absent from most conversations about American music.

CULTURAL GEOGRAPHY AND THE MULTICULTURAL MIX

The United States is home to people from across the entire world, creating a particularly rich and complex cultural landscape. On the West Coast the influence of immigrants from all over Asia is obvious, particularly in urban areas like Los Angeles and Seattle. The southernmost states form a "border culture" where the music, fashion, and food from Mexico, Central America, and the Caribbean permeate every stratum of society. In the so-called heartland of our country (the American Midwest), African Americans, as well as people of Northern European and Scandinavian heritage, share the map with Middle Easterners and people from Eastern Europe. The Northeast, home to populations of "old world" Europe, such as Italian and Irish Americans, also welcomes new families from Africa. With the help of various aid agencies, political and economic refugees find new homes in cities and towns across the country. Every large city in the United States, from Boston to San Francisco, is a complicated cauldron of ethnicity, race, nationalism, class, religion, and social affinity. *The Music of Multicultural America* challenges its readers to develop an enhanced awareness of American musical life that matches the diversity and complexity of the American population.

The study of America's musical diversity not only provides a method for understanding our multicultural population; it also reveals the ways that peoples and cultures move around within the United States and between communities in various international locales. The movement of Mexican American peoples from the Southwest throughout the country has introduced a number of important

Mexican American styles, including for example, *conjunto*, mariachi, and *tejano*, which are now readily heard in the North and East. As people of Norwegian, Swedish, Finnish, Czech, and Bohemian background permanently leave their northern homes and become full-time "snowbirds," they bring with them the polka bands and dances that find new audiences in places like Arizona and Florida.

The popularity of Cajun culture and music illustrates that certain types of regional or ethnic music become trendy and undergo waves of popularity that extend beyond their place and community of origin. Looking into the history of Cajun music and culture reminds us of this community's original migration from France to eastern Canada and then from these Maritime Provinces to present-day Louisiana and, as described in this volume, to California. Beginning in the 1960s and rapidly gathering momentum over the past twenty years, gumbo, button accordions, and two-stepping became chic. Hundreds of miles from the bayou, throughout much of the United States, not only have the sheer number of Creole, Cajun, and New Orleans–style restaurants increased dramatically but the interest in Cajun music and dance has mushroomed. The Washington, D.C., area, for example, supports weekly dances that feature creolized music. Nevertheless, even with today's nationwide and international fascination with things Cajun, we rightly associate Cajun music and culture with southwestern Louisiana and southeastern Texas. Even though music always seems to be on the move, styles like Cajun, polka, or mariachi (to name just a few examples) are inseparable from the places and the histories of their origin. The power of music to refer to these places and histories is one of the things that makes music so compelling.

For those who identify their heritage as originating outside of the United States, and others who are learning about their heritage through community performance, music *invents* homeland. Collections of essays on the performative power of festivals edited by Falassi (1987), and on the use of music in the construction of place edited by Stokes (1994), for example, along with many other studies of music and identity offer examples of the power of music, dance, festival, and ritual to actualize community through referencing its sights, sounds, smells, customs, and worldviews. George Lipsitz in *Dangerous Crossroads* (1994) extends the discussion to embrace mediated popular music in a global postmodern context and its power to communicate a "poetics of place." Edited collections on music and diaspora confirm that music and musicians are ever on the move and that their networks are both local and global (see Witzleben 2013; Turino and Lee 2004; Um 2005; Ramnarine 2007; see also Clifford 1997). Whether remembered from "over there" or learned here, music has the power through lyrics, instruments, ornaments, scales, intonation and a host of other features to reference time and place in special ways. Furthermore, because listening, playing, and moving to music are all physical activities, the poetics of place, the sense of belonging, or the complex feelings associated with identity are activated through performance and experienced and remembered in both the mind and the body.

ETHNOMUSICOLOGY AND THE STUDY OF THE WORLD'S MUSIC

The study of "world music" has played an increasingly important role in college curricula, particularly since the field of ethnomusicology developed as an academic discipline in the mid-1950s. In liberal arts colleges, large universities, and schools of music, courses in world music and ethnomusicology have contributed to a more comprehensive study of music of all the world's peoples. Such courses expand and challenge the focus of music programs on the select cultures of Europe. Courses that include music cultures of the world have also done much to satisfy the increasing demand within college and university-wide curricula for attention to histories and cultures outside the Western tradition.

Those of us who teach world music courses are challenged and excited by our assignment to teach "the world" in one or two semesters. Yet we can be frustrated by the marginalization of world music by some who consider western art music superior and any kind of global studies as extra, exotic, faraway, foreign, or mostly for fun. Although its influence is waning as many academic institutions address the need for a more global perspective in the areas of art, history, literature, philosophy, and religion, the dichotomy between "the West and the rest" remains an important principle for the ordering of knowledge in the academy.

The world music classes that fulfill the non-Western, global, multicultural, or world history requirements for students in colleges and universities across the country tend to survey select musical traditions of Asia, the Middle East, Eastern Europe, Latin America, Africa, and Native America. For various reasons, the serious consideration of world music traditions in the United States (for example Chinese music in America, or Chinese American music) has lagged behind. Over the past two decades, however, ethnomusicologists have expanded the purview of their discipline to include not only musical practices characterized by age, place, and "purity," but also those rich with the complexities of the contemporary, the mediated, the transnational, and the postmodern, phenomena that have been identified and theorized by contemporary thinkers. In other words, scholars are increasingly looking within the United States to discover and explore the music of the world's peoples.

Ethnomusicologists then, among others, have reinforced the fact that the "New World" is as rich a field of study for contemporary scholars as the "Old World" has been for historical and comparative musicologists and their colleagues. Thanks to the time and energy ethnomusicologists have invested toward the understanding of multiple musical languages in our increasingly interconnected world, they have much to offer contemporary study of American music. In the twenty-first century the discipline of ethnomusicology itself is characterized as much by theoretical and methodological approach as by geographical orientation. Taking a nod from anthropology, ethnomusicologists look at music *in* and *as* culture, as a fundamental activity of humankind, and they concern themselves with trying to understand the ways people use, practice, and ascribe meaning to music. Ethnomusicologists aim to gain insight into native systems of musical practice and aesthetics and to adopt a relativistic view of musical sounds and systems.

Some college students gain an interest in world music because of related coursework in anthropology, history, languages, religions, and literature. Or, they come into world music classes because their interest has been piqued by international artists and pop stars, such as Algerian rai singers Cheb Khaled and Rashid Taha or Nigerian juju musician King Sunny Ade, or Youssou N'Dour from Senegal, or Wyclef Jean of Haiti. Thanks to a variety of media like Spotify or Smithsonian Global Sounds, world music is now widely available. Students often recognize their own experiences in our classes because they have heard some so-called world music in their own backyard—a *conjunto* band on a Texas radio station, a salsa group performing at a New York City nightclub, klezmer music at a friend's wedding, or the religious and holiday songs that accompany their own family celebrations.

MUSIC, ETHNICITY, AND IDENTITY

Building upon the interests of such sociologists and anthropologists as Melville Herskovits (1945), Milton Gordon (1964), and Frederick Barth (1969), studies of ethnicity as a profound and enduring social construct of humankind gained momentum in the mid-1960s. Scholars in fields ranging from music to political science developed a keen interest in ethnicity and race as keys to understanding the development of an "American identity." Writers initially examined the old customs and modes of behavior that were passed down and inherited from generation to generation with an eye toward understanding the process of assimilation and acculturation in the New World. Their view was that these processes, together, served as a catalyst for the erosion of "authentic" old world traditions that resulted in the gradual meltdown of ethnic distinctions into the American pot.

As the civil rights movement and the modern feminist movement of the early 1960s legitimized difference, new academic paradigms emerged that focused not on the meltdown of tradition but on the constant reworking and re-articulation of tradition through idea and action. In the 1980s and 1990s, studies of race and ethnicity as social constructions were extended by numerous scholars from within ethnic groups, who, writing as insiders, gave voice to the complexity and richness of the process of identity formation. The establishment of numerous interdisciplinary programs and departments such as Women's Studies, Africana Studies, or Ethnic Studies resulted from their work.

We now accept that categories of ethnicity, identity, and even race are far from static and largely constructed through social process. In spite of the fact that we are born into families, into socioeconomic classes, and into religious groups, our identities are largely constructed through the daily processes of personal interaction, choosing associates, and through participating in a wide range of social activities that include music and dance. Morelli's interpretation of American women and the Indian classical dance world in San Francisco, and Scales and Desrosier's presentation of intertribal powwow both get to the heart of ideas about race and ethnicity as they are embodied by practitioners and perceived by audiences and communities. Along with many of our case studies, theirs show how the sense of who we are is not entirely predetermined at birth; rather, it is invented throughout the life cycle and reinterpreted from generation to generation. Ethnic and community identity are fluid, vigorous, and to a certain extent voluntary, and it is through and with music that processes like exposure, enculturation, and embodiment, all of them key to the formation of identity, are set into motion.

With this volume, we extend and revisit the theoretical attention to "the construction of community" and view this extraordinarily resilient but very natural human process through the lens of performance. We believe that the agents that are at work for an ethnic group in their construction of community through music and dance are at work for any community, however self-identified. Certainly a community-generated festival at the Los Angeles Thai Temple stands in sharp relief to an African American go-go dance held at a skating rink in the Anacostia section of Washington. But are the fundamental processes of choosing ways to dance, which clothes to wear, how to worship, what to eat, or when to sing really that different for Thai Americans of Los Angeles and the thousands of Americans who gather each weekend at go-goes? We suggest that the answer is no. Participation in music, whether as a player, a dancer, or a listener, implies making choices, choices that are sometimes made in the light of ethnicity and heritage but at other times may be made according to a political or social affiliation or to a professional or artistic agenda.

Switching codes between American popular music at a school dance at the gym and, for example, Mexican American mariachi at a family graduation party are part and parcel of multicultural America. The process of code switching that might happen every day between school and work and home, may also occur over a longer span of time: during the life cycle, as has been the case with Linda Ronstadt, profiled in Dan Sheehy's chapter; or from generation to generation, as is discussed by Susan Asai in her chapter on Japanese American music making. In the context of a mid-1990s wedding, young Americans of Arab heritage in Dearborn, for example, moved easily between *Casey Kasem's Coast to Coast* (in 2004 the show became *American Top 40 with Ryan Seacrest*) and the most recent Arab hits from Lebanon. That Kemal Amin "Casey" Kasem (1932–2014) was himself a Lebanese American and a highly visible supporter of Arab American social causes and cultural events is indicative of the complex web of multiple identities that Americans may negotiate within the course of a day or their life span. In their own way, each of the communities profiled in *The Music of Multicultural America* defiantly and proudly proclaims—in the words of *Polka Happiness* authors, Keil, Keil, and Blau—a resounding "No!" to monoculture (1992).

Our collection is rife with examples of the ways in which musical practices and processes powerfully articulate individual and community identity. For the Riot Grrrls described by Cateforis and Humphreys, music was the most visible emblem around which that community could coalesce. Romero writes that the Pueblo themselves invest the performance of matachines with such a sense of authenticity that it is absurd for the scholar to even evaluate continuity and change in what is obviously a very old but also quite flexible performance complex. Pen suggests that religious and cultural impulses, many of which are steeped in decades of tradition, underpin the singing from the shape-note books used by people in central Kentucky. Spinney, who explores the Irish American music scene in Boston, suggests that the presentation of their music in twenty-first-century "kitchen rackets" is a response to changes in the older societies that had supported the music over the previous decades.

The ability of music to consistently generate powerful symbols of social alliance, tradition, heritage, place, love, hate, nationalism, xenophobia, and a host of other emotions is a key feature of America's musical diversity. A profound sense of spirituality may permeate certain audience members at a gospel quartet performance who normally may not articulate their religious orientation. At a civic festival of Arab culture in Detroit, spirited nationalism may rise unexpectedly among individuals who are normally ecumenical in their view of the Arab world. In a contrasting example, the sense of intertribal solidarity as an integral aspect of the American Indian sense of self may be something that is actually fostered by the intertribal powwow phenomenon common to the upper Midwest. Thus, what may not be even hinted at in spoken and written discourse, for example, may be vividly obvious or subtly encoded in a music event. In addition to describing the power and beauty of the sound of music, this team of authors looks to musical activity as a rich repository of information about cultural and social issues and as a generative force in forging individual and community identities.

Every essay in *The Music of Multicultural America* exemplifies the way in which music making contributes to the creation, maintenance, and transfer of individual and group identity. For example, reliving Carnival every year in the streets of New York brings Caribbean Americans together in an almost obligatory celebration that reaffirms their heritage and their solidarity as a people, however dispersed are their residences in America. For communities such as these, the musical event may be the only time during which group members—of disparate ages, income levels, and educational backgrounds—gather together. For other communities, such as the gospel quartet community in Memphis, Yemeni Americans in Detroit, Native Americans participating in an Upper Plains powwow, or transplanted Cajuns gathering to dance in Oakland, interaction may occur in a number of domains (at home, at school, or in the workplace), but the musical event may be the time during which bonds are especially strong. Rather than merely reflecting and repeating a community's pre-established ideology and practice, however, the creation and performance of music can generate (to borrow a phrase from

Rudolph Vecoli, longtime director of the Immigration History Research Center at the University of Minnesota) "a sense of peoplehood."

DEFINING AMERICAN

As wonderfully eclectic and inclusive as Vecoli's notion of Americanness sounds, membership in the American peoplehood can be fragile and fickle. Since the publication of our first edition in 1997, several events have occurred that have challenged the ways we, as Americans, view ourselves. The events of September 11, 2001, dramatically altered our cultural landscape, igniting vigorous debates about what it means to be "American" and inspiring laws, rules, and ideas, both formal and informal, that impact American citizens, people who live within our sovereign borders, visitors to our country, and the circulation of travelers the world over.

In November 2001 an act of Congress created what is now known as the Transportation Security Administration (TSA) within the US Department of Homeland Security, a completely new federal agency created in the wake of 9/11. The TSA is best known for its security officers, who daily check tens of thousands of airline passengers through checkpoints set up at all airports in the United States. Obtaining visas to visit, study, and perform in the United States also became more difficult, and although the process may have lightened up within the past decade, the expense of expediting visas for artists from abroad can be prohibitive for presenters who want to feature foreign artists in their series or to facilitate collaboration and education among artists, students, and audiences. Further and tangentially related to the post 9/11 impetus to tighten up the borders of our homeland, US Immigration and Customs Enforcement (better known by its acronym ICE) gained sweeping new powers in light of the cobbled-together series of legislation devoted to regulating what used to be called "undocumented aliens." The various theatrics of security, while targeting dangerous people from outside of our homeland, particularly through new waves of anti-immigration initiatives, had the collateral damage of making certain kinds of Americans, some of who had lived in the United States for generations, suddenly feel unwelcome.

Another major event to shake the foundation of the notion of America as the land of the free and the home of the brave was the natural disaster Hurricane Katrina. In late August 2005, Katrina wreaked widespread destruction all along the Gulf Coast and devastated large sections of one of the most important musical capitals in our country, New Orleans, Louisiana. The shoddy response to Katrina, the costliest natural disaster in American history, brought American realities of socioeconomic and racial inequality into sharp relief. Although Katrina put New Orleans and its uniquely American music culture in the spotlight, celebrated through projects such as the HBO television series *Tremé*, the city of New Orleans still struggles to regain its economic and social footing, and some sections of the city, most notably the largely African American Ninth Ward, scarcely resemble their pre-Katrina landscape. Indeed, it seems that New Orleans, the so-called birthplace of jazz and a cauldron of musical creativity and collaboration, may have been irreversibly changed by Hurricane Katrina.

As a last example of the fluidity of the debate on Americanness, the topic at the core of America's musical diversity, we cite the election of Barack Obama in 2008 and his 2012 reelection. For some, the election of the first African American, truly multiracial president represented liberation from the yoke of racial inequality that has harnessed American society, in spite of the Emancipation Proclamation that freed slaves from bondage more than 150 years ago. But Obama's election has also inspired some of the most racist vitriol among certain populations who point to his multiracial and international heritage as proof of his ineligibility to lead the nation.

These three wrinkles in time of American history have increased the volume of the refrain that some people, like some musics, are more American than others.

CLOSING THOUGHTS

The Music of Multicultural America broadens the horizons of those interested in music found in the United States. We hope that these fifteen case studies also stimulate students to more carefully explore the multitudinous musical communities untouched by this collection. We anticipate that our readers will become more acutely aware of the diversity of music making in the United States and understand that our musical heritage extends far beyond the familiar folk, rock, pop, jazz, and country genres to encompass an enormous range of music that is built upon the bedrock of immigration, regionalism, race, and ethnicity and fueled by innovation and creativity. Additionally we wish to stress that musical taste and cultural identity in the United States is really a matter of choice. People of Jewish heritage may cringe at the sound of klezmer; African Americans may never have experienced a Sunday afternoon gospel program; Americans with a Caribbean background living in Kansas may simply be too far from the New York Carnivals to truly appreciate this scene. At the same time, people connected to various subcultures through affinity and not heritage may be deeply committed to the production and preservation of America's musical diversity.

Moreover, it is important to understand the intellectual history of the United States of America and the many emotional and ideological shifts in perspective that our nation has undergone and continues to experience regarding the very notion of cultural diversity. The popularity of the familiar melting-pot metaphor has waxed and waned with movements toward nationalism and xenophobia on the one hand or toward proud promotion of cultural diversity on the other. Consider for instance the immigration quotas of 1924, which reflected the concern to limit the racial and ethnic contamination of America by immigrants from Asia and Eastern Europe. Recall, for example, Alex Haley's influential 1976 novel *Roots* and the numerous, publications, television programs, and trips to Ellis Island to check the passenger records for an ancestor that his powerful book inspired in its wake. Contrast the inclusive messages of multiculturalism in popular media and corporate advertising with the defensive rhetoric of the harsh Arizona immigration laws that were largely struck down by the United States Supreme Court in late June 2012.

Whichever way the winds of ideology, politics, and policy may blow in America, it is clear that people are hooked on musical diversity. When commercial jingles are tinged with world percussion and harmonies and when people are dancing to Cajun music in the North and polka bands in the South, it seems that individuals are searching for ways in which they can listen to and participate in an increasingly diverse set of musical options. The musics profiled in this collection, in addition to hundreds of other American musical scenes and subcultures, have provided these options. There is little doubt that these American musics, whether in the mainstream or under the radar, will continue to play on and flourish, providing powerful catalysts for artistically creative and socially positive experiences.

Notes

1. Deborah Wong contributed a chapter to the first edition of this project titled *Musics of Multicultural America: A Study of Twelve Musical Communities* (Schirmer 1997: 287–316). Wong's chapter, "Just Being There: Making Asian American Space in the Recording Industry" was republished in her subsequent volume, *Speak It Louder: Asian Americans Making Music* (Routledge, 2004).

2. In December 2013, pop star Beyoncé surprised her fans by releasing her new album *Beyoncé* digitally rather than through the usual medium of the CD recording. While other groups, for example Radiohead, have made their new music available online in limited editions, Beyoncé's entire album, fourteen audio tracks and seventeen videos, became available as a download to fans through iTunes, thus turning the tables on the process and economics of music production.

For Further Reading

Alba, Richard D. 1990. *Ethnic Identity: The Transformation of White America*. New Haven, CT: Yale University Press.

Alcoff, Linda Martin, et al., eds. 2006. *Identity Politics Reconsidered*. New York: Palgrave/Macmillan.

Anderson, Benedict. 1983. *Imagined Communities: Reflections on the Origin and Spread of Nationalism*. London: Verso.

Appadurai, Arjun. 1990. "Disjuncture and Difference in the Global Cultural Economy." *Public Culture* 2, no. 2: 1–24.

Appell, Glenn, and David Hemphill. 2005. *American Popular Music: A Multicultural History.* New York: Schirmer Books.

Barron, Robert, and Nick Spitzer. 1992. *Public Folklore.* Washington: Smithsonian Institution Press.

Barth, Frederik. 1969. *Ethnic Groups and Boundaries: The Social Organization of Cultural Difference.* Boston: Little, Brown.

Bergeron, Katherine, and Philip V. Bohlman. 1992. *Disciplining Music: Musicology and Its Canons.* Chicago: University of Chicago Press.

Berlin, Edward. 1980. *Ragtime: A Musical and Cultural History.* Berkeley and Los Angeles: University of California Press.

Bloom, Alan. 1987. *The Closing of the American Mind: How Higher Education Has Failed Democracy and Impoverished the Souls of Today's Students.* New York: Simon & Schuster.

Briggs, Vernon M., Jr. 1992. *Mass Migration and the National Interest.* Armonk, NY: M. E. Sharpe.

Caraveli, Anna. 1985. "The Symbolic Village: Community Born in Performance." *Journal of American Folklore* 99 (289): 260–86.

Carney, George O. 1994. *The Sound of People and Places.* 3rd ed. Lanham, MD: Rowman & Littlefield.

Charters, Samuel. 1975. *The Country Blues.* Reprint, New York: Da Capo. Original edition, 1959.

Chase, Gilbert. 1992. *America's Music: From the Pilgrims to the Present.* 3rd ed. Urbana: University of Illinois Press.

Ch'maj, Betty E. M., ed. 1993. *Multicultural America: A Resource Book for Teachers of Humanities and American Studies.* Lanham, MD: University Press of America.

Clausen Bernd, Ursula Hemetek, and Eva Saether. 2009. *Music in Motion: Diversity and Dialogue in Europe.* New Brunswick and London: Transaction.

Clifford, James. 1997. "Diasporas." In *Routes: Travel and Translation in the Late Twentieth Century.* Cambridge, MA, and London: Harvard University Press. 244–78.

Cohen, A. P. 1985. *The Symbolic Construction of Community.* London: Tavistock.

Cohen, Norm. 2007. *Ethnic and Border Music: A Regional Exploration.* Lanham, MD: Greenwood Press.

Cromwell, Grant H., and Eve Walsh Stoddard. 2001. "Introduction: National Boundaries/Transnational Identities." In *Global Multiculturalism: Comparative Perspectives on Ethnicity, Race and Nation.* Ed. Grant H. Cornwell and Eve Walsh Stoddard. Lanham, NY, Boulder, and Oxford, UK: Rowman & Littlefield. 1–28.

Epstein, Dena. 1977. *Sinful Tunes and Spirituals: Black Folk Music to the Civil* War. Urbana: University of Illinois Press.

Erikson, Thomas Hylland. 1993. *Ethnicity and Nationalism: Anthropological Perspectives.* London: Pluto Press.

Evans, David. 1982. *Big Road Blues: Tradition and Creativity in the Folk Blues.* Berkeley and Los Angeles: University of California Press.

Falassi, Alessandro. 1987. *Time Out of Time: Essays on the Festival.* Albuquerque: University of New Mexico Press.

Georges, Robert A., and Stephen Stern. 1982. *American and Canadian Immigrant and Ethnic Folklore: An Annotated Bibliography.* New York: Garland.

Glazer, Nathan, and Daniel P. Moynihan, eds. 1975. *Ethnicity, Theory, and Experience.* Cambridge, MA: Harvard University Press.

Gordon, Milton. 1964. *Assimilation in American Life: The Role of Race, Religion, and National Origins.* New York: Oxford University Press.

Gronow, Pekka. 1982. "Ethnic Recordings: An Introduction." In *Ethnic Recordings in America: A Neglected Heritage.* Ed. Richard Spottswood. 1–31. Washington: Library of Congress.

Hamm, Charles. 1979. *Yesterdays: Popular Song in America.* New York: W. W. Norton.

———. 1983. *Music in the New World.* New York: W. W. Norton.

Handler, Richard, and J. Linnekin. 1984. "Tradition, Genuine or Spurious." *Journal of American Folklore* 97, no. 385 (July-September 1984): 273–90.

Heilbut, Tony. 1985. *The Gospel Sound: Good News and Bad Times.* 2nd ed. New York: Simon & Schuster.

Herskovits, Melville J. 1945. *Acculturation and the Study of Culture Contact.* New York: J. J. Augustin.

Hitchcock, H. Wiley. 1988. *Music in the United States: A Historical Introduction.* 3rd ed. Englewood Cliffs, NJ: Prentice Hall.

Humphrey, Theodore C., and Lin T. Humphrey. 1988. *"We Gather Together": Food and Festival in American Life.* Ann Arbor: U.M.I. Research Press.

Jackson, George Pullen. 1964. *White Spirituals in the Southern Uplands: The Story of the Fasola Folk, Their Songs, Singings, and "Buckwheat Notes."* Reprint, Hatboro, PA: Folklore Associates. Original edition, 1933.

Kiel, Charles, Angeliki Keil, and Dick Blau. 1992. *Polka Happiness.* Philadelphia: Temple University Press.

King, Joseph. 2001. "Songs in a Strange Land: Dual Consciousness and the Narrative of African American Identity in the United States." In *Global Multiculturalism: Comparative Perspectives on Ethnicity, Race, and Nation.* Ed. Grant H. Cornwell and Eve Walsh Stoddard. Lanham, New York, Boulder, and Oxford: Rowman & Littlefield. 143–68.

Kingman, Daniel. 1990. *American Music: A Panorama.* 2nd ed. New York: Schirmer.

Kirshenblatt-Gimblett, Barbara. 1983. "Studying Immigrant and Ethnic Folklore." In *Handbook of American Folklore.* Ed. Richard M. Dorson. Bloomington: Indiana University Press.

Klymasz, Robert B. 1983. "Folklore of the Canadian American Border." In *Handbook of American Folklore.* Ed. Richard M. Dorson. Bloomington: Indiana University Press.

Levine, Lawrence W. 1988. *Highbrow/Lowbrow: The Emergence of Cultural Hierarchy in America.* Cambridge, MA: Harvard University Press.

———. 1996. *The Opening of the American Mind: Canons, Culture, and History.* Boston: Beacon Press.

Lipsitz, George. 1994. *Dangerous Crossroads: Popular Music, Postmodernism and the Poetics of Place.* London: Verso.

Lomax, Alan. 1960. *The Folk Songs of North America in the English Language.* Garden City, NY: Doubleday.

———. 2012. *Cultural Equity.* An online archive of the Lomax Collection of Field Recordings. http://research.culturalequity.org/home-audio.jsp.

Lomax, John A. 1938. *Cowboy Songs and Other Frontier Ballads.* Rev. ed. New York: Macmillan.

Lornell, Kip. 1989. "The Early Career of Whoopee John Wilfahrt." *John Edwards Memorial Forum*, vol. XXI, no. 75/76 (Spring 1989): 51–54.

———. 1995. *"Happy in the Service of the Lord": African American Sacred Vocal Harmony Quartets in Memphis.* 2nd ed. Knoxville: University of Tennessee Press.

———. 2002. "Virginia Traditions: Non-Blues Secular Black Music." In *American Musical Traditions*, eds. Jeff Todd Titon and Richard Carlin. New York: Schirmer Reference. 42–49.

Loza, Steven. 1993. *Barrio Rhythm: Mexican American Music in Los Angeles.* Urbana and Chicago: University of Illinois Press.

Malone, Bill, and Jocelyn R. Neal. 2010. *Country Music, U.S.A.* Third rev. ed. Austin: University of Texas Press.

Marks, Craig. 2011. *I Want My MTV: The Uncensored Story of the Music Video Revolution.* New York: Dutton.

McCready, William C., ed. 1983. *Culture, Ethnicity, and Identity: Current Issues in Research.* New York: Academic Press.

Naficy, Hamid, and Gabriel Teshome. 1993. *The Making of Exile Cultures: Iranian Television in Los Angeles.* Minneapolis: University of Minnesota Press.

Oliver, Paul. 1974. *The Story of the Blues.* Reprint, New York: Chilton. Original edition, 1969. Boston: Northeastern University Press.

Omni, Michael, and Howard Winant. 1994. *Racial Formation in the United States: From the 1960s to the 1990s.* 2nd ed. New York: Routledge.

Palumbo-Liu, David, ed. 1995. *The Ethnic Canon: Histories, Institutions, and Interventions.* Minneapolis: University of Minnesota Press.

———. 2002. "Multiculturalism Now: Civilization, National Identity, and Difference before and After September 11th." *Boundary 2* vol. 29, no. 2: 109–27.

Peña, Manuel. 1985. *The Texas-Mexican Conjunto: History of a Working-Class Music.* Austin: University of Texas Press.

Peterson Royce, Anya. 1982. *Ethnic Identity: Strategies of Diversity.* Bloomington: Indiana University Press.

Porterfield, Nolan. 1979. *Jimmie Rodgers: The Life and Times of America's Blue Yodeler.* Urbana: University of Illinois Press.

Ramnarine, Tina K. *Musical Performance in the Diaspora.* 2007. London: Routledge.

Ramsey, Frederic, Jr., and Charles Edward Smith. (1939) 1977. *The Jazzmen.* Da Capo.

Rasmussen, Anne K. 2004. "Mainstreaming American Musical Multiculturalism." *American Music* 22, no. 2: 296–309.

Spaeth, Sigmund. 1977. *Read 'em and Weep: The Songs You Forgot to Remember.* New York: Da Capo. Original edition, 1926.

Schuller, Gunther. 1989. *The Swing Era: The Development of Jazz, 1930 through 1945*. New York: Oxford University Press.

Seeger, Ruth Crawford. 1953. *Animal Songs for Children*. Garden City, NY: Doubleday.

Simonson, Rick, and Scott Walker, eds. 1988. *Multicultural Literacy: Opening the American Mind*. St. Paul, MN: Greywolf Press.

Slobin, Mark. 1993. *Subcultural Sounds: Micromusics of the West*. Hanover, NH: Wesleyan University Press.

———. 1982. *Tenement Songs: The Popular Music of the Jewish Immigrant*. Urbana: University of Illinois Press.

Spottswood, Richard K., ed. 1990. *Ethnic Music on Records: A Discography of Ethnic Recordings Produced in the United States, 1893-1942*. Champaign-Urbana: University of Illinois Press.

Sollors, Werner, ed. 1989. *The Invention of Ethnicity*. New York: Oxford University Press.

Stern, Stephen, and John Allan Cicala, eds. 1991. *Creative Ethnicity: Symbols and Strategies of Contemporary Ethnic Life*. Logan: Utah State University Press.

Stokes, Martin, ed. 1994. *Ethnicity, Identity, and Music: The Musical Construction of Place*. Oxford: Berg.

Takaki, Ronald. 1993. *A Different Mirror: A History of Multicultural* America. Boston: Little, Brown.

Tawa, Nicholas E. 1982. *A Sound of Strangers: Musical Culture, Acculturation, and the Post–Civil War Ethnic American*. Metuchen, NJ: Scarecrow Press.

Thernstrom, Stephan, ed. 1980. *Harvard Encyclopedia of American Ethnic Groups*. Cambridge, MA, and London: Belknap Press of Harvard University Press.

Titon, Jeff Todd, ed. 1992. "Special Issue: Music in the Public Interest." *Ethnomusicology: Journal for the Society of Ethnomusicology* 36, no. 3.

Toll, Robert. 1974. *Blacking Up: The Minstrel Show in Nineteenth-Century America*. New York: Oxford University Press.

Solis, Ted. 2004. *Performing Ethnomusicology: Teaching and Representation in World Music Ensembles*. Los Angeles and Berkeley: University of California Press.

Starr, Larry, and Chris Waterman. 2009. *American Popular Music: From Minstrelsy to MP3*. New York: Oxford University Press.

Turino, Thomas, and James Lea, eds. 2004. *Identity and the Arts in Diaspora Communities*. Warren, MI: Harmonie Park Press.

Um, Hae-Kyung, ed. 2005. *Diasporas and Interculturalism in Asian Performing Arts: Translating Traditions*. London and New York: RoutledgeCurzon.

US Commission on Immigration Reform. 1994. *U.S. Immigration Policy: Restoring Credibility*. Report to Congress by the US Commission on Immigration Reform, chaired by Barbara Jordan. Washington: US Government Printing Office.

Walker, Rob. "On YouTube Amateur is the New Pro." *New York Times*, July 1, 2012. www.nytimes.com/2012/07/01/magazine/on-youtube-amateur-is-the-new-pro.html?_r=1&nl=todaysheadlines&emc=edit_th_20120630.

Waters, Mary C. 1990. *Ethnic Options: Choosing Identities in America*. Berkeley, Los Angeles, and Oxford: University of California Press.

Witzleben, J. Lawrence. 2013. "Review Essay: Music and Diaspora." *Ethnomusicology* 57, no. 3: 525–32.

Websites

Alan Lomax Collection online at the American Folklife Center, Library of Congress. www.loc.gov/folklife/lomax/

Alan Lomax Collection: www.research.culturalequity.org

Center for Traditional Music and Dance: www.ctmd.org

City Lore: http://citylore.org

Folkstreams: Folkstreams.net

Lomax, Alan. 2012. *Cultural Equity*. An online archive of the Lomax Collection of Field Recordings. http://research.culturalequity.org/home-audio.jsp.

Smithsonian Folklife Festival: www.festival.si.edu.

Smithsonian Folkways: www.folkways.si.edu.

Society for American Music: www.american-music.org.

Society for Ethnomusicology: www.ethnomusicology.org.

Urban Gateways: www.urbangateways.org.

- 2 -

CZECH AMERICAN POLKA MUSIC IN WISCONSIN

James P. Leary

In this essay, James Leary, a folklorist who teaches at the University of Wisconsin at Madison, examines the evolution of one strand of polka music in the Dairy State. Although he briefly mentions the German, Polish, and Slovenian communities of the region and the love for polka music that they share, the author specifically focuses on the Czech enclaves, especially those in eastern Wisconsin. Leary traces the history of Czech American polka music from its origins in the 1850s, with a special emphasis on the changing contexts in which the music has been performed: from the Bohemian halls built by Czech fraternal organizations during the late nineteenth and early twentieth centuries, to Depression-era ballrooms, to contemporary polka festivals. These settings and the close-knit Czech American communities of Wisconsin have helped to bridge the gulf between the old world and the new while contributing to the Slavic, German, and Scandinavian cultural pluralism that distinguishes Wisconsin and the Upper Midwest. Leary addresses one strand of the multiethnic polka community that until the 1980s, barely received serious attention from scholars in American vernacular music—despite its mainstream status among so many citizens of the United States from Texas to Minnesota. Today, because of the work undertaken by Leary, Richard March, Victor Greene, Charles Keil, Manuel Pena, Robert Walser, and a handful of others, polka music is finally being treated with respect.

POLKA MUSIC, AMERICAN MUSIC

Polka is the vernacular music of rural and working-class ethnic Americans whose ancestors emigrated from Europe in the nineteenth and early twentieth centuries to labor in factories, in lumber and mining camps, and on farms. Incorporating not only the polka, but also such other nineteenth-century couples dances as the waltz, the schottische, the ländler, the mazurka, and assorted "mixers," polka music is typically played by small ensembles consisting of some combination of brass, reed, percussion, and stringed instruments. Most at home in community halls and amidst weddings and local festivals, polka music has, from the nineteenth century through the present, entered into every form of mass media. Not surprisingly, it

2.1. Tuba Dan Jerabek, with his wife Corky on drums, at the Midwest Folklife Festival, Dodgeville, Wisconsin, August 20, 2011. Photo by Jim Leary.

has been influenced by and has occasionally contributed to American popular music. And it has affected and intermingled with such other American folk traditions as the Cajun and zydeco music of southwest Louisiana, the Mexican American *conjunto* music of south Texas, and the *waila* or "chicken scratch" music of Arizona's Tohono O'odham peoples.

Prominent in the industrial cities of southern New England and the Middle Atlantic states, the farming communities of the eastern Great Plains, the mining towns and alpine resorts of the Rocky Mountains, the ports and valleys of the Pacific Northwest, and the retirement havens of the Sun Belt, polka music is practiced most vigorously in the Midwest. In 1994, for example, the Wisconsin legislature designated the polka as the official state dance.[1] The genre's recognition was particularly appropriate since, because of Wisconsin's long history of cultural pluralism, the state's borders encompass a greater variety of polka substyles than anywhere else in the world.

For self-described "polka people," ethnicity has been the primary feature in distinguishing among the Dairy State's profusion of polka sounds. Austrians, Belgians, Croatians, Finns, Irish, Italians, Jews, Mexicans, Norwegians, Swedes, and Swiss have all made contributions within their respective enclaves. Czechs (Bohemians), Germans, Poles, and Slovenians, however, have done the most to shape Wisconsin's polka music. Indeed this quartet of ethnic American polka styles, each with its innovative practitioners and evolving substyles, dominates the nation's polka scene (Leary 1991).

Despite its diversity, ubiquity, longevity, and clear contribution to the peculiarities of American musical life, polka music has received scant attention from folklorists, ethnomusicologists, and other students of American folk and vernacular music, especially in comparison to the considerable research devoted to America's Anglo-Celtic and African-derived musical traditions. There are several obvious reasons for this neglect, most of them descendent from the conservative, Anglophile, implicitly xenophobic, upper-class, academic origins of scholarship concerning American life and culture, including American folk music.

First, as the music of Germans, Italians, Jews, Slavs, Scandinavians, and other non-English-speaking immigrants, polka has been regarded as "foreign," a survival from the old country, and therefore less worthy of full musical citizenship than folk performances by those of "old stock" Anglo-Celtic heritage. Second, as a European American genre, polka has, for the European Americans who dominate folk-music scholarship, lacked the exoticism of African American and Native American musical traditions. Third, as a multifaceted, pluralist, and widely dispersed genre, polka music—in terms of style, community, and place—has been far less geographically circumscribed, and consequently far less easy to definitively study than the music of such otherwise comparable ethnic-regional Americans as Cajuns and Hispanics. Fourth, as a musical movement whose brief flirtation with American popular music was swept away in the early 1950s by the emergence of rock 'n' roll, polka music and, by association, the accordion have been regarded by the nation's tastemakers as hopelessly square.[2]

Happily, however, scholars have begun to discover polka music in increasing numbers since the 1980s (see especially Greene 1992; Keil, Keil, and Blau 1992; Spottswood 1990). Part of this turnabout stems from the reassessment and broadening of canons in many fields, including folk music, since the late 1960s (Bohlman 1988; Slobin 1993). Part is attributable to a parallel expansion of the number and backgrounds of scholars researching American folk music: as more people do more work, they draw from a greater range of experience, and invariably some have grown up amidst the polka scene. Finally, the robust emergence of public folklore in the late 1970s, with its emphasis on culturally diverse folklore practitioners in every state (Feintuch 1988; Baron and Spitzer 1992), has provided both mandate and opportunity for the study of such previously neglected genres as polka music.

My own experience is instructive. I was born in 1950 in Rice Lake, an ethnically diverse farming and logging community in northwestern Wisconsin. While growing up in the 1950s and 1960s, I heard or heard about local Bohemian, German, Norwegian, Polish, Slovenian, Swedish, and Swiss polka bands performing live on WJMC radio, and at the Moose Club, Sokup's Tavern, the Pines Ballroom, Virgil's Bunny Bar, the Bohemian Hall, the Barron County Fair, Mount Hardscrabble's ski chalet, and an occasional wedding or barn dance. The music was everywhere.

In the early 1970s, however, when I began studying folk music as a graduate student, I could discover almost nothing about my hometown's polka scene and its broader American context. Neither course syllabi nor academic publications so much as acknowledged the genre's existence. Determined to learn more, in the late 1970s I began to buy polka recordings by Wisconsin bands, hang out at dances, and photograph and interview musicians. About the same time, Richard March—a fellow folklorist with polka roots and Wisconsin connections—and I began to get research contracts from various public folklore agencies for the purpose of documenting regional folk music traditions. For more than thirty years, in collaboration or working on our own, we have been responsible for the inclusion of polka music in numerous festivals, documentary sound recordings, videos, radio programs, exhibits, and folk artist award ceremonies.[3] Along the way, we have learned a great deal about polka music, especially through the musicians themselves, and we have published steadily on the subject (for example, Leary and March 1996; Leary 2006). Our commitment to the polka music of America is likewise a commitment to a pluralist vision of American folk music. This essay draws upon my work, Richard March's, and that of other polka scholars in an effort to illuminate one more rich territory on America's polka map—that occupied by Wisconsin's Czechs.

CO ČECH, TO MUZIKANT

> There were so many great bands in a small area . . . It's the Bohemians. They all love music and they love to show off. They either played or wanted to.
>
> —"TUBA DAN" JERABEK[4]

On a summer's night in 1988, Dan Jerabek took a break from playing at Americano's, an old wooden ballroom slated for razing in the modernizing paper-mill city of Appleton. An all-star lineup of polka bands and a floor full of dancers were sending the place off. We stepped outside into the parking lot, I propped a tape recorder on my car's hood, and—with brass and reeds blending in the background—Dan offered an old-world proverb that recalled a past and plotted a future guaranteed to withstand urban renewal: "Co Čech, to muzikant" (every Czech is a musician).

These words and sentiments have long echoed throughout Wisconsin's Czech communities: Hillsboro and Yuba in the lower Wisconsin River watershed; Ashland on the shores of Lake Superior; Haugen and Phillips in the northern cutover; and the Manitowoc and Kewaunee area along Lake Michigan. Here, music has been as vital as bread. Here, playing a tune has been no less important than ploughing a field. Here, the hard play of dances and weddings has been regarded as the natural complement of the hard work on farms and in factories.

One of nine children, Dan Jerabek was raised on a forty-acre farm near Kewaunee. "My dad wanted to keep us on the farm and out of mischief, so he gave us instruments." Jerry played piano, concertina, and bass clarinet; Bill was on drums and the button accordion; John favored the cornet; Joe and Ann switched off on clarinet and saxophone; while Dan blew the tuba. In the early 1950s the Jerabeks played variety shows in Manitowoc and Kewaunee Counties. "We didn't make any money, but we could start and end together. And the old people liked us," recalled Dan.

When Dan Jerabek was fifteen, a local musician needed a tuba player and offered eight dollars for a wedding job. Over the next two decades Dan played with over forty bands, either as a full-time or a fill-in player. By the late 1970s he had formed the Polkalanders, eventually known as the Tuba Dan Band, which originally included himself as the energetic bass horn player, his wife, Corky, on drums, and their son, Danny Junior, on the clarinet, saxophone, and button accordion. Versatile enough to perform country music, rock, and some jazzy pop, the Tuba Dan Band of the twenty-first century remains, at heart, a polka band with a Czech soul. Meanwhile, Danny Jerabek and his wife Michelle, who was raised within a Wisconsin German polka tradition, have gone on to form a polka-rock band, Copper Box, fusing their Czech and German repertoire with the hot squeezebox sounds of Cajun, zydeco, and conjunto genres (Rake 2011).

FROM OLD WORLD TO NEW

The roots of the Tuba Dan Band extend across nations and centuries. While some Czech immigrants found work in America as factory hands, tradesmen, and domestics in such urban centers as New York, Cleveland, and especially Chicago, more than half, like Dan Jerabek's ancestors, sought land. Most came from the German-dominated province of Bohemia (hence their designation as "Bohemians"), while others were from Moravia. Whether Bohemians or Moravians, Czechs constitute America's largest population of rural Slavs. Accordingly, their old-world village traditions have evolved more slowly than has been the case for their urban counterparts. Immigrant farmers arrived in Wisconsin first in the 1860s, but they were soon coming to agrarian east-central Texas in large numbers, sailing from the German ports of Bremen and Hamburg to Galveston. Today Texas outranks all other states in the total number of Czech Americans, with Wisconsin, Nebraska, Iowa, and Minnesota next in line. Settling in sufficient numbers to form their own cultural institutions, and often coexisting with immigrant Germans and Poles (their old-world neighbors), rural Czechs tempered the assimilative forces of Anglo-America to establish distinctive regional and ethnic identities (Leary 1995).

The fact that seven-eighths of America's four hundred thousand Czech immigrants arrived between the liberal revolutions of 1848 and the onset of World

War I had an enormous impact on their music. That period coincided with the emergence and pan-European popularity of the polka, the flowering of brass-band music, the career of František Kmoch, the invention and mass production of the accordion, an interest in folksongs among intellectuals, and the association of folksongs and new songs in a folk style with nationalism—all of which profoundly influenced what has become Czech American polka music (Leary 1987a).

Performed by a couple executing a hop-step close-step pattern in 2/4 time, the polka emerged around 1830 in northern Bohemia near the German and Polish borders. Although the dance draws upon earlier ethnically diverse forms, its oft-printed legend of origin, suffused with the era's romantic nationalism, suggests that Anna Slezak, a Bohemian peasant girl in the village of Elbeteinetz, improvised a tune and steps one summer afternoon. The local schoolmaster noticed Slezak's invention, taught it to his students, and sparked an international dance craze (Shaw 1948, 67–69). Certainly the polka had entered the genteel ballrooms of Prague by the mid-1830s; by the mid-nineteenth century, dancing masters had pupils dancing the polka in Vienna, Paris, London, and New York City. Like its couple-dance contemporary, the waltz, the polka was the perfect dance for an immigrant people to carry to new surroundings: rooted in the soil of peasant life, yet valued by the upper classes; an extension of old-world village customs, yet the fashionable rage in modern ballrooms; distinctly Czech, yet internationally adapted (Keil, Keil, and Blau 1992, 10–14).

Although perhaps first played on some combination of fiddles, clarinets, *cymbaly* (hammer dulcimers), or bagpipes, Czech folk instruments of the early 1800s, polka melodies were popularized through military brass bands. A Bohemian regimental brass band was playing polkas in Vienna, the Hapsburg seat of imperial power, as early as 1840. The military influence, technological innovations enabling the mass production of relatively inexpensive standardized instruments, and musical literacy prompted the formation of many late-nineteenth-century village bands, whose members donned military garb and scanned musical staffs while blowing their horns for Sunday afternoon concerts and dances.

František Kmoch, the "Czechoslovak March King," wrote roughly four hundred marches and polkas for brass ensembles during a lifetime extending from 1848 to 1912. A trumpeter who combined traditional melodies with peasant themes and nationalist sentiments, Kmoch popularized his compositions, beginning in the 1870s, through European tours with his own brass band. Sheet music versions of such Kmoch compositions as "Koline, Koline," "Andulka Šafářová," and "Muziky, Muziky" were carried to America by immigrants or purchased here from Midwestern ethnic entrepreneurs. In an era when the martial winds of John Phillip Sousa swayed all Americans, Czech Americans could draw similar inspiration from one of their own (Greene 1992, 50–51).

More humble than the booming brass band, the diatonic button accordion and its instrumental relatives, the concertina and the piano accordion, likewise prospered in the late nineteenth and early twentieth centuries when German and, later, Italian companies produced inexpensive models in quantity. Most of the musicians who strapped on so-called squeezeboxes learned by ear rather than through formal training. With a voice that simultaneously replaced and sustained the reedy bite of bagpipes, the accordion could either accompany a clarinet, a violin, a *cymbalum*, or it could stand alone, a veritable one-man band, as its player punched out melodies with the right hand while articulating bass patterns with the left. Absent on the nineteenth-century village bandshell, the accordion became the central instrument for taverns, house parties, and weddings where revelers sang folksongs in polka and waltz tempos.

The period of Czech immigration to America was, finally, an era when intellectuals throughout Europe documented and celebrated the folksongs of peasants as exemplary of their people's essential spirit. Valued for their indigenous "natural" poetry, these folksongs were also elevated for their proto-nationalist sentiments—sentiments that Slavic foes of the Germanic Hapsburg empire expressed overtly in folk-inspired anthems like "Kde Domov Můj" (Where Is My Home), with its declaration that the old province of Bohemia is "God's country" and the rightful home of Czechs. The patriotic veneration of Czech folksongs was furthered in old world and new by the emergence of liberal-thinking Sokol organizations that, like the German Turners, established halls for the promotion of artistic, athletic, and political activities (Kolar 1979).

As a consequence of their common cultural history, the first generation of Czech Americans shared a fondness for polkas, waltzes, and related couple dances; they formed brass bands that often relied on arrangements written down by composers like Kmoch; they numbered many accordionists among them; and they sang traditional songs in homes and ethnic halls that merged peasant memory with ethnic allegiance.

BRASS BANDS AND BOHEMIAN HALLS

The early experiences of many Wisconsin Czechs exemplify the foregoing musical pattern. Consider Martin and Ludmila Stangle, both born in Bohemia, who immigrated to Ashland, Wisconsin, in 1905 (Leary 1988). Ludmila played harmonica and button accordion by ear. Martin, a clarinetist, could read music. Martin's immigrant baggage, in the recollection of his son, Stanley, included "green books, red books, blue books. And they all had categories of music in each one . . . little notebooks with printed staffs on them . . . schottisches, and waltzes, and polkas." During a three-hour interview in the music room of his Ashland home, Stan Stangle enthusiastically recalled his first instrument, a baritone horn imported from Czechoslovakia, and his dad's improvised instructions.

> I'll never forget that first lesson my dad gave me. He just had a piece of paper, I think it was the back end of a calendar. He made the staff out and

> he wrote the scale for me. I was as tall as the doorknob and that's where he made a slit in the paper and hung it on the doorknob. And he said, "Get this note." And he'd sing it: "Da." Then the next note, first and third valves . . . from there on it was nothing to it. . . . And I loved to practice. There were times when he'd work nights and he'd have to sleep during the day. I'd go out to the woodshed and sit on a coal pile or a stump, or close the barn door, and go to it.

The family soon had a band with Ludmila on button accordion, Martin on clarinet, Stan on trumpet, and a brother and sister on baritone horns.

Besides encouraging the talents of his children, Martin Stangle was a driving force behind his community's Bohemian Brass Band. Ashland in the early twentieth century was a patchwork of ethnic working-class neighborhoods—Norwegian, Swedish, Finnish, Polish, and Czech—stitched east to west near the sawmills and iron-ore docks that hugged the shores of Lake Superior (Leary 1984). Each enclave had one or several organizations. These collective entities, created to sustain ethnic and ideological solidarity, not only offered life insurance, athletic training, cultural programs, and social events, but also erected halls. Ashland's Bohemian Hall, "the jewel of the east side," was erected in 1910 by the ZCBJ or Západni Česko-Bratrská Jednota (Western Fraternal Life Association). It had an ample basement kitchen, a stage with painted backdrops of old-world scenes, and an open space that doubled as gymnasium and the best dance floor in town. Stangle's Bohemian Brass Band, garbed in militaristic, black uniforms and visored caps, held forth in the hall from 1910 through the late 1920s.

In the band's final years, Stan, his brother, and other youngsters filled in for the old timers. Stan Stangle recalled: "about seven members. There was usually two cornets, two clarinets, baritone, tuba—there were no drums, no piano—and peckhorn, maybe two peckhorns. Peckhorn is an upright alto that gives that 'oooh aaah' for rhythm."

With tuba and twin alto horns oompahing a powerful rhythm, and clarinets, baritone horns, and cornets weaving melody and harmony, the band set dancers swirling until the floor shook. "We usually started out with a polka. That gets 'em out on the floor. Oh boy, they can hardly wait. Then a nice waltz. And then there was another type of waltz called the ländler. It was similar to a waltz, almost in the time of a waltz, but it had a different feeling to it. Then we'd go into another polka. We'd even play marches and they'd dance around to that." The band also played the galop, a cousin of the march that is distinguished by its rollicking promenade. Similarly, many polkas and waltzes featured residual elements of marches in introductions and bridges framing the dance melodies.

Dances at the Bohemian Hall welcomed entire families. Before Stan Stangle was old enough to perform, he squirmed with other kids on chairs surrounding the dancers. Parents and grandparents frequently pulled their offspring onto the floor for impromptu lessons. And whenever musicians took a break, Stan and his peers capered and slid across the waxed wood floor, an experience he still relished half a century later: "WHOOSH! We'd skid on our bellies, our new clothes. Our parents didn't think anything of it, because we were having a good time. As long as we behaved, they were having a good time dancing, so we could have a good time too."

Good food and cold beer were always plentiful at Bohemian Hall dances. Band members slaked their thirst by pulling bottles from an iced tub at the back of the stage. Sometimes drink brought mischief, as Stan recalled filling a baritone-horn player's instrument with brew. Beer also inspired songs from the dancers. Braced by several draughts in the hall's basement, old gentlemen, especially, would ascend and crowd in front of the stage singing:

> Má roztomila Baruška" [my beloved Barbara] . . . Oh it was fun. And the old guys would sweat. They'd be all dressed up in the suit they're going to die in and get buried in. And their ties would be over here [askew], you know. And the women would be sitting there staring because the men wouldn't be dancing with them. . . . They'd get their [Stan sings] "Pivo, pivo, pivo červený" [beer, beer, red beer] and they'd down it.

Besides "Baruška" and "Pivo Červený," favorite songs included "Louka Zelená" (Green Meadow), "Červený Šátaček" (Red Handkerchief), "Modre Oči" (Blue Eyes), and "Švestková Alej" (The Prune Song).

The latter, with its typical peasant setting, universal theme, reliance on natural metaphors, and subtle shifts from familiar (Anca/Annie) to formal (Andula/Ann) terms, is perhaps the best-known Czech American song. [Listen to the classic version by Romy Gosz on the website hosting the audio examples.]

> Za naší vesničí, na hlavní silnici, Bosenský rostou švestky. Bájó!
> Ančou jsme hlídali švestky jsme jídali bejvalo, to moc hezký.
> Vždycky jsme sědeli vedle sebe, na hvězdy čučeli a na nebe,
> A tedko sám a sám, na všecko vzpomínám, chtěl bych být blizko tebe.
>
> CHORUS:
> V tej naši aleji, švestky se váleji
> Já dneska nehlídam, oči mně páleji.
>
> Za naší vesnicí, na hlavní silnici, švestky jsou jako pěsti. Bájó!
> Anča nic neřekla, ode mně utekla, ted nemám žad ne štěstí.
> Andula s jiným ted švestky hlídá, už naše providla neuhlídá.
> Dřív tady hvězdičky vidali věcičky, o tom se nepovídá.
>
> CHORUS

Za naší vesnicí, na hlavní silnici, švestky jsou očesány. Bá jó!
Šaty mám v almaře a sjinou na faře, máme to podepsaný.
Snad až se oženim zapomenu, pak ti to Andulo připomenu.
Co jsi to provedla žejsi mně provedla švestky ted nemanj cenu.

CHORUS

Behind our town on the main road, Bosenky, grow plums. Ba jo!
We looked for plums, Annie, we ate plums; it was real nice.
We sat together, we looked at the stars in the sky.
And now, all alone, I remember. I'd like to be close to you.

CHORUS:
In our alley, plums are lying around.
Today I'm not looking, my eyes are burning.

Behind our town on the main road, plums grow as big as fists. Ba jo!
Annie said nothing and ran away, now I have no luck at all.
Ann is looking for plums with someone else, she'll not look on our familiar places anymore.
And little stars of former times saw what happened, nothing more can be said.

Behind our town on the main road, the plums are picked. Ba jo!
I have clothes in the closet and have signed the banns at the parsonage with another girl.
Perhaps when I marry I'll forget, perhaps I'll tell you Ann:
What did you mean when you said that plums have no price?[5]

Just as "Švestkova Alej" has been sung repeatedly, the Stangle family's experiences have been replicated, with slight variation, again and again throughout Wisconsin's Czech enclaves. In the 1940s Helene Stratman-Thomas of the University of Wisconsin's Music Department journeyed for the Library of Congress into the Czech communities of southwestern Wisconsin.[6] In family kitchens and community halls she recorded such standards as "Švestkova Alej," "Baruška," and František Kmoch's "Koline, Koline" from a cappella singers and squeezebox players, as well as polkas and marches from the brassy Yuba Band. [Stratman-Thomas's recording of the wedding polka by the Yuba Band is included on the same website.]

Founded in 1868 by Martin Rott, Sr., who had emigrated from Bohemia to the Richland County hamlet of Yuba, the Yuba Band persisted through the mid-1950s (Levy 1987). The band's performances for life cycle and seasonal events—characteristically complementing religious ceremonies in this overwhelmingly Catholic community—included funerals as well as weddings, and winter frolics as well as summer picnics. Regarding funerals, Helene Stratman-Thomas offered the following in her 1946 journal:

> I was told that the band would precede the hearse and march from the church to the cemetery, a distance of a mile and a half. When I asked the band if they would record one of their funeral marches, they selected "Bohemul," which was the march played for the funeral of . . . Martin Rott [Sr.] in 1932. Although this custom is passing, one elderly lady who was standing near me remarked, "When my husband died, the children didn't think we should have the band, but I insisted. I knew their father wouldn't think it right to be buried without playing the funeral procession." (Peters 1977, 33)

Beyond musical funeral processions, Czech and Catholic performance traditions merge during Masopust, the Czech Mardi Gras: a two-day celebration that precedes the prolonged abstinence of Lent (Barden 1982; Kallio 1987).

Literally translated as "without meat," Masopust occurred on the Monday and Tuesday prior to Ash Wednesday. During a 1991 interview in his Yuba home, Raymond Liska, born in 1913, told me that the festivity's Monday night dance was always a masquerade. "Before midnight everybody paraded around, then three judges would pick out the best." In keeping with old-world village traditions of animal and cross-gender disguise amidst moments of seasonal transition, Ray once deceived even close neighbors by masquerading as a young woman. "I won first prize that year," he told me with mischievous chuckle.

The party continued all day and into the night on Tuesday, especially if there were "no cows to milk." But as the clock struck twelve, music and dancing ceased. Then the revelers blackened each other's faces with burnt corks in rowdy parody of the ashes to be marked on foreheads by the priest the following morning.

POLKA BANDS AND BALLROOMS

Masquerades and ashen faces have vanished from Yuba winters. The custom of musical funeral processions, "passing" in the 1940s, ceased a decade later with the Yuba Band's demise. The gradual decline of Czech speakers and family farms, together with the out-migration and Americanization of younger generations, loosened the venerable hold of seasonal custom and community hall. Yet Yuba's Masopust continues, albeit with a shift to weekend nights in recognition of the participants' clock-bound schedules. Similarly, descendants of Yuba Band members still play Czech music for a new, self-consciously ethnic festival, Český Den (Czech Day), that emerged in the 1970s. Wisconsin's Czechs generally, and its musicians in particular, have found ways to accommodate the changes in American life through the creative transformation of their cultural heritage.

As early as 1870, southwestern Wisconsin Czechs, perhaps some of them members of Martin Rott's Yuba Band, participated in their region's musical ferment with an eclectic fervor that combined the dance repertoires of continental Europeans, Anglo-Celts, and African Americans. As Franco-American Charles Mon Pleasure, a fiddler and sometime house painter, observed in his autobiography:

> When winter [1870] set in, I did not do any painting, but organized a quadrille band of six pieces. At that time we used the old-fashioned post horns [i.e., small European horns that were coiled in a circle and used to announce the arrival of mail coaches] and bugles, so we had the first violin, second violin, double bass, post horn, clarinet, and bugle. They were all Bohemians but myself. I guess we would look like monkeys nowadays [1910] with such a band, but it was all right in those days. The first ball that we played for was for old George F. Switzer, a big old fat Dutchman, a darned good fellow too . . . I had the only quadrille band in Prairie du Chien. Jim Williams, a negro, had a band across the [Mississippi] river at South McGregor [Iowa]. He sometimes played in Prairie du Chien and I would play in McGregor. (Mon Pleasure 1910)

By the early twentieth century, the northeastern Wisconsin Czechs of Manitowoc and Kewaunee Counties had embarked upon musical innovations that rivaled the interest paid to French quadrilles and black performers by Mon Pleasure's Bohemian cohorts.

As was the case in the hinterlands of Ashland and Yuba, these Czechs included squeezebox and brass players, they established ethnic halls, they held Masopust dances, and they observed weddings and funerals with musical processions. In contrast, however, they also drew considerable musical inspiration from their Lake Michigan neighbors in Chicago, where Czechs occupied a niche within that cosmopolitan metropolis.

Exporting such treasured rural commodities as goose down for feather pillows and dried mushrooms for cookery to their ethnic kin in Chicago, northeastern Wisconsin Czechs were recompensed with instruments, sheet music, and sound recordings. Situated on West Eighteenth Street in Chicago's "Little Bohemia," Joseph Jiran's store, established in 1898, was the first of a succession of Czech music businesses operated by such immigrant entrepreneurs as Anton Grill, Louis Vitak, and Joseph Elsnic (Greene 1992, 51–55). Czech musicians from Chicago traveled to New York City in 1911 to make recordings for Columbia. Four years later that label made its first Czech recordings in Chicago, and by the 1920s Chicago bands led by Vaclav Albrecht, Anton Brousek, Vaclav Fiser, Anton Grill, and others had cut scores of 78 rpm discs (Spottswood 1990, vol. 2, 602–8,612–17,625–27,632–33).

Grounded in old-world village traditions, the sheet music and sound recordings of Chicago Czechs were simultaneously urbane, often incorporating elements of American popular music and of Chicago's emergent jazz scene. The influence of these innovations on northeastern Wisconsin communities accelerated in the mid-1920s, when radio stations like Chicago's WLS bombarded the region with a broad musical spectrum. The Manitowoc-Kewaunee area's numerous brass bands began an instrumental transformation: reed players supplemented clarinets with saxophones, the afterbeat of dual alto horns was replaced by a piano or piano accordion, while the new addition of trap drums emphasized dance rhythms. Seven-piece bands became the standard: a front line of two trumpets and two reeds, with reed players switching from clarinet to saxophone, and a rhythm section of piano, drums, and bass horn. The remnants of military band music were diminished by the abandonment of marches and promenading galops. Some bands rejected their old-world repertoire entirely to embrace the popular music of the day. Others performed an occasional "modern" fox trot while grafting a jazzy feel onto older Czech polkas, waltzes, and ländlers (Janda 1976). Like their traditional yet modern southern Anglo-Celtic counterparts, these northern Czech Americans self-consciously promoted their hybrid sound as "old-time music" and, eventually, as polka music.

From the 1930s through the 1950s in particular, many of them made recordings, performed for live radio broadcasts, and traveled a widening dance hall circuit. With the end of Prohibition in 1933, dance halls proliferated throughout ethnic Wisconsin. Typically "mom and pop" operations, they largely superceded the old ethnic halls by combining the functions of a tavern, weekend eatery, and community hall. Despite fierce competition, there were enough musicians and dancers to keep the floors filled. When interviewing the area's Czech musicians in 1988 for a Wisconsin Public Radio documentary on their musical scene, I heard many poetic testimonies of the sort offered by Jerome Wojta, a polka disc jockey on Kewaunee's WAUN and the leader of a Czech polka band, the Two Creeks Farmhands:

> We'd go to country dances. And a typical country dance would consist of people of all ages. This was everyone from the grandchild to the grandmother. You could go to a dance each night of the week.
>
> It's really hard to tell someone who hasn't experienced it what it was really like. When you get a group of people going, and happy, and dancing, it would be just like watching big waves on the sea.

Wojta's home Manitowoc County, likewise the territory of Tuba Dan Jerabek, boasted twenty such dancehalls, with evocative and personal names like Terrace

Gardens, Peterson's Modernistic Ballroom, Forst's New Hall, the Maribel Ballroom, and Romy's Ballroom.

JUMP AND TOSS WITH ROMY GOSZ

Romy's Ballroom, situated at a crossroads called Polivka's Corners, was run by Romy Gosz, the leading exponent of northeastern Wisconsin's updated Czech American polka sound. Roman Louis Gosz was born in 1911 in Rockwood, north of Manitowoc. His father, Paul, ran a family band that sometimes doubled as a basketball team, playing for both local sporting events and dances in the early 1920s. By 1928, Romy had taken over the band, and he made his first recordings in 1931 for Port Washington, Wisconsin's Broadway label. Gosz was recording in Chicago two years later.

From his first session to his death in 1966, Romy Gosz recorded roughly 170 tunes on the Broadway, Brunswick, Columbia, Decca, King, Mercury, Mono, OKeh, Polka King, Polkaland, and Vocalion labels. Playing for countless dances in the Manitowoc area, Gosz also barnstormed throughout Wisconsin: south to Milwaukee and Watertown, north to Green Bay and Wausau, and west to Stevens Point. He performed on radio and television and was pronounced the "polka king" by both his followers and such national magazines as *Coronet* and *Time* (Greene 1992, 164–67; Janda 1976, 6–7; March 1991, 391–93).

Originally a piano player, Gosz won admirers with his trumpet. Czech bandleader Jerome Wojta, himself a trumpet player, expressed awe: "Romy Gosz had a style all his own. His tone was clear and penetrating. He had a very good lip, a lip of steel. His music was smooth, it was humorous. A fellow like Romy comes along once in every five hundred years." The overall Gosz style was distinguished by a slow tempo, a dignified pace, and a heavy feel anchored by a stolid tuba. A piano, or increasingly the more portable piano accordion, contributed rhythm and fills but seldom took a lead voice. Gosz's trumpet, often in chorus with a second trumpet and saxophones, introduced the melody, with clarinets frequently answering a phrase or chiming in with a countermelody. Ethnomusicologist Charles Keil has written of "Romy's buttery tone, vibrato, [and] loose surging phrases," aspects of instrumental articulation that folklorist Richard March suggests draw upon a prior Czech folk aesthetic that emphasizes rather than minimizes the natural slurring "whaaa" of the trumpet and the tendency of clarinets toward reedy quavering, not clear bell-like tones (Keil 1982, 55; March 1991, 392; March in Leary and March 1996, 76–78). [Listen to "Švestková Alej" on the website hosting the audio examples.] In this way the rough, passionate old-country edges of Gosz's instrumental attack merged with the hot, bluesy intonations of African American jazz. In keeping with Jazz Age conventions the Gosz band played chiefly instrumentals or sang truncated versions of traditional songs in the latter half of a given performance. The singers' harmonies, like those of jazz brethren, were at once well conceived and imbued with a loose feeling echoing the horns' controlled abandon.

Much to the chagrin of the region's high school band teachers—who have favored round notes and square rhythms, while valuing external rather than local traditions—Romy Gosz inspired young musicians throughout northeastern Wisconsin, and his influence remains powerful thirty years after his death. Like Kentucky's Bill Monroe, whose pioneering Blue Grass Boys provided both a standard and a training ground for subsequent bluegrass generations; like Muddy Waters, who inspired legions of urban performers with his amplified update of Delta blues, Romy Gosz and his band spawned fervent disciples. Since the 1930s a succession of bandleaders, some of them former sidemen, have built upon the Gosz sound.

Many of them—Larry Hlinak, Dan Jerabek, Mark Jirikovic, Jimmy Nejedlo, Rudy Plocar, Jerome Wojta, Louie Zdrazil—have been of Czech heritage, but perhaps more have been German Americans: Elroy Berkholtz, the Greiner Brothers, Gene Heier, Joe Karman, Ludger Karman, Quirin Kohlbeck, Bob Kuether, Gordy Reckelberg, Don Schliess, Harold Schultz, Tom Siebold, Jerry Voelker. Such cross-ethnic affinity for Czech music may be partially attributed to old-country roots in the mixed Czech and German villages of southwestern Bohemia (Rippley 1992, 5–8). When nineteenth-century German immigrants settled northeastern Wisconsin in tandem with their old-world Czech neighbors, their already established musical synergy persisted. The wind-driven Pilsen Brass Band, for example, was northeastern Wisconsin's most prominent old-style Bohemian band in the decades prior to the modern transformations wrought by Romy Gosz (Janda 1976, 2). Its members' surnames balance the Czech (Janda, Nejedlo, Sladky) with the German (Altman, Schliess, Suess).

More than anything else, however, Gosz's sound and his memorable public performances inspired allegiance irrespective of ethnicity. As Russ Zimmerman, a Swiss American, explained in liner notes for the album *Old Bohemian Memories* (K-2039), recorded in the 1960s for Sauk City, Wisconsin's Cuca Records: "This album is truly a collection of good-time Bohemian melodies that were originally recorded many years ago by the famous 'Polka King' and were accepted by the public, nationwide, as the most popular songs of the era." With its insular assumption that all readers will understand the royal reference to Romy Gosz, its equation of an ethnic sound with American popular music, and its hopeful expansion of a regional fan base to include the entire nation, Zimmerman's comments amply demonstrate the power of Gosz, at least in his home territory, to command loyalty and transcend boundaries. The Gosz legacy came to be the collective heritage of all the people of northeastern Wisconsin.

Consider the experience in the 1960s of a youthful Cletus Bellin, a Belgian American, who, like fellow ethnics Marvin Brouchoud and Gene LeBotte, was charmed by Gosz-inspired music. Growing up in that northeastern Wisconsin "border country" where Czechs and Germans intermingle with members of

America's largest settlement of Walloon Belgians, Clete Bellin learned to speak his ethnic elders' Walloon French dialect as well as English. His region's musical language and lineage, however, was decidedly Czech.

> I first started playing polka music with a local band, and we used to play in the Czech villages and Czech settlements in my neighborhood. Especially if we played one of the popular Czech songs . . . people would come to the bandstand and say, "Why don't you sing it? You have a beautiful voice." I used to tell them, "I don't know the Czech language?" Well, they told me, "You should learn?" So from that point on, I made it a kind of a life endeavor.

Bellin sought out a Kewaunee County tavernkeeper, Ella Warczyk, who came "from a family of exceptionally good Czech musicians and singers" in the hamlet of Slovan. He asked her to teach him the correct pronunciation of Czech songs; she was delighted to comply, and Bellin proved a dedicated student. From the 1990s until his death in 2010, the Clete Bellin Band, featuring its leader's vocals, was northeastern Wisconsin's premier Czech polka band.

A REAL CZECH ORCHESTRA

While Clete Bellin and his contemporaries sustained the Gosz legacy, they also departed from it in ways that matched the changing context of Czech polka music in Wisconsin—and beyond. Romy Gosz's modernization of Czech music beginning in the 1930s was paralleled by other performers throughout Czech America. In eastern Nebraska, for example, a greater number of Czechs worked the button accordion into their bands, and they were far more likely than the jazz-smitten Gosz to sing full, not incidental, versions of Czech songs. In Texas Czech communities, polka bands likewise favored singing, and they often fused their sound fascinatingly with the western swing and honky-tonk music of Anglo-Celtic neighbors (Machann 1983). Like Wisconsin's Romy Gosz, many Nebraska and Texas Czechs made recordings and, branching out on radio and the ballroom circuit, expanded their local followings to the surrounding territory.

Not surprisingly, Czech bands from distant American regions began to cross paths. Contact was, at first, largely through recordings and radio airplay. But beginning in the 1970s, the growing phenomenon of polka festivals regularly lured fellow polka travelers from around the country. Attributable both to an ongoing ethnic revival movement that gained momentum during America's 1976 bicentennial and to the new mobility of retirement-aged ethnic Americans raised on polka music, the polka festival also filled the void created by the gradual decline of ballrooms from their zenith in the early 1950s. Trans-regional musical exchanges accelerated between Czech polka bands. Vocalist Clete Bellin, for example, was attracted by the singing Nebraska bands, incorporating elements from their repertoires to treat his Wisconsin audiences to something new.

During the 1980s and early 1990s, the gradual dissolution of the "Iron Curtain," Czechoslovakia's "velvet revolution," and the eventual creation of the Czech Republic resulted in an increase of transatlantic cultural exchanges. Czech Americans traveled to the old country and Czechs visited America. Some American polka bands organized tours to their ancestral homes, while state-sponsored Czech musical aggregations launched extensive tours to the mostly rural communities of Czech America. Recruited from the most virtuosic of village performers, garbed in generalized regional folk costumes and expertly playing an "authentic" repertoire sanctioned by ethnologists, such all-star groups as Moravanka made a powerful impression on their new-world kin through highly structured concert performances intended to conjure the essence of Czech folkness.

The impact of such culturally imbued showmanship on Czech American audiences and musicians, including those in Wisconsin, was immediate. Clete Bellin concurred when I interviewed him just after a festival gig in October 1995: "Moravanka, when they toured the country, were a big popular hit, so people asked me, 'Clete, will you do some of those songs?'"

It was not enough to do them, they had to be done right. Soon Bellin was not only buying the group's recordings but incorporating critical elements of its style into the musical attack of his own band. "I wanted a real Czech orchestra like the Czech country bands in Europe. I wanted to play the Czech music as close to the original style as you possibly can, with the Czech tempos and the Czech vocals." Unlike many Czech American bands who favor shortened renditions of old country originals, or whose performances fuse several styles, the Bellin Band was committed to the characteristic Czech emphasis on full versions that frame familiar melodies with distinct introductions and choruses.

Clete Bellin's emulation of such polished contemporary old-world troupes as Moravanka won him followers beyond the normal sphere of Czech American polka enthusiasts. Like any other ethnic group, Czech Americans include upper-class or upwardly mobile members with rigid notions of authenticity and quality. For them, Czech American compositions are akin to the bastard offspring of noble stock: of questionable lineage since they did not originate fully in the Czech homeland. For them, folk music, whether Czech or Czech American, is likewise crude stuff, rendered worthy only through the refined transformations of classical composers like Antonín Dvořák and Bedřich Smetana, or through the more populist, but no less carefully arranged, works of "march kings" like František Kmoch.

From this strongly held, albeit not widely shared, perspective, the Clete Bellin Band stood at the tip of the Wisconsin Czech polka pyramid—a point brought forcefully to my attention in the spring of 1995. The Smithsonian Institution was preparing for the summer Festival of American Folklife, which would include participants from the Czech Republic for two weeks on the national mall in Washington, D.C. Aware of my work in Wisconsin, and wishing to include a Czech

American band, the Smithsonian's senior ethnomusicologist, Tom Vennum, asked for my advice. I recommended the Clete Bellin Band *and* the Tuba Dan Band as the leading candidates. Vennum wondered if one was playing soon, so that he might hear for himself. As it happened, the Tuba Dan Band was playing near my home that weekend. Tom flew out, was delighted, and booked the group. He was also very impressed with the tape I played of the Clete Bellin Band. Yet, given the logistical complications of organizing a festival, the serendipitous face-to-face encounter with Tuba Dan carried more weight. Within a few weeks, however, after word of the invitation had circulated, Vennum received a letter from the head of a small Wisconsin Czech cultural organization. Citing classical music credentials, the writer offered his services regarding who ought or ought not be included in the Festival of American Folklife. He went on to laud the authenticity and quality of Clete Bellin's Band, while deriding Tuba Dan's music as a crude hodgepodge.

Tom Vennum called for my advice before declining the writer's help with polite firmness. From my own point of view—I told Vennum as I would tell anyone—the Tuba Dan and Clete Bellin bands were both equally remarkable, equally legitimate. Both moved in musical directions that were simultaneously fresh and familiar. Like polka bands throughout America, and certainly in Wisconsin, both approached the twenty-first century with their sonic coordinates fixed on the old-world past and the new-world present.

Indeed, Czech American polka music, like any other vibrant musical tradition, flows in more than one direction. Drawing upon the exuberant brass bands and village songs of immigrants, the jazz-tempered innovations of Romy Gosz, and the classicized memorialization of folk music by those who stayed in Europe, Wisconsin Czech polka bands, each in their own way, not only persist but continue to evolve.

Notes

1. Legislation was sponsored by State Senator Gary Drzwiecki, a Polish American from Pulaski in northeastern Wisconsin and a polka musician proficient on the German or Chemnitzer concertina.

2. Lawrence Welk, whose television program persisted through reruns four decades after its origin in the 1950s, came to represent in the popular media all that is cornball and saccharine about polka music. It is worth pointing out, however, that, although Welk's roots *were* in the German-Russian polka traditions of North Dakota, he was not really a polka musician, but essentially a practitioner of "sweet" jazz and pop music.

3. Some of the research for this essay was conducted from 1978 through 1996 in connection with public folklore projects undertaken or funded by the Cedarburg Cultural Center, the Minnesota Historical Society, the Folk Arts Program of the National Endowment for the Arts, the Smithsonian Institution's Office of Folklife and Cultural Studies, the Wisconsin Arts Board, the Wisconsin Folk Museum, and the Wisconsin Humanities Council. I thank these organizations for their support.

4. Unless otherwise indicated, all quotations from musicians are drawn from tape-recorded interviews conducted by the author. Full citations appear in the list of interviews that follows.

5. Czech lyrics and translations are by Clara Belsky Sveda of Ashland, Wisconsin; originally published in Leary 1986.

6. On August 19, 1941, Stratman-Thomas recorded Czech musicians in Prairie du Chien; Archives of Folksong (AFS) discs 5020-5022, 5025. She also recorded musicians in Yuba on September 25, 1946; AFS 8436-8439 (see also Leary 1987b; Peters, 28, 33).

Chapter 2: Musical Examples (access through companion website)

Chapter 2. Track 1. Romy Gosz, "The Prune Song."
Chapter 2. Track 2. Yuba Bohemian Band, "Wedding Polka."

Interviews (All interviews were recorded by James P. Leary)

Bellin, Cletus. 1995. Cedarburg, Wisconsin, 7 October.
Jerabek, Dan ("Tuba Dan"). 1988. Appleton, Wisconsin, 4 May.
———. 2011. Dodgeville, Wisconsin, 21 August.
Liska, Raymond. 1991. Hillsboro, Wisconsin, 9 March.
Stangle, Stanley. 1980. Ashland, Wisconsin, 6 November.
Wojta, Jerome. 1988. Two Creeks, Wisconsin, 3 May.

References Cited

Barden, Thomas. 1982. "The Yuba Masopust Festival." *Midwestern Journal of Language and Folklore* 8, no. 1: 48–51.

Baron, Robert, and Nicholas Spitzer. 1992. *Public Folklore.* Washington: Smithsonian Institution Press.

Bohlman, Philip V. 1988. *The Study of Folk Music in the Modern World.* Bloomington: Indiana University Press.

Feintuch, Burt. 1988. *The Conservation of Culture: Folklorists in the Public Sector.* Lexington: University Press of Kentucky.

Greene, Victor. 1992. *A Passion of Polka: Old-Time Ethnic Music in America.* Berkeley: University of California Press.

Janda, Robert. 1976. "Entertainment Tonight: An Account of Bands in Manitowoc County Since 1900." *Occupational Monograph* 28. Manitowoc, WI: Manitowoc County Historical Society.

Kallio, Sandra. 1987. "In Yuba, It's Masopust." *Wisconsin State Journal*, 18 February, section 3:1.

Keil, Charles. 1982. "Slovenian Style in Milwaukee." In *Folk Music and Modern Sound*, ed. William Ferris and Mary L. Hart. Jackson: University Press of Mississippi. 32–59.

Keil, Charles, Angeliki V. Keil, and Dick Blau. 1992. *Polka Happiness.* Philadelphia: Temple University Press.

Kolar, Roger. 1979. "Early Czech Dance Halls in Texas." In *The Czechs in Texas: A Symposium*, ed. Clinton Machann. College Station: Texas A&M University College of Liberal Arts. 122–27.

Leary, James P. 1984. "Old Time Music in Northern Wisconsin." *American Music* 2, no. 1: 71–88.

———. 1986. "Accordions in the Cutover." Booklet to accompany the double LP listed below. Ashland, WI: Northland College.

———. 1987a. "Czech Polka Styles in the U.S.: From America's Dairyland to the Lone Star State." In *Czech Music* in *Texas*, ed. Clinton Machann. College Station, TX: Komensky Press. 79–95.

———. 1987b. *The Wisconsin Patchwork: A Companion to the Radio Programs Based on the Field Recordings of Helene Stratman-Thomas.* Madison: University of Wisconsin, Department of Continuing Education in the Arts.

———. 1988. "Brass Bands and the Bohemian Hall." *Folklife of the Upper Midwest* 4, no. 3: 4–5.

———. 1991. "Polka Music, Ethnic Music: A Report on Wisconsin's Polka Traditions." *Wisconsin Folk Museum Bulletin* 1. Mount Horeb, WI: Wisconsin Folk Museum.

———. 1995. "Poppies, Pillows, and Polkas: Czech American Folk Culture." In *1995 Festival of American Folklife*, ed. Carla M. Borden. Washington: Smithsonian Institution Center for Folklife Programs and Cultural Studies. 58–59.

———. 2006. *Polkabilly: How the Goose Island Ramblers Redefined American Folk Music.* NYC: Oxford University Press.

Leary, James P., and Richard March. 1996. *Down Home Dairyland: A Listener's Guide.* Madison: University of Wisconsin-Extension.

Levy, Marcella. 1987. "Richland Ramblings." *Richland Observer*, three-week series: 12, 19, 26 February.

Machann, Clinton. 1983. "Country Western Music and the 'Now' Sound in Texas-Czech Polka Music." *JEMF Quarterly* 19, no. 69 (Spring): 3–7.

March, Richard. 1991. "Polkas in Wisconsin Music." In *The Illustrated History of Wisconsin Music, 1840-1990*, ed. Michael Corenthal. Milwaukee: Yesterday's Memories. 385–97.

Mon Pleasure, Charles W. 1910. *Adventures of a Violinist: The Autobiography of Charles W. Mon Pleasure.* Originally serialized in the *Platteville Witness and Mining Times*, typescript copy courtesy of Alan D. Goff, Fort Wayne, IN.

Peters, Harry. 1977. *Folksongs Out of Wisconsin.* Madison: State Historical Society of Wisconsin.

Rake, Jamie Lee. 2011. "Copper Box's Polka Fusion." *Shepherd Express*, April 6.

Rippley, LaVern J. 1992. *The Whoopee John Wilfahrt Dance Band: His Bohemian-German Roots.* Northfield, MN: St. Olaf College German Department.

Shaw, Lloyd. 1948. *The Round Dance Book.* Caldwell, ID: Caxton.

Slobin, Mark. 1993. *Subcultural Sounds: Micromusics of the West.* Hanover, NH: University Press of New England.

Spottswood, Richard K. 1990. *Ethnic Music on Records: A Discography of Ethnic Recordings Produced in the United States 1893-1942.* Vol. 2. Urbana: University of Illinois Press.

Additional Recommended Recordings

Deep Polka: Dance Music from the Midwest. Smithsonian Folkways CD 40088.

Deeper Polka. Smithsonian Folkways CD 40140.

Down Home Dairyland. Half-hour radio programs on "The Manitowoc Bohemian Sound" and "Czech and Slovak Music in Wisconsin." University of Wisconsin Press.

Golden Horns on Green Fields: Czech Polka Music from the Midwest. Polkaland Records CD 639.

Texas Czech: Historic Recordings 1929-1959. Arhoolie CD 7026.

- 3 -

KITCHEN RACKET, CÉILÍ, AND PUB SESSION

Traditional Irish Music in Boston, Massachusetts

Ann Morrison Spinney

Although its genesis is most strongly felt along the Eastern Seaboard from Boston down to Philadelphia, Irish American music is among the oldest and most widely spread forms of vernacular music in the United States. As early as the seventeenth century, Irish music became incorporated into our musical vocabulary and remains an inspiration for artists as varied as Bill Monroe and the Dropkick Murphys. This essay focuses on Irish music in Boston, both as an historical artifact and as a vital musical and cultural expression in the twenty-first century. Throughout her essay, Spinney carefully examines and emphasizes the support this ever-evolving music receives from local cultural and educational institutions as well as the importance of informal community-based music making that occurs in contexts as varied as informal sessions held in people's homes to the semi-formal ones hosted by clubs and bars in and around Boston.

Note: All the Irish musical terms are defined, with audio clips of correct pronunciation, on the website of Comhaltas Ceoltóirí Éireann, http://comhaltas.ie/glossary/

INTRODUCTION

Irish folk music is one of the oldest European traditions transported to North America. Its dance tunes and song airs were among the popular musics brought over by settlers beginning in the seventeenth century, and many of these pieces contributed to American musical genres such as old-time and bluegrass. The tune "Soldier's Joy" is an example: the American version has diverged from the Irish version but both are part of what scholars call "a tune family."

Performances of traditional Irish music in America are not well documented before the middle of the nineteenth century. By the 1870s, activities of local Irish social organizations were reported in the society pages of Boston newspapers. However, the folk music tradition, because it had been associated with the lower

3.1. Musicians at the Green Briar Restaurant (Brighton, MA) session, spring 2014. Photo by Deb Carleton.

economic classes in Ireland, was dismissed until antiquarians and then Irish nationalists took an interest in it. Because the majority of Irish immigrants to the Boston area were of low status—servants, small farmers, and itinerant tradesmen—their cultural contributions were ignored until famines in the 1840s forced large numbers of Irish to migrate across the Atlantic as passengers or ballast on British shipping routes (Handlin 1991, 49–50). The destitute condition of these migrants provoked a good deal of social and political commentary, and soon stereotypes of Irish people flourished in North American popular culture. Names such as Paddy (from Pádraig) were attached to cartoon and stage characters, who spoke in brogue, were dressed in rags, and behaved foolishly.

Traditional music was one of the cultural characteristics most lampooned, which (ironically) also made it popular. For example, the music hall song "Tim Finnegan's Wake" included a vignette of dancing in its chorus and vocables imitating the driving fiddle style:

Whack fol the da, now, dance to your partner
Welt the floor, your trotters shake
Wasn't it the truth I tell you
Lots of fun at Finnegan's wake

This song, popular on both sides of the Atlantic from the mid-nineteenth century to the present, codified a widespread assumption that, in Irish culture, music, drinking, and fighting were bound together and considered good sport

(Williamson 1996, 75); and since the song text describes a funeral it mocks the religious practice of Irish folk as well. Contemporary bands including the Dropkick Murphys and Great Big Sea have recorded the song recently, and many versions can be found on YouTube.

My Morrison ancestors came to the area in a small group of farmers, fleeing the severe famine of 1840. They departed from the port of Belfast in Northern Ireland, and settled together in "the North Parish" of Bridgewater, which became Brockton, Massachusetts. The original group probably kept to themselves, although their children intermarried, a pattern of migration and settlement typical of the time (K. Miller 1985, 151–55).[1]

So many Irish emigrants came to Boston that it became known in Ireland as "the next parish over." Even The Beatles' 1964 film *A Hard Day's Night* contains a scene in which John Lennon advises Paul McCartney's film grandfather, "You should have gone west to America. You would have been a senior citizen of Boston." In fact, during the twentieth century people traveled back and forth, creating a transnational Irish musical culture in Boston. Interviewees recalled returning to Ireland every few years by boat or plane to maintain family ties. Musicians who resided in Boston for a significant time before returning to Ireland include Joe Cooley (accordion), Paddy Cronin (fiddle), and Tommy Peoples (fiddle). Singer Simon "Frank" Forde recounted his family's experience:

> Ballinasloe . . . that's where I was born [in 1926]. I had four brothers and four sisters, and myself, nine . . . Andy, he was the youngest. He's out here . . . I came here [for the first time] the tenth of June 1949. My father was an American citizen, because he came out here in 1912. He came back [to Ireland] in 1921, and he got married to my mother. She was much younger than him. I forget now, she was twenty—twenty something, he was fifty something. (Forde 2011)

By the mid-twentieth century, the term "Boston Irish" was synonymous with an ethnic enclave centered in South Boston. Their political shenanigans were captured in the song lyrics "Vote early and often for Curley," about mayor James Michael Curley. Their image as a tight-knit community was reinforced by the school busing crisis of the 1970s, when predominantly Irish neighborhoods resisted school integration, and the spectacular career of gangster James "Whitey" Bulger, who was on the FBI's "Most Wanted List" from 1995 until his arrest in 2011. Yet this tight-knit community also served as a launching pad for the careers of national politicians: the Kennedys and Thomas "Tip" O'Neill.

In the 2010 Federal Census, 15 percent of the population in the City of Boston claimed Irish ancestry. In several of Boston's suburbs, the proportion ranged between 45 and 49 percent. These figures show that the Irish were assimilated to the extent that those who became citizens followed the post–World War II migration of upwardly-mobile European Americans to the suburbs.

With their long presence, proportionally large numbers, and strong sense of identity, Boston's Irish American community seems ideally situated to have created a distinctive musical sub-style as they adapted their inherited traditions to their new situation. One of the features of this musical sub-style are regional identities emphasized both in Irish culture and in the music, as the many songs mentioning specific places attest, for example, "Galway Bay" and "Rose of Tralee." Features that define a regional style within traditional Irish music include the emphasis of certain instruments, for example the concertina in County Clare; certain types of tunes, such as the slides associated with County Kerry; "switches" or "sets" (habitual groupings of tunes as in a classical music suite), that differ from place to place; the "feel" or "groove" of the rhythm patterns, which are short and driven in County Donegal; and a preference for specific melodic ornaments over others, such as the "rolls" players from County Sligo will add where others play single-tone "cuts" in front of a main tone. (Examples of these ornaments are given at the end of this chapter.)

While many point to these musical details as distinctive of a particular place and its musicians, none of these features, individually or in combination, are sufficient to define the style, because the existence—or nonexistence—of a regional style is as much a social fact as a musical one (O'Shea 2008, 53–77). Nevertheless, during the last century recordings, broadcasts, and travelling performers demonstrated that the music as played in Kerry, Clare, Galway, Sligo, Donegal, and other geographic regions such as Sliabh Luachra (a mountain range) could be distinguished. Irish government cultural initiatives have helped support these local traditions, and the variety of traditional music that can be experienced across the island is publicized by the Irish tourism industry.

Further, these regional styles were established in different American locations, either through large numbers of immigrants from one part of Ireland settling there together or through the residence of an influential player. Thus in the area of St. John's, Newfoundland, one can hear the legacy of settlers from Waterford (Osborne 2013); while in New York City the Sligo style is prominent, passed down from fiddler Michael Coleman to American-born Andy McGann and from him to another generation, who have in turn taught it to their students.[2]

So, we might wonder, is there a particular style of traditional Irish music associated with Boston? This question was the focus of interviews I carried out between 2009 and 2012. Boston's most celebrated Irish American accordionist Joe Derrane had titled his 2004 album *The Boston Edge*, a phrase with which a listener described his playing. However, he considers its implications somewhat of a joke, and many of the musicians, singers, dancers, and listeners whom I interviewed for this study pointed out elements specific to traditional Irish music in Boston without drawing the conclusion that there is any particular style associated with Boston, either indigenous or imported. Some, like Joe, flatly rejected the idea of a Boston style. But arguably, these "non-findings" show how important conceptual components are in maintaining a traditional music. They reveal that the concept "what we are doing is Irish" has shaped traditional Irish music as a regional, national, and transnational practice.

The two other generally acknowledged components in maintaining a traditional music are behavior and sound.[3] In these domains we can demonstrate that features of the traditional Irish music played in Boston are the product of this city's peculiar history and social structure. Most notable is the impact of Boston's highly regarded university music departments and conservatories on traditional Irish musicians. This was emphasized by many of the people I interviewed. Two developments from this influence are now evident in Irish music worldwide.

First, several generations of musicians active in traditional Irish music in Boston trained at these institutions, and brought skills such as arranging to the traditional music bands that were hired for weddings and community events. Recently, academic and conservatory teachers have been encouraging their students to blend classical music and various traditional ethnic musics including Irish. Currently some of the leading traditional Irish musicians are on the faculty at Boston-area conservatories and colleges. The players trained here bring some of these influences with them wherever they play. This newly conscious mixing of style elements only continues the effects of immigration to Boston, which placed earlier generations of Irish musicians alongside French Canadians and Scottish Cape Bretoners in the Catholic parishes, neighborhoods, and kitchens where they collaborated to produce recreational music all could appreciate.

Second, over decades Boston has been known for its large open "sessions," rather than for specific Irish bands such as flourished in New York City (Joyce 2009). This peculiarity of the music in Boston was extended into "slow sessions" to accommodate learners at the Gaelic Roots summer school of Boston College, and it immediately took root in local pubs (Connolly 2013). There is now an international network of slow sessions.

A session (or seisiún, in Gaelic) is a gathering of traditional Irish musicians to play music together. Sessions are the principal site where tunes and styles of playing are shared. They fulfill social functions primarily—reinforcing connections between individuals and families, and community norms—although participating may also fulfill an individuals' needs for self-expression.[4] A session may include singing, usually solo or with the group joining in on refrains; story telling; and dancing sometimes accompanies the instrumental music if there is space.

The instruments played in sessions are emblematic of Irish music: fiddle, flute, tin whistle, accordion, concertina, and the bodhrán drum. Also likely to be played are instruments more recently adapted to Irish music, such as six-stringed guitar, tuned DADGAD; banjo with only four strings; and the Greek bouzouki, modified with a flattened back. The uilleann pipes and harp, formerly associated with the Irish aristocracy and requiring more maintenance and commitment to play, are now often used in sessions although traditionally these were played solo. The "small instruments"—harmonica, one-handed bones, and spoons—may be played as well.

The repertory played in sessions consists of reels, jigs, slip jigs, hornpipes, marches, waltzes, polkas, mazurkas, and barn dances. Like the instruments used, some of these dance genres originated outside of Ireland but have been taken over into the traditional music. Irish musical genres are distinguished by specific meters and rhythm patterns. Most tunes are in two or more sections, each section usually made up of eight bars or measures; each section is repeated, then the whole will be repeated two or three times. The tunes then are strung together in sets of two to four, usually all of the same type, for example all jigs or all reels. The melody is played continuously by everyone in a loose unison with little or no harmonies or chords. There are no solo "breaks" as in bluegrass. One or two players may play the entirety of a slow air, however; these melodies are drawn from the old songs in Irish known as sean-nós (old style).

What all participants—listeners and players—seek in a session is the transcendent, trancelike experience of losing their sense of self in the melody. When musicians achieve this, whether they are playing slow or fast, it is magical for all present. It can inspire a sense of connection to the immediate community, to the homeland, to ancestors, to historical events and legends; these are some of the feelings expressed in interviews. Clearly, sessions fulfill an important psychological function for Irish and Irish Americans, and for the musicians of other heritages who have adopted and mastered the music.

Today in Boston, self-identity is what drives the majority of participants in traditional Irish music, even though their Irish ancestry may be fractional. Children are most likely to participate because of family ties to the music, however they may learn—even master—styles from their teachers that are not directly connected to their ancestral roots in Ireland. Emphasizing the adaptation to locale that I find to be a constant in traditional Irish music, one American interviewee described the challenge of playing music in her family's home town, and her delight at finding compatibility with players from her teacher's home town: "I started learning . . . we'd be playing céilídhs [i.e., dances], all those polkas and stuff, all Leitrim and Sligo waltzes and everything. My Dad was from [another county] . . . in the summers we'd go over there. I wouldn't fit in. Sat down in a session first time in Sligo, said, 'O my God!' Felt so good. I knew all the switches, all the tunes" (Anonymous A, 2009).

Sessions are not an ancient phenomenon, however strongly they are associated with Irish traditions; and the word is possibly borrowed from American jazz, which reached Ireland via American Armed Forces Radio during World War II. Writing about Ireland, Colin Hamilton notes: "the session developed at the same time as the pub became an important feature in Irish social life, this essentially a post-WW2 phenomenon" (Vallely 1999, 345). Sessions in public accommodations first supplemented gatherings in homes, then largely replaced them as the working classes moved from the country into city apartments, or became migrant workers.

In Boston, sessions did not become a phenomenon until the 1960s, when bars in the Irish neighborhoods started promoting them to accommodate small groups of dancers. This occurred as the ballroom dance halls clustered around Dudley Square were closing due to changing popular music tastes (Reynolds 2009). By the 1970s sessions were flourishing in immigrant neighborhoods, attracting many high-caliber traditional musicians to the area.

It was not until the 1990s that sessions became ensconced in the restaurants and bars central to Boston's tourist and nightlife districts as a primary means for outsiders to experience "Boston Irish" culture. As traditional Irish music gained more exposure, partly driven by broader cultural trends such as the popularity of the touring show *Riverdance*, sessions proliferated, resulting in the different types of traditional Irish music sessions operating in Boston today that will be described below. I moved to Boston in 1989 for graduate study, and this is how I reconnected with the tradition I was raised in. Though I grew up playing the tin whistle and singing along at social gatherings, and my father taught a course on "Folklore of the British Isles" and advised the folk music club at the college where he taught anthropology, I did not study traditional music or ballads seriously until my peers began attending sessions.

Many elements are required in order for sessions to thrive in a community, including venues willing to host them, transportation options to the venues, participants with time and resources to play music, and a group of people with a common repertory and compatible styles of playing. Sessions in Boston have been supported by a social and economic network that developed over the several centuries Irish people have lived and settled here. Cultural changes, economic shifts, technological developments, and influential individuals have all shaped traditional Irish music in Boston. Since many of these elements are part of the social structure of Boston, the history of the city, as well as of its Irish residents and their American descendants, provide important data for understanding this musical community.

HISTORICAL CONTEXT

Historians generally agree that the Irish people and their descendants faced peculiar constraints in the Boston area (Kenny 2000, 228). The city, and surrounding Massachusetts Bay Colony, were established and developed in the early 1600s, contemporaneous with brutal conflicts between the English and the Irish. Historical documents show that the colonial governors did not welcome Irish people and few were allowed in, even as servants (See Edmonds 1916).[5] The colonies were forced into more open policies by their need for workers.

English laws did not give full citizenship to people who were not members of the established church, and they were often forced into separate settlements (see Lilley 2002).[6] This precedent was followed even in the American colonies, and placed Irish Catholics and Presbyterians into lower social ranks. The Catholic Church became a focal point of criticisms directed at Irish immigrants to the

Boston area, stoked by nearly a century of wars between the English and French colonies in America. The first Mass in Boston was in 1788, at the establishment of a parish for French and Irish Catholics, after the French had proven to be good allies in the War for Independence. Previous to this it was illegal to conduct Catholic services in Boston, though they were held in private (Shea 1857).[7]

Before their War for Independence the position of the American colonies was similar to Ireland's in relation to Great Britain. Trade restrictions limited what the colonies could export, and to where; manufacturing also was curtailed in order to bolster British industries. Thus, Irish interest in the American conflict is well documented by historians, and evidence even appears in music, with tune titles such as "The Rights of Man" and song lyrics that borrow the American symbol of the Liberty Tree—an actual tree in Boston (Zimmermann 2002, 38–41). However, Irish efforts at rebellion came to a chaotic, unsuccessful head in 1798 that left the country politically divided. The War of 1812, which ended in February 1815, firmly established independent American industries that were attractive to restive Irish workers. The almost simultaneous end of the Napoleonic Wars in Europe threw Britain and Ireland into an economic recession, sending many unemployed artisans across the Atlantic (Handlin 1991, 31–32; Kenny 2000, 50–52). Even unskilled laborers were needed for construction projects around Boston (O'Connor 1995, 35).

Shipping records and census figures for Boston show the ebbs and flows of Irish immigrants to Boston from the early nineteenth century to the present. The effects of famines in the 1840s caused a tremendous swell, especially in unskilled people and poor families, which strained Boston's charitable institutions and caused social backlash. The historian Thomas O'Connor argues that Federalist political opponents of Andrew Jackson, who proclaimed his Irish heritage, were active in Boston cultivating anti-Irish and anti-Catholic public feeling; this erupted spectacularly in the burning down of the Ursuline convent in Charlestown in August 1834. Another outburst was the Broad Street Riot between firefighters and an Irish Catholic funeral procession in June 1837. O'Connor suggests that the anti-immigrant violence of the early 1800s convinced the majority of Boston's Irish to stick together in neighborhoods like South Boston (O'Connor 1995, 38–54). (The geography of Boston is important to understanding its Irish culture, and can be seen on the interactive map maintained by the Metropolitan Area Planning Council: trailmap.mapc.org.)

The general musical life of Boston in the eighteenth and early nineteenth centuries was typical of American cities founded by the English. There were professional church musicians, teachers, dancing masters, and theatrical performers. Military regiments had bands. Amateurs at all levels of society sang, played instruments, and danced for entertainment and to celebrate special occasions (see Lambert 1980). Ballads were composed and printed to spread news, often set to traditional tunes and airs, including many found in Ireland. In an 1850 census, twenty-four Irish-born residents of Boston were counted as professional actors or musicians alongside a majority of laborers and domestic servants (Handlin 1991, [250]).[8]

During the nineteenth century Irish music and musicians achieved prominence in Boston's cultural life. This social change accompanied the mainstream popularity of Thomas Moore's songs and other expressions of Irish nationalism. Local militias seem to have adopted Irish music as their ranks swelled with Irish men and their descendants. Several music books from Massachusetts regiments in the Civil War era include traditional Irish tunes.[9] Particularly popular were band arrangements by Patrick Sarsfield Gilmore, who came to Boston from Galway in 1849 and became a nationally celebrated band leader. Gilmore wrote many popular songs and marches, including "When Johnny Comes Marching Home," which is based on a traditional Irish song.[10] An analogy can be drawn to the pipe bands sponsored by fire and police departments today, not only in Boston but in other American cities.

Irish immigrants who had become comfortably established in Boston organized charitable institutions to support other Irish people, such as the Charitable Irish Society, founded in 1738, and the Eire Society. The balls, recitals, and lectures about Irish culture that these organizations sponsored were covered by the *Boston Globe* starting in the late nineteenth century (see the *Boston Globe* Archives, available online). The Charitable Irish Society's balls included society dances of all types, including genres popular in Ireland, and the newspapers also advertised all sorts of dancing and music academies. The Feis competitions (from feis cheoil, "music festival") instituted by the Gaelic League (Conradh na Gaeilge) in Ireland became an important focus of Boston students' training in music and dance. Feiseanna (plural) began in 1897 and originally included performances in many styles of music. In 1929 the Gaelic League established the Irish Dancing Commission (An Coimisiún le Rincí Gaelacha), which codified Irish dances—declaring some to be non-Irish—and began to license dance teachers. Thus the term Feis is also used for official dance competitions. In largely Irish American Roxbury, the Irish Social Club began as a booster organization supporting young dancers aiming to compete at the Feis in New York City.[11]

TRANSNATIONAL INSTITUTIONS AND ORGANIZATIONS

The Boston area boasts many certified teachers at academies teaching Irish step dance and group céilí dancing. However, instruction in traditional music was handled more informally until the establishment of a Boston branch of the Irish Music Organization (Comhaltas Ceoltóirí Éireann, or CCÉ) in the 1970s.

CCÉ, usually spoken of as Comhaltas, was organized in Ireland in 1951 to pass on the traditions of Irish music, song, and dance. Their regional and national competitions (fleadheanna), begun the same year, have always included sessions at which master players mingle with each other and with students. In part, this counteracts criticisms—which the organization takes seriously—that competitions take the music out of its traditional contexts. Local Comhaltas branches around the world sponsor classes for children and adult learners.[12] Winners of regional Feiseanna dance competitions go on to national competitions. Winners in the regional Fleadheanna are eligible to compete in Ireland at the "All-Ireland" Fleadh, which—since some branches abroad have the same "provincial" status as the regions in Ireland—is now international. Administrative elements of the local branches similarly report to regional, provincial, and ultimately central offices in Ireland.

When Comhaltas began sending its champion players on tour in 1972, Boston was soon added as a stop. After their tremendously successful visit in 1975, Larry Reynolds organized the Hanafin-Cooley Boston branch of CCÉ. Both namesakes—fiddler Michael Hanafin, "the first to be recorded in the early days of the phonograph industry," and accordionist Joe Cooley—spent part of their lives in Boston (CCÉ Boston website). Following the death of Larry Reynolds in 2012, this was renamed the Reynolds-Hanafin-Cooley branch.

Until the CCÉ branch was founded, Boston did not have a central institution organizing the teaching of traditional music, although this was an essential part of maintaining the style. There were no published standards of playing, as Comhaltas has set in its competition judging criteria; but through "Irish music clubs" skilled players like Tom Senier organized sessions that welcomed junior players to learn by playing alongside them. Senier's son recalled those held regularly at the Ancient Order of Hibernians hall in Roxbury (Senier n.d.; Gedutis 2004, 16). Other cities such as Philadelphia, Cleveland, and Chicago had similar music clubs before Comhaltas became transatlantic (Noonan 2009; McCullough 1978, 305–6).[13] This was the way the music was taught before Comhaltas in Ireland, too, recalled Larry Reynolds:

> Where I came from, there was a good corps of players. I learned a lot. They wouldn't be teaching you, you'd be listening . . . this would be close to 1940, in the 1940s, the early '40s . . . I lived about four miles away from Paddy Fahey. I used to hear him a lot. Paddy Kelly was another one. These guys played with the Aughrim Slopes Céilí Band. They were really top class musicians. So we'd be listening to them as much as we could. Whenever they would come to the dance hall in Ahascragh we would be always there. Another band was the Moate Céilí Band. The Killimer Céilí Band. There were a number of céilí bands within about ten miles. (Reynolds 2009)

The first Comhaltas classes were held at the Reynolds's house in Waltham on Saturdays. Séamus Connolly, ten-time fiddle champion at the All-Ireland Fleadh Cheoil, recalls that Larry Reynolds drove down to where he was living in Connecticut to persuade him to spend weekends teaching in Boston. Within a year, the classes had moved into the Canadian American Hall, and Connolly's then wife Frances, a champion dancer, was teaching céilí dancing.

The Comhaltas Boston branch school was chartered in 1997, with a particular commitment to maintaining instruction in uilleann pipes and harp (Kennedy 2012). Current classes are in the traditional instruments plus Gaelic song and extend to more recently adopted instruments such as mandolin. Students are of all ages, from retirees to children; and although the majority claim Irish descent, many do not. Some parents take classes too, or use the time and facilities to play music together. One of the school's goals is to prepare students for competitions, usually the New York Fleadh.

The school has always tried to foster a community by selecting teachers who are leading players in the local scene and "have camaraderie" (Kennedy 2012). Instructors encourage students to play together and make sure to teach tunes that are called at the local sessions. Several of the staff and students are also involved at the Irish Cultural Centre in the suburb of Canton, which sponsors weekly sessions, special events, and an annual Irish festival that focuses on music. This festival originated at Stonehill College, an outgrowth of its Irish Studies program, and is another example of support from local academic institutions.

Another way instruction in traditional Irish music has become institutionalized is through state and federal arts grants. Boston's own Joe Derrane (accordion) and West Clare–born Séamus Connolly (fiddle) are National Heritage Fellows. The Massachusetts Arts Council funded Irish American singers studying the Connemara sean-nós style with Bridget Fitzgerald, and two Americans, fiddler Laurel Martin and dancer Kíeran Jordan, have received similar grants.

Beneath this formal vein, traditional Irish music style continued to be transmitted by amateurs in kitchen rackets, rent parties, mortgage burns, and celebrations of life cycle ceremonies like weddings and funerals. The latter two events might be held in parish halls; the others were informal and held in private homes. Although the presence of traditional musicians has always been essential, not much formality was extended to them: interviewees recalled musicians being given food and drink instead of monetary payment, and Joe Derrane tells a story of performing from the kitchen sink (Derrane 2004; Gedutis 2004, 30; d'Entrement 2009).

Households have been central nodes in the web of support for Irish musicians in the Boston area. During the twentieth century Irish American families held close connections to Ireland through letters, phone calls, and visits back. Visitors and immigrants from Ireland were welcomed into the American homes of their own relations or neighbors' relations. According to Kitty d'Entrement, a pianist active in Boston's Comhaltas branch, "People from the same counties hung out together," helping each other find work—including playing music (d'Entrement 2009). Most people came over as economic migrants, and traditional music was not considered a profession until the folk revival. Good players could be drafted into bands or session groups from house parties and playing might become a second job for them. Larry Reynolds did not bring his fiddle when he first came to Boston, but when he demonstrated how skilled he was at parties, "a fiddle was found" for him (Reynolds 2009). Although he was out nearly every night playing, Reynolds had a regular job as a union electrician.

The Irish County Associations in Boston formerly played a greater role than at present. These social clubs each welcomed immigrants (and descendants) from a specific county of origin (Galway, Clare, etc.). In them, familial roots and networks back home were emphasized. Today only a few remain active, but according to Larry Reynolds, in the 1950s and 1960s they had their own halls and sponsored regular dances for which they hired musicians:

> Of course you had the sets [dances] from Kerry and Galway here. They'd do them not at the regular dance, but at the club dance, the county that was doing it. So after awhile, they were doing it all here. You had big county clubs, Galway, Cork, Kerry, Mayo, Sligo, and Clare. . . . Some of them like the Cork Club is like a hundred and four years old. St. Brendan's Kerry Club the same. So they'd bring their own players. Most of the clubs leaned a little more towards modern music. (Reynolds 2009)

The musicians played what the dancers wanted, the Irish content (as now) mainly sets of reels, jigs, and polkas to fit the figures of quadrilles, Lancers, Siege of Ennis, and so forth, with a few sentimental songs to provide breaks.[14] These were not sessions, but many of the current session players learned in these formats (Reynolds 2009).

The neighborhoods into which immigrants settled supported broadly Irish social clubs as well, where people from all counties mixed. There are half a dozen Hibernian Halls still operating in Massachusetts as meeting places for the Ancient Order of Hibernians, a fraternal organization founded to support and protect Irish Catholics. The Hibernian Hall in Roxbury became a famous place for dances in the 1940s and 1950s. Hibernian Hall in Watertown is rented out for an Irish musical session once a month. Watertown also has a Canadian American Club that hosts Irish, Cape Breton, and French-Canadian events, including the twice monthly Comhaltas dances.

Church parish organizations also hired traditional musicians for their social dances. These church and neighborhood networks overlapped with charitable organizations that had been established in the eighteenth century to support all Irish immigrants. Recently, many parishes in the Boston Diocese have been consolidated, particularly those built to serve particular ethnic communities. Many of the social clubs are challenged by aging membership, as illustrated by the Irish Social Club of Boston, which was forced to close in April 2011.

During the same period that these clubs flourished, Boston supported a number of commercial dance halls catering to young Irish and Irish Americans with a mix of traditional and popular music. The halls were clustered around Dudley Square in Roxbury, where there was an elevated train station that brought people from around the city. The music was a combination of traditional Irish music and Canadian folk musics unique to Boston: Dudley Square has been described as "the cross roads of Celtic culture."[15] The height of this scene was from after World War II to the early 1960s (Gedutis 2004).

The dance halls were busiest on weekends, beginning with "maid's night out" on Thursday evenings. This term was an anachronism by the end of World War II, as in the postwar economic boom many of the Irish immigrants were getting jobs above the station of maids. Simon "Frank" Forde, who came over from Ireland in 1946, was not unusual in splitting his working life between yard maintenance jobs and a union job with the Massachusetts Transit Authority. The ensembles that played in Dudley Square were a melding of Irish céilí bands and American swing bands. They included fiddles, accordions, banjos, saxophones, and brass. Besides the different orchestration, there was less emphasis on harmonizing between instruments than found in American dance orchestras. Many of the musicians had learned by playing Irish tunes with their parents and teachers in parish halls and clubs, but several notable players had no Irish heritage: "We had Germans—Walter Diess was of German extraction. Mike Portenova, he was Italian. They were fabulous musicians. They were interspersed with the Irish musicians. They adapted to the Irish dances, they played jigs, reels. They could read" (Reynolds 2009).[16]

The roster of players included several who moved on to lead traditional music sessions after the halls closed in the 1960s. This seems to have shaped the collective memory of these bands as traditional: their repertoire actually included more contemporary than traditional tunes.[17]

TRADITIONAL MUSIC SESSIONS AROUND BOSTON

Today's patrons of traditional Irish music head to Boston's pubs, especially those that are Irish-themed, for music sessions advertised to tourists and locals alike.[18] Several of these are part of hospitality groups: multiple venues owned by one local conglomerate, although the atmosphere of the sessions in each pub is distinct. The Green Briar pub in Brighton that hosts the Monday night sessions described below is part of the Briar Group, along with ten other pubs in greater Boston and affiliated with Boston Event Solutions, a company that handles special events around the city. Through such links, traditional musicians get hired to play for corporate receptions. These connections are also international: the Burren in Medford and the Skellig in Waltham are owned by Tommy McCarthy and Louise Costello, who also co-own the Shaskeen in nearby Manchester, New Hampshire, with Matt Molloy, flautist in the groundbreaking Irish supergroup the Chieftains.[19]

Support for traditional music sessions outside the Irish community in Boston had to be built up, although Boston already had a thriving folk music scene that was more eclectic. Compared to the ballroom dance bands, sessions in pubs and restaurants were not a reliable source of income for traditional Irish musicians in Boston, and some players like Joe Derrane simply did not want to play in bars. But by the late 1970s Séamus Connolly recalls:

> There was an income to be had playing in the pubs; mostly accompanying singers. [Interviewer: Was this folk songs or a more commercial style?] It was a more "commercial" style, Irish American. There were pubs all over the place, there was dancing in some of them. There were lots of "commercial" bands that played, like Noel Henry's Band. We stood all night, 9:00 to 1:00. Lots of modern dancing too. (personal communication, 25 March 2012)

Many musicians active in the early 1980s reference this as another "golden era" that the contemporary scene does not match. A particularly important venue during that time was the Village Coach House in Brookline, which closed in 1988. There, musicians who had met at the dance halls mingled with the new generation of musicians involved with Comhaltas and their students. Connolly explains:

> One of the first places I remember where musicians sat down and played was the Village Coach House. [Interviewer: The difference was that you were playing for each other?] Everybody who came to Boston sought it out, everybody and his mother as you say over here. I heard it described as THE place in America! People have said there has never been anything like it. (personal communication, 30 November 2012)
>
> The musicians were from all over! There was Gene Preston from Sligo, Gene Frain—he was American, his dad played in Dan Sullivan's Shamrock Band. The Kelly family, they had music at their houses. There were a lot of musicians coming down from Canada, Jerry Holland, Bill Lamey, John Campbell, Joe Cormier. Great Cape Breton players. (personal communication, 25 March 2012)

His description echoes Larry Reynolds's description of the dance hall bands in the 1950s:

> Paddy Cronin, Frank Neylon from Clare, there were quite a number of other Clare people around. Gene Preston from Sligo, there were a number of Sligo players here, and of course Joe Derrane he was all the go then, his brother played banjo you know . . . you had Johnny Maloney, a great banjo player. Quite a few Cape Bretoners and Nova Scotia and some from PEI [Prince Edward Island]. (Reynolds 2009)

The combination of Irish, Irish American, and Canadian players in the 1980s sessions thus continued the amalgamation that had occurred in the Dudley Street dance halls. There were at least two generations of Irish immigrants involved in the sessions, represented by Larry Reynolds, who had come over from Galway in 1956, and Séamus Connolly, who came from Clare in 1976. The session leaders organized a recording session in 1981, funded by a private donor, under the auspices of Boston's Comhaltas branch. This resulted in an album titled *We're Irish Still.*

The establishment of traditional Irish music sessions in greater Boston's entertainment economy during the 1980s can be directly correlated to social changes. First was the rise of "young urban professionals" (nicknamed "yuppies") who came to work in Boston's financial, medical, and high-tech industries. Among them were Irish Americans—and Irish—who had achieved a high level of skill in traditional music and dance through Comhaltas, the Irish Musicians Association, and other formal institutions. Due to the stagnant economy in Ireland at this time there was an influx of young adults from Ireland to America, seeking jobs in trades, with Boston being an attractive destination because of its existing Irish American community. Many of the young Americans had experienced sessions in Ireland on visits to family "back home." This generation is largely responsible for moving the music into bars and pubs as an attraction. These were places where young adults gathered after work, in part because many were putting off getting married and starting families, and therefore had the energy and income to support playing or listening to the music sessions.

Jimmy Noonan, a flute player and session leader who moved to Boston in 1985 and has played four to five sessions a week ever since, recalls: "When I came here, the Boston sessions, would be like forty musicians, all good players. The bars would also have bar bands, they would be coming on and the session musicians would try to keep going" (Noonan 2013). These Irish bar bands played mostly ballads, featuring a singer and backup, perhaps a guitar player and accordion or fiddle player, who might play a few tunes in between the songs.

Noonan grew up in Cleveland and had played sessions in Ireland, Toronto, and New York City. "The large group sessions was always a Boston thing. The smaller sessions are like conversations. Five to six people, that's perfect" (Noonan 2013). He formed such a group and they began to play in the same venues that were hosting the ballad bands, but emphasizing instrumental tunes for the majority of the night. These were sessions, but the musicians played into microphones and thus were not open to everyone to sit in and play.

> It was hard work. We played all over, in the Black Rose, Purple Shamrock, Cape Cod. We went to New York; we played at Tommy Makem's in New York. We'd play in Falmouth [Cape Cod] on like a Wednesday night, 10 [p.m.] to 1 [a.m.], we'd come back and go to work the next day. (Noonan 2009)

> You had to get the staff into it. You had to make it so the whole bar was waiting for the session. The crowd would drive in from the suburbs. (Noonan 2013)

Although traditional musicians were traveling all around the greater Boston area to play in the Irish venues, Noonan says that "There was a downtown session scene: O'Leary's, the Black Rose, the Purple Shamrock, the Littlest Bar" (Noonan 2013).

Noonan, who has held a demanding day job in finance throughout this time, emphasized that sessions weren't—and aren't—as lucrative for the bar owners as other types of entertainment. He never made much money from playing. Everyone was in it for love of the music. Among those who supported these developments were Tommy McCarthy and Louise Costello, serious session players from Ireland who opened the Burren in 1994.

Comparing sessions in the present to the 1980s, Noonan pointed out that immigration restrictions since 2001 have "really affected it. If you meet someone who is really into the music, they might come over and say two words to you, but if you know they're listening, it gives you a lift" (Noonan 2013). Traditional music was part of Irish working-class culture, but because in Boston all socio-economic classes are united in supporting it, the whole community has been diminished by declining numbers of Irish immigrants in technology, trades, service, and labor jobs.

Sessions remain in the weekly entertainment at many venues, but their nature has changed to reflect the desires of new cohorts of traditional music enthusiasts. The rising demand for group set dancing—a phenomenon exploding in Ireland in the 1970s—dampened the enthusiasm of some musicians for playing in Boston's Irish social venues. This is a sensitive point, because in the early twentieth century the Gaelic League had banned set dancing from schools and competitions as foreign. "Sets" are complex figures that squadrons of dancers move through in time to a specific order of reels, jigs, and polkas similar to square dancing. The figures, with intriguing names like "house around" and "show the lady," are largely derived from continental dances such as quadrilles; but an outsider might not be able to distinguish set dancing from céilí dancing.[20] In any case, some musicians did not enjoy being asked to play continually, with little time to visit—which is the literal meaning of "céilí." One stated:

> In the seventies and eighties there could be forty to fifty musicians [at a Comhaltas Sunday céilí]. Now the music is all based on set dancing, you have to play at their speed. Even when the musicians are just playing a tune for each other, the dancers will be right back on the floor, waving their hands, "faster faster!" I remember someone saying to me, "This is too much like a job." (Anonymous B, 2009)

Yet a member of the Comhaltas céilí band declared, "It is a great privilege to play for dancers." The complex figures and increased speed of set dancing may engage dancers to a degree that they cannot pay mutual attention to the musicians playing for them. However, the Boston Comhaltas branch embraced sets as well as céilí dancing, including both in their twice-monthly dances at the Canadian American Hall in Watertown, accompanied by their junior and senior céilí bands. Most of the dancers are older people, though some families involved with the Comhaltas school participate.

The popularity of sessions without dancing may reflect the general shift in focus within traditional Irish music toward tunes and songs in their own right, for listening and study, which is a product of the folk revival. Boston was a center of this, and it took root in the city's collegiate culture. Contradicting the association of traditional music with "backward" rural people, the community of traditional Irish players in Boston includes many with advanced degrees. When asked about his own background, one session leader—a retired school administrator—noted: "I think you'd find many of the people here tonight work in tech and the sciences." Overlapping with the folk music revivalists are the many historical re-enactment societies (Historical Highlanders, brigades from the Revolutionary militia and "Redcoats," the War of 1812, and Civil War), which include musicians and singers. Many have Irish examples in their repertory.

As it is my own instrument, I am aware that Boston also offers unique resources for harp players. The Museum of Fine Arts has important historical harps in its collections (such as an Egan Royal Portable Irish Harp), and has commissioned replicas like that of its Bunworth harp at the center of a 2011 conference and concert.[21] Historical harps and harp music are features of the annual Boston Early Music Festival. Mary O'Hara, a leading figure in restoring the Irish harp and its repertory to popularity, donated her collected papers and 1953 Briggs harp to Boston College. The New England Irish Harp Orchestra rehearses in Boston and Exeter, New Hampshire, under the direction of Regina Delaney. NEIHO plays arrangements similar to those of the Belfast Harp Orchestra, with whose director, Janet Harbison, Delaney studied.

The tremendous number and variety of traditional and eclectic "folk music" groups in the Boston area can be experienced at the annual New England Folk Festival Association meeting. At most Irish sessions today, some participants are involved in other "folk music" groups. For example, Frank and Jane Horrigan, who have led the "slow session" at the Green Briar pub for over a decade (see below), first got interested in Irish music through attending eclectic folk dances and workshops in Cambridge in the 1960s and 1970s. Although Frank's Irish American family has deep roots in the very neighborhood where this pub is located, he jokes: "It was my Swedish–French Canadian wife who pointed out that this is my heritage" (Horrigan and Horrigan 2012).

Club Passim in Cambridge is an important folk music venue, the descendant of Club 47, where Bob Dylan, Joan Baez, and other luminary singer-songwriters got started. Passim's concert series feature established touring artists and younger folk and traditional players studying at Berklee School of Music, New England Conservatory, and other academic music programs in the Boston area. Passim sponsors a Boston Celtic Music Festival every January, with Celtic Music Mondays held throughout the year to raise funds for it. The term "Celtic" implies the kind of musical hybrid encouraged by the conservatories. But traditional Irish music is always a major part of "BCMFest," and in 2010 the festival's moving finale featured the oldest generation of active Irish musicians playing with the youngest students.

An important factor contributing to the vitality of traditional Irish sessions in Boston is the exciting combination of punk rock and traditional music that developed during the 1980s. Arguably, this was an extension of the folk-rock movement of the late 1960s and 1970s; but the raucous style of the Pogues (based in England) and Black 47 (based in New York City) appealed to a younger generation.[22] Boston, being saturated with college students and college radio stations, had a large punk community that overlapped its Irish population. A signal of this overlap was the scally caps worn by men in the Boston punk scene; this is the Irish name for a flat wool cap with a short, stiff brim favored by working-class men. Young people discovered it was now widely considered "cool" to play tin whistle or bagpipes. I saw several bands in this subgenre of "Celtic punk" cross the stages of venues like the Rat in Kenmore Square before the Dropkick Murphys became their home town's favorite band. They took their name from a sort of counseling center in South Boston run by a local character.[23]

Recent developments in indie rock such as "New Weird America" and "Psycho-folk" have kept younger generations of Bostonians interested in traditional Irish music, and inspire some to join sessions or take lessons. Others are drawn in by more commercial musical acts from Ireland purveying elements of traditional music such as Enya, Riverdance, and Celtic Woman. When these touring acts peak in popularity, I have observed that the songs and tunes they feature are more often called for and sung at Boston area sessions.

The Hub is a colloquial name for Boston, as in "the hub of the universe." Also, this well describes its transportation infrastructure, which looks like a wheel when mapped (trailmap.mapc.org). The old neighborhoods are at the center, and "spokes" of highways and trolley and train tracks lead out to Route 128, the "technology highway" encircling the city, and beyond. Sessions that are thriving outside of Boston have been located at important junctions, such as Davis Square in Medford (the Burren), Moody Street in Waltham (Skellig), and downtown Ayer. Public transportation made Dudley Square a center for the music in the 1940s and remains an important factor in session participation despite the extension into online groups, email lists, and so forth.

The multitude of sessions currently held regularly in the Boston area, and the constant shifts in available venues and lead players, means that no description can be more than a snapshot of part of the scene, part of the time. As explained below, locating sessions in Boston is best done by word of mouth; no one website or newspaper carries an accurate list.[24] But examining in detail some of the longest running will exemplify the features of traditional Irish music in Boston.

THE SOCIAL SYSTEM OF BOSTON SESSIONS

Although there is at least one session every evening in Boston, all have slightly different protocols. They can be classified into presentational sessions and participatory sessions,[25] with some toward the middle of this spectrum. These general concepts for understanding occasions of music making are enacted in ways particular to Boston's Irish community.

The presentational sessions involve musicians who are paid to entertain patrons in pubs and restaurants as a regular job and at special events. They perform with a relatively high degree of skill, and usually have experience playing together; in some cases they have a band name or are hired as a group. Other players might join by invitation, usually extended prior to the session. They play tunes for and with each other, usually ones that they know are known to all. They may take requests from the venue's patrons, who may be familiar to the musicians. There are relatively few surprises in these sessions, which can be identified by the presence of microphones in the area where the musicians play, assigned seats, or a small stage. Such sessions provide reliable ambiance for the venues that support them. An example is the Gan Ainm pub near Fanueil Hall,[26] which engages a house band for daily sessions and other musicians for short terms. This is a restaurant and bar serving Irish and American fare: shepherd's pie, burgers, Guinness, and Samuel Adams beer. The patrons are a mix of tourists and regulars, and the house band even conduct sing-alongs. Although such occasions are advertised as sessions, and accepted by patrons as sessions, Séamus Connolly points out: "Musicians call it a 'gig.' They are getting paid to play, and they are entertaining."

The sessions that emphasize participation are also held in pubs and restaurants, but the musicians may not be formally contracted to attend, and the quality of the playing fluctuates from week to week and even hour to hour. They may or may not have microphones. In some of these situations a few lead players are paid or given free food and drink, in exchange for attracting other musicians and creating a communal ambience. At many of the sessions that cater to learners, the participants feel obliged to patronize the establishment in exchange for the provision of a place to gather and play.

Traditional musicians use the terms "closed session" and "open session" to designate the expectations governing those who attend. Both lie on a continuum between the presentational performances of a house band and the participatory learners' slow session. In a closed session, people do not join in unless invited. The invitation may be extended as the result of a pre-existing social contact outside the session context, for example, if a musician is visiting Boston. It is expected that many people will attend a closed session just to listen to the players. At an open session anyone who shows up with an instrument is welcome to participate, and social introductions often follow joining in. Concepts of session etiquette have filtered into folk musicians' consciousness, spread in part by the Internet, so that rarely does anyone embarrass herself by trying to sit in with players beyond her skill. But it does happen, as in this remembrance of a session led by Larry Reynolds:

> One night at the Briar a guy showed up, and he was just terrible: I mean, when he joined a tune it didn't sound like anything anyone else was playing. I wondered, "How is Larry going to handle this one?" Well, after a few tunes, when everyone took a break, Larry came over and started talking to him, asking him lots of questions about where he learned to play, where he grew up, his family, and on and on. The music started up again without either of them. Larry kept the guy occupied so he wouldn't ruin the session for anyone else. (Anonymous C 2012)

Whether the regularly held sessions in Boston are open or closed is a topic of discussion on traditional Irish music websites and forums. The slow sessions are open, but players who have progressed may find themselves caught between the continual influx of new learners and the closed circle of master players. Jimmy Noonan, who was inducted into the CCÉ North America Hall of Fame for his work as a session leader and teacher, expressed his philosophy:

> The secret is to find public places to play with people at your own level, so you're supporting each other. It's about getting together. You aren't trying to do your thing, you are trying to keep it going. Although everyone comes in with their party pieces. We go hard at it. I don't want you coming in late. Put all your effort into the first hour; the second and third hours will take care of themselves. You have to keep the entertainment value. There's a lot to running a session. You don't get credit for it—if it was good, it was just a great session that people remember. (Noonan 2013)

The open participatory sessions operate under a different set of expectations from the presentational occasions, even if some of the same musicians are involved. While there is usually a recognized leader who calls tunes and a core group of players, participants come and go during the session, unexpected visitors are welcomed, and if a player drops in with tunes no one else knows, he will be asked to play them alone. All levels of skill are welcomed and supported, and anyone who shows up with an instrument will be pressed to play something; even travelers who have stopped in to listen are often requested to sing a song. Traditional Irish music sessions in most other places are not so open, and many participants attribute that to Larry Reynolds, who led sessions in Boston from the 1960s until his death in 2012. His role as chairman of the Boston branch of Comhaltas may have set this expectation.

The slow session held at the Green Briar in Brighton is part of a network of slow sessions that extends across North America, and beyond, supported by an Internet presence.[27] These are open to visitors and beginners in an extension of the effort to maintain and grow traditional Irish music, although there may be no formal connection with organizations such as Comhaltas.

Several other learners' sessions are supported in the Boston area, including two weekly at the Irish Cultural Centre in Canton, which has significant overlap in membership and leadership with Comhaltas, the Gaelic League, and other Boston Irish institutions. Canton is a suburb southwest of Boston that attracted many families from the old inner-city neighborhoods. Also notable is the session held once weekly in affluent Groton, northwest of Boston. This session was conceived by a recent Irish immigrant as a learning experience for her children, and its leaders subsequently organized workshops with master teachers, providing tune notations and recordings for study. They have a well-developed website where these materials are archived. The session has moved to a downtown restaurant in nearby Ayer, but the current leaders have carried on the teaching legacy by hosting a "reely slow session" for beginners before their main event gets started. The relatively easy access to both of these locations is an important factor.

A different level of support for traditional music in Boston is provided at the closed sessions around Boston. For example, because the Burren pub in Medford attracts a high caliber of players, touring traditional musicians will stop by to play with locals. Recording release parties are often held here as well.

Sessions at the Green Briar

The Monday evening sessions at the Green Briar pub in Brighton are one of the Boston area's longest running. This family-friendly establishment serves full lunch and dinner menus of Irish and American fare. Traditional Irish musicians from around Boston have been gathering here at 9 p.m. since the 1990s for a session led by the Comhaltas branch. In 2000, a slow session was added to the evening by beginning adult players who had been attending the Gaelic Roots summer school at Boston College, a few blocks away in Chestnut Hill. The school began in 1993 and director Séamus Connolly, in response to student requests, created a slow session as part of the summer school activity. An alternate origin story is that the Briar's slow session was an outgrowth of the Comhaltas school. Since the two student populations overlapped significantly, both claims may be true. In any case, the students named themselves Boston's Original Slow Session (BOSS) and began to meet for two hours before the 9 p.m. session. They were almost immediately joined by accomplished players such as accordion player Joe Joyce, who wanted to encourage them. Many of the original players now join in the late session as well, which was their goal; and new learners often stay after the slow session just to listen. Larry Reynolds used to invite individuals from the slow session to join the master players, often assigning them a seat; but many position themselves at the margins, joining in as they are able.

Because the slow session is held before the master session, players arrive and join in throughout those two hours. A core group arrive before the publicized starting time of 7 p.m. to make sure it gets off to a good start. Leadership roles naturally developed, such as keeping track of tunes played, keeping track of newcomers (now an elected position), and keeping time during the playing (Horrigan and Horrigan 2012). A moderated BOSS Yahoo Group online keeps participants in touch through email announcements; the group site includes an archive of messages, a historical sketch of its activities, and lists of tunes played at various times.

Both sessions continually attract newcomers even as some players drop out. Musicians visiting Boston will come by, attracted by the online presence of BOSS or having heard through word of mouth that leading players in Boston will be there. Some former participants who have moved away make return visits, heartily welcomed; and the deaths of players in both groups have been poignant milestones. They are still remembered as their names and idiosyncrasies are often invoked. Longtime Comhaltas flute teacher Andrea Mori recalls: "Joe Joyce always used to sing along at the third section of Dingle Regatta. He'd sing 'Heigh ho, Heigh ho' and it annoyed Larry [Reynolds]. So Larry stopped playing it! When I was playing for the céilís and Joe was there, I would always have to watch carefully in the second part to see what Larry was going to do" (personal communication, 21 April 2012).

Discussion on the traditional Irish music website thesession.org indicates that shenanigans associated with this tune are widespread, and extend to standing up at this point in the tune. Séamus Connolly recalls the Liverpool Céilí Band, who were the All-Ireland champion band, doing so, and suggests that Joe Joyce may have seen their act as well. In any case, at the Green Briar session, people sing and stand during this tune, remembering Joe, who died in 2007.

The Green Briar slow session is no longer actually slow, and many participants now call it "the early session," yet it still goes under the acronym BOSS (Horrigan 2013). Yet new learners are always welcomed, encouraged, and indeed keep coming. Over more than ten years I have observed participants graduate from this session to others. Its legacy as a teaching session is evident in the "tune of the month" program, devised to inspire participants to learn more tunes. Nominations are suggested during the sessions and through the email list, complete with linked notation and audio files, and a vote is held at the beginning of the month. The tune is then called at each session during that month, and enters the session repertory. A complete roster is posted on the BOSS Yahoo Group site. Some of the tunes have been drawn from the *Foinn Seisiún* books published by Comhaltas, but many come from outside sources, such as recordings by well-known players and teachers at music camps like Catskills Irish Arts Week.[28]

At the slow sessions some players use notation to facilitate their participation, drawing on the Comhaltas publications, traditional music websites, and online archives. Two types of notation are used, standard staff notation and ABC, which notates the melodic pitch names from the staff system with rudimentary rhythmic markings. Notation is not a traditional method of learning tunes, though many accomplished players now use it.[29] Many musicians cannot read either system, and rely on audio recordings, a method becoming more prevalent with increasingly easy devices such as smartphones. Everyone's goal is to play by ear, as is done in the other sessions without exception. Singers at sessions do not use lyrics sheets as a general rule; songs may be sung in truncated versions as a result, and prompts are given when needed by the audience.

Participation on non-melody instruments at any session will be limited, because too many drums and chording instruments constrain and drown out the other musicians. Bodhrán and bones players therefore take turns, and guitarists and harpers play melody or take turns playing chords. Instruments playing bass lines were never included in the Boston area sessions I have attended—perhaps due to a general consciousness that they are not appreciated. In his *Field Guide to the Irish Music Session*, Barry Foy specifically lists as unwelcome instruments "Electric bass, stand-up bass, washtub bass, any damn bass at all" (Foy 1999, 20). This is despite the presence of bass players in traditional music supergroups like Lúnasa, whose recordings and tours are extremely popular.

Unless specifically advertised as a singing session, songs are usually sung only on request, accompanied by loud calls for quiet ("Ciúnas!"), because if started spontaneously they easily will be drowned out by musicians chatting or practicing licks between tunes. Rowdy patrons are occasionally a problem for singers, even at venues hosting publicized singing sessions. The Greater Boston Folk Song Society—whose members include amateurs, people who make money singing, and scholars—is one of many groups sponsoring regular weekly "sings" around the city, at which Irish songs are popular but not the focus as they are in Irish music sessions. Larry Reynolds was always careful to include singers at the Green Briar, and a weekly session he led at the Skellig pub in Waltham used to decamp to its back room to join the monthly sing held there by the Greater Boston Folk Song Society. Since Larry's death, singing has not diminished at the Briar.

The layout of these pubs contributes to their accommodation of sessions, even two in one evening. The Briar, the Skellig, and the Burren have a "back room" which can be closed off from the area close to the bar where patrons gather to drink, talk, eat, and watch Boston or Irish sports teams on multiple televisions while the sessions go on. Over the years sessions at the Green Briar have been moved around the pub. Currently the slow session is held in the back room but the advanced players are now in the main room under the biggest TV screen, indicating that the management sees them as the main attraction on Monday evenings.

STYLE FEATURES OF IRISH MUSIC IN BOSTON

The introduction outlined some basic style elements of traditional Irish music. A more detailed analysis of its expected features includes modal rather than tonal melodies—that is, tunes revolving around pitches other than "doh" or skipping important tones in the seven-tone scale used in European art music. An Irish tune, being constructed of repeating sections, may be in more than one mode and the rules of tonal harmony may not work. However, Boston's younger musicians are more likely to add harmonies to traditional tunes, and to experiment with rhythmic accompaniments such as the "chop"—a percussive bowing technique—in sessions.[30] Recordings by the group HaLaLi, featuring three young fiddlers trained at Boston conservatories and active in area sessions, are exemplary. Such extensions of traditional style would not be welcome in all sessions, and players are sensitive to this. They are features of the "Boston Urban Céilidh" events that blend Irish, Scottish, Cape Breton, and old-time American music and dances with innovative American contra dances. Signifying this Celtic blend, the dancers' footwear ranges from traditional dance shoes to cowboy boots to the Doc Martens boots associated with punk rock; and men may wear Utilikilts®.

The rhythm patterns previously mentioned as characterizing traditional Irish music include triplet and dotted (unequal) rhythms. Because traditionally Irish tunes are played in unison rather than in harmony, "feel"—the handling of the rhythms—is of paramount importance in the sense of cohesion among players. This style element is much discussed, with loads of ink spilled on the topic in "session etiquette" hints for players and in scholarly analyses.[31] Session etiquette advisories usually stress listening to the other players, not pushing the speed, keeping ornaments to a minimum at first, and so on. The importance of feel to a player's comfort in a session is evident, from rank beginners, who may be able to play tunes quite well alone but get thrown off when playing with others, to professional players who joke about it.[32] Although several musicians noted, in the words of one, that younger players in Boston "are doing some interesting things with rhythm," these appear in solo performances rather than when playing in sessions; and as harper Regina Delaney pointed out, "you can't do that if you're playing for dances" (Delaney 2012). Very important in traditional Irish music is the way players vary melodies and rhythms, unconsciously as well as consciously, just as their speech patterns vary: that is, with divergences and similarities that reflect their social contacts and situation. A significant technique of variation is the use of ornaments: adding one or more tones to a melody. Ornaments are an important element of phrasing, creating a sense of motion and marking off points of rest in a melody. They can be considered part of articulation—how a tone is begun, sustained, and ended—being physiologically linked to players' breathing and bowing patterns, and to singers' pronunciation of lyrics. Ornaments are emphasized in scholarly discussions of Ireland's regional styles and are also idiosyncratic, often passed from teacher to student. As notated in Example 2, ornaments used by

3.2. Ornaments used by traditional Irish players.

traditional Irish players include rolls, long and short; cuts; trebles; and the crann, a series of cuts associated with piping technique.

It is possible for players to play well together without applying the same ornamentation, a musical texture that is described as melodic heterophony. Some ornaments are idiomatic to specific instruments: the treble (striking one tone three times) is impossible on the pipes, but a feature of fiddle and harp playing; a slide (bending the pitch from one tone to another by sliding the finger along the string of a fiddle or off the tone hole of the pipes or tin whistle) is impossible on the harp. In Boston area sessions, sub-groups of players can be discerned who use the same ornaments—learned from each other, the same teacher, or the same recording.

Another kind of ornamentation takes place when players habitually hold a tone and omit its neighbor, as when simplifying a reel (see Example 3.3). This happens in many of the learners' or slow sessions, but is used by sophisticated players as well to vary repetitions. Séamus Connolly emphasized that this is not merely a technique for simplification: "The 'long note'—John Joe Gardner, he played with [James] Morrison [and] I toured with John Joe on the first Comhaltas tour [when] he was 78 years old—John Joe recommended to put long notes in from time to time. 'It steadies up the music' he said" (personal communication, 30 November 2012).

When playing in the loose unison typical of traditional Irish music, it is possible to discern some musicians holding the main melody tone while others play through passing tones or ornaments. As long as everyone moves together on the main pulses a comfortable feel can be maintained.

Another factor contributing to local style is that specific tunes wax and wane in popularity within the groups of players who gather regularly for sessions. While traditionally players are famous for favorite tunes, which often take their name (like "Morrison's jig"), these have changed over the years in the Boston sessions. For example, "South Wind"—so popular it was chosen as the name for a

3.3. Simplified Reel: "Miss Monaghan" (Traditional; version heard in the Green Briar slow sessions. In measures 1 and 5, after the initial quarter note where most notated version have a triplet, musicians play all eight notes to match the rhythms in measures 2.3 and 6.7; and in measure 14, they play two initial quarter notes instead of the eight notes or triplets given in notated versions.

Boston showcase album produced by Peter Johnson[33]—was regularly called at the slow session in the Green Briar in 2003 but by 2010 it was rarely played. While Boston boasts more than one notable composer of tunes accepted into the "Trad" canon—for example, "Brendan Tonra's Jig" is in the *Foinn Seisiún* collection published by Comhaltas—these are not emphasized in the sessions I have attended. Mr. Tonra was honored at the Comhaltas Ceoltóirí Éireann Cultúrlann in Ireland in 2002 for his work in traditional music.

Flutist Jimmy Noonan pointed out that which tune follows another in a set is also an important feature of regional difference in Ireland, to an extent that it can be disorienting for an outsider. The different sessions in the Boston area have created sets of tunes linked by constant association in addition to emphasizing certain tunes. Some of these sets are named for, or associated with, participants who enjoyed playing them ("Amanda Cavanaugh's Favorite"); others have mnemonic names, like "the Maids Set" ("Sligo Maid," "Wise Maid," and "The Maid Behind the Bar") played at the Green Briar slow session. The leader of another area slow session noted that when a visitor is asked to call a set and names tunes that the regular attendees do not usually play together, they often "correct" the visitor, although he personally felt that any tunes which go well together can be paired. Musicians who play at multiple sessions still reserve these habitual combinations of tunes for specific gatherings.

The repertory at the Green Briar slow session, and those at the Irish Cultural Centre and Groton sessions, is mostly drawn from the *Foinn Seisiún* books or other teaching publications; but the sets—as well as phrases of specific tunes—are not always played as given in the source. At these sessions, someone regularly takes notes on what tunes are called, and lists are posted on the group websites so that participants and potential participants can find recordings or notation and practice.

Many individuals show the strong influence of their teachers when they perform alone, in the way they phrase melodies, in their bowings, articulations, ornaments, and even their active repertory of tunes. The tunes I learn from my harp teacher include arrangements learned from her teacher, and so on. When asked about teachers, several interviewees mentioned that Séamus Connolly's students sound like him, and they pointed to bowing techniques. Similar lineages are often drawn between flute and whistle players, who instinctively use the phrasing and breathing patterns of players they learned from. The connections between teacher and student are perhaps most striking in singers, because the regional accents of the lyrics as sung in Connemara, Kerry, or Donegal determine melodic phrasing and will be stable across different performance contexts.

CONCLUSIONS

In an article based on his fieldwork in Chicago, L. E. McCullough concluded that style in traditional Irish music depends on the choices individual players make, and that players draw on the music played around them. Other writers have pointed to factors in the present day that have eroded regional and personal distinctions in traditional Irish music and led to a homogenization of style. These include recordings, Comhaltas's publications and competitions, players travelling to perform all over the world, and the increasingly cosmopolitan musical culture of cities such as Dublin or Boston. Players of traditional Irish music in Boston regularly interact with all these influences. And yet, even while disavowing a "Boston style," they point out and exemplify features that are unique to its instantiation here. My conclusion is that McCullough's observation is as true now as it was in the seventies when he did his fieldwork; but that "drawing on the music played around them" now includes exposure to specific teachers, competition standards, concerts, recordings, and online tune banks. Through interviews we can document these influences, though there are more of them, and they are more disparate, than in the kitchens and pubs where traditional Irish music flourished in the past.

Making music together is still the crucial factor distinguishing this musical community as it ever was. By playing together regularly, session participants accumulate style elements that add up to what might be called a micro-style characteristic of the session group. This is happening throughout the Boston area. Individuals carry some of these style elements with them when they play in other contexts. Because listening to each other and adapting to the prevailing feel, phrasing, and repertory of surrounding players are fundamental requirements of Irish session participation, elements of an individual's playing style will be flexibly applied and sometimes repressed, depending on the context. The dynamic between individual experience and group expectation is most evident when someone is asked to sing or play alone. Group cohesion is desirable in other musical styles, of course, as in any collective endeavor; but in the context of an Irish music session it is significant because of the spontaneous flow of events from playing tunes to conversing to singing, with musicians joining in gradually and dancers joining in sporadically. The formation of micro-styles is not unique to Boston. Because of the group nature of traditional Irish music, wherever it is being played in the world today such micro-styles are probably developing. If the local influences become too obvious, the music will sound less traditional.

The particular migration patterns of Boston's Irish community have provided multiple sources of traditional authenticity, some of which remained intact within Boston's musical culture. Continuous waves of migrants from Ireland keep the musical style refreshed; esteemed traditional players are accessible in sessions to be studied and copied; return visits to family homes in Ireland provide opportunities to experience music there. Connections to Ireland are highly valued, yet after several generations of intermarriage, a broadly Irish identity better suits the experience of Boston's Irish Americans than specific regional associations because many have ancestors—or teachers—from different places. As harper Regina Delaney mused, "There is no geographic style [here] because it's *all* geographic styles" (Delaney 2012). For these reasons, none of the traditional Irish musicians in Boston I have encountered emphasize the local features of their music. Despite the popularization of a Boston Irish socio-cultural identity, there has never been a need to define a corresponding musical style. Perhaps doing so would contradict the open attitude carefully cultivated here.

Notes

1. My genealogical information is from Moses Cary, *A Geneaology of the Families who have settled in the North Parish of Bridgewater* (Boston: Bannister and Marvin, 1824).

2. See the obituary for McGann http://comhaltas.ie/music/treoir/detail/new_york_fiddling_icon_andy_mcgann/.

3. See Alan Merriam, *The Anthropology of Music* (Evanston, IL: Northwestern University Press, 1964), 32–33.

4. Some participant-observers have discerned sexism as a norm operating in sessions; see O'Shea 2008, 105–18. There is also a preference for older musicians.

5. See John Henry Edmunds, "Dorman Mahoone alis Mathews: An Early Boston Irishman." Boston: s.n., 1916. Open Collections Program at Harvard University. Emigration and Immigration. http://nrs.harvard.edu/urn3:FHCL:877090.

6. See Keith Lilley, "Imagined Geographies of the 'Celtic Fringe' and the Cultural Construction of the 'Other' in Medieval Wales and Ireland." In David C. Harvey, Rhys Jones, Neil McInroy, and Christine Milligan, eds. *Celtic Geographies: Old Culture, New Times* (New York: Routledge, 2002), 21–36.

7. See John Gilmary Shea, "Journal of an Embassy from Canada to the United Colonies of New England in 1650 by Father Gabriel Druillettes of the Society of Jesus." *Collections of the New-York Historical Society*, Second Series, vol. 3 (1857): 303–28. New York: D. Appleton.

8. This data was drawn by Handlin from local and federal census reports. As Handlin explains, these were taken at various times, did not have standardized reporting categories, and required extensive analysis.

9. A partial list of tunes from the 25th Massachusetts Regiment, 1861 can be found on the website www.1stbrigadeband.org/website/1_home.html?musicpg3.html.

10. See the website of the Patrick Sarsfield Gilmore Society: www.psgilmore-society.org/.

11. At that time, New York City's United Irish Counties Association was holding its own feis, including musicians. It was an annual event begun in 1933. See their website, www.uicany.org, which maintains an archive.

12. Branches currently operate in North and South America, France, Italy, Luxemburg, Finland, Japan, and Australia.

13. The Irish Musicians' Association was an American organization founded in 1956 with branches in several cities.

14. These are all specific dance genres. Choreographers analyze these dances by figures—such as "star" or "house around," which are movements of the entire body in time to the phrases—and steps, which are movements of the feet in time to the beats of a jig, reel, etc.

15. Joe Derrane, interview, RTÉ Channel TG4 "Se Mo Lach."

16. The Italian and German players were also Catholics, and had some exposure to Irish music through church social functions.

17. See the discussion of repertory in Gedutis op. cit., 61–70.

18. See the website of the Boston Irish Tourism Association, an organization directed by traditional Irish flute player and historian Michael Quinlin: www.irishmassachusetts.com.

19. Matt Molloy's pub in Westford, County Mayo, is famous for its sessions, as immortalized on the recording *Music at Matt Molloy's* (Real World, 1993). This is an excellent introduction to the variety and ambience of session music.

20. The terminology is confusing, too. Traditional Irish dance steps (jig, reel, and so forth) were done to the set dancing figures historically taught by European dancing masters (professional social dance teachers). "Ceili dances" were derived from group folk dances and codified by the Gaelic League and Irish Dance Commission. However, "Ceili bands"—distinguished by a drum set with snare and bass drums—now play for "set dancing" and are often associated with this repertory. Adding to the confusion, a few solo step dances done to specific tunes ("St. Patrick's Day," "The Blackbird") are called "set dances" because the tunes are irregular in form.

21. "A Voice from the Past: Replicating the 1734 Bunworth Irish Harp," lecture and concert, Museum of Fine Arts Boston, June 12, 2011. Early Gaelic Harp Conference, Boston Conservatory, June 11–12, 2011. Nancy Hurrell is harp consultant to the museum, restringing and recording some of their instruments. The museum website's searchable collections includes images and sound files: www.mfa.org/collections.

22. Ireland's punk scene spawned several notable bands who drew on Irish topics or traditions; see Gerry Smyth, *Noisy Island: A Short History of Irish Popular Music* (Cork University Press, 2005).

23. For more on the original Boston punk scene, see Brett Milano, *The Sound of Our Town: A History of Boston Rock & Roll* (Boston: Commonwealth Editions, 2007).

24. Visitors might start with the websites of the Boston *Irish Reporter*, the Boston Irish Tourism Association, and the Boston Comhaltas chapter.

25. For an explanation and discussion of these terms, see Thomas Turino, *Music as Social Life: The Politics of Participation* (Chicago: University of Chicago Press, 2008).

26. Gan Ainm (No Name) is a pseudonym for one of the many Irish pubs in this location.

27. See the webpage www.slowplayers.org.

28. This is a summer "school" offering classes in all traditional instruments, step, set, and céilí dancing, storytelling, and other arts during the day; nights are devoted to sessions. Teachers are drawn from Ireland, the United States, and Canada. Entire families attend. It is held in the town of East Durham, New York, on the Hudson River, a resort area for New Yorkers in the late nineteenth and early twentieth centuries.

29. Master fiddle player Séamus Connolly learned to read and write western staff notation in order to analyze his own playing and become a better teacher. He wanted to be able to explain, "What did I do on a quarter note, what kind of note did I do five note roll on?" Connolly is famous for his ability to recognize by ear a massive repertoire of tunes, as well as specific players. He has published one notated tune collection and is working on another.

30. See Laura Risk's extensive study of the chop, tracing its diffusion from player to player back to the Turtle Island String Quartet, who learned it from a Bluegrass player (Risk 2011).

31. See Foy 1999, 40–41, 78–80; O'Shea 2008, 95–101 and notes.

32. As when Jackie Daly joked, at a workshop during Catskills Irish Arts Week in 2006, that his former bandmates in De Dannan being "Galway boys" didn't know how to play a polka.

33. Peter is a legendary character in Boston folk circles. He attended Harvard College and maintained affiliation with its Celtic Studies program. Now retired, he produced concerts and recordings, and claims to have married Margaret Barry, a famous Irish Traveller singer and banjo player, so that she could play Carnegie Hall.

Chapter 3: Musical Examples (access through companion website)

Chapter 3, Track 1. Excerpts from sessions at the Green Briar

Chapter 3, Track 2. Regina Delaney demonstrates ornamenting a tune on the harp

Chapter 3, Track 3. Field recordings of a house party at the Kellys, 1950s. Muise Collection, Boston College, Irish Music Center Archives

Interviews

Note: Interviews were conducted in 2009 and 2011–13, in person and via email. Some interviewees requested they be cited anonymously in publications.

Séamus Connolly gave me valuable input at every stage of this project, credited as dated Personal Communications in the text. He bears no responsibility for any errors herein.

d'Entrement, Kitty. Interview with Ann Spinney and Sara Goek, 3 December 2009. Boston College, Irish Music Center archives.

Delaney, Regina. Interview with Ann Spinney, 25 September 2012.

Derrane, Joe. Class presentation, Boston College, 3 May 2004. Boston College, Irish Music Center archives.

Forde, Simon "Frank," and Henry, Kevin. Interview with Ann Spinney and Elizabeth Sweeney, 9 May 2011. Boston College, Irish Music Center archives.

Horrigan, Frank and Jane. Interview with Ann Spinney, 6 September 2012.

Horrigan, Frank. Email to Ann Spinney, 16 March 2013.

Joyce, Karin. Interview with Sara Goek, 15 December 2009. Boston College, Irish Music Center archives.

Kennedy, Frank. Email to Ann Spinney concerning Comhaltas Boston school, 7 May 2012.

Noonan, Jimmy. Interview with Ann Spinney and Sara Goek, 3 November 2009. Boston College, Irish Music Center archives.

Noonan, Jimmy. Personal communication, 12 February 2013.

Reynolds, Larry. Interview with Ann Spinney and Sara Goek, 29 October 2009. Boston College, Irish Music Center archives.

Senier, Richard "Dick." Undated email to Ted McGraw, Boston College, Irish Music Center archives.

References Cited and Additional Sources

Boston Irish Tourism Association: www.irishmassachusetts.com/.

Comhaltas Ceoltóirí Éireann. 2007. *Foinn Seisiún: Favorite Irish Traditional Tunes Arranged in Session Sets.* Compiled by Brian Prior. Volumes 1–3. PDF download: http://comhaltas.ie.

Comhaltas Ceoltóirí Éireann, Reynolds-Hanafin-Cooley Branch, Boston Massachusetts, USA: www.cceboston.org.

Foy, Barry. 1999. *Field Guide to the Irish Music Session.* Niwot, CO: Roberts Rinehart.

Gedutis, Susan. 2004. *See You At the Hall: Boston's Golden Era of Irish Music and Dance.* Boston: Northeastern University Press.

Hamilton, Colin. 1999. "Session." In Fintan Vallely, *The Companion to Irish Traditional Music.* New York: New York University Press. 345–46.

Handlin, Oscar. 1991. *Boston's Immigrants, 1790-1880.* Fiftieth anniversary edition. Cambridge, MA: Belknap Press.

Kenny, Kevin. 2000. *The American Irish: A History.* New York: Pearson.

Lambert, Barbara, ed. 1980. *Music in Colonial Massachusetts, 1630-1820*. Publications of the Colonial Society of Massachusetts, vols. 53–54. Boston: The Society.

McCullough, Lawrence E. 1977. "Style in Traditional Irish Music." *Ethnomusicology* vol. 21, no. 1: 85–97.

———. 1978. *Irish Music in Chicago: An Ethnomusicological Study*. PhD diss., University of Pittsburgh.

Miller, Kirby. 1985. *Emigrants and Exiles: Ireland and the Irish Exodus to North America*. New York: Oxford University Press.

O'Connor, Thomas. 1995. *The Boston Irish: A Political History*. Boston: Back Bay Books.

O'Shea, Helen. 2008. *The Making of Irish Traditional Music*. Cork: Cork University Press.

Osborne, Evelyn. 2013. *The Most (Imagined) Irish Place in the World? The Interaction between Irish and Newfoundland Musicians, Electronic Mass Media, and the Construction of Musical Senses of Place*. PhD diss., Memorial University, Newfoundland.

Risk, Laura. 2011. "The Chop." Paper presented to the joint meeting of the International Council for Traditional Music and the Canadian Society for Traditional Music, Memorial University, Newfoundland, July 20, 2011.

Shea, John Gilmary, 1857. "Journal of an Embassy from Canada to the United Colonies of New England in 1650 by Father Gabriel Druillettes of the Society of Jesus." *Collections of the New-York Historical Society*, Second Series, Vol. 3: 303–28. New York: D. Appleton.

"Teaching with Historic Places: Saugus Iron Works." National Park Service, United States Department of the Interior: www.nps.gov/history/NR/twhp/wwwlps/lessons/30saugus/30saugus.htm.

Turino, Thomas. 2008. *Music as Social Life: The Politics of Participation*. Chicago: University of Chicago Press.

Vallely, Fintan. 1999. *The Companion to Irish Traditional Music*. New York: New York University Press.

Williamson, William. 1996. *'Twas Only an Irishman's Dream: The Image of Ireland and the Irish in American Popular Song Lyrics, 1800-1920*. Urbana and Chicago: University of Illinois Press.

Zimmermann, George Denis. 2002. *Songs of Irish Rebellion: Irish Political Street Ballads and Rebel Songs, 1780-1900*. 2nd ed. Portland, OR: Four Courts Press.

Recordings Cited and Recommended Listening

A Clareman's Music (CD). Jimmy Hogan. Chestnut Hill, MA: John J. Burns Library Boston College, 2005.

The Egan Irish Harp (CD). Nancy Hurrell. Nancy Hurrell, 2011.

The First Star: Christmas with the New England Irish Harp Orchestra, Directed by Regina Delaney (CD). RDP Music, 2010.

HaLaLi (CD). Hanneke Cassel, Laura Cortese, Lissa Schneckenberger, Flynn Cohen. Footprint Records, 2003.

The Maple Leaf: Irish Traditional Music from Boston (CD). Jimmy Noonan, Chris McGrath, Michael Shorrock, Ted Davis. Boston: Windjam Records, 2001.

On the Road with the Dropkick Murphys (DVD). Los Angeles: Hellcat Records DVD 804629, 2003.

Sé Mo Laoch: Joe Derrane. TG4 (Teilifís na Gaeilge) series, episode available on YouTube.

South Wind: Traditional Folk Songs from Concerts, Ceilidhs, and Studio Sessions. Produced by Peter Johnson. Belmont, MA: Living Folk Records LFR 102, 2003.

We're Irish Still (LP). Comhaltas Ceoltóirí Éireann Hanafin-Cooley Branch. Needham, MA: Vogt Quality Recordings CRSV 2696, 1981.

- 4 -

KLEZMER MUSIC

The First One Thousand Years

Henry Sapoznik

When it comes to studying and performing klezmer music, Henry Sapoznik is a musical insider. The son of a cantor, Sapoznik, a music practitioner, was initially attracted to "old-time" country music, mostly as a researcher and banjo player. In the middle 1970s, however, he became increasingly interested in klezmer, the music of his Jewish heritage. Using the life story of the master clarinetist Dave Tarras, Sapoznik looks at the development of klezmer music in the twentieth century. Although Tarras was not the sole proponent of klezmer music in America, he has clearly emerged as a key figure in the transmission of klezmer to the New World in the early part of the century, as well as a major contributor to its dynamic renewal beginning in the 1970s. This chapter underscores the importance and impact that one individual can have within a specific musical genre. In looking at the longer evolution of klezmer music, Sapoznik also makes the connection between itinerant Jewish musicians in the Middle Ages and their counterparts in contemporary urban settings in the United States. It is a story that explores the marginalization of Jewish culture in the old world followed by its near extinction under the Nazi regime. Ironically, although klezmer gains a foothold in the American context, it subsequently dissipates, a phenomenon fueled in part by the Jewish American experience of post–World War II prosperity and the rise of suburban American lifestyles. Sapoznik's musical choices and experience prior to his (re)discovery of klezmer are in some ways conditioned by that era of post–World War II, pre–civil rights "Americana." The transformation of his musical identity from American folk musician to klezmer musician reflects a characteristic of American identity politics, whereby "ethnic" identities may be "born into," rejected, discovered, created, and embraced at various stages of a person's life. Sapoznik's story narrates his own arrival on the scene as one of a select group of musicians who inspired a renewal in the klezmer tradition that has not only taken America by storm, but that has also reached back to the roots of Jewish culture in Europe.

INTRODUCTION

It would seem nearly impossible. A music born during the dark years of the Middle Ages by a people deprived of a homeland, buffeted by persecution, dispersion,

4.1. Dave Tarras performing in the 1940s.

wars, revolutions, assimilation, and the Holocaust makes a dramatic worldwide comeback in post-Woodstock America. In a nutshell, that is the story of klezmer music, the traditional instrumental music of the Jews of Eastern Europe. And no life story better exemplifies this near millennium of musical and cultural history than that of clarinetist Dave Tarras.

Tarras, trained in Europe, arrived in New York to enter the tumult of the Yiddish music world. By sheer dint of technique, intuition, and presence, he managed to shape the way people heard the distinctive sound of the klezmer clarinet from that moment on. Tarras's playing transformed the second generation of Jewish clarinetists with its new sense of style, interpretation, and orchestration and completely overwhelmed the previous European approach to the music.

The revival of klezmer music, which I helped stimulate, had as its inspiration veteran players like Dave Tarras. When I formed Kapelye in 1979, there were only two other bands in the United States. Since then more than 150 groups have sprung up across North America and half that number again in Europe, most amazingly in Germany, the place where the Jewish presence was nearly extinguished half a century ago. The function of new bands like the Klezmatics in New York, Nisht Gerferlakh in Montpelier, Vermont, the Mazeltones in Seattle, among others, is to act as the cultural conscience for communities that have lost touch with their folk identities. The 1970s so-called roots movement that began in the African American community had great resonance with other minority cultures who were struggling to reconnect with their own identities. The expression "the children try to remember what the parents tried to forget" aptly describes the process of those of us who reunited our community with a vibrant part of its history.

This is a history that most music historians have ignored. It is a history that until recently existed only in the anecdotes and memories of elderly musicians who had run out of people with whom to share them. Someone like myself. The quotes featured here by Dave Tarras were collected by me over a period of years in a variety of venues: at his little kitchen table while we munched on cookies and sipped endless glasses of tea; in the hospital, where I visited Dave after his heart attack; on the boardwalk on Coney Island; at my parents' house when Tarras came for a Sabbath dinner. Most times my tape recorder was there, quietly humming as Dave's vision turned inward and he became misty and wistful or harbored anger over a wrong done him long ago. At times, a tape recorder was not available and I had to concentrate on memorizing his fleeting recollections. I need not have worried: his voice, his words, his whole demeanor are as fresh and present to me now as they were when we first began our chats in 1977.

"IN THE BEGINNING . . .": MUSIC IN THE OLD WORLD

Yiddish music may be described as the informally accumulated history of the Jews of Eastern Europe and America. In numerous forms, from folk songs to fiddle tunes, a clear picture emerges of the people through their music. The Yiddish language and its culture sprang from the Western European Jewish communities that had settled and grown during the Middle Ages along the river Rhine in Germany (*Ashkenaz*). It was the success of Moses Mendelssohn's *Haskalah* (Enlightenment) movement in the late eighteenth century that gradually ended the use of the Yiddish language and its attendant culture in Germany, while it continued to grow and thrive in Eastern Europe. The most influential form of musical expression within the Jewish community was the singing of the *khazn* (cantor). No aspect of Jewish music remained unaffected by the performance and content of this principal form. The centrality of this vocal style is due to a formative and historic chapter in Jewish musical life. After the destruction of the Second Temple in Jerusalem (70 C.E.), the rabbinate (the association of religious authorities), then in mourning, banned instrumental music. Following this profound event, the only officially sanctioned music was unaccompanied liturgy. Even with the cantors' commitment to the content of the prayers, there are examples of rabbinical reprimands against them because of their beautiful voices, which—it was claimed—distracted the worshippers from the piety of the prayers. In addition to his role as a leader in the dynamic performance of community prayer, the khazn was also responsible for training the future generations of *khazonim*. The apprentices (*meshoyr'rim*) would learn the rudiments of the special prayer modes to accompany the cantor; some of them might later become cantors themselves. In smaller towns that had no khazn, prayers were led in the synagogue by such talented amateurs as the *ba'al tfile* (master of prayer) and the *ba'al koyre* (master of reading), or community services were led by one of many traveling khazonim. Religious music also thrived in the *kheyder* and *yeshiva* (primary and secondary schools), where the whole of Jewish law and traditions were taught to students with the help of specific mnemonic melodies. (In the study of religious texts, the writings are set to simple modal melodies to help students remember them.)

Also influential were the myriad forms of unaccompanied folksongs that reflected the broad diversity of East European Jewish life. These included songs of love and marriage, lullabies and children's songs, work songs, and ballads detailing natural and national disasters. Sung in a plain manner—as opposed to the more florid and virtuosic khazonic style of singing—they would, by the beginning of the twentieth century, form a rich source for music of the Yiddish theater. Most of these songs were learned through an oral tradition, that is, from family and friends and, later, from theater performances, recordings, or the radio.

The Hasidim, a charismatic religious sect, developed a spiritual interpretation of piety encouraging song and dance, as opposed to religious texts, as a valid approach to prayer. Their fervor accorded a great value to compositions called *nigunim* (wordless songs), whose melodies bypassed the "burden" of words in the quest of a oneness with God. These tunes, sung on holidays and celebrations, would build in intensity as they progressed, accompanied by clapping, stamping, and enthusiastic dancing. Because of the religious mandate of separation of men and women, there was no mixed dancing; thus, specific men's and women's dance traditions were created.

All of these forms were to have a profound influence on the instrumental music of the klezmer. The term *klezmer* (plural, *klezmorim*) is a Yiddishized contraction of two Hebrew words, *kley-zemer*, meaning vessel of melody. Although the original Hebrew meaning connotes the musical genre, klezmer, the Yiddish meaning refers to the musician himself, a *klezmer*, or a group of them, *klezmorim*. Though looked down upon by the rabbinate for promoting "frivolity," instrumental music was an important part of both sacred and secular events in Jewish life.

The influence of the khazn could be heard in the music of the klezmer. Not only did the klezmer emulate the vocal stylings and inflections of the khazn but also the specific modes and scales used by the khazn in their performance of his religious duties. The *meshoyrer* system, whereby young boys would be apprenticed to older, experienced khazonim, also found a parallel in the klezmer world, where children would be inaugurated into local *kapelyes*, who played in the back row while they learned, slowly moving to the front.

Using instruments popular in their particular region, klezmorim played fiddle, flute, bass, *baraban* (drum), *tsimbl* (hammered dulcimer), and *tats* (cymbals). By the nineteenth century other instruments such as clarinets, trumpets, and tubas were also added. The repertoire reflected the wide diversity of classes and communities with which the klezmer interacted.

Music was heard at weddings, balls, market days, village inns, and other celebrations. The Jewish repertoire was characterized by a large number of tunes tied to the *khasene* (wedding). General dances such as the *sher* (scissors dance), which closely resembles an American square dance, the *hora* (or *krimer tants*, "limping" dance, so called because of its 3/8 limping rhythm) and *freylekhs* (lively) were joined by ritual dances, such as those for the bride (*badekn*), the groom (*khusnmol*), and the mothers-in-law (*broyges tants*, "dance of anger and reconciliation"), among others.

Jewish musicians would also learn local peasant dances like the polka (*karobishke*, *kamariske*, or *oberek*), and in fact these non-Jewish dances were often played at Jewish weddings; for that matter, Jews and gypsies, both at the bottom of the Eastern European social scale, would often play together. For the more cultured patrons, klezmorim would be expected to play salon dances, such as the gavotte, quadrille, or lancers, or even light classical overtures. It was through the forum of klezmer music—more than any other medium—that Jews and Gentiles could share their art and economics.

In addition to playing dance music, the musicians would accompany the improvisatory rhymes and songs of the *badkhn*. The badkhn combined the talents of a poet, satirist, Talmudist, and social critic. His pithy and sly insights into the nature of life and religious responsibilities made him an integral part of any Jewish wedding. The vocal style used by the badkhn was also derived from the religious chanting heard in the synagogue, while the klezmorim, in accompanying him, adapted a Rumanian musical form called *doina*, a free-metered rhapsodic form emphasizing improvisatory skills within a set mode or scale. Doina was favored by star soloists as a showcase for their virtuosity and usually also contained a hora followed by a freylekhs.

The life of the klezmer musician was far from easy or honored. In addition to the rabbinical dictates against the "excessive frivolity" that dance music produced, there were also numerous restrictions placed against Jewish musicians throughout the many non-Jewish municipalities through which the klezmer traveled. The enforced second-class status of Jews was clearly seen in the laws passed against Jewish musicians. Limitations on when, where, and how many klezmorim could play in certain towns were common, and in some cases Jewish musicians were banned entirely.

By the 1870s a new development was taking place in the burgeoning Yiddish world. From the wine cellars of Jassy, Rumania, came the Yiddish theater of Abraham Goldfadn (1840–1908). Until Goldfadn's time, the rabbinate discouraged any kind of theater as antithetical to proper Jewish behavior and only tolerated amateur plays that were presented on certain holidays. (On Purim, *purimshpilers*—or schoolboy actors—through song, dance and skit, presented the story of the foiling of a plot against the Jewish community of Persia.) By borrowing from all the sources available to him in the late nineteenth century from grand opera to biblical tale, Goldfadn crafted a musical theater whose future influence was little imagined in its humble birthplace.

Within a few years of the theater's inception, a number of traveling companies had sprung up, bringing Yiddish variants of everything from the works of Shakespeare to contemporary plays based on the pages of daily newspapers, as well as episodes from the annals of Jewish history and popular and trendy music-hall performances. Singers, comics, composers, artists, and musicians joined the growing numbers of these traveling theater troupes. Like their fellow performers the klezmorim, acting companies too suffered at the hands of belligerent local and national governments that instituted restrictive measures against their performances.

Motivated by social and political upheavals in Eastern Europe, some three million Jews emigrated between 1880 and 1924. The ultimate destination for many of these Jews was the United States and among them were numerous musicians, composers, singers, actors, and dancers. They and their children would soon provide the creators, performers, and audiences for the Yiddish American cultural experience. Chief among them was Dave Tarras.

FROM OLD WORLD TO NEW: THE LIFE OF DAVE TARRAS

Early Training

> We were a family of musicians; we knew we were good musicians. My cousins were, my father, my brothers. One was a concert master in the Philharmonic—he played in Leningrad by the symphony. My grandfather was a fiddler; I had an uncle, a fiddle player . . . one of the greatest. In our town, Teplik, was a Count Pototski, the large landowner. So he played for him an affair. Count Pototski told him to come and take wood and pick himself a spot and build himself a house for nothing. He built a two-story house, when there were no two-story houses in Teplik. And he had four sons, also good fiddle players, and clarinet; they played all instruments. They were in my time. My father was the second generation.

Dave Tarras was born in the Ukrainian *shtetl* (town) of Ternovka, where the family had only recently moved from the nearby town of Teplik. The family's professional involvement with music went back several generations by the time Tarras was born, in 1897: When Tarras was nine, his father, a trombonist and a badkhn, taught him to read and write music. At the same time, Tarras began instrumental lessons, first on the balalaika, then on the mandolin and flute. The following year his father took him to play his first wedding. "The first lesson I got was the notes: a, b, c . . . There was a flute player in my father's band, so he started teaching me a little. And then he got himself a girl in town, so he stopped teaching me because he was afraid if he teaches me to be a flute player, he wouldn't have . . ." What he "wouldn't have" was a corner on the flute market and a more secure way to support himself and his bride-to-be. What he would have, and recognized it, was a competitor in the talented young Tarras.

This incident, and the fact that the sound of the instrument did not express his musical ideas, caused Tarras, at age thirteen, to become dissatisfied with the flute. "I went to [the city of] Uman for three, four weeks and . . . a certain clarinet player taught me how to play a little bit—just three weeks. So I come home from the holidays, I went to play already a *goyishe khasene* [non-Jewish wedding], my father, on the clarinet, and then I just picked up by accident a nice tone. He was very impressed."

The training that the young Tarras received as a member of the family *kapelye* would also be the underpinning of his later success in New York: the willingness to travel, the technical ability to produce both the repertoires and correct style of various genres of music, and a dignified and professional mien. That the family's kapelye was obligated to perform the repertoires of diverse communities—secular and Hasidic Jews as well as non-Jewish peasants and aristocracy—and was able to play them in a convincing stylistic manner presupposed a meticulous attention to technical skills and deep knowledge of the repertoire.

> My father kept ten men: two fiddles or three, one was a *secunda* (chord-playing second fiddle), flute, clarinet, trumpet, trombone, tuba, and drums with the tats in the right hand and another played a small drum. We traveled for a hundred miles . . . those days landowners, the Poles, counts, barons. We used to go play weddings, banquets, they used to make every time balls, you already had to play different music: waltzes, mazurkas, and once in a while an overture like [von Suppé's] "Poet and Peasant." So my relatives were good musicians and they were prepared. And I learned from them to read music and I played with them.

They were successful in learning the art and salon music repertoire from music published in the big cities, such as Kiev; the Jewish music was an entirely different matter: "Mostly on Jewish weddings we didn't need arrangements: we knew hundreds of waltzes by memory, *shers, freylekhs, bulgars*. Each instrument knew exactly what they should do, how to fill in."

The ugliness of the anti-Semitism rife among the peasantry, and always just beneath the surface in most day-to-day relationships, did not emerge in their dealings with the Polish nobility: "They had for us the greatest respect: they used to come for us with a wagon with four big horses, and give us good seats, and take us. After two or three days [at the wedding] they gave us along a sack of potatoes, and chickens, and bread, and brought us back to the door. Maybe they were anti-Semites, but it never came out. They had respect."

With his future as a musician in his father's kapelye all but assured, the outbreak of World War I dramatically changed his plans. Though Tarras was conscripted into the Czarist army, he was luckily recognized as a musical talent and transferred to the military band, where he continued to sharpen his musical skills. In 1917 the Bolshevik Revolution eliminated Russian involvement in the war. In the chaos and confusion, Tarras returned home to Ternovka to find the war, the revolution, and the subsequent counter-revolution (all with their attendant anti-Jewish pogroms) overwhelming. In 1921, after having written to his older sister, who lived in New York with her husband, he left for America, his clarinet in his satchel.

On to America

His arrival at Ellis Island, however, was less than auspicious: "From the ship we walked off, I had my clarinet with me in a satchel. They wanted to fumigate and I wanted to tell them that I had a clarinet, but before I started to explain what I want, the clarinet was fumigated and was to pieces."

Nevertheless, even had the instrument not been ruined, Tarras would initially not have been disposed to playing music in America. Instead, the recently married Tarras had his brother-in-law find him work in the fur trade.

> I thought that in America to be a musician one has to have—he must be something—I didn't think I'm good enough to be a musician. I went to work in a factory and I swept the floor. I got ten dollars the first week, I figured it was worth twenty rubles in Russian money. They taught me to be an operator; I got fifteen, twenty, fifty dollars a week with overtime I worked fifty hours. I was happy with it.

Tarras worked at that job for almost a year before he bought a new clarinet and began taking small wedding jobs booked through his cousin, a trumpet player.

Tarras's First Big Break

Soon word began to spread about the new clarinet player who worked weddings. Tarras's first important break came through the drummer Joe Helfenbein, who remembered a job they worked together in 1923: "I heard this guy play and I said 'This guy is terrific.' So I says: 'I played a job the other day and I worked with a player he plays Jewish beautifully. And a gentleman!'"

Helfenbein arranged an audition for Tarras with Joseph Cherniavsky, a composer and conductor who led the popular Yiddish vaudeville act the Oriental American Syncopators. Tarras recalled: "I had an appointment to see Cherniavsky. His wife was a very fine pianist and [I] brought my clarinet and played for her.

'Very good. Could you read music?' 'I try.' So she put out a couple of songs and I swallowed it down. So Cherniavsky booked me for a job in Philadelphia."

Tarras's first outing with Cherniavsky was a success. The fact that he was a fast and accurate reader who had both a great command of the Yiddish style and a clean "legitimate" sound made him a natural choice. At the conclusion of the concert, Cherniavsky made Tarras an offer:

> "I have one week to play in the Bronx, next week all I can pay you is $110." He thought I would ask for more and when I heard $110, I nearly fainted. So I accepted and saw that I can make a living here. I went to my brother-in-law and his two partners in the furriers and I said: "Thank you very much for giving me a job—I'm quitting." He was glad too, to see that I'm doing good.

"I went, I make": On the Stage and in the Recording Studio

The Yiddish theater that Tarras came in contact with in New York was a far cry from the simpler one Goldfadn had founded back in Rumania. By the time Tarras arrived in the United States there were over fifty theaters in the New York City area alone—with dozens more peppered across the United States, making for a widely rooted circuit for traveling performers—each presenting its own brand of show from high art to low music hall. For a while, the Yiddish theater eclipsed its non-Jewish uptown cousin, Broadway, as the preeminent showcase of cutting-edge theater. Non-Jewish patrons and critics flocked to Second Avenue (called the "Jewish Rialto") to witness the latest Yiddish plays in addition to American premieres—albeit in Yiddish—by such contemporary playwrights as Ibsen and Strindberg and to witness the introduction of modern acting techniques, such as the Stanislavsky Method.

Though there were many "art" theaters that played these highly dramatic plays, it was the musical theater that was closest to the hearts of its patrons. Many of the composers who wrote for the stage had studied to be meshoyr'rim and brought with them not only a knowledge of the broad spectrum of Jewish musical modes and scales but also a profound understanding of the spirituality inherent in the music and sense of community experienced by Jews who attended the synagogue. By recontextualizing the prayer modes into popular songs, the composers—and the singers and musicians—encouraged a deep response from their enthusiastic and loyal audiences.

One of the other by-products of Tarras's association with Cherniavsky and the Oriental American Syncopators was his introduction to the recording world. In the spring of 1924, Cherniavsky was approached by a representative from the Pathé record company.

Pathé, like Columbia, Victor, and other major labels of their day, produced a wide assortment of records. In addition to pop and classical titles, these companies maintained large catalogs of foreign and domestic traditional musics. Yiddish records had been recorded in the United States since the earliest days of commercial recording in the early 1890s.

It may have been due to the success of his first recording with the Cherniavsky orchestra that word got out about Tarras and his studio skills. The Columbia record label approached Tarras about recording for them. Tarras was contacted by Moe Nodiff, the A&R (Artist and Repertoire) man for foreign recordings:

> Nodiff calls me up and books me to play a record . . . four sides, two recordings. He says, "Mr. Tarras, I'm giving you forty dollars and make me a session. And then if it's all right I'll give you more."
>
> Forty dollars? I would've done it for nothing. I was so . . . I was making a record!
>
> "Can you play a Russian session?"
>
> "Yeah."
>
> "Good, so you'll come down next week and make a Russian session."
>
> So I went; I make. Two weeks later I make another Jewish session with Schwartz; whatever Nodiff gave me: Russian, Polish, Greek. . . .
>
> A recording session consisted of four records—eight songs—so writing the songs was no problem for me. They'd let me know, "Two weeks from today we'll need . . ." I sat down for a day or two to write the numbers; I wrote for the piano the chords, the violin or trumpet melody. The drums he knew; I didn't write. My part, I knew by heart. I had the four numbers in a couple of days. But the names, I had with them trouble; I gave family names: my daughter, my grandfather . . .
>
> We never rehearsed. All the music was done in the studio. The whole pay was fifteen dollars a musician to play three hours and make four sides. We came in at nine and by twelve o'clock we were out. If we had to stay later, he paid us overtime. We played through the number, and if anything we needed to change—so the engineer took a test and he played it back right away, he played through the test. If the test was good, we went through to the next.

As soon as it became clear that Tarras was a rapid sight-reader who could coolly improvise a stylistically appropriate musical accompaniment on the spot, his rank as a session musician rose. Listen to Chapter 4, Track 1 for an example of Tarras playing with Abe Schwartz. In 1927 Tarras was invited to join the Boiberiker Kapelle, a popular Yiddish music act that made broadcasting history in 1929. Together with Molly Picon, Irving Grossman, and other stars of the Yiddish theater, Tarras appeared on the newly created CBS radio network's *Jewish Day Radio Concert*, the first—and last—network Yiddish radio show.

It was about this time that Tarras met Irving Gratz, who would be his longtime drummer. Gratz, who was sixteen when he came to the United States in 1923, was encouraged to become a musician by his father. Before joining Tarras, Gratz, a classically trained percussionist, gained experience with other New York Jewish bands, including that of fiddler Abe Katzman, with whom he began his career. Gratz and Tarras would continue to work together on and off until Tarras's death.

The haphazard scheduling of jobs in the Jewish music world required a willingness to travel and an ability to play various repertoires—those same skills Tarras had learned in Ternovka. His description of a Saturday night from the mid-1930s, when he played with bandleader and composer Alexander Olshanetsky, illustrates this point:

> I played with Olshanetsky a job for the Baker's Union in the Bronx till about five o'clock in the morning . . . so we went from that job to his hotel where we showered and he had to finish one of the arrangements for the "Forverts Hour" at WEVD. And we go straight to the radio to make rehearsal, and I got through with the job at twelve o'clock. I went from the radio, I went to the Paramount in the Bronx—I had an afternoon there—and at night I had at the DeLuxe Palace on Howard Avenue back in Brooklyn. See what I mean?

The Catskills

By the time he had established himself as a full-time professional, another venue for his performing had established itself as well. The Catskill region of New York State was transformed from a series of former farmhouses that sheltered tubercular Jewish New York sweatshop laborers at the turn of the century, to one of the most developed and influential resort areas in America.

By the 1920s the Borscht Belt, as it later came to be called, boasted scores of hotels that catered to a Jewish clientele; hotels in other parts of the Catskills region routinely restricted the admission of Jews. The Hotel Majestic, the Pineview, the Normandie Hotel, and Echo Lodge, among others, competed to bring to the newly emerging Jewish leisure class a full palette of cultural and culinary offerings.

Though many of the professionals in the Yiddish theater would vacation in the Catskills during the theatrical off-season, entertainment was not the original attraction at these resorts. Later, however, as resort culture came of age, so too did stand-up comedy, now a standard fare of American entertainment. Like the badkhn of old, who was hired to liven up Jewish weddings, so too was the *tumler* at Jewish hotels. The *tumler* (literally someone who makes a *tuml*, a big racket) was supposed to be quick, inventive, and above all, funny, anything to divert the guests, who, in a generation, had gone from "recuper-ation" to "recreation." In time, the tumler was transformed into the modern emcee, who epitomizes the contemporary stand-up comic. Well-known entertainment personae Jerry Lewis, Sid Caesar, Joan Rivers, Buddy Hackett, and dozens like them took the styles they originally perfected in the Jewish resorts during the 1930s and adapted them from the small cozy stages in the Jewish hotels to the more gaudy—and lucrative—stages of Las Vegas and television.

For musicians, the development of this new performance context was not as profound as it was for the comics. For them, playing the Borscht Belt was just another gig. At its peak, the Catskills circuit required a combination of the rigor of playing for the theater and the flexibility of a wedding reception—and sometimes the worst aspects of both. What made the comics so successful was the dream of all performers: to cross over into the American mainstream. And for a brief moment the crossover dream *was* possible for Dave Tarras.

The Rise of "Jewish-Jazz"

When the Yiddish theater season reopened in 1932, Tarras was there too, featured as a soloist in the Yiddish musical *I Would If I Could*. Despite billing top actors and actresses and a wonderful score, it closed after a few weeks. One of the songs from this show, "Bay Mir Bistu Sheyn," was sold for forty dollars by composer Sholem Secunda and in 1938 became a huge hit for the newly formed non-Jewish Andrews Sisters vocal trio. The immense popularity of this song meant that this was the first Jewish tune to become popular in American music, thus beginning a short but furious fad of "Jewish-Jazz" hits.

In an age when "making it" in American entertainment meant that the children of immigrants would change their names, such personalities as Detroit Tiger star Hank Greenberg and swing clarinetist Benny Goodman were heroes to the immigrants for not changing their names. Proclaimed the King of Swing, Goodman used jazz to create a bridge between black and white performers and audiences. Though Jewish, Goodman had no interest in playing klezmer style, preferring the newly emerging jazz coming up in his Chicago hometown. When Goodman wanted a "Jewish" solo he would turn to trumpeter Harry ("Ziggy") Elman (born Finkelman), as he did on their recording of "Bei Mir Bist Du Schoen." The first solo record Elman was to make upon entering the studio in late December 1938 was a tune that would push the Jewish/jazz crossover even farther along.

Elman crafted an imaginative and thrilling arrangement of a solid old Yiddish dance chestnut that had earlier been recorded under the title of "Der Shtiler Bulgar" (The Quiet Bulgar). Calling it "Frailach in Swing" (And the Angels Sing), Elman's version wove back and forth between sophisticated swing trumpet skills and the driving meat-and-potatoes style of Yiddish dance music, exhibiting his experience in both genres. Once again, Goodman saw the potential of a crossover, and two months later, in February 1939, recorded "And the Angels Sing" with Martha Tilton as the vocalist and with words by Johnny Mercer. And again, there was a big "Jewish" hit, a trend that would continue for several more years.

If Dave Tarras was the improved, Americanized version of the rougher-hewn, old-country klezmer, then Goodman represented the next generational development. Because of this inevitable comparison, Tarras was considered redundant and dubbed the "Jewish Benny Goodman," a term he found bizarre but complimentary nonetheless.

On the Air: Radio Reaches Out

It was also in 1939 that the piano-playing son of a Yiddish theater veteran approached Tarras about appearing in his radio orchestra. Young Sam Medoff—whose father was the Yiddish-Russian recording pioneer David Medoff—was impressed by the great success of using Jewish music as a wedge into the popular mainstream and saw his opportunity. Medoff recognized that his generation—those born in America of European parents—felt a cultural allegiance to both communities; and the radio show, *Yiddish Melodies in Swing*, effectively addressed that loyalty in its choice of musical repertoire and its mixed English-Yiddish script. Although radio station WHN had a regular orchestra, Medoff's agreement with the station allowed him to bring in his own band. Tarras was his first choice.

Accelerating the assimilation of foreign-born Jews while simultaneously engaging younger American-born Jews in older Yiddish culture was a formidable and seemingly hopeless task. The program continued on the air long after swing ceased to be the cutting-edge music for the younger generation (and saw its orchestra shrink from eleven to five musicians). Tarras's long-term involvement with the show ended when *Yiddish Melodies in Swing* went off the air in 1955.

This was not Tarras's only outlet in broadcasting, for at the same time he was the music director at the small WBBC ("The Brooklyn Broadcasting Company"), a competing Brooklyn station, and at WARD and WLTH, housed in the Yiddish Second Avenue Theater.

THE HOLOCAUST AND THE NEXT GENERATION

The post–World War II years brought a decline in Jewish audiences despite the small, temporary influx of Yiddish-speaking Holocaust survivors. American anti-immigration laws aimed at eastern and southern Europeans in the middle 1920s effectively shut the doors to Jews attempting to flee Hitler in the 1930s. The genocide of six million European Jews meant that the fertile birthplace of Yiddish culture was forever destroyed and now only its offshoots—like the one in America—would continue the traditions of the older Jewish communities.

Yet despite this shrinking of venues for performance, the 1920s' American-born generation of clarinetists who had grown up emulating Dave Tarras were now ready to enter the fray full-time. Among them were Danny Rubinstein, Rudy

Tepel, Howie Leess, Marty Levitt, and Sid Beckerman. Chief among them, however, was a tenor-sax player in the Gene Krupa band: Sammy Musiker.

In the postwar years, Musiker, who was born in 1916 and whose name means musician in Yiddish, worked with Dave Tarras regularly. He developed a sound that was so much like Tarras's that, when he wanted to, he could play so that no one could tell them apart. But Musiker's strong ego would not let him merely imitate someone else's style or sound, and he pushed further to explore his own interpretation, incorporating all the lessons he had learned from both Tarras and from big band drummer and bandleader Gene Krupa, in whose orchestra he played. The results were extraordinary. More recording opportunities were in store for Tarras and the young Musiker.

In 1946 Savoy, a jazz and popular label, contacted Dave to record for them: "Savoy came to me. They wanted a band that mixed Jewish and jazz . . . And I arranged for a big band and I made Sammy do the arrangements. He made beautiful arrangements."

The two sessions, in 1946 and 1947, produced five discs. Musiker effectively constructed arrangements around Tarras's strengths—and avoided his weaknesses. Knowing Tarras's jazz playing to be virtually nonexistent, he had him play in the ensemble (or sit out) until the arrangement blossomed forth in the "Jewish" section—where he soloed brilliantly.

This ternary sectional form (ABA)—jazz, Jewish, jazz—is based on the structure used by Ziggy Elman on his ". . . Angels Sing" recording. Yet, as Tarras recalled, "The stores said: 'It's a good record, it's beautiful, but if jazz we want, we got Benny Goodman.' It's not Jewish 'cause it's mixing in too much jazz, and it's not jazz 'cause it's mixing in too much Jewish. It's what killed it."

They were just too late. "Hot" swing had finally surrendered its place of honor to the "sweet" bands, whose lush orchestrations became the standard for mainstream pop music until the unexpected phenomenon of rock 'n' roll in the 1950s.

The postwar period engendered an immense upheaval in the Jewish community. The Holocaust ended forever the fertile source of new Yiddish-speaking audiences and performers, with a definite shift of focus from European Jewish culture to Israeli Jewish culture. With the founding of the state of Israel in 1948, the increasing popularity of all things Israeli also meant that for the first time in his playing career, Dave Tarras—and many of his contemporaries—would be approaching a form of Jewish music as a stranger. Tarras neither liked nor was challenged by the pseudo-folk music coming out of Israel, as much of it was a merely a simplification of the music he already played and mastered.

This was also the time of the rising Jewish middle class: the emergence of the suburbs with its attendant easy access to assimilation—a generation that forsook the Catskills for the Caribbean, the Yiddish theater for Broadway.

If, however, bourgeois assimilation was happening in some quarters of the American Jewish community, at the same time a separatist ultra-Orthodoxy was rising in others. The Hasidic communities, which had for the most part not migrated to America before the war, did come en masse after the destruction of the European towns from which they originated. Early on, the growing Hasidic communities sought out Dave Tarras to play for them. But he was not long for this scene because of its rigorous physical requirements (weddings usually lasted all night) and his growing disinterest in the current simplified repertoire demanded by this community.

Tanz!: The Klezmer Supernova

In 1956 Epic Records, a budget label at Columbia, brought Dave into the studios. The album *Tanz!* was conceived by Sammy Musiker, and it emerged as the most musically sophisticated fusion of Yiddish and American music forms to that time. Musiker's brilliant arrangements, played in a masterly fashion with their foreshadowing of melodic elements and precise attention to interesting voicings, are matched by a unity of overall construction, giving this record a thematic coherence that puts it many years ahead of its time. He utilized a wide variety of harmonies culled from modern jazz, show music, and classical and traditional Jewish music sources, creating a unique bridge between the styles. To achieve that, he needed the best players.

In spite of the presence of some of New York's top Jewish musicians ("Red" Solomon on trumpet; Seymour Megenheimer on accordion; Moe Wechsler, piano; Mac Chopnick, bass; Irving Gratz, drums; and Sam and his younger brother, Ray Musiker, on clarinets and saxophones), CBS did not pursue an aggressive outreach with *Tanz!* and sales foundered. Within a few years it was impossible for the record-buying public to find a copy. Although there have been several inquiries to CBS to produce a rerelease, there are no plans to reissue *Tanz!* on CD; nonetheless, it is now available as a download.

Though this was the era of be-bop, rock 'n' roll, and folk music, there were still young Jewish musicians who found themselves gravitating to the Jewish music world. Chief among them was reed-player-turned-pianist Pete Sokolow.

In 1959, three years after he had turned professional, Pete Sokolow played his first job with Dave Tarras. They were co-occupants in the sax section of the Ralph Kahn big band at New York's swanky Hotel Astor. Sokolow recalls: "At this time Tarras had a tremendous reputation, he was the absolute king of the Jewish world—an icon. People spoke to him in deferential tones. Kahn had him there to play a specialty: go out on the floor, play a *doina*, a *bulgar*. He introduced himself to me: 'I am Dave Tarras. I am teacher of clarinet!' As if I weren't intimidated enough!"

As the demand for klezmer music waned, so did its major proponent, Dave Tarras. He kept active with occasional gigs in hospitals or old-age homes, and music union "trust fund" jobs with his old sidemen. Now and then he would hear a record of his played on radio station WEVD, or receive an occasional fan letter. Fewer and fewer people were stopping him on the street to ask if he was indeed Dave Tarras.

After the death of his wife, he reacted by throwing out many photographs, records, and memorabilia from their early days together in America—much of it related to his career—a response to grief that he later regretted. He was, by his own account, at the lowest ebb of his life.

THE REBIRTH OF "KLEZMER": MY OWN REAWAKENING

Nevertheless, while Tarras thought that recognition of his work was all behind him, another event outside his control was taking shape. Almost as gradually as the postwar interest in Yiddish culture faded, a renewed interest in it emerged in the 1970s.

In the early 1970s, I played Appalachian string-band music ("old-time music") in a group called the Delaware Water Gap String Band, spending part of each year collecting traditional music and playing with local older musicians in the Blue Ridge Mountains of North Carolina. But what was I doing there? I didn't come from six generations of Scots-Irish settlers. My family were Holocaust survivors who came over after World War II and were steeped in Eastern European Yiddish culture. My father was not a renowned square-dance fiddler and caller but a renowned khazn in whose choirs I began singing at the age of six, learning the time-honored modes, scales, and vocal skills required for the traditional synagogue services.

In my quest as a child of immigrants, I resolved to become even more conscious of authentic American music than many Americans. I came to old-time music through folk music that was generated by the anti–Vietnam War movement. From there it was not very difficult to make the transition to the rural music that inspired urban folk singers like Pete Seeger and Bob Dylan.

It was through the generosity and help of the veteran Appalachian music collector Ray Alden that I was introduced to the world of the music of the Blue Ridge Mountains, and veteran fiddle and banjo players Fred Cockerham and Tommy Jarrell. These older men were hospitable and gracious hosts and guides who, taking me under their wings, shared the accrued artistry of their family's musical heritage as if I were one of their own.

Yet, they were also a bit puzzled. I was not the only one who had beaten a path to their doors seeking insight into one of America's most exciting musical forms. Others preceded me, and not a few of them were also Jews from urban areas. At one point, several years into my trips to Tommy Jarrell's home and knowing I was Jewish, he asked "Don't your people got none of your own music?" I was surprised but intrigued. Did we have a music as simple and powerful as the fiddle tunes Fred and Tommy played? Was there an unbroken line in Yiddish music that was as easily definable as the one Tommy bridged from his fiddle-playing father, Benjamin Franklin Jarrell, to his fiddle-playing son, Benjamin Franklin Jarrell? I did not know. But I was determined to find out.

The Old Records Have Something New to Say

Consulting the renowned folklorist Barbara Kirshenblatt-Gimblett, I was introduced to the holdings of period 78 rpm records at New York's YIVO Institute for Jewish Research. Collected but never listened to here—I would have to bring in my own turntable to play the records!—were hundreds of Jewish 78s recorded from the turn of the century up to the post–World War II era. I was, for the first time, able to hear the records that were made in my community at the same time that Tommy's father had made his recordings in the mid-1920s.

And there it was. That same directness. The same ease of understanding about how to play simple and powerful music and project a sense of the moment. But instead of Charlie Poole and the North Carolina Ramblers or Uncle Dave Macon and the Fruit Jar Drinkers, I was listening to Abe Katzman's Bessarabian Orchestra and the Boiberiker Kapelle. What I had loved about the singularity of old-time music, I was now discovering in the music I grew up with; it was there in klezmer. (Interestingly, during its heyday, this music was never referred to as klezmer, but as *tants muzik*, dance music; *khasene muzik*, wedding music; *freylekhs;* or simply "Yiddish music." In many ways the term *klezmer* was a demeaning one, connoting either shtetl "hick" music of a crude and untutored character, or a romantic image of a wandering, passionate, tragic artist. In either case, the revivification of the music form in the 1970s also elevated the term *klezmer* to a new and respected status.)

Though I had never before heard these old records, there was a strong sense of familiarity about them. Apart from the reassuring hiss of the 78 rpms with their sepia-toned sound of yesterday, the music, the voices, and the presence all jumped out at me at once. And none more so than those of Dave Tarras. There was something about his records that seemed even more familiar than the others. I asked my father, who, as a professional khazn, had sung at all the major synagogues and hotels, about Dave Tarras. Tarras, my father reminded me, was an old friend of his, whom we knew from the hotels where my father conducted the religious services. It was a standard situation: during the days my father led the singing of prayers in the synagogue, I sang in the choir, and Dave was one of the members of the congregation. At night, Dave played onstage and everyone listened and danced to his music.

I Meet Dave . . . Again

That was Dave Tarras? As a kid, he seemed older than music itself. This was the guy I dubbed "a round man playing square music"? How could I have missed the power in his playing? I had been so intent on becoming part of American culture, so adept at ignoring and dismissing my heritage, that I had blocked out my own primary and deep interaction with a living folk culture. It was the rediscovery of Dave's 78s—and the man himself—that reminded me what I had very nearly thrown away.

Through my father, I began visiting Dave and thus began a rich and mutually enlightening relationship. Dave, like Tommy Jarrell, was a genial host, allowing me into his home and life. Unlike Tommy, Dave had seen me grow up and could not resist reminding me of just that fact. He had a profound sense of self and had, in many ways, been waiting years for someone to come to him to get "The Story." He was ready and so was I.

The most interesting adjustment for me was to learn how to do fieldwork in my own community. Even though I already understood the language (I had spoken Yiddish before English), I had to learn to make myself a stranger in order to ask and understand basic questions and to assume nothing. Through Tarras, I was able to contact many of the surviving veteran klezmer musicians in New York, such as Joe Helfenbein, Irving Gratz, and Louis Grupp, all of whom were generous and equally startled that anyone, let alone a young American-born kid, would take an interest in music that had ceased being relevant in the Jewish world years ago.

It was at this time that I created and then directed the Archives of Recorded Sound at the YIVO, building the collection in thirteen years from several hundred to several thousand discs, the most important collection of its kind in the world. (The vast number of 78 rpms that Dave recorded— somewhere over five hundred—have given me the pleasure of reuniting Dave with recordings of performances that he had forgotten.) Soon, the work that I was doing at the YIVO—reissuing these classic recordings, lecturing on and writing about the history of the performances of Andy Statman, who was a student of Tarras's, and the Klezmorim—began to stimulate an interest in this music. Part of the impetus was the location and identification of authentic old-time klezmer players. No one fit that bill better than Dave Tarras.

Tarras's home in the Coney Island section of Brooklyn became a klezmer mecca. It was now not unusual for TV or documentary filmmakers to set up shop in his living room and record this last of the old-world klezmorim. Klezmer was hot and Dave Tarras was its Godfather.

A steady stream of well-wishers and klezmer fans came to him bearing recordings, publicity kits, and videos of their groups, looking for insights (and endorsements) from this man whom many had known only through his 78s or hard-to-find LPs. His influence, once so powerful for earlier generations of musicians, was again transforming the young players who came to klezmer from rock, jazz, country, classical, and other ethnic musics—from musics an earlier generation had sought out in order to get away from klezmer. He was real continuity—to be in his presence was to be part of the historic transmission of tradition, a chain of transmission that was growing more and more fragile. He was a 78 rpm come to life.

Enter Kapelye

During this time in 1979, I formed Kapelye to feed my passion for mixing Yiddish music research and playing hot dance tunes. For a performance by Kapelye, refer to Chapter 4, Track 2. The group was instantaneously acclaimed—making four records and two Hollywood film scores and touring the United States. Buoyed by the general influence of the "roots" movement, we were in the vanguard of a resurgence of interest in secular Yiddish culture that generated a community-based desire to re-establish a link with this cultural heritage.

In 1984 Kapelye had the singular distinction of being the first band to bring traditional Yiddish music back to Europe. Among the countries we played were France, Switzerland, England, Belgium, and Germany. It was in Germany that I experienced some of the most profound and unsettling feelings I have ever felt. Here, in the birthplace of the most massive campaign of organized genocide in history—where Yiddish culture was born and very nearly destroyed—Yiddish music found a new and enthusiastic audience.

The stark contrasts of wanting to share my music with those who loved it as much as I did was tempered by a belief that cultural ownership might claim certain boundaries. Could the children and grandchildren whose community orchestrated the Holocaust take part in the revivification of a culture that was almost obliterated? Had they abrogated their right—or, as I've also thought, who better—to make cultural amends for the mass murder by reanimating this nearly annihilated civilization? It is a conflict that I still harbor.

Dave's Last Years

In 1984 Tarras received a National Heritage Folklife Award from the Folk Arts Division of the National Endowment for the Arts. The significance of the award profoundly moved Tarras, but the happy moment was marred by near tragedy. While performing at the awards ceremony in Ford's Theater in Washington, D.C., Tarras was stricken on stage with a massive heart attack. It was because of this near-death experience that Dave and I stepped up the documentation of his life and thus, among other things, produced our seminal CD-biography *Dave Tarras: Father of Yiddish American Klezmer Music.*

The following year I founded KlezKamp: The Yiddish Folk Arts Program, which was dedicated to reviving the "apprentice" environment. We created an intensive intergenerational workshop of music and cultural activities, including language, folklore, poetry, dance, visual arts, song workshops, instrument classes, history seminars, all in a supportive atmosphere of learning and performance. What started as a modest local event of 125 people soon blossomed into an international outpouring of hundreds from around the world. (As of 1995, nearly five thousand people have participated.) In December 1988, Dave Tarras was selected as the first recipient of the newly inaugurated Lifetime Achievement Award from KlezKamp. Due to his ever-weakening condition, however, he was unable to attend KlezKamp to accept his award.

Dave Tarras died on February 14, 1989, but the music scene that his masterful music helped inspire shows no signs of slowing down. Tarras was the necessary element common to all in the Jewish world—from the glorified performers of the Yiddish stage, screen, and radio, to the factory worker who hired him for his daughter's wedding—the career of Dave Tarras is the history of the Yiddish American culture. It is a testament to the power of Tarras's great gift that a man born in the nineteenth century and who blossomed in the twentieth might extend his influence into the twenty-first century.

Glossary

(Note: KH sounds as "ch" as in "Bach")

Ashkenaz (ASHkenaz) (pl. ashkeNAZim). Yiddish: literally, Germany. Those Jews of Western and Eastern Europe who are descendants of Jews who originally settled in Germany and then migrated elsewhere, as well as any others whose language and basic cultural forms derive ultimately from the old German Jewish settlement.

Ba'al Koyre (ba'al KOYRE). Heb.: literally, "Master of Reading." Lay reader of the Torah in the synagogue.

Ba'al Tfile (ba'al TFIle). Heb.: literally, "Master of Prayer." Lay leader of prayer in the synagogue.

Badkhn (BADkhn). Heb./Yid.: Improvisatory poet and emcee at traditional Jewish weddings.

Bar Mitzva (bar MITSva). Heb.: Confirmation of Jewish thirteen-year-old boy. Bas Mitzva (fem.)

Freylekhs (FREYlekhs). Heb./Yid.: "Lively." Group of Yiddish dance tunes played in 2/4 time.

Haftora (hafTOra). Heb.: Selection from the Prophets, which is read after the Torah portion on Sabbath and holidays. Thirteen-year-old boys and girls will generally read it at their *bar* or *bas* mitzva.

Hasid (HASid) (pl.: hasIDim). Heb.: Follower of Hasidic movement.

Hasidism (HASidism). Heb.: Eighteenth-century Jewish charismatic religious movement.

Haskala (hasKAla). Heb.: Enlightenment. Nineteenth-century Jewish reform movement.

kapelye (kaPELye). Yid.: Band.

khasene (KHAsene). Heb./Yid.: Wedding.

khazn (KHAzn) (pl.: khaZONim). Heb.: Synagogue liturgical singer.

kheyder (KHEYder). Heb.: Primary Jewish day school.

klezmer (KLEZmer) (pl.: klezMORim). Heb./Yid.: Traditional instrumentalist.

meshoyrer (meshOYrer) (pl.: meshOYr'rim). Heb.: Apprenctice cantor; also chorister.

nigun (NIgun) (pl.: niGUnim). Heb.: Wordless song associated with Hasidim.

pogrom (poGROM). Yid.: Organized mass violence against Jews.

Purim (PUrim). Heb.: Holiday that celebrates the foiling of the plot to destroy the Jews of Persia in the fifth century C.E.

shtetl (SHTETl) (pl.: SHTETlakh). Yid.: A small town.

Chapter 4: Musical Examples (access through companion website)

Chapter 4, Track 1. Dave Tarras, "Second Avenue Square Dance" from *Music from the Yiddish Radio Project*, Shanachie SHA -6057

Chapter 4, Track 2. Kapelye, "Berditchever/Mazel Tov." *On The Air*, Shanachie LC 5762.

Additional Sources

Discography

Historic Recordings (All historic recordings contain extensive notes)

Abe Schwartz. *The Klezmer King*. Columbia/Legacy CK 86321.

Cantors, Klezmorim & Crooners 1905-1953: Classic Yiddish 78s From the Mayrent Collection. JSP-CD5201.

Klezmer Music: Early Yiddish Instrumental Music: The First Recordings: 1908-1927, From the Collection of Dr. Martin Schwartz. Arhoolie/Folklyric 7034.

Klezmer Music, 1910-1942. Smithsonian-Folkways FSS 34021.

Dave Tarras. *Yiddish American Klezmer Music*. Yazoo 7001.

Klezmer Pioneers: European and American Recordings 1905-1952. Rounder 1089.

Naftule Brandwein. *King of the Klezmer Clarinet*. Rounder 1127.

Yikhes: Early Klezmer Recordings, 1911-1939. Trikont US-0179.

Contemporary Recordings

Andy Statman. *Avodas Halevi*. Tzadik 8101.

Dave Tarras. *Master of the Jewish Clarinet*. Ethnic Folk Arts US 1002.

Kapeleye. *Future and Past*. Rounder FF249.

———. *Levine and His Flying Machine*. Shanachie 21006.

———. *Chicken*. Shanachie 21007.

———. *On the Air*. Shanachie 67005.

Klezmatics. *Rise Up! Shteyt Oyf!* Rounder 11661-3197-2.

Klezmer Conservatory Band. *Dance Me to the End of Love*. Rounder 613169.

Klezmer Plus! Featuring Sid Beckerman and Howie Leess. Rounder FF 90488.

Radio

www.yiddishradioproject.org/ is the home for a multi-part radio program aired on NPR's *All Things Considered* in 2002.

Films

A Jumpin' Night in the Garden of Eden. 1988. Directed by Michal Goldman.
Fiddlers on the Hoof. 1992. BBC. Directed by Simon Braughton.
The Klezmatics: On Holy Ground. 2010. Directed by Erik Greenberg Anjou.
The Last Klezmer. 2008. Directed by Yale Strom.
The New Klezmorium: Voices Inside the Revival of Yiddish Music. 2001. Directed by David Kaufman.

Bibliography

Idelsohn, A. Z. 1967. *Jewish Music in Its Historical Development*. New York: Schoken Edition.
Sapoznik, Henry. 2005. *Klezmer: Jewish Music from Old World to Our World*. New York: Schirmer.
———. 1998. *Klezmer! A Very Social History of 100 Years of Yiddish Music in America*. New York: Schirmer.
———. 1990. *The Klezmer Plus Folio*. New York: Tara.
———. 1987. *The Complete Klezmer*. New York: Tara.
———. 1986. "Dave Tarras." *New Grove's Dictionary of American Music*, ed. H. Wiley Hitchcock and Stanley Sarlie. London: Macmillan.
———, ed. 1992. "Yiddish Music." *Encyclopedia of Jewish American History of Culture*. New York: Garland.
Slobin, Mark. 2003. *Fiddler on the Move: Exploring the Klezmer World*. New York: Oxford University Press.
———, ed. 2001. *American Klezmer: Its Roots and Offshoots*. Berkeley: University of California Press.
———. 1984. "The Neo-Klezmer Movement." *Journal of American Folklore*.
———. 1982. *Old Jewish Folk Music: The Collections and Writings of Moshe Beregovski*. Philadelphia: University of Pennsylvania Press.
Spottswood, Dick. 1990. *Ethnic Music on Records: 1895-1942*. Urbana: University of Illinois Press.
Yale Strom. 2011. *The Book of Klezmer: The History, the Music, the Folklore*. Chicago: Chicago Review Press.

- 5 -

THE MUSIC OF ARAB DETROIT

A Musical Mecca in the Midwest

Anne K. Rasmussen

Anne Rasmussen is an ethnomusicologist and musician who specializes in the music and culture of the Middle East. Although she has done research and fieldwork within the Arab American community throughout the United States, the focus of this chapter is the multilayered and diverse Arab American community around Detroit, Michigan. With her focus on Arab Detroit, Rasmussen makes the point that ethnic groups that seem homogenous to outsiders are in fact multicultural and multifaceted. Following a historical survey of the musical life of the Arab community in the United States, the author turns her attention to three wedding celebrations in Yemeni, Lebanese, and Iraqi subsections of Detroit's Arab American community. She then takes us to a large city festival and a formal concert as she considers how music patronage works differently on the family level, in the larger community, and with civic arts agencies. Through the analysis of ethnographic scenarios from her fieldwork experience, Rasmussen demonstrates how aspects of ethnicity, class, region, religion, tradition, and innovation are played out through the process of musical performance. Rasmussen views the musicians of Arab Detroit as the cultural and ritual specialists of a community, transporting their family and friends to a time and place that is distinct from that of mainstream America through the powerful medium of music and dance. While giving us some very practical and specific guidelines for understanding and appreciating this "Arab sound," she also suggests a number of points that are crucial to understanding the relationship between music making and community life in any context.

INTRODUCTION

Arab American music culture has been a part of American life since at least the beginning of the twentieth century. In spite of the hegemony of American popular music, Arab music continues to thrive in the many Arab American communities of the United States—from Maine to California and from Washington to Florida. This chapter opens with a historical overview of Arab American musical

5.1. *Tabl baladi* player Wa'el Zazigy plays to the line of dabkah dancers at a Lebanese wedding.

life the Unites States and then focuses on the dynamic contemporary musical scene in one region of the country, Detroit, Michigan, where the Arab American population is most highly concentrated and multifaceted.[1]

The Arab American community includes both immigrants to the United States and people of Arab heritage and numbers around three and a half million. People of Arab heritage trace their family ties to the Arab world—a collection of twenty-two nations that spans from Morocco, across North Africa through Egypt, continuing east through Saudi Arabia and the United Arab Emirates, and extending north from Egypt through the Eastern Mediterranean countries of Palestine, Lebanon, Jordan, Syria and Iraq, and south to the Sudan. The term *Arab world* is a collective term, coined to facilitate social and political solidarity. Although Arabs may differ in ethnicity, religion, race, and nationality, they are unified by language and by various aspects of culture, such as cuisine, folklore, and music. Arab Americans are, by background, Jews, Christians, and Muslims, and may be highly educated professionals in white-collar jobs, university students, owners and operators of family businesses, or unskilled laborers. Large concentrations of Arab

Americans live throughout the United States, most notably in California, New York, Texas and the South, New England, and around Detroit, where the community numbers close to a quarter of a million people.[2] It is important to note at the outset that Arab Americans are all individuals and there is a certain danger in discussing them as a group of people all of whom are passionately involved in the music and culture of their heritage. In fact, many Americans whose families originally came from the Arab world may be completely uninvolved and disinterested in Arab expressive culture as it transpires here in America or in the Arab world itself. At the same time, hundreds of non-Arab Americans, people of diverse heritage, have also been involved in the study and performance of Arab music, and particularly of Middle Eastern dance, since the early twentieth century. These so called affinity learners and advocates are an important component of any American ethnic or community music scene; but they have been particularly important for Arab music in the United States, which has been confronted with numerous challenges due to political conflict in the Middle East and wars involving Arab, Middle East, and US people.

While music is often thought of as a mirror of society that refracts and comments on every social and political ripple of history, it is fair to say that the Arab music scene in the United States operates independently of the chaotic and violent accounts of the region that we hear about daily in the news. Context for musical performance can in fact be a refuge from daily life, whether dull or devastating. At the same time, political unrest, violence, and death in certain Arab world countries, and the way such events are reported in the mainstream American press, can cast a long shadow on the celebrative nature of community life, a factor that certainly affects the livelihood of the community's musicians. Nevertheless, it is the ambiance of exuberance during contexts for musical performance that originally pulled me into the Arab American community. And in spite of the many conflicts that have encouraged emigration from the Arab world and that have disrupted transnational networks of economy and kinship, many people of Arab heritage in America are involved in a thriving and exciting musical subculture.

The ethnographic scenarios discussed below are intended to show that Arab American musical life, a small piece in the mosaic of multicultural America, is in itself multicultural and multifaceted. Although the descriptor *Arab American* indicates that this population is a homogenous group, Arab Americans themselves make multiple distinctions among each other. These distinctions may be based on such obvious qualities as nationality ("I am from Lebanon and you are from Egypt"), on religious orientation ("I am Christian, you are Muslim"), on generation ("My family has been in America since 1915, and your family just arrived"), or on regional provenance ("We are from the north and you are from the south"). Such cultural distinctions, which are often completely invisible to the outsider, may be of paramount importance inside a particular community. Furthermore, and of particular interest for this endeavor, such cultural distinctions may actually be heard, played, sung, and danced during the course of a music event.

Musicians of various heritage—Lebanese, Palestinian, Yemeni, Syrian, and Iraqi—are showcased in this chapter in an attempt to emphasize the central role of individuals as they bring to their community the sounds of culture. In an immigrant or subcultural setting, where the invasion of the mainstream America knocks at every door, the proactive efforts of musicians to learn, teach, perform, and create the repertoires that amalgamate their communities have a phenomenal impact on the expressive culture of a community. Although music making and all that goes with it—dance, food, ritual and the display of cultural custom and social order—may seem to be a collective endeavor, I argue that it is individual musicians who are the lifeblood of any music culture. I hope my work begins to convey that whether recorded or live, music has the power to move people to different times and places, and is thus one of the most compelling agents in the definition of community and individual identity.

A BRIEF HISTORY OF THE MUSICAL LIFE OF ARAB AMERICANS

We know from family memoirs and photo albums that, at the beginning of the century, music making was part of most family gatherings and that no wedding or picnic was complete without singing and dancing. The people who made up the first wave of Arab immigration to this country were, for the most part, Christians from Greater Syria, an area sometimes referred to as the Levant, which now comprises the countries of Syria, Lebanon, Jordan, and Israel and the Palestinian territories of the West Bank and Gaza (formerly Palestine). This first wave of immigrants to "the new world" were looking for a haven from the turmoil of the Ottoman occupation of their homeland, and, when they settled in America their music, along with their cuisine, their language, and to some extent their professions, settled here with them. By 1914 the community numbered about 110,000 (Hoogland 1987). In the early 1920s the United States government began to control the number of foreigners who could come into the country by instituting a quota system that limited immigration from all parts of the world, including Greater Syria. In spite of the Immigration Act of 1924, also known as the Johnson-Reed Act, which restricted the arrival of Middle Easterners to the United States, the Arab American community continued to expand, with new generations of American-born children, and the consistent, if infrequent, arrival of family and friends from overseas.

The photographs and stories of older musicians and clippings from the Arab American press indicate that the first part of the twentieth century was an exciting time for Arab music in the United States. From the mid-1920s through the early 1960s, two primary contexts for music making developed and flourished in the community: the *haflah* (pl. *haflat*), a formal music party; and the *mahrajan* (pl. *mahrajanat*), a weekend-long gathering to which some people traveled from hundreds of miles away. During my interviews and discussions with elderly professional instrumentalists (all men) and singers (both male and female), they remember how busy their schedules were when, particularly during the summer, they traveled up and down the East Coast to perform for audiences that sometimes numbered in the thousands. Haflat and mahrajanat were usually sponsored by church or community groups or by a prominent philanthropist. These large-scale social and musical events were usually organized to raise money for some kind of good cause, such as the building or renovation of a church (remember the overwhelming majority of Arab immigrant families were Christian), or the financial and social support of newly arrived immigrants, orphans, or even family members still living in the Middle East.

Although many of the Arab Americans who attended these events spoke English well and were completely integrated into American society, the music, dance, and food at a haflah or mahrajan was, according to community memory, completely Arab. The combination of aromatic Syrian and Lebanese cuisine, Arabic song lyrics, the sights and sounds of musical performance, and the movement of dance created an ambiance and experience of the homeland. Such celebrations brought the qualities of Arab place and time into American place and time through a process that is certainly not unique to the Arab American community.

Yet in addition to being a time and a place where "the old country" was invented in the space of a few hours, haflat and mahrajanat were also affirmatively Arab American events. These music parties and festivals that became such a conspicuous feature of Arab American life were sponsored by social organizations that evolved according to the needs and interests of the immigrant community. The musicians played to an audience that was connected not only by their place of birth, but more immediately, by their journeys to the New World and the challenges that faced them here.

During this same time period, roughly the first half of the twentieth century, the Arab American music media, an equally dynamic context for artistic expression, developed in complement to the live performance culture of the community. Beginning in the second decade of this century, Arab immigrant musicians began recording their music on 78 rpm discs at the invitation of such American record companies as Columbia, Victor, and Standard. These record companies were searching for, and found, new musics and new markets in the myriad ethnic communities in America. By the 1940s, however, Arab Americans had taken charge of their own recording industry and several Arab American record labels emerged. Thus, recording music, as both an artistic and a commercial endeavor, made up part of the professional activities of the many musicians of the community. When we listen to these old, scratchy three-minute-long Arab songs, we can only imagine what the live music scene might have been like.

Listen to Chapter 5, Track 1 on the website, an improvisation on the Arab lute, *'ud* (also *oud*), by Jalil Azouz, a Palestinian musician who immigrated to the United

States in 1947. You will hear an announcement of the title, artist, and record label, *Orient Records*, which precedes Azouz's exquisite solo. (See also Rasmussen 2002, and *The Music of Arab Americans*, under Recordings and Films.)

The instruments that musicians brought with them and later imported and crafted here include:

ud	A fretless pear-shaped lute with a round belly, a bent neck, and eleven strings, ten of which are in double courses.
qanun	A plucked zither with 72 to 78 strings in triple courses, which are fine-tuned during performance with a series of small levers that are moved up and down.
nay	A reed flute, heard rarely at first in the United States, but then, more frequently, as professional musicians from the Arab world came to this country to perform.
violin	Formerly an Arab upright fiddle called *rebab*, the Western violin was adopted into the Arab ensemble by the early twentieth century.
riqq	A tambourine with heavy brass jingles, also called *daff.*
darabukkah	A vase-shaped ceramic drum with a single head; sometimes the Turkish/Armenian metal *dumbek* was also used.
mizmar	A double-reed folk oboe usually associated with folk and village music. The *mizmar* is a loud instrument used in combination with the drum called *tabl baladi* for celebrations.
mijwiz	A double-piped, single-reed folk "clarinet" known in countries like Lebanon, Syria, and Palestine and associated with folk music and especially the *dabkah* dance.
tabl baladi	Literally *country drum*, a double-headed drum played on one head with a beater and on the other with a thin willow branch or stick. One head is thicker than the other, giving the drum two distinct pitches. The drum is suspended from the neck of the player, who is free to roam around the floor and play directly to the dancers. Paired with the *mizmar*, the dynamic performance style of *tabl* players gives the dancers tremendous energy.

This early era of Arab American music featured a repertoire that musicians have described as "traditional," "classical," or "listening" music, also commonly referred to as *turath*, the Arabic term meaning heritage. The repertoire performed included a mix of urban music from such cities as Beirut, Lebanon; Aleppo, Syria; Istanbul, Turkey; and Cairo, Egypt. Musicians laced their performances of listening music with a sprinkling of folk music for dance and an emergent popular music, which by about the 1960s overshadowed and engulfed the listening music of the past.

SAVORING THE MIDDLE EASTERN SOUND: INGREDIENTS IN THE MIX

What makes Arab music sound like it does? Like all musical systems of the Middle East, and Central and South Asia, Arab music is based on a number of melodic modes called, in the Arabic language, *maqam* (pl. *maqamat*). Two examples of maqamat are shown in Figure 5.2. In addition to a scale of specific notes, each maqam is characterized by particular musical phrases and gestures as well as by a particular emotional character. In performance practice, melodic lines may be played with flashy ornamentation or subtle nuance. Harmony is largely absent from Arab music. Each musician plays the same melodic line, yet each musician embroiders his or her part with trills, slides, turns, the addition of a flurry of notes here, the absence of others there, collectively enriching the sonic texture of a performance, creating what ethnomusicologists refer to as *heterophony.*

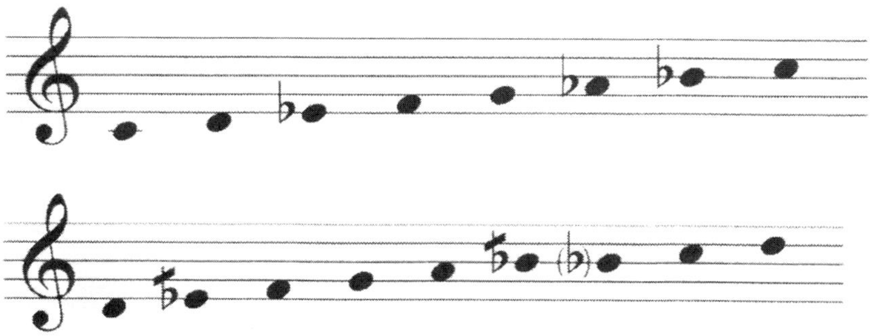

5.2. Two modes of Arab music. *Maqam Nahawand* employs the same notes as the Western minor scale (top), and *maqam Bayyati* employs the notes E half-flat and B half-flat; the latter is most often used in an ascending passage (bottom).

To the uninitiated, Arab music may at first sound "out of tune." It is, however, the tuning system of Arab music that gives it a unique character. While some of the maqamat have the same notes as the Western major and minor scales, other modes differ in terms of both the collection of pitches and the intonation of each pitch. Arab music uses notes that fall between the cracks of our tuning system. In other words, several modes use what are referred to as quarter-tones or neutral notes (neither sharp nor flat) that cannot be reproduced on Western instruments with fixed pitch, such as the piano. For Arab music to sound Arab, it should be played on traditional Arab instruments, which are built with the capability of playing the pitches of the maqam system.

The melodic modes of Arab music are complemented by a set of rhythmic patterns called *iqa'* (pl. *iqa'at).* Rhythmic patterns are recognized by their duration: they may be 3, 4, 7, 8, 10, or 14 beats long (to cite only a few examples), and

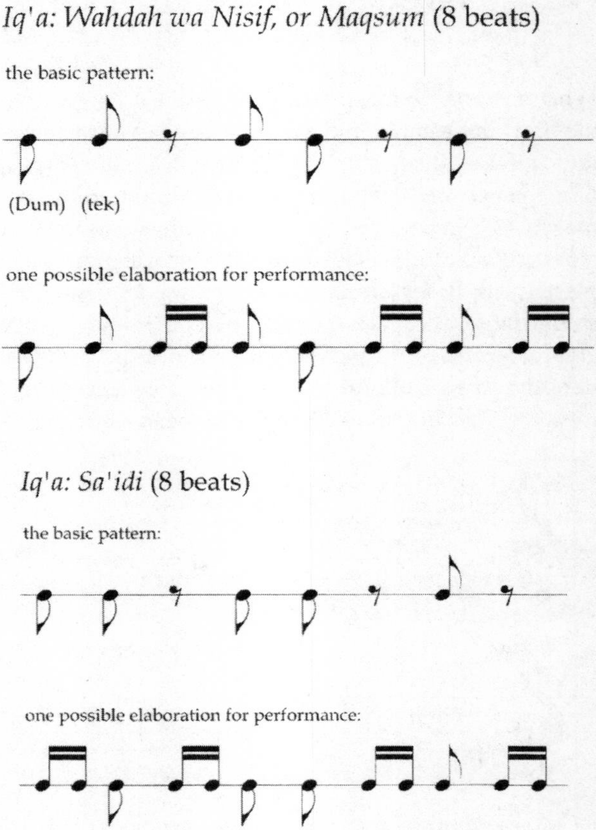

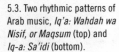

5.3. Two rhythmic patterns of Arab music, *Iq'a: Wahdah wa Nisif, or Maqsum* (top) and *Iq-a: Sa'idi* (bottom).

they comprise a pattern of beats of different tones or emphasis, and rests. Two examples of iqa'at are shown in Figure 5.3.

In performance practice, each beat has a particular timbre, the most important sounds being the *dumm*, a low-pitched tone produced by striking the middle of the head, and the *tek*, a high, drier sound produced closer to the rim of the drum (or on the jingles in the case of the *riqq* or tambourine). Thus two iqa'at, each eight beats long, may have completely different patterns of beats and rests and therefore different names and functions. Like Arab melodies, Arab rhythmic patterns are decorated and varied in performance, producing a musical product that is far more sophisticated and interesting than the theoretical models described on paper.

In addition to metric music, in which rhythmic patterns provide a regular temporal structure in complement to the melody, Arab music features lots of performance in free rhythm, or nonmetric music. Instrumental and vocal improvisation, one of the hallmarks of Arab music, often occurs in free rhythm, and it is this juxtaposition of metric and nonmetric performance, or sometimes even the simultaneous combination of the two, that distinguishes Arab music. My second musical example accessible on this book's website is a field recording I made in the living room of Detroit musicians Rana and Naim Homaidan. The recording was made so that I could better understand the Lebanese folk music that I heard at all of the Detroit area weddings. Rana sings, Naim plays 'ud, and I play violin in an impromptu performance of Lebanese folk genres "Mijana and 'Ataba," followed by a lively song for the *dabkah* dance "'Ala Daluna."

Although Arab music of the Levant and Egypt has been accompanied by a written theoretical discourse (see Marcus 1989), it is practiced by many without reference to books and without extensive knowledge of music theory. This was especially true in the United States during the early days when musicians learned their craft without the conservatories, music lessons, method books, and other pedagogical institutions and devices that are more readily available in Arab world cities. This is less the case today, when musicians have access to the discourse of Arab music theory, through formal and informal music pedagogies, ethnomusicologists teaching and publishing in the field, and camps and retreats where master musicians pass on their knowledge (see references for a list of such institutions). Nevertheless, and particularly in Detroit, there is no formal school for music and most young musicians are acculturated into the music scene through a combination of listening, playing, dancing, and singing. In spite of the absence of organized music pedagogy, many of the rules of melody, rhythm, and form that are written in theoretical works and passionately discussed by musicians, professors, and ethnomusicologists may exist in a musician's practice—the way they play the music—but not conceptualized in their intellectual understanding of the music—the way they explain the music (see also Davis 1992; Racy 1991; Marcus 1992; Rasmussen 2010, chapter 3; and Schuyler 1990).

When we take the distinguishing features of Arab music together—the unique timbres of traditional instruments; the particular approach to intonation; a melodic texture that foregrounds improvisation, decoration, variation, and nuance; the exciting meters and rhythms of the music and the sounds of the percussion instruments that play them; and the affection for the juxtaposition and combination of metric and nonmetric music—we might begin to understand some of the reasons why we are "turned on to" or "turned off by" the Arab sound. Middle Eastern music has been a source of fascination in the West, and this can be heard throughout the history of Western music. Composers of Western "art music," for example, Mozart and Tchaikovsky, have been inspired by music of the Middle East or the "Orient." During the early years of this century, the popular music of vaudeville and Tin Pan Alley included numerous songs inspired by foreign places and newly arrived immigrants in America, for example "The Sheik of Araby" and "Lena from Palestina." Music and the contexts for belly dancing, an American craze with roots in the 1893 Columbian Exposition in Chicago that reached its peak in the 1960s and 1970s, was created by American-born musicians of both

Middle Eastern and non–Middle Eastern heritage. Rooted in real traditions, this music also capitalized on the sounds and sights of an Oriental fantasy (see Rasmussen 1992). And countless Hollywood film scores for movies that depict stories from biblical epics to James Bond adventures feature music that, through instrumentation, rhythm, and melody, references a musical Middle East. The contemporary interest in Arab or, more broadly, Middle Eastern music rings out in such "world beat" or "world music" projects as Peter Gabriel's soundtrack for *The Last Temptation of Christ* and the later-released recording *Passion Sources*, Yemeni singer Ofra Haza's popular recordings (in a Jewish tradition related to Arab Yemeni music), or Robert Plant and Jimmy Page's collaboration, tour, and audio and video recording *No Quarter* with musicians from Egypt and Morocco. Sting and Shakira have collaborated with Arab musicians and dancers. And with YouTube, popular musicians from the Middle East and its diaspora are just a click away. These few examples of contemporary world music demonstrate that the sound of Arab music, with its unique style and performance practice, is meaningful to a population that extends far beyond Arab America.

ARAB AMERICAN COMMUNITY AND CULTURE IN THE DETROIT AREA

There is no place in America, and perhaps in the world, that better approximates the ideological notion of the Arab world mosaic than Detroit and the adjacent city Dearborn. In order to gain insight into the Arab music scene in Detroit, we consider, first, music making at the family level by looking at three wedding celebrations; second, music sponsored by a large community festival in Detroit; third, a concert sponsored by an Arab American cultural arts agency. An appreciation of the interface between contexts for musical performance that are grounded in the "natural" life of the community and those events that are sponsored by larger community, city, or national organizations and institutions is the key to understanding the forces at work behind the Arab American music scene specifically and, by extension, any American music scene in general.

Detroit's Arab American community numbers about 250,000 with a statewide population of about 500,000. It is reportedly the largest community of Arabic speakers outside the Arab world. Arab Americans have been in the area for more than one hundred years. Small groups migrated from New York and New England to the area along peddling routes that were established at the beginning of the twentieth century. Many more followed with the economic revolution facilitated by the Ford automobile plant and related industry, which created jobs requiring few English-language skills or previous technical training (see Naff 1985).

The nature of the Arab American community changed dramatically during the 1960s in Detroit and throughout the United States. First, immigration quotas enacted in 1924 that restricted Arab immigration were lifted in 1965, effecting a surge of emigrants from the Arab world. Second, while the Arab American community, in the middle of the twentieth century, was a stable group of primarily of Christians from Syria and Lebanon and their American-born families, the newly arriving Arabs were from all over the Arab world, including Yemen, Iraq, and the Arabian Peninsula. Third, while many of these new immigrants sought educational and economic opportunity in the United States, they were also escaping the reverberations of tumultuous conflicts in their home countries, including the Arab-Israeli wars (1948 and 1967), twelve years of civil war in Lebanon (beginning in 1975), continuing warfare and invasions in Beirut and South Lebanon, the Palestinian uprising or Intifadah (beginning in 1988), and the second Al-Aqsa Intifadah (beginning in 2000), and war in Iraq (1991 and 2003).

In Detroit, many from the first wave of immigration have moved out to the suburbs. These early immigrants and subsequent generations of American-born family members are well established and well assimilated. This old community stands in sharp contrast to many of the newer communities of people that have immigrated within the past thirty years, many of them refugees of war, who are continuously welcoming new members from "back home." At this writing (2015), situations in Syria, Iraq, and Palestine foreshadow the continuous migration from parts of the Arab world.

Fieldwork

Before turning to three scenarios of music making on the family level, let me place myself in the picture. I began doing fieldwork in the Detroit area during the summer of 1988 as a part of the research for my dissertation in ethnomusicology (Rasmussen 1991). Over the past two and a half decades, my original set of contacts has blossomed into an ever-expanding network of musicians, community members, and their families. Between 1988 and 2000, I traveled to Detroit nearly every summer. Beginning in 1996 I also began to do fieldwork in the southeast Asian country of Indonesia, in a completely different context but on a project that still concerned Arab music—the Arab music of the Indonesian Muslim community. Much more recently, in 2010 I began a new fieldwork project in the Persian Gulf country of Oman, where, to my surprise, I found transnational connections between musicians of the Iraqi diaspora who were working as musicians in both the Gulf and the United States. Although I have traveled to Detroit much less frequently since the year 2000, I am still very much in touch with the Arab music scene, primarily through the many musicians who have become colleagues and whom I have invited to perform with the Middle Eastern Music Ensemble that I direct at the College of William and Mary. Although two wars in Iraq, consistent turmoil in Lebanon, and, at this writing, Syria, and unending escalating tension in the occupied Palestinian territories have cast one dark cloud after another over the Arab American community, the music scene is thriving, perhaps in part to counterbalance all of the tragedy in the Middle East, and certainly because the

United States offers a safe haven for both music and music making. In fact, some of the most exciting Arab music anywhere happens in the United States.

Let me describe my fieldwork. My point of entrée into Arab American culture in the Detroit area is almost always with musicians. I meet musicians at their gigs and greet the members of the band; I sit with the band at the musicians' table. Sometimes I "sit in" with the band and play either 'ud or riqq on stage. In the course of the several hours of a music event, I circulate and meet a variety of people: participants, young and old; videographers; caterers; the host of the party; the mother of the bride; festival organizers; a belly dancer. People come to know me in a variety of roles: friend, friend of friend, professor of music, ethnomusicologist, music student, fellow musician, or even "that strange American woman who plays the 'ud." I always ask permission to photograph or to make audio or video recordings and explain that my intentions are for the purposes of documentation and education. Communication transpires in a combination of English and Arabic; although I have a working knowledge of written and spoken Arabic, I am less than fluent in the language. I do not deny that many things may escape my understanding.

In addition to attending weddings, parties, and festivals and dropping in at nightclubs, I visit people in their homes to discuss their musical experience in general and to learn from musicians by playing music for and with them. I have been studying and playing Arab music since 1985 and I believe that this is a source of fascination, curiosity, and pride for many of my informants, people who we ethnomusicologists also refer to as consultants, interlocutors, collaborators, colleagues, or friends. Often when I am invited to someone's home, other family and friends are present, a meal is generously prepared and served, music is played live and recorded performances are shared, people dance, the television is on, kids come and go, phones ring.

One of the greatest challenges since beginning my fieldwork among Arab Americans has been to sharpen my perception and understanding of the multicultural Arab music scene in the Detroit area. So, in order to gain insight into the sights and sounds of music making in Arab Detroit on the family level, I offer these experiences—a Lebanese wedding party, a Yemeni wedding party and an Iraqi-Italian wedding party—as points of departure.

A Lebanese Wedding Party

We are in a modest but large banquet hall in suburban Detroit. I am seated at the musicians' table where we are wolfing down our dinner to fuel up for the three-and-a-half hour set of nonstop music that is to come. The bride and groom and the bridal party have already ceremoniously entered the hall to the accompaniment of special processional wedding music supplied by the band and the singer Mahmoud Beydoun. This special procession, called *zaffah*, knows many variations, but is a prerequisite part of every Arab American wedding. The bride and groom sit on a raised platform on special throne-like chairs opposite the band's stage. They do not eat with the guests; rather, they appear as if on display for the rest of the guests to admire. A group of old women clad in long *jalabayyahs* (a traditional straight, long-sleeved, ankle-length woman's dress) approach the stage and perform *awiyyah*—stylized little poems of welcome and blessing that are called out in a high voice. The genre of awiyyah is probably hundreds of years old. Another guest half reads and half sings a special poem in the classical or formal Arabic language (*fusha*) that he has composed for the bride and groom. At our table, the musicians, including three whom I have known for years and several whom I am meeting for the first time tonight, eat and visit, paying little attention to the action in the banquet hall. For them, this is a "gig"!

The crowd, and especially the women, are dressed in fancy attire. My subtly colored suit pales in comparison. Women wear jeweled gowns and sequined party dresses, many with matching veils. The families of both the bride and the groom come from a predominantly Muslim village of Northern Lebanon. The majority of the attendants are also from that village—many have immigrated recently, some within the past ten years; almost everyone is speaking Lebanese Arabic.

When given our cue, we musicians take our place on the stage. For the remainder of the evening, we provide a kind of temporal structure that frames each set of wedding guests with music, through dance. The musicians take their cue from the master of ceremonies who, throughout the evening, consults a list of guests, and from the singer, who launches into song after song after song, demonstrating his knowledge of an apparently unlimited repertoire of lively, danceable tunes.

The emcee calls out: "The grandmother and grandfather of the bride and all of their family, please come up, it is your turn." At this point the members of this part of the family come to the dance floor and dance exuberantly. As they dance, money is tossed into the air. A dancer, perhaps a young man or a child, is hoisted upon the shoulders of other dancers. More money is thrown. Young boys, from about five to ten years of age, race around and gather up the bills that are thrown on the floor, stuffing them into cardboard boxes. The throwing of money is both a public display of generosity and a contribution to the new couple. Although the money is tossed into the air in a carefree manner, the bills are fastidiously collected, counted, and later presented to the newlyweds.

At this particular wedding, group after group is called to the dance floor, until every part of the extended family and every guest has been recognized. Sometimes the emcee identifies prospective dancers by their profession. "Let's call up Ali, the engineer!" or "Let's call up the Barda family, the owners of the Caravan restaurant!" Two musicians, Nadeem Dlaikan, who plays the *mizmar*, and Wa'el Yazigi, who plays the tabl baladi, spend much of their time out on the dance floor playing among the celebrants. The singer, too, often descends from the stage onto the dance floor. He and the other band members whoop and holler, shouting exclamations, calling out the names of the family members who are out on the floor, and urging the dancers on.

The last segment of this wedding evolves into a huge collective line dance called the *dabkah*. Eventually a line of one hundred or more people forms around the perimeter of the dance floor. The line comprises primarily men, who are at the beginning of the line, followed by women and children at the end. Various men take turns leading the dabkah line and performing their own fancy variations. Throughout the party, the performance of spirited dancing seems to be almost an obligation of the celebrants in their public expression of joy for the couple.

The singer and musicians are an excellent match for this crowd, whose energy never wanes for even a moment of the long evening. During the dabkah segment, Mahmoud Beydoun summons from his memory or invents from his imagination verse after verse and song after song. His tireless singing is supported by Nadeem, playing nay and mizmar, Wa'el on the floor with the tabl baladi, and Ghassan Shaito, who with his keyboard synthesizer, can imitate the timbre and tuning of nearly any Arab instrument. The drummers, one on trap drums with electronic pads and one on the traditional vase-shaped *darabukkah*, push the sound system to its limit. Although the musicians complain about the length of the wedding as we are packing up—we played for four and a half hours without a break—they nevertheless seem to enjoy themselves thoroughly as they infuse the crowd with one burst of musical energy after another. In addition to providing a menu of primarily Lebanese folk and pop music for their patrons, they have structured the progression of the evening, from the ceremonial zaffah procession of the bridal party to the facilitation of kin-group dancing, accompanied by the important financial transaction of gift money to the bride and groom; and they have provided a kinesthetic climax with the long set of dabkah music, which is exciting even for those who choose to sit on the sidelines and watch.

A Yemeni Wedding Party

As we pull into the parking lot of the Crystal Palace Banquet Hall in South Detroit, Sammiah hurries me along, worried that we have already missed the zaffah, the initial procession of the bride and groom and their attendants into the public space of the party. Sammiah and her husband agreed to take me along to a Yemeni wedding, just the day before. I had naively anticipated an exotic traditional wedding in a private home, where men and women celebrated separately, each gender dancing their own dances to their own group of musicians. I worried about what to wear and whether to cover my head. I was aware that the Yemeni population in Detroit is known to be conservative, reserved, and Muslim. As we walk into the wedding, I am greeted by the familiar wedding party setting. Round tables, balloons, large platters of green beans, roast beef, chicken, and salad with Italian dressing, pitchers of orange pop and cola: American food at its most mediocre. There are more than three hundred guests in attendance, a typical size for a Detroit wedding party. All but one or two others, like myself, are Arab American, and the majority of these people are of Yemeni heritage. As I become more comfortable with the surroundings and with my new Yemeni American friend, Sammiah, at my side, my perception sharpens.

Sammiah directs me to the "family side." Here men, women, and children sit together at tables. Women are variously dressed; many wear the traditional headscarf, yet others are attired in sleeveless, tight-fitting evening gowns. Sammiah has led me away from the men's side of the banquet hall. The celebrants on this side of the room are young men who have come to America and who work, primarily in Detroit's automotive industry.

At the front of the hall is an elaborately decorated tiered stage where the bride and groom will sit. In the front corner of the family side, a stage is set up for the Lebanese group, the Rana and Naim Band. In the corner of the men's side, the Yemeni band Afrah al-Yemen tunes up. Suddenly, the celebrants move toward the center aisle and crowd toward the door. I have been granted permission to photograph and videotape but am uncomfortable wielding the equipment through the dense crowd.

"Move closer, move up Anne, because you're missing a lot! Just push your way up!" encourages my companion Sammiah. Just then, a booming announcement penetrates the soundscape:

"And now will the beautiful bride and groom enter, they're going to do the zaffah with Rana and Naim."

Rana, a Lebanese American singer, is poised at the front of the procession that is about to ensue. She announces the entrants with a traditional wedding song. With her powerful, controlled alto voice, Rana belts out the melismatic, nonmetric melody, called *mawwal*, which serves as an introduction to the song that will bring the celebrants into the public space of the party. Naim, Rana's husband and partner, stands behind her, supporting her song on his instrument, the 'ud. As they lead the procession of bride and groom, bridesmaids, groomsmen, and children and family members, Rana and Naim continue their performance. They work with remote mikes, somehow communicating tempos and transitions through the dense crowd to the rest of the band members, who remain on their stage back in the corner of the hall. As Rana escorts the couple down the middle aisle between the family side and the men's side of the hall, she sings, claps, and dances with the handsome, but naturally shy couple. Two belly dancers, hired especially for this ceremonial zaffah procession, assist the musicians by dancing with and around the members of the bridal party. Meanwhile, Naim performs crowd management, directing people in the zaffah line, encouraging them to approach the dance floor at the front, all the while playing 'oud. The celebrants crowd around the couple. Money is tossed into the air and later collected and counted. As soon as there is a critical mass on the dance floor and all the key players of the wedding party are dancing, Rana and Naim "work the tables," greeting the guests, who do not make it to the front, in song. Perhaps twenty or twenty-five minutes after the onset of the zaffah, Rana has woven her way through all of the tables on the family side of the hall. Rana and Naim then join the newly married couple on a special tiered stage, where they will sit on throne-like chairs with their "court" of about a dozen child bridesmaids. Rana and Naim wave to all before they leave the couple alone and at the center of attention. In a gesture of closure, the musicians exit the hall, taking the same path the bridal party had traveled during the zaffah. There is a break in the action, but their work for the evening is hardly over.

Throughout the rest of the evening Rana and Naim (who bill their music as "Arabic Pop") share the party with Afrah al-Yemen, a group of three young Yemeni men who in the late 1990s constituted the only regularly working ensemble of Yemeni musicians in Detroit. Their main singer, Abd al-Nour, plays the 'ud, the other two play darabukkah and bongo drums. As they play their traditional music on the men's side of the banquet room, the men dance a graceful line-dance; sometimes they break off into couples and, while supporting each other by grasping their arms, plunge down to the ground and spring back up again without missing a beat. Listen to my third musical example accessible on the website for this book, a live field recording of Afrah al-Yemen.

The repertoire of Afrah al-Yemen is distinct from that of the Rana and Naim band. The melodies and rhythms they play are Yemeni and similar to the rhythmic grooves of the Arabian Gulf countries. Their vocal timbre is tight and nasal; their Yemeni dialect and accent is different from the pan-Levantine Arabic one hears in much of Detroit. Rana and Naim comment later, while we sit together listening to Afrah al-Yemen, that they understand little of this music. "It sounds like they're just playing the same rhythm all night long," one comments.

Although both bands at the party play Arab music, their repertoire comes from two related but very different Arab musical languages. That they are combined in the time and place of this party is worthy of explanation. The Yemeni families who celebrate the wedding have naturally sought out Yemeni music for this auspicious occasion. The band, Afrah al-Yemen, is positioned on the men's side of the hall, and provides the sonic environment for the most traditionally Yemeni aspects of this community of celebrants. The Lebanese and Arab popular music that Rana and Naim perform might be referred to as the musical *lingua franca* of Arab American Detroit. Their songs and musical style are the most commonly heard music in the area. The zaffah they lead is beautiful and exciting. Although very few of the hundreds attending this party are Lebanese, they seem to enjoy both styles, and are able to switch between the musical and cultural codes of Yemeni and Lebanese performance.

An Iraqi-Italian Wedding Party

This evening I am at an exquisite banquet hall in the northern suburbs of Detroit, at the invitation of Majid Kakka and the Bells Band, whose three members, manager, and combination soundman/"roadie"/disc-jockey are of Chaldean, Christian, Iraqi heritage. The Bells Band shares the stage with an Italian band whose front man, Pino Marelli, hails from Italy. Among the guests are, not surprisingly, a number of Americans of both Iraqi and Italian heritage. The Detroit Iraqi community is clustered in the northern suburbs and is generally quite well off, especially when compared to Iraqi Americans who are refugees of the series of wars that have plagued this country. The majority of Iraqi Americans in the Detroit area are Caldean (also Chaldean), and their religion is an ancient form of Catholicism. The Italian contingent at the wedding is also Catholic. An Italian-Iraqi mixed marriage makes "sense," one musician told me, because their religions are compatible—"both are a brand of Catholicism."

Like the Yemeni community, the Iraqi community in Detroit is culturally unique. For example, in addition to the Arabic language, Caldeans speak neo-Aramaic, a language believed to have been spoken by Jesus Christ. As a result, contemporary Iraqi music features a repertoire of songs and lyrics that are specifically Caldean, as well as rhythms and dances that are completely distinct from the Lebanese/Egyptian traditional and popular music that forms the main staple of Arab music culture in Detroit. Although Iraqis take great pride in the ancient roots of their language and culture, their music is, ironically, the most modern-sounding and technically "hip." Very few young Iraqi musicians use any traditional instruments. Rather, they represent the sounds of traditional instruments with keyboard synthesizers, drum machines, and sampling devices (listen to Chapter 5, Track 4 accessible on the website for this book).

Unlike Yemeni music, which remains on the margins of the Detroit music scene, the distinctive Iraqi branch of Arab American music is part of the local musical mainstream. The growing popularity of Iraqi music and dance may be attributed in part to the large number of Iraqis here but also to the fact that these folks are good patrons: they have money to spend on music and dance events for which musicians are hired. As one American-born musician of Palestinian heritage told me: "You've got to play Iraqi [music]. Everybody plays Iraqi. If you don't play Iraqi [music]? You starve!!" My friend's comments reflect both the popularity of Iraqi music in the Detroit/Dearborn area as well as the robust patronage of the Iraqi community.

On this particular evening, the Bells Band has already played for the zaffah procession as well as performed a set of dance music featuring primarily Iraqi songs with a smattering of mainstream Arab music thrown in. The Bells' front man, Majid Kakka, plays three keyboards, sings, and controls the band's impressive rolling rack of computer and digital technology. Kakka is flanked on either side by two fellow musicians, both of whom play electronic drum pads. Acting as a kind of operations manager, a young man named P-Nice, also of Iraqi heritage, is responsible for getting all of the equipment to the gig, setting it up, running sound, and spinning discs during the band's breaks. While the Bells Band played and P-Nice worked off stage, the wedding guests, holding hands and in a line formation, danced a bouncing Iraqi dabkah dance, as well as Oriental-style dancing in groups or couples.

But now the energy has shifted. Pino Marelli (on tour from Italy) and his six-piece band are playing a set that includes Italian hits, the tarantella, American favorites, and now the ridiculous and fun "chicken dance" in which the participants intermittently act like chickens flapping their wings while moving in a circular procession. I am hanging out on the sidelines with the Bells Band, now on break. The hall is splendidly appointed. A huge ice sculpture graces the cake table; the cake itself looks like a miniature palace. The dessert table is laden with fruits and petit fours. Dinner included seafood and steak and the guests have enjoyed an open bar all night.

I have been captivated by the Iraqi, Italian, Catholic, and American array of expressive culture—music, dance, food, prayer, language, and gesture—that has evolved over the evening. As I try to take in the commentary of my hosts combined with all that I observe, a moment occurs that seems to summarize the multicultural essence of this exhilarating scene.

Suddenly, there is a power outage. Pino's sound goes dead. Dancers on the floor gasp but continue to frolic about as we are well into the party. P-Nice checks the Bells' sound on the right side of the stage. Their equipment checks out. The Bells go into standby mode. Then, Pino's sound is back on. "Come on everybody! Let's continue with the Chicken Dance!" calls Pino. But, as soon as the dancing celebrants begin to flap and squawk, the power is out on Pino's side once again.

At this moment, P-Nice springs into action, headphones around his neck, one phone to his ear as he cues up two vinyl discs on twin turntables. He teases the audience with the summer's salsa-flavored hit "Hot! Hot! Hot!" P-Nice scratches the mix and eases into the introduction of another hit of that summer, "Rhythm of the Night." As if they had been rehearsing for weeks, the dance floor shrieks with delight and a wave of free-form disco dancing ensues. P-Nice is in his world, mixing and scratching, choosing up new discs for the rest of his set. But just as the dancers are in the groove of "Rhythm of the Night," the power comes on again on Pino's side of the stage and the band is up and running. The rhythm reverts to the square and corny European polka-based chicken dance. The crowd happily complies and continues partying to Pino Marelli's selection of Italian-flavored and international hits. Later the Bells Band steps into the limelight for a last set of their exciting, digitized ethnic sound. A quick YouTube search results in numerous recordings by this ever-popular band.

These three scenes evoke the sound of Arab America in Detroit, all of it virtually invisible to mainstream America. Weddings are the mainstay of a professional musician's livelihood, especially during the summer months when there may be five or six every weekend. Musicians are not only the artistic specialists for their community, they are also cultural and ritual specialists. Through their sound, they provide a regionally specific cultural language that gives meaning and emotional impact to community gatherings. Through the ways in which they arrange their performance, they structure the time of the wedding celebration ritual by directing the sequence of events and the corresponding actions of the participants. In the next two sections of this chapter, we will look at contexts for musical performance that bring together Arabs from all nations, religions, regions, and socioeconomic classes of Detroit in ecumenical events organized by multicultural committees that are interested in presenting Arab American culture to general, public audiences.

AN AFTERNOON AT THE ARAB WORLD FESTIVAL

This afternoon we are enjoying a midwestern heat wave in downtown Hart Plaza, where the Arab World Festival takes place every summer as part of a series of weekend ethnic festivals in downtown Detroit. At the time of my research, the festival was organized every year since the early 1970s by an ad hoc committee of community members who take an interest in Arab American arts and social causes in general. The festival is free, open to the public, and eminently accessible, and several thousand people, from the Arab American community and the general public, are in attendance today. If the Arab world festival is no longer a Detroit tradition today, other similar festivals have taken its place. Just check the website www.arabamerica.com for an ongoing list of concerts, festivals, classes, and other events in the area. This year's festival opened ceremoniously, with a few words from Detroit and Dearborn politicians and from Muslim and Christian religious leaders of the Arab American community. In the course of the afternoon we are treated to a fashion show of traditional Arab dress as well as performances by two dance troupes. One of the troupes comprises about twelve Arab American young men and women wearing coordinated costumes of shiny gold and black fabric. To the accompaniment of recorded music, they dance fancy choreographed variations of a folk dance, the dabkah. The second dance troupe, which consists of mostly non–Arab American women, presents solo and group "Oriental" dances. The crowd seems to enjoy everything.

Part of the fun of the Arab World Festival is to wander around and visit the many booths and tables that are set up and around this cement, urban fairgrounds. The Arab World Festival also brings great visibility to businesses, social organizations, and clubs, which have set up booths where one may purchase Arabic food and imported products, or simply pick up information about the services available in the community.

Musicians view this as an excellent venue for both established and emergent bands. The singers who are featured in the much-coveted evening time slots are greeted with the cheers and applause of a crowd that matches—in size and volume—that of a rock concert. When evening falls, thousands descend on Hart Plaza, and it seems that at least that many crowd toward the front of the performance space to dance and be a general part of the action. The concentration of people, from the newly arrived grandmother who speaks nary a word of English to the wealthy, smartly dressed plastic surgeon, the loud music, and the boisterous dabkah dancing combine to supercharge the atmosphere of the event with the collective current of the Arab American community.

Today the notion of unity and diversity is honored not only by the myriad groups who participate but also by their musical repertoires and, in some cases, the particular songs that are chosen to represent and recognize all groups. Singers, who are able to perform songs from a variety of countries, carefully string together a medley of songs from Iraq, Egypt, Lebanon, Jordan, and so forth. Today, however, one singer, a popular performer at the Arab World Festival, revises the lyrics of "Ya Saree Saralay," a Jordanian song about the happiness of the wedding night, to welcome each subset of the Arab community.

Lubnan baladna, Beirut ʿasimitna
Lebanon is our country, Beirut is our capital
Filistine bakadna, al-Quds ʿasimitna
Palestine is our country, Jerusalem is our capital
Urdun baladna, Amman ʿasimitna
Jordan is our country, Amman is our capital
Al-Yemen baladna, Sana'a ʿasimitna
Yemen is our country, Sana'a is our capital

As they hear the vocalist sing out the names of their countries and capital cities, each section of the crowd cheers and waves.

While Yemeni, Palestinian, Lebanese, Syrian, Egyptian, Jordanian, and Iraqi populations may remain relatively endogamous in their private and professional lives, they will come into contact with one another through such civic organizations as the school system and events as the Arab World Festival, at which presumably all sections of the community are represented. The unified Arab world, however, may exist for only a fleeting moment of the festival. In general, Arab Americans, even those who describe themselves as completely Americanized, tend to derive their identity from the unique cultural qualities of their national, regional, and religious heritage rather than from the collective and expansive notion of the Arab world. Music in Detroit references these cultural differences with elegant precision. With respect to Arab American culture in general and music specifically, the Detroit area is in fact unique in its ability to support so many Arab musical subcultures.

FANN WA TARAB: A CELEBRATION OF ARAB AMERICAN ART, MUSIC, AND POETRY

This afternoon we are gathered in a lovely atrium in downtown Detroit's premier art museum, the Detroit Institute of Arts. Waiters serve us wine, and we choose from a colorful variety of Middle Eastern appetizers and snacks. The trickle of the fountain combines with the polite conversation and excited chatter of the eclectic crowd. Several hundred people have already toured a special exhibit in one of the museum's galleries and are now eager to meet and congratulate the six Arab American artists whose paintings are on display. Members of the Detroit arts world, politicians, and Arab American community leaders and their families seat themselves in informal configurations at the iron tables in the atrium or mill about enjoying the refreshments before the concert begins.

Attendance at this event is open to the public for the ticket price of twenty-five dollars; the audience seems select. "*Fann wa Tarab*, A Celebration of Arab American Art, Music and Poetry" has been in the planning for more than a year. In this case, the patronage behind the event does not come from a Lebanese or Iraqi family group but from an ecumenical, voluntary civic organization of artists and patrons called the Arab American Arts Council. An excerpt from the sixteen-page program booklet illuminates the mission of the council and sets the tone of the evening:

> Hoping to stimulate creativity and insight, the Council showcases the classical, folk, and contemporary Arab arts in unconventional contexts, for culturally diverse audiences. The Council cultivates young talent and ancient art forms alike. It supports local writers, visual artists, and musicians by encouraging arts programming of the highest quality. The Council also strives, through a variety of collaborative programs, to bridge the distance between Arab American artists and the larger arts community of Metro Detroit and beyond.

The Arab American Arts Council was created under the auspices of the Cultural Arts Program of ACCESS, the Arab Community Center for Economic and Social Services. The Cultural Arts Program of ACCESS, for many years under the directorship of Sally Howell, has worked to recognize master musicians in the community by commissioning their performance and collaboration for special events. ACCESS's Cultural Arts Program regularly brings in guest artists from other parts of the country and sponsors formal concerts of traditional music and musical fusion projects. ACCESS has organized teaching workshops, research and fieldwork projects, lecture series, and exhibitions. Through all of these activities, and many others, ACCESS aims to bring together various factions of the local Arab American community and non–Arab Americans that might naturally remain separate. Such efforts in Arab cultural arts programming, now assumed by the National Arab American Museum, which opened in 2005, stand in sharp relief to the "natural life" of the music scene in Detroit, which is largely driven by popular and folk music, in the context of private family celebrations, nightclubs, or parties.

The festive reception comes to an abrupt finish, and we are encouraged to take our assigned seats in the adjacent theater. Formal announcements precede a thirty-minute reading by Lebanese American poet David Williams. Finally, seven musicians, clad in tuxedos, take their seats in a semicircle on the small stage. The selection of Arab classical, traditional, and "serious popular" music has been carefully planned and rehearsed under the authoritative guidance of the New York artist Simon Shaheen, an extremely accomplished and well-respected Arab American who is the premier guest artist of the evening. With the exception of the vocalist, Ghada Ghanem, also visiting from New York, the other musicians have been hand picked by the patrons of the event. All of the musicians are profiled in the program with a bio and publicity photo. Of the perhaps 150 professional musicians in Detroit's Arab American community, these men are considered the most seasoned and the most capable of playing serious music of, in the words of the Arts Council statement quoted above, "the highest quality."

The program proceeds as planned, with the exception perhaps of an encore. The audience, a combination of musical connoisseurs and newcomers to the "Arab sound," responds with enthusiastic appreciation. Although the exuberant dancing, singing, and clapping of the wedding parties and the festival described above is absent, members of the audiences may be heard offering vocal kudos of praise, especially during the long solo improvisations, *taqasim*, which are a hallmark of Arab traditional music performance. For many of those who attend this event, including the musicians, the serious, formal presentation of Arab arts—music, poetry, and painting—is a great source of pride. Normally Arab American musicians depend on the demand of public audiences from within their own ethnic community; the opportunities to formally rehearse a program of serious music for an attentive audience are few, although that has changed significantly in the past two decades as more Arab music moves into university settings and more serious Arab musicians draw upon universities, museums, and performing arts centers for patronage.

The patronage of ACCESS differs in a number of ways from the hiring of musicians by families, nightclubs, and community groups. Cultural programs at ACCESS are carefully conceived and organized. They are always funded in part by such granting agencies as the National Endowment for the Arts, the Doris Duke Foundation, or the Lila Wallace Reader's Digest Foundation, groups that support the arts and artists throughout the country. In order to receive such funds, ACCESS must submit carefully written grant applications describing its plans to present Arab American arts and artists. The application process is fiercely competitive and the language of a grant application must reflect clear vision and purpose. Often, in order to convince granting agencies of the merit of their proposed programs, letters of support are solicited from artists, politicians, cultural leaders, and academics from throughout the country, who are thought to be familiar with the people and the arts involved. Because outside supporters have the appropriate credentials, their opinions are usually respected. While it may be unfair to generalize about granting agencies, they tend to fund projects that showcase arts that are considered traditional, classical, or new works. "Pop" music is often disqualified.

Official support, both financial and moral, for Arab American music fills an important gap in the patronage structure of Arab American musical life. Whereas in the home countries of Arab Americans and other immigrant communities, their music and musicians had the support of local conservatories, theaters, universities, and radio and television stations, in the United States support for their art by such institutions is rare if it exists at all. Thus the health of their musical culture depends to a large extent on the multicultural programming efforts of such agencies as ACCESS and the support of foundations.

There is some irony in this mix, because community musicians are rarely involved in the fundraising process. Owing perhaps to a cultural gap between the musicians of Arab Detroit and mainstream America, musicians do not speak the same language as the agencies that might be able to help them the most. Instead, such cultural agents as folklorists, anthropologists, and ethnomusicologists serve as liaisons between the music and the money. In fact, although there may be very little academic prestige attached to work within the public sector (as opposed to pure research and scholarly publication), many people trained in these fields, including perhaps some of the authors of this book, believe that bringing "subcultural" artists into the limelight of mainstream America is our most significant mission.

CONCLUSIONS

What are some of the issues that emerge from the consideration of Arab American music culture that resonate with and extend to other subcultural music scenes in the United States? As mentioned at the outset, Arab American musical culture is in and of itself multicultural and multifaceted. Distinctions, both obvious and subtle, are a feature of many and perhaps all American communities, and it is through music, dance, food, and language that such distinctions are articulated. In order to "read" social, cultural, and aesthetic issues in music and dance events, it is important to know something of the specific history and contemporary life of the people involved. For immigrant groups, understanding patterns of immigration to the United States, as well as settlement and migration within the country, is crucial to understanding the evolution, flowering, or withering of a particular music scene.

Individual musicians, who look both to their own musical heritage as well as to the artistic currents of the "host" culture in the creation of an expressive voice, have phenomenal impact on the construction and activation of community through performance. By extension, the patronage of sociocultural organizations, from the family to grass roots community centers, religious institutions, and even the national government, directs the path of musical life within a community as they support some artists and art forms and ignore others. It is because of these multitudinous variations in music patronage that some of the activities of a particular musical subculture, such as the neighborhood street fair or the multicultural arts festival, may be easily visible and of great interest to the American mainstream, while others, such as the family wedding, remain completely invisible and/or irrelevant. It is also important to note that for Arab Americans or, for that matter, any community, the continuous use of mass media—including, at first, 78 rpm discs and, later, radio, television, records, cassettes, videotapes, and cable television, social media, live streaming, and file sharing—plays a huge role in collapsing distance in the Arab diaspora, among communities across the country, and between nations separated by oceans, political boundaries, and government travel bans. The idea that culture transpires only in particular geographical spaces is completely irrelevant when it comes to issues of expressive performance. Whether recorded or live, music moves people to different times and places and is thus one of the most compelling agents in the definition of community and individual identity. In the course of a twenty-five-year involvement with musicians and audiences of the Arab American community, I too have been powerfully affected by the sound and spirit of their musical performance. As is the case with any ethnographer, I bring to my work a unique and selective perspective that is dependent on my relationships with friends and consultants in the community and what I have experienced in the process of research and fieldwork. While I may be able to interpret and describe some aspects of this musical subculture, I no doubt remain ignorant of others.

In this chapter, I have attempted to highlight some of the issues that are central to an understanding of the musical life of Arab Americans and the relationship of this musical subculture to music culture of the United States as a whole. Furthermore, I believe that such issues—the power of performance, the initiative of individuals, the relationship of musical performance to ritual structure and social process, the effects of patronage, an understanding of community history, a consideration of mass media, and the rich experience and inevitable limitations of ethnographic fieldwork—are also germane to the consideration of the nearly infinite musical microcosms that constitute our American musical landscape.

Notes

1. This chapter reflects research and relationships that have been ongoing since 1987. For this particular project I am indebted to many musicians, community members, and colleagues in the Detroit-Dearborn area. Among them I thank Pete Arabo, Mahmoud Beydoun, Nadeem Dlaikan, Naim and Rana Homaidan, Sally Howell, Mahsin and Samia al-Jabri, Majid Kakka, Maher Mejdi, Saleh Najar, Abd al-Nur, Ghassan Shaito, Andrew Shryock, Wa'el Yazigi, and Mufadel Yaser. Fieldwork focusing specifically on weddings in Arab Detroit was carried out during the summers of 1993 and 1994 and was supported in part by Michigan State University, which featured the expressive culture of Arab weddings at the 1996 Michigan Folklife Festival that was produced by the university. I must also

acknowledge my ongoing involvement in the Arab American music scene and continuous interaction with numerous artists across the country and abroad, and particularly the forty-some who have been guest artists at the College of William and Mary with the Middle Eastern Music Ensemble that I direct there.

2. The term *Arab world* was one used by former Egyptian president Gamal Abd al-Nasser beginning in the 1950s. Arab world countries include (starting from the western coast of North Africa): Mauritania, Morocco, Algeria, Tunisia, Libya, Egypt, Sudan, Jordan, Lebanon, Syria, Iraq, Kuwait, Saudi Arabia, Yemen, Djibouti, Somalia, Oman, United Arab Emirates, Bahrain, and Qatar.

3. The number of clubs and social organizations in the Arab American community is overwhelming. There are church groups and groups from Islamic centers. (It should be mentioned that although there are significant numbers of Arab Americans of the Jewish faith, very few of them live in the Detroit area.) Some groups have political agendas and others provide medical or translation services. Some are based around an activity such as dabkah dancing, others around a common affiliation with a region. Some Arab American organizations, for example the Ramallah Club for people who trace their roots to the Palestinian town of Ramallah, have branches throughout the United States. When these clubs and social organizations hold events—often fundraisers—they can be an excellent source of patronage for musicians. The Palestine Democratic Youth Organization, the Union of Lebanese Women, the American Islamic Institute, the Arab American Chaldean Council, Beit Hanina Social Club, and the Syrian American Council of North America are just a few of the clubs that might establish a presence at the Arab World Festival. Numerous and varied businesses sell their wares, from calligraphy, to insurance, to tabouleh (a delicious salad made with bulgur wheat, parsley, and tomatoes).

Chapter 5: Musical Examples (access through companion website)

Chapter 5, Track 1. "Taksim 'Ala al-'Ud (Improvisation on the 'Ud) by Jalil Azouz. *Istiwanat Al-Chark* (Orient Records), 590A.

Chapter 5, Track 2. Rana and Naim Homaidan and the author perform Lebanese folk genres 'Ataba, Mijana, and 'Ala Daluna. Rana's family is heard clapping, dancing, and singing along in this spontaneous afternoon performance m their living room.

Chapter 5, Track 3. A brief excerpt of the Yemeni America group Afrah al-Yemen performing at a wedding during the summer of 1994. Group members include vocalist 'Abd al-Nur and Salah Najar and Mufadal Yaser on percussion.

Chapter 5, Track 4. A brief excerpt of the Iraqi American group the Bells Band at a wedding during the summer of 1995. Salam Kakka and Johnny Sana play percussion synthesizers. Majid Kakka is the group's director, lead singer, and keyboard player. Kakka continues to perform among Arab Americans in Michigan and throughout the United States. A quick YouTube search will bring you to a number of his contemporary recordings and videos.

References Cited

Davis, Ruth. 1992. "The Effects of Notation on Performance Practice in Tunisian Art Music." *World of Music* 34, no. 1.

Hoogland, Eric, ed. 1987. *Crossing the Waters: Arabic-Speaking Immigrants to the United States before 1940*. Washington and London: Smithsonian Institution Press.

Marcus, Scott L. 1989. *Arab Music Theory in the Modern Period*. PhD diss., University of California, Los Angeles.

———. 1992. "Modulation in Arab Music: Documenting Oral Concepts, Performance Rules and Strategies." *Ethnomusicology* 36, no. 2: 171–96.

Naaf, Alexa. 1985. *Becoming American: The Early Arab Immigrant Experience*. Carbondale: Southern Illinois University Press.

Racy, A. J. 2003. *Making Music in the Arab World: The Culture and Artistry of Tarab*. Cambridge, UK: Cambridge University Press.

———. 1991. "Creativity and Ambiance: An Ecstatic Feedback Model from Arab Music." *World of Music* 33, no. 3: 7–28.

———. 1981. "Music in Contemporary Cairo: A Comparative Overview." *Asian Music* 13, no. 1: 4–26.

Rasmussen, Anne K. 1996. "Theory and Practice at the 'Arabic Org': Digital Technology in Contemporary Arab Music Performance." *Popular Music* 15, no. 3: 345–65.

———. 1998. "The Music of Arab Americans: Aesthetics and Performance in a New Land." In *Image and Performance of the Middle East*. Ed. Sherifa Zuhur. Cairo: American University in Cairo Press. 135–56. (A revised version of "The Music of Arab Americans: Performance Contexts and Musical Transformation," *Pacific Review of Ethnomusicology*, 1989.)

———. 2005. "An Evening in the Orient: The Middle Eastern Nightclub in America" and "Epilogue: Middle Eastern Music and Dance since the Nightclub Era." In *Belly Dance: Orientalism, Transnationalism, and Harem Fantasy*. Ed. by Anthony Shay and Barbara Sellers-Young. Costa Mesa, CA: Mazda. 172–206.

———. 2002. "Popular Music of Arab Detroit." In *Garland Encyclopedia of World Music*. Vol. 6: The Middle East. Ed. by Virginia Danielson, Scott Marcus, and Dwight Reynolds. New York and London: Garland. 279–88.

———. 2001. "Middle Eastern Music." In *Garland Encyclopedia of World Music*. Vol. 3: The United States and Canada. Ed. by Ellen Koskoff. New York and London: Garland. 1028–41.

———. 1991. *Individuality and Musical Change in the Music of Arab Americans*. PhD diss., University of California, Los Angeles.

Schuyler, Philip. 1990. "Hearts and Minds: Three Attitudes toward Performance Practice and Music Theory in the Yemen Arab Republic." *Ethnomusicology* 34, no. 1: 1–18.

El-Shawan Castelo-Branco, Salwa. 1984. "Traditional Arab Music Ensembles in Egypt since 1967: The Continuity of Tradition within a Contemporary Framework." *Ethnomusicology* 28, no. 2: 271–88.

Touma, Habib Hassan. 1996. *The Music of the Arabs*. Expanded with compact disc. Translated by Laurie Schwartz. Portland, OR: Amadeus Press.

Vigreux, Pierre, ed. 1989. *Musique Arabe: Le Congres du Caire.* Proceedings of colloquium on the documents of the First Congress on Arab Music in Cairo, 1932, held in Cairo, May 1989, under the direction of Scheherazade Qassim Hassan. Cairo: CEDEJ.

Recordings and Films

Abdo, George, and his Flames of Araby Orchestra. 2002. *Belly Dance!* Produced and compiled with a twenty-four-page booklet of notes by Anne K. Rasmussen. Washington: Smithsonian/Folkways, SFW CD 40458.

el-Bakkar, Mohammad. 1957. *Port Said: Music of the Middle East.* Mohammed el-Bakkar and his Oriental Ensemble. Audio Fidelity AFSD 5833.

———. 1958. *The Magic Carpet: Music of the Middle East.* Vol. 4. Audio Fidelity AFSD 5895.

"Caravan." 1937. Composed by Juan Tizol and Duke Ellington, words by Irving Mills.

Dabis, Cherien. 2009. *Amreeka.* Feature film. 96 minutes. National Geographic Entertainment.

Elias, Fred. n.d. *Artistic Moods for Dance.* Vol. 2. Ultrasonic IS-2003.

Gabriel, Peter. 1989. *Passion: Music for the Last Temptation of Christ.* Geffen CD 24206-2.

Haza, Ofra. 1988. *Fifty Gates of Wisdom: Yemenite Songs.* Shanachie (World Beat/Ethno Pop) 64002.

Kochak, Eddie "the Sheik." 1970s. *Strictly Belly Dancing*, Vols. 1–6. Ameraba 2500 senes.

Mandell, Joan, director. 1995. *Tales from Arab Detroit.* 45-minute documentary film. Detroit: ACCESS and Olive Branch Productions.

Rasmussen, Anne K. 1997. Producer, compiler, author of notes. *The Music of Arab Americans: A Retrospective Collection.* A collection of performances by Arab American artists originally recorded on 78-rpm disc. Rounder Records 1122.

Page, Jimmy, and Robert Plant. 1994. *No Quarter (Unledded).* Atlantic 2 CD 82706-2.

"Palesteena." 1918. Composed by Con Conrad and Jay Russel Robinson. Introduced by the Original Dixieland Jazz Band and popularized by Eddie Cantor.

Passion Sources. 1989. [Music by various artists from India, Africa, and the Middle East used as source material for the soundtrack for *The Last Temptation of Christ*, compiled by Peter Gabriel.] Real World Carol 2301-2.

Additional Resources

Abraham, Sameer Y., and Nabeel Abraham. 1983. *Arabs in the New World: Studies on Arab-Amencan Communities.* Detroit: Wayne State University Press, Urban Studies Center.

Ahmad, Ismael, and Nancy Adadow Gray, eds. 1988. *The Arab American Family: A Resource Manual for Human Service Providers.* Detroit: ACCESS (Arab Community Center for Economic and Social Services) and Department of Social Work, Eastern Michigan University.

Captan, Kareem Habib. 2008. "Constructing the Arab: Orientalism in American Popular Culture, 1893–1930." Masters thesis, University of California, Long Beach.

Fa'ik, Ala. 1994. "Issues of Identity in Theater of Immigrant Community." In *The Development of Arab American Identity*, ed. Ernest McCarus. Ann Arbor: University of Michigan Press. 107–18.

Habib, Kenneth S. 2007–13. "Arab American Music." Oxford Music Online. http://oxford musiconline.com.proxy.wm.edu/subscriber/article/grove/music/A2223688. Accessed September 1, 2013.

Hitti, Philip. 1924. *Syrians in America.* New York: George Doran.

Houwat, Igor N. 2011. "Maintaining a Musical Tradition in Arab-America: An Oral History of Abdel Karim Bader." Masters thesis, Michigan State University, East Lansing, MI.

Howell, Sally. 2014. *Old Islam in Detroit: Rediscovering the Muslim American Past.* New York: Oxford University Press.

Kayal, Philip M., and Joseph M. Kayal. 1975. *The Syrian-Lebanese in America: A Study in Religion and Assimilation.* Boston: Twayne.

McCarus, Ernest. 1984. *The Development of Arab-American Identity.* Ann Arbor: University of Michigan Press.

Malek, Alia. 2009. *A Country Called Amreeka: Arab Roots, American Stories.* New York: Free Press.

Orfalea, Gregory. 2006. *Arab Americans: A History.* Northampton, MA: Olive Branch Press.

Oweis, Fayeq S. 2008. "Resources on Arab American Artists and Arab Culture in the United States." In *Encyclopedia of Arab American Artists.* Westport, CT, and London: Greenwood.

Rasmussen, Anne K. 2008. "The Arab World." In *Worlds of Music: An Introduction to the Music of the World's Peoples.* Ed. Jeff Todd Titon. Belmont, MA: Schirmer Cengage. 473–530 (with ten recorded performances on the accompanying CD set).

Swedenburg, Ted. 2004. "The 'Arab Wave' in World Music after 9/11." *Anthropologica* xlvi: 177–88.

Zuhur, Sherifa, ed. 2001. *Colors of Enchantment: Theater, Dance, Music, and the Visual Arts of the Middle East.* Cairo: University of Cairo Press.

Arab American Organizations and Internet Resources

Arabic Music Retreat: www.simonshaheen.com/arabic-music-retreat

Mendocino Middle Eastern Music and Dance Camp: www.middleeastcamp.com/Mendocino.html

Al Bustan Seeds of Culture: http://albustanseeds.org

University of California, Santa Barbara Middle Eastern Music Ensemble: www.music.ucsb.edu/mee/

College of William and Mary Middle Eastern Music Ensemble: www.wm.edu/as/music/ensembles/nontraditional/meme/

University of California, Los Angeles, Near East Ensemble: www.ethnomusic.ucla.edu/music-of-the-near-east-ensemble

ACCESS: Arab American Center for Social and Economic Services: www.accesscommunity.org

Arab American National Museum: www.arabamericanmuseum.org

ADC: American-Arab Anti-Discrimination Committee: www.adc.org

- 6 -

MEXICAN MARIACHI MUSIC

Made in the U.S.A.

Daniel Sheehy

As former director of the Smithsonian Center for Folklife and Cultural Heritage and current director and curator of Smithsonian Folkways Recordings, Daniel Sheehy produces and oversees dozens of projects to promote the Center's mission of promoting understanding and sustainability of traditional cultures in the United States and around the world. His original and continuing work as both an ethnomusicologist and a musician, however, is in the area of Mexican mestizo music, including music of the mariachi. In addition to being a well-recognized symbol of "Mexican-ness" for non–Mexican Americans, mariachi remains an important expression of culture of people of Mexican heritage. As such, this music has become part of the curriculum of schools and universities across the Southwest and in a select few other parts of the United States, where Mexican Americans are widely represented. As he traces the evolution of mariachi music in Mexico, Sheehy highlights the ties mariachi has had as with the evolution of Mexican nationalism, a relationship that has been fueled by mass media and one that is perceived not only from within the Mexican American community but by the American population at large. Unlike many of the musics profiled in this book, mariachi is well known in America for a number of reasons. The music (along with a host of other symbols of Mexico) has been featured in countless Western movies, national television specials, Mexican eateries, major concert halls, and even at Disney World and Disneyland. The use of such Western European instruments as trumpets and violins in the mariachi ensemble has helped to make this music more acceptable to the mainstream in the United States. And because Spanish is the second most frequently spoken language in the country, the Spanish-language lyrics of mariachi are far more accessible to Americans than any other non-English-based music. Sheehy's chapter on the history of mariachi in Mexico and its transplantation and performance in the United States is especially timely with the rise of popularity and legitimacy of mariachi in the United States, a phenomenon that may be attributed to the continually expanding presence of Mexican Americans and the performance of mariachi music by such well-known popular singers as Linda Ronstadt.

6.1. Mariachi violinist Matías Gutiérrez (far right), father of Margarito Gutiérrez, pictured with Mariachi Vargas de Tecalitlán, ca. 1940. Courtesy Margarito Gutiérrez.

INTRODUCTION

What is mariachi? Many Americans think of it as the stereotype so colorfully portrayed on television, in the movies, or on Linda Ronstadt's *Canciones de mi Padre* tour—a dozen Mexican musicians in big hats and silver-studded pants, playing trumpets, violins, and Mexican guitars, backing up a Mexican country singer crooning beneath a moonlit hacienda balcony. For others, it is a popular music like any other—they buy the latest *música ranchera* (literally, "country music") CD with a well-known singer backed up by a mariachi group, go to large-scale concerts by those same artists, and learn the words to many of the songs. For still others, mariachi music is a potent symbol of their deeply felt identity. As you will read below, over its 160-year history, mariachi has been all of these things and more. It is symbol and stereotype, ancient and modern, glorified and scorned, profession and avocation, a form of musical expression, and a way of life.

The term *mariachi* may mean a single musician, a kind of musical group, or a style of music. In addition to the music itself, three dimensions of mariachi musical life—cultural, commercial, and social—are key to understanding it fully. Since the 1930s, the mariachi ensemble and its music have been an emblem of Mexican identity, a cultural icon to anchor a Mexican culture in transition.

> In contemporary cultural dynamics—dominated by modern electronic communication—particular regional traits are debated in the face of a

> worldwide homogenizing culture. At the same time a society accepts outside influences, it bases its identity on the perseverance of the values, forms, and rhythms that preceding generations established as their own: the mariachi will continue as the symbol of the Mexican people to the extent that we conserve our national character. (Jesús Jáuregui 1990, 169; my translation)

A similar statement might be made about the symbolic importance of the mariachi ensemble and its music to the culture of many Mexican Americans, particularly those of the recent several generations of immigrants from west Mexico.

For nearly as long, music linked to the mariachi sound has been an important niche in the Mexican popular-music industry, and since the 1980s has made important gains among North American consumers as well. And as long as the mariachi's history has been documented, Mexican middle-class and elite society has been ambivalent in its attitude toward mariachi musicians and their music, which is associated with rural and working-class people. A stanza from Mexican singer and songwriter Cuco Sánchez's classic *canción ranchera* "No soy monedita de oro" (I'm Not a Gold Coin) illustrates this attitude:

> In your house they do not want me
> because I love singing.
> They say I am a mariachi
> and I don't have enough
> to buy you a wedding dress,
> that I am wasting your time. (my translation)

On any weekend or holiday, particularly during the fair-weather months, hundreds of Mexican mariachi ensembles may be heard performing across the United States. In Los Angeles, San Jose, San Francisco, San Diego, Tucson, Phoenix, Las Vegas, El Paso, San Antonio, Houston, Chicago, Orlando, Washington, New York, and dozens of other American communities, the sound of trumpets, violins, and guitars enlivens weddings, birthdays, baptisms, parties in homes, festivals, restaurants, bars, and many other social events.

Here is a glimpse of mariachi life, based on a visit in the 1990s to two mariachi performance venues in Los Angeles. On a Sunday afternoon, musicians Margarito Gutiérrez and his brother Salvador sat on two ramshackle chairs situated comfortably in the shade of the donut shop at the corner of Boyle and First Streets in East Los Angeles. They and most of their immediate family came to the United States from their hometown of Ciudad Guzmán in the Mexican state of Jalisco thirty-five years earlier, looking for greater opportunities for work. Most days of the week, this is where they may be found, passing the time trading jokes and jibes with their fellow musicians. Like most *mariacheros* (another term for mariachi musicians), they were known among their comrades by their nicknames "Santa Claus" and "Jeremec," respectively. The donut stand sat on a small triangle of concrete and asphalt recently named Plaza de los Mariachis by the City of Los Angeles. The Boyle Hotel across the street and several crowded apartment buildings and boarding houses in the surrounding neighborhood are packed with musicians. At peak business hours on weekend evenings, there may be as many as two hundred itinerant *mariacheros*, most dressed in silver-adorned black suits, waiting for clients in need of their services.

An approaching car slows and, like a magnet, attracts the musicians. The elderly driver sees the Gutiérrez brothers, whom he has hired before, and he beckons them over. He wants a group to play at his wife's birthday party in two hours. They agree on a price, number of hours of music, and number of musicians, and the client speeds off to prepare for the festivities. Margarito calls the other five members of their seven-piece group—two other brothers and three nephews—to let them know where to be and when.

Their group, Mariachi San Matías (Mariachi Saint Matthew), is named after the brothers' late father Matías Gutiérrez, also a mariachi musician, as was his father before him. The name is in part an insider, tongue-in-cheek, double entendre witticism. To the unknowing, "San Matías" could refer to a little-known town or to the Christian apostle, but it is in fact a half-humorous, half-reverent gesture at beatifying their late father as a saint. For Mariachi San Matías, this would be a typical Sunday.

Two hours later, the group is at the client's home, shoulder to shoulder with a lively gathering of his wife, children, grandchildren, extended family, and friends. Men and women try to out-yell one another to request their favorite pieces, and when they recognize the first few notes of a popular *canción ranchera*, the entire gathering erupts in a chorus of *gritos* (traditional yells). When the partygoers feel like dancing, Mariachi San Matías plays fast *polcas* (polkas) and *cumbias*, as well as slower *valses* (waltzes) and romantic *boleros*. When the two hours of music that they had agreed upon ends, the client negotiates for an additional hour, and all present gather around to sing the birthday greeting song "Las Mañanitas" for the family matriarch. At the end of the final hour, the client pays Margarito a roll of bills, and the musicians return to the time-worn station wagon of one of their members to divide up their pay. Then, since the night is young, they decide to go to a nearby bar to *talonear*, that is, to look for clients who will pay by the song to hear them play (from the word *talón*, "heel," which refers to the walking around from one place to another). At the bar it is a busy night, and they rove from customer to customer, playing five pieces for two *compadres* out on the town, three songs for a lonely-looking man on a barstool, ten more for two pairs of lovers at a table, and so forth, charging eight dollars per song. After several hours, the crowd thins out, the demand for music is exhausted, and the members of Mariachi San Matías split up their earnings and retire to their homes.

At the moment the client had arrived at the East Los Angeles plaza, several miles across town at La Fonda restaurant in the more upscale Wilshire district, the thirteen members of Mariachi Los Camperos, led by Natividad "Nati" Cano, were beginning to rehearse several new arrangements for an upcoming show. In a week, they would perform at the annual Tucson International Mariachi Conference before a sellout audience at the Tucson Convention Center. At this year's appearance, they will accompany guest artists Linda Ronstadt and the Chicano music pioneer Lalo Guerrero (now deceased), both Tucson natives. At their rehearsal, the group's musical arranger, Jesús Guzmán, passes out music for the seven violinists, who begin work on the parts and agree on precise violin bowings; the *guitarronero* (bass player), *vihuelero* (rhythm guitarist), and guitarist coordinate the piece's rhythmic and harmonic accompaniment, and the two trumpet players retire to a corner to practice so that they will not disturb the others. After about an hour, they decide to try the piece out during this evening's performance at La Fonda.

At 6:30 p.m., most of the audience arrives for the first of the evening's five forty-five-minute shows—two busloads of Japanese tourists and a small group of middle-class Mexican Americans and other diners—a typical night at La Fonda. At 6:45, the Camperos take the stage and play a forty-five-minute program of tightly arranged medleys of popular tunes. Between medleys, the group's violinist and spokesman says a few words in Japanese and sings the well-known Japanese song "Sakura" (Cherry Blossom) to the delight of the tourists and to the amazement of most of the audience who, before then, had never heard a mariachi sing in Japanese. Near the end of the set, two colorfully dressed folkloric dancers take the stage to perform the "Jarabe Tapatío"—announced as the "Mexican Hat Dance"—the stage lights go out, and the musicians retire to their dressing room. The length of each show and the break that follows is designed to correspond with the time it takes for the diners to order, eat, pay their bill, and leave, so that others may attend the next show. As the night wears on, the audience consists of fewer and fewer tourists and more Mexican American "regulars," many of whom have been coming to La Fonda since it opened in the late 1960s.

EARLY MARIACHI: FROM RURAL ROOTS TO URBAN MARKETPLACE

It is remarkable that not until the 1960s did music scholars apply their skills to charting an extensive history of the mariachi, a musical complex that had been a widely accepted icon of Mexican culture since at least the 1930s. Part of the reason for this neglect may have been that during the 1930s, 1940s, and 1950s, when Mexican researchers were intensifying their efforts to discover and to document their nation's rural folk traditions, mariachi musicians and their music had already migrated to urban Mexico City, where it merged with the popular, commercialized música ranchera of the radio and cinema, and was consequently outside particular interests of scholars. Since the late 1960s, however, numerous younger Mexican and American ethnomusicologists, ethnographers, historians, and linguists have delved into the origins of the mariachi tradition.

In the United States, the revival of interest in Latin American folksong, the heightened cultural awareness stimulated by the Chicano movement, and the rise of ethnomusicology all invigorated scholarly attention to the mariachi and its music. In the 1960s, UCLA graduate student Don Borcherdt did fieldwork in Jalisco, collecting ethnographic recordings and cultural history of the mariachi. Building on his work, the Institute for Ethnomusicology at the University of California, Los Angeles, hired mariachi violinist Jesús Sánchez, a native of Zacoalco in the Mexican state of Jalisco, who had been laboring as a farm worker in California, to lead a student mariachi ensemble at the university. With the volunteer assistance of Professor Timothy Harding, of California State University at Los Angeles, this ensemble thrived and attracted many other young scholars to mariachi music, including Mark Fogelquist (see Fogelquist 1996) and myself. In the period since the late 1960s, dozens of student mariachi ensembles at high schools and universities have emerged throughout the American Southwest, reinforcing the intellectual attention to mariachi history and cultural significance.

The renewed attention to Mexican folkloric dance that coincided with the Chicano movement beginning in the mid-1960s also reinforced interest in the mariachi music that usually accompanied the dance. Several dance groups cultivated student mariachi groups as part of their companies. Later, in San Jose, California, Jonathan Clark, who had performed mariachi music regularly with the Los Lupeños dance group in the 1970s, began documenting early mariachi history through interviewing living senior musicians and collecting rare historical recordings and photos. His collaboration with the owner of the Arhoolie recording company, Chris Strachwitz, produced four of the most important publications on mariachi music during its years of transition from rural to urban life (Clark 1992; 1993; 1994; 1998).

The 1970s and 1980s saw renewed attention among Mexican scholars, as well, to the documentation of regional musical traditions and a sharpened eye toward the anthropological analysis of national cultural symbols. The *Serie de Discos* (Record Series) of the National Institute of Anthropology and History, directed by historian Irene Vázquez Valle, produced recordings of "roots" mariachi music from small towns in Jalisco (Vázquez Valle 1976). Jalisco native and anthropological ethnographer Jesus Jáuregui published the major comprehensive work on mariachi history, *El Mariachi: Símbolo Musical de México* (The Mariachi: Musical Symbol of Mexico) in 1990, highlighting both the music's exploitation by commercial interests and its ongoing folk roots. These three decades of scholarly research shed much light on the evolution of the mariachi tradition and its place in contemporary life. They also showed us that there is much yet to be revealed about early mariachi history. The precise origin of the term *mariachi*, for example, is still not clear.

An official letter of May 7, 1852, from the Catholic priest Cosme Santa Anna, of the town of Rosamorada (located in the western Mexican state of Nayarit), contains the first known reference to the mariachi in connection to music. Writing to his archbishop in Guadalajara, the priest complained of the unrestrained music making, drinking, and gambling that occurred outside his church on Holy Saturday, offending his religious sensibilities. He had pressed the local civil authorities to end this type of annual event—called *mariachi* in that region of the country—but the mayor, instead of stopping it, contributed money to bring new musicians for a *fandango* dance party that lasted from Holy Saturday to the following Tuesday (Jáuregui 1990, 15–16). In his visit to Guadalajara in 1875, General Ignacio Martínez reported the presence of a three- or four-piece orchestra called *mariage* at a serenade in the main plaza, though the musicians may have been from the region's rural areas (see Martínez 1884; Jáuregui 1990, 21). In his book *Paisajes de Occidente* (1908), Enrique Barrios de los Ríos, writing of his observations on life in the coastal region of the territory of Tepic, describes a platform called *mariache*, on which people danced "joyful *jarabes* to the sound of the harp, or of the violin and *vihuela*, or of the violin, snare drum, cymbals, and bass drum in a deafening quartet" (43–44, my translation). The jarabe is an indigenous dance form that was first documented around 1800 and seen as an important cultural expression tied to the rise of Mexican *mestizo* (a mix of Spanish, Amerindian, and African) culture and the movement for Mexico's independence erupting in 1810. "Up to four people at once dance on the [mariache], and the loud tapping of the clamorous *jarabe* resounds through the plaza and nearby streets . . . The mariaches are surrounded by a pleasantly entertained crowd absorbed in that joyful and noisy dance" (ibid., 44).

The historical evidence uncovered so far tells us that in the nineteenth century mariachi meant more than merely a musical group. It might have described a local festive event with music, or a dance platform, for example, as well as a two-, three-, or four-piece group comprising such string instruments as the violin, vihuela, and harp. Overall, its use circumscribed a varied but discernible, widespread musical/choreographic tradition found in the western Mexican states of Jalisco, Nayarit, Colima, Michoacán, and Guerrero and parts of other neighboring states. In the rest of Mexico, the mariachi tradition was little known, that is until several enormously important national trends propelled its rise to national and international prominence in the decades following the Mexican Revolution (1910–17).

Intellectual and political nationalism, massive migration from rural areas to urban Mexico City, and the growth of a large-scale Mexican electronic media industry were powerful forces directing the evolution of Mexican society, including the mariachi. Before the revolution, the mariachi and its music had begun in a limited way to cross deeply rooted geographic, class, and cultural lines, becoming more widely known. In the late 1800s and early 1900s, piano arrangements of important traditional songs and dance pieces, rooted in western Mexico and most likely part of the mariachi's repertoire, were published for performance by Mexico's growing middle class. The most prominent of these was the "Jarabe Tapatío," *tapatío* indicating that the dance was from Guadalajara, capital of the state of Jalisco, and the surrounding region. In 1905, Justo Villa's four-piece mariachi was brought from the town of Cocula in Jalisco to Mexico City to perform for the celebrations of President Porfirio Díaz's birthday and Mexican Independence Day on September 16 (Clark 1993, 9). In 1907, on an occasion in Mexico City's Chapultepec Park honoring the American Secretary of State on a goodwill tour, an eight-piece mariachi ensemble and four folkloric dancers from Guadalajara presented a stage performance of their regional music and dance (October 3, 1907, in the newspaper *El Imparcial*, quoted in Jáuregui 1990, 31). The first known recordings of mariachi music were made on wax cylinders in 1907 and 1908 by three American recording companies. They were made by Justo Villa's group, called Cuarteto Coculense for these recordings (Clark 1993, 9). These emerging roles of the mariachi as a symbol of an important regional grassroots culture, as a part of a staged *espectáculo* (spectacle or show), and a music with commercial potential were early portendings of what would follow.

The Mexican Revolution brought with it an upheaval in cultural values. While Mexico's elite had looked to Europe for their cultural models and guidance, many post-revolution intellectuals and government officials praised the value of the homegrown cultural accomplishments of Mexico's *mestizo* and Indian inhabitants. Rural, regional cultural traditions were promoted as building blocks for a new, more nationalistic Mexican identity. In 1920, for example, Mexico's Secretary of Public Education José Vasconcelos unveiled a version of the regional folk dance "Jarabe Tapatío"— subsequently known as the *Jarabe nacional* (national jarabe)— that was to be taught in schools throughout Mexico. In a massive performance in Mexico City's Chapultepec Park, three hundred dance couples performed a choreography (Saldívar 1937, 9) that had been influenced by the stage production *Fantasía mexicana* (Mexican Fantasy), a production of the visiting Russian ballerina Anna Pavlova in 1919.

In the 1930s the nationalist President Lázaro Cárdenas included mariachi groups in political events, and in 1940 he personally ordered the commander of the Mexico City police "not to bother the mariachis any more" (Gabaldón Márquez, 284) and to lift the prohibitions barring them from performing in the plazas and streets (Jáuregui, 48). At Cárdenas's behest, a mariachi group that came to Mexico City in 1934 from Tecalitlán, Jalisco, led first by Gaspar Vargas and later by his son Silvestre Vargas, destined to be the most influential of all mariachis, was given employment lasting two decades representing the Mexico City police department in public performances.

In 1920 Dr. Luis Rodríguez brought the Mariachi Coculense, led by a *guitarrón* player named Cirilo Marmolejo from Tecolotlán, Jalisco, to Mexico City to perform for a group of post-revolution politicians (Sonnichsen 1993, 2). Many of Mexico's new revolutionary elite, who themselves came from rural backgrounds, viewed the mariachi and its music as an important representation of Mexican culture. Marmolejo and his group stayed in Mexico City and found a new, urban clientele for his music, playing for customers in bars and for parties and other special events. His group, "the first mariachi to appear in a stage show in a legitimate theater in Mexico City (the famous Teatro Iris); the first to appear in a 'sound' [Santa 1931] film and, above all, the first to make 'electric' recordings, initiated the era of the dominance of the mariachi style in radio, film and, especially on records, which has endured over fifty years" (3). In 1925 Marmolejo and his group, which included his compadre from Cocula and mariachi leader Concho Andrade, were performing regularly at the Tenampa Bar located on Garibaldi Plaza in Mexico City, beginning the plaza's longtime popularity as a center for mariachi music.

Both Marmolejo and Andrade were important pioneers in transplanting mariachi music to Mexico's capital, placing it in a position of significant influence in the enormous societal changes that followed. Little did anyone suspect that this modest seed, planted in the fertile ground of a rapidly urbanizing Mexican society and later transported northward by massive migration, would make its unmistakable mark on the culture of the United States.

The 1920s saw rural musicians from all parts of the country flocking to Mexico City. This movement was part of a large and steady migration that would continue throughout the twentieth century and that would make greater Mexico City the most populous metropolitan area in the world, with well over twenty million inhabitants. At the same time the capital was becoming more of a modern urban metropolis, the constant influx of rural people who maintained family ties created a demand for music that reflected and renewed connections to their rural, regional identity. Popular media of entertainment—radio, recordings, film, variety shows in major theaters, and live music in restaurants and other public venues—responded to this demand, featuring musics rooted in the provinces. This, in turn, had an unprecedented influence on popular musical tastes throughout the country and beyond.

Mexico's powerful radio station, XEW, inaugurated in 1930 in Mexico City, by mid-decade broadcast live music—including mariachi and other rurally rooted music, along with urban musics more related to international popular tastes—to all corners of the Mexican Republic and neighboring areas. Throughout most of the 1930s and 1940s, Mariachi Tapatío and other groups were heard regularly on XEW and other stations, assuring the mariachi and its music a place in the musical life of the broad Mexican public (Moreno Rivas 1989, 182–83).

In the 1930s, 1940s, and 1950s, Mexico's "golden age" of film cultivated noble, idealized images of country life that were epitomized by famous actor-singers performing pseudofolk songs that appealed to the Mexican public's desire to identify with an idyllic rural past. The 1936 film *Allá en el Rancho Grande*, featuring Tito Guízar, was the first of these. Soon others followed; for example, superstar actor singer Jorge Negrete made his first film in 1941 as a singing *charro* (cowboy) in *Ay Jalisco, No Te Rajes* (Oh, Jalisco, Don't Give Up). Negrete had already launched a career as actor, singer, and nightclub entertainer and had worked in New York and Hollywood before he found his lucrative niche in the Mexican counterpart of American westerns. He and such other singer actors as Pedro Infante, Flor

Silvestre, and Javier Solís played a major role in bringing mariachi music to national and international attention. These films also circulated among Spanish-speaking communities of the United States, and in fact many became film classics that are still shown regularly on Spanish-language television, especially in the American Southwest. The impact in the United States of over half a century of popularity of the mariachi through film and television has been widespread and profound.

Professional songwriters applied their skills to writing *canciones rancheras* (country songs) and, later, the more suave *boleros rancheros* (country boleros) that evoked sometimes idealized images and values that struck deep emotional chords in the rural and urban "common man" alike. In the late 1940s, a singer and songwriter from the state of Guanajuato, José Alfredo Jiménez, launched an enormously influential career that endured until his death in 1973. Many of his more than four hundred published compositions have dominated the *canción ranchera* repertoire of mariachis everywhere for decades following his death, and his statue looms over Mexico City's Garibaldi Plaza as testimony to his preeminence. Nearly all of the most fervently requested melodies at the birthday party in East Los Angeles that was described above were written by "José Alfredo," as he is affectionately called by Mexicans and Mexican Americans alike.

Thus, a mutually reinforcing cycle arose, in which rural tastes influenced the popular media, and then in turn were influenced by popular creations appealing to those tastes. As this came about, certain rural musics were successful in breaking into the media mainstream and others were not. Those that were not included often languished or faded away entirely in the shadow of a powerful "mainstream" Mexican life—in both Mexico and the United States—shaped largely by the popular media. Those that were included were inevitably transformed to suit the demands of the commercial market. The mariachi and its music became by far the most universally recognized and commercially dominant of these rurally derived musics. And its expansion through the popular media became the first major step toward the music's widespread acceptance, especially among those of Mexican heritage, in the United States.

THE EVOLUTION OF THE MARIACHI: CREATIVITY, COMMODIFICATION, AND MARIACHI VARGAS DE TECALITLÁN

At the end of the nineteenth century, the mariachi of west Mexico, like most regional mestizo musical ensembles, derived from stringed instruments imported from Spain in the early colonial era (1521–1810). Harp, violin, and different shapes and sizes of guitar were combined in various ways, with particular localities preferring certain combinations. In mariachi culture, the deep-boxed, percussive *guitarra de golpe* and/or smaller *vihuela* were paired with the harp and/or violin. These were the combinations of instruments that were brought to Mexico City in the early decades of the 1900s. The early Mariachi Vargas, for example, embodied the Tecalitlán preference for harp, guitarra de golpe, and two or more violins, while the Cuarteto Coculense (from the town of Cocula) that made the first mariachi recordings reflected the local custom of combining the vihuela and two violins with the five-string guitarrón (later modified by adding a sixth string). In the new context of Mexico City, in which mariachi groups from different local origins intermingled and were in commercial competition with other styles of music, the distinctive local styles merged over time into a more standard instrumentation and, at the same time, incorporated certain innovations that allowed mariachi groups a greater range of musical possibilities.

Early on in the Mexico City environment, violins dominated the melody in the mariachi and the size of the ensemble expanded, both factors diminishing the importance of the harp as a melody instrument in its higher range. The guitarrón, preferred in the style of performance associated with the town of Cocula, Jalisco, began to displace the harp as the bass instrument, a trend that continued until all but a few ensembles included a guitarrón as the exclusive bass instrument. That the harp has persisted in a small number of urban mariachis is largely due to its inclusion in Mariachi Vargas de Tecalitlán, with its large instrumentation of twelve or more musicians and its roots in Tecalitlán, an area with which the harp has long been associated.

In the 1940s the trumpet's place in the mariachi was established. Experimentation with non-stringed instruments, the trumpet in particular, had been of interest for decades during the mariachi's transition to urban life. Yet, only when Silvestre Vargas invited Miguel Martínez to become the group's first permanent trumpet player in 1942 (Martínez 2012, 75) was the trumpet's destiny as an integral part of the mariachi sealed. Martínez's exquisite technique, tasteful style, and inventiveness in later adding a second trumpet set the standard for the mariachi's future. By the early 1950s the urban mariachi had taken the basic form that today is considered standard—guitarrón, vihuela, guitar, two trumpets, three or more violins, and, occasionally, the harp. The standard size of mariachi ensembles ranges from seven to eleven musicians, though major show groups may comprise thirteen or more (customarily adding violins and a guitar), and many groups smaller than seven abound, usually for economic reasons—many clients cannot afford larger groups. In all cases, the guitarrón, vihuela, violin, and trumpet are considered to be the minimum-sized core of a genuine mariachi moderno (modern-day mariachi).

A strong influence leading to the standardization of the mariachi's instrumentation was its evolution as a commodity, a commercial product to be packaged, marketed, sold, and consumed by large numbers of people. The expansion of the instrumentation offered greater musical possibilities, but it also allowed the mariachi a broader range of repertoire and thus a competitive edge over other folk-rooted ensembles that did not adapt to the marketplace. The real competition in the urban marketplaces of Mexico and its northern neighbor, undoubtedly, was the Afro- and Euro-American popular music of the United States—dance-band music, popular songs, and their Spanish-language imitation—with "slick" arrangements and aggressive marketing. While the types of music played by the mariachi expanded greatly in the second half of the twentieth century, commodification led to an opposite trend, the standardization of repertoire. The commercial music industry came to dominate musical life, and when music consumers listened to a mariachi, they expected to hear their favorite songs with arrangements like those they had heard over the radio, in the movies, or on recordings. Just as the music in the media of the 1930s and 1940s had eclipsed those that were not included, in the 1950s and afterward, the musical marketplace rewarded a relatively small number of musicians, requiring others to imitate the "stars" in order to please the consuming public so that they might fare well in their profession. Since at least the 1950s, the mariachi that has enjoyed this position of preeminence and influence has been Mariachi Vargas de Tecalitlán, often known—most would agree, with good reason—as "El Mejor Mariachi del Mundo" (The Best Mariachi in the World).

The farsightedness of Silvestre Vargas in adapting his group to urban, commercial, and musical demands, his insistence on a consistently high technical level of performance, his incorporation of extraordinarily talented musicians into the Vargas ranks, and his acceptance of the need for tight, polished, and innovative musical arrangements accounts for much of the success of Mariachi Vargas. In 1937 they appeared in their first film, *Así es mi tierra* (My Land Is Like That), and they would appear in more than two hundred others over the following decades (Clark 1992, 5). Violinist Rubén Fuentes joined the group in 1944 (ibid., 6) and later became the most prominent mariachi arranger and innovator. Mariachi Vargas and Fuentes backed up virtually all of the most famous singers on their major recordings of música ranchera and made dozens of their own recordings as well. In working with José Alfredo Jiménez, for example, the musically unlettered songwriter would sing his melodies to Fuentes, who would then create an arrangement (Moreno Rivas 1989, 194). Fuentes experimented with the mariachi sound, adding such instruments as flutes and French horns, inventing new rhythmic techniques for the vihuela, and incorporating contemporary chords and harmonies. He created original compositions with a strikingly new sound. For more than half a century, Mariachi Vargas and Rubén Fuentes set the standard for mariachi music everywhere, inspiring others to expand its creative possibilities, evolving ever more complex instrumental techniques and precise arrangements, and adapting it to the ever evolving commercial music market, while preserving in it a Mexican musical sensibility.

MARIACHI REPERTOIRE AND PERFORMANCE CONTEXTS

In its earlier rural setting, the mariachi repertoire had at its core the older, lively *sones* and jarabes that are imbued with a vigorous rhythm suited for the often percussive footwork of the traditional *zapateado* dance style. The *son* "El Cihualteco"

(The Man from Cihuatlán)" exemplifies this style. Other social dance rhythms that rose to popularity in the nineteenth century—the waltz, schottische, and polka, for example—also left their mark on the repertoire of many musicians. A body of instrumental music called *minuetes* (no relation to the minuet) was used exclusively for religious events in western Mexican rural life. When the mariachi moved into the urban sphere, the repertoire and corresponding performance style changed. As the mariachi became more closely associated with música ranchera, it increasingly emulated the image of the singer actors of the cinema and the recording superstars. The high-intensity, emotion-packed canción ranchera and more suave bolero ranchero moved to the fore, leaving the sones and jarabes in a secondary, though nevertheless important role. The religious minuetes did not survive the transition to urban life, although a few of the older style rural groups still remember them.

Today, the common mariachi repertoire still draws from the more stylized forms—sones, rancheras, boleros, polkas, and such folkloric classics as "Jarabe Tapatío"—but a wide variety of others have crept into the repertoire as well. The *danzón*, a dance of Cuban origin popular in the first half of the twentieth century; the cumbia, rooted in Colombian-Panamanian folk music and popularized in the 1960s and later; folk-based melodies from other Mexican regions, such as "La Bamba" from Veracruz and "Las Chiapanecas" from Chiapas; more recent *baladas* (ballads) crooned by pop singers; novelty pieces, such as "Poet and Peasant Overture," "Orange Blossom Special," and bilingual versions of "Before the Next Teardrop Falls"; the (now passé) "Macarena" dance craze; and many other kinds of music have been taken up by mariachi groups.

Even as the mariachi repertoire reflects both a deep sense of grassroots Mexican tradition and an adaptation to evolving musical and commercial trends, so do the contexts for mariachi performance. As we observed in the opening vignette about Mariachi San Matías, the mariachi remains an important part of Mexican social life. As they were a century ago, mariachis today are a part of important social occasions—birthday celebrations, wedding receptions, baptisms, and so forth.

Notably, another context for mariachi performance is the Catholic Mass. In the several decades since the Catholic Church in the 1960s began encouraging the use of vernacular music in religious ceremony, a new repertoire of music for the mass has come into existence. The "Mariachi Mass," begun in Mexico and now quite popular in many Catholic churches with large Mexican congregations, offers mariachi arrangements of all the major parts of the mass, as well as hymns for regular or special occasions, such as the annual celebration of the Virgin of Guadalupe on December 12. This Catholic commemoration of the sixteenth-century apparition of the Virgin Mary on Tepeyac Hill in what is now Mexico City is a major event in the calendrical cycle of Mexican Catholicism, as the Virgin of Guadalupe has become an important symbol of Mexican cultural identity on both sides of the border. Mariachi masses often attract large numbers of worshippers and tourists, especially in such large cities as San Antonio or Los Angeles. A mariachi mass has become a popular way of marking a special occasion, and it is not unusual for a mariachi to perform at a mass for a wedding, an anniversary, a funeral, or a *quince años* ("coming-out" party for fifteen-year-old girls) and then move to the church hall or client's home to play at the social celebration that follows.

At the same time that the mariachi expanded into many social and religious contexts, it also made its way into major public venues packaged as a "show." Such groups as Nati Cano's Mariachi Los Camperos of Los Angeles, and Mariachi Sol de México, of Orange County, California, Mariachi Cobre (copper, after the ubiquitous mineral of Arizona, the state of the group's origin) at EPCOT Center in Florida, and Campanas de America (Bells of America) from San Antonio, Texas, have developed complex arrangements and performance sets fit for such occasions. Consequently, there is a wide range of performance styles and settings for the mariachi. In the United States, the special character of the American cultural and social context has had an interesting effect on mariachi repertoire and performance contexts in recent years.

THE MARIACHI IN THE UNITED STATES: A CHANGING FRAME OF REFERENCE

During the twentieth century, large numbers of Mexican people immigrated to the United States. Particularly in the decades following World War II, a demand for inexpensive labor on the American side and population explosion and high unemployment on the Mexican side stimulated a dramatic surge of immigration. At the beginning of the century and long before, the United States–Mexican border had meant little in terms of cultural barriers between the two countries. People along the border moved with relative ease back and forth, and as a consequence shared a more or less common culture. But culture then was strongly regional, and as the mariachi and its music came from central western Mexico and not from the north, it was not a significant part of border life. When in the late 1930s mariachi music began to be an important part of the growing pan-American experience largely as a result of the expanding media industry, it only then began to play a larger role in Mexican life north of the border. Large Mexican American communities in California, Texas, and other communities of the Southwest had long maintained strong cultural ties to Mexico, ties that were further strengthened by the popular media, and one of those ties was the mariachi and its music.

Perhaps the strongest flow of new immigration in the years following World War II was from the agricultural regions of western Mexico, also the traditional stronghold of mariachi music. New immigrants, of course, further bolstered a demand for mariachi music.

> As it came to the United States, it was in the *cantina* [a bar that served as the principal gathering place for blue-collar men] that the music first took hold. Musicians followed immigrants and were able to assuage feelings of isolation and loneliness at the end of the work-day or week. While major groups in Mexico generated their income from tours, recordings, and the accompaniment of "star" singers (*artistas*), groups in the United States, like the lower echelons of mariachi in Mexico, were almost entirely employed in the cantina, with supplemental income derived from *chambas* ("casuals"): performances at weddings, baptisms, birthdays, and small-scale family celebrations. (Fogelquist 1996a, 3)

In general, these two main contexts of mariachi music—local social occasions attended to by cantina-based groups and Mexican-based shows on tour to American venues—were transplanted whole cloth into the American setting and accounted for virtually all occasions for mariachi performance.

Since the late 1960s, though, the American setting has seen many important changes in this pattern, as mariachi music has found a place in school programs and more genteel middle-class performance settings. At the same time, the changing metaphorical "frame" around the performance—the specific context—has been accompanied by a changing set of meanings about and attitudes toward the music. In the late 1960s, mariachi music began to be taught in school settings in the Southwest, a trend that accelerated in the 1970s and 1980s.

By the 1990s there were several university-level mariachi music programs in California, Arizona, New Mexico, and Texas and dozens of middle and secondary school programs throughout the West. The primary promoters of these programs at the middle and secondary levels were advocates of multicultural education and of the inclusion of music instruction that was culturally representative of Mexican American student populations. One of the first such efforts was in Texas, where multicultural education expert Belle San Miguel Ortiz of the San Antonio Independent School District launched an ambitious, multi-school program of after-school mariachi instruction at both middle and secondary levels. Ortiz's conviction in the educational and human development value of the mariachi-in-schools program led her to organize the first International Mariachi Conference, held in San Antonio in 1979, that combined instructional workshops with performances by Mariachi Vargas de Tecalitlán. The festival's model of matching youth-oriented instruction with an inspirational concert by the most renowned of mariachi ensembles was a resounding success. The students, awestruck by the presence and extraordinary musicianship of the Vargas performers, were highly motivated learners, and in following years the San Antonio festival attracted new attendees from as far away as Arizona and California.

Festival organizers in Arizona were the first to replicate Ortiz's idea, organizing what came to be the largest of these festivals, followed by many others in California, New Mexico, Nevada, and other Texan cities. Middle and secondary mariachi instructional programs have also multiplied, most of which have been inspired by the festivals themselves or by a greater awareness sparked by the festivals of other model school programs. In any given year, there may be as many as fifteen major mariachi festivals in the United States and many dozens of ongoing school programs nationwide.

At the university level, a similar trend, as well as the emergence of several programs in ethnomusicology that emphasized the performance of many styles of music from around the world, was the principal motivating force for the inauguration of mariachi ensembles. Such programs "have provided unprecedented opportunities for young performers to study with outstanding mariachi musicians, establishing continuity with the roots of the traditions and a forum for the exploration and expression of cultural identity" (Fogelquist 1996, 23). They also led to the formation of new, professional ensembles of American origin. The student group humorously named Los Changuitos Feos (The Ugly Little Monkeys) from Tucson, for example, evolved into the Mariachi Cobre that has performed at the Epcot Center in Florida for decades.

At the same time, during the late 1960s, a second development took place: in Los Angeles, Natividad Cano and his Mariachi Los Camperos established La Fonda, the first night club where mariachi music was presented on a stage as a dinner show (Fogelquist 1996a, 3). The restaurant–dinner show context provided an inviting environment to middle-class non-Mexicans and others who did not frequent the male-dominated (primarily first-generation immigrant) cantinas. The idea caught on, and by the 1990s, there were numerous similar situations in Los Angeles, Tucson, Albuquerque, Denver, Houston, San Antonio, and many other cities in the Southwest. These contexts played upon the notion of a Mexican music "show," but they foregrounded the mariachi itself, in contrast to the long-standing tours of big-name Mexican singers in which the mariachi was relegated to the role of an anonymous backup group.

Through the years, these changing frames of reference in the learning, performance, and appreciation of mariachi music have had many noticeable effects—social, contextual, musical—on mariachi musical culture. The social view of music is changing. In Mexico, mariachi musicians were often victims of class prejudice. In the words of one senior musician: "I know that they say 'the mariachi is the heart of Mexico'; and that's an odd thing, because I've also seen that in Mexico there are people who scorn us. . . . I understand from my years as a child on the ranch, how the rich scorn the poor, but it is impossible for me to accept that they feel that way about us, who are the music and the happiness of Mexico" (Gabaldón Márquez 1981, 360).

The change in performance context from the cantina to the restaurant and in role from backup musician to featured performer is tied in the minds of some musicians to their desire to elevate the social status of the music and the musicians who play it, distancing them from these old prejudices. The late mariachi pioneer Natividad Cano would tell of how, in his earlier career in Mexico, there were signs on cantinas with the warning "No Dogs, Women, or Mariachis Allowed," and how he was determined to change this form of prejudice through maintaining an extraordinary level of musicianship and through advocating his musical tradition to the widest public possible. Cano has had great success in his efforts; he has performed regularly to sold-out houses in major performance venues, was featured in two national public television shows (including a performance with Linda Ronstadt at the White House), received a prestigious National Heritage Fellowship from the National Endowment for the Arts, and earned a Grammy nomination (2006) and a Grammy award (2008).

With the change in performance contexts has also come a change in the social prohibitions governing mariachi performance. In particular, as the schools, dinner-show restaurants, and other public performance venues have moved the mariachi further away from the male-dominated cantina context, women instrumentalists have increasingly taken on a role on par with male performers. Historically, while a few all-women mariachis existed, the vast majority of mariachi groups were composed exclusively of men, partly in keeping with the social prohibitions against women participating as musicians in cantinas and other libertine circumstances. More gender-equal school programs and stage concerts have changed this, making the presence of women more of an asset to the groups' showmanship. The addition of Chicana violinist Rebecca Gonzales to the ranks of Los Camperos in the early 1970s set the stage for many other female musicians to follow her example and perform with top-notch show-oriented ensembles. Gonzales had previously been a member of Mariachi Uclatlán, the UCLA student group that had become an independent, professional mariachi. As the influence of mariachi school programs and festivals is felt across the Southwest, many more women musicians are becoming professional *mariacheras* (mariachi performers). The "Viva el Mariachi" festival in Fresno, California, has featured the growing role of women in mariachi music, showcasing the all-female groups Mariachi Reyna de Los Angeles (Queen of Los Angeles) and Mariachi Mujer 2000 (Women Mariachi 2000) from and Mariachi Femenil "Las Perlitas Tapatías" (The Mariachi Tapatía Pearls) from Guadalajara. In addition, a growing number of male and female non-Mexicans, having discovered the music mainly through school and university programs, have played more of a role in both amateur and professional mariachi performance.

Mariachi music's popularity has clearly been on the rise in the United States. An important spinoff of the mariachi festival movement—the Tucson International Mariachi Festival in particular—that added great impetus to this trend was popular-music singer Linda Ronstadt's two recordings, *Canciones de mi Padre* (Songs of my Father) and *Más Canciones* (More Songs), and her national tours of mariachi music. Ronstadt made the recordings following her performance at the Tucson festival, in which she recalled her Mexican American musical heritage during her years growing up in Tucson. The boost in esteem and popularity the music enjoyed both among Mexican Americans and non-Mexicans alike as a result of Ronstadt's efforts were widespread and profound. David Gates, writing for *Newsweek* magazine in 1988, reported that "[Linda Ronstadt's mariachi album] 'Canciones de mi Padre'—Songs of My Father—has gone gold and is at 55 on *Billboard*'s Top Pop album chart: hardly unusual for a Linda Ronstadt LP, but pretty impressive for a record whose words most *norteamericanos* can't understand" (Gates 1988, 66).

Several years later, the late Mexican American superstar vocalist from Corpus Christi, Texas, Selena Quintanilla-Pérez, recorded similar arrangements of several of the "classic" melodies selected from Ronstadt's *Canciones de mi Padre* album, taking mariachi music to still greater audiences and inspiring adoring imitators nationwide.

The show context has had a noticeable influence on the mariachi repertoire. Compared to the cantina and other contexts with more social interaction, the musical repertoire performed in the contexts of restaurant dinner shows and major concert performances is significantly more standardized and narrow in range (Pearlman 1984, 7–8). As these new show contexts proliferate, and as young American musicians perform more in these situations and less "*al talón*" (paid-by-the-song) in cantina settings or for other social events in which the audience expects the musicians to play the repertoire that they request rather than a fixed show repertoire, the overall effect may be to narrow the range of music played. This is not to say that the more intimate and demanding situations in terms of repertoire are destined to fade out; they are not. More likely, the two principal subclasses of mariachi musician and ensemble will be more differentiated, reflecting the particular demands of their respective performance situations. Ideally, many musicians will possess both the technical capability demanded for the show setting and the breadth of repertoire required for more intimate settings and will be equally adaptable to both.

Today, mariachi music is performed frequently in all regions of the United States. New York, New Jersey, Massachusetts, Maryland, Washington, D.C., Virginia, North Carolina, Georgia, Florida, Tennessee, Michigan, Illinois, Kansas, Idaho, Washington, Oregon, California, New Mexico, Arizona, Texas, Nevada, Utah, Colorado, and many other states are home to mariachi ensembles. And as the mariachi has become more a part of the broad cultural landscape of the United States, so have musicians of many cultural backgrounds taken up the guitarrón, vihuela, violin, or trumpet to play the sones, rancheras, boleros, and other musical genres at the heart of mariachi tradition.

This Saturday was a normal day for our mariachi, Mariachi Los Amigos, based in the Washington, D.C., area. I had helped organize the group in 1978 when I moved from California, where I had studied Mexican music at U.C.L.A. and played trumpet with Mariachi Uclatlán. Made up of another non-Mexican Californian who had played violin in her university's mariachi in Santa Cruz, two musicians from Mexico who knew the basic repertoire and techniques of guitarrón and vihuela, a trumpet player from Bolivia, a violinist from Guatemala, and a Chinese American violinist and ethnomusicologist from Cleveland, our mariachi had committed to memory a repertoire of about two hundred tunes. This, along with our respectably polished style, was more than enough to get by playing for the general American audiences that hired us for house parties, fundraisers, ethnic concert series, and the like. Today, though, we were going to Fredericksburg, Virginia, to play an outdoor mass and party celebrating the quince años (fifteenth birthday) of our friend Rafael's daughter, and we expected that there would be lots of recent immigrants from Mexico who had come to northern Virginia to work in construction and agricultural jobs and who would be requesting plenty of tunes that we did not know from the "talón"-style mariachi's repertoire of at least a couple thousand tunes. Thus, we recruited our friend Pedro, who had arrived a couple years before from El Salvador and who worked al talón in the cantinas of the Washington area's burgeoning Latino (mainly Central American and Mexican) neighborhoods, to come along with us and fill in as needed.

In a field next to Rafael's mobile home, two Spanish-speaking priests said the mass as we played the Kyrie, Gloria, Alleluia, Sanctus, and other parts of the mass. *Papel picado* (colorful paper cuts) were strung over the altar and platform that would later serve as a dance floor. The reverent audience, about 150 *mexicano* immigrants, mostly men, many of whom wore Mexican-style Western hats and boots, were reserved and silent. When the mass ended, the party began, with the unveiling of tables full of enchiladas, carne asada (grilled beef), *birria* (western Mexican goat stew), and beer. When we started the classic son "La Negra" (The Dark Woman), *gritos* (yells) erupted from all sides, and after the final note, we were surrounded by people who requested hits from the latest compact-disc recording by mariachi superstar Vicente Fernández, along with the obscure classic rancheras favored by grassroots mexicanos. Halfway through the party, the skies opened, and the rain poured down, wilting the papel picado and soaking partygoers and musicians alike. But the requests continued, and a few determined men and women kept dancing, until the rain, mud, darkness, and fatigue brought the event to a close and we piled in our cars to return home.

Before we left, we made plans to rendezvous the next day for a performance at a "food fair" that would be put on by local restaurateurs who had hired our mariachi, a German folk music trio, a Japanese koto player, and a bluegrass band to represent stereotypes of the ethnic diversity of the Washington restaurant cuisine. As it would be presented in the shallow, Disneyland theme-park style of "It's a Small, Small World" there, we would not need Pedro to help us out. The non-Latino public usually asks for the same dozen or so pieces, and we know them all.

In the course of time, the people who make music, the audiences for whom it is made, and the contexts in which it is played have a powerful effect on the music itself. As mariachi music becomes more a part of life north of the US-Mexican border, it both changes and remains the same, in order to suit the musical tastes, social needs, and lifestyles of people in its new homeland. This dialectic between tradition and change has brought a particular kind of creative tension to mariachi culture in the United States, resulting in a broad degree of change in the music and its meaning. While mariachi music has changed little in Mexican American communities that are strongly rooted in traditional Mexican cultural ways, some groups have attempted to reach broader audiences through crowd-pleasing pop fusions by playing, for example, arrangements of tunes from the Broadway show *A Chorus Line* (with choreography) or salsa music. In the middle are "innovative traditionalists," epitomized by Nati Cano, who embraces both change and tradition. "Music is a constant evolution I never cease to enjoy," he once said (Lopetegui 1996, F1). "I can't see why you can't create valuable music while remaining traditional. It is such a rich music." The seeds of mariachi music have been firmly planted in North American culture. The future of mariachi music in the United States and the course of its evolution will undoubtedly be determined by musical leaders such as Nati Cano, the enthusiasm of American audiences, the support of educational institutions, and the continuing interest of the entertainment industry.

AFTERWORD

More than fifteen years have passed since this I wrote this chapter. Mariachi music in the United States has continued to evolve, and it has continued to stay the same. The Boyle Street donut shop was torn down by the city in favor of a Mexican-style bandstand (*quisco*), and a Mariachi Plaza light rail metro station links the plaza to further reaches of Los Angeles. Salvador "Jeremec" Gutiérrez passed away, and a younger generation of Gutiérrez musicians—male and female—have followed in the footsteps of their fathers and uncles. Beepers were replaced by cell phones and then smart phones, allowing musicians to text and "Facebook" one another, and giving musicians instant access to lyrics and YouTube performances of songs from the Web. In 2008, Mariachi Los Camperos appeared in the popular movie *Sex and the City.* They earned a Grammy nomination in 2006 for their album *¡Llegaron Los Camperos!* and a Grammy award in 2008 for *Amor, Dolor y Lágrimas.* That same year, the all-female Mariachi Divas won their own Grammy for the CD *Canciones de Amor.* This marked the first time that a mariachi ensemble—as opposed to the star singer they accompanied—won a Grammy. La Fonda is under new management, with a different mariachi delighting its clientele, as Mariachi Los Camperos mainly performs concert events and tours. In 2012 First Lady Michelle Obama presented a National Arts and Humanities Youth Program award to the Mariachi Master Apprenticeship Program of San Fernando (Los Angeles area), a program launched by Nati Cano and his musicians to instill a high level of mariachi musicianship in local youth.

From this point in time, one thing is clear—mariachi music has established a solid niche in the musical life of the United States at the grassroots level. Mariachi ensembles are found in the majority of US states, and more groups are comprised of US-born musicians than a generation previous. While some of the older repertoire—waltzes, schottisches, and particular songs of many rhythms failing to withstand the test of time—have faded from popularity, new pieces and new styles of artists replace them. Overall, musicianship continues to rise, and mariachi pioneers following in the footsteps of Nati Cano (who passed away in 2014) take satisfaction in the fact that the music they have cared for so deeply has reached a position of social, cultural, and artistic respect.

Chapter 6: Musical Examples (access through companion website)

Chapter 6, Track 1. "Las mañanitas," from *Mariachi Águilas de Chapala: Mariachi Music from the Mexican State of Jalisco*. Folkways Records FW8870, 1960. http://www.folkways.si.edu/"www.folkways.si.edu.

Chapter 6, Track 2. "El cihualteco," from *¡Viva el Mariachi!: Nati Cano's Mariachi Los Camperos*. Smithsonian Folkways SFW 40459, 2002. http://www.folkways.si.edu/"www.folkways.si.edu.

References Cited

Barrios de los Ríos, Enrique. 1908. *Paisajes de Occidente*. Sombrerete, Zacatecas (Mexico): Imprenta de la Biblioteca Estarsiana.

Clark, Jonathan. 1992. *Mexico's Pioneer Mariachis*, vol. 3: *Mariachi Vargas de Tecalitlán: Their First Recordings, 1937-1947*. Descriptive notes to Arhoolie Folklyric CD 7015.

———. 1993. *Mexico's Pioneer Mariachis*, vol. 1: *Mariachi Coculense de Cirilo Marmolejo*. Descriptive notes to Arhoolie Folklyric CD 7011.

Fogelquist, Mark. 1996. "Mariachi Conferences and Festivals in the United States." In *The Changing Faces of Tradition: A Report on the Folk and Traditional Arts in the United States*. Washington: National Endowment for the Arts. 18–23.

———. 1996a. "Mariachi Conferences and Festivals in the United States: A Report." Unpublished manuscript on file with author.

Gabaldón Márquez, Edgar. 1981. *Historias Escogidas del Mariachi Francisco Yaíñez Chico, Según los Apuntes de Edgar Gabaldón Márquez*. Mexico City: J. M. Castañón.

Gates, David. 1988. "A Rocker Reclaims Her Roots." *Newsweek*, 29 February, 66–67.

Greathouse, Patricia. Mariachi (Layton, Utah, 2009). A fan's book that emphasizes interviews and biographical sketches, and includes lots of nice photos.

Jáuregui, Jesús. 1990. *El Mariachi: Símbolo Musical de Mexico*. Mexico City: Banpaís.

Lopetegui, Enrique. 1996. "Still Making Music with a Legendary Enthusiasm." *Los Angeles Times*, 26 December, F1, F4.

Moreno Rivas, Yolanda. 1989. *Historia de la Música Popular Mexicana*. Mexico City: Editorial Patria.

Pearlman, Steven Ray. 1984. "Standardization and Innovation in Mariachi Music Performance in Los Angeles." *Pacific Review of Ethnomusicology* 1: 1–12.

Santa. 1931. Director: Antonio Moreno. Producers: Joselito and Roberto Rodríguez Ruelas. Studio: Compañía National Productora de Películas.

Saldívar, Gabriel. 1937. *El Jarabe: Baile Popular Mexicano*. Mexico City: Talleres Gráficos de la Nación.

Sonnichsen, Philip. 1993. *Mexico's Pioneer Mariachis*, vol. 1: *Mariachi Coculense de Cirilo Marmolejo*. Descriptive notes to Arhoolie Folklyric CD 7011.

Vázquez Valle, Irene, series director. 1976. *El son del sur de Jalisco*. Vols. 1, 2, 18, and 19. Instituto Nacional de Antropología e Historia. Serie de Discos. Mexico: Instituto Nacional de Antropología e Historia.

Additional Resources

Braojos, Ricardo, Director. Eugene Rodríguez, Producer. 2008. *Pasajero: A Journey of Time and Memory*. Ryko Distribution DVD

Clark, Jonathan. 1994. *Mexico's Pioneer Mariachis*, vol. 2: *Mariachi Tapatío de Jose Marmolejo "El Auténtico."* Descriptive notes to Arhoolie Folklyric CD 7012.

———. 1998. *Mexico's Pioneer Mariachis*, vol. 4. Arhoolie Folklyric 7036.

Fogelquist, Mark. 1975. *Rhythm and Form in the Contemporary Son Jalisciense*. Master's thesis, University of California, Los Angeles.

Fogelquist, Mark, and Patricia W. Harpole. 1989. *Los Mariachis! An Introduction to Mexican Mariachi Music*. Danbury, CT: World Music Press. Twenty-page booklet, illustrations, cassette tape.

González, Al, producer. *Viva el Mariachi! The History, the Culture, the Instruments of Mariachi Music*. 2004. Vision Quest Entertainment. DVD, 50 minutes.

Gradante, William. 1982. "'El Hijo del Pueblo': José Alfredo Jiménez and the Mexican Canción Ranchera." *Latin American Music Review* 3, no. 1 (spring–summer): 36–59.

Jáuregui, Jesús. 2007. *El Mariachi: Símbolo Musical de Mexico*. Mexico City: Santillana Ediciones Generales, S. A. de C. V., Editorial Taurus, and Instituto Nacional de Antropología e Historia.

Koetting, James. 1977. "The *Son Jalisciense:* Structural Variety in Relation to a Mexican *Forme Fixe*." In *Essays for a Humanist: An Offering to Klaus Wachsmann*. New York: Town House Press. 162–88.

Mariachi México de Pepe Villa. *Más Mariachi*. CD. Mediterráneo MCD-10130. Contains twenty-three classic polkas, *pasodobles*, folk dances, and songs.

Mariachi High. 2012. PBSDVD MAHI601. This documentary presents a year in the life of the champion mariachi ensemble at Zapata High School in Zapata, Texas.

Mariachi Vargas de Tecalitlán. *El Mariachi*. CD. Polygram Discos, Polydor 839 332 2. Contains mainly new arrangements of older mariachi favorites.

Martínez, Miguel. 2012. *Mi vida, mis viajes, mis vivencias: Siete décadas en la música del mariachi*. México: Consejo Nacional para la Cultura y las Artes.

Nati Cano's Mariachi Los Camperos. *Tradición, Arte y Pasion.* Smithsonian Folkways SFW CD 40559. Last recording of the stellar mariachi ensemble while under the direction of Nati Cano.

———.2008. *Amor, Dolor y Lágrimas.* SFW CD 40518. Grammy-winning recording with various genres of mariachi music.

———. 2005. *Llegaron Los Camperos.* Smithsonian Folkways SFW40517. A Grammy-nominated release by one of the genre's best groups.

———. 2002. *¡Viva el Mariachi!* Smithsonian Folkways SFW CD 40459.

Nati Cano's Mariachi Los Camperos, Mariachi Chula Vista, Jesús "Chuy" Guzmán, and Mark Fogelquist. 2010. *The Sounds of Mariachi: Lessons in Mariachi Performance.* Smithsonian Folkways SFW DV 48008. A DVD with demonstrations by musicians and words of instruction from three leading mariachi educators.

Ronstadt, Linda. 1989. *Canciones de Mi Padre.* Arranged and conducted by Rubén Fuentes. Compact disc recordings with Spanish texts and English translations. Asylum 9 60765-2.

- 7 -

"NIMIIDAA!" [LET'S ALL DANCE!]

Music and Dance of the Northern Intertribal Powwow

Christopher A. Scales and Gabriel Desrosiers

This chapter is part of an ongoing collaborative musical and scholarly partnership between Chris Scales and Gabe Desrosiers. Scales is an ethnomusicologist who has been researching and writing about powwow music for fifteen years and has also participated in powwows as a singer (as part of the Ojibwa singing group the Spirit Sands Singers, from Swan Lake First Nation in southwestern Manitoba) and as a recording engineer who has produced numerous commercial CDs of powwow music for Arbor Records and War Pony Records, independent record labels that have specialized in the recording and distribution of powwow music. Gabe Desrosiers is an Ojibwa singer, songmaker, Grass dancer, and educator who has been participating in powwow culture since childhood. Gabe rose to prominence in the 1980s singing and composing songs for the Whitefish Bay Singers, a powwow group from the Whitefish Bay Reserve in northwestern Ontario. In 1991 he formed his own singing group, the Northern Wind Singers, and has been performing regularly with that group since that time, serving as the leader of the group, the lead singer, and the principal songmaker. He is also well known throughout the powwow world as a champion grass dancer (see Fig. 7.1), winning competitions across North America, and he has toured Europe and the Middle East as part of a professional Native American dance troupe. More recently he has participated in powwows as head singing judge, head dancing judge, arena director, and in several other administrative capacities for powwows across the United States and Canada. Mr. Desrosiers is also an Anishinaabe language instructor and the Coordinator of Cultural Programs and Outreach at the University of Minnesota–Morris.

While the voices of the two authors are often demarcated through the use of direct interview quotation, the entire content of this chapter represents a jointly produced picture of Northern competition powwow culture and is the result of dozens of formal interviews and informal lengthy conversations about powwow singing and dancing and powwow culture more generally.[1]

7.1. Gabriel Desrosiers, in his grass dance regalia, performing on a hand drum. Photo by Christopher Scales.

POWWOW TIME: "NIMIIDAA!"

On the first weekend of August 2011, the Saginaw Chippewa Indian Tribe of Michigan was hosting its 27th annual intertribal competition powwow. The pow-wow grounds are conveniently situated near a campground on the Isabella Indian Reservation in Isabella County in central Michigan, near the city of Mount Pleasant. The event has become known as one the biggest competition powwows in Michigan and typically attracts singing groups and dancers from throughout the Midwest and Northern Plains of the United States, as well as a number of visitors from Canada.

When you enter the campground by a narrow gravel road, you come to a larger clearing on your right where visitors can park their cars. From there it is only a short walk to the powwow grounds proper. At the center of the grounds stands the "dance arbor." This is a large circular area surrounded by a number of free-standing canopies. Some of these canopies shelter booths for powwow committee business, such as singing and dancing contest registration, while others provide shade for the singing groups, who set up their drums all around the arbor. Importantly, some of this seating is also reserved for elder audience members who want a comfortable seat (protected from sun and rain) and a good view of the dancing. At the center of the arbor is a wooden shelter, under which a number of large P.A. speakers point out in all directions, providing amplification for the singing groups as well as the announcements of the emcees. Another permanent, raised wooden shelter is situated at the eastern end of the circle, where the emcees for the event oversee the proceedings, talking to the crowd, telling jokes, announcing upcoming dance events, communicating with the arena directors (one or two individuals who work in the dance arena and take care of all of the organizational and logistical challenges of a powwow), and generally keeping the event moving along.

Surrounding the arbor on all sides are a number of craft, food, and vendor booths, small, independently operated businesses that travel from powwow to powwow every weekend selling their products. Many of the booths sell commercially produced Native American craft items oriented toward tourists, such as dream catchers, silver jewelry, and beadwork. Others are dedicated to servicing the powwow community and supply beads, jewelry, bells, jingles, leather, feathers, fans, and other items that dancers use to make, enhance, or repair their dance outfits for themselves and their family. Still others sell CDs of powwow music and books on various Native topics. Many more sell food to visitors, dancers, and singers, with menu items like wild rice soup, bannock (frybread), "Indian tacos" (frybread and chili), and as well as hamburgers, hot dogs, soda pop, and coffee.

The powwow begins in earnest at 7 p.m. on Friday evening with the commencement of the first "Grand Entry," an event that features an organized procession of all of the participating dancers into the dance arena to the accompaniment of a powwow "Grand Entry song," rendered by the "host drum" (a singing group hired by the powwow organizers to provide music for the weekend). This group is led by a "color guard," a number of highly respected dancers, elders, and military veterans, the latter of which carry several flags into the arbor, including American, Canadian, and tribal flags as well as a number of "Eagle Staffs" (decorated staffs that represent particular families or communities). The next group to follow includes honored guests such as powwow "princesses," who are school-age girls that have been selected to represent their home communities. Then come all of the dancers, who enter in groups according to their age and dance style. Each of these styles is distinguished by both dancers' clothing/outfit and by their unique movements and footwork. Once all the dancers have entered the arena, the emcee requests that everyone in attendance stand and remove their hats while a "flag song" is rendered. Often referred to as a "Native American national anthem," a flag song is meant to honor all of the flags carried by the color guard and the various communities they represent. Following this, an elder from the community, selected by the powwow organizing committee, takes to the emcee stand and delivers an "invocation." Speaking first in Anishinaabe (Ojibwa), then in English, the speaker welcomes all the visiting singers, dancers, and families to the event and then offers a short prayer, asking the Creator to watch over all in attendance. While all remain standing, a "Veterans song," is performed, which is intended to honor all of the military veterans in attendance (both in the dance arena as well as spectators). After all of these songs have been completed, the emcee acknowledges all of the flag carriers, thanking them by name as each, in turn, walks the flag to the arena director, who then posts it near the announcer's booth. Visiting powwow "royalty" (princesses) are also acknowledged at this time. These final formalities mark the end of the Grand Entry and the emcee exclaims "OK, intertribal time! *Nimiidaa!*" and a long night of singing and dancing begins . . .

CHRIS SCALES: What exactly is a Grand Entry song? What distinguishes this kind of song from other powwow songs, and what features make a "good" Grand Entry song?

GABRIEL DESROSIERS: You know, back in the day when I was younger, there used to be just one or two songs that were used. And they're still being used today up in the Lake of the Woods area [in Northwestern Ontario, Canada], where I'm from. They were composed specifically for use in the Grand Entry. And we still sing them in my group too. And other powwow singing groups use them too. Ojibwas, or whoever, they still use these songs. And they have Ojibwa lyrics. And they are used for Grand Entry only. That's the only time you'll hear them. So when we are called upon to do a Grand Entry we typically go to those songs. And there were two of them that were specifically composed. I can't tell you who composed them. They've just been around a long time. You know, ever since I was a kid they've been used in that way.

CS: What makes them good Grand Entry songs?

GD: It's just the lyrics. I can't say what specifically makes a good Grand Entry song, because they have different types of meanings. Some [singing] groups, like even myself as a composer, have made songs that we only use for Grand Entry. So I use lyrics about dancers dancing into the dance arena. But you could do a slower song, or a faster song. All different kinds of songs can be used. And in different communities, they do it different ways. I've seen in the northwest [United States] they do what's called a "Double Beat" song for Grand Entry. The Crow people do this. And it's the ladies—they have a certain [ceremonial] society there where it's the women who wear the headdresses and they dance in the Grand Entry to what's called a "Crow Hop" song or a "Double Beat." And that's their Grand Entry. I don't know the history of that society, but it's pretty awesome to see. They dance in with all these war bonnets and they lead the other dancers in. So the Grand Entry is different in some areas. Traditionally, there was no Grand Entries at all in the Lake of the Woods area. Or anywhere. That is a more "contemporary" thing that was first introduced with Buffalo Bill and the Wild West shows from back in the day. It was just a show, you know. And as time went on it was adopted into the regular powwow protocol or process. Today, for modern times, it's important because it's a time to honor veterans who have served in the armed services and went overseas in these different eras of war. So now veterans are being honored at powwows as part of the Grand Entry.

CS: So Grand Entry songs now are just songs that singing groups feel are appropriate.

GD: Nowadays, yeah. It has just changed through time. As I said, when I was a kid, singers felt like you had to sing those songs, you know, because they were originally made for Grand Entry. But as time went on, things changed. So even in the 1980s, when I was singing with [the] Whitefish Bay [Singers], we introduced a different way of singing for a Grand Entry where—back then if you were the host drum, you were solely responsible for providing songs for the whole Grand Entry. And back then sometimes Grand Entry would take forever. There'd be a lot of dancers dancing in to the arena. So what we did was, we would change up songs. We would sing one song through four times and then switch to another song. Then sing that one four times through. Sometimes we'd sing four or five different songs in one Grand Entry. So that was a new thing also. So nowadays Grand Entry songs can be any song you want to sing.

A HISTORICAL SKETCH OF POWWOWS

The people known as Native Americans—also sometimes called American Indians or, in Canada, First Nations peoples—represent hundreds of different tribal and community groups across the North America. There are over five hundred different federally recognized tribes in the United States alone. While these communities are understood by both the federal government and by each other to be distinct cultural and political entities, they may also be understood as a large and very diverse "ethnic" community that share some political and cultural similarities. Powwows are large, social, and generally secular weekend-long events held year round by both urban and reservation Native communities across the United States and Canada. Held in abundance during the summer months, powwows are opportunities for Native American peoples from many different tribal communities to come together to create, renew, or strengthen social relationships and friendships through a celebration of singing, dancing, camping, honoring elders and veterans, "feasting," visiting, and "relative making." Because powwows bring together so many different communities and the cultural practices are so widely shared across many different tribes, both scholars and Native Americans themselves often refer to these events as "intertribal."

It is generally thought that the term "powwow" originates from the Algonquian language family of the northeastern United States and Canada, descended from the Naragansett words "pau wau" (he/she dreams) and originally associated with healing and medicine men. Its association with Indian dancing began approximately in the 1880s (Browner 2002, 27–28). Today the term "powwow" denotes a wide variety of celebrations and dance events within and between Indian communities. The roots of the modern powwow celebration may be found in the late nineteenth and early twentieth centuries and involve a confluence of historical forces, including the nineteenth-century Southern Plains warrior society dances, as well as tribal and community fairs, exhibitions, and other social gatherings.

Scholars of Native American music have typically traced the origins of many of the modern day powwow singing and dancing styles to the tribal warrior/military societies of the Southern Plains, which used songs and dances to maintain important cultural and social practices (Ellis 2001, 357).[2] For example, it is widely believed that the modern powwow grass dance style of dancing is distantly related to the ceremonial outfit and movements of the Iruska dance of the Pawnee (see Wissler 1916; Browner 2002, 20–27; Ellis 2003, 29–54). The Iruska dance was part of a larger set ceremonial events associated with a warrior society, the Iruska society. Versions of this dance and its accompanying ritual practices were shared among many different plains tribal communities during the nineteenth century, which eventually became known as the Omaha dance/Omaha society. The dance and ceremony's relationship to warriors and warfare perhaps explains in part why the dance became popular at powwows in the early part of the century. After World War I powwow events increasingly began to celebrate and honor returning WWI military veterans (de Shane 1991). As noted by Gabe above, the practice of publicly honoring and acknowledging war veterans is an important feature of powwows that continues to this day.

Many of the formal, organizational elements of the modern powwow are also drawn from a variety of historical tribal and intertribal practices. For example the Grand Entry that begins every powwow dance session over the course of a weekend event is widely believed to have been adopted from the Wild West shows and other traveling carnivals and vaudeville-type shows that were popular during the turn of the twentieth century. These shows, the most well known of which were Buffalo Bill's Wild West Show and Pawnee Bill's show, both featured grand entry parades that included all of the performers, including Native American dancers. While these shows were mainly concerned with presenting stereotypical and romanticized images of cowboy life (including bronco riding, roping, and trick shooting as well as staged battle scenes between "cowboys and Indians"), they also presented unique economic and cultural opportunities for Native American dancers, who were hired by these shows to perform unique "traditional" styles of

Indian dancing. During this time the federal government had formally outlawed all forms of "Indian dancing" as part of a larger initiative to suppress traditional Native American religious practices, in a misguided and ill-conceived attempt to assimilate Native peoples into mainstream American society. These shows were one of the only venues in which Native Americans could openly dance in styles that were inspired by more traditional forms of dancing (see Ellis 2003). Several scholars have also suggested that the modern-day fancy dance (see below) style of powwow dancing was first developed by Native American dancers who performed in these shows. Because many of the dances performed by these individuals were based on more ceremonial and "non-presentational" styles of dancing (Browner 2002, 30), they were encouraged to incorporate more "flashy" and spectacular choreography into their performances. The spirit of these performance innovations, if not the actual dance steps themselves, have influenced both the performance practices and the dance outfits (called "regalia," which refers to both clothing and accessories) of modern fancy dancers.

Most elements of the modern-day powwow began to take form and solidify after WWII, in the 1950s. During this time federal Indian policy encouraged many Native Americans to move from their homes on the reservations to major cities across the United States. In these cities intertribal Native American social clubs formed that would often sponsor powwow events in order to bring together urban Indians from many different tribes and communities. Because powwow styles of singing and dancing were by this time widely performed by many different Native communities, it was thought to be a relatively "neutral" form of celebration that did not favor or emphasize any particular tribal practices or customs. The powwow thus became an ideal social event for generating and strengthening "intertribal" social solidarity—a way of celebrating a common "Native American" heritage, rather than (or along with) a specific tribal heritage.[3]

Since the 1970s powwows have only grown in size and popularity across North America, with the song and dance styles and powwow event format spreading beyond the Northern and Southern Plains communities to both the East and West Coasts. Powwow events can now be found from California to Maine and all points in between. While powwows are more far more prevalent during the summer months, these events are now hosted year round by different reservation and urban Native communities.

Presently, there are two major powwow "circuits" in North America, each characterized both by geographic region as well as singing and dancing styles. The Northern style powwow began in the Northern Great Plains and Great Lakes region of the United States and these powwows are now found throughout the Midwest and Northern Plains of the United States (stretching from Michigan and Illinois through North and South Dakota, to Montana, Idaho, and Wyoming) as well as the Central Plains of Canada. Southern powwows are those typically found in Oklahoma, although these events may be found throughout the Southwest as well. Native American communities found on the East and west Coasts also host powwows, but often these events are inflected by local song and dance practices and many times feature enough stylistic hybridity that they do not easily fall into one or the other of these two paradigmatic types of events.

The distinctions between Northern and Southern powwows also manifest in performance style, as each features a unique style of singing (unsurprisingly known as "Northern style singing" and "Southern style singing"), different song genres and categories, as well as different dance styles. While the general form and structure of these events remain consistent enough across North America that Native dancers and singers from any tribal community are able take part in any particular event, participants recognize significant differences in the overall tenor and purpose of different powwows. Thus the terms refer now to broadly defined powwow styles—different styles of singing and dancing and different orders of events—as well as to geography.

Throughout the summer months, powwow participants—singing groups, more commonly called "drum groups" or simply "drums," and dancers—travel across North America within and between the Northern and Southern powwow circuits, often competing for sometimes quite large cash prizes. Powwows in the twenty-first century are perhaps best thought of now as an important and unique kind of Native American popular culture. There are several large, international, highly commercialized powwow events like the Denver March Powwow and the Gathering of Nations powwow in Albuquerque, New Mexico, that draw the best singers and dancers from across North America. These events are not unlike some of the big summer rock and pop music festivals. There are also several record labels that are dedicated to the production and distribution of the latest and most popular powwow music groups. And while many powwows emphasize intergenerational participation, with all ages being welcomed and encouraged to dance, powwows are increasingly becoming associated with Native American youth culture.

NORTHERN POWWOWS: TRADITIONAL AND COMPETITION

> GD: Well, typically if you go to either type of a powwow—contest or traditional—you're going hear pretty much the same kind of music, the same repertoire of music, Native American music. So take for example our powwow back home on Northwest Angle [Reserve in the Lake of the Woods area]. What we do there is we first try and do our own ceremonial teachings that we've been always been taught. And with that I'm saying we smoke the [traditional] pipe and sing on traditional drums. We make sure that the ceremonial part, and the protocols of the process, that those spiritual things are taken care of. And that happens on Friday night. When the traditional drums come in there, we sing traditional songs that belong to those traditional drums, and we feast those drums. And we have a little "giveaway" [a formal session of gift giving] and then we smoke the pipe and take care of our four directions.

CS: How do you feast the drums?

GD: We smoke the pipe and then offer food to people: relatives, friends, whoever is there. That way we bless the grounds so good things will happen during the festivities and the powwow. We take care of all the spiritual things that we're supposed to take care of, the way a traditional powwow is supposed to be. And then we have elders talking and holding the pipe, walking around the arbor doing teachings, talking to the people. Making sure everyone understands what a powwow is about. That's how we open our powwows. And then Saturday comes and the powwow changes into a more intertribal powwow where everyone can expect the common practices of an intertribal contest powwow: Grand Entry, specials, the whole process. So the powwow changes and turns into an intertribal powwow where everyone's invited to participate. Different songs and different dances are performed.

CS: So is it fair to say that basically all contest powwows are like that. Not that they necessarily split the powwow into two separate kinds of events like that, but in the sense that powwow committees try to balance local traditions with intertribal contest powwow protocols.

GD: I know that's how Sisseton does it. [The Sisseton Wahpeton Oyate is a Dakota community located on the Lake Traverse Reservation in Northeastern South Dakota, where Gabe and his family make their home.] They bless the grounds the week before. And then they sing the traditions of the grass dance society. Grass dancers come in and flatten the [grass on the] ground and bless the ground before they dance. And then they do their prayers there.

CS: So sometimes it happens even out of sight of the visitors.

GD: Yeah. In the background of a powwow you might see something going on. Or prior to when the powwow is actually taking place. And then the visitors start coming in and it's, all of a sudden, like a regular intertribal [competition] powwow. Where all these different Native nations come in and every one of them understands the common, modern-day practice of a contest powwow.

CS: So probably even at a very contemporary kind of contest powwow, like the Mount Pleasant powwow, the powwow committee and the community are still following some local ceremonial traditions?

GD: Blessing of the ground, smoking of the pipe. I'm sure of it. I'm sure they do that.

CS: So maybe that's a good way to think about the similarities and differences with all the different powwows across the Northern Plains and the Midwest?

GD: First they take care of their local belief systems and culture. They take care of that. And then it turns into a more intertribal event when people start arriving. I think that's why you can look at powwows as both a social but also as a spiritual event.

Within the Northern powwow circuit there is a widely recognized difference between what are known as "competition" or "contest" powwows and "traditional" powwows. As their name suggests, competition powwows feature formal song and dance competitions and (sometimes large) cash prizes for participants, while traditional powwows do not. Several other differences exist as well. Competition powwows are generally much more structured proceedings with fairly strict adherence to a schedule of events. Due to the schedule of competitive events, more emphasis is placed on the strict division of dance and song categories, and competitive powwows do not regularly emphasize community and tribal concerns or local dance traditions. At these powwows, both singers and dancers are judged by their peers, other singers and dancers chosen by the head singing and dancing judges, although, as a rule, one is disqualified from judging if they are related to any of the competitors.[4]

Conversely, traditional powwows typically (although not always) operate on a much smaller budget and emphasize community and intertribal friendship over formal competition. Instead of holding formal contests, each participating dancer or singer receives a modest sum of money from the powwow committee to help offset the expense of travel, food, and lodging for participants. These powwows will, more often than not, offer a feast for all participants and spectators each evening as a way to honor and welcome visitors and community members alike. Dancing and singing activities are undertaken informally, and the proceedings will often feature a number of giveaways, "honor songs," and other events that highlight or emphasize local community concerns. Friendship and camaraderie are emphasized over contests and competitiveness.[5]

As Gabe indicated in the interview excerpt above, another important difference distinguishing traditional and competition powwows is the degree to which local religious or ceremonial practices are incorporated into the events. In many Ojibwa communities in the Lake of the Woods area where Gabe grew up, the music is performed almost entirely by what are known as "traditional drums."[6] This term refers both to the instrument itself and to the group of singers who perform with the drum. These instruments are approximately the size of the bass drum of a marching band with wooden frames and animal hide (typically deer, moose, or buffalo) stretched across both sides. Traditional drums are understood to be sacred objects and are treated with the utmost respect and care. They are typically owned by chosen "drumkeepers" whose job it is to care for the drum and observe all of the ritual practices associated with it, including, for example, "feeding" the drum with offerings of food every season and caring for and smoking a pipe that is part of the ritual paraphernalia connected to the drum and its use. Drumkeepers are also responsible for memorizing, maintaining, and performing a collection of songs that are sung only with that instrument. Such drums rarely travel outside of the community and are typically only used for traditional powwows or other ceremonial events.

Traditional drums, and the drumkeepers who care for them, typically provide the music for the weekend of dancing at traditional powwows. Many times drumkeepers do not necessarily have a regular group of singers with whom they perform. Instead, they simply show up at a traditional powwow and rely on other singers from the community (or sometimes from outside of the community) to come together around the drum and sing when called upon. Singing at these powwows often feature a larger number of songs that "belong" to a particular community and thus many singers from the community will know them. This shared community repertoire allows for the maximum number of participants to join in and sing with a number of drums. Other traditional drums may feature only singers from a particular extended family.

There are no contests at traditional powwows, and as such, no cash prizes awarded for the different styles of dancing. Instead, an emphasis is placed on "intertribal dancing," which is a time when all dancers at the event, regardless of dance style or dance regalia, are welcomed to dance in the dance arena. Participating dancers and singers are often paid a small amount of money by the powwow organizing committee through what is known as a "drum split" and a "dance split." Powwow committees will set aside a certain amount of money to pay the singers and dancers who attend the powwow. This money is usually a modest sum, intended only to help offset the cost of travel. In order to be eligible for the dance and drum splits, participants must register as a participating singer or dancer (or both). Drum and dance splits are important ways that communities show hospitality. When inviting someone to one's home, there is an obligation to make sure that the guests are comfortable and do not suffer any hardship as a result of their visit. Drum and dance splits, as well as feasts, are mechanisms by which local communities welcome visitors and reflect the interpersonal host–guest obligations that occur more generally in everyday reservation life.

In contrast, competition powwows can be very large, colorful, boisterous, and sometimes highly commercialized events. The competition powwow circuit began to form in the 1950s as a loosely related aggregate of song and dance events that offered modest cash prizes to participants. This circuit became larger and more structurally coherent by the 1970s as more and more reservations began holding annual celebrations open to intertribal participation. The 1980s and 1990s saw the emergence of "mega-powwows," with such events as the Gathering of Nations in Albuquerque, the Denver March Powwow, the Mashantucket Pequot's Schemitzun, and Coeur d'Alene's Julyamsh. Drawing thousands of participants from across North America and fueled in part by the large injection of capital generated through the proliferation of reservation-based casinos, competition powwows began offering cash prizes on the order of thousands of dollars for dance events and tens of thousands for singing contests.

The 2011 Mount Pleasant powwow, described at the beginning of this chapter, was typical in this regard. Funded in part by the Soaring Eagle Casino and Resort, a tribally owned and operated business, the advertising for the powwow boasts that it is the home of the "Midwest world class singing and dance championships." Contest prizes for the event were extravagant, with an open singing contest that paid $10,000 for a first place finish with seven places in total offering cash prizes, and the rest of the drums sharing a drum split. Similarly, the first place prize for all the adult dance categories was a generous $1,400 per dancer, with lesser prizes awarded to second through fifth place finishes. There were also a number of unique contests sponsored by the powwow organizing committee including a fry bread contest, a baby parade (for children under twenty-four months dressed in special dance outfits), and a number of special dance contests held throughout the weekend.

The host drum for the powwow that year was the Grammy Award–nominated powwow singing group and local favorite Bear Creek, a group of singers who hail from Sault Ste. Marie, Ontario, a town just across the northern Michigan border between the United States and Canada. A number of other popular groups were also competing in the singing competition that weekend, many who had traveled long distances from their homes across North America, including Crazy Spirit, Young Kingbird, Southern Boys, Ho-Chunk Station, Dusty Bear, Elk Spirit, Tha Tribe, Meskwaki Nation, and Pipestone.

While singing and dancing styles at competition and traditional powwows are ostensibly the same, competitions have inspired a much higher degree of professionalization among participants. Some dancers (and even a few singing groups) can even earn enough money through constant participation in competitions every weekend to support themselves throughout the year. For most however, the money earned through competition is simply enough to help offset the cost of a summer of traveling to powwows across the Northern Plains and beyond.

NORTHERN POWWOW DANCING

GD: I think there are certain things that you have to like about contest powwows. I enjoy going to contest powwows because, for one thing, it gives me the opportunity to participate as both a singer and a [grass] dancer. It

> also gives me the opportunity to be fortunate enough to serve as a head staff dancer, or an arena director, or a singing judge, or a dance judge [Gabe served as the head male dance judge at the 2011 Mount Pleasant powwow]. You know, it gives me those opportunities, and I enjoy that a lot about contest powwows. I also like to dance—just to dance, you know. I really enjoy myself when I'm just dancing to good quality music. And when that happens, when you're dancing to a good, quality-sounding group, then a lot of good feelings just come out. The good feeling of just being able to dance, you know. And it's a good physical workout. I like that. It keeps you in shape. And I feel good about myself, being able to dance to two, three contest songs. It's a very fulfilling feeling for me. Yeah it's—it's an energizer for me . . . and it brings out the competition part of me. Knowing that you are able to dance with all these young guys. I can dance with these guys for three or four songs in a row and I feel good about it. And I don't care if they beat me or not but I'm—I'm feeling good about dancing. And when you go to contest powwows, that's what defines me as who I am as a dancer.

The Mount Pleasant powwow is a well-established and well-known competition powwow, and a regular part of the powwow schedule for many competition dancers and singers who travel the powwow trail all summer long. Tara Browner (2002), a Choctaw Jingle Dress dancer and ethnomusicologist, has rightfully noted that dance events may be separated into three broad categories: intertribals, specials, and competitions. The 2011 Mount Pleasant powwow committee made sure to schedule a variety of each kind of dance event every session in order to keep all the participating dancers dancing regularly (without long breaks between dances) and keep audience members engaged and interested. There were three scheduled dance sessions over the course of the weekend. Each session began with a Grand Entry, the first beginning on Friday night at 7 p.m., and other two scheduled for 1 p.m. on Saturday and Sunday. However, inclement weather played havoc with the scheduling over the weekend and because of heavy rain the entire powwow (all of the singing groups and dancers and vendors' booths) had to be moved from the powwow grounds to a large performance area inside the Soaring Eagle Resort complex. Saturday's Grand Entry was delayed until 2:30 p.m., pushing all the other scheduled dance events back and forcing the powwow to continue into late Saturday evening as they tried to squeeze all the scheduled competitions into the compressed time frame. All of the dancing on Sunday took place indoors as well.

Intertribal dancing is open to general participation and has no special footwork or regalia requirements (although it is customary for women at least to wear a shawl over their shoulders when entering the arena). During these dances, all who are attending are welcome to dance, including singers, spectators, and, upon invitation, even non-Natives. During an intertribal dance it is common to see a wide variety of dance styles and footwork. For many dancers, it is a time simply to circle the dance arena using the basic "tap-step" dance pattern. Many of the footwork patterns for the dances derive from this basic form: a four-beat pattern in which the right foot moves forward, taps the ground, and then lands flush to the ground and weight is shifted onto that foot. The left foot then follows exactly as the right foot did: tap-step, tap-step. As almost a kind of stylized walking step, this footwork pattern allows dancers to leisurely move around the dance arena and visit and talk with fellow dancers or other friends who are in the dance arena. For other dancers, particularly those who are registered to participate in a dance competition, it is a time to warm up and practice their own dance steps for their upcoming dance event. For those who are not in "regalia" (the term preferred by powwow dancers when referencing their dance outfit), it may simply be a time to join the dance circle and participate in the event in a more active way. At the Mount Pleasant powwow, each Grand Entry was followed by a number of intertribal dances as a way to warm up the dancers and get everyone immediately involved and participating.

"Specials" refer to any number of dance events that are held apart from either intertribals or the regular dance category contests. These could involve competitions or exhibitions of any of the major dance categories, as well as tribally or regionally specific dances that may not be regularly performed at powwows, as well as more participatory dances that do not necessarily involve any dance experience and are used to generate audience participation. For example, the 2011 Mount Pleasant powwow featured a number of "committee specials" throughout the weekend, specific dancing and singing contests that were sponsored (funded and run) by the powwow organizing committee for that year. Friday night featured an "iron man" contest, where fancy dancers competed by dancing for as long as they could without a break. Saturday's session featured a smoke dance special (the smoke dance is a style unique to the Haudenosaunee people of the eastern United States) as well as a hand drum contest, where groups of three singers, generally from the same drum group, performed on small, handheld frame drums and sang unique "round dance" songs that are closely associated with that instrument. Throughout the weekend there was also a "Men's All-Around" contest where dancers who registered had to dance in all three of the main male dance categories: men's traditional dancing, men's fancy dancing, and grass dancing.

Competition dancing comprises the majority of dance events that takes place at competition powwows. Competition events are organized according to age group, sex, and dance style category: Tiny Tots (five years old and younger, mixed dance categories and gender), Junior Boys and Junior Girls (ages 6–12), teen boys and girls (13–18), Adult Men and Adult Women (ages 19–54, although this category is sometimes further split into two different categories: 19–34 and 35–54), and Senior Men and Senior Women (ages 55 and older). In this way, dancers are always competing with their age peers.

Northern competition powwows feature six standard competition dance styles, distinguished by gender, choreography, and regalia, with each style constituting a separate contest category. There are three men's styles: men's traditional dance, men's grass dance, men's fancy dance; and three women's styles: women's traditional dance, women's jingle dress dance, and women's fancy shawl dance. While a high degree of variation is the norm, both between tribally specific styles and according to the tastes of individual dancers, some general comments can be made.[7]

Traditional style dancing in both the male and female form is descended from many pre-reservation, tribally specific dance forms (mainly the Dakota and Lakota Sioux tribes). The men's traditional dance features a unique regalia (dance outfit) distinguished by a circular or U-shaped single feather bustle made of wing or tail feathers and fastened around the waist of the dancer. A "roach," often made of porcupine hair and featuring (most commonly) two feathers, is worn on the head. Many other features of the regalia will reflect the tribal affiliation of the dancer, but other common elements include a ribbon shirt, bone breastplate, neck choker, a cloth or leather breech cloth, bells around the ankles, and beaded moccasins. Traditional dancers often carry a range of objects in their hands, commonly a wing fan or pipe. The choreography of this dance is typically said to re-enact the movement of a warrior hunting an animal or searching out an enemy.

A women's traditional dancer's regalia is either of the Northern buckskin style or the Southern cloth style. The buckskin outfits are decorated with intricate bead designs and a fringed shawl draped across one arm. Breastplates are made from hair bone pipe, and glass beads may hang to the waist, or all the way to the ankles. The choreography of this dance is one of elegance and grace and features subtle, smooth, and flowing movements. Dancers either move forward, lightly stepping to every other beat of the drum, or stand in one spot, feet together, gently bobbing to the rhythm of the song with the long fringe of their sleeves swaying in time. As a standard practice, these dancers will raise their fans in honor of the drum during the "honor beats" (see below) of the songs.

The men's and women's fancy styles both emphasize athleticism, intricate footwork, and complex, free-form choreography. The men's regalia is marked by two feather bustles worn around the waist and the shoulders, often color-coordinated, with copious beadwork displayed on the outfit and displaying large amounts of feather "hackles" (a feather plume) dyed in coordinating colors. Small matching hackle bustles are sometimes worn as armbands as well. Accompanied by fast-tempo dance songs, this dance style emphasizes highly kinetic choreography and often tests a dancer's reflexes and stamina as well as their creativity in creating unique dance moves.

The women's fancy shawl dance developed in the 1950s and is the counterpart to the popular male style. This regalia is relatively simple with a decorated cloth dress, leggings, and a shawl worn over the shoulder comprising the basic elements. Like the men's dance, the women's version of the fancy dance features a great degree of latitude and variation in footwork and choreography. Sometimes called the "butterfly dance," the movement of the dancers must be light and graceful and usually incorporates a spinning motion, arms spread wide, draped in a shawl, with arm motions characteristic of the movement of butterfly wings.

The men's grass dance (see Fig. 7.1) is one of the most popular styles of the contemporary Northern Plains powwow circuit. The outfit does not feature a feather bustle but consists of shirt, trousers, and apron, to which yarn fringe, sequins, and beaded designs are attached, a possible simulation of a much older outfit style that featured dried grass tucked in the dancer's belt. A beaded or otherwise decorated belt, armbands, cuffs, and front and back aprons with matched headband and moccasins, and a feathered roach complete the outfit. A common story associated with the dance maintains that it evolved from the tradition of young boys tying grass to their outfits and stomping down the long prairie grass so that a dance could begin. The unique choreography of this dance reflects this activity (see Wissler 1916; Howard 1951; Powers 1966, 1990; Browner 1995, for more about the historical development of the dance).

It is commonly agreed among powwow participants that the women's jingle dress dance originated with the Ojibwa people in the Lake of the Woods area of Ontario. Various origin stories currently exist in oral history, but they all fall within a basic narrative pattern. A medicine man's daughter became very ill and, in a dream, his spirit guide told him to make a jingle dress for her and to instruct her in the unique steps of the dance. In doing so, his daughter would be healed. Upon making the dress and giving it to his daughter, the girl indeed recovered. Consequently, the dance continues to be associated with healing and is often referred to as a "medicine dance." According to oral history, the jingle dress dance diffused into the modern Northern powwow complex in the 1960s and 1970s. The outfit itself consists of a dress decorated with a large number of rolled-up snuff can lids attached with ribbon in various patterns. The basic footwork consists of the graceful bouncing on the dancer's toes in a right/left alternation to the steady beat of the drum. An alternate dance step, known as the side step, involves dancing to a quick triple-meter song with the dancer executing quick slide steps to the left, hands on hips.

NORTHERN POWWOW SONGS AND SINGING GROUPS

GD: I don't know what made me create my first songs. I started when I was with the police force, when I was about twenty years old. I would cruise around in my cruiser by myself and I found one day that I could make a song. And I just recorded it on tape. And that was the beginning. And so I started carrying around a cassette player with me, recording whatever songs I would make. I would put them right onto that tape recorder. And then from there, whenever I had a weekend off, we [the Whitefish Bay Singers, Gabe's powwow singing group at the time] would go off to a powwow, and we'd sing them. We'd sing those songs that I made. And that's how that all started.

CS: Now, when you were making them did you did you come up with a lead [the first musical phrase] first and then compose the rest of the song from that, or did the whole song just come to you all at once?

GD: Well I have found out through the years that there are three ways that a song comes to me. One of them is, I make them outright. Getting a lead [to build from, and then] getting the rest of the tune. Then you put it together. Or sometimes I start with the words, and I just build off that. You build the melody from how the words are going to sound within the song. I get the words first. I figure out what words I want to sing for a particular dance style, or what words are appropriate. Or I think about who the song is going to be made for when I make a song outright. So if it's a jingle dress song, for example, I'll look for the words that are appropriate for those dancers. And then I'll just put them together. Or if it's for someone, if it's an honor song for a specific person, I'll just use appropriate words for that person. And then create the lead and then create the rest of the song. And usually it just all comes together, until I'm finished with it. Sometimes I'll put it aside and I'll come back to it and I'll change it maybe a little bit. And then sometimes I think, "oh, it sounds too much like this other song" and then I'll change it. I usually change some parts of it. But sometimes a song will just come to me if I'm alone, or something. I just start singing, and I'll think, "wow I've never heard this before," you know. And I just put it on tape. Yeah. Those are the songs that kind of come to me. That's the second way I compose. Songs just come to me during . . . whatever I'm doing in my daily life. And then the third way is—and these are the sacred ones—through dreams. I dream of a song. That doesn't happen much, but when it does happen, I wake up in the middle of the night and then I hear that song that I was singing in my dream. When I wake up it's still there. And when that happens I run down and get my tape recorder and then sing it. Those are the special songs for me. And they come with words and everything. Sometimes they're straight songs [songs that use vocables only]. But a lot of times they're with words and there's a deeper meaning behind it.

At its most basic level, Northern style singing features unison singing accompanied by a steady drumbeat, performed by all the musicians sitting around the drum. The texts of these songs are either a series of vocables (e.g., hey ya wey ya yo wey), lyrics in a Native American language, or some combination of the two. Several other stylistic features are also typical of Northern singing. The first is a high, tense, somewhat nasal vocal production. These timbral and vocal-register features are actually typical of many different kinds of singing across many different tribal groups that live or hail originally from the Northern Plains. As such, it is not surprising that this kind of vocal production would be featured in a song style that is as widely dispersed and as intertribally varied as powwow music. Northern songs are also performed with a noticeable amount of vocal vibrato. While the depth and amount of vibrato used varies from singer to singer, all Northern style singing requires at least some vibrato, and absence of vibrato alters the music on a fundamental level. Another regular feature of powwow songs are melodies that have a terraced and generally descending melodic shape. The highest notes of a powwow song are found in the opening phrase of the song, and each successive phrase features collections of notes that are generally lower than those found in the previous phrase.

Another important and unique stylistic hallmark of Northern style singing is a subtle rhythmic displacement that exists between the sung melody and the steady pulsing of the unison drum beating. Powwow singers refer to this technique as "off the beat" singing. Singing "off the beat" refers to two distinct but equally important kinds of rhythmic displacements. The most noticeable way that singers will sing off the beat is by making sure a melodic phrase begins in between drum beats, a technique that creates syncopation between the rhythmic structure of the melody and the steady drumbeat. Singers who sing "on the beat" (who begin their melodies at the same time that they are beating the drum) are typically considered to be "just beginners," meaning that they have not yet absorbed and mastered this essential element of style.

However there is also a second, more subtle kind of rhythmic displacement that takes place during the performance of a Northern style powwow song. Singers typically sing slightly ahead of or slightly behind the regular pulse or subdivision of the pulse of the drum accompaniment. As such, the melody sounds as if it is floating above the drumbeat, connected to but not entirely aligned with the steady rhythm of the drum. Powwow participants recognize that different drum groups will sing more or less "off the beat," and the degree of rhythmic displacement between melody and drumbeat is often a matter of individual or sometimes tribally or regionally defined aesthetic preference. However, most would agree that in order to sound like a powwow song, singers have to be able to sing "off the beat." From my own experience, acquiring the ability to sing off the beat—singing a melody that is rhythmically connected but displaced from the rhythmic framework that one is performing on the drum—is the single most challenging aspect of learning this style of singing.

Finally, perhaps one of the most noticeable and consistent traits of powwow songs is the remarkable regularity of their musical form. A "push-up" is the general term for a single verse of a powwow song. Each push-up is divided into two sections. The "lead" section refers both to the opening melodic phrase of the push-up and to the fact that it is almost always performed by a single singer. The "seconds" section is comprised of all of the remaining phrases of each verse, sung by the entire group in unison. Because of this division of singing labor, these terms are also used to refer to the singers. "Lead singers" are those members of a group who can be counted on to perform solo lead phrases, and "seconds" is the term used to refer to all the other members of the group. The most common rendition of a powwow song will feature four repetitions of a single verse/push-up, and while it is not unusual for performances to last longer than four push-ups, depending on the context and function of the song within a powwow, a song will almost never be shorter than four push-ups.

Many non-Native scholars of this music have described the structural divisions of powwow song form by outlining phrase structure. Within this literature, powwow songs are categorized as a kind of "incomplete repetition" with a phrase structure that is represented as AA'BCBC or AA'BCDBCD, with each letter representing a unique melodic phrase. There is generally a high degree of motivic relationship between the different phrases; the A' phrase is a repetition of the A phrase with an extended ending, while the B, C, and possibly D phrases all may share a great degree of melodic material with the A phrase and with each other.

The repetition of the BC or BCD phrases is also marked by performers through the use of "honor beats," which are also sometimes called "hard beats" or "check beats," performed on the drum. Honor beats refer to a series of louder, accented beats that occur on alternate drum strokes numbering between four and eight (or more, depending on the aesthetic preferences of the performer). These drum strokes are performed by specified members of a drum group who strike the drum closer to the center and with a marked increase in force while the other members of the group simultaneously reduce the force and volume of their drumming. Honor beats are often said to honor the four directions (north, south, east, and west). These drum strokes are usually initiated at some point during the repetition of the B phrase and may last into the opening notes of the C phrase, and, apart from their spiritual significance, they are a signal to the dancers that the end of the push-up (or complete verse) is drawing near.

This standard song form is used for the vast majority of both newly composed and older and more traditional Northern powwow songs. Remarkably, despite the incredible regularity and ubiquity of song form, powwow musicians and composers that I have spoken with rarely talk about their compositions in terms of phrase structure. While it is clear they are fully aware of this formal structure, they simply do not consider it particularly useful or illuminating when talking about how a powwow song is put together. (I have often thought that one reason for this may be that the phrase structure is so fundamental to what makes a powwow song sound like a powwow song that it seems silly to even mention it. It would be akin to making special mention of the fact that powwow songs feature a melody.)

When explaining the remarkable regularity of powwow song form to my students, I have often compared powwow songs to twelve-bar blues songs. Like powwow, blues music uses a very restricted set of musical forms, the most common by far being a twelve-bar blues, which features a standard number of bars, chord progression, and poetic form. Yet within this seemingly very limiting set of compositional requirements, there is room for an almost infinite amount of subtle compositional and improvisational variation. So it is with powwow songs. Rather than developing or experimenting with new compositional forms, powwow music is kept musically interesting (for performers, dancers, and fans) through more subtle forms of variation, such as playing with the degree to which one sings "off the beat," or varying the amount of vibrato used when singing, or using asymmetrical sets of sub-phrases that are articulated through the emphasis of certain vocables within a larger phrase. Formal variation is also not desirable because powwow music is primarily "dance music" and is performed primarily and essentially in the service of the dancers. Dancers often have specialized and formalized movements and steps that that are performed at very specific points in the musical form. Too much formal innovation could possibly cause the dancer to lose their place in the song, which would create all kinds of choreographic confusion.

All of the stylistic and formal elements just discussed may be heard on the Northern Wind Singers' recorded performance of the song "November Winds" (commercially available for download from iTunes or Amazon.com) from their 2008 CD of the same name (Arbor Records AR-13032). This song, composed by Gabe Desrosiers, uses vocables only and features a medium tempo suitable for intertribal dancing. While maintaining a strict adherence to the typical AA'BCBC form, Gabe has given this song a unique compositional shape through the symmetrical subdivision of each phrase into two fourteen-beat melodic sub-phrases. A gradual increase in the tempo and volume of the drumming, beginning at the start of the third push-up, also help give the performance a dynamic shape as the energy of the song slowly builds until the honor beats are performed at the end of the fourth and final push-up.

Powwow singing groups are typically comprised of between five and fifteen male singers, all of whom sit around the drum in a circle. Each singer holds a drumstick and is responsible for both drumming and singing at the same time. While singers may sometimes stop singing to clear their throats, catch their breath, or perform "honor beats," singers are typically expected to always share equally in the labor of singing and drumming. However, there are also some specialized musical roles for individual drum group members. A group must have at least one lead singer, someone who can sing the lead phrases of a song (the A parts of the AA'BCBC form) by himself. Lead singers are typically thought to be the best singers in the group. To be a successful lead singer requires not only a strong, clear, and loud voice but also the confidence to sing by oneself. A good lead singer must also have a good musical memory and be able to recall the lead melody to a song at a moment's notice. Those singers who do not sing any lead phrases are known as seconds, and as their name suggests, they are responsible for singing all of the other phrases, apart from the lead, within a push-up. Most singers begin as seconds within a drum group, and as they become stronger, more confident singers, they may graduate to singing leads. This division of labor, combined with the typical unison singing required to render a powwow song, makes powwow singing a fairly participatory activity that allows for singers from a wide range of skill levels, from rank beginner to the most experienced lead singer.[8] Most powwow people recognize, appreciate, and value the skill and talent of highly accomplished singers; however, there is also a shared sentiment that anyone is welcome and able to become a singer. Learning to sing is typically undertaken informally and one learns through aural/oral transmission. One starts by simply being invited to sit at a drum and beginning to sing.

While powwow singing is generally understood to be the domain of men, women have a particular musical role that, while narrowly restricted and proscribed, is nonetheless highly valued. During a performance, women singers form a secondary circle, standing just behind the seated male singers, and render the BC or BCD phrases of the melody an octave higher than their male counterparts. While musicologists would call this octave unison singing, powwow performers refer to the women's part as "harmonizing" and women singers are known as "harmonizers."

The repertoire of modern drum groups who perform at competition powwows like the Mount Pleasant powwow typically consists of a majority of newly composed songs. Novelty and "newness" are highly valued at competition powwows and drum groups are expected to have a new and original set of songs to perform each new powwow season. Thus drum groups must also have at least one composer or "song maker" in their group. While song composition may sometimes be a group activity, most songmakers create songs on their own and then bring them to their group. Like the ability to sing, the ability to compose powwow songs is considered to be a natural talent or gift, but one can also work to become a good song maker and all are welcome to try to develop their compositional skills.

POWWOWS AS POPULAR CULTURE

> GD: Now we're living in a time where, within the powwow world, there's a huge influence from the [non-Native] dominant culture and dominant society. For example, there's this idea that everything should be equal [between men and women—that men and women should be able to do the same things and have the same kinds of responsibilities]. And that's Western philosophy, Western teachings.[9] Or there's the fact that a lot of tribes have adapted to Christianity and Christian religious teachings. It just kind of changes the way people think about the powwow. For me, I think about how to correlate Anishinaabe [Ojibwa] beliefs and philosophy with Western teachings, you know? And I think, as a community and as a people, we need to think more about that. I think sometimes that we've become too assimilated, in a lot of ways. So people forget, I think, in my opinion, about these old teachings and that should be maintained. But you know, you'll go to a powwow and you'll always hear, "this is the twenty-first century," you

know. "We need to keep on going." That's why you see so many changes in powwow. It's always changing. There was even a time when drum groups were dressing like African American gangster rappers, with chains and hats. Flipping their hats around or wearing them to the side or something. It's just . . . I don't know. I don't know how to explain that. It's too much for me. It becomes a picture of confusion. And these changes are still going on really strong. Facebook plays a really huge part in powwow now. After every powwow someone's posting: "Here are the winners from this powwow. These are the drums that won." People are requesting results on their Facebook page. And people are posting YouTube videos of music from their favorite drum groups. So social media is playing a huge role. And now you have all these websites like powwows.com. And everybody's keeping track of one another. Who's winning first, who's placing in the contest. And it's all this modern-day technology that is changing the context, and the mindset, of what powwows are actually supposed to be.

CS: So do you think new singing and dancing trends are happening faster now because everybody can see all of this new stuff, these new and different practices on YouTube and Facebook and all of these other social media?

GD: Now it's all actually happening even faster, in "real time." People are posting videos from their phones of what's going on at this powwow, what's happening at this other one. Who's there [which drum groups and which dancers]. And it's always going. It's a constant stream of information. And on to the next powwow. Taking videos with your phone. And these videos are also incorporating what's going on after the powwow. What they're [the dancers and singers] doing. This is a whole different vision of what a powwow is. I don't know where it's going to end, you know. It's going to keep on going. I don't know what else is going to come in next. And so, with contest powwows, sometimes I wonder if the spirituality of singing and dancing is still there, you know. I often wonder about that. Then again, I hear a lot of the dancers, they say, "well, I'm not going to go to this powwow next week because I'm going to go to the Sun Dance."[10] Or "I have to be at a ceremony, so I won't be able to make to Red Earth [powwow]," or something like that. So it gives you the idea that some of the dancers are still practicing their traditional ways, their traditional teachings. They're still trying to maintain that balance for themselves, their spirituality. I've heard some drum groups say these kinds of things too, like some of the Mille Lacs [Indian Reservation in Minnesota] drum groups. I often hear them say, "Well, we can't make this powwow because our drum ceremonies are happening then so we're not gonna be there." And like I said, it gives me the idea that some people are still practicing their cultural ways.

Powwows in the twenty-first century are an important site of Native American cultural and social innovation and experimentation. As Gabe's comments above indicate, one of the central challenges for both powwow organizing committees and participating singers and dancers is how to most successfully and satisfyingly merge traditional community and tribal values and lifeways with the twenty-first-century communications and media technologies that have become increasingly ubiquitous and popular, particularly with Native American youth culture. There are similar concerns and discussions about the role of prize money at competition powwows: how much money can and should a community be spending on its annual powwow? Some formerly very large and lavish casino-sponsored powwows have begun to scale back their prize money and size of their powwow considerably. Other powwows, like the Saginaw Chippewa Mount Pleasant powwow, continue to grow in both size and contest dollars. In 2013 the Saginaw Chippewa completely renovated their powwow grounds, installing permanent covered seating for spectators and drum groups around the entire arbor with a raised announcer's booth and another permanent covered structure in the center of the dance arbor where drum groups can set up and perform. A state-of-the-art public address system has also been installed. The 2014 event boasted prize money in excess of $90,000.

Powwows have the remarkable ability to adapt and transform, continually incorporating new ideas, new protocols, new tribally or intertribally developed song and dance styles, and many other trends. Some may enjoy popularity for only a year or two; others will become more permanent or perhaps even standard parts of a powwow that become adopted by powwow committees across the country (like the Grand Entry). For those people who dedicate their summers to the powwow trail, singing and dancing is a lifelong vocation that they take very seriously. Thus, these changes are often carefully evaluated and passionately debated. But engagement with these questions—how tradition and the past can and should play a role in the present and future of powwows—are a sure sign of vitality. This commitment is evidence of the ongoing importance of powwows as social and artistic practice in the lives of Native Americans in the twenty-first century.

Notes

1. Throughout this essay I use the terms "Native," "Native American" (used mainly in the USA), "First Nations" (used mainly in Canada), and "Indian" (used throughout North America, most often by Native Americans themselves) somewhat interchangeably. All these terms refer to the same segment of the larger indigenous population in North America.

2. Within anthropology, The "Great Plains" refers to both a geographic and cultural area that stretches approximately 1,500 miles across the heartland of North America, from southern Canada to central Texas, and from east of the Mississippi River to the eastern edge of the Rocky Mountains (Sutton 2004, 258). This area is often subdivided into the Northern Plains, which includes the southern part of the prairie provinces of Canada as

well as Montana, Wyoming, North Dakota, South Dakota, and parts of Minnesota and Wisconsin, while the Southern Plains covers territory from Iowa and Nebraska through Oklahoma to Texas. The Northern Plains are home to tribal groups such as the Plains Cree, Blackfoot, Crow, Santee Sioux, and Yankton-Yanktonai Sioux (among others), while the Southern Plains tribes include, for example, the Comanche, Pawnee, Kiowa, and Plains Apache.

3. In many cities there simply were not enough people from any one tribe or community to create strong and supportive social networks, and so it was vital for urban American Indians from many different tribes and geographical areas to come together as a larger community in order to support each other in this new and challenging social setting (see Fixico 2002).

4. Typically, the powwow committee will select and appoint head song judges and head dance judges for a competition powwow. The duties of these individuals include overseeing all of the competitive events, choosing new judges for each round of contests, and tabulating all of the scores. Thus it is imperative that these judges are very familiar with, and well known within the powwow community so they can be sure they are choosing judges who will act impartially.

5. A giveaway is a public and formalized session of gift giving. Giveaways are organized and sponsored by individuals, families, or other social or political groups. Families generally must plan these public spectacles months in advance, slowly accumulating the various blankets, shawls, articles of clothing, housewares, tobacco, and other homemade and commercially produced products to be given away. At the behest of the family organizing the event, gifts are given to particular individuals or particular groups (e.g., all the male traditional dancers) who are in attendance at the powwow. These events serve both to honor specific community members, family members, or groups of dancers or singers as well as to help forge, maintain, and strengthen social relationships within a community.

6. See Thomas Vennum's (1982) excellent ethnohistorical work for more details on this type of Ojibwa "traditional" drum.

7. A great deal of attention has already been paid to dance styles and dance outfits in the ethnographic literature. As such, only very cursory descriptions of these dance styles will be presented here. For further details, see Browner (2002), MacDowell (1997), and Powers (1966), among others; www.powwows.com also features reliable and accurate descriptions and photographs of the different regalia styles.

8. Ethnomusicologist Thomas Turino (2008) has written extensively on the differences between participatory and presentational modes of musical performance. According to Turino, an important feature that distinguishes participatory musical styles is the ability of the musical performance to accommodate a wide variety of musical skill levels. While powwow performances certainly display this feature, I would hesitate to call powwow music true participatory music in Turino's sense of the word. Powwow groups' increasing participation in singing competitions has actually caused a level of professionalization among certain groups, which are far more reminiscent of Turino's definition of presentational forms of music.

9. Ethnomusicologist Anna Hoefnagels (2012) has also written about the larger conversations taking place within the powwow social world concerning the role of women at powwows and the degree to which these roles are influenced by Western/non-indigenous attitudes and expectations.

10. The sun dance is an indigenous religious ceremony widespread among tribal groups that live in the Northern and Southern Plains. While there is a wide range of tribal variation in how the ceremony proceeds, self-sacrifice for the common good of the community is a common theme.

Chapter 7: Musical Example

Chapter 7, Track 1. Northern Wind Singers, "November Winds" (commercially available for download from iTunes or Amazon.com) from their 2008 CD of the same name (Arbor Records AR-13032).

References Cited

Browner, Tara. 1995. "A Reexamination of the *Peji Waci*." *American Music Research Center Journal* 5: 71–82.

———. 2002. *Heartbeat of the People: Music and Dance of the Northern Pow-wow*. Urbana: University of Illinois Press.

de Shane, Nina. 1991. "Powwow Dancing and the Warrior Tradition." *Studia Musicologia* 33: 375–99.

Ellis, Clyde. 2001. "'We Don't Want Your Rations, We Want This Dance': The Changing Use of Song and Dance on the Southern Plains." In *American Nations: Encounters in Indian Country, 1850 to the Present*. Ed. Frederick Hoxie, Peter Mancall, and James Merrell. New York: Routledge. 354–73.

———. 2003. *A Dancing People: Powwow Culture on the Southern Plains*. Lawrence: University Press of Kansas.

Fixico, Donald L. 2000. *The Urban Indian Experience in America*. Albuquerque: University of New Mexico Press.

Hoefnagels, Anna. 2012. "Complementarity and Cultural Ideals: Women's Roles in Contemporary Canadian Powwows." *Women and Music: A Journal of Gender and Culture* 16, no. 1: 1–22.

Howard, James H. 1951. "Notes on the Dakota Grass Dance." *Southwest Journal of Anthropology* 8: 82–85.

MacDowell, Marsha, ed. 1997. *Contemporary Great Lakes Pow Wow Regalia:* "Nda Maamawigaami *(Together We Dance)*." East Lansing: Michigan State University Museum.

Powers, William K. 1966. *Here Is Your Hobby: Indian Dancing and Costumes*. New York: G. P. Putnam's Sons.

———. 1990. *War Dance: Plains Indian Musical Performance*. Tucson: University of Arizona Press.

Sutton, Mark Q. 2004. *An Introduction to Native North America, 2nd Ed.* New York: Pearson.

Turino, Thomas. 2008. *Music as Social Life: The Politics of Participation*. Chicago: University of Chicago Press.

Vennum, Thomas, Jr. 1982. *The Ojibwa Dance Drum: Its History and Construction*. Smithsonian Folklife Studies no. 2. Washington: Smithsonian Institution Press.

Wissler, Clark. 1916. "General Discussion of Shamanistic and Dancing Societies." *Anthropological Papers of the American Museum of Natural History* 11, no. 12: 853–76.

Selected Discography

Bear Creek. 2013. *Kaagige—"Forever": Pow-wow Song Recorded Live in Rocky Boy*. Canyon Records CR-6507.

Black Lodge Singers. 2010. *Kids' Pow-wow Songs*. Canyon Records CR-6274.

Northern Wind. 2006. *Medicine Dress*. Arbor Records AR-12462.

Northern Wind. 2008. *November Winds*. Arbor Records AR-13032.

Tha Tribe. 2013. *Stoic*. Canyon Records CR-6510.

Various Artists. 2013. *Gathering of Nations Pow-wow: GON 30 Celebration*. Gathering of Nations 13GONCD.

Additional Sources

Browner, Tara. 2009. "An Acoustic Geography of Intertribal Powwow Songs." In *Music of the First Nations: Tradition and Innovation in Native North America*. Ed. Tara Browner. Urbana and Chicago: University of Illinois Press.

Desrosiers, Gabriel, and Christopher Scales. 2012. "Contemporary Northern Plains Powwow Music: The Twin Influences of Recording and Competition." In *Perspectives on Contemporary Aboriginal Music*, ed. Anna Hoefnagels, M. Sam Cronk, and Beverley Diamond. Montreal: McGill-Queens University Press.

Ellis, Clyde, Luke Eric Lassiter, and Gary H. Dunham. 2005. *Powwow*. Lincoln: University of Nebraska Press.

Hatton, Orin T. 1986. "In the Tradition: Grass Dance Musical Style and Female Pow-wow Singers." *Ethnomusicology* 30, no. 2: 197–222.

Lassiter, Luke E. 1998. *The Power of Kiowa Song: A Collaborative Ethnography*. Tucson: University of Arizona Press.

Mattern, Mark. 1996. "The Powwow as a Public Arena for Negotiating Unity and Diversity in American Indian Life." *American Indian Research Journal* 20, no. 4: 183–204.

Scales, Christopher A. 2012. *Recording Culture: Powwow Music and the Aboriginal Recording Industry on the Northern Plains*. Durham, NC: Duke University Press.

- 8 -

WAILA

The Social Dance Music of the Tohono O'odham

James S. Griffith

Jim Griffith is an anthropologist and folklorist with strong interests in topics as diverse as Uncle Dave Macon and mariachi music. Through his work at the University of Arizona Southwest Folklife Center and the annual festival "Tucson, Meet Yourself," Griffith has been a tireless advocate for local traditions, including the music and dance of the Tohono O'odham. The factors that he discusses in relationship to the development and performance of waila music, also called "chicken scratch," in southern Arizona, include the physical and cultural isolation faced for decades by the Tohono O'odham (also known as the Pima Indians). Modern (post–World War II) waila music, largely unknown outside of its hearth area, has been shaped by several musical forces, both Native and non–Native American. As an example, Griffith describes the influence of religious continuity, specifically the Catholic Church, in shaping the lives and rituals of Tohono O'odham. Similarly he explores the role of educational institutions, and boarding schools in particular, in their lives and music (in the "Indian School" marching bands). In the light of these disparate factors, it is not surprising that many members of waila bands are members of the same, often extended families. This sense of community and family is reinforced by the standard performance contexts for waila: local dances and the religious ceremonies around which they are often built.

SETTING THE SCENE

It is dusk on the Arizona desert, about one hundred miles west of Tucson. We are in a small village on Tohono O'odham Nation, an almost three-million-acre tract of land formerly called the Papago Indian Reservation. The village, which could be any one of twenty or more similar settlements, is about twenty miles north of the Mexican border, and we have traveled for almost two hours from Tucson by paved and dirt roads in order to reach it. Although the village normally contains perhaps ten families, there seem to be at least one hundred fifty people gathered here, standing around the church, saying a rosary in the chapel, eating in shifts in

8.1. The shield of the Papago Midnighters waila band. Tumacacori Fiesta, December, 1981.

a nearby outdoor dining room. In front of a small white-painted Catholic chapel is a cement dance floor festooned with paper streamers suspended from wires overhead. To one side of the floor is a small, three-sided house. The side facing the dance floor is open to the elements.

Five Indian men in Levis and T-shirts enter this building. One sits behind a drum kit, the others pick up their instruments: electric guitar and bass, saxophone, button accordion. The tuning process over, the accordion player nods to the others and the band bursts into a recognizable polka. The music is strictly instrumental and promises to remain that way; although the group is amplified, no voice mikes are in evidence. Couple by couple, the people who have been standing and sitting nearby move onto the floor and start to dance, moving with small steps around the floor in a counter-clockwise motion. The dance—the *waila*—has begun and will probably last until dawn the next morning. The following essay is an attempt to explain waila music and dance and to show how these art forms arrived in Tohono O'odham culture and how they fit into the world of the O'odham.

REGION, PEOPLE, AND HISTORY

The American Southwest is a very large region consisting of Arizona, New Mexico, and west Texas; it extends north into Utah and Colorado and west into California. Physically it is marked by extreme dryness and a warm climate; its most important cultural characteristics stem from the fact that, long before it became the southwestern portion of the United States, it was the Northwest. By the end of the eleventh century, it had become the northwesternmost extension of the high native cultures of Central Mexico; from the 1540s on, it was northwestern New Spain, and after 1821 it was northwest Mexico. This "northwestishness" has marked the region strongly and provides many of the cultural features that make it seem exotic and fascinating to the rest of the country.

The Southwest is not, however, a unified region, either physically or culturally. This fact may be difficult to discern from a distance, for its shared characteristics—dryness verging on desert conditions, warm climate, a large Native American population that has preserved many aspects of its traditional cultures, and a strong Spanish, and later Mexican, presence—tend to obscure the intraregional differences.

Yet the Southwest is in fact a region of highly distinctive subregions. The major cities of the region, notably Albuquerque and Santa Fe in New Mexico, El Paso, Texas, and Phoenix and Tucson in southern Arizona, differ from each other in environment, history, and character. Northern New Mexico is ecologically and culturally distinct from southern New Mexico. The Arizona deserts are separated from Arizona's high plateau by several thousand feet of elevation and the White Mountains. The Native American peoples of these different regions have distinctive cultures. The Pueblo and Navajo people of the Four Corners area (where New Mexico, Arizona, Colorado, and Utah meet) are very different from the O'odham and Yaquis of the Arizona borderlands (Byrkit 1992; Griffith 1996; Wilder 1990).

These subregional distinctions are important to bear in mind, for this essay will focus on a kind of music which, though related to other musics of the Southwest, is unique to Southern Arizona. This music—waila (pronounced to rhyme with "pile-a")—is played by Native peoples whose home is in the desert and river country stretching from approximately Phoenix to the Mexican border. It is *a* Southwestern music but by no means *the* or even the best-known Southwestern music. Waila is the traditional social-dance music of the Tohono O'odham and the Akimel O'odham—the peoples who since their first contact with Europeans have been called by outsiders the Papago and Pima Indians but who now prefer to be called by the traditional names of their own language. While this essay will deal primarily with the music of the Tohono O'odham (Desert People, formerly the Papago Indians), the music and dance traditions are much the same for the Akimel O'odham (River People, or Pimas) as well (Fontana 1981; Russell 1975).

O'odham means *people* in a language that is spoken throughout much of south central Arizona and in small pockets in the Mexican states of Sonora and Durango. The earliest known contact between O'odham and Europeans occurred when the Spanish explorer Cabeza de Vaca arrived at a village of those people in the Sonora River valley in 1539. The earliest permanent contact between Europeans and the northern O'odham—ancestors of today's Pimas and Papagos—occurred in 1687, when Father Eusebio Francisco Kino, S.J., arrived in what was then called the *Pimería Alta*, Upper Pima Country, to start his labors as a Catholic missionary and emissary of the Spanish crown.

Kino and the missionaries who followed him—members of the Jesuit order until 1767, and of the Franciscan order from then to the 1840s—brought a series of profound changes to the peoples of the desert. The region and its people ceased being independent units and became connected with ever-tightening political, economic, and cultural bonds to Mexico, to Europe, and eventually to the entire globe. This process of connection to the outside world continues to this day as the region becomes steadily ever more integrated into the life of the "global village."

The missionaries, who initially came from many different parts of Europe, brought with them new crops and domestic animals, such as wheat and cattle. They brought membership in the Spanish Empire and in the Catholic religion. They brought European architecture, European dress, European worldviews, and European music.

Most of these commodities were brought only to the river valleys in the eastern portions of O'odham country. In these valleys—the Santa Cruz, in what is now Arizona; and the Magdalena, Concepción, and Altar, in what is now Sonora, Mexico—the newcomers erected mission churches and established a continuing presence among the O'odham. Many of these churches still stand, and one, San Xavier del Bac, just south of present-day Tucson, is still surrounded by its O'odham village.

The rest of the O'odham did not survive as well in their mission communities, however. Ravaged by new diseases and subject to the forces of acculturation and intermarriage, the native peoples slowly disappeared from all of the mission communities save San Xavier. Only in the north, along the Gila and Salt Rivers, and in the desert to the west—both areas where permanent missions were never established—did the O'odham remain undisturbed on their traditional lands. And finally, by the 1830s, the missionaries had withdrawn as well, and the remaining O'odham, along with their Mexicano neighbors, were left in semi-isolation to work out their own destinies. This did not mean that the O'odham were isolated in an idealized kind of static, traditional culture. O'odham and Europeans had been in some sort of contact since the 1680s, and such imported foods as wheat and cattle were well established in O'odham country. Rather, the O'odham were sufficiently isolated and could select the concepts and practices that made sense to them and adapt them to O'odham culture.

This gradually changing scene lasted until a new people appeared on the horizon, this time speaking English and coming from the north and east. Following the Gadsden Purchase of 1853, an international border was drawn from east to west across O'odham country and the area north of that border became a part of something new—the American Southwest.

Change, though still slow, inevitably accelerated in O'odham country, especially after 1886, when Geronimo's final surrender ended two hundred years of warfare between the Apaches and their European and Indian neighbors. By around

1915, two institutions were in place that would bring the Desert and River People closer than ever to the mainstream of American life. One of these was the United States government–sponsored boarding school. Beginning in the late nineteenth century, it became US government policy to separate Native American children from their parents and culture and raise them in English-speaking boarding schools, usually organized along military lines. This policy was to have the effect, believed to be salutary and possible at the time, of turning Native American children into mainstream American farmers and laborers. As has been the case with many other acculturation schemes, however, things simply did not turn out the way the government expected. Human cultures do not change on demand, and the plan of efficiently turning members of one culture into full participants of another failed.

The other institution was the modern-day Franciscan mission. Setting out from Phoenix, Franciscan missionaries, many of whom were German Americans, worked among the O'odham, initially the River People, and then, beginning in 1909, among the Desert People south of Phoenix and west of Tucson. By 1913 Franciscan missionary priests had taken up residence in Tohono O'odham villages. These men said mass, offered religious instruction, set up day schools, and mediated with outside state and federal agencies on behalf of the Papagos, the Desert O'odham. In fact the very shape of the Papago Indian Reservation—which was established in 1916, and nowadays is called Tohono O'odham Nation—and the fact that its organization reflects at least some of the realities of O'odham culture, is due to the intervention of sympathetic missionaries.

When the twentieth-century Franciscan missionaries first came to many of the Papago villages, they were surprised to discover what appeared to be Catholic chapels. During the late nineteenth century, many O'odham on both sides of the border had absorbed a kind of folk Catholicism from their Mexican neighbors—a Catholicism that had developed along specifically O'odham patterns, with emphasis on the maintenance of the health of people and animals in the village.

This health maintenance was, and is, accomplished through the accumulation of power-charged holy pictures and statues, annual trips to the great regional pilgrimage center at Magdalena, Sonora, and the holding of village saint's day feasts. These feasts include such activities as praying, marching in processions, feasting on special foods, and couple-dancing to European-style music (Bahr 1988; Griffith 1992, 67–93).

O'ODHAM MUSIC THROUGH TIME

Where is O'odham music in this historical portrait? The Jesuit and Franciscan missionaries of the eighteenth and nineteenth centuries took pains to teach their Indian charges how to play such European instruments as the violin, the guitar, and the European bass and side drums. This was done so that the Indians could provide music for the mass and other church occasions. Thus there were probably violinists, guitarists, and drummers in such communities as the one at San Xavier, south of Tucson, through which the American "49'ers" traveled on their way to the California Gold Rush and camped in order to repair their gear and "water up" before embarking on the brutal desert journey ahead. It may have been in this sort of context that O'odham musicians learned such new, fashionable dances as the polka, mazurka, and schottische. By the late 1860s, an O'odham band consisting of fiddles and guitars was playing at Tucson's annual Fiesta de San Agustin. Here is how the band looked and sounded to John Spring, a pioneer Arizona educator. In this passage, Spring remembers a fiesta from around 1869:

> In the middle of the square stood a wooden platform, an improvement over the earth floor and here the rabble danced as of yore, and to the same music and tones I had first heard twelve years before. In fact, the music, which was for years produced by the same Papago Indians upon their home-made fiddles, consisted of only two recognizable airs. One did service for polka, schottische, waltz, and quadrilles [sic] by simply adapting its "tempo" to the faster or slower movements of each dance. The other was the so- called "pascola," a distinctively Papago dance. What these active musicians lacked in tuneful accomplishments, they made up by perseverance, for they daily played these two tunes consistently from four P.M. until long after midnight, during the nineteen days that the feast lasted. Upon the platform only low-caste Mexicans, half-breeds and Indians danced, and only women of questionable (or rather unquestionable) reputation. (Gustafson 1966, 301)

It is extremely likely that Mr. Spring's perception that only one tune was played in different tempos for different dances may reflect his personal view of the music rather than what the musicians were actually playing. One frequently hears such comments as "it all sounds the same" from those who describe music that is unfamiliar to their ears. Aside from Spring's casual remarks about the music itself, this is a valuable description of a performance of an old-style waila band.

According to older O'odham musicians, ensembles such as that described by Mr. Spring remained active until after World War II, when they were gradually replaced by modern waila bands. These groups have instrumentation modeled after that of the popular *conjunto norteño* of the Mexican American borderlands: button accordion, saxophone, guitar, bass, and drum kit (Peña 1985). During the 1960s most reservation villages had electricity, and electric instruments became practical. As a result, most waila bands use electric guitars and bass guitars, and accordion and saxophone players play into microphones.

One impetus for the new instrumentation, in addition to the highly popular norteño music that was flooding Southern Arizona at this time, may well have been the boarding school program mentioned earlier. Bands were important features of these schools, and apparently many students enjoyed playing in them.

In fact, in the decades after World War II, all-Indian marching bands composed of boarding-school veterans appeared in many of the Southwestern cities that were adjacent to reservations. The saxophone may well have entered O'odham culture via this route. If so, it would confirm that modern waila music derives from the two great historical acculturative programs that have been directed at the O'odham: the Spanish mission system and the Indian boarding school of the late nineteenth and early twentieth centuries.

WAILA TODAY

This brings us back to where we started—the band is warming up to play polkas at an all-night dance in a village on Tohono O'odham Nation. The music is called waila, from *baile*, the Spanish word for "social dance." More specifically, waila means polka as well as the whole genre of music. Another name for waila is "chicken scratch," which is a reference to an older dance in which the dancers kick up their heels behind them like chickens scratching in the dust. The name is more accepted by the River People than it is by the Desert People, many of whom feel that the term *chicken scratch* is slightly derogatory and used only by whites. A guitar and saxophone player, Philip Miguel, recently remarked at a workshop, "We are not chickens; we're O'odham, and this is O'odham *waila* music" (Miguel 1995).

The line-up of a contemporary waila band consists of button accordion, saxophone, or both, as lead instruments supported by bass guitar, electric guitar, and drum kit. All of the musicians are males, with very few exceptions. The music consists of three main music and dance genres: the polka (waila in O'odham), two-step (*cho:di*, in O'odham; *chotis*, in local Spanish), and the *cumbia*, a Caribbean genre that originated in Colombia but that has been extremely popular in the US–Mexico borderlands since the 1970s. *Mazurkas* or fast waltzes and tunes in 6/8 are also heard, although more rarely.

The button accordion and saxophone function as the melody or lead instruments. Not all bands have both; in some there is only an accordion, in others, the accordion player doubles on second sax, and in still other bands there are two saxes. But in all cases, these instruments supply the melody. Sometimes they play together in unison, sometimes in harmony; occasionally they will trade solos. The guitarist usually plays a strum on the off-beat. The drummer maintains a steady, heavy beat on the bass drum and may drop occasional "bombs" on his other percussion instruments to accentuate the rhythm.

Waila tunes come from many sources. A large number are borrowed from the norteño repertoire and from the repertoires of other Mexican musical traditions. Many are popular mainstream American pieces, old and new. I have heard tunes from American popular and vernacular music, such as "Blue Tango," "Turkey in the Straw," "The Beer Barrel Polka," "Clementine," and "It's a Small World," all played by waila bands. One veteran waila musician told me that there are three ways of inventing a "new" song: revive an old-time tune that no one plays anymore; play a well-known tune in a new key, thus changing its character; or take bits of other songs and recombine them into a new tune. The waila repertoire is highly eclectic and constantly expanding (Enis, Mike 1974–80; Joaquin 1976–80).

Waila tunes do not necessarily have titles. The best way to request a certain tune from a band is either to hum a few bars or to refer to some memorable occasion on which the band played that tune. This system of tune reference serves dancers and musicians perfectly well until a band has cut a tape and needs to assign titles to each song for liner notes. Under these circumstances, the group will usually work out titles by suggestion and consensus. Occasionally, someone will remember a name for the tune in English or Spanish, or, if not, the tune frequently takes its name from a member of the band or some other person who especially likes it—as, for example, "John's Special"—or after a village where the piece went over particularly well, as in the case of the "Pisinimo Two-Step." Both of these titles appear on an LP recorded by the band the American Indians in March 1974 (The American Indians 1974, A-3, A-5).

Several years ago, I accompanied the Enis Company from San Xavier Village to the National Folk Festival at Wolf Trap Park outside of Washington, D.C. The band felt that one of their polkas was especially well received during the festival, and so the tune was known thereafter among band members as "The D.C. Polka." At about the same time, in the mid-1970s, I was in the habit of requesting the Mexican waltz "Las Nubes" of the band whenever I danced to their music. I learned later that this tune, which had previously been known as "That Old Waltz" had started to be called "Jim's Waltz" (Enis, Marvin 1976).

Waila is almost entirely instrumental. One musician, Virgil Molina, who played with a waila band in the 1970s and 1980s, recorded a few vocal numbers that included one of his one compositions in the O'odham language; but he stands alone (The Molinas 1972, A-1, B-1; 1976, A-3, A-5, A-6). Few other singers have yet followed his lead, although I have occasionally heard musicians say that they were thinking about working up some songs in O'odham. On August 25, 1996, at the Tucson Historical Society's San Agustin Fiesta, I heard the Cisco Band from Sells, the capital of Tohono O'odham Nation. They featured harmony duets sung in English—but this is only the second time in more than twenty years that I have heard a band sing.

Waila is primarily dance music. On those occasions when waila bands played at folklife festivals and other culturally mixed events, some attempt has usually been made to accommodate dancers. The average waila tune is certainly much longer then the traditional three-minute-plus duration of the record single or LP cut. Once a band has started to play a tune, there is little change. Musicians seldom "take off" in solo variations; the melody is simply played over and over by one or both lead instruments until the band is finished. This may be slowly changing, as in the case of contemporary groups like Southern Scratch, who are more accustomed to playing for non-O'odham audiences, but it still seems to be the rule more often than not.

Waila is very well integrated into and contained within O'odham culture. Although a number of commercial recordings are available on the Phoenix-based Canyon label, waila is not often played over the air, and waila bands are seldom invited to appear at culturally mixed occasions. But this is changing also. Since 1974 a waila band has been featured at the annual Tucson Meet Yourself Festival, and, more recently, waila bands have become regular additions to other multicultural celebrations. Since 1994 a group of Tucsonans who are interested in various kinds of traditional dance has sponsored annual waila dance workshops. Finally, since 1989 an annual waila festival, conceived and organized by a Tohono O'odham, has been sponsored in Tucson by the Arizona Historical Society.

Waila, as I have said, is first and foremost a dance music. Moreover, at an O'odham waila, everybody dances—elders, little children, teenagers, young adults. The local version of the polka is, however, quite different from the two-step used by many immigrant European communities, and even farther from the athletic one-two-three-HOP favored in other parts of the United States. Throughout the borderlands, the regional polka step is a walking one-step, in which the dancer moves a foot with each beat of the music.

Within this general style, which is practiced by Native Americans and Mexicanos alike, there seem to be certain distinctly O'odham characteristics. Where a Mexicano male dancer will balance on the balls of his feet, leaning forward into the dance, an O'odham man will have his weight centered on his heels, leaning even slightly backwards. A Mexicano couple's polka stance seems to dramatize a traditional set of gender-based expectations, with the man assuming an aggressive stance and the woman leaning either slightly away from him or crushed against him. Left-arm positions may accentuate this sense of tension. O'odham couples, on the other hand, often dance close to each other, with a more passive, cooperative body language.

Movement around the floor is inevitably counterclockwise. (This is the same direction taken by the traditional O'odham *keihina*, or circle dance, and opposite from the direction used by many other Native American peoples.) Couples move lightly around the floor, taking small steps and turning to the left and right. Rarely, if ever, will an O'odham couple separate and promenade side-by-side or engage in hand swings, as Mexican American couples will. The dance, like the music, is solid and matter-of-fact. The visual aesthetic, as it is all along the border, is one of smoothness, with little or no vertical movement.

Performance of the cho:di, or two-step, in the O'odham context reveals fewer variations, although I have seen O'odham couples deliberately dance the "step-close-step-pause" pattern *across* the phrasing of the tune. The cumbia is danced in couples, each partner dancing alone, with hands raised above the waist and fists lightly clenched. Once again, the O'odham cumbia, in both music and dance, is a little more solid, a little heavier, than it usually is in its Colombian home.

Finally, waila tends to be a family music. It is not uncommon to find three generations of male musicians in the same family, and many waila groups comprise brothers or cousins who play together. In fact, at a recent workshop designed to bring together teenaged waila novices and seasoned veteran musicians, not only did all of the youngsters have parents who were waila musicians, but, almost without exception, so did the veterans!

THE VILLAGE FEAST, A CONTEXT FOR WAILA

Although waila is featured at all kinds of celebrations—weddings, graduations, birthday parties, first Holy Communions, and the like—perhaps the most typical setting for waila is still the village feast. These feasts occur on the assigned day that a particular saint is venerated in the village. If possible, the priest will come by and say the mass in the morning. (There are currently three missionary priests serving about forty active villages on the nearly three-million-acre main reservation of Tohono O'odham Nation, second only in size to the 19.7-million-acre Navajo Nation. They visit outlying villages by automobile on a regular monthly schedule.) Before or after the mass, a procession will form at the Catholic chapel, and men, women, and children of the village carry all of the holy statues and pictures from the chapel to a stationary cross that stands some distance to the east or south of the chapel door. As they walk along, they sing religious songs in O'odham and Spanish. After a pause by the cross, during which each participant establishes a personal contact with each sacred object, the procession returns to the chapel.

After the mass and procession are over, the feasting starts. One or more steers have been slaughtered, butchered, and cooked in an outdoor kitchen near the chapel. The cooking is done in huge pots over a series of adobe firepits, under a *ramada* (see Glossary).

Traditional feast foods include shredded beef stewed with red chile, beef and beef bones cooked with corn, squash and other vegetables, pinto beans, potato salad, locally made flour tortillas and wheat bread that has been baked in a communal, outdoor oven, and Kool-Aid, coffee, and cake. Other, optional dishes include *menudo* (a stew of tripe, hominy, and cows' feet), the local flat enchiladas (fried cakes of corn meal and chile, served in a red chile sauce), and sometimes macaroni salad.

Interestingly enough, none of these foods, except for some of the vegetables in the beef stew, were eaten by the O'odham before the missionaries arrived. This is almost a completely borrowed diet, even as the occasion is a borrowed, Christian celebration. Beef and wheat were brought to the O'odham in the seventeenth century by Spanish missionaries; tortillas, pinto beans, and coffee were also introduced during the Spanish period, and potato salad, Kool-Aid, and iced cake are all twentieth-century contributions (Bahr 1988).

Guests are fed in shifts through the night until shortly after dawn, when the dance concludes. The men and women of the village serve the food, clean and reset oilcloth-covered tables after each group finishes, and place serving bowls along the middle of the table. The guests sit at long, homemade benches to eat their food, getting up to thank the cooks and servers when they are finished.

During the feast day, some of the celebratory activity takes place in the chapel. This sacred activity may include the recitation of a rosary or other prayers in Spanish or O'odham, which is led by a villager who specializes in reciting sacred Catholic texts. Unlike Roman Catholic churches, the Tohono O'odham folk chapels have the specific purpose of protecting the village supply of holy pictures and statues. These sacred objects have been acquired during the annual October pilgrimage to Magdalena de Kino, a colonial mission town on the main north-south highway, about sixty miles south of the border in Sonora, Mexico. The objects are placed next to a particularly miraculous statue of St. Francis Xavier, which, it is believed, charges them with spiritual power. The acquisitions from the pilgrimage are then brought back to the village, spiritually aligned with the needs of the villagers and their animals through a ceremony of baptism, and placed on home altars or in the village chapel. Here the pictures and statues serve to maintain the balance that protects villagers and livestock from illness and misfortune.

This religious and philosophical system, with its emphasis on healing and the maintenance of health and spiritual balance, is as much, if not more, O'odham than it is Catholic, and has over the years been called "Sonoran Catholicism" and "O'odham Catholicism" by Anglos, and *santo himdag*—"saint way"—by O'odham. It is a dynamic religious and philosophical system, changing with each generation of O'odham in order to accommodate their needs. It is in this context—a context rich in ideas and customs that have been borrowed from Mexican and other neighbors and then reinterpreted by the O'odham—that music may best be understood.

THE OLDER FIDDLE MUSIC: WAILA, *KWARIYA*, AND *PASCOLA*

Related to modern waila music is the music played by old-style fiddle-based bands. Related in turn to the fiddle music (and often played by the same men) are two forms of strictly ritual music and dance: the *pascola* and *matachinis* complexes. So that waila and its place in O'odham culture may be fully understood, a brief explanation of these three violin-based forms of dance music follows.

The older violin-based bands of an earlier period have not disappeared entirely from the desert scene. These groups, which typically consist of two violins, one or more guitars, and a bass drum and snare drum—each played by a different musician—have undergone a revival since the mid-1980s, when for several years an All-O'odham Old-Time Fiddle Orchestra Contest was featured at the annual Wa:k Pow Wow in March. As a result of the interest generated by these contests, older musicians started playing again, and three bands have produced commercial cassettes. These are the San Xavier Fiddle Band from the San Xavier District, the Gu Achi Fiddlers from the middle of Tohono O'odham Nation (listen to Track 18, "Libby Bird Mazurku" to hear this music), and the Gila River Fiddlers from the Gila River Pima (Akimel O'odham) Reservation. The first two groups recorded for the ubiquitous Canyon label, while the latter tape was self-produced (San Xavier Fiddle Band 1989; Gu Achi Fiddlers 1988; Gila River Old-Time Fiddlers 1990).

Closely allied to the older fiddle band sound is a distinct kind of dance, known in O'odham as *kwariya*, a version of the Spanish *cuadrilla* or quadrille. Oddly, the kwariya is not a quadrille at all, but rather a circle dance in which couples promenade, reverse direction, do a grand chain, and then form into two-couple sets for such well-known Anglo-American square dance figures as "duck for the oyster," "birdie in the cage," and "around that couple you take a little peek." Figures are called by one of the dancers, and the couples are likely to exit the floor by promenading under a bridge of hands.

Music for the *kwariya* is provided exclusively by old-time fiddle bands and consists of various tunes played in 6/8 time. Each village seems to have its special *kwariya* tune, the one from San Xavier Village being a six-eight version of the tune known to Southeastern Anglo-American fiddlers as "Flop-Eared Mule." This piece is known all the way from Eastern Europe to Arizona. The tempo varies from place to place: in New Mexico, for instance, the tune is played as a schottische, while Southeastern fiddlers play it as a fast reel—but it keeps its general melodic outline and two-key structure wherever it is found.

Another kind of traditional O'odham music commonly played on violins and guitars are the *pascola* tunes that, as John Spring mentioned, were distinct from the European social dances of the mid-nineteenth century. *Pascola* is a loan word from the Yaqui Indian language. The Yaquis, whose homeland is in southern Sonora, Mexico, and who moved to the United States around the turn of the century to escape persecution, have a rich tradition of Native Christian ceremonialism that was developed through several centuries of contact with European missionaries.

In Yaqui, *pahko o'ola* means "Old Man of the Fiesta," and the Yaqui *pas-cola* is the ritual host of every religious feast and ceremony. Yaqui pascolas open and close the feast with speeches, prayers, and fireworks. They act as hosts, passing out cigarettes and water to spectators. They serve as clowns, engaging in humorous dialogue and pantomime. And they perform step dances to two kinds of music—for violin and harp and for flute and drum—both kinds played by one man. Judging from the types of tunes and melodies heard in Yaqui pascola performance, the violin and harp music appears to be based upon relatively old European models, preserved in the community through oral tradition since the early eighteenth century. It is this violin music that has been transmitted to the O'odham, along with the pascola dance (Griffith and Molina 1981).

At some time in the past, the Tohono O'odham seem to have borrowed the pascola dance and its music from the Yaquis. As long ago as the 1750s, a Jesuit missionary described Yaqui pascolas dancing at O'odham feasts in what is now northern Sonora, Mexico. Since about the turn of the century, there have been colonies of Yaquis living and performing their traditional ritual dances in and near Tucson and at various sites near Phoenix. At some point, apparently before the 1860s and John Spring's experiences at the San Agustín Fiesta, O'odham learned their pascola music and dances.

Unlike their Yaqui neighbors, who wear masks and breechcloths, O'odham pascolas wear ordinary feast clothes—Levis and a dress shirt. Each man wears a belt with several metal jingle bells (preferably brass ones) dangling from it. A string of rattles made from the dried cocoons of the giant silk moth (*Rothschildia jurulla*) is wrapped around each ankle. The pascola's feet are bare.

Pascolas usually dance in a small ramada erected to one side of the chapel. A small altar with images of one or more saints stands at the rear of the ramada. The musicians—one or more violinists and a guitarist—sit to one side of the cleared, swept dance floor. When they commence playing the first pascola tune or son (pronounced to rhyme with "bone"), the pascolas kneel before the altar and cross themselves, quietly reciting a short prayer. Then each pascola, in order from the youngest to oldest, takes his turn at dancing. There may be as many as four pascolas at any given feast. The dance is an elaborate step-dance performed in a slightly stooped stance, with head lowered and arms hanging loosely at the sides. The leg rattles accentuate the complex rhythm of the son, thus allowing the pascola to become a third musical instrument.

Pascolas dance at the feasts all night until around dawn, when they close the ceremony by dancing several times in unison up to the altar and back, kneel and cross themselves once more, and recite a closing prayer. The dance music is traditionally regulated by the time of night at which it is played. Typically, there is one body of tunes for the early evening, one for the hours just after midnight, and one for the early morning. In many villages, the instruments are retuned to a different pitch at midnight. Sometimes there is a special son for the hour of midnight and another for the dawn.

The other great body of Yaqui violin-based music that has been borrowed by the O'odham is used to accompany the matachines dancers. Among the Yaquis, matachines are men and boys who perform European-derived contradances as an act of devotion to Our Lady of Guadalupe. Wearing paper crowns and carrying trident wands decorated with feathers, they march and wheel in three lines, going through their intricate figures in time to music played by several violinists and guitarists. Among the matachin figures danced by Yaquis is the winding and unwinding of a maypole (Painter 1986, 157–83).

I know of one group of O'odham matachines dancers, based in the Gila River Reservation. Once again, their dance and music is very similar to those of the

Yaquis, and the Pima (as the River O'odham were formerly known) undoubtedly learned this dance complex from their Yaqui neighbors.

SACRED OR SECULAR DANCE MUSIC?

I have pointed to the most traditional context for waila music and dance as being the village feast, itself an occasion for various kinds of European-based behavior, much of which has been modified and reinterpreted by the O'odham to suit their own cultural needs. One more detail should be mentioned. Just as Yaqui and O'odham pascolas have the custom of setting aside specific tunings and melodies for specific times of night, so the traditional waila bands seem to have had specific songs for such times as midnight and dawn. After midnight, they would retune their instruments in order to play at a higher pitch. One O'odham who discussed this with me added that few musicians know these conventions anymore. All tunes are the same for the musicians nowadays, to be used whenever they feel like it. "And that's why," he told me, "you'll sometimes hear some of the old people sitting by the dance floor listen to a song and then say something like 'Dawn is sure coming early tonight'" (Juan 1980). This parallel with the overtly sacred pascola music and dance complex suggests strongly that there is an important ritual component to waila.

It seems evident to me that, with a music like waila, the oft-made distinctions between the sacred and the secular simply do not apply. Yes, waila is similar to and derived from a music and dance form that in its original, European-based context is secular. Yes, its use has spread to celebrations other than village feasts—weddings, first Holy Communions, baptisms, birthdays, graduations, even to bars and dance halls outside the reservation. But only one of the family occasions that I have mentioned is itself purely secular, and the lines that may be drawn between the sacred and the secular do not sit comfortably on O'odham culture.

I recall being instructed by an O'odham man of about my age in how to do the *keihina* or traditional round dance. "Stomp your feet hard down on the ground to bring in the rain clouds," he told me, "and get yourself between two big women and dance with your elbows out." So even the courtship and flirtation aspects of European-style social dancing may not appear as secular to O'odham eyes as they do in European-derived cultures, where generations of young people have been told in one way or another that the Devil himself lurks on the dance floor.

At a recent waila workshop that offered school-aged musicians an opportunity to work directly with older players, the phrase "make people happy" was used over and over by the older men to describe their function as musicians. In mainstream American culture, this may legitimately be understood as a reference to entertainment, pure and simple. In traditional O'odham culture, with its emphasis on spiritual balance and its need for full cooperation among small groups of people in isolated villages, the phrase may well mean a good deal more. I suggest that waila bands operate ideally within O'odham culture as a means of maintaining community health and good feelings. Thus, the waila occasion becomes a little less secular than it may appear at first and a little more involved with the sacred purposes of life.

WAILA BEYOND THE O'ODHAM

Waila music has been exported beyond the O'odham community since at least the 1860s, when John Spring witnessed waila music and dance at the San Agustin fiesta in Tucson. With the end of the Apache Wars in 1886, however, Papagos (the Desert O'odham) were no longer valued allies of the whites, and in most cases simply stopped being noticed. Over the course of the twentieth century, they increasingly became regarded as providing a sort of local color, and their music, because it did not fit the stereotype of Indians singing with drums and rattles, was largely ignored by middle-class, mainstream Arizonans.

Waila music became better known outside of O'odham culture after January 1972, with Ray Boley's Canyon Records Company recording of Tohono O'odham waila band Mike Enis and Company, in the dance ramada at San Xavier Village. This resulted in the LP record *Chicken Scratch: Popular Dance Music of the Indians of Southern Arizona* (Enis Company 1972).

This was not the first time waila music had appeared on record. A 78 r.p.m. single of an old-style fiddle band—Harry Marcus and Orchestra—was produced as a fund-raiser for the St. Johns Indian School at Komatke, Arizona, in 1951 (Marcus 1951). But the 1972 Canyon disc was the first waila recording to be made available to the non-Indian world. It also stimulated me to become interested in waila, especially as I discovered that members of the Enis band were my next-door neighbors. Thus I became a part of the waila scene, at first as a dancer, and later as a writer and a concert and festival presenter.

Since 1974 I have been active in studying waila music and presenting it to a wider audience. That first year I was able to secure invitations for the Enis band to the San Diego Folk Festival and the National Folk Festival outside of Washington, D.C. Also in 1974 I produced the first edition of the Tucson Meet Yourself folklife festival, which was to become an annual event until 1994, and which featured a waila band (and later on, an old-style fiddle band) each year. Waila bands made subsequent appearances at several festivals around the country, including the National Folk Festival and the Smithsonian Festival of American Folklife, and even appeared at Carnegie Hall in New York.

The first Canyon Record was swiftly followed by more LPs and cassettes, as other bands approached Boley and requested recordings. In September 1995, the Canyon catalogue included fifty waila tapes—with more new and reissue recordings in production—and three cassettes of old-time fiddle bands. Although there is some crossover trade into the mainstream world, an attempt at marketing waila music to Mexican American fans of norteño music was unsuccessful. Consequently, most recordings of waila music are confined to sales within the Native American market.

All of this recording and festival activity gradually drew waila music into the consciousness of the local middle classes and people connected to universities in Tucson and elsewhere. When the Arizona Historical Society revived the San Agustin Fiesta as a cultural event in the 1980s, it seemed only right to feature a waila band. Then, in 1989, Angelo Joaquin Jr., son of the founder of the highly popular Joaquin Brothers band and veteran festival volunteer at national, regional, and local folklife festivals, founded the annual Waila Festival, held each Spring at the Arizona Historical Society headquarters and museum in Tucson.

By 1996 waila music had moved, not into the mainstream of American culture, but into a state of contact with and recognition by that mainstream. With the exception of one group of New Mexico musicians who studied with the late Elliott Johnson of the Gu-Achi Fiddlers, no non-O'odham to my knowledge have tried to learn waila or to form a waila band. In 1994 and 1995, workshops were held on how to dance waila for the Tucson Friends of Traditional Music, a local contradance and old-time music organization that comprised mostly college-educated, middle-class young adults. People from many cultural traditions attend the festivals at which waila is played and dance enthusiastically to the music when the opportunity arises. However, they tend not to seek out opportunities for waila dancing at strictly O'odham social occasions.

Waila has also begun to make an appearance in print through the media of scholarly and other writing. Beginning with an article in *Country Music Magazine* in 1976 (Miller 1976), waila has sporadically come to the notice of popular music fans (Wilson 1995); occasional scholarly articles discuss the music, usually in the broader context of O'odham Catholic practice (Griffith 1979; Griffith 1988, 71–84). The archives at the University of Arizona Library's Southwest Folklore Center contain a few waila interviews, copies of all commercial waila recordings, and tapes of waila performances at Tucson Meet Yourself and other public festivals.

Despite this broadening of horizons and audience, however, waila continues to be an O'odham music. Most waila is still played in a thoroughly O'odham context—at village feasts and personal celebrations, such as weddings, baptisms, and birthdays. (In the 1970s and 1980s, a few Tucson bars, catering to a predominantly working-class clientele, featured waila for dancing on weekend evenings; however, this trend did not make it into mainstream musical life in Tucson.) Waila musicians continue to eschew vocals, and continue the O'odham tradition of enthusiastic tune borrowing. Some innovations occur; two or three of the twenty or more waila bands have experimented with electronic keyboards, for instance, and in the 1970s and 1980s Big John Manuel of waila band the American Indians played his button accordion with a wah-wah pedal, somewhat in the style of norteño innovator Esteban Jordan. Women are slowly entering waila, and there is an all-woman band playing on the reservation.

But these innovations seem to be well within the mainstream of waila music, which has long reflected the various kinds of musical influences available to the O'odham. The basic nature of the music—an instrumental dance music played mostly by men, with a repertoire consisting mainly of polkas, two-steps, mazurkas, and cumbias—seems unchanged, nor does it seem likely to change radically. Waila lacks the excitement and the high-energy rhythm that might propel it to follow zydeco and the various world-beat musics into the floodlight of mass popularity. It possesses a certain conservatism and solidity that seems to ensure that, for awhile at least, it will remain what it has been—the traditional dance music of the O'odham of Southern Arizona.

Notes

1. The First Young Waila Musicians' Workshop was held at the Southwest Center for Music in Tucson on Saturday, August 12, 1995. It was sponsored by the Waila Festival Board and partially funded through a grant from the Folk and Traditional Arts Division of the National Endowment for the Arts.

2. The Anglo musicians mentioned in this sentence are Ken Keppeler and Jeanie McLerie of Albuquerque, New Mexico. Their band, which specializes in various kinds of traditional dance music, is called Bayou Seco, although for their recording of O'odham fiddle tunes they renamed themselves Bayou Eclectico. They have also recorded O'odham music under the name o-a-machetah/Bayou Eclectico. The word *o-a-machetah* is a phonetically spelled O'odham name bestowed on the group by the late O'odham fiddler Elliott Johnson, from whom they learned most of their waila music. The word means fry bread, a favorite O'odham foodstuff. For the sake of convenience, their commercial recordings are listed under the name Bayou Seco. Bayou Seco recordings are available from 2824 Sierra Vista, N.W., Albuquerque, New Mexico 87107.

Glossary

baile. Spanish word that refers to "social dance."

conjunto norteño. Popular music of Mexican Americans who live along the US-Mexican border.

cumbia. Dance from Colombia that has been popular along the US—Mexican border since the early 1970s.

keihina. Traditional O'odham circle dance.

kwariya. Local version of a quadrille, which is actually a type of circle dance.

mazurkas. Fast waltzes (played in 6/8 time).

pascola. Religious ritual and ceremony held by the Yaqui Indians.

ramada. Common word in the Southwest referring to a roof that is supported by four or more posts.

son. First tune played at a *pascola* and distantly related to the Cuban dance of the same name.

Sonoran Catholicism. Also called *santo himdag*, or saint way, by the O'odham. A religious and philosophical system that blends O'odham beliefs with Catholicism.

Chapter 8: Musical Examples (access through companion website)

Chapter 8, Track 17. Southern Scratch, "First Stop Waila"
Chapter 8, Track 18. Gu Achi Fiddlers, "Libby Bird Mazurka"

References Cited

Bahr, Donald. 1988. "Pima-Papago Christianity." *Journal of the Southwest* 30, no. 2: 133–67.

Byrkit, James W. 1992. "Land, Sky, and People: The Southwest Defined." *Journal of the Southwest* 34, no. 2. Entire issue.

Enis, Marvin. 1976. Conversation with the author.

Enis, Mike. 1974–80. Conversations with author.

Fontana, Bernard L. 1981. *Of Earth and Little Rain.* Flagstaff, AZ: Northland Press.

Griffith, James S. 1979. "Waila: The Social Dance Music of the Indians of Southern Arizona: An Introduction and Discography." *JEMF Quarterly* 15, no. 56: 193–204.

———. 1988. *Southern Arizona Folk Arts.* Tucson: University of Arizona Press.

———. 1991. *Beliefs and Holy Places: A Spiritual Geography of the Pimería Alta.* Tucson: University of Arizona Press.

———. 1996. "The Southwest." *American Folklore: An Encyclopedia.* Jan Harold Brunvand, ed. New York and London: Garland. 681–82.

Griffith, James S., and Felipe S. Molina. 1981. *Old Men of the Fiesta: An Introduction to the Pascola Arts.* Phoenix, AZ: Heard Museum.

Gustafson, A. M., ed. 1966. *John Spring's Arizona.* Tucson: University of Arizona Press.

Joaquin, Daniel. 1976–80. Conversations with author.

Juan, Blaine. 1980. Conversation with author.

Miguel, Philip. 1995. Public Comment at First Annual Young Waila Musicians Workshop, Tucson, August 12.

Miller, Tom. 1976. "Papago Indians are Chicken Scratching . . ." *Country Music* 4, no. 8: 16.

Painter, Muriel Thayer. 1986. *With Good Heart: Yaqui Beliefs and Ceremonies in Pascua Village.* Tucson: University of Arizona Press.

Peña, Manuel C. 1985. *The Texas-Mexican Conjunto: History of a Working-Class Music.* Austin: University of Texas Press.

Russell, Frank. 1975. *The Pima Indians.* Tucson: University of Arizona Press.

San Xavier Fiddle Band. 1989. San Xavier Fiddle Band. Phoenix: Canyon CR-8085.

Wilder, Joseph, ed. 1990. "Inventing the Southwest." *Journal of the Southwest* 32, no. 4.

Wilson, Sule Greg C. 1995. "Dancing in their Ancestors' Footsteps." *Rhythm Music* 4, no. 4: 36–38.

Recordings Cited

Bayou Seco. *Following in the Tuneprints.* UBIK UB-25. Cassette and CD, containing seven waila cuts.

Bayou Eclectico. *Memories in Cababi.* UBIK UB-27. Cassette; all waila music. One cut, "First Choice Two-Step," is no. 21 on Rounder CD-0391, *Old-Time Music on the Air*, vol. 2.

o-a-machetah/Bayou Eclectico. Cut no. 1, on Rounder CD-0379, *American Folkies*, vol. 1, is a waila piece named "Squash Fields."

Gila River Old-Time Fiddlers. 1990. Gila *River Old-Time Fiddlers.* Phoenix, AZ: Akina Productions.

Gu-Achi Fiddlers. 1988. *Gu-Achi Fiddlers.* Phoenix, AZ: Canyon CR-8082.

Marcus, Harry. 1951. *Harry Marcus and Orchestra:* "Honor y Patria" (A), "Nos Fuimos" (B). 78 r.p.m. Phoenix, AZ: Komatke ARP 132/133.

Mike Enis and Company. 1972. *Chicken Scratch: Popular Dance Music of the Indians of Southern Arizona.* Phoenix, AZ: Canyon C-6085, Side B.

The Molinas. 1974. *The Molinas: Super Scratch Kings Number One.* Phoenix, AZ: Canyon C6128.

The Molinas. 1976. *Scratch Encores with Virgil Molina.* Phoenix, AZ: Canyon C-6161.

Additional Resources

Canyon Records began operations in 1952 and remains the oldest, largest purveyor of Native American music, including a healthy selection of chicken scratch. www.canyonrecords.com/.

Erickson, Winston P. 2003. *Sharing the Desert: The Tohono O'odham in History.* Tucson: University of Arizona Press, 2003.

Rock-A-Bye Records has released twenty-four waila recordings, including performances on DVD, since their founding in 2004. 3676 South Whispering Sands Drive, Casa Grande, AZ 85193. (520) 510-6721 or 421-7037. http://rockabyeaz.tripod.com/index.html.

Waila Music Association and Museum: The recently founded Waila Music Association honors and recognizes waila artists, musicians, composers, and any other persons who have contributed to the awareness and entertainment of the Waila Culture. http://rockabyeaz.tripod.com/id15.html.

Waila! Making the People Happy is a thirty-minute documentary film about the genre produced and directed by Daniel Golding in 2009. www.itvs.org/films/waila.

Waila: the Music of the Tohono O'odham featuring Gertie Lopez and the TO Boyz. This 45:30 documentary film about chicken scratch was directed by Stephen Nugent and released in 2009. For more information go to http://anthrofilm.onlinefilm.org/en_EN/film/47403.

CULTURAL INTERACTION IN NEW MEXICO AS ILLUSTRATED IN LA DANZA DE MATACHINES

Brenda M. Romero

Brenda M. Romero is an ethnomusicologist who has a long-standing involvement with Native American and Mexican American traditions of New Mexico. In her essay on matachines, a music and dance drama performance complex with significant spiritual and historical overtones, she examines the cultural interaction between two prominent minority populations in the American Southwest—the Native American Puebloan[1] and Mexicano[2] (or Indohispano[3]) of New Mexico and southern Colorado. A unique cross-fertilization of their cultures has produced a complicated genre that integrates music, dance, and theater. Romero traces a variety of musical forms to eighteenth-century Mexico and even further back, to twelfth-century Spain, through a complex musical and cultural history of tune families. Implicit in this discussion is a quest for that which is "authentic." Romero concludes that authenticity is defined not by the scholar, who searches for the ultimate original version of a tune or a tale, but by the community itself, which imbues the performance, however fresh its elements, with the weight of tradition and authenticity. Romero's simultaneous insider and outsider perspectives further heighten the long and complicated history of matachines music. As a scholar and a musician who has played an active role in the perpetuation of the matachines fiddle repertoire, Romero demonstrates the potential of the scholar to both objectively "study" a cultural phenomenon and to positively affect its course.

INTRODUCTION

When North Americans talk about Latino musical culture in the United States, they are most likely to mention the norteño tradition of the Texas-Mexican border area or the salsa music of the sizeable Cuban and Puerto Rican populations in New York City. Yet, the longest continuously Latino-populated areas in the United States are Northern New Mexico and Southern Colorado, where music has always been an integral part of daily life for those who traditionally describe themselves in Spanish as *Mexicanos*, one of the terms that is used in this chapter. Although the

9.1. Pueblo of Jemez Matachina dance in Ponderosa, NM on August 28, 2010, to commemorate the memory of Adelaido Martinez, fiddler of thirty years.

Spanish first scouted the region between 1540 and 1542 under Francisco Vásquez de Coronado and initiated colonization under Don Juan de Oñate in 1598, the area has been continuously inhabited by American Indian Puebloan peoples, who have sung and danced sacred ceremony into the earth and sky for thousands of years. The greatest significance of this rich cultural area lies in the close interaction of Spanish, then Mexican, peoples with the nineteen New Mexico Pueblo groups, as with Navajo, Apache, Ute, and Comanche nations, and, more recently, the interaction of these groups with other United States citizens and residents of various birthrights. Of some significance is the fact that the first schools of music and luthiery (instrument making) in the area now called the United States were not in Massachusetts but in New Mexico (Lozano 2007, 606).

While I describe Mexicano and Puebloans in general terms, in this essay I focus specifically on the Towa-speaking people of the Pueblo of Jemez, who live about fifty miles northwest of Albuquerque, and the Tewa-speaking peoples who live in six Pueblos north of Santa Fe along the Rio Grande. Ohkay Owingeh is the largest of these Pueblos.[4] The Mexicano towns I describe are Bernalillo and Alcalde, small towns in close proximity to their Puebloan neighbors in Jemez and Ohkay Owingeh, respectively.

New Mexico, the "Land of Enchantment," continues to captivate outsiders with its rich heritage, both ancient and recent, and with the strong sense of Native and Mexicano pride in its political and social life. The state capital, Santa Fe, has emerged in this century as a center of architectural beauty, a place where builders have developed the possibilities inherent in adobe Pueblo and Spanish/Moorish forms. With inspirational blue skies, mystical sunsets, and the allure of traditional culture, Santa Fe and Taos have become international centers of fine art. Santa Fe has hosted one of the premier opera houses of the world since 1957, and the hundreds of art galleries and numerous music and art festivals in New Mexico attract aficionados and tourists year round.

Why do we group Mexicano and the Puebloan in this chapter? Simply because these communities have shared the same space for hundreds of years. The reality of the US experience is that we cross over each other's cultural spaces every day. While daily newspapers report water and land disputes between Native Puebloans and local non-Natives, only minutes away from the large cities and towns the Puebloans open some of their ancient ceremonies to their neighbors and to an increasingly international public. Among these public ceremonies, one of the best known and least understood is the *Danza de matachines*, unique by virtue of being the only Pueblo ceremony—which the Puebloans call Matachina—that uses European instruments and music.[5] Almost as an accident of fate, the matachines—a performance complex involving music, dance, story, and ritual—took on a devotional quality in both cultures and survived in Mexicano and Pueblo settings, where it is typically associated with Catholic saints' days. Although there is evidence that the clergy taught the danza, its profane origins in Old Spain gave the matachines troupes a certain autonomy, allowing the ceremony to be in the hands of the people. For this reason, the matachines genre provides an excellent medium through which to observe the processes of cultural interaction that have defined New Mexican existence for centuries (see also Rodríguez 1996; Lamadrid 2003).[6]

ETHNOMUSICOLOGICAL METHOD AND APPLICATION

Western musicology has focused primarily on questions relevant to the understanding and development of Western art music. Since membership or identification with a Western European worldview is implicit in this discipline, musicology has rarely concerned itself with questions of cultural significance. Ethnomusicology differs from musicology's traditional history and score reading emphasis in that it is "studying the music of our time" (Porter 1995, 26), or better, the "musics" of our time. The emphasis is synchronic (of our time), with diachronic (historical) study as a means of better understanding contemporary musical phenomena. The discipline requires firsthand observation and experience, and thus fieldwork is an essential aspect of ethnomusicological methodology. Change has been so fast and furious in the past century that at times a historical approach is irrelevant and only fieldwork reveals the nuances of a musical phenomenon.

Puebloan resistance to passing their spiritual knowledge into the wrong hands does not undermine the importance of fieldwork as a tool for understanding more clearly what happens in and with Pueblo music. Puebloans, like many other American Indian societies, believe in witches and the power of those who are capable of taking sacred knowledge and using it for their own interests, with potentially devastating consequences for others (see Toelken 1995). One does not, then, enter the Pueblo with notebook, camera, and tape recorder in hand. It is essential to direct a written request to conduct fieldwork research to the governing Pueblo authority. Additionally, one must contact each newly elected governing tribal authority to keep the Pueblo informed of what you have done and what you are now doing. In every case, in order to continue to conduct research, verbal information must be formalized in a "letter of request."

Photographs have always adorned the walls of the front rooms of most Pueblo households. Puebloans increasingly own cameras and the latest visual recording technologies and usually only Pueblo members are allowed to photograph ceremonies. Sometimes, however, not even they are allowed take photographs. Outsiders, should they be ignorant of the community's sensitivity to photography, are in danger of having their equipment or cellphone confiscated. Exceptions to the rule may be made when ceremonial dances take place outside of designated sacred spaces. Usually one is allowed to take pictures only after purchasing a permit, and even then, only in some Pueblos, only of particular ceremonies, and only during certain years. One is most likely to be allowed to take pictures in such public settings as the state fair or a cultural center; however, asking for permission is still a common courtesy in these situations.

It is often easier to conduct fieldwork among the Mexicanos, who have seemed to be as open to ethnographers as the Puebloans are closed to them. Recently, however, some Mexicano groups have barred photography even in public matachines settings. One example of a *persona non grata* is a photographer who, during the 1970s, photographed matachines *danzantes* and masks, then displayed and sold his photographs internationally without compensating the groups from whom he profited. The influence of the Pueblo sensitivity to outsider documentation is having an impact in Mexicano sites like Bernalillo, where only designated individuals are now allowed to record.

For all involved, issues of appropriation for commercial profit are significant concerns. A desire to control the outcome of outside research so that the Pueblos benefit is clearly seen in recent Pueblo tribal rulings. While Mexicano community organization is not as formalized as Pueblo government, there is a growing awareness among Mexicanos of a need for community guidelines that will help to protect community and individual rights and cultural property. For both communities, cultural appropriation is potentially tied to religious desecration.

"WITHOUT YOU WE CAN'T DANCE": APPLIED ETHNOMUSICOLOGY

I was born in Santa Fe but grew up along the Rio Grande just north of Ohkay Owingeh. Much of my childhood was spent in close proximity to the Puebloans, who have exchanged customs with rural descendants of the Spanish colonists for centuries (see also Romero 2011). I began to conduct fieldwork on the matachines in 1987 out of a desire to know my own cultural music and traditions, and to understand how the matachines danza functions as a medium for cultural interaction. When I began my study, the folk violinist with whom I wanted to work, Adelaido Martinez, was terminally ill. After his death, I gained assurance from the governor of the Pueblo of Jemez that if I learned the repertoire, I could play in the ceremony, which might then continue. Since I was trained primarily as a composer, singer, and guitarist, learning to play the fast pieces on the violin was a challenge. As a result, the focus of my fieldwork was turned upside down; now, much of my time at the Pueblo was spent as a participant who concentrated on being a credible violinist. Despite occasional involuntary variations in the melody, I was able to keep the rhythm going. The lead dancers and my Puebloan consultants, Randolph Padilla and Stanley Waquie, encouraged me often and praised me highly for good performances, for "without you we can't dance," as Waquie once said.

While my role as the necessary and trusted musician seemed to be generally accepted, the regularly changing Pueblo authorities viewed my role as an academic researcher with suspicion. The unethical use of Pueblo religious information by such anthropologists as Elsie Clews Parsons in the 1920s is still fresh in the minds of the elders, and a Jemez governor told me in 1993 that Pueblo elders determined that her publications on the Pueblo of Jemez would never be reissued. Luckily, when I was a graduate student, my mentor, Cherokee ethnomusicologist Dr. Charlotte Heth, introduced me to the concept of applied ethnomusicology and the importance of giving something back to the communities I was working with in exchange for the knowledge I gained from them. Dr. Heth recommended I read Susan Guyette's *Community-Based Research: A Handbook for Native Americans* (1983). It was gratifying to be able to do something for the Pueblo while I grew in my understanding of the people and their music culture. I began to view myself as an applied ethnomusicologist, a scholar who both identifies and responds to the needs of a people. At the same time, the Puebloans were able to see the ways that scholarly work could be of benefit to their community.

Among my questions were the following: In what ways have Mexicano and Puebloan mediated hostility over time? How have these cultures that are in close proximity negotiated difference? What defines identity for each community? What constitutes authenticity when people perform ceremonies borrowed or received from other peoples? Before exploring the matachines, let us acquaint ourselves with the musical cultures of Puebloans and Mexicanos (see also Romero 1993). As a preface, bear in mind that the societies under discussion have been engaged in a constant struggle to overcome poverty over the course of the twentieth century to the present day. Nevertheless, both Puebloans and Mexicanos have made significant economic gains as their cultural art forms have become known. Today the Pueblos are also owners of large gaming facilities that have strengthened their economies. Music and dance, especially in the Pueblos, have resisted commercialization, in large part because of their spiritual importance to the people involved.

THE SIGNIFICANCE OF MUSIC IN THE PUEBLOS

The sense of place is of central importance for the Puebloan cultures. Ideals of worldview, such as that documented by the late Ohkay Owingeh Tewa anthropologist Alfonso Ortiz, delineate the Pueblo as a special place in the universe (1969). This place is defined by sacred hills and mountains on which special shrines mark places for spirits to come and go between this world and an unseen place of origin that is also the individual's ultimate spiritual destination. Tewa Pueblo society is traditionally stratified into three distinct social classes. Those with the highest status, including the medicine men and women, conduct the business of the ceremonial societies and thus carry the greatest responsibility for the physical and spiritual well-being of the people. Secondary status is assigned to those who define the core of the Tewa political organization. The lowest status is assigned to those who serve no official capacity in the political or ceremonial system. After death, a person's spirit enters a spiritual reality commensurate with his or her earthly position (Ortiz 1969, 17).

The ceremonial cycle follows regional ecological patterns, functioning in part to regulate the inconsistencies of the ecosystem with regard to subsistence, thus assuring the survival of the entire population. Food sharing is a regular feature of public ceremonials; and, not surprisingly, ceremonies are most frequent during the times of the year when fresh food is least available (Ford 1972, 11–12).

Song is the medium of communication with the spiritual forces that govern life. *Kachinas*[7] are intermediaries between this reality and non-empirical reality. Individuals who dress as kachinas transform into them, and their participation in ceremony is highly desirable. Songs accompany all aspects of ceremony, representing an active force that can affect the order of things in the universe. Thus, the Puebloans emphasize formulas, ritual, and repetition (Ortiz 1972, 143). Functioning as the heartbeat of the deities, it may be said, "the drum beat, plus rattles sounding with up- as well as downbeat accents, bring the deities to life" (Romero 1993, 166). Rattles recall the sound of falling rain; accompanying the drum, together they establish the tempo. Against the steady beat, singers must be able to sing seemingly independent rhythms and pulsations. The vocal text does not align itself in an exact correlation with the rattle or drum beat (see also Scales's chapter in this volume). "The soundscape is a complex and subtle interweaving, and most importantly, it is profoundly alive" (166). The engaging of the unseen forces assures a plentiful harvest and prosperity for all. For this reason, the term *embodiment* is more useful than the term *symbolism* to describe the process of spiritual representation in the Pueblos.

Music is always sung and almost always paired with dance, an essential component of communal ceremonies. Dance helps to demonstrate the interdependence of man, nature, and the spiritual world. The corn plant is considered a model for this concept of interdependence: all parts of the plant work together to produce the corn that brings life to the people—an ancient philosophy that was shared by many pre-Columbian peoples throughout the Americas. Participation in communal ceremonies is imperative to the well-being of the group, and precision is necessary to ensure the participation of the Unseen.[8] Except for cures and society initiations, Pueblo ceremonies do not call much attention to individual-centered rites (Ortiz 1972, 140). As a result of this emphasis on group cooperation, traditional Pueblo song is typically monophonic, accompanied by a single drum, although the use of multiple drums is becoming more and more common. It is the men's job to provide a tight, well-rehearsed chorus, as if in a single voice. Unless they are dancing in communal dances, the women are busy with many other aspects of ritual organization, including the all-important job of food preparation and distribution.

Roberts (1972, 251) categorized the Rio Grande Pueblo dances into six basic classifications: kachina dances, maskless kachina dances, animal dances, corn dances, borrowed (or "received") dances, and social dances. Due to the prohibition of masks by the Spanish colonial government, which viewed them as idolatrous, masked kachinas are largely missing from most of the Rio Grande Pueblo dances, with a few exceptions. Masked kachinas do continue to be prominent in the Zuni and Hopi Pueblos, where the Spanish theocracy exerted less influence. Animal dances honor the human relationship to birds and animals, at the same time as they function as sympathetic prayer magic for the perpetuation of species important for subsistence (Romero 1993, 161). Corn dances are essentially fertility dances. Hundreds of men, women, and children dance, sometimes under intense sun, usually barefoot, to a well-rehearsed male chorus and drum.

The Puebloans practice a two-part social organization, dividing their community into two halves, or two moieties. They divide their ceremonial tasks into ceremonial units called *kivas.* The Tewa moieties are Summer and Winter kivas and the Towa moieties are Turquoise and Squash kivas. Kiva is also the name of the subterranean ceremonial space where ceremonies are rehearsed or conducted indoors in some Pueblos.

Like most public communal dances in the Pueblos, the corn dance, the best known of the public dances, takes place on Catholic saints days, as Spanish Catholic practices survive alongside traditional religious traditions. This is because the Pueblos were under strict Spanish rule from 1598 to 1680, and again from 1696 until 1821, when the Mexican government won independence from Spain. At the time of "Americanization"—under control by the United States government—in 1848, Pueblo citizens were winning cases in Mexican courts against their Mexicano neighbors, a clear sign that the Puebloans understood and were participating in the mainstream Spanish-Mexican legal system. Pueblo social dances typically incorporate humor and other aspects that also reflect a dynamic interaction with the world outside the Pueblos.

MATACHINA AS A RECEIVED OR BORROWED TRADITION

The Spanish matachines is one of the most recently received music/dance forms in the Pueblos, who call it *Matachina*, the term used in this chapter when referring specifically to Pueblo versions. The Puebloans have a long-standing tradition of borrowing or receiving songs and ceremonies (Ellis 1964, 57; Humphreys 1984, 29–56; Ortiz 1972, 147; Romero 1993, 148, 154). Whether from other native tribes or from the Spanish, "borrowed traits were usually adapted to existent patterns and tended to add rather than substitute religious traits" (Ellis 1964, 57). This practice of adaptation (a process of syncretism) is crucial for understanding traditional American Indian worldview, which underscores respect for the power inherent in song, dance, and ceremony per se. Recognizing only one Creation composed of a myriad of peoples and languages, American Indians in general perceive no conflict between different tribal belief systems. The people were eager in the past to acquire a song or ceremony known to be powerful in hunting, healing, or other ritualized activities. For instance, the Pueblos also have a buffalo dance, received from Plains groups, for whom religious ideology revolves around the buffalo. Reciprocal sharing or payment of some kind would normally accompany the adoption of a new ceremony from the outside.

No doubt in the past some ceremonies were "received" along with entire bands of extended families subdued in battle or otherwise adopted. In that case a leader of that group could become the head of the particular Pueblo society responsible for the new ceremony, a strategic cooptive practice. The Pueblo kivas take great care to perform and observe all of a ceremony's attending requirements.

It is not known when the Spanish first introduced the Matachina pantomime (that is, without song texts or lyrics), and it remains the only pantomime of its kind performed in the Pueblos.

But, while the Spanish may have believed that they were replacing traditional beliefs by allowing matachines as the only masked dance, the Puebloans more likely believed that they were being given the source of spiritual power that the matachines ceremony gave to the Spanish. Today, the Pueblo of Jemez Turquoise Kiva Matachina is also an example of how a music/dance ceremony received from a highly divergent foreign source may be reinterpreted, or tailored, to fit existent ceremonial Pueblo formats. In spite of the Puebloans having learned Spanish polyphony in the early colonial period, the Matachina is the only ceremony of the Pueblos that uses European music and instruments. The Pueblo of Jemez Pumpkin Kiva Matachina version has reinterpreted the tradition to the extent that it no longer resembles the "Spanish" version that uses the violin and guitar; instead, it uses male chorus and drum accompaniment. Nonetheless, the Iberian-rooted choreography is very similar in these two versions, requiring stamina and an agile solo dancer, in addition to more typical group dancing. Like the corn dance, the Matachina dance in some Pueblos involves an animated crowd and a highly charged atmosphere. Friends and relatives visit at this time, and food as well as arts and crafts vendors line the peripheral areas of the sacred plaza in evergreen-shaded booths, as is often the case for celebrations that are open to the public. Many visitors will feast with the families of friends and relatives who are dancing on that day, however, as is customary.

The Matachina is not always an occasion for which vendors appear. One such is a less celebrated third version of Matachina now performed in the Pueblo of Jemez, said to have originated in San Felipe Pueblo. It features three drums and a male chorus, dressed with Mexican serapes and wearing big, colorful mariachi hats. The matachines (males) accompany young women dressed in ballroom gowns and wearing moccasins. They hold one side of their skirts as they dance. All of the songs are sung in Spanish or Spanglish in Pueblo musical accents, and often quoting mainstream Hispano/Chicano hits like Selena's "Biri biri bom bom" and the Texas Tornados' "Hey Baby ¿Que Pasó?": "Thought I was your only vato." This version of Matachina is especially fun during the long, dormant winter season, as it makes for great entertainment. One of the sequences on October 21, 2012, featured couples dancing a two-step in the sacred plaza. For this sequence only, spectators may join in as people do in round dances at powwows.

In addition to the public enactments, like the Matachina just described, social dances often have "home" contexts (i.e., they are performed in homes) and are part of the general festivities at special times of the year, such as Christmas or New Year's Day. While an atmosphere of merry-making, including burlesque, dominates such social dances, they seem to conform to certain ritual requirements of producing an atmosphere of well-being and happiness—assuring all good things for the forthcoming year. Alfonso Ortiz (1972, 147) described this idealized worldview thus:

> Among human beings the primary causal factors are mental and psychological states; if these are harmonious, the supernaturals will dispense what is asked and expected of them. If they are not, untoward consequences will follow just as quickly, because within this relentlessly interconnected universal whole the part can affect the whole, just as like can come from like.

Typically, elderly women enact the Matachina in front of the Infant's House on New Year's Day, incorporating a great deal of burlesque. As such, it closely resembles home dances on that particular occasion. The Infant's House is a site for feasting, and is lavishly decorated: scarves and blankets cover the ceilings and walls, which are adorned with paintings, baskets, and ceremonial items of various kinds. Tinsel and fringe suspend from above in colorful synergy, suggesting the falling rain. The Infant is the statue of the Baby Jesus, who sacralizes the space it inhabits in the Pueblo, and so the Infant goes to a different home each year. Many visit to honor the Infant with songs and dances, including Mexicano musicians from surrounding towns and even international musicians, such as a Colombian duo in 2013.

THE ESSENCE OF PUEBLO MUSIC

Pueblo life revolves around the idea that the Pueblo is a special and unique place in the universe. Song, story, and dance accompany ceremonies that assure the Puebloan's harmony with the natural world, which is continuous with the world of the Unseen. In this belief system, the combination of music and dance embodies spiritual forces, which in turn give life to the people by ensuring abundance of all good things. Community participation in ceremonies, reflecting the cooperation of all parts of the corn plant, is important in order to gain the goodness of the Unseen. The ideal chorus sings together in a single voice, accompanied by double-headed drum whose steady, heartbeat-like beats are not strictly tied to melodic accents.

Since Native Americans honor ceremonies for their inherent spiritual power, dances from foreign groups or peoples form part of the annual cycle of ceremonial events. Among other uses, words in songs embody beliefs about the living world and sometimes function as a way of remembering something about the ceremony itself; vocables reinforce the idea that sound itself is sacred. While commonly described by non-Natives as "meaningless syllables," vocables are often laden with connotations. For instance, sometimes vocables announce, if not evoke, particular deities or a particular ceremony—as, for example, in the San Juan Turtle Dance (LaVigna 1980, 86)—as if recalling the sacredness of sound itself. Because of this, vocables are best described as words without a dictionary or lexical meaning. Sometimes vocables originated as words in ancient languages that are no longer spoken and are preserved only in ceremonies. In other instances, vocables serve a variety of functions, including framing texts to enhance musical forms or recalling the sounds of the "animal nations." Vocables also make it possible for different tribes to join together in song even when they do not speak the same language. Songs among Native North Americans, in general, use both words and vocables, but sometimes a song uses only vocables, as in the Taos Pueblo Round Dance Song discussed below.

Among the Tewa, words tend to be arranged in highly rhetorical forms that reflect the process of mediation of such opposite forces as day and night, youth and old age, male and female. Words reflect different aspects of meaning and beliefs in various ways. For example, the word *old* might imply age, wisdom, eternity, and the like.

Humor is an essential aspect of ceremonial life, for in order to be effective, a ritual must be undertaken with the right heart. Thus, all ceremonies include one or more clown figures, among the most sacred of the kachinas. This influences social practices, and humor accompanies all aspects of everyday life and interactions (see also Romero 2000).[9] As a researcher close to this community it still took several years for me to recognize all the inside jokes, parodies, and the joy and lightness in Pueblo interactions.

New Media in the Pueblos

Until recently, electronic media were low-key in the Pueblos, where community life continues to be an imposing force. While radio, television, video, and DVD players might be absent during the two weeks a home is converted into the Infant's House, electronic media or the modern apparatus of a mediated society are part of many Pueblo households. The Internet has rapidly become a source of YouTube videos that represent many "First Nations" (a term coined in Canada), largely from insider perspectives. Rather than romanticized versions of Natives, they provide real connections to communities and their music cultures, including Puebloan.

Like music everywhere, American Indian music responds to contemporary life and today Native musicians use performance and recording technology and bring their music to concert venues. Telephones (including cellphones) are still not necessarily a part of all Pueblo households, but some kind of recording equipment is always handy when a new song is being created and learned. Commercial Native American recordings are now available that demonstrate the use of synthesizers and other electronic equipment. The Taos Pueblo Round Dance Song (Rainier et al. 1992) demonstrates that innovation in one area of Native music today often implies innovation in other areas as well. The Round Dance is a friendship dance usually danced in a circle by both men and women and is most often sung by a male chorus, unlike this recording, which features both men and women singing.[10] The mixed chorus sings vocables alternating with the flute, traditionally a courtship instrument played by men. Finally, a synthesizer is used, sounding Western harmonies in a drone-like effect. Both harmony and the use of a drone are absent in traditional Pueblo and Native American music in general. Recording the music is itself an innovation that in many cases also implies the equally innovative idea of concert performances.

Non-Natives might be surprised to learn that various categories of commercial American Indian music have emerged over the past fifty years. Country western, and mainstream rock styles have long been popular in Pueblo households, and as more Pueblo and American Indian music in general is available commercially, it too forms a significant part of individual recording collections. Overall, however, new Native music in the Southwest, constantly being created by a variety of Pueblo, Navajo, Apache, and Ute composers and musicians, appears to be missing from more than local circulation. Notable exceptions include Taos composer-flutist-singer Robert Mirabal and Navajo-Ute composer-flutist R. Carlos Nakai, as Native flute music is among the categories that have gained international attention.

Borrowing from popular mainstream music trends, direct social commentary is often heard in contemporary urban Native musical contexts. A good example of this, and of crossing over into each other's spaces (discussed below), comes from New Mexican activist singer A. Michael Martinez. Elsewhere I have discussed his founding role in the Native rock group XIT, dating back to the 1960s (see Romero 2011). Raised in Albuquerque, New Mexico, Martinez's background includes ancestors from Laguna Pueblo, Ireland, and Spain. Among his various musical projects, he provided original songs—including the title cut—and lead guitar and/or vocal accompaniment to the CD *unioNation™: Machinists Music Project*. The *unioNation™* project (www.unionation.com), directed by Henry Bagwell, features musical union members and underscores the importance of unions for Native Americans, Hispanos, and Caucasian workers, the vast majority of whom hold blue-collar jobs. Listening example Chapter 9, Track 1 on the accompanying website features Martinez on lead guitar and vocals on his song "unioNation™":[11]

UnioNation™, Union proud, tell all the world, shout it out loud
Brothers and Sisters, we all stick together,
To form an unbreakable chain
Brothers and Sisters, we all stick together,
One family that are all one and the same
Chorus
UnioNation™, Union proud, tell all the world, shout it out loud
Brothers and Sisters, it's our God given right
To uphold rights to bargain as we please,
Brothers and Sisters, it's our God given right
To demand fairness and solidarity
God bless America, God bless the Union,
Together we will succeed, God bless America, God bless the Union,
One nation without corruption or greed
(A. Michael Martinez, cited with permission)

THE SIGNIFICANCE OF MUSIC AMONG THE MEXICANOS

Much Hispano folk music was already old when the Spaniards settled New Mexico in the early seventeenth century. Spaniard and self-proclaimed troubadour Tomás Lozano has documented various negotiations in which early European instruments were ordered for or formed parts of the inventories of New Mexico's Roman Catholic mission churches. Such evidence suggests that in New Mexico, as elsewhere in the Americas, Flemish polyphony sounded in the Pueblos during the seventeenth century in vocal and instrumental forces.[12] This colonial musical institution, including polyphony and European instruments, ended abruptly with the Pueblo Revolt of 1680, with few traces of the music culture left in the Pueblos. There is no other known evidence that European colonial music influenced traditional Pueblo formats (Roberts 1972, 243), except for the instruments and music for the Matachina discussed below. A formal music tradition was never reestablished among the poor Hispano commoners either. Rather it was the thriving troubadour tradition that fared much better over time. Hispano music traditions survived in the Latin-language Gregorian chant that the religious Mexicanos perpetuated in all Catholic churches until Vatican II (1962–65), in the laments on the suffering of Christ, the *alabados* and *alabanzas* of the *Penitente* male sect (not included in this chapter), and in the troubadour songs recorded in *cancioneros*, song books.

The following folk songs, collected in New Mexico between 1930 and 1960, date back to Western Europe in the twelfth century and some are still older.[13] They represent many different genres, including narrative ballads (*romances*), topical songs (*canciones*), and children's game songs. The entire Robb Field Recording Collection is now available online,[14] with the corresponding transcriptions—he hired many helpers to transcribe the songs and the lyrics. The transcriptions provided below sometimes deviate from Robb's, however, as I have re-transcribed some of them for greater accuracy or, as in the case of "La Delgadina," to reflect my performance on the CD accompanying this book. Please note that the Spanish language often uses elision between two vowels, creating a diphthong. I have indicated elisions with ’. Another resource is the second edition of John D. Robb's *Hispanic Folk Music of New Mexico and the Southwest: A Self-Portrait of a People* (2014), a comprehensive compilation of the vast amount and types of music he recorded, primarily among Hispanos, in New Mexico.

For centuries, folk singers took out their *cancioneros* in the evening hours, after the day's work was done. They entertained themselves and taught songs to their children and relatives in extended families. This is notable insofar as similar practices resulted in the preservation and maintenance of the same or similar folksongs throughout the Spanish-speaking Americas south of New Mexico all the way to Argentina and even Brazil. Among those Mexicanos who continue to perform the old music today, this style of musical transmission is much the same as it used to be. Oral transmission within kinship groups is not unusual for non-traditional music like rock and roll either, and many local bands are comprised of family members. Some of the older Spanish/Mexicano music has survived alongside, if not because of, the advent of electricity and the availability of radio and television, and such older music is still the musical foundation for many contemporary New Mexican styles (see Romero 2011).

One of the oldest Mexicano genres is the *romance* (pronounced rohmáhnseh), or ballad, the early forms of which featured two rhyming sixteen-syllable lines, each a complete thought. Sometimes a refrain (called *estribillo*) was added, as in the following variant of "La Delgadina":

> Delgadina se paseaba en una sala cuadrada (Quí din, qué don, qué don, don, don)
> Delgadina was walking in the great hall
> con una mantona de oro que la sala relumbraba. (Quí din, qué don, qué don, don, don)
> wearing a golden shawl that made the room shine.

In the past, long before the days of television and other forms of mass media, the romance featured many verses with much detail and could last a long time, for this was popular evening entertainment. Contemporary Spanish troubadour Tomás Lozano, addresses the romance's origins as a song of honor and *geste* (correct deportment, gesture), a heroic, epic ballad; or as a news bulletin and something of the masses, popular but only later valued:

> When the *romance* is composed as an autochthonous Spanish epico-lyrical genre, new original poems are created, at the same time that tales from the repertories of other European gests are adopted, especially those from French and Provençal traditions. Nevertheless, romances continue to maintain the primary function of a *chanson de geste*; they are still essentially news bulletins. Intellectuals and the learned, by contrast, scorned *romances* until the late fifteenth century when they begin to transcribe and collect them. (433)

By the time of the Spanish arrival in present-day New Mexico in 1540, the romance, or ballad, was well known and appreciated, with French, Provençal, Irish, and English counterparts. The romance is often set in the royal courts of medieval times, preserving significant historical accounts. The oldest romance recorded in New Mexico, "Gerineldo, Gerineldo, mi camarero aguerrido" ("Gerineldo, My Veteran Steward"), dates back to the early ninth century in the Carolingian era (ninth century) in Europe (see Robb, 74–79, items A12, A12a–A12g). "Gerineldo" is a story of forbidden love between the *infanta*, the princess Emma, the daughter of Charlemagne, king of the Franks and Holy Roman Emperor, and Eginhard, the king's chamberlain. Charlemagne, hearing his daughter's plea, cannot bring himself to execute them and instead allows them to marry (Mendoza 1986, 134; Espinosa 1985, 85).[15] Undoubtedly, it is the symbolical bridge between nobility and commoner that made this song so popular for centuries on the Iberian Peninsula and even in New Mexico, far from its original setting (Romero 1993, 2008). Additionally, it is one of a few instances in which fatherly tenderness toward a daughter is openly expressed. Women are more typically punished or killed in traditional patriarchal genres, as in "La Delgadina."

Del-ga-di-na se pa - sea-ba, en u-na sa - la cua-dra-da, con u-na man-
7
to - na d'o - ro, que la sa-la re - lum-bra - ba Y le di-ce'el rey su
13 "Aye, que lin - da Del-ga
pa-dre "Aye que lin - da Del-ga - di - na" (que din, que don, que don, don, don)
di-na pue-de ser mi'her-mo-sa da ma" (que din, que don, que don, don, don)

9.2. *La Delgadina* using two melodic variants (Robb, 31, 38).

The most widely disseminated romance in the New Mexico and Southern Colorado area was "La Delgadina" (The Thin Maiden, Chapter 9, Track 2 on accompanying website), also well-known in Mexico and other parts of Latin America. Like "Gerineldo," the song is set in the European royal courts. "Delgadina" is the tale of an incestuous king who locks his daughter in the castle tower when she refuses his indecent advances. The bell-like *estribillo* (refrain)—Robb's "mournful tolling of bells" (31)—is also a play on words that idiomatically mocks the *don*, usually a Spanish term of honor for a man. For my performances, I sing two of the many melodic variants found in New Mexico and Colorado. The older variant divides the form into two complete thoughts, each followed by the refrain, as described above. I sing this version that Próspero S. Baca sang for Robb in 1944 (Robb, 28–31; A2, R2), preceded by the version Connie Dominguez sang for V. Acosta in Arizona in 1947 (Robb, 37–38; A2d, RB534), without estribillo, as in Figure 9.2.

In the end Delgadina dies, surrounded by angels, while her father's bed is tormented by devils for the rest of his life and beyond. Still performed in the 1950s, this ballad functioned to discourage incest in the isolated Spanish-Mexican villages. Remnants of Jewish versions of "La Delgadina" found in New Mexico reveal another ethnic and religious influence among the descendants of the Spanish colonists (Romero 1993, 217), reminding us that the Sephardim (Sephardic, or Spanish Jews) lived in Spain continuously since the first century CE until their expulsion in 1492, and that many came to the New World as *conversos* (converts). Some converted in order to escape the Inquisition and continued to practice Judaism clandestinely (often a female-centered activity) in colonial New Mexico (see Jacobs 1995; Tobias 1990). In the Sephardic versions Delgadina never gives in, emphasizing self-determination as opposed to divine intervention in the Christian versions (Benmayor 1979).

Although Muslims were not officially expelled from Spain until 1609, little if any of their cultivated Mudejar period music made it to the Americas, although the Mudejar style is still evident in intricate and decorated wooden ceilings in churches, patios, or central courtyards, and enameled tiles in Mexico and

9.3. Verses 1 and 3 of *Palomita que vienes herida* (Robb, 216).

elsewhere in the Americas. I have noted some similarities between New Mexican alabados (religious laments) of New Mexico's Catholic penitent male sect and Arab-language laments. These likely date from a time earlier than the Mudejar period, however.

Among other genres that survived the colonial period were hundreds of *canciones*, soulful lyrical songs, such as "Palomita que vienes herida" (Little Dove that Comes Wounded). The dove is a symbol of love, in this case wounded love. Two singers from La Jara, New Mexico, Celao Trujillo and Fidel Romero, sang this song for Robb in 1944. With folk music there is always a gradual "editing" process that takes place over time. In this case, I completed the musical-lyrical form in order to sing the song myself, in the style of most folk singers within a tradition.[16] As the second line is missing from the third verse of the fragments that John Donald Robb recorded, for my contemporary performances I composed a line that is now sung by other New Mexicans who perform this song, such as the group Bayou Seco. Figure 9.3 includes lyrics for the first and third verses, including my composed second line in the third verse (see Robb, 216). The English translation follows the transcription:

Little dove that comes wounded
At the hands of a good hunter,
Go and tell him to lay down his arms
While my love sleeps and rests.

Where is my beloved to be found?
Where is that flower of my desire?
But you not even for an instance,
nor a moment remember me. (My translation)

Songs like "La Delgadina" and "Palomita que vienes herida" eventually transformed into songs that reflected life in New Mexico and southern Colorado. They often retained an ancient modal structure, a feature that Gregorian chant no doubt reinforced, as was common in the region until the mid-1960s, as previously mentioned.[17] Gradually, the *copla* (also referred to as *verso*) became the most pervasive

A - ño de mil o - cho cien - tos o - chen - ta'y nue - ve pa - so___ que'el
6
dí - a cin - co de Ju - lio mi Dios lo de - ter - mi - nó

9.4. *Corrido de la muerte de Antonio Maestas* (Robb, 527).

form in both Mexican and New Mexican folk song. It utilizes four eight-syllable lines with an abcb rhyme or assonance scheme (Robb, 869). The copla is the form preferred for lyric songs and was traditionally a popular form for improvised song duels, although a more complex ten-line form, the *décima*, was also used in such *trovos* (song contests). For an idea of what these contests sounded like, one might listen to contemporary song contest traditions of the Basque peoples of Spain, whose song styles are reminiscent of the old Mexicano styles of New Mexico (for the New Mexican texts, see Robb 2014; Lamadrid 1994).[18] Most notably, the copla is the form of today's *corrido*, a contemporary ballad that describes events in detail, typically beginning with the date and often the time and place of the event. The corrido, most often associated with Mexican music, is often commemorative, commissioned in memory of an important person or event, and frequently appears following a tragedy, as if in protest.

The oldest archival example of a New Mexican corrido is the "Corrido de la muerte de Antonio Maestas" (Corrido of the Death of Antonio Maestas), composed by Higinio Gonzales in 1889 (Robb, 523). It fits the textual characteristics of the Mexican corridos as described above, but is markedly modal, unlike contemporary Spanish-Mexican corridos, which are usually in a major key. The use of melodic and rhythmic modes (each with its own name and musical character) has roots in medieval music, and modal music was common in Western Europe, particularly in church music, at the time of the conquest, beginning in 1492, of what we know today as the Americas. In the early eighteenth century, however, the French composer John-Philippe Rameau (1683–1764) codified the major-minor system that had developed since 1600, in part due to the change to calibrated equal temperament instead of natural tunings that supported ideas surrounding modality. The codified system is often referred to as "functional tonality," because ideas of tension and release dictate chordal progressions. This system characterized Western music practices for roughly three hundred years, until around 1900, and eventually came to dominate Western-derived music everywhere. Modal structures are thus remnants of an older layer. The "Corrido de la muerte de Antonio Maestas" also exemplifies a typical practice of irregular metrical divisions that is common to the old Mexicano music. In this case, the meter includes a 3/8 measure in what is otherwise 6/8 meter, as shown in Figure 9.4.

9.5. *La Indita de Manuelito.* Although the key signature is G major, this is in Dorian mode with A as the tonic note. The chords provided are those I use in performances to emphasize the modal character.

An interesting trend in New Mexico is that the term *indita* came to designate a narrative ballad very similar to the version of the corrido just described. Elsewhere I have argued that the indita is the regional designation for an early, feminine, and Native-identified corrido style (Romero 2002). The Mexicano song genre referred to as the indita (the diminutive of "Native woman"), which emerged during the nineteenth century in Mexican theater and radiated out from there, also utilizes indigenous musical or textual themes. An example of this genre in New Mexico is the "Indita de Manuelito," which Esteban Torres sang for Robb in Tomé, New Mexico, in 1957 in the Dorian mode (Robb, 434; F9a, R1517). This is also an example of a typically New Mexican and Mexican style, where the dead come back to speak through song in temporally convoluted ways.[19] "La Indita de Jesús María Sánchez" (ibid., 424) and "La Indita de Amarante Martínez" (Robb 1954; 19) both of which date themselves in the lyrics at around 1900, also exemplify this practice. The words to the "Indita de Manuelito" suggest that the composer was Native, and died when Charles and Captain Grey betrayed him, alluding to intercultural regional conflict following the Euro-American colonization of the Southwest region. My transcription (see Fig. 9.5) differs from Robb's in significant ways, as it highlights an old practice that continues to be widespread in the Americas, that of alternating twos and threes in succession or in combination, a practice commonly known in Spanish as *sesquiáltera* or *hemiola* (see also Robb 1954, 434).

Other, similar narrative ballads that I have classified as inditas might not be called indita in the title, but might include the word in the refrain, as in "Aye indita, y eso no" (Oh, Indita, not that), mentioned just once in the refrain of "Nos quemaron el rancho" (They Burnt Our Ranch). This indita focuses on regional conflict, when a gringo mob with gunnysacks over their heads attempted to burn out the Mexicanos. Perhaps the use of the term "indita" signified a greater identification with Native people, once Hispanos were themselves victims of oppression. Although inditas seem to have been primarily composed around the turn of the twentieth century, local scholars also tend to classify ballads with themes of captivity as inditas even though they probably emerged earlier than the inditas so named (Romero 2002). The theme of captivity had precedents on both sides. For instance, the lingering war between Moors and Spaniards prior to 1492 revolved around the taking of captives for ransom, and Natives in the Americas also took captives.

To a degree, isolation from the rest of the Spanish-speaking world was a condition of the Spanish-Mexican colonies that became New Mexico and Colorado. Such isolation was reinforced when political boundaries were formalized between Mexico and the United States in 1848. Consequently, many song genres that developed into modern, major-minor key styles in Mexico continued in an older modal style in New Mexico until the introduction of radio and television in the early 1950s. Contemporary New Mexican corridos follow the Mexican styles closely. These include one about the Challenger disaster that killed seven astronauts on January 28, 1986, "El Corrido de los Astronautas," which appeared on the radio only one week after the accident and, after that, "El Corrido del 720," which is dedicated to the members of the 720th Transportation Company and their families. The latter aired in 1991 during Operation Desert Storm in the Persian Gulf, where the 720th Company were stationed. Both corridos were written by the late legendary composer and musician Roberto Martinez (1929–1913) and recorded by Los Reyes de Albuquerque, his local mariachi group. Mexican mariachi orchestras began to arrive in New Mexico in the 1930s, and Roberto Martinez was playing mariachi music in New Mexico and Colorado by the 1950s (see Romero 2001).

Many other vocal genres existed in the past and survived through the 1950s, including children's game songs that taught numbers or colors or that added a new animal or event in the same style and format as "Old McDonald," the children's nursery rhyme. In celebrations, however, it was the dance music that took center stage. The baile, or social dance, originally was set in the front room of a large house, in which furniture was rearranged to create a large space for dancing. (This tradition died out among Mexicanos as dancehalls became popular—but the large living room is an architectural feature that has survived in Pueblo homes, and is particularly important for the social and political elite Puebloans whose families assume leadership roles in the community, and who must be able to host large gatherings.) Young Mexicano women were always accompanied by chaperones, and the virtue of women was protected even in the dances, where men and women often held opposite ends of handkerchiefs rather than each other's hands. Most were group dances, some of which originated in the Spanish courts before the colonial period. Following the French occupation of Mexico in the 1860s, the list included quadrilles, pavannes, schottisches, waltzes, and the famous polka and other dances of pan-European distribution. Inditas were sometimes played as dance pieces; their words, occasionally vulgar, are usually not sung today or are lost. Hispano tradition bearer Arsenio Córdova of Taos provided the melody seen in Figure 9.6.

9.6. *La Indita de Taos.*

Because of indigenous traditional beliefs that value the natural world over the unharmonious world humans have created, I can surmise that Mexicano households may have more telephones and greater access to electronic media than do Pueblo households. Nonetheless, computers and cellphones are increasingly part of both Mexicano and Pueblo households. Mexicanos show a marked preference for Spanish-language media, to the extent that much New Mexican popular music is in Spanish (see Romero 2011). Electric instruments and amplifiers have been in common use since the 1950s, and many popular Mexicano dance bands, such as the family-oriented Blue Ventures and the all-female group Sparx, own the latest sound equipment. Technology typically enhances traditional and popular forms rather than dominating them. The matachines, an outdoor ceremony, is one example of this, since the guitar and violin are often amplified. The matachines in Alcade, New Mexico (and perhaps others) play the matachines repertoire acoustically when a quieter setting makes amplification unnecessary (Garcia 2014).

THE MATACHINES DANZA

Although ritual dance dramas are common among the Puebloans, the masked matachines danza is the only such ritual dance drama among the Mexicanos. A symbiotic relationship between the Puebloans and Mexicanos developed as a result of the need for Mexicano violin and guitar players in the Pueblos and the need for an organizational role model with regard to ritual dance dramas, among the Mexicanos. Over the years, each culture reinforced the continuing performance of matachines and influenced each other's beliefs and practices in different ways.

The matachines danza is an ancient pantomime that enacts the spiritual victory of a king, although the specific details of this interpretation vary depending on the beliefs of the interpreter. The word matachines may derive from an obscure Arabic term for masked dancers; it is also associated, however, with the Italian term *mattaccino*, meaning jester or strolling player. Each part of the enactment features a dance sequence accompanied by a particular melody played on the violin and guitar. Some of the melodies bear likeness to those of Arbeau's *Buffons* and *Morisque*, documented in 1543 (Romero 1993, 28–39; Arbeau [1588]

1925, 156–62; Lozano 2007, 405). Among the earliest predecessors of the matachines in Western Europe were Roman sword and stick dances, perhaps derived from the Greeks (Lozano 2007, 405); these had evolved by the thirteenth century into ceremonial dances for religious processions and public festivals. According to the folklorist John Forrest (1984), the Morris dance (from *moresco*), which uses sticks, is the English version of matachines. Burlesque elements that accompanied such profane dances as the matachines often served as vehicles for social commentary (similar to the function of ritual clowns in Pueblo ceremonials). For this reason the Church, which was then also the state, censored such displays as early as the sixteenth century; and even as late as 1780 they were prohibited in church processions (Romero 1993, 76). A sacred version without burlesque elements, known as the *auto sacramental*, or religious play, survived as a symbol of the subduing of the Turks and the Moors, both major historical events for Christian Europeans (see also Lozano 2007, 7). The *auto sacramental* developed in Spain and was transported across the ocean, to survive in the Americas with more burlesque elements in some locations (Colombia, for example) where Carnival traditions flourished. In Mexico as in New Mexico, matachines comprising more religious than carnival aspects have survived, although some burlesque elements are always prominent.

The matachines danza (which refers to the entire ceremonial dance drama, as opposed to the individual dances of which it consists) of New Mexico typically features four central characters, the *Monarca*, the *Malinche*, the *Abuelo*, and the *Toro*, as well as from eight to twelve matachines dancers in a double file. In the past someone would read a narrative that accompanied the pantomimed dance drama. The Monarca, or king, struggles toward spiritual conversion; in Picuris Pueblo he symbolizes Moctezuma, a narrative that is closely related to the Mexican Nahua version called la Danza de Moctezuma.[20] In New Mexico *La Malinche* symbolizes the first Indian convert to Christianity, or Christ's Virgin Mother as a child. The Abuelo symbolizes the wisdom of old people. He assists the Monarca and the Malinche during the Monarca's struggle. The Abuelo (grandfather) also cues the musicians, who play a different dance melody (in Mexico generically called *son*) for each sequence of the *danza*. The Abuelo, together with the vaqueros (cowhands), help control the unruly Toro (Bull), who distracts the Monarca and the Malinche from their spiritual mission. John Donald Robb believed that the Toro symbolizes man's lower nature, and this has resonated with ancient Roman beliefs such as those of the cult of Mithra, in which soldiers slayed a bull as a sacrificial offering and a symbol of the victory of good over evil. But the sweet young boy that peers out from under the bull headdress in the Pueblos is honored rather than killed, as in Hispano contexts.

The central characters dance between and around the double file of matachines, who symbolize Christian foot soldiers, or Christ's twelve apostles, although in many places there can be fewer or more than twelve danzantes; the masked headdress also evokes images of subdued Moors. An Abuela (Grandmother), usually a man dressed as a drunk old woman, often features in the burlesque, serving to exemplify socially unacceptable behavior, through symbolic reversal (the opposite of what is intended). This burlesque may also ridicule old women unfairly and is not a feature of the Pueblo Matachina. In the Pueblo of Jemez, old women often parody the Matachina dancers during the official Matachina dance in front of the Infant's House for the January 1st celebration of New Year's Day. January 1 is also the feast day of St. Manuel, and those named Manuel, or Manuela also offer feasts in their own homes that day.

THE MATACHINES AMONG THE MEXICANOS

The matachines genre was introduced in Mexico as a means of evangelizing indigenous populations and Spanish and mestizo (mixed) "commoners" (today a contested term). Because the Natives resisted Spanish attempts at complete colonization, the matachines dances of New Mexico often include obscure sequences that can only be explained through Mexican indigenous symbolism.[21] A strong Mexican indigenous influence is apparent in the character of the Malinche, said to be the first female convert to Christianity in the Americas.[22] Formerly, women did not dance the matachines; thus a boy, usually dressed in a white dress, enacted the part of La Malinche in both Puebloan and Mexicano versions. Social roles of men and women have gradually become less rigid, and today women are seen dancing along with men in Bernalillo and other Mexicano villages, or as the *mayordoma* (steward), who is usually a man (*mayordomo*) appointed by the community to be responsible for the danza on any given year. The Rainbow Dancers of Alcalde, New Mexico, are a matachines troupe comprised entirely of young women.

For most Mexicanos, the matachines danza no longer implies the conversion of the Natives, but rather, it is perceived as a dance for honoring patron saints (each village celebrates its own saint's day throughout the year) or the Holy Child during the Christmas season.[23] The Catholic Church no longer governs everyday life and local priests do not spend their time organizing community activities. Neither does the mayor of a town organize the matachines dance merely because he is mayor. Charles Aguilar, who, as the mayor of Bernalillo, organized their matachines danza, was himself a matachines dancer and violin player long before he became mayor. The matachines danza has gained importance through its survival. Always through the efforts of individuals, the impact of dancing and preserving the tradition is a renewed faith. Euro-American New Mexican citizens want to participate in matachines as well, however, and in some places in New Mexico, they too are beginning to perpetuate this tradition (see Lamadrid 2008).

Most importantly, matachines is an emblem of the pride of a people struggling for freedom from imposed colonization as well as from internalized colonization. As the Hispanos colonized the Pueblos for 250 years, so Anglo- and other Euro-Americans subsequently colonized both the Pueblos and Hispanos in 1848.

As a result of socio-historical processes, many Hispano and Pueblo peoples, who constitute two-thirds of the state's population, have experienced colonization in recent memory.

MATACHINES IN THE PUEBLOS

Because the Pueblos have sovereign status (as do all First Nations), they have their own governing bodies and laws, which are separate from the New Mexico state authorities and laws that apply to non-Indians. Within the Pueblo structure are both ancient and civil forms of government. The head of the ancient governing body is the *cacique*, the spiritual leader of the community. The head of the civil government is the Pueblo governor, who is usually assisted by two lieutenant governors. Although it is an honor to serve, there are many social and religious obligations attendant to holding office.

Dance organization is part of a systematic and coordinated effort supported by Pueblo social structure. Social and ceremonial obligations are regulated in part by dividing the Pueblo into moieties (halves). In the Pueblo of Jemez, a War Chief takes responsibility for each kiva, including organizing its public ceremonies for the year. War Chiefs for the Pumpkin and Turquoise kivas organize all aspects of the Matachina. It is the War Chief who appoints dancers, notifies them about rehearsals, and makes sure that everything is done and at the right time. The Tewa Pueblos, along the Rio Grande in northern New Mexico, elect both a Summer Chief and a Winter Chief who is also the Hunting Chief. In Ohkay Owingeh, however, the Matachina is the responsibility of the civil authorities, or governor's office. Here a man demonstrates honor by dancing the Matachina, which has been closely associated with civil government (imposed by the Spanish in the early seventeenth century), and seems almost to constitute a prerequisite for civil office. While in office, however, pressing responsibilities tend to preclude dancing in any ceremony.

CROSSING INTO EACH OTHER'S CULTURAL SPACES

For Mexicanos and Puebloans, crossing into each other's cultural spaces has historically been limited primarily to social dance and church contexts. Throughout the early colonial period, Natives mostly observed the *bailes*, or social dances, when they occurred in church contexts on saints' days, at trade fairs, or as a result of being laborers for the Spanish Mexicans. In the post-colonial period, prominent Anglo-American settlers, such as Kit Carson and Charles Bent, were known for inviting Natives to their fiestas, for which Mexicano musicians provided the music. Over time, Native individuals grew familiar with the dances, which utilized group-dance choreographies similar in some ways to Native ceremonials.

Native resistance to outside cultural hegemony—including to the Catholic Church—has been the rule, so that once Spanish control of the missions was lost in 1680, the Puebloans abandoned the polyphonic liturgical Latin music they reportedly had learned so well. Like most Judeo-Christian Euro-Americans, the Mexicanos (mostly mestizos) held to superstitions regarding Pueblo traditional religious beliefs. For the most part, they observed Pueblo ceremonies with little, if any, understanding or appreciation of them, although today Native online media resources increasingly help foster a greater understanding and appreciation. Matachines survived in Mexicano and Pueblo settings as an expression of Catholic devotion in the honoring of the saints. The lively and cheerful matachines dance sequences have elements of the old bailes (social dances); the ceremonial matachines elements blended with Pueblo formats, and many adopted and maintained the matachines and their attendant events. The strength of ceremonial practices in the Pueblos no doubt helped reinforce the matachines among the Mexicanos after 1848, when Mexicanos in a gigantic landmass extending from California to Louisiana were severed from Mexico following the United States takeover of the area.

Because the matachines is performed to honor Catholic saints in both cultural settings, the danza provides an ongoing context for the interaction of Mexicano and Puebloan musicians and peoples. Saint's day celebrations tend to be big events, beginning with the Mass, and many Mexicanos attend the Pueblo Matachina. And, although the Puebloans and Hispanos live largely separate existences, a great deal of visiting and feasting at each other's homes occurs when the matachines dance. At first the music required Mexicano musicians. Gradually, an increasing number of Pueblo musicians have begun to play the violin and guitar, although Mexicanos are still hired to play in some Pueblos that feature the danza. In the Pueblo of Jemez, for example, Lawrence Trujillo currently performs the lead violin. His grandfather, Adelaido Martinez, a Mexicano from the nearby town of Ponderosa, played the violin for the Matachina for thirty years before his death in 1988. (Adelaido's father and grandfather had also played the violin for the Matachina as for Hispano matachines.) For the last eighteen of those thirty years, Daniel Culacke accompanied Adelaido on the guitar. Daniel was a member of the Jemez Pumpkin kiva, but played for the Turquoise kiva Matachina. He continued to play the guitar, accompanying me on the violin, until his death in 1994.

The accompanying recorded examples are from the Pueblo of Jemez Turquoise kiva Matachina repertoire. First is the "Son de la Malinche," featuring Adelaido Martinez on violin and Daniel Culacke on guitar in a recording collected on December 29, 1979, by John Donald Robb (Chapter 9, Track 3). The following performance is also the "Son de la Malinche," featuring Gabriel Casiquito, a member of the Pumpkin kiva at Jemez Pueblo, on January 1, 1993 (Chapter 9, Track 4). This is followed by the "Son del Toro"—a favorite of Adelaido Martinez—again featuring Martinez on violin and Culacke on guitar, from the same recording collected on December 29, 1979, by John Donald Robb (Chapter 9, Track 5). The Malinche and Toro melodies (see Figs. 9.7 and 9.8) are related motivically in that they both use

9.7. *La Malinche* sequence of the Matachina in the Pueblo of Jemez.

9.8. *El Toro* sequence of the Matachina in the Pueblo of Jemez. Note the use of *sesquiáltera* as part of the character of this melody.

the same fast ornamental slide. In the "Son del Toro," the gesture expresses the mischievous nature for which the *Torito* (little bull) is known.

The final example, "The Fast Monarcha," or "The Jemez Man Song" (Chapter 9, Track 6), features the author on the violin and Daniel Culacke on guitar, performing at the Infant's House on January 1, 1993.

Moving beyond the components of performance, the matachines danza allows a glimpse into the ways that the Puebloans negotiate difference and define identity. A few Pueblos perform two different versions of the Matachina. A "drum" version, said to have originated in Santo Domingo Pueblo, uniquely substitutes male chorus and drum for the "Spanish" version, which uses violin and guitar. One group immediately follows the other in the same ceremonial space on the sacred plaza. The choreography remains almost exactly the same, although the Pumpkin kiva ceremonial dress is completely Puebloan. Instead of dress trousers and leather boots, for example, the dancers wear traditional Pueblo leggings and moccasins. Instead of a prepubescent Malinche in a white, Holy Communion dress, she is a young teenager, who wears a traditional Pueblo maiden's dress, with one shoulder bared. One is a symbol of virgin chastity and the other a symbol of latent fertility or potential. The song that is sung for the latter is in the Keres language of the Santo Domingo Pueblo; the words describe the ceremonial dress she wears.

In the Pueblo of Jemez, the Turquoise kiva enacts the Spanish version and the Pumpkin kiva (the more conservative and traditional of the two kivas) enacts the drum version. The Pumpkin kiva danza has been effectively reinterpreted into the traditional male-chorus-and-drum format, which reinforces the resistance to foreign cultural hegemony, while obvious ties to Mexicano culture are maintained in the Turquoise kiva, as if in recognition of the intermixing of bloodlines through the centuries. Both versions are performed to honor the Virgin of Guadalupe on December 12, as well as St. Manuel, whose feast day happens to be on January 1, when the elder Pueblo women participate in humorous parodies and burlesques of Matachina simultaneously with the serious Matachina's enactment.

While some may say that Matachina is not authentically Puebloan, time and circumstances, as well as its ritual practice, have authenticated the ceremony by reinterpreting its meanings to conform to local traditions (the process of reinterpretation). Although aware that the Spanish Mexicans introduced the ceremony, most Puebloans claim ownership, incorporating into it various general ceremonial practices common to the more traditional Pueblo dances, and adapting Spanish Mexican practices in unique ways. In Ohkay Owingeh, the Matachina dancers dance to fulfill a sacred *promesa* (promise), a Spanish practice, but highly compatible with traditional Pueblo ritual obligations that ensure sufficient rain and a plentiful harvest. In contrast, the Mexicano Malinche is strikingly similar in concept to the idea of the White Corn Goddess, the female winter deity for the Tewas. White Corn Goddess is highly mystical and is only impregnated by the sun, much as the Virgin Mary is believed to have been impregnated by a spirit. Mystical Puebloan beliefs surround the Matachina and its characters; for instance, in Ohkay Owingeh when the Malinche is from the winter moiety, she is believed to bring snow to the village. Although the Pueblo Matachina and the Hispano matachines outwardly resemble each other, the dance ritual event evokes different worldviews in its deeper significances.

Mexicanos who participate as matachines musicians often feel a spiritual calling, perhaps in part because of the extremely cold conditions in which one is usually required to perform. When I became the violin player at the Pueblo, I had dreamt of Adelaido after his death—although I was not aware then that he had died. After I learned of his death, I interpreted that dream as a sign for me to learn the repertoire and play for the Pueblo—and the Pueblo governor agreed to allow me to do so. Adelaido Martinez never required payment from the Pueblo of Jemez for playing on December 12, when the Pueblo celebrated the sacred feast day of the Virgin of Guadalupe. On New Year's Day, however, the *vaquero* (cowboy) characters collect donations for the musicians from the audiences throughout the day. Pueblo influences are felt among Mexicanos most strongly in a sense of renewal that accompanies the entire ceremony, from the simple rituals of making their own ceremonial crown (*corona*) to the repetitive dance steps on the cool, sacred earth. The concept of *tierra sagrada*, or sacred earth, is perhaps the most profound reflection of the Puebloan mark on Mexicano beliefs.

Among the Mexicano musicians who play in the Pueblos, I am particularly moved by the ritual of sprinkling sacred corn meal—sacred because of the ancient provenance of the seed used to grow it—in the prayers for life. Many Pueblo practices serve to teach a simple yet magical humanity. The warmth and caring of family relationships in the Pueblos is significant, especially obvious in the largess displayed on feast days, which belies the fact that few are wealthy. In the Pueblo of Jemez, for two weeks, from December 24 to January 6, one house is designated the Holy Infant's House, in which food is served every day from dawn until 2 a.m. the following day. Everyone in the Pueblo who is able to do so contributes a delicious dish every day. No one goes hungry; all, including outsiders, are welcome.

IN CONCLUSION

When communities cross over and share each other's cultural spaces, opportunities are provided for interaction that may alter how they feel and think about each other. Mexicano and Puebloan have interacted in limited, yet profoundly spiritual ways for over four hundred years. Negotiating differences has not meant abandoning ethnic and cultural identities. Rather, the two cultures have maintained a ceremony in common, sharing its music and its musicians freely, learning from and gradually influencing each other. Authenticity is subject to change, for what gives musics authenticity is not open to quantification as much as to cultural and spiritual intent. The matachines in New Mexico illustrate a sharing of spiritual intent that is mutually expressed in musical/artistic forms, and which helps bridge cultural distance.

As an ethnomusicologist with significant ties to my New Mexican field sites, I found a way of giving back that fulfilled personal desires to help to create that "bridge over troubled waters" that Simon and Garfunkel sang about on the airwaves when I was a teenager. After Daniel Culacke died in 1994, Adelaido Martinez's grandson, Lawrence Trujillo, who played guitar in a local country and western band, began to fill in as Matachina guitarist. Soon he began to play his grandfather Adelaido's violin and I began to coach him on the pieces. In September 1998 Lawrence (on guitar) and I (on violin) played for the Jemez Turquoise Matachina for an event at the University of New Mexico in Albuquerque. At one point that day, Lawrence played through all of the pieces for me. The one really tough piece was shaky but passable and I said, "You're playing this December." That December I took off for the Borderlands to conduct fieldwork on matachines, guided by UNM documentary photographer Miguel Gandert. In 2000–2001 I held a Fulbright García-Robles award to conduct fieldwork on matachines in Mexico, then learned from New Mexico state folklorist Claude Stephenson (himself a matachines violinist for Bernalillo) of matachines in Colombia. I began fieldwork in Colombia in 2007, and in spring of 2011 I held a Fulbright Colombia award to teach a class on ethnomusicology and to conduct fieldwork on matachines in Colombia. I have since learned that matachines is even more widespread, found in Guatemala, Bolivia, Puerto Rico, Brazil, and no doubt many other locations where the Iberians left their mark. In each site the danza tells a different tale, much as the Jemez Turquoise kiva Matachina differs from the Jemez Pumpkin Matachina, and how they both differ from the Bernalillo Matachines, and so on it goes. As in New Mexico, the matachines elsewhere have served to unite disparate communities in artistic musical endeavors.

Notes

1. *Pueblo* is the Spanish word for village, widely used as a designation for the multi-apartment-style adobe villages of the Native peoples in New Mexico and the Hopi in Arizona. All have sovereign rights and thus their own governing bodies, as do all recognized Native populations in the United States.

2. I use the contemporary spelling, Mexicano, of *Mejicano*, the term the elder generation used to refer to themselves in Spanish. For the most part they did not use the English equivalent, *Mexican*, which was used pejoratively by Anglo and other white Euro-American settlers (see also Briggs 1988). Older culture members might refer to themselves as "Spanish," which reflects Spanish ancestry and governance of this area until 1821, or "Mexican American," which reflects Mexican governance from 1821 until 1848 and ancestral ties to Mexico. Some, starting with the baby boomer generation refer to themselves as "Chicanos," a politicized term coined during the civil rights movement in the late 1960s. The term *Chicano*, literally "children of the earth" or "red people" in Nahuatl, denotes the same respect for the indigenous contributions to the community as has always been given to the Hispano contributions. Most recently I have identified traditional New Mexican Hispano descendants of the colonists as *'Manitos* (see Romero 2011). Some (but not all) 'Manitos call themselves Chicanos. Many others still self identify as "Spanish."

3. According to Enrique Lamadrid (2014), the term *hispano* began with the historic term "hispano americano" in the first half of the twentieth century. The Chicano land grant activist Reies López Tijerina is credited with initiating the term "indo-hispano." Although the term "Hispanic" was better accepted in New Mexico than elsewhere, many scholars are critical of "Hispanic" as an outsider term imposed by the US Census beginning in 1980. It labels everyone from the Americas, including the Caribbean, as having a connection to Spanish, and thus misses many linguistic and cultural markers in an immense geographical region. Not only is "Hispanic" an imposed term, but also sounds like the pejorative "spic." "Hispano" (or "hispana") is a proper Spanish term for someone of Spanish ancestry, who presumably speaks the language. New Mexican activist scholars embraced the term "Indo-Hispano" as opposed to the more generic "mestizo" (mixed indigenous and Spanish) in the 1990s because the term explicitly differentiated mixed-race New Mexican ancestries (using the term "Indo" rather than the pejorative *indio* for indigenous). See, for instance, Jack Loeffler, *La música de los viejitos: Hispano Folk Music of the Rio Grande del Norte* (1999), and Enrique Lamadrid, *Hermanitos Comanchitos: Indo-Hispano Rituals of Captivity and Redemption* (2003).

4. The 400-year commemoration of the Spanish presence in New Mexico in 1998 resulted in new efforts among the Pueblos to correct old wrongs perpetuated by the colonizer Juan de Oñate. Among those efforts, in 2005 a general election reclaimed the place name Ohkay Owingeh, or "Place of the Strong People," the pre-Hispanic name for the Spanish Pueblo de San Juan (San Juan Pueblo or St. John's Village).

5. The term danza implies ceremonial dance drama. *Matachines* is the name of the particular type of dance drama under discussion; when used alone the term matachines refers either to the dance drama (the performance complex) or to the ceremonial line dancers, the danzantes.

6. Other kinds of Chicano music in the United States exemplify the crossover between cultures: Tex-Mex and norteño styles have incorporated the German, Polish, and Czech polka styles with Mexican, and more recently with Cajun musical styles. Afro-Cuban and Puerto Rican styles reflect the mixing of black and white musical styles. Such satisfying musics belie the presence of intercultural hostility.

7. Most non-Natives are familiar with the doll-like kachina representations sold commercially throughout the Southwest. These small representations, usually carved out of cottonwood, preserve the features associated with particular kachinas. When displayed at home, the kachinas are considered spiritual guardians. The Jemez artist Jose Rey Toledo has this to say about kachinas:

> They are creatures in that [spiritual] world that are very much like creatures here that act as negotiators and mediators. It's so precious to people, [kachinas] are considered very special and very much a part of [us] and should not be watered down to where it has only fun value and not sacred value. The tourist is always looking for appetites that he has of fun and fantasy . . . They look more for something theatrical all the time. That's where we differ in our religious concept. (unpublished manuscript 42)

8. Ed Valandra, Lakota political scientist, objects to the use of the words *supernatural* and *deities*, since the Lakota worldview, and indigenous worldviews in general, do not distinguish between natural and supernatural phenomena.

9. In the earlier edition of this book, I cited Acoma and Laguna Pueblo singer and lyricist Harold Littlebird's "Navajo Love Song" for its clever use of insider Pueblo/Navajo humor.

10. Traditionally, Native Americans have well-specified gender roles. Among the Lakota Plains people, the reason men dominate ritual is not necessarily because they consider themselves superior to women. In societies that focus on human harmony with natural forces, women are considered to be naturally in greater harmony. Evidence for this is seen in women's ability to bear children, and by monthly purification cycles. Men, who are most often in touch with forces in opposition to life, through war or hunting, for instance, constantly need to be reaffirmed in the cycles of life, and thus require ritual intervention. This is not to undermine the fact that women in the Pueblos may have become, in some instances, victims of imposed Eurocentric ideas of male domination.

11. From the liner notes: "unioNation™ Band was inspired by Cody Wilder, writing and performing the song 'United We Stand, Divided We Fall' as a class project in Leadership I at the International Association of Machinists & Aerospace Workers (IAMAW), William W. Winpisinger Education & Technology Center (W3). Music breaks down many barriers. Could the IAMAW use music to organize, inspire, and motivate our Union members to create and communicate workers' issues in new and different ways?" (Henry Bagwell, W3 Education Representative, goiam.org).

12. The period of Spanish Flemish polyphony and a general flowering of the arts came about as a result of a noble marriage alliance in the early seventeenth century between Princess Isabella Clara Eugenia, daughter of Spain's King Philip II, and the Archduke Albert of the Netherlands.

13. In 2008 I published a CD titled *Canciones de mis Patrias: Early New Mexican Folksongs*, on which many of the songs discussed in this chapter may be heard.

14. The original recordings are now available online by searching for "UNM CSWR John Donald Robb Field Recordings": http://econtent.unm.edu/cdm/search/collection/RobbFieldRe.

15. Nonetheless, Robb collected a version (A12) from the folklorist Espinosa that ends with Gerineldo marrying "the daughter of Charles the Fifth."

16. I recorded my arrangement of this canción as Track 1 of my 2008 CD recording, featuring accompanying musician Tomás Lozano (originally from Andalusia, Spain), on *bandurria* and lead guitar on other tracks as well, and his wife Rima Montoya (originally from Costa Rica), on the Western transversal flute. Since this recording celebrates the different nations—Spanish, Mexican, and indigenous—that inform New Mexican music, this same song, "Palomita que vienes herida," as Track 15 of my CD features Mexican musician-ethnomusicologists Guillermo Contreras Arias (on violin), Gonzalo Camacho Díaz (on mandolin), and Rubén Luengas Pérez (on *bajo quinto*) accompanying on the first take of the musicians' spontaneous arrangement.

17. With changes initiated by Pope John and Vatican II in the early 1960s, the liturgy of the Mass gradually became dominated by vernacular musics. A new wave of local and regional church compositions arose, modeling or using mostly Mexican folk melodies. In 1996, the Church again revived the use of Gregorian chant in the Mass, juxtaposed with vernacular hymns.

18. Song duels, called *Zajal*, are also currently practiced in many places in the Arab world, from Lebanon to Saudi Arabia. The practice is thought to have originated in the Moorish courts at Córdova and Granada during the Arab occupation of Spain from 711 to 1492 (Anne Rasmussen, personal communication).

19. The Mexican ethnomusicologist José Luis Sagredo Castillo categorizes these as *Despedimientos* (Farewells).

20. *Moctecuzoma* is the original spelling in the Spanish codices (Salvador Rodriguez del Pino, personal communication, 1996). Montezuma is a popular English mispronunciation of Moctezuma.

21. An example of this is the Monarca's (Monarch's) sequence, in which he extends an ailing leg to the Abuelo (Grandfather). A possible explanation is that this part of the dance was taken from an Aztec dance that honored Tizoc, who ruled the Aztecs in the late fifteenth century. Tizoc was known for bleeding his leg with cactus spines, for which the Spanish named him *Pierna Enferma*, or Sick Leg. One recalls that the Aztecs in authority had many self-bleeding practices to ensure order in the universe.

22. In Mexico, Malinche, the multilingual Nahua slave woman given to Cortez as his wife, is maligned as a traitor to indigenous cultures, but she is not portrayed this way in New Mexico.

23. In the town of Bernalillo, the matachines danza commemorates the return of the Spanish to New Mexico following the great Pueblo Revolt of 1680. Here the danza honors an ancient *promesa* (promise) to dance on August 10, the feast day of San Lorenzo, and the day on which many Spanish colonists were killed or fled New Mexico.

Chapter 9: Musical Examples (access through companion website)

Chapter 9, Track 1. *unioNation™: Machinists Music Project*
Chapter 9, Track 2. La Delgadina.
Chapter 9, Track 3. Malinche no. 1.
Chapter 9, Track 4. Malinche no. 2.
Chapter 9, Track 5. Son del Toro.
Chapter 9, Track 6. Fast Monarca.

References Cited

Arbeau, Thoinot. (1588) 1925. *Orchesography*. London: Cyril W. Beaumont.

Benmayor, Rina. 1988. *Romances judeo-españoles de Oriente: Nueva recolección*. Musical transcriptions by Judith H. Mauleón. Madrid: Cátedra-Seminario Menéndez Pidal: Gredos.

Briggs, Charles. 1988. *Competence in Performance: The Creativity of Tradition in Mejicano Verbal Art*. Philadelphia: University of Pennsylvania Press.

Ellis, Florence Hawley. 1964. "A Reconstruction of the Basic Jemez Pattern of Social Organization, with Comparisons to Other Tanoan Social Structures." *University of New Mexico Publications in Anthropology*, no. 11. Albuquerque: University of New Mexico Press.

Espinosa, Aurelio M. 1985. *The Folklore of Spain in the American Southwest*. Norman: University of Oklahoma Press.

Ford, Richard. 1972. "An Ecological Perspective on the Eastern Pueblos." *New Perspectives on the Pueblos*. Alfonso Ortiz, ed. Santa Fe: SAR Press. 1–17.

Garcia, David. 2014. Personal communications with the author.

Forrest, John. 1984. *Morris and Matachin: A Study in Comparative Choreography*. Sheffield, UK: Centre for English Cultural Tradition and Language, University of Sheffield.

Guyette, Susan. 1983. *Community-Based Research: A Handbook for Native Americans.* Los Angeles: Regents of the University of California.

Humphreys, Paul. 1984. "The Borrowing and Adapting of Songs among the Pueblo Indians of the Southwest United States." *Pacific Review of Ethnomusicology* 1: 29–56.

Jacobs, Janet. 1995. Unpublished manuscript.

Lamadrid, Enrique. 2003. *Hermanitos Comanchitos: Indo-Hispano Rituals of Captivity and Redemption.* Photographs by Miguel A. Gandert. Albuquerque: University of New Mexico Press.

———. 2008. "Moctezuma and the Elders, the Virgin and the Bull: the Matachines Dance of Greater Mexico." In *Matachines: Essays for the 2008 Gathering.* Claude Stephenson, ed. Albuquerque: New Mexico Arts, 11–14.

———. 1994. *Los Tesoros del Espiritu: A Portrait in Sound of Hispanic New Mexico.* Bilingual, with set of three compact discs or cassette recordings. Researched and written by Enrique Lamadrid. Recorded and produced by Jack Loeffler. Photographs by Miguel A. Gandert. Embudo, NM: El Norte/Academia Publications.

———. 2014. Personal communications with the author.

LaVigna, Maria. 1980. "Okushare, Music for a Winter Ceremony: The Turtle Dance Songs of San Juan Pueblo." In *Selected Reports in Ethnomusicology* 3, no. 2, ed. Charlotte Heth. Los Angeles: Regents of the University of California. 77–99.

Lozano, Tomás. 2007. *Cantemos al Alba: Origins of Songs, Sounds, and Liturgical Drama of Hispanic New Mexico.* Edited and translated into English by Rima Montoya. Albuquerque: University of New Mexico Press.

Mendoza, Vicente, and Virginia R. R. de Mendoza. 1986. *Estudio y Clasificación de la Música Tradicional Hispánica de Nuevo Mexico.* Mexico: Universidad Nacional Autónoma de Mexico.

Ortiz, Alfonso, ed. 1972. *New Perspectives on the Pueblos.* Albuquerque: University of New Mexico Press.

———. 1972. "Ritual Drama and the Pueblo World View." *New Perspectives on the Pueblos.* 135–61.

———. 1969. *The Tewa World.* Chicago: University of Chicago Press.

Porter, James. 1995. "Eth-no-mus-i-co-lo-gy." In *Rhythmmusic* 4, no. 5: 22–26.

Robb, John Donald. [1980] 2014. *Hispanic Folk Music of New Mexico and the Southwest: A Self-Portrait of a People.* Norman: University of Oklahoma Press.

Roberts, Don. 1972. "The Ethnomusicology of the Eastern Pueblos." *New Perspectives on the Pueblos.* 243–55.

Rodriguez, Sylvia. 1996. *The Matachines Dance: Ritual Symbolism and Interethnic Relations in the Upper Río Grande Valley.* Albuquerque: University of New Mexico Press.

Romero, Brenda M. 2001. "La Creciente popularidad del mariachi en los Estados Unidos" (The Growing Popularity of Mariachi in the United States). *De Occidente es el mariachi, y de México . . .*, ed. Álvaro Ochoa Serrano. Zamora, México: El Colegio de Michoacán, 171–80.

———. 2002. "*La Indita* of New Mexico: Gender and Cultural Identification." In *Chicana Traditions, Continuity and Change*. Olga Najera-Ramirez and Norma Cantu, ed. Chicago: University of Illinois Press. 56–80.

———. 1993. *The Matachines Music and Dance in San Juan Pueblo and Alcalde, New Mexico: Contexts and Meanings*. PhD diss., University of California, Los Angeles.

———. 2011. "New Mexico and *'Manitos* at the Borderlands of Popular Music in Greater Mexico." *Transnational Encounters: Music and Performance at the U.S.-Mexico Border*. Alejandro Madrid, ed. New York: Oxford University Press. 287–311.

———. 2000. "Soundscapes of the Native Southwest." *Plateau Journal*, Grand Canyon Association and the Museum of Northern Arizona (Winter 2000-2001): 42–56.

Sagredo Castillo, José Luis. 2014. Personal communications with the author.

Stephenson, Claude, ed. 2008. *Matachines: Essays for the 2008 Gathering*. Albuquerque: New Mexico Arts.

Tobias, Henry J. 1990. A *History of the Jews in New Mexico*. Albuquerque: University of New Mexico Press.

Toelken, Barre. 1995. "Enlightened Fieldwork." *Parabola* (summer): 28–35.

Toledo, Jose Rey. Forthcoming. *Morning Star: The Autobiography of a Jemez Pueblo Indian Artist*. In collaboration with Susan Scarberry-Garcia. Albuquerque, NM: University of New Mexico Press.

Additional Sources

Campa, Arthur L. 1979. *Hispanic Culture in the Southwest*. Norman: University of Oklahoma Press.

Champe, Flavia W. 1983. *The Matachines Dance of the Upper Rio Grande*. Lincoln: University of Nebraska Press.

Dozier, Edward P. 1970. *The Pueblo Indians of North America*. New York: Holt, Rinehart, and Winston.

García, Nasario. 1987. *Recuerdos de los Viejitos: Tales of the Rio Puerto*. Albuquerque: University of New Mexico Press.

Gutierrez, Ramón. 1991. *When Jesus Came, the Corn Mothers Went Away*. Stanford, CA: Stanford University Press.

Loeffler, Jack. 1999. *La música de los viejitos: Hispano Folk Music of the Rio Grande del Norte*. [Compiled by] Jack Loeffler with Katherine Loeffler and Enrique R. Lamadrid. Photography by Jack Parsons. Albuquerque: University of New Mexico Press.

Sweet, Jill. 1985. *Dances of the Tewa Pueblo Indians: Expressions of New Life*. Santa Fe, NM: School of American Research Press.

Weigle, Marta, and Peter White. 1987. *The Lore of New Mexico*. Albuquerque: University of New Mexico Press.

Yeh, Nora. 1980. "Pogonshare: The Cloud Dance Songs of San Juan Pueblo." In *Selected Reports in Ethnomusicology* 3, no. 3: 1.01–45.32

Recordings Cited

Martinez, Roberto. 1991. *Ayer y Hoy: New Mexico's 720th Bound for War.* Dedicated to the members of the 720th Transportation Company and their families. Los Reyes de Albuquerque. MORE Records 0814.

Martinez, Roberto. 1995. *Treinta Años de Grabaciones.* Los Reyes de Albuquerque. MA-0827.

Ranier, John Jr., with Lillian, Verenda, Howard, and John Ranier Sr., and P. J. McAfee. 1992. "Taos Pueblo Round Dance Song." *Music of New Mexico: Native American Traditions.* Liner notes by Edward Wapp Wahpeconiah. Smithsonian/Folkways CD SF 40408.

Romero, Brenda M. 2008. *Canciones de mis Patrias: Early New Mexican Folksongs.* With explanatory notes as enhanced content. Featuring special guests Tomás Lozano, Rima Montoya, Guillermo Contreras Arias, Gonzalo Camacho Díaz, and Rubén Luengas Pérez.

unioNation™: Machinists Music Project. 2013. Liner notes by Henry Bagwell. Recorded, mixed, mastered, engineered by KMH Recording Studio, Keith Harancher, Lusby, Maryland.

Additional Recommended Listening

Cipriano con Música Folklórica. 1994. Cipriano Vigil. Catalina Records, P.O. Box 747, El Rito, NM 87530; (505) 581-4520.

Ditch-Cleaning and Picnic Songs of Picuris Pueblo. 1972. Indian House 1051-C.

Martinez, Roberto. 1993. Lo Mejor de Lorenzo Martinez y Sus Violines. CD-MO 0823.

Music of New Mexico: Hispanic Traditions. Smithsonian/Folkways, 1992. CD SF 40409.

Music of New Mexico, Native American Traditions. Smithsonian/Folkways, 1992. CD SF 40408.

The Tewa Indian Women's Choir of San Juan Pueblo, Songs from the Tewa Mass. 1994. Tewa Indian Women's Choir, P.O. Box 27, San Juan Pueblo, NM 87566.

Turtle Dance Songs of San Juan Pueblo. 1972. With explanatory notes. Indian House 1101-C.

- 10 -

TRIANGLES, SQUARES, OVALS, AND DIAMONDS

The "Fasola Folk" and Their Singing Tradition

Ron Pen

In his chapter on the "fasola folk," music professor and Sacred Harp singer and teacher Ron Pen narrates the history and contemporary life of an American singing tradition that represents the confluence of white, Anglo-Celtic ethnicity with other European immigrant and African American styles. Prior to American independence, colonists developed a musical performance practice for religious worship that was distinctly different from that of their European forebears. Pen traces the development of psalm singing from its first manifestations in New England and the Mid-Atlantic states through the migration of singing schools to the western and southern frontiers, the rise of white spirituals, gospel hymnody at camp meetings, and the evolution of revivalism and traditionalism in shape note singing today. These distinct singing styles and their respective communities of performers are tied to different shape note tunebook publications, including *The Southern Harmony* and *The Sacred Harp.*

The musical tradition has been marked by a continuously evolving repertoire, a "singing school" approach to pedagogy and dissemination, and a uniquely American version of music theory and performance practice. In his analysis of two tributaries of the same stream, Pen points to the continuity of the family- and community-perpetuated tradition of *The Southern Harmony,* in which the "authenticity of practice" is surely, if tenuously, guaranteed by the fragile line of oral transmission dating at least back to 1884. The practice of *The Sacred Harp,* on the other hand, is a vibrant example of a revivalist musical subculture in America, whose proponents may have little or no connection to the family, community, and religious background of the authentic tradition. Contemporary Sacred Harp singings, which are held regularly throughout the nation, hold attraction for Americans because of the powerful sound and experience of *The Sacred Harp* and the creation of a community through musical performance.

In the years since this chapter was initially published, the Benton Big Singing Day has demonstrated persistence and renewed vitality. Although a new, modern courthouse was constructed outside the center of town, the old courthouse continued its role as the site of the annual singing. Females were permitted to lead for the first time in 2005 and the social dinner on the ground was re-established. The Kentucky State Singing continues to flourish as well at the Pisgah Presbyterian Church. There are also regular monthly singings

10.1. An invitation to sing in May 2010.

connected with the Appalachian Association of Sacred Harp Singers in Louisville, Berea, and Lexington, Kentucky. Scholarship has produced important new critical studies and new tunebooks have appeared that introduce new compositions that complement traditional tunes and texts. These new publications include *The Norumbega Harmony* (2003), *The Missouri Harmony* (2005), *The Georgian Harmony* (2012), *and The Christian Harmony* (2010). Future generations of shape note singers now receive training at Camp Fasola (four-shape books) in Alabama and at Camp Doremi (seven-shape books) in North Carolina. Despite the popularity of social networks and the prevalence of new "cloud" technologies, anachronistic shape note singing has not only survived into the twenty-first century, but it is also flourishing and covering the country like kudzu.

BIG SINGING DAY IN KENTUCKY

The day dawns bright and beautiful this fourth Sunday in May in the cozy town of Benton, Kentucky. Located in the far western part of the state in a remote and rural area known as the Jackson Purchase, Benton, with a population of 3,899, is the seat of Marshall County and home to the venerable Big Singing Day. As you stroll along the quiet, tree-shaded street on the way to the courthouse, you glance at the bronze marker stating, "The Big Singing in Benton is the oldest musical tradition in the United States." Then you enter the red-brick courthouse and climb the stairs to the spacious main courtroom where you see generations of friends, family, and visitors milling about in animated conversation—a scene that has been reenacted every year since 1884.

At ten-thirty in the morning, with his well-worn copy of *The Southern Harmony and Musical Companion* grasped firmly in hand, Frank Nichols strides purposefully to the front of the judges' bench and calls out "Number 103, Holy Manna." Nichols is president of the Bank of Benton and a member of an extended family that has been intertwined with the singing for generations. His warmly resonant voice sings out the introductory *fa-la-so-la-fa* syllables that provide the singers with the pitch of the opening chord. Slowly gathering vocal steam, like a train rolling out of the station, the assembled singers join in, the words resounding round the old courthouse like distant thunder. "Brethren we have met to worship, and adore the Lord our God. Will you pray with all your power, while we try to preach the word." It is "Big Singing Day" again in Benton, Kentucky, and compliant with the 113-year tradition, the "fasola folk" have met to sing the shape-note hymns whose roots stretch back to the earliest days of the American colonies.

KENTUCKY SACRED HARP CONVENTION IN WOODFORD COUNTY

The day dawns bright and beautiful this Saturday in May at the Academy Building of Pisgah Presbyterian Church in the rolling countryside of Woodford County, Kentucky. Located in the central Bluegrass region, Pisgah Church, built in 1784, is the home of the Kentucky State Sacred Harp Convention, hosted by the Appalachian Association of Sacred Harp Singers. As you drive up the country lane to the church you pass the oak-shaded old graveyard where Revolutionary War soldiers, farmers, and former governors alike now rest. Carrying your copy of the *Sacred Harp* and a covered dish for the noontime "dinner on the grounds," you enter the old stone academy building and see friends and visitors milling about in animated conversation—a scene that has been reenacted every Saturday before the second Sunday in May since 1980.

At nine o'clock, with his well-worn copy of the *Sacred Harp* grasped firmly in hand, the author strode to the middle of the hollow square, welcomed the fifty singers gathered in the resonant meeting hall, and called out "Number 58, Pisgah, in honor of this lovely church where we are meeting today." After pitching the song with the traditional *fa-so-la*, the singers join in with the syllables indicated by the triangle, square, circle, and diamond shapes of the notes. Like the loud rush of a Kentucky mountain stream, the heartfelt words of the hymn gain force and tumble throughout the old hall, "Jesus, thou art the sinner's friend, As such I look to thee." The Kentucky Sacred Harp Convention is meeting again at Pisgah Church.

COLONIAL AMERICAN ROOTS

Musical culture in the New England colonies was heavily influenced by Protestant Calvinist theology, which considered the 150 Biblical psalms of David the only proper music for worship. These psalms were intended to be sung simply, in unison with every voice on the same melody, and without instrumental accompaniment so that the words were clearly understood. Because of the general illiteracy and scarcity of books in eighteenth-century America, however, colonists adopted a performance technique called *lining out*, in which communities sang in a call-and-response manner. The leader, or deacon, would call out a line of the text, for example, "When I can read my title clear to mansions in the skies," and the congregation would then slowly echo the line by singing it as a group. Even though the congregation was supposedly singing a single unaccompanied version of the melody, individuals personally ornamented and varied the melody in a musical texture known as *heterophony.* After years of such alteration, the psalm tempos became incredibly slow and melodies were transformed by quantities of added notes. Consequently, psalms took ten times as long to sing as they had formerly and the original tunes were distorted beyond recognition. Thomas Walter, a contemporary writer, described the process as follows: "For much time is taken up in shaking out these turns and quavers, and besides, no two men in the congregation quaver alike, or together; which sounds in the ears of a good judge, like five hundred different tunes roared out at the same time" (Walter 1721, 4–5).

Harvard-educated clerics who were greatly upset by the style of this singing called it "a horrid medley of confused and disorderly noises" and "the uncouth noise of untuned ears." Writers such as Thomas Symmes called for an end of lined out singing and a return to "regular" singing through a return to reading music notation. As a result, in 1721 Boston witnessed the first *singing school* devoted to teaching members of a community how to read music and sing in harmony. Popular as both an educational and recreational experience, singing schools soon spread throughout New England. By the end of the century, singing schools had traveled down through Pennsylvania and west along the Shenandoah Valley into the western frontiers of Virginia and Kentucky.

SINGING SCHOOLS

Singing schools were taught by a traveling *singing-school master* who settled in a community for a period of two or three weeks. Singing masters seldom had any formal musical training; instead, they generally apprenticed through participation in singing schools themselves—all that was required was a keen ear, a strong voice, and a burning desire to travel in order to spread this music. In compensation for his instruction, the teacher would customarily be provided with meals and lodging and given a small fee for each student. Amzi Chapin (1768–1835), a singing-school master working in Kentucky, had the following agreement: "We the subscribers do promise to pay unto Amzi Chapin nine shillings for each person whom we subscribe to instruct them in the Art of Music. Twenty six days. Payment to be made at the expiration of the term."

Meeting in the evening, after the day's chores were completed, the singing master would begin by instructing the class in the rudiments of music theory, teaching the students how to read rhythms and how to follow steps of the scale by reading the pitches on the music staff. After the class gained enough proficiency in the rudiments, he would then lead them in singing parts to some of the less complex hymns. First, the class would learn the air, or melody, which was in the tenor voice, and once they had mastered that, they would begin reading the other parts—treble (soprano), counter (alto), and bass. As the students gained confidence in their ability to read music at sight, they proceeded to learn more challenging music until the final *singing lecture*, a graduation ceremony in which they presented a public concert to demonstrate their achievements. The purpose was pedagogical, the atmosphere was morally uplifting, but it is clear from this Yale student's journal entry of 1782 that the singing school also provided a much-needed social outlet: "At present I have no inclination for anything, for I am almost sick of the world and were it not for the hopes of going to the singing meeting tonight and indulging myself a little in the carnal delights of the flesh, such as kissing and squeezing etc., I should willingly leave it now" (Lowens 1964, 282).

SINGING SCHOOLS

The early lined out psalm singing style required only a book with the words of the psalms printed for use by the song leader. Because the congregation merely echoed the leader's line of text and followed the well-known melodies by ear in lined out style, a single copy of a book was all that was really needed for performance. Singing schools, however, required a book for every participant since each singer was sight reading the words and music for their individual harmony lines.

John Tufts (1689–1750) printed the first book suitable for use with the singing schools. His *A Very Plain and Easy Introduction to the Singing of Psalm Tunes* (ca. 1714) was a short, twelve-page volume containing thirty-seven tunes written for treble, tenor, and bass voice parts. As the book's purpose was to teach illiterate colonists to read music, Tufts sought an innovative system that would be more clear and easy to read than conventional European notation. He placed letters of a *solfege* system on a five-line staff rather than the usual "round notes." Thus, he used the letter *F* for the pitch *fa*, the letter *S* for *so*, *L* for *la*, and M for *mi*. Today, we commonly use seven syllables—*do*, *re*, *mi*, *fa*, *so*, *la*, *ti*, *do*—to teach students how to read music, but Tufts employed an earlier English system that only used the four syllables *fa*, *so*, *la*, and *mi* to indicate the pitches of the scale and show the distance, or *interval*, between one note and the next.

The rhythms were also represented by a simple, yet innovative, system. The letter alone was worth a quarter note (F), a letter with a period following it was a half note (F.), and a letter followed by a colon was a whole note (F:). The inventive notational solutions of Tufts were typical of the American process of cultural adaptation in which we retained aspects of "old world" British culture and transformed them to suit our new situation. Psalmody may still have been "music in America" rather than "American music," but the rise of the singing school soon led to the first distinctive musical expression of the American colonies.

NEW ENGLAND AND THE MID-ATLANTIC STATES

Tufts's book opened the floodgates to a whole generation of New England and Mid-Atlantic singing masters who composed their own original music as well as collected and arranged earlier music in their publications. In addition to the psalm tunes inherited from Britain, such Yankee singing masters as William Billings added new *plain tunes*, vigorous *fuging tunes*, and extended *anthems* that explored the expressive relationship between words and music. Plain tunes were short "chorale style" works in which all the voices moved *homophonically* (rhythmically together) to complement metrical strophic texts of repeated verses. Fuging tunes began with a section in which all the voices sang rhythmically together in four-part harmony followed by an imitative section in which the voices chased each other as in a "round." Anthems were more extended compositions with changes of tempo, different rhythms, and key changes that painted the meaning of the words through musical expression. This was a new American music suited to the temperament and needs of a new American people.

This new singing-school music clearly reflected the important question that was at the heart of America's experiment in participatory democracy: how was this country going to reconcile the tension between individual freedom and the constraints of social order? Each vocal line was fiercely independent in following its own path. William Hauser, author of *The Hesperian Harp*, stated that each part should be "so good a melody that it will charm even when sung by itself" (Hauser 1848, xviii).

Tenors, trebles, counters (altos), and basses all possessed their own melodic direction that coexisted with the other independent parts in a loose confederation of harmony. The bass was not content merely to plod subserviently below the soprano melody and the counter refused to be relegated to the supportive role of doubling harmony notes. Each part had its own distinct melody that contributed a unique perspective to the total sound. Democracy can sometimes be a messy process, and occasionally the independent vocal parts clashed discordantly or tripped over themselves as they crossed paths with another part, but they always did so within a framework of collective order.

SHAPED NOTES

Despite the efforts of John Tufts to develop a clearer system of music notation, musicians continued to use the conventional round notes for all singing-school tune books through the eighteenth century. In 1798, however, William Little and William Smith of Philadelphia invented an entirely different way of indicating pitches, using various shapes to represent notes. Taking the four-syllable fasola system used earlier by Tufts as the basis, Little and Smith substituted differently shaped note heads for the letters as a visual aid in reading music. Thus, a triangle was used for *fa*, an oval for *so*, a square for *la*, and a diamond for *mi*.

Unlike the common *do-re-mi* system where each of the seven pitches of the scale corresponds to a different syllable, this shape-note fasola system has to repeat three of the syllables and their corresponding shapes twice within a scale; thus the entire scale would be sung *fa, so, la, fa, so, la, mi, fa*. This is not really confusing, however, since the note shapes are placed on a five-line staff and it is easy to distinguish the pitches by their relative height on the lines and spaces of the staff. It is also important to remember that the shapes only indicate the relative placement in a scale and the interval between tones. The shapes do not represent fixed pitches as do notes on a piano. For instance, fa is the root and fourth of any major scale—in the key of C major, the fa corresponds to the notes C and F, while in the key of D major fa corresponds to the notes D and G. Rhythms were indicated the same way as with round notes, with hollow or shaded note heads and stems and beams.

The combination of fasola syllables and the shape-note notation proved to be highly successful. Between the printing of Little and Smith's *The Easy Instructor* in 1798 and the publication of *The Social Harp* in 1855, there were at least thirty-eight different tune books in circulation that all used the four shapes. Singing masters compiled and printed books for use in their own schools that typically included an assortment of the most popular hymns excerpted from other books as well as original compositions and arrangements of vernacular melodies that were matched with sacred texts and adapted for hymn use. In this way, the collective compiling work of various singing masters increased the singing school repertoire beyond the original British psalm tunes through the inclusion of original American compositions and adaptations. Like a living organism, shape-note repertoire evolved in response to the changing tastes of musical America. Now as singing-school masters followed the growing tide of migration to the southern and western frontiers, another rich layer of new shape-note hymnody, known as white spirituals, would further enrich the repertoire.

WHITE SPIRITUALS

During the first decades of the nineteenth century, musical life in New England was altered by the rise of public school music education, an emphasis on European "classical" music, and the immigration of trained professional European musicians. Singing schools and their folksy, homegrown music became an endangered species in the urban centers of New York, Boston, and Philadelphia. Such reformist musicians as Lowell Mason, who condescendingly called shape notes "dunce notes," established more formalized organizations—the Boston Handel and Haydn Society, for example—and forced the singing schools to retreat to rural areas of New England and down through Pennsylvania into the wilderness areas of Virginia, North Carolina, and Kentucky.

Kentuckians were especially receptive to singing schools. The first school was recorded in Lexington in 1797, and shortly thereafter subsequent singings spread throughout the Bluegrass region and into the mountains to the east and the Purchase area of the west. Southern singing-school masters also began compiling and publishing their own tunebooks. Incorporating the contributions of Lucius and Amzi Chapin, who were living in Fleming County, Kentucky, John Wyeth published the *Repository of Sacred Music* in 1810. Six years later Ananais Davisson, who lived in the Shenandoah Valley, printed his *Kentucky Harmony*, and the following year Samuel Metcalf of Shelbyville, Kentucky, issued the *Kentucky Harmonist* in Lexington.

These first southern books were important because they popularized a whole new type of shape-note hymn based on indigenous music. Called *white spirituals* by scholar George Pullen Jackson, the new hymns married sacred texts of such authors as Isaac Watts, John Newton (author of *Amazing Grace*), and Charles Wesley with melodies drawn from secular ballads, fiddle tunes, and lyric songs. For example, the hymn "Sawyer's Exit," found in the *Sacred Harp*, couples the words "Flow bright is the day when the Christian receives the sweet message to come" with the bouncy Irish jig melody called "Rosin the Beau (Bow)." White spirituals blurred that fine line between sacred and secular since the same tune sung at Saturday night's frolic might be heard at Sunday morning's worship as well.

The tunes are pungently striking, with melodies often based on five-note *pentatonic* or *modal scales*, that impart a high, lonesome sound reminiscent of the sound of Scottish bagpipes. Often composed for only three voice parts, by eliminating the counter line, they have a distinctively "hollow" quality that sounds more "ancient" than the rounded chordal sound characteristic of classical harmonic practice. White spirituals were enthusiastically embraced by the fasola folk because the words contained vivid and colorful imagery, the tunes were exciting, and the melodies were already familiar to many southerners through square dances or back-porch singings.

CAMP MEETINGS

At the turn of the nineteenth century, a religious fervor known as the Great Revival, or the Second Great Awakening, swept through the country. In 1801 approximately twenty thousand people flocked to Cane Ridge Meeting House in Bourbon County, Kentucky. Twenty thousand people drawn by wagon and mule and on foot along dirt roads, praying, loudly singing, barking like dogs, dancing wildly, weeping, and jerking uncontrollably in the throes of religious ecstasy arrived for this revival, perhaps making it the Woodstock of its day. Presbyterian, Methodist, and Baptist ministers gathered and preached fire and salvation to the crowds from wagon beds and tree stumps. The excitement kindled by this first huge camp meeting spread throughout the South and carried with it a new type of gospel hymnody that was added to the constantly expanding repertoire of shape-note music.

Singing was an important means of exciting the passions of the crowds at a camp meeting. The rhythmic propulsion and melodic surge of repeated refrains had the effect of simultaneously reinforcing key ideas as well as introducing an out-of-body trance experience. Since people could not read words or music notation from books at a camp meeting, songs that were easily learned had to be chosen so that people could immediately participate. Therefore, camp meeting gospel music had limited vocal ranges, catchy tunes, infectious dancelike rhythms, short verses, and choruses that could be repeated forever. Often the same verse could be repeated over and over simply by changing a few words. For instance, "Hebrew Children," found in *The Sacred Harp*, has a repeating line, "Where are the Hebrew children," that may be changed to "Where are the twelve apostles" or "Where are the holy Christians," to stretch out the song for numerous verses.

THE SOUTHERN HARMONY AND *THE SACRED HARP*

Approaching the middle of the nineteenth century, when Southern fasola singing was at the zenith of its popularity, two shape-note tune books, *The Southern Harmony* and *The Sacred Harp*, appeared. Although similar in appearance and contents, they were destined for very different fates. *The Southern Harmony* would become frozen in time, preserved for the most part in a single traditional annual performance, Big Singing Day at Benton, Kentucky, while *The Sacred Harp* would become a living history told through various revisions and editions performed in hundreds of contemporary singings held throughout the United States to this very day.

SOUTHERN HARMONY ORIGINS

The two books had curiously intertwined origins. William "Singin' Billy" Walker and Benjamin Franklin White, both of Spartanburg, South Carolina, were brothers-in-law through their marriage to the Golightly sisters. The two men compiled *The Southern Harmony* together, but in 1835 Walker evidently took the book to New Haven, Connecticut, to get it printed and somehow failed to credit White with his share of the authorship. The story may merely be fiction, but to this day the legend is still the source of good-natured bantering back and forth between adherents of the different books as though the schism between Walker and White were just a recent family unpleasantry.

Walker was much in demand as a singing-school teacher and his *Southern Harmony* was the most popular tune book of the nineteenth century, selling approximately six hundred thousand copies, with a revision in 1847 and a final revision in 1854. Unfortunately, the book's further development was disrupted by the Civil War and Walker's subsequent decision to publish a new book, *The Christian Harmony*, in the seven-shape solfege system that was supplanting the four-shape notation. The life of a singing is tied to the life of a book. With the final *Southern Harmony* published in 1854, the book would have become extinct were it not for a single community event sparked by the enthusiasm of James R. Lemon, editor and owner of the Benton *Tribune*.

As a child, Lemon traveled from North Carolina with his family over the Blue Ridge and Cumberland Mountains to Marshall County, Kentucky, in 1852. Packed away in the family's covered wagon was a copy of the *Southern Harmony*, perhaps acquired directly from a singing school led by William Walker himself. Lemon began teaching in singing schools as a young man and maintained a lifelong devotion to fasola music. Observing that the music of his youth was rapidly disappearing, Lemon used the public forum of his paper to propose a general gathering in Benton that would be devoted to singing from *The Southern Harmony*. Following that first Big Singing Day in 1884, the countywide family reunion, coupled with the *Southern Harmony* singing, has become a local tradition tenaciously maintained in the face of many cultural changes that have threatened its existence over the years.

One of the greatest challenges to the survival of the tradition was the scarcity of books. By the 1930s there were scarcely thirty of the precious and tattered 1854 editions still available. Many people were singing from memory. In 1931 George Pullen Jackson noted: "The *Southern Harmony* singings at Benton are probably the last of their kind anywhere and dissolution stares them in the face. The only thing that can lengthen their life is a new supply of the song books with which the tradition is inseparably bound up. Will some worshipper at the shrine of 'old-time songs' provide that supply?" (Jackson [1933] 1965, 67–68).

Fortunately, that "worshipper" appeared close at hand. The book that is the lifeblood of the tradition was reissued in 1939 by the Young Men's Progress Club, and subsequently local singer Dr. Glenn Wilcox published his Pro Music Americana edition in 1966. The book is still in print today through a 1987 facsimile edited by Wilcox and published by the University Press of Kentucky.

SACRED HARP ORIGINS

B. F. White moved to Georgia and collaborated with Elisha J. King to publish his own tune book, *The Sacred Harp*, in 1844. White's book shared many of the same tunes as Walker's with the usual representation of New England composers, such as William Billings and Daniel Read, and white spirituals by Davisson and the Chapins. In addition, nearly a quarter of the tunes in the book were written by, or at least attributed to, Georgia singers including White, King, and White's nephew J. T. White. The success of a book depended on the compiler's ability to choose the best and most popular hymns for inclusion. Obviously White chose well, for *The Sacred Harp* has enjoyed a 150-year publishing history marked by the appearance of various revisions and many printings. The popular 1991 edition is currently in its third printing of three thousand copies.

Popular in its time but nearly extinct today, *The Southern Harmony* would come to represent fasola as it was in mid-eighteenth-century South, while *The Sacred Harp*, with its continuous history of growth and change, would evolve to reflect the state of fasola singing at the end of the twentieth century. Folks at Benton talk of the "purity" of their singing and complain about *Sacred Harp* innovations, such as "those ragtimey rhythms" and "that added counter part," but it is exactly that element of change that doomed *The Southern Harmony* to museum status and contributed to *The Sacred Harp*'s role in the rise of shape-note revivalism.

For that reason, a comparison of Big Singing Day and the Kentucky Sacred Harp Convention represents a comprehensive portrait of community traditionalism and revivalism characteristic of shape-note singing in American culture. Let us briefly define *tradition* as culture that is "bred in the bone," passed on through oral transmission within an identifiable community. *Revivalism* consists of participation in a tradition by people who are not born into the traditional community yet who consciously choose to participate in that community.

BIG SINGING DAY

The day dawns bright and beautiful this fourth Sunday in May as you enter the red-brick courthouse and climb the stairs to the spacious wood-paneled courtroom. At about ten o'clock folks dressed in their Sunday finery begin to gather. Soon, excited knots of people form, catching up on all the news and stories since they were last together. Patriarchal figures, such as Dr. Ray Mofield and Dr. Glenn Wilcox, are busy with last-minute organizational details, making introductions and drawing up a list of the morning's song leaders. Mrs. Tula Nichols and Miss Margaret Heath, resplendent in their "go-to-meeting" hats, are engaged in conversation with a young graduate student who is making her first visit to Benton. Young children dart between legs of parents, a sound engineer from Texas is adjusting microphones, luncheon plans are discussed, area politicians shake hands with potential voters, recipes are traded, golf games recounted, and family and visitors alike are drawn into the social fabric woven at that first singing gathering of 1884.

It is a tight social fabric, woven from a narrowly circumscribed geographic region and limited social context. The community is defined by a common evangelical Protestant heritage—chiefly Primitive Baptist, Church of Christ, and Baptist. The singing itself is a secular event and is not associated with any church, although there is a strongly moral foundation since all the song texts are scriptural, and invocation and benediction prayers frame the day.

Members of the singing represent a homogenous ethnic stock that is almost exclusively Anglo-Celtic in origin. Most of the singers are members of families that have been associated with the singing for generations, such as the Nichols family. Marshall County is essentially an agricultural economy with little industry capable of either retaining younger residents or luring new inhabitants to the area. As a result, few singers who did not grow up with the tradition are permanently integrated into the Big Singing Day community.

As is characteristic of farming communities, home and family are at the core of the values system. The concept of homeplace is itself firmly rooted in the Big Singing. Family members may be dispersed far beyond the region, but on Big Singing Day they religiously return home for the weekend, drawn by the bonds of family, community, and identity. Big Singing Day is actually more of a family reunion than a musical event. The singing would surely have died off years ago if it had not been closely intertwined with homecoming and community identity.

THE DAY CONTINUES

You walk over to the benches on the left-hand side of the judge's chair and sit with a group of men that look as though they might be basses. Shortly after ten-thirty, the singers have seated themselves in their accustomed places in the area before the bar while community members and visitors who are present merely to listen have arranged themselves in the audience area. The courtroom looks crowded with approximately fifty singers and several hundred audience members. It is hard to imagine how the building and square outside would have looked back in the 1920s and 1930s when ten thousand people regularly attended the event.

With his well-worn copy of *The Southern Harmony* grasped firmly in hand, Frank Nichols rises and an expectant quiet settles over the gathering. After a short greeting, Nichols announces "Holy Manna" (Chapter 10, Track 1), pitches the song by ear, and exclaims "by the note," directing people to sing the syllables. Beating time simply with his right arm, he cautions the singers to observe the two beats of rest at the beginning by calling out "down left." With books open on their laps and rapt expressions on their faces, the singers slowly and gravely make their way through the syllables. After the shapes have been sung through once, Nichols says "by the line," which signals the singers to sing the music with the words. Following "Holy Manna," an invocation is delivered that is always succeeded by the singing of "New Britain," more commonly known as "Amazing Grace." The hymn always concludes with the verse beginning "When we've been there ten thousand years," which are the only words sung by the Benton community that are not printed in *The Southern Harmony.*

Each year a senior and highly respected member of the singing community is charged with convening the sessions and moderating the day's activities. In recent years this role has been entrusted to university professors Ray Mofield and Glenn Wilcox, both now deceased, and Frank Nichols, who is currently president of the Society for the Preservation of Southern Harmony Singing. The decorum, tone, and organization of the entire day are set by the moderator, who is a link in the unbroken lineage stretching back all the way to Walker himself.

The rest of the morning is structured according to a simple, recurring pattern. Each singer who is willing to lead comes forward and chooses two of his favorite tunes. Calling out the number and title of the song, and perhaps prefacing it with a few comments—such as "Raymond Lay always loved this song. He was a fine gentleman and a wonderful singer"—the leader pitches the song and sets the tempo with simple conducting gestures. In between songs, there may be a little conversation among singers commenting on the tempo or sharing an anecdote from past years, but the orderly process of singing proceeds almost like clockwork until noon.

After all the experienced community members have had an opportunity to lead, younger singers and visitors are encouraged to come forward and participate. In this way, novices have the opportunity of first observing the model of veteran singers before participating themselves. The singers are supportive of these unfamiliar leaders, but if one chooses a fast tempo, beats with an unclear pattern, or chooses a difficult and unfamiliar number, the singing can quickly disintegrate and even cease altogether. If this happens, the singers feel perfectly comfortable with starting again by altering the pitch or gently correcting the tempo. The day is viewed as a singing school and not a polished performance. They are singing with one another, not performing for the public, and the courtroom audience is merely an extension of the singers themselves.

By tradition, only men are permitted to lead. This has caused quite a bit of controversy in recent years, but tradition is a strongly conservative force, and the weight of 113 years of custom have defined the role of men and women at Big Singing Day. Women are certainly treated as equals in all other respects, in fact, they hold many of the elected positions within the Society for the Preservation of Southern Harmony Singing, but they never lead the singing itself. Leadership within the community is based on singing ability, knowledge, experience, and family relationships without respect to gender, but the leadership role on Big Singing Day is reserved for the men of the community.

THE AFTERNOON SESSION

At noon the singers quickly disperse and head for various homes, where dinner is served. At one time, Courthouse Square was the scene of a huge "dinner on the grounds," with family picnics sprawling out in all directions. In recent years, most families gather at home to eat, although several picnics are customarily held upstairs in the court building itself. Since it is Sunday, most of the restaurants in town are closed, so guests are cheerfully welcomed into various families for the "potluck" meals. The hospitality of Mrs. Tula Nichols is legendary, and after a dinner of the wonderful vinegary barbecued mutton accompanied by an array of vegetable casseroles and a host of home-baked desserts washed down by gallons of iced tea, it seems scarcely possible that people will be able to sing again that afternoon.

By one-thirty people have returned to the courthouse. Frank Nichols rises and opens the session again with "Holy Manna." Following a welcoming address that notes the history of the singing, eulogizes prominent singers who have passed away during the year, and acknowledges visitors, the singing commences. The afternoon session is more formal than the morning, with a printed program listing the probable song choices for likely leaders. There are 341 songs in the book, but singers usually choose from a core repertory of thirty-seven tunes that are most familiar to the community—songs with evocative titles like "Happy Land," "Thorny Desert," and "Sweet Rivers." In the same way that "Holy Manna" has become identified with the entire Big Singing Day, certain hymns become strongly associated with certain leaders or families who may have led the song for years. It is considered a mild breach of etiquette for a song leader to knowingly "trespass" on another person's song. Songs are not repeated, although the same song may be chosen at both the morning and afternoon sessions.

The tempos are characteristically slow and deliberate, as though the participants are lingering with a cherished friend whom they will not see again for at least another year. The balance features strong tenor and bass sections with fewer penetrating treble voices than might be found at a Sacred Harp singing. Singing style is full and natural, complemented by the pitching, which is low, often as much as a third below the note indicated on the music. The overall sound is haunting, powerful, and unhurried.

The afternoon passes in much the same way as the morning session, with each leader rising to lead two songs. As you glance down at your watch, you realize that you have been lulled into a timeless moment that has all too quickly passed.

At three-thirty Frank Nichols calls for the final song in the book, "The Christian's Farewell," which traditionally closes the singing. There is a final benediction, and then you find yourself wandering through the crowd, saying good-bye to new friends and promising to return again next year. Another Big Singing Day has passed into history, but the gathering has again served to bind the community together with the shared song of an unbroken lineage stretching back into the past and forward into an uncertain future.

Urbanization, mobility, and the rise of media technology separated most of a generation from participation in singing schools. Only the most rural and isolated areas of the Deep South retained their Sacred Harp singings and passed them on to the next generation. Ironically, the same media and technology that threatened the existence of fasola singing also reintroduced the revivalist generation to Sacred Harp music through recordings, radio, and television exposure. The same mobility that drew families from their homeplace roots also facilitated travel to singings. The same urbanization that fragmented communities throughout migration has provided a favorable climate for singings in large cities of the Northeast and Midwest. The very same cultural changes that severed a generation from traditional fasola singing have also served to reconnect that generation to the Sacred Harp community.

THE SINGING BEGINS

Seated in your chair in the treble section, you observe the moderator striding into the middle of the square to convene the morning session of singing at the old Presbyterian Church. After some brief opening remarks welcoming folks and familiarizing singers with local customs, he cradles his *Sacred Harp* in the crook of his left arm and calls for number 103, "Pisgah." Sounding pitches of the opening chord, the leader starts the singing by beating time with a simple up-and-down motion of his right arm. Tentative at first with the syllables, the music gains in confidence and volume by the time the singers begin the words. Soon the old meeting hall is ringing with the loud, rushing sounds of *The Sacred Harp.*

PERFORMANCE STYLE

The style of performance is very different from that of the Benton gathering. Songs are taken at brisk tempos—not as fast as the deep southern Georgia and Alabama singings, but in many cases, twice the speed of Big Singing Day. The tempo emphasizes the surge of the rhythm and, noticeably, many people are tapping their feet or beating time with their hand in unison with the leader. While pitch is different according to each leader (there are no tuning forks or pitch pipes), pitches tend to be higher than those at Benton in order to emphasize the tension between the tenor and treble parts. The intonation is not absolute and is shaded toward modal inflections in which the pitch notated in the music is not the pitch that is actually sung (for example, note the raised sixth that is sung instead of the D6 that is notated in the melody line of "Wondrous Love").

Voices tend to be wide open, without vibrato, somewhat nasal, and strained at the top register. The sheer volume of the sound is striking. If the Big Singing can be characterized as a nostalgic reminiscence, then the Kentucky Convention is an exultant shout. There is little dynamic contrast except for a few places where the singers customarily grow quiet, as in the second emotional utterance of "Oh my son" in "David's Lamentation." The musical force of *The Sacred* Harp is manifest in the words and in the rhythmic drive of the melody lines—there is little desire for the expressive subtleties found in art music.

The morning unfolds in a pattern similar to Big Singing Day. The leadership rotates, with each person, in turn, guiding the singers through two songs. However, unlike Benton, the women and men are both encouraged to lead. The relationship between gender and power is not really an issue at the singing. Women and men share the leadership as well as kitchen duties equally, and while the two moderators for the convention have both been male in recent years, the elected song leader of the Appalachian Association of Sacred Harp Singers is currently female. Female and male leaders are judged according to the same criteria—their ability to lead a song by pitching it correctly, to set an appropriate tempo, and to lead the singers through difficult passages and problematic repeats through the strength of one's voice and personality. (Listen to Chapter 10, Track 2, "Promised Land.")

Before the noon recess for dinner there is a Memorial Lesson, at which time deceased members of the singing community are remembered with brief comments and a song dedicated to their memory. One especially emotional Memorial Lesson at a Kentucky Convention involved the observance of a longtime female member who had been brutally murdered. The song given in her memory was "Stockwood," whose words have been permanently etched in this community's memory of the young woman.

Sister, thou wast mild and lovely,
Gentle as the summer breeze,
Pleasant as the air of evening,
When it flows among the trees.

Peaceful be thy silent slumber,
Peaceful in the grave so low;
Thou no more wilt join our number,
Thou no more our songs shall know.

AFTERNOON

At noon "Old 100" is sung as a blessing, and the session adjourns for dinner on the grounds. Sacred Harp singing provides an excuse for cooks to parade their favorite recipes, and soon plates are piled high with home-baked bread, sweet potato casserole, spring garden salads, countless variations on fried chicken and corn bread, and a host of home-baked pies and fresh strawberry shortcake. Nothing forges a community more tightly than shared song, conversation, and a good meal.

At one o'clock the afternoon session is convened and the singing continues in the same vein as the morning. Approximately forty hymns, fuging tunes, and anthems are attempted before the afternoon draws to an end with "Parting Friends," the song the Appalachian Association traditionally uses to conclude its singings: "Farewell my friends, I'm bound for Canaan, I'm trav'ling through the wilderness / Your company has been delightful."

It has been a long day. Empty casserole dish and *Sacred Harp* in hand, you climb in your car and head back down Pisgah Pike. Fragments of songs, bits of stories, a haunting melody, a new face, and the taste of fresh strawberries are all woven together in a memory quilt that accompanies you down the highway home.

FINAL THOUGHTS

Big Singing Day and the Kentucky Sacred Harp Convention are tenuous survivals of the past that have lingered into the end of the twentieth century. The original function and context of singing schools has been permanently altered by contemporary culture, but the infusion of revivalist energy flowing into the steady stream of tradition has invested this uniquely American heritage with meaning and vigor. In a fragmented modern society, family has been preserved and community established through shared song.

Singers in Benton are born into shape-note singing early in life through a traditional family background. Singers may chose to become involved in Sacred Harp singing later in life, through a revivalist introduction. Either way, at some point the singer must make a conscious choice to identify herself or himself with the tradition, and in so doing, they become yet another voice in the unbroken lineage of fasola singing stretching back to the American colonies.

Chapter 10: Musical Examples (access through companion website)

Chapter 10, Track 1: The Southern Harmony, led by Ray Mofield,, "Holy Manna."
Chapter 10, Track 2: The Sacred Harp, led by Ron Pen, "Promised Land."

References Cited and Additional Sources

Bealle, John. 1997. *Public Worship, Private Faith: Sacred Harp and American Folksong*. Athens: University of Georgia Press.

Clawson, Laura. 2011. *I Belong to This Band, Hallelujah!: Community, Spirituality, and Tradition Among Sacred Harp Singers*. Chicago: University of Chicago Press.

Cobb, Buell E., Jr. 1978. *The Sacred Harp: A Tradition and Its Music*. Athens: University of Georgia Press. Paperback, 1989.

Hauser, William. 1848. *The Hesperian Harp*. Philadelphia.

Jackson, George Pullen. 1933. *White Spirituals in the Southern Uplands*. Chapel Hill: University of North Carolina Press. Reprint, New York: Dover Publications, 1965.

Loftis, Deborah Carlton. 1987. *Big Singing Day in Benton, Kentucky: Study of the History, Ethnic Identity, and Musical Styles of the Southern Harmony Singers*. PhD diss., University of Kentucky.

Lowens, Irwin. 1964. *Music and Musicians in Early America*. New York: W. W. Norton.

Miller, Kiri. 2007. *Traveling Home: Sacred Harp Singing and American Pluralism*. Urbana: University of Illinois Press.

Steele, David Warren, and Richard Hulan. 2010. *Makers of the Sacred Harp*. Urbana: University of Illinois Press.

Walker, William. 1987. *The Southern Harmony and Musical Companion*. Facsimile of the 1854 edition. With an introduction by Glenn C. Wilcox. Lexington: University Press of Kentucky.

Walter, Thomas. 1721. *The Grounds and Rules of Musick Explained: Or an Introduction to the Arts of Singing by Note*. Boston: J. Franklin for Samuel Gerrish.

White, Benjamin Franklin, and Elisha J. King. 1991. *The Sacred* Harp. Ed. Hugh McGraw et al. Bremen, GA: Sacred Harp Publishing Company. Original edition.

Videography

Awake My Soul: The Story of the Sacred Harp. 2006. By Matt Hinton, Erica Hinton, John Plunkett. Atlanta: Awake Productions.

Audiography

White Spirituals from the Sacred Harp: The Alabama Sacred Harp Convention. 1992. New World 80205-2. CD remastered from original 1959 recording made by Alan Lomax at Fyffe, Alabama.

Companion CD to *The Southern Harmony*. 1987. CD-9354. In *The Southern Harmony*, published by the University Press of Kentucky. This recording presents live performances from Big Singing Day between 1966 and 1992.

Holy Manna. LP recorded by Society for the Preservation of Southern Harmony Singing. Available from Benson Blackie, 1615 Dunn Cemetery Road, Benton, KY 42025.

The Social Harp: Early American Shape-Note Songs. 1977. Rounder CD 0094. Performed by singers from Georgia and Alabama, led by Hugh McGraw.

The Colored Sacred Harp. 1993. Rounder CD 80433-2. Performed by the Wiregrass Singers of Ozark, Alabama. Led by Dewey Williams, this is a recording of the African American Sacred Harp tradition.

Sounding Joy. 1990. CD available from Ted Mercer, 1807 West North Ave., Chicago, IL 60622. This recording of the United Sacred Harp Musical Association is representative of current Sacred Harp singing style and features northern and southern singers.

- 11 -

THE MEMPHIS AFRICAN AMERICAN SACRED QUARTET COMMUNITY

Kip Lornell

Kip Lornell, an American vernacular music historian with strong ties to cultural geography, folklore, and ethnomusicology, works on music-related projects for the Smithsonian Institution and teaches at George Washington University. Based on fieldwork accomplished over a three-year period in Memphis, Tennessee, this chapter focuses on a tradition that had been previously underexplored by African American music scholars. Lornell examines the importance of families in maintaining musical continuity and the role of quartet trainers (who are viewed as very particular musical specialists) in shaping the sound of quartets. The importance of transmitting religious values and religiosity in general is another theme explored in this chapter. The contexts for quartet performances: churches, community halls, and contests and the relationship (and tension) between this religious expression and popular music provides a backdrop to the entire article. Finally, Lornell discusses the reasons for the decline in popular interest in quartets and why some of the groups have persisted in singing in this style.

PROLOGUE

The genesis of this study may be traced back to 1979, when I moved to Memphis to become one of the first students in the newly founded doctoral program in Southern Regional Music and Ethnomusicology at the University of Memphis. With my interest in fieldwork-oriented projects and African American music, I soon decided that it would make sense to choose a local subject for research and, ultimately, as a dissertation topic. I knew Memphis as the focal point for early country-blues activity, rockabilly in the middle 1950s, and the "Stax Sound" of soul in the 1960s (Gordon 1995). Two major, black gospel composers the Reverend William Herbert Brewster and Lucie Campbell lived in Memphis and contributed many important compositions to the canon beginning in the 1920s and continuing through the 1950s (Reagon 1992). Such nationally known jazz musicians as pianists Phineas Newborn and James Williams, in addition to the saxophonist

11.1. This local quartet sang throughout the Mid-South in the early 1950s.

George Coleman, were born and trained in Memphis. Important blues artists like B.B. King and Howlin' Wolf made Memphis or West Memphis, Arkansas, their home in the late 1940s and early 1950s.

I was familiar with the work that had been done on vernacular music in Memphis and felt compelled to conduct research in some area that had been overlooked. My previous work on blues and other related forms of music by African Americans had been expanded by a recent one-year stint in Tidewater Virginia, which has a long and complicated history of sacred quartet singing among its black residents. I had undertaken the modest project of interviewing older quartet singers in Tidewater, and I wondered if this music was, or had been, widely performed in Memphis too. After less than two months of preliminary research, including a quick survey of local black newspapers and some brief conversations with singers, it became evident that the topic of sacred quartets in Memphis was ripe with promise.

The fact is that very little of the history and development of this community of singers had been collected, analyzed, and written about. The singers themselves, or members of their families, held the key to understanding the history of quartet singing in Memphis in the twentieth century. My dissertation and subsequent publications based on this research are largely built on the oral histories and interviews undertaken between 1979 and 1983 (Lornell 1995). In addition to speaking with members of the quartet community, which included not only singers but also radio personalities, record executives, and concert promoters, I attended many rehearsals and some programs in churches.

This essay focuses on not only sacred quartet singing in Memphis but also two of its specific aspects. The introduction presents the historical background of quartet singing; the first part of the essay, "A Family of Singers," looks at the diverse nature and relationships among members of the quartet community; the concluding section, "Training Quartets," will explain how the quartets themselves are formed and directed as well as the types of venues in which these vocal harmony groups performed.

HISTORICAL BACKGROUND

African American sacred quartet singing is a pan-southern tradition that can be traced back to the Reconstruction era that followed the end of the Civil War. This musical phenomenon is most closely tied to the newly founded colleges, such as Fisk and Hampton, that sponsored "jubilee" groups as well as to traveling minstrel shows and community-based groups that emerged near the dawn of the twentieth century. Community-based quartets, in particular, proved to be so popular that they helped spread this style of singing among the black population in general. In reminiscing about his Florida childhood during the 1890s, the noted African American writer James Weldon Johnson wrote:

> Pick up four colored boys or young men anywhere and the chances are ninety out of a hundred that you will have a quartet. Let one of them sing the melody and others will naturally find parts. Indeed, it may be said that all male Negro youth of the United States is divided into quartets. When I was fifteen and my brother was thirteen we were singing in a quartet which competed with other quartets. In the days when such a thing as a white barber was unknown in the South, every barbershop had its quartet and the young men spent their leisure time "harmonizing."[1]

Such groups as the one described by Johnson were predominately male. They featured four voices, which included a bass singer, two tenors, and one alto. The lead singer was chosen according to the song's arrangement; "Roll, Jordan, Roll," an antebellum spiritual that could still be heard in the 1990s, almost always features a tenor singer. The first musical example for this chapter (Chapter 11, Track 1) is an a cappella (without instrumental accompaniment) version of this song from the Harmonizers, a Memphis group. "Wade in the Water," on the other hand, is usually performed with the bass singer fronting the group. These pioneering quartets almost always sang a cappella and utilized a repertoire that relied heavily upon traditional songs, especially spirituals.

At the beginning of the twentieth century the interest in quartet singing continued to grow, and the music was often incorporated into the everyday lives of many working-class, blue-collar black Americans. This trend continued with great vigor well into the 1920s as sugar refinery workers, railroad pullmen, and family members formed quartets that sang in local Baptist or Methodist churches, for neighborhood gatherings, and at other social functions. Barbershops, as James Weldon Johnson intimated, often served as a center for male blacks' social life in general and for quartet singing in particular (Abbott 1992).

These trends were directly related to the increasingly urban character of the South's black population. Many African Americans were leaving their agrarian roots behind and moving to cities in search of economic advancement. Following the end of World War I, the Hampton Roads section of Virginia, and Jefferson County (especially Birmingham), Alabama, emerged as the best-known centers for gospel quartet singing. Significantly, these were two areas with large numbers of blue-collar jobs that were becoming increasingly available to blacks. In Hampton Roads, the ship-building industry was booming, while the burgeoning coal and iron industry attracted nearly one hundred thousand blacks to greater Birmingham between 1890 and 1920. The singing from these two centers was disseminated not only by the quartets that began to tour for performances, but especially through commercial phonograph records by such groups as the Birmingham Jubilee Singers, the Norfolk Jubilee Quartet, the Silver Leaf Quartette of Norfolk, and the Bessemer [Alabama] Melody Boys (Seroff 1980).

Since the 1920s at least, Memphis has been home to a thriving gospel quartet community. In nearly all respects, the development of sacred quartets in Memphis mirrored the trends in other parts of the United States. The earliest documentation of sacred quartet singing comes not from a school or a community-based group but from an ensemble that, along with the Orval Brothers (Construction Company) and the S. and W. (Construction Company), was affiliated through work. The I.C. [Illinois Central Rail Road] Glee Club Quartet was organized around 1927 and lasted for approximately ten years. Haywood Gaines, a retired Illinois Central employee who performed with the second I.C. Quartet in the early 1930s, quite literally sang with the quartet on the trains as they moved passengers from Memphis to points north and south. Performances by quartets helped attract passengers back to the railroads, which had lost business because of the growing automobile trade and the Depression:

> Folks thought little of the railroad at that time [the passenger service] and to get them to come and ride with us, we had booster clubs and singers. The booster club was . . . an organization that gave different parties or entertainment. They would entertain and invite the general public. When we got them there, we would impress upon them the necessity to use the railroad as transportation. We sang, held dances . . . had five or six hundred people! That brought business back to the railroads.[2]

The overwhelming majority of Memphis quartets, however, were affiliated with neighborhood groups or with specific churches. North Memphis and South Memphis have long been bastions for black residents of the city. The Harmony Four was perhaps the premier sacred quartet from the southern part of Memphis during the 1930s; in the northern section both the Royal Harmony Four and the Old Rose Quartet sang frequently at local churches. Church groups were equally important, as, for example, the Lake Grove [Baptist] Specials and the Middle

Baptist Quartet, who performed during the Depression and afterward, into World War II. In the days prior to full-time professional quartet singing, which began around 1938, the members of these and other groups worked at full-time extra-musical jobs. These groups generally rehearsed one evening each week and sang publicly in church at least once on Sunday.

Without a doubt the best-known group to emerge from the city during the early years of quartet singing was the Spirit of Memphis Quartette. (This old-fashioned spelling of the word quartet was often used by groups in the late 1920s and into the 1930s.) The roots of the Spirit of Memphis are in the T.M. and S. Quartet, a name derived from the initials of the three churches Tree of Life, Mount Olive, and St. Matthew's Baptist attended by its founders about 1927. The revamped name came about two years later in honor of Charles Lindbergh's 1927 flight across the Atlantic in the *Spirit of St. Louis*. According to founding member James Darling:

> When the group was named . . . it was named after the initials of the churches and when we decided to organized into a quartet we had to bring in some names. The night we had to bring in some names, I hadn't thought up a name until we almost got to [the house at] Looney and Second Street. I had a pocket handkerchief, had the "Spirit of St. Louis" in the corner. That's where the name really originated.[3]

The Spirit of Memphis eventually became the city's first fully professional quartet. After nearly two decades of singing in Memphis and the Mid-South, the group followed the rapidly growing trend toward full-time professional status that began some ten years earlier. In fact, the Spirit of Memphis routinely booked, through a co-sponsorship arrangement, the Famous Blue Jay Singers of Birmingham, Alabama, and the Soul Stirrers, who originated in Houston, Texas. Because the quartet attracted such large audiences and were not a part of the Sunday worship service, their programs were held in one of the large churches or in the downtown City Auditorium. The onset of World War II all but stopped this movement because of wartime restrictions on rubber (tires) and gasoline limited travel for all citizens of the United States, but after the war, opportunities for performance soared. Spurred by the ability to travel once again and by the evolution of independent record companies willing to take a chance on both the better-known and the obscure groups, many quartets began to hit the road in an attempt to cash in on the widespread interest in four-part vocal harmony singing.

In 1949 the Spirit of Memphis contained all of the ingredients to make the daring leap from a highly respected, semiprofessional quartet to full-time status. It had added two important out-of-town members (lead singers Silas Steele and Wilmer Broadnax, best known as "Little Ax") who had sung with such well-known groups as the Famous Blue Jay Singers. The Spirit of Memphis also benefited from its first commercial record release, "I'm Happy in the Service of the Lord"/"My Life Is in His Hands," on Hallelujah Spiritual, a small Birmingham,

Alabama-based label. The record had only regional impact, but it led to a contract with the far-larger independent King Records, which was based in Cincinnati and specialized in hillbilly, rhythm and blues, and gospel music. These elements allowed the group to book enough programs to quit their day jobs and become full-time quartet singers. The success of the Spirit of Memphis helped inspire two other local groups, the Southern Wonders and the Sunset Travelers, to take the same leap.

Around 1950, black sacred quartet singing was at its height of popularity not only in Memphis and the mid-South but across the entire country. The number of quartets performing on all levels—community-based, semi-professional, and fully professional—was at an all-time high. Professional groups as diverse as the extremely popular "jubilee" ensemble the Golden Gate Quartet and the Dixie Hummingbirds (a "hard" gospel quartet featuring the dramatic lead singing of Ira Tucker) enjoyed great success as recording artists and radio performers as well as through live programs. The elite status of these, perhaps sixty, professional groups was augmented by hundreds of semiprofessional quartets and thousands of community-based groups that formed the backbone of the black vocal sacred-quartet tradition (Abbott 1983).

The music had evolved into two related styles with relatively fluid boundaries. The "hard" quartet style uses alternating lead vocalists, whose arsenals include falsetto, wordless moans, and extended sections of improvised singing drawn from the well of the African American musical vocabulary. This style is perhaps best characterized by the dramatic singing of Claude Jeter of the Swan Silvertones, the Dixie Hummingbird's Ira Tucker, and Silas Steele of the Spirit of Memphis Quartet. The jubilee style, on the other hand, featured an even more syncopated style, with a prominent bass part, a cante-fable (half spoken half sung) lead vocalist, and texts often taken from the New Testament of the Bible. The Golden Gate Quartet is the archetype jubilee quartet, and from the late 1930s through the early 1950s they became the model for other groups, particularly in the Southeast and Middle Atlantic states, who wished to explore this style (Grendysa 1976).

While the professional quartets that toured both locally and nationally may have gained the greatest attention, it was the community-based groups that continued to provide most black Memphians with the music they heard each week. The community quartets in Memphis, to some degree, followed the lead of their professional counterparts; identical uniforms often replaced the neatly tailored suits of an earlier era, and by 1950 most groups had added at least a guitar to a genre that began a cappella. In addition to the traditional stockpile of songs, local Memphis groups were sometimes able to introduce the new compositions of Lucie Campbell and Reverend Herbert W. Brewster who, as mentioned earlier, published many gospel songs between the early 1920s and the early 1960s (Reagon 1992). Among local quartets, Reverend Brewster's compositions, in particular "Old Landmark" (1948) and "Surely, God is Able" (1950), are longtime favorites. Lucie Campbell's most popular and widely performed composition was undoubtedly

"The King's Highway" (1923), which continued to be performed by quartets and other religious ensembles in the 1990s.

Local community-based quartets for example, the Campbellaires (named after Lucie Campbell), the Friendly Brothers Quartet (fronted by John and Robert Maddrie), the True Friends Gospel Singers, and such female groups as the Golden Stars and the Harps of Melody performed regularly in local churches during the 1940s and into the 1950s. They existed as an outlet for Memphis singers who had talent and commitment as well as a desire to sing for other black Christians who attended the same mainstream Protestant, primarily Baptist and Methodist, churches. These quartets served the community well and could be counted on to provide sacred vocal harmony singing whenever it was called for.

While quartets sometimes sang during the Sunday worship services, they also performed at special song programs that were typically held early Saturday evening or late Sunday afternoon. Such programs, which proliferated in the early 1950s, offered not only quartet enthusiasts but everyday churchgoers an opportunity to hear the music they loved. It also provided black Christians with another occasion to worship the Lord in song.

The popular interest in quartet singing began to fade in the middle 1950s. Some of the more conservative church members felt that the music and culture was become too secular. Harry Winfield, a Memphis keyboard player who was active in the 1950s, suggested that the quartet singing . . .

> was traveling more towards rock and roll music. They were changing their style and they were dancing on stage. They were now, more or less, giving performances. They were now walking on benches and getting sort of ridiculous. Quartet singers were now processing their hair and riding in Cadillacs, doing very much of the things that the gospel people attributed to the world, you know, drinking. We see you now on stage, can't hardly stand up . . . Church people [soon] felt that they were being deceived. Lots of things happened that started people totally against what was happening in the gospel field, as far as quartets was concerned.[4]

This sea change in the popularity of quartets was by no means restricted to Memphis. Even such popular groups as the Pilgrim Jubilees and Soul Stirrers fell upon financial hard times. Among Memphis groups, the Spirit of Memphis were on the road full-time into the late 1950s, several years longer than the Sunset Travelers or the Southern Wonders remained fully professional quartets. Local semiprofessional groups, such as the Jubilee Hummingbirds, the Dixie Wonders, and the Southern Jubilees, began to emphasize their lead singer(s) and perform even more contemporary gospel songs to the accompaniment of a full rhythm section. In spite of new trends, older community-based groups have continued to perform, with ever-changing personnel, for several decades. In the early 1980s, the roots of at least three community groups, the Royal Harmony Four, the Gospel

Writers, and Harps of Melody, extended back to the 1940s and continued to represent the quartet tradition in its oldest form.

A FAMILY OF SINGERS

Since its inception in the 1920s, the community of African American gospel quartet singers in Memphis has evolved into a highly complex social unit analogous to the so-called extended family, a family related through birth, marriage, geographical proximity, religious affiliation, social values, and economic status. The group encompasses not only the singers themselves but disc jockeys, preachers, record-company officials, and fans. The singers themselves, the organizers of local gospel quartet unions, and those who train quartets constitute the core of this unique community, and it is the interaction among these groups that will be described in the rest of this essay.

In the course of my fieldwork among the Memphis gospel quartet singers, the term "family of singers" took on literal meaning. Of the forty-five singers interviewed for this study, 60 percent were married to others who had been affiliated with quartets. Cleo and Louis Satterfield, for instance, first met in 1941 at a gospel quartet program; Louis sang with the True Friends Gospel Singers, while Cleo sang with the Union Soft Singers (in Memphis, the word "Soft" designates a quartet as female). Both in their early twenties, the singers married within two years. Another couple in the Memphis family, Elijah Jones and his first wife, Jimmie Martin, became acquainted in the late 1930s when he led the Gospel Writers and she performed with the Gospel Writer Junior Girls. Some of the most influential singing couples in Memphis, for example, Jethroe and Shirley Bledsoe, James and Elizabeth Darling, and Floyd and Florence Wiley, were involved with gospel quartets both before and after their marriages.

Patterns of kinship within the gospel quartet community are not limited only to married couples; many siblings have also been involved with singing. Willie and Rochester Neal began their careers in the late 1940s as members of the Gospel Writer Junior Boys, which was under the direction of their stepfather, Elijah Jones. The brothers have continued to sing together throughout most of their lives. During the 1950s their first group became the Dixie Nightingales, but when the group switched to secular music in the middle 1960s, they left to join the Pattersonaires, with whom they remained into the mid-1980s. Clara Anderson, founder and leader of the Harps of Melody in the late 1940s, began singing with her sister, Essie, around 1935 in the Busyline Soft Singers, then briefly with a neighborhood quartet until Essie's death in 1938.

Familial involvements in black gospel music have certainly not been limited to quartets or to Memphis (Burnim 1985; Heilbut 1985). The Staples Singers, for example, is a family group that began in Mississippi and later moved to Chicago; and one of the most popular groups from the 1980s, the Winans, are led by the sisters Bebe and Cece Winans. Nevertheless, it is in Memphis that kinship systems are most strikingly pervasive.

Despite Memphis's size, its position as a transportation hub, and its importance as a destination for migrants in the Mid-South, the quartet community in Memphis remains largely insular and thus free of outside musical influences. This may be attributed not only to the factors previously cited but also to the continued importance of families in shaping the sound of indigenous quartets. As most of the in-migration consisted of people who had moved to Memphis from nearby counties in the Mid-South in particular, from northern Mississippi, eastern Arkansas, and west Tennessee, the familiar styles of singing and the favorite songs in the repertoire of quartets tended to remain intact.

QUARTET UNIONS

Beyond the kinship systems described above, the formation of unions helped cultivate and promote quartet singing in Memphis. The National Convention of Gospel Choirs and Choruses, founded in 1932 by the famous composer, entrepreneur, and performer Reverend Thomas A. Dorsey, worked with vocal ensembles, which included some quartets, to promote gospel music across the United States (Harris 1992; Stebbins 1972). In the late 1930s the first quartet organization in Memphis, the City Quartette Union, was established by "Doctor" Frost, who was not a singer himself but simply a man who loved singing and was friends with many of the community's members. The City Quartette Union, a cooperative and nonprofit venture, helped organize and promote weekly programs in and around Memphis, with Frost himself often serving as the master of ceremonies. After Frost migrated to Detroit in 1943, he was succeeded by James Darling, one of the early members of the Spirit of Memphis Quartet, and then by another local singer, Huddie Moore, who held the job until its dissolution in 1953. Moore explains that the idea behind the City Quartette Union was "to get a lot of singers together and cooperate, and have more people participate on your program. When you had the City Quartette Union and the quartets, you had your program all you had to get [was] the church and render your program. We had the City Quartette Union [chorus] open the program and let the quartets come on later."[5]

Two other organizations, the South Memphis Singing Union and the North Memphis Singing Union, briefly augmented the work forwarded by the City Quartette Union. They existed in the early 1940s but were so short- lived and ephemeral that nothing more than their names remain. Directly after World War II, Lillian Wafford organized the United Singing Union, which quickly emerged as a significant force in organizing Memphis quartets. Although it nominally existed until the early 1980s, the United Singing Union was strong for only its first decade. With Mrs. Wafford's death in 1982, the city's last gospel quartet cooperative disbanded.

Quartet unions served several important functions: to encourage solidarity among its members, to assist groups in booking their programs, and to promote quartet singing. While the goals of the unions were concrete and their leadership stable, the organizations themselves were less stable. According to Mary Davis, cofounder of the Majestic Soft Singers in 1944, the ranks of the United Singing Union was always in flux: "The original group was the Majestic Soft Singers plus the Spiritual Pilgrims. Then came the Wells Spirituals . . . then the Morris Special Singers . . . [and] four or five years later, the Brewsteraires. Then we had the Walker Specials to join in. In other words, we had several groups to going in, but several of them didn't stay too long."[6]

During its prime in the early 1950s, the United Singing Union served a useful and important function for members of the Memphis gospel quartet community. Mrs. Wafford devised a simple formula for splitting the monetary honoraria, or "donation," between the group and the church that hosted them. (Quartet musicians prefer these more neutral-sounding terms because they suggest that their motivation for gospel singing is not tainted by the lure of money.) Basically, for programs held in Memphis, 50 percent of the money went to the group(s) and an equal amount was donated to the church. Programs held outside of Memphis or in neighboring Shelby County were split differently, with 60 percent going to the musicians and the rest helping to fill the church coffers.

This spirit of cooperation and mutual assistance that characterized these cooperatives was emblematic of a more general sense of a synergetic partnership that permeated the black American gospel quartet community in Memphis. Although singing remained the focal point for their energies, nearly all of the union members were also involved in service to the community at large. In this sense, the quartet singers were simply fulfilling their role within the family, extending their role to encompass the city's entire black population, not merely those in their own nuclear family or in their own neighborhood (Burnim 1980; Dyen 1977; Jackson 1988). The city's black religious community, the church and its many allied support services, in fact had served as the unofficial center of black social and community life long before President Johnson's presidency passed the so-called Great Society bills with its more highly codified welfare system and Aid to Dependent Children.

Cleo Satterfield spoke at length about the importance of the union within the community at large:

> Frost [founder of the City Quartette Union around 1939] was the type of person who could keep a program so alive that everybody wanted to hear him talk after the singing. He was nice about helping someone if he know they were sick or somebody in the group of the church was sick. If somebody tell him about it, he would raise an offering for them . . . they would always reach out and give a helping hand. We never had that much, but what we had, we'd give it freely.[7]

Huddie Moore echoed these sentiments and recalled that the City Quartette Union "would do a program for somebody who had gotten burned out or something like that. We would put on programs to raise money to help that family or for somebody who was in necessity."[8]

This aid included spiritual sustenance as well, particularly in the form of free programs presented in rest homes and senior citizens' centers where the word of God could be preached to a captive, and often willing, audience. Some quartets even performed in local prisons and jails, the idea being simply to spread the ministry of God in song. Etherlene Beans explains how she and her group, the Willing Four Softline Singers, worked:

> They contacted us because they found that we were just a group that liked to sing. We didn't sing for finances . . . [but because] we like to sing and we always want to share what we had with other people. We was really a spiritual group [that] like to sing and get happy and let other people get happy [reaching an ecstatic state of direct communication with God]. We would go to the workhouse and sing . . . also sing for sick people, cripple[d] children's hospitals, and to help people.[9]

The relationship between quartet singing and spirituality cannot be overstated. Since most quartet singers are devoutly religious, their intent is clear: to provide their fellow singers and their audience alike with a Protestant Christian message through words and songs. In this regard, quartet musicians and preachers share similar roles that of delivering the message of God's love and salvation. Instead of preaching a sermon, quartet singers deliver their message through song (Allen 1992; Franklin 1982; Jackson 1988). Hershall McDonald, of the Harmonizeers, told me: "We believe that we carry the gospel in a number of ways. One is the direct teaching of principles, which we carry through in our songs. In singing, our work is twofold to edify and serve as inspiration for those who are members of the body and as a source of inspiration and a way to draw those who are not members of the church."[10]

TRAINING QUARTETS

Sacred quartet trainers helped shape musical direction, agents of both continuity and change. Their role in shaping the sound of sacred quartets in Memphis was unique and their influence was profound. To the best of my knowledge, there was no parallel to quartet trainers in any other form of black American vernacular music, either sacred or secular.

At first glance, the primary role of gospel quartet trainers appeared quite simple: they teach songs. Quartet training, however, was very demanding, requires extremely specialized skills, and is critical to the preservation of the genre because it is one of the principal means by which repertoire, style, and innovation are transmitted. By preserving specific aspects of performance practices traits—most importantly, vocal timbre and the approach to rhythm and harmony—quartet trainers also provided a crucial link between one generation of musicians and another, as well as links among groups within the city.

The functions of trainers in a community were actually quite complex, and they have long been regarded by quartets as specialists. A quartet trainer is asked by groups to indoctrinate new members and to help them learn new songs or change an arrangement that needs a complete overhauling, updating, or merely tinkering. If a trainer developed an innovative arrangement that proved popular, other local groups often asked him to provide a similar service for them, tailored to their particular strengths. Trainers were sometimes called upon to locate new singers for groups, though most groups recruit members themselves. Elijah Jones, who worked with Memphis quartets for forty years beginning in the middle 1930s, served as the unofficial coordinator for local groups looking for new singers.

Although they were very busy assisting quartets in a variety of ways, trainers were usually not motivated by the prospect of financial gain. The most influential Memphis trainers, Elijah Jones and his mentor Gus Miller, sang with several local quartets but supported themselves through other means: Miller survived with the help of a veteran's pension that was given to him after he was severely wounded in World War I; Jones worked at a series of blue-collar jobs. Trainers were occasionally offered money for their services; however, this was strictly a free-will offering or an honorarium. Etherlene Beans notes that Jones "never did get money from us. Now [in the late 1970s, just before Jones's death] we give him a little transportation money, but he never made money off us. He just likes singing . . . and he was always willing to assist us in singing."[11]

This observation provides the key to understanding the motivation of quartet trainers: these talented men (nearly all of them male) not only loved harmony singing, they freely shared their special abilities with their fellow singers. George Rooks, who knew and sang with Elijah Jones off and on for nearly forty years, stated that Jones always stood at the nexus of the quartet community. Most weekends found him singing or attending a quartet program or a rehearsal. During the week he might receive a telephone call asking him to help a group locate a new tenor singer or to judge an upcoming quartet contest (see discussion below).

Recognition by one's peers as a trainer denotes a special status within this closely knit musical community. Gospel quartet trainers are thought to be blessed with unusually perceptive ears and keen minds as well as the ability to communicate their knowledge. That groups regularly come to certain individuals asking for assistance acknowledges and underscores the community's respect for talents that have been honed through years of practical application rather than formal education. Elijah Ruffin, who worked with about a dozen groups throughout a career that stretched from the early 1930s into the middle 1980s, considered his training ability a natural gift.

Males have dominated quartet training in Memphis, but it is not precisely clear why this trend was so pronounced. Except for a handful of women, such as Clara Anderson, who trained her own groups the Harps of Melody and the Golden Stars, female quartet trainers were an anomaly. The number of women who have participated in quartet singing in Memphis is less than the number of men. None of the female groups became fully professional, and only the Songbirds of the South reached semiprofessional status. The rest of the female quartets were either community-based or affiliated with a local church. From the 1920s through the 1950s, women were expected to assume the responsibility for child rearing and other obligations that tended to keep them close to home, and this may be the reason why fewer women than men participated in quartet singing.

The fundamental process of training quartets appeared straightforward: the trainer merely sang each part to the singers in turn and then they blended the parts in four-part harmony. This meant though, that the trainer must take upon himself the difficult task of learning and remembering all four parts. Jack Miller of the Royal Harmony Four, who trained a dozen or so groups during a career that spanned nearly five decades, offered these general tips:

> The first thing is the voice. Check the voice out; see if it is fitted for a tenor, baritone, lead, or bass. . . . You have four voices to get the pitch of the song, to teach it. Then you work on the time of the songs, how long you should go with it. Some people are quick to catch on, some are not. If they got the talent to catch on and the voice, then you can train them in a couple of months.[12]

Although the basic process sounds simple, it demands an unusual knowledge as well as specialized skills. First, the trainer must be able to sing each of the four voices. Many trainers, in fact, fulfill the role of "utility" singer in their own quartet, as does a utility player in baseball, who fills in as a shortstop, left fielder, or catcher with equal skill. The trainer also intuitively conceives harmonies, rhythms, and tempos, a process that is refined and then adjusted as the parts are taught to the group. Finally, because they do not use musical notation, trainers work entirely through oral means, relying entirely upon tonal memory and sheer repetition. Training a quartet requires not only an immense amount of skill but also a willingness to invest a great deal of time, concentration, and energy.

The most renowned and influential trainer in Memphis, Elijah Jones, worked with countless groups during his career. Etherlene Beans describes how Jones helped the Willing Four Soft Singers during the late 1940s:

> He would train you how to control your voice, how to keep your voice with the next singer, not to get too loud for the next singer, not to get too loud for your music [instruments], not to get your music too loud for you . . . He always teach you to sing words distinctly, and . . . you cannot really sing a

song unless you know it. He helped us a whole lot; it was just remarkable what he could do with singers.[13]

Memphis trainers are also notable for giving suggestions about vocal and tonal qualities or techniques. For instance, a trainer might advise that the featured singer affect a more raspy timbre or sing in falsetto. The trainer might also make the arrangement of a song distinctive by altering the tempo during the chorus or by having the background sung more staccato. Working with a new song or rearranging a well-known quartet piece could take several evenings of work, or at least several hours of exhausting work.

The role of quartet trainers has diminished since the 1960s; people who might have trained quartets probably now work with choirs or choruses. Many of the first generation of trainers retired, moved from the area, or died. With the diminishing interest in quartet singing, fewer people stepped forward to take their places and fewer groups sought the help of a trainer. The era when quartet trainers flourished corresponded with the height of interest in quartets. By the 1990s, the art of quartet training had all but been lost in Memphis.

Performance

Live performances, usually called programs, provided the most common forum for the public to hear and see these singers. On Sundays and nearly every Saturday since the 1920s, Memphis gospel quartets have appeared in churches and auditoriums throughout the city. Although all quartets have some direct affiliation with churches, either as church-related groups or simply as members of a church, they have not always appeared as part of the worship service itself. More often, it is congregational singing, choirs, or choruses, rather than quartets, that present the musical offering during the regularly scheduled church service.

In Memphis, quartets usually performed on special musical programs that are held during the afternoons or evenings and feature more than one ensemble. Quartet programs were similar to the Sunday morning worship service, the difference being the programs' emphasis on music and the lack of a sermon. These programs were promoted within the black church community by way of placards, posters, notices in the church bulletins or newsletters, announcements from the pulpit, over the radio, during other programs, and by word of mouth (Cantor 1992).

Programs have almost always been held at local churches in the predominately black sections of Memphis, such as Orange Mound, North Memphis, or Whitehaven. Occasionally programs are held in private homes, usually by groups just beginning to sing together, though this was more common in the past. Huddie Moore describes the early appearances of the Spiritual Four in the late 1930s: "When you first getting started, you be a little shy about going out and facing public. We would rehearse and set up programs at different one's houses. Just say you gonna have a program, we invite other groups and set up chairs and sing in the house. We would get ready to get out on the stage at the church. We used to have a nice time at a house program."14

All quartet programs featured at least one local group, but it was not uncommon to have one or more quartets from outside of the city, especially for a program held in a larger venue, such as a community hall. Programs featuring non-Memphis quartets fell into two categories. The first comprised nonprofessional, community-based groups much like nearly all of the quartets from Memphis. These ensembles were nearly always from the Mid-South or more northern towns and cities, such as St. Louis, Chicago, or Milwaukee, to which Memphians had migrated. These quartets frequently "trade" appearances back and forth, especially when groups celebrated their founding through an anniversary program that might last up to ten hours. The other category encompassed performances by well-known professional groups that were held in larger venues such as the City Auditorium or Mason Temple. In years past, the Soul Stirrers, Pilgrim Jubilees, or Golden Gates drew thousands of people; in the 1980s and 1990s the Mighty Clouds of Joy or the Jackson Southernaires attracted hundreds of listeners to one of the large churches in the city. By 2015, however, quartet programs in Memphis were a thing of the past.

Performance events by groups in either category were not radically different, and all ceremonies by quartet singers had religious praise as their primary goal. Such events were complex and are structured according to a clearly established format with three essential "players": the MC (master of ceremonies), the quartets, and the audience. The programs usually opened with a well-known song that is led by the emcee, a minister, or a quartet member and performed by everyone in the audience. This helps establish a feeling of fellowship among the participants. A prayer offered by one of the ministers then followed (Allen 1992).

The job of the MC was to move the program along so that each group has a chance to sing. This person was also responsible for making certain that the quartets appear in the announced order and providing proper introductions. The MC (who is often, but not always, male) also filled in the time between groups while the equipment is being changed and the quartets are getting set up with announcements about future programs, family-oriented jokes, recognitions for people attending the program, and general observations about life. He makes it as friendly and down-home as possible, partly in deference to previous role models but mostly because the MC knew most of the other participants quite well. MCs, especially for anniversary programs or ones featuring major out-of-town groups, were specialists—usually disk jockeys who hosted one of the local gospel musical radio programs, or someone who had some other type of media connection. For strictly local programs, one of the group members or a clergyman may serve in this capacity.

Song Battles

In Memphis two related types of programs, known locally as quartet contests and song battles, emerged as early as the middle 1930s and continued for twenty years. Such contests, which simply pitted one group against another, have also been reported in Birmingham, Alabama, and the Hampton Roads section of Virginia. These programs, featuring local ensembles, were held in local churches and billed themselves as "quartet contests" in order to build interest in a specific program. The format called for each group to perform from four to six selections, whereby the quartet giving the finest performance was declared the winner. Judges for these contests, who were chosen from the ranks of veteran and respected singers not participating in this program, evaluated the finer points of singing and then determined the winners by assigning points to each group. Although the criteria were inherently subjective, they usually included rhythmic precision, enunciation of words, inventiveness, accuracy of harmony, and the ability of the singers. Elijah Jones, who served the quartet community as a trainer, singer, and judge, talked about his experiences in the 1930s:

> I always liked judging 'cause so many folks didn't know singing. You got three judges that know singing, then you got fairly seeded [rated]. They would look for time, music, don't miss no minors or sharps. The one that makes the most points, that's the one that wins. During that particular time, we didn't have but four voices: leader, tenor, baritone, and bass, and we would listen to each voice.[15]

Money was, he added, the impetus for local churches to hold a quartet contest. The winning group received a modest share of the donations, collected at the door, but perhaps more importantly, the quartet members' performing ability was acknowledged by their peers. To be the champion of a local contest meant both prestige and greater respect, which is one of the reasons why along with fund raising the contest gained in popularity into the 1940s. During the late 1940s, quartet singing became even more popular, more groups turned professional, and a shift occurred in the format and style of these competitions: they became known as "song battles" and were frequently staged in large auditoriums.

In Memphis most of the major songs battles took place in the Mason Temple or in the City Auditorium. These performance events were a manifestation of popular culture and a local evolution of the earlier contests. The audience's applause, rather than a small number of specialists, decided the winner of the song battle. Elijah Jones observed that "we started having audiences judging in the fifties. Then you just get out there hoopin' and hollerin' and if they like that, then you be the man."[16] Jones's dislike for the event reflected a clear movement from a program overseen by the quartet community itself to one dominated by popular trends and opinion. Julius Readers, who was most active as a semiprofessional quartet singer during the 1950s, told me:

> It sort of worked like the group that get the most shouts of the most applause you know what the favorite group was. You didn't need judges then because if you were tough, when you hit the floor you knowed who had it then, because two to one if you were a favorite in town, when they call your name, everybody go wild! Then you get up there, their hands clap, and you know who was the winner![17]

Quartet programs tend to start slowly and build in intensity, similar to the momentum gained as the spirit moves those in the church during the delivery of a chanted sermon or a Pentecostal service. Much of the success of this kind of musical performance depends upon the interaction between the quartet and the audience. By the 1950s, almost all Memphis quartets, and certainly each of the more highly regarded out-of-town ensembles, stressed their stage presentation along with a well-choreographed and well-planned performance. Seemingly small things, such as a singer's gesture toward the audience or a particularly well-chosen spoken commentary, perhaps about a topical event such as a tragic plane crash or the unexpected death of a community member, could help ignite a performance. The possibilities brought on by this type of interaction is vividly recalled by Tommie Todd, who sang with the Gospel Writers in the decade following the close of World War II:

> When we would go and render our programs, a lot of times we'd get converts. A lot of times people would join the church on our singing. That's the reason I liked it, because there was something in it I could feel, that other people could feel. So many people would come to hear us because we would give them something that was a help to them. We would have our prayer service just like a revival, then we'd go from there. When we got into our singing, people would be shouting. One time they got shouting so bad until a lady got hold of the wrong end of my tie and pulled and choked me! When we got singing like that they'd be shouting and throwing pocketbooks and like that.[18]

Before such black popular singers as Little Richard or James Brown gained the limelight in the middle to late 1950s, professional quartet singers like Silas Steele and "Jet" Bledsoe of the Spirit of Memphis Quartet were highly respected for their ability to "work" an audience. Their performances combined a dramatic stage presence and singing calculated to motivate and engage the crowd (Allen 1992; Burnim 1988). It became acceptable for singers to crawl along the floor or walk on the floor, behavior that strongly contrasted with the more sedate programs held in the 1920s or 1930s, before full-time professional groups began touring the United States.

The frantic and colorful nature of post–World War II professional quartets sometimes bothered older quartet singers, such as Leon Moody, who began singing in the late 1930s and had a different sensibility regarding the performance of sacred music:

> Every song we sung, we tried to tell a message. We figured that in every song we sung, if we couldn't give them something to think about, that song wasn't worth singing. But some people just get up and go for a lot of "Hallelujah!" Most generally they go for guitars and a whole lot of noise. They do a lot of performing, a lot of show. I think if it is supposed to be a religious program, it should be a service.[19]

It would be easy, however, to simply dismiss certain on-stage mannerisms as mere stylized antics. Professionalism undeniably changed the character of black gospel quartet performances, but the singers still draw some of their inspiration and role models from older traditions. Unquestionably, some of these characteristics dramatic body gestures, emotional vocal styles, and flamboyant behavior may be partially attributed to the Pentecostal movement, in which holy dancing and speaking in tongues is part of worship. Memphis has been home to the Church of God in Christ, one of the largest black American Pentecostal churches since the early 1900s (Burnim 1989). The ecstatic speech heard in ring shouts, which remained part of a few of the West African–inspired religious services of the coastal islands of Georgia and South Carolina well into the late twentieth century, provide another probable role model for Pentecostals.

Despite the controversies regarding performance practices and song battles in the 1950s, even the most conservative members of the quartet community agreed that singing comes from the spirit and helps promote religious feeling. These spiritual impulses were, in fact, at the core of the community of quartet singers from Memphis. Gospel quartet singing, after all, helped express religious convictions and is one of the many ways that Christians communicated their message of salvation through a belief in God. Etherlene Beans of the Willing Four Softline Singers spoke for many of the community members when she told me: "we like to sing and we always want to share what we had with other people. I like to sing quartet singing because I am a Christian person and I believe in feeling spiritually. I sing until I feel good and feel like I've helped somebody. I want to try and save a soul through my singing [and go where] the spirit is needed."[20]

POSTSCRIPT

In some significant ways very little has changed in the world of gospel quartet research since the writing of this chapter in 1996 (and updating it in 2014), which in itself is based on research and fieldwork accomplished in the late 1970s and early 1980s. Scholars still overlook and underplay the importance and impact of African American gospel music, in general, and quartets, in particular, much to my frustration. But the scene is not entirely barren. Robert Darden wrote a well-researched, easily accessible overview of black gospel music, *People Get Ready*, which was proceeded, five years earlier, by Horace Boyers's *The Golden Age of Gospel Music*. Both books covered similar territory and both men give quartets their due.

At least one book, *Cleveland's Gospel Music*, by Frederick Burton is sharply focused on the local quartet scene and is based on Burton's decades-long career as a quartet singer. The same year, 2003, Oxford University Press published Jerry Zoltan's study of a very important group, the Dixie Hummingbirds. Perhaps most importantly, 2013 saw the publication of Lynn Abbott and Doug Seroff's important historical study, *To Do This, You Must Know How*, about the development of a pedagogy for teaching the black gospel quartet tradition that emerged in the 1870s and flowered in the 1920s.

Since the publication of my book about black gospel quartets in Memphis, virtually all of the research has been published to accompany sound recordings. And some very important collections have been issued since 1997. The most comprehensive set was issued in 2012 the UK by JSP Records in the form of a four compact-disk set, *Memphis Marvels: Memphis Gospel 1927-1960*, which includes a somewhat flawed set of notes by Opal Louis Nations and several dozen great sides by local quartets. In 1999 Zu Zazz reissued some of the gospel quartet sides recorded by small labels in the 1960s and 1970s on a disc provocatively entitled *The Assassination: A Stunning Collection of A Cappella Gospel Music from Memphis*. In between these two collection came *Happy in the Service of the Lord*, a nice compilation of sides by the Spirit of Memphis that includes all of their King records. My own recordings of Memphis quartets from the early 1980s were reissued on two compact discs that once again used the title *Happy in the Service of the Lord: Memphis Gospel Heritage—The 1980s, Vol. 1 and Vol. 2* in 2000.

In retrospect, I came to Memphis and my quartet research at a propitious time. I contacted and interviewed singers such as Elijah Jones, Clara Anderson, and Elijah Ruffin who had direct links back to the pre–WWII period when the local scene was more eclectic and less under the sway of groups like the Soul Stirrers. Within several years of my leaving Memphis in 1983, many of the important singers had died, making this particular project all the more timely.

As I write this in the summer of 2014, I am struck by how few scholars have undertaken fieldwork projects focused on Memphis or the Mid-South. Aside from Theodore Edward Fuller's important dissertation, "The Blackwood Brothers:

A Southern Family and the Commercialization of Southern Gospel Music" (University of Memphis, 2005), one could further examine the thriving southern gospel scene or the local impact of the Church of God in Christ, the huge Pentecostal sect based in the Bluff City. But most scholars default to examining better-known secular entities, such as Stax Records or Elvis Presley. Despite the interest in popular music in Memphis and the various writings about Sun Records, I am still awaiting the definitive book about the local rockabilly scene or a critical assessment of Jim Dickinson's role in shaping the sound of Memphis music, particularly from the late 1960s until his death in 2009. The fact remains that there are so many topics and so little time.

Notes

Much of this essay first appeared as parts of three chapters in *"Happy in the Service of the Lord": African American Sacred Vocal Harmony Quartets in Memphis*, 2nd ed. Copyright 1995 by the University of Tennessee Press. Used with permission.

1. James Weldon Johnson, "The Origins of the 'Barber Chord,'" *The Mentor* (February 1929): 53.

2. Haywood Gaines, interviewed by Kip Lornell, June 24, 1982. Unless indicated otherwise, all interviews were conducted by the author in Memphis, Tennessee. Transcript copies and tapes are on deposit at the Mississippi Valley Collection, Brister Library, University of Memphis.

3. James Darling, telephone interview by Kip Lornell, July 21, 1982.

4. Harry Winfield, interviewed by Kip Lornell, July 14, 1982.

5. Huddie Moore, interviewed by Kip Lornell, February 2, 1982.

6. Mary Davis, interviewed by Kip Lornell, May 10, 1982.

7. Cleo Satterfield, interviewed by Kip Lornell, June 7, 1982.

8. Huddie Moore interview.

9. Etherlene Beans, interviewed by Kip Lornell, July 3, 1982.

10. Herschall McDonald, interviewed by Kip Lornell, February 22, 1982.

11. Etherlene Beans interview.

12. Jack Miller, interviewed by Kip Lornell, February 1980.

13. Etherlene Beans interview.

14. Huddie Moore interview.

15. Elijah Jones, interviewed by Kip Lornell, October 1979.

16. Ibid.

17. Julius Readers, interviewed by Kip Lornell, May 28, 1982.

18. Tommie Todd, interviewed by Kip Lornell, August 11, 1982.

19. Leon Moody, interviewed by Kip Lornell, February 8, 1981.

20. Etherlene Beans interview.

Chapter 11: Musical Examples (access through companion website)

Track 1: The Harmonizers, "Roll, Jordan, Roll."
Track 2: Spirit of Memphis, "I Saw John."

References Cited

Abbott, Lynn. 1983. *The Sproco Singers: A New Orleans Quartet Family Tree*. New Orleans: National Park Service.

———. 1992. "'Play That Barbershop Chord': A Case for the African American Origin of Barbershop Harmony." *American Music* 10 (Fall): 289–326.

Allen, Ray. 1992. *Singing in the Spirit: African-American Sacred Quartets in New York City*. Philadelphia: University of Pennsylvania Press.

Boyer, Horace, and Lloyd Yearwood (Photographer). 2000. *The Golden Age of Gospel*. Champaign: University of Illinois Press.

Burnim, Mellonee. 1980. "The Black Gospel Music Tradition: A Symbol of Ethnicity." PhD diss., Indiana University.

———. 1985. "Cultural Bearer and Tradition Bearer: An Ethnomusicologist's Research on Gospel Music." *Ethnomusicology* (Fall): 432–37.

———. 1988. "Functional Dimensions of Gospel Music Performance." *Western Journal of Black Studies* 12: 112–21.

———. 1989. "The Performance of Gospel Music as Transformation." *Councilium: International Review of Theology* 2: 52–61.

Burton, Frederick. 2003. *Cleveland's Gospel Music*. Mount Pleasant, SC: Arcadia.

Cantor, Louis. 1992. *Wheelin' on Beale*. New York: Pharos.

Robert Darden. 2005. *People Get Ready: A New History of Black Gospel Music*. New York: Continuum.

Dyen, Doris. 1977. "The Role of Black Shape-Note Music in the Musical Culture of Black Communities in Southeast Alabama." PhD diss., University of Illinois.

Franklin, Marion Joseph. 1982. "The Relationship of Black Preaching to Black Gospel Music." PhD diss., Drew University.

Gordon, Robert. 1995. *It Came from Memphis*. New York: Faber and Faber.

Grendysa, Pete. 1976. "The Golden Gate Quartet." *Record Exchanger* 5: 5–9.

Harris, Michael. 1992. *The Rise of Gospel Blues: The Music of Thomas Andrew Dorsey in the Urban Church*. New York: Oxford University Press.

Heilbut, Tony. 1997. *The Gospel Sound: Good News and Bad Times, 25th Anniversary Edition*. Milwaukee: Hal Leonard Reference Books.

Jackson, Joyce. 1988. "The Performing Black Sacred Quartet: An Expression of Cultural Values and Aesthetics." PhD diss., Indiana University.

Lornell, Kip. 1995. *"Happy in the Service of the Lord": African American Sacred Vocal Harmony Quartets in Memphis*. 2nd ed. Knoxville: University of Tennessee Press.

Reagon, Bernice Johnson, ed. 1992. *We'll Understand It Better By and By: Pioneering African American Gospel Composers*. Washington: Smithsonian Institution Press.

Seroff, Doug. 1980. Brochure notes, *Birmingham Quartet Anthology*. Clanka Lanka Records CL 144.
Seroff, Doug, and Lynn Abbott. 2009. *Out of Sight: The Rise of American Popular Music, 1889–1895*. Jackson: University Press of Mississippi.
———. 2013. *To Do This, You Must Know How: Music Pedagogy in the Black Gospel Quartet Tradition*. Jackson: University Press of Mississippi.
Stebbins, Robert. 1972. "A Theory of the Jazz Community." In *American Music: From Storyville to Woodstock*, ed. Charles Nanry. New Brunswick, NJ: Transactional Books.
Young, Alan. *The Pilgrim Jubilees*. 2001. Jackson: University Press of Mississippi.
Zoltan, Jerry. 2003. *Great God A'Mighty! The Dixie Hummingbirds: Celebrating the Rise of Soul Gospel Music*. New York: Oxford University Press.

Additional Sources

Selected Audiography

Broadnax, Willmer. *So Many Years*. Gospel Jubilee RF-1403.
Spirit of Memphis Quartet. *When Mother's Gone*. Gospel Jubilee 1404.
Spirit of Memphis Quartet. *Traveling On with the Spirit of Memphis*. High Water LP 1005.
Spirit of Memphis Quartet. *"Happy in the Service of the Lord."* Acrobat.
Various Artists. *Bless My Bones: Memphis Gospel Radio: The Fifties*. Rounder 6032.
Various Artists. *Happy in the Service of the Lord: Memphis Gospel Quartet Heritage in the 1980s*. High Water LP 1002.
Various Artists. *Happy in the Service of the Lord: Memphis Gospel Heritage: The 1980s, Vol. 1 and Vol. 2*. High Water/HMG6516/7.
Various Artists. *Memphis Marvels: Memphis Gospel 1927-1960*. JSP.
Various Artists. *The Assassination: A Stunning Collection of A Cappella Gospel Music from Memphis*. Zu Zazz ZCD 2019.

Selected Videography

A Singing Stream: A Black Family Chronicle. www.folkstreams.net/pub/FilmPage.php?title=2.
The Living Legends of Gospel, Vol. 1: The Quartets. Good Times Video 05-81872.
The Living Legends of Gospel, Vol. 2: The Quartets. Good Times Video 05-81884.
Soul of the Church. Infinity Video IEG2187.

- 12 -

"PAN IS WE TING"

West Indian Steelbands in Brooklyn[1]

Gage Averill

Gage Averill paints an exciting picture of the music, dance, food, and language of Caribbean New York. His chapter concentrates on the musicians of steelbands in Brooklyn as they practice and prepare for performances in competitions at the annual Labor Day Carnival parade, as well as on the instruments and the music they play. Looking back to colonial Trinidad, Averill traces the development of the steel drum, or pan, and the creation of a repertoire and context for its use in performance. Like many American musics, the establishment of West Indian steelbands in this country began with a handful of innovative individuals who possessed the expertise to construct and tune the various pans that are used in an ensemble and who served as energetic ambassadors for the music and the instrument. Today, for youth of Caribbean heritage in Brooklyn, most of whom are American-born, steelbands are rich institutions of art, culture, and mutual aid that demand rigorous rehearsal and musicianship from their players. Averill's interviews with members and directors of Brooklyn-based Caribbean organizations reveal the positive role steelbands play in giving members a sense of direction, self-esteem, and Caribbean identity. Averill, a musician and ethnomusicologist who lived and taught for many years in the New York area, was deeply involved not only in fieldwork and research on West Indian steelbands but also in rehearsing in the panyards, judging at competitions, and bringing Wesleyan Pandemonium, the university-based ensemble that he directed, into the ring of competition.

> We take an empty oil drum and we tune it
> Creating an instrument of beautiful music
> Whenever I hear a pan
> Ah feel so proud of my land
> Pan is we ting [thing], doh [don't] stop jamming.
> —"PAN IN YUH PAN," DENNIS "MERCHANT" WILLIAMS, 1993

Leaving a record store that prominently advertises and loudly plays West Indian recordings (soca, calypso, reggae, dancehall) alongside Haitian *konpa*, I head over

12.1. Steel pans as they appear on a Brooklyn stage in the mid-1990s

to the travel agency on the opposite corner of Flatbush Avenue that specializes in booking discount charter flights to Trinidad's Carnival. Around the block, one can stock up on salt fish for *accra*, a kind of fried spicy fish cake, and *dasheen* bush for the popular Trinidadian stew called *callaloo*. Haitian Creole, Jamaican patois, and various inflections of Eastern-Caribbean vernacular English are the languages and dialects that rule the street and shops in this neighborhood, where men and women have gathered in small groups to *lime* (hang out and chat) in the early evening. It is still two weeks before Brooklyn's Labor Day Carnival, but banners already flutter over Flatbush Avenue proclaiming the names and locations of nearby *mas* (short for "masquerade") camps where the Carnival costumes are made. On side streets throughout the neighborhood, parking lots have been transformed into temporary *panyards*, temporary rehearsal spaces and homes for the instruments of the steelband.

Well away from New York's better-known Latin Caribbean barrios like Loisaida (the Lower East Side), Washington Heights, and the original El Barrio (Spanish Harlem), the West Indian and Haitian districts of Brooklyn—concentrated in the Flatbush, East Flatbush, Crown Heights, and Bedford-Stuyvesant neighborhoods—contain some of the highest immigrant populations of any area in the country.[2] This fact of cultural geography is partly responsible for the emergence of steel pan as one of the most important instruments in Brooklyn's multicultural music scene. "Pan" refers to the various instruments fashioned from 55-gallon oil barrels, which have the barrels cut at different heights and the bottom of the barrel pounded down and shaped into multiple note heads. The pan or steeldrum is often heard as a part of large ensembles, called steelbands, which combine other percussion instruments with an array of pans with ranges from bass to tenor. Housed in outdoor panyards where performers practice in the weeks before Carnival, they are a typical sonic feature of some Brooklyn neighborhoods during Carnival season, serving as a noisy reminder of the presence the West Indian community. In North American popular culture and in the media, the pan has become an icon of Caribbean fun in the sun—an auditory symbol used to sell fruit juices and tropical vacations. The Brooklyn steelband movement, however, reflects a deliberate strategy to maintain cultural links to the Eastern Caribbean and to promote West Indian identity in North America. Steel pan and the Carnival on Brooklyn's Eastern Parkway are part of a set of transnational practices joining cultural systems in the Caribbean diaspora to those at home in an ongoing, dynamic fashion. This chapter examines the steel drum or pan, and its ensemble, the steelband, and the role that this music plays among West Indians in New York City in constructing ethnic solidarity, transmitting values to younger generations, and serving as a locus for ongoing interaction and feedback between Brooklyn's West Indian diaspora and the island nations of the West Indies.[3]

My interest in these issues was in part a result of my decades as a pannist. Beginning in 1989 and continuing sporadically for a decade and a half, I was involved with the steelband movement in Brooklyn, documenting Carnival and speaking with organizers and participants. I paraded with both Haitian and Trinidadian bands and videotaped Carnival parades from inside the road march and as a spectator. The steelband that I directed at Wesleyan University, Wesleyan Pandemonium, competed against a number of the Brooklyn steelbands at Lincoln Center in 1991 and returned to Lincoln Center to open for Trinidad's Trintoc Invaders in 1992. I served as a judge for the 1994 Brooklyn Panorama steelband competition, an experience I wrote about in the steelband publication *Pan-Lime*, and I played mas (took part in the costumed Carnival parade) and *jouvay* (an all-night parade before the main road marches) in Trinidad in the 1990s and in 2011. Panorama is a steelband competition, featuring lengthy and demanding arrangements of that year's Carnival calypsos and soca tunes (these arrangements are called "panorama arrangements"). In the 1990s, I "beat" pan with the Silhouettes Steelband, in the Panorama competition and in Brooklyn's version of *jouvay*. Panorama and *jouvay* are events from Trinidadian Carnival that have been incorporated into Carnival in Brooklyn. My own forms of participant-observation in these events have helped reveal otherwise inaccessible elements of the musical world in question and have given me some insight into the debates and even conflicts within the West Indian community over musical issues. The experience of training in the panyards and playing in the Panorama steelband competition, and even adjudicating the competition, has involved me directly in the discourse about these events in ways that simple interviews and observation could not have, and these experiences have deepened my understanding of West Indian music in the diaspora.

WEST INDIANS IN BROOKLYN

West Indians settled in New York City throughout the twentieth century, but migration reached new levels after American immigration laws were liberalized in 1965. There are no reliable statistics on the number of legal and illegal West Indian immigrants (and their children) residing in New York City or in the borough of Brooklyn, but by extrapolating from available census data, it might be assumed that this figure is larger than half a million for the city as a whole, with perhaps half of that number residing in Brooklyn.

With so many West Indians living in a single urban area, businesses prosper by catering to an exclusively West Indian clientele, something that allows the community to resist rapid and wholesale acculturation. American race relations also play a role in the resistance to acculturative pressures. While West Indian Americans like Marcus Garvey or even Roy Innis were long involved in the struggle of black peoples in North America and promoted black solidarity, they were also motivated to differentiate themselves from African Americans (a group that West Indians see as structurally disadvantaged in America) at the level of ethnicity in order to pursue the American dream as Caribbean Americans. Black West Indians have had little reason to lose their accents or the other markers of cultural distinctiveness that confer on them a more generous reception by white America than they would have as "unmarked" African Americans.[5]

The first West Indian Carnival balls in New York were held in the 1920s in Harlem. When an outdoor parade was organized in 1947, the organizers chose to parade on Labor Day rather than before Lent to take advantage of the warm summer weather. Calypsonian "Lord Invader" (Rupert Grant) penned a 1950s calypso called "Labor Day" on the theme of this Carnival:

> Labor Day I felt happy
> Because I played Carnival in New York City . . .
> From 110th to 142nd, we had bands of every description . . .
> This is the first time New York ever had
> Carnival on the streets like Trinidad (Grant 1956)[5]

This parade on Seventh Avenue in Harlem was held annually until 1964, when the event encountered opposition from African American neighbors radicalized by the civil rights struggle and wary of the happy, festive image that the parade projected. The Carnival idea persisted, however, and in 1969 organizers (later called the West Indian American Day Carnival Association, or WIADCA) obtained a permit to parade on Eastern Parkway in the heart of the new West Indian neighborhood of Brooklyn, an event now known as the West Indian American Day and Parade (but commonly called Brooklyn Carnival).[6]

Pan pioneer Ellie Mannette[7] was invited to the United States in 1967 at the behest of Murray Narell, the father of the well-known pan soloist Andy Narell, to build and tune pans for inner-city youth groups in New York City, and within five years he had started over ten bands in the New York area. Narell and Mannette hoped to use steel pan to inspire African American and Caribbean American youth to get involved in positive activities and to help them avoid gangs, drugs, and violence. Other bands were started by the first generation of pannists in Trinidad and Tobago who had migrated to New York City in the 1960s and early 1970s, with the bands Silhouettes, Sonatas, and Moods all performing by the early 1970s. By the 1980s, many of the bands had come so far in size and quality that they could perform complex Panorama arrangements. Accordingly, a Panorama competition was added to Brooklyn's Labor Day Carnival in 1985.

Trinidad and Tobago's Carnival provided the initial model for diasporic West Indian Carnivals. The most prominent of Eastern Caribbean Carnival arts are recognized as having been developed in Trinidad and Tobago, but this collection of Carnival practices has become something akin to a multi-island lingua franca, that creates an overarching notion of West Indian identity in New York City.[8] As Mighty Sparrow (Slinger Francisco) sang in "Mas' in Brooklyn":

> New York equalize you
> Bajan, Grenadian, Jamaican, tout moun
> [Creole for "everybody," from the French *tout le monde*]
> Drinkin' they rum, beatin' they bottle an' spoon
> Nobody could watch me and honestly say
> They don't like to be in Brooklyn on Labor Day (Francisco, 1969)

Mighty Sparrow points out that the leveling process comes both from without (from Americans who cannot distinguish between different island peoples) and from within (from the various groups sharing cultural features and celebrating together). This is not to deny the various expressions of nationalism present in Carnival: in response to demands of certain constituencies, a Friday night Jamaican reggae concert and a Thursday night Haitian concert were added in the late 1980s to the roster of official Carnival events.

Annual Carnival celebrations in Brooklyn are only one example of the seasonally accentuated ethnicity that is practiced by many ethnic groups in America. Seasonal ethnic holidays such as St. Patrick's Day, Chinese New Year, or Cinco de Mayo often feature and reinforce the invented traditions of nostalgic immigrant communities. West Indians are at a distinct advantage in having a model at home of a seasonal event that is already a peak outpouring of local cultural expression with performances of calypso, soca (an up-tempo dance form of calypso), masquerade, and pan. Trinidad's Carnival is a rich context for the expression and exploration of identity, community, hybridity, and social and political commentary, and so it has proven to be an effective template for seasonal ethnic festivities throughout the West Indian diaspora.[9]

Some features are unique to festivals in the West Indian diaspora; for example, the crowds are much more eclectic than they would be at home, and the summer schedule of festivals outside the Caribbean tends to be disconnected from the Catholic calendar (whereas Trinidadian Carnival proper takes place on the three days before Lent). The three largest of these diasporic Carnivals are, in order of occurrence, Toronto's Caribana, London's Notting Hill Carnival, and Brooklyn's Labor Day Carnival, all of which take place between July and early September. This schedule of events has helped create a West Indian Carnival "circuit" with opportunities for calypsonians, arrangers, costume designers, and other West Indian Carnival professionals to find work during Trinidad's off-season (see Manning 1990, 49). Interestingly, the music in diasporic Carnivals tends to be derivative of *last* winter's Caribbean Carnivals, while the *mas'* camp designers often use the diasporic carnivals as a chance to try out designs for *next* winter's Carnival in Trinidad and Tobago.

Carnival arts play a special role in West Indian immigrant identity by virtue of the cathartic nature of the Carnival experience, allowing participants to *leggo* (let go) or to *breakaway* (lose control), to throw one's *hands in the air*, to *jump up* (join in the festivities), to *wine* the waist (to roll the waist and buttocks in a figure eight motion), to *get on bad*, or to improvise playful dancing that Trinidadians call *dingolay*. The terminology employed in the West Indies for this exuberant, bodily response and surrender of control is strikingly similar to that employed in Haiti and in Brazil (Averill 1994a). Calypsonian David Rudder has provided a poetic link between the bodily experience of Carnival and how Carnival functions as a political event, singing that calypso music is "a living vibration rooted deep within my Caribbean belly / Lyrics to make a politician cringe and turn a woman's body to jelly" (Rudder 1987). The same respect for the power of music is evident in Lord Kitchener (Aldwin Roberts)'s description of a Panorama crowd in "Pan Dingolay":

> People jumping up
> Oh Lord and don't want to stop
> Then as Cordettes [a steelband] start to play
> And the whole place breakaway
> A man say, "On Earth
> We done get our money's worth!" (Roberts 1990)

Hearing pan music, calypso, and soca in New York is often described by West Indian immigrants in just such ecstatic terms. Their full-fledged participation in the experience, jumping up with the music or engaging in breakaway, invokes a compelling set of feelings and confirms for many of them their Caribbean identity at a profoundly affective level. These kinds of experiences are often overlooked in the literature on ethnicity and immigration, but I believe they play a critical role in easing the transition of West Indians within different social and cultural systems.

IN A BROOKLYN PANYARD

Members of Silhouettes Steelband trickle into the parking lot serving as a temporary panyard on Church Avenue in Brooklyn. Inside the gates, there are still cars left in spaces for long-term storage, but there is enough room to set up the band's racks, the mobile frames that carry the pans through the street (typically pulled by trucks) and onto the stage. Many of these racks have plywood floors on which the pannists stand, but sometimes the pannists walk directly on the street as they play.

Brooklyn's steelbands are not commercial enterprises. A Miller Beer banner on the fence advertises the Silhouettes Steelband, but other than the banner, Miller's sponsorship extends only to giving the group beer to sell in the panyard. Without a major sponsor, the group must rely on its members to defray the costs of renting the panyard ($1,000 per month in this case), building and tuning the pans, building racks, buying tee-shirts, and paying the arranger's fee. The pannists play for the love of music, for the thrill of competing against other bands, and for the camaraderie and socialization afforded by a panyard.[10] Here, as in Trinidad, yards serve as seasonal gathering spots where neighborhood pannists and their friends hang out.

There is an undeniable fever for pan in the Brooklyn panyards that is fueled by a growing consciousness of the important postcolonial history of pan and of the instrument's role as a symbol of Caribbean hybridity and creativity. Following the abolition of slavery in the English West Indies in 1834, Trinidadians of African descent helped convert the European celebration of pre-Lenten Carnival into an Afro-Trinidadian emancipation celebration, replete with African-style drumming ensembles, stick fighting, the carrying of burning cane, obscene Carnivalesque parodies, masquerades and stilt dancers, and the singing of topical calypsos. The colonial elite lashed out at this lower-class *jamet* Carnival, a derogatory term deriving from the French *diametre*, referring to activity that took place outside the "diameter," or periphery, of proper behavior. The authorities banned many Afro-Trinidadian Carnival components in a series of ordinances in the mid to late nineteenth century that culminated in the Carnival riot of 1881. Due to the prohibitions, Carnival musicians replaced their neo-African drum ensembles with *tamboo bamboo* instruments, using different lengths of bamboo tubes struck together and pounded on the ground to produce tones. Business sponsorship of Carnival activities at the turn of the century and governmental patronage promoted the European-style *fancy mas* costume bands and attempted to move calypsonians onto the stages of commercial "tents" where they could compete against each other for prizes in the months prior to Carnival. And yet the popular mas activities continued to run in parallel to the more refined Carnival.

In the 1930s, tamboo bamboo bands began incorporating such makeshift metal instruments as dustbins, pitch-oil pans, garbage-can lids, and automotive brake drums, culminating in raucous bands made entirely of metal percussion instruments. This process of conversion accelerated when it was discovered in the late 1930s that multiple surfaces pounded out of the metal pans (originally biscuit bins) could produce multiple pitches. When Carnival bands took to the streets after World War II, simple melodies were beaten on these new instruments. Ellie Mannette of the Woodbrook Invaders steelband experimented using fifty-five-gallon oil drums for this purpose, pounding down the bottom of the drum to produce a concave bowl that allowed additional space for notes. Over the next couple of decades, more notes were added to the drums; tuning was improved; drums were joined together into sets that were differentiated from other instruments by their ranges; and an orchestra took shape using oil drums as its raw material.

The steelband spread quickly from Trinidad and Tobago throughout the Eastern Caribbean. In the 1950s, pannists (formerly looked on by the upper classes as disreputable *badjohns*) earned a level of respectability. In fact, the colonial ministries even helped institutionalize and sponsor pan competitions and export steelbands as cultural ambassadors for Trinidad and Tobago. Middle-class schoolboys (and later girls) increasingly joined in and identified with the steelbands, even over the objection of their parents. With Trinidad's independence, and with a cultural nationalism supported by Prime Minister Eric Williams, came pan programs in the schools, a Panorama contest at Carnival, and a pan component within the annual classically oriented Trinidad and Tobago Music Festival. Steel pan came to be embraced as the national instrument of Trinidad and Tobago (a status contested by Indo-Trinidadians in subsequent years, who saw this as evidence of Afro-Trinidadian dominance).[11]

But let's step back into Sunday night in the Silhouettes' panyard, where the fruits of the technological development of the steel pan are in full flower. A line of tenor pans occupies the front center rack of the band; these pans carry the melody of the arrangement and, despite their name, possess a soprano register. The tenors have a deep bowl, a very shallow skirt, and approximately thirty note heads raised from out of the bowl for a range of approximately two and a half fully-chromatic octaves (see Fig. 12.2). The tenors, like all of the higher pans in the yard, have been dipped in chrome to help preserve their tuning and to resist rust. Arranged behind and to the sides of the tenors are a few rows of double tenors and double seconds.

The double tenors and double seconds consist of sets of two pans together on a stand, with ranges below that of a tenor. The double tenors primarily play harmonizations of the tenor lines, while the double seconds often "strum," hitting two notes on the pans in a rhythmic pattern to fill in the chords in the arrangements. Lower pans, such as the double guitar pan and the quadraphonic, also concentrate

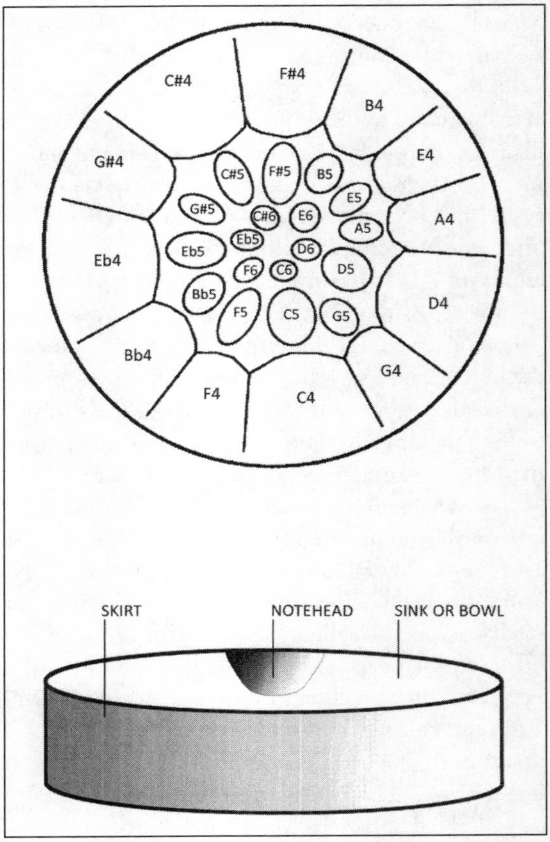

12.2. Diagram of a tenor-C pan (a lead pan with C as the lowest note), shown first from a top-view, demonstrating the placement of the note heads on the bowl of the pan, and second from a front elevation, with the key components of the instrument labeled.

principally on strum patterns. The quadrophonic has four pans, two of which are suspended vertically while the other two are hung horizontally. The cellos, consisting of a low-pitched set of three and four pans—the latter often called a four-pan—can play countermelodies, bass lines, or strums. Basses have the longest "skirts" in order to help their low-pitched notes resonate; these pans are made from entire barrels, and they are arranged in sets of six, nine, or twelve. Bass pans, not surprisingly, carry the bass lines of the arrangements, usually reinforced by the cello pans. The "sticks" used to play all of these instruments are merely different lengths of wood and metal tubing with the ends wrapped in varying thicknesses of rubber. A glance at the sea of concave steel playing surfaces in any panyard will confirm that the British former colony of Trinidad and Tobago has succeeded in fashioning one of the world's largest and most complex orchestras. See Figure 12.3 for an example of the layout of the Brooklyn steelband Pan Rebels as they arrange themselves on the Panorama stage,[12] and listen to this chapter's musical example for their version of "Fire Coming Down." I have provided a description of this performance with a timeline at the end of this chapter.

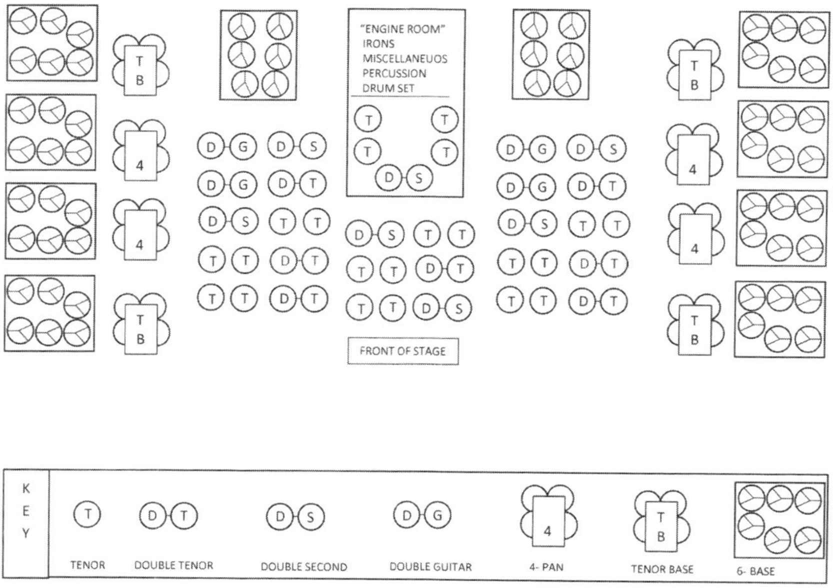

12.3. The layout of the Pan Rebels Steel Band on the Panorama stage at Brooklyn Carnival, 1995.

In the Silhouettes' yard, all of the pans are already arranged in moveable racks that will be rolled on stage for Panorama. The engine room (drum set, congas, timbales, and scraped and shaken instruments that provide the band with its rhythmic propulsion) is clustered in the middle of the band. One can glean immediately the complexity of the orchestra as well as the difficulty of moving such an orchestra rapidly on and off stage. The spatial configuration preferred by Pan Rebels helps separate out for the listener various voices of a pan orchestra without completely segregating the sections (which would produce an exaggerated stereophonic separation). It allows all musicians to hear the engine room (rhythm section) on its elevated rack in the center of the orchestra, and it also allows them all to hear the basses, which are distributed around the periphery. The configuration has the added advantage of permitting the audience to view a number of differently sized instruments—from basses to double seconds and tenors—arrayed across the front of the stage.

One of the chief instruments of the engine room is the iron, a humble automotive brake drum struck with iron rods and played along with a variety of cow bells to provide a rhythmically dense and insistent clanging central to the orchestra's sound. In a steelband, the engine room creates a layered, composite sound, a rhythmic counterpoint to the chords and melody of the pans (see Fig. 12.4.)

The arrival of the band's arranger, Earl La Pierre, marks the start of the formal rehearsal. Many of the points awarded at Panorama competitions are for the

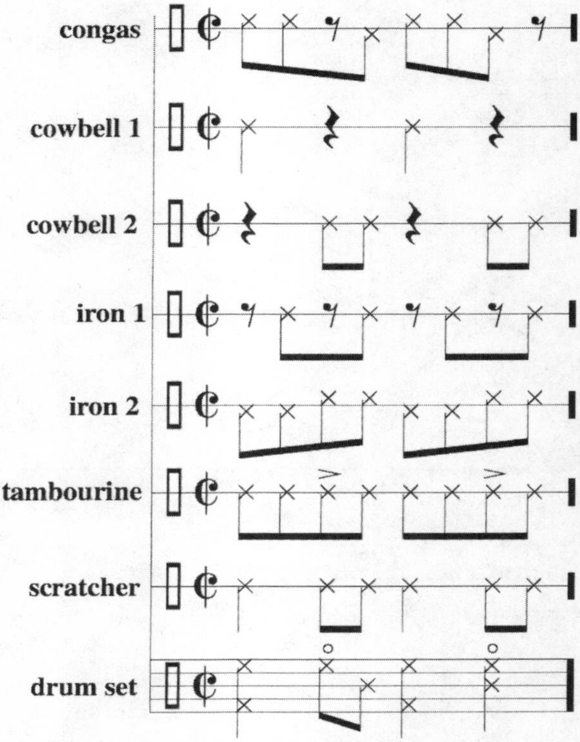

12.4. Typical engine room parts. The rhythms played by the engine room vary from band to band and from piece to piece, but this diagram represents common parts that one would hear accompanying a Panorama arrangement of a soca or calypso tune. The two pitches in the conga transcription refer to the two conga drums (high- and low-pitched) played with mallets. For the drum set, I have chosen to show (from top to bottom of the staff) the high hat, snare, and bass-drum strokes. The small "o" over two of the strokes designates an open stroke on the high hat.

quality of arrangement and interpretation, so the work of the arranger is critical. La Pierre has chosen one of the year's calypsos that adapts well to a steelband arrangement, "Mind Yuh Business," written by the Trinidadian arranger and pannist Len "Boogsie" Sharp (who is, himself, working on an arrangement of this same tune with the Pan Rebels a few blocks away). Panorama arrangements are based on commercial recordings of calypsonians that must receive airplay in the months before Carnival and be popular among the public if the Panorama arrangement is to have any chance of success. Without this prior exposure, an audience will be unable to follow the variations on the calypso that the arranger has built into his steelband arrangement. A week before Panorama, La Pierre has nearly completed the ten-minute, multi-part orchestral arrangement using "Mind Yuh Business" as his raw material. Like all good Panorama arrangements, it is essentially through-composed, although individual sections sometimes repeat. The skill of the pannists is showcased in rapid, chromatic passages and in intricately syncopated strum patterns. Tonight, the double tenors and seconds are running through the introduction, which has a call-and-response dialogue with the basses. This short musical fragment for double tenors and seconds is included as Figure 12.5. Note the syncopation (off-beat accentuation) and the melodic phrasing that

12.5. The introduction as played by the doubles (double tenors and double seconds) to Earl La Pierre's arrangement of Len "Boogsie" Sharpe's "Mind Yuh Business." Note the use of offbeat phrasing (especially the rests at the beginning of measure) characteristic of calypso and soca melodies. Each pannist, using two "sticks," is capable of playing two notes simultaneously, either in a single stroke or as a sustained roll. Rolls are shown here with double lines through the stems of the noteheads.

begins after the downbeat of the measure, techniques that are both used throughout this arrangement and commonly heard in the genre of calypso as a whole.

For a winning Panorama performance, the pans must be "blended" (tuned) sweetly,[13] the tune has to be popular and appropriate for pan, the arrangement has to sustain interest over the length of the performance (in Brooklyn, anywhere from five to twelve minutes), and the playing must be precise and energizing. Tempi are extremely fast (cut-time markings of "half note = 132 beats per minute" are not uncommon). In their size, density, and overall form, panorama compositions bear similarities to Western classical symphonic movements based on sonata-allegro form, although they draw extensively from theme-and-variation form as well. These similarities to classical structures are not accidental; steelbands performed pieces from the classical repertory as early as the 1950s, and classical music has exerted an influence on the Carnival competition treatments of calypsos ever since.

Figure 12.6 is a short passage from the original arrangement to a 1994 Panorama performance of "Fire Coming Down," composed and arranged by Robert Greenidge. This is the same song (but in a different arrangement) as the audio example for this chapter. The arrangement starts off in the key of G, modulates to A, then to A minor, back to A major, and finally returns to the original key of G for a coda. The excerpt in Figure 12.6 is taken from the return to A major near the end of the composition. The top three voices—tenor, double tenor, and double second—provide the melody and harmonize it (this melodic motif is taken from the latter part of the verse of the original calypso). The guitar pans provide a syncopated harmonic grounding for the chord progression of B minor to A major. This arrangement was created and taught orally at first and later transcribed for publication (Greenidge 1994).

12.6. A six-measure passage from "Fire Coming Down," composed and arranged by Robert Greenidge. This passage begins the 31st section of the song (we see measures 541–547) in the key of A, whereas the arrangement starts in G and is about to transition back to G. This passage features a melody in the tenor part that is a variation of the second half of the verse of the song. The length, difficulty, and number of arranged parts are typical of Panorama arrangements. I should emphasize that most such compositions are produced without notation and are taught orally to the band members. Transcription by Steve Popernack, edited by Steve Popernack and Shelly Irvine, copyright 1994 by Ro Gree Publishing [ASCAP], all rights reserved, published by Panyard, Inc., Akron, Ohio.

An arranger seldom comes to the first practice with an entire arrangement in his or her head. Instead, he or she will compose sections day by day, working ideas out with the pannists and revising them as needed. This challenges the memorization skills of even the most virtuosic pannists. Some pannists devise their own notation systems, such as listing the names of the notes in sequence, and some carry tape recorders to capture the complexities of the arrangement, but the most common means employed to memorize arrangements is simply to play them over and over. Anxious arrangers, however, have been known to rearrange extensive sections of the tune only days before the competition. As I work on my own (double-tenor) part, La Pierre moves over to the basses where he directs one of the players, "No, it's A to E, ba-dum-bum. You've got to hear the melody." From there he turns around, picks up some sticks and demonstrates the entire double tenor part to my section, and then returns to the middle of the band, taps on a drum to silence the players, and lectures them on stage presence: "I look around the band and I see everybody looking *so serious.* The whole band should be moving and having fun. You are performing, you are presenting something to the people, and you should be *enjoying* yourselves!" In the same night, La Pierre composes new lines for the tenors; admonishes a pannist on his bad panyard manners; tries to lift the band's morale; and sings, talks, and demonstrates many of the instrumental parts. The role of a steelband arranger is, as one can see, extraordinarily complex and demanding in musical, organizational, and personal skills.

A small audience has collected inside the panyard, and they applaud the final two run-throughs of the piece (minus the two minutes of additional material that La Pierre still wants to write for the band). This rehearsal breaks at 11:00 p.m. in deference to the neighbors, but it will be repeated every night until Panorama.

The arranger's and captain's personal skills are tested regularly in maintaining the discipline and unity of the band under many pressures, disagreements, and differences in perspective that may be musical, generational, political, or social in nature. For example, one band was deeply divided over the decision by the band captain to kick out five pannists only a week before Panorama. The pannists—some of the best players in the group—were playing with more than one band and were missing rehearsals as a consequence. Although this practice is increasingly frequent in steelbands in Brooklyn and Trinidad, the captain held to an older ethos about commitment to a single panyard and about team competitive spirit that was incompatible with the new attitude. In another incident, an arranger and a pannist (with a distinctly American accent and attitude) clashed over a perceived breach of respect and authority. The arranger complained publicly, "I'm not paid enough to take this crap. I'm here to do a job, not to be second guessed." The offending pannist said privately later, "I had too much of this shit with those old Trinidadian headmasters when I was a kid at school, you know what I mean? All I did was ask him what it was I was doing wrong. Just, 'Tell me, what am I doing wrong?!' This is America—I don't have to take orders and disrespect from nobody." These social dramas reveal clashes of values and worldviews that often take shape around generational fault lines and that have profound implications for the steelband movement.

BROOKLYN PANORAMA AND THE ROAD MARCH

In the cool Brooklyn night air, steelband racks roll into the enclosure behind the Brooklyn Museum while a calypsonian on stage sings, "On the Parkway, we get down, On Labor Day Monday, we get down." The arriving steelbands position themselves at different corners of the lot to do some last-minute practicing. The growing crowd samples the food for sale in the tents ringing the enclosure, including such West Indian delicacies as doubles, palourie, goat roti, and roasted corn, washing it all down with drinks like Carib beer, Malta, champagne cola, ginger beer, sorrel, and mauby.

The Brooklyn Panorama is a scaled-down version of the competition held at Carnival in Trinidad every February or March. In Trinidad, Panorama is the final stage of weeks of regional and semifinal competitions; eleven bands in each of the two major categories (large bands, and small bands) make it to the finals to compete for the title of Panorama champions on the stage at the Queen's Park Savannah in Port-of-Spain. In Brooklyn, however, there is only one competition with merely enough large orchestras, known as "conventional bands," for the finals. Selected steelband performances at Brooklyn Carnival have been recorded since 1994 by a Brooklyn-based company, Basement Recordings.[14] The stakes and media attention may be small in comparison to Trinidad—where an international satellite broadcast carries Panorama to various parts of the world—but New York–area pannists take their competition very seriously.

First with its racks on stage is *C.A.S.Y.M. Steelband* (Caribbean American Sports and Youth Movement), a youth-oriented steelband that gigs extensively outside of the Caribbean community, under a banner that reads: "Drugs are a bust, education's a must." The tune is "Pan by Storm," by Professor Ken Philmore, and the banner gives the customary names of arranger, band captain, and tuner. The kids are dressed in black, as are the flag boys and girls. Those carrying flags dance on the front of the stage to entertain and work up the crowd.

C.A.S.Y.M.'s arranger sets the tempo with a few taps on the side of a pan, the racks begin to shake, and the metallic fringe on the tops of the racks shimmers in the bright stage lights. Behind the front row of tenors, the engine room plays on a raised central platform, also framed by fringes. The overall effect is of an entire stage—animate and inanimate objects together—dancing, swaying, and sparkling. In front of the stage sit the five judges; behind them, members of the audience raise their arms and dance in place. The climactic final passages, with a shouted part for the pannists, brings the remaining seated audience members to their feet.

Sonatas, next up, unfurls their flags and launches into their own treatment of Philmore's "Pan by Storm." It is not uncommon for a number of bands to select the same calypso for a panorama arrangement. Sponsored by British West Indies Airlines and dressed in yellow, the pannists in Sonatas dance and play their way through the piece with the audience in tow. And on it goes into the night as every band (Pan Rebels, Silhouettes, Moods, and others) has their fifteen minutes or so on stage. Soon after the previous band's final chords fade, another group is rolling onto the stage to take their place. Somewhere just past 4:00 a.m., the last band clears the stage and the judges begin adding up their scores. The judges' decisions are often contested by the losing bands and their supporters; in fact the judges are often booed when the results are announced. Indeed, during my stint as a judge, the panel of judges was pelted by food launched by disaffected audience members, a not-uncommon form of audience censure!

Following the Panorama on Saturday and the calypso contest on Sunday, Carnival hits Brooklyn's Eastern Parkway on Labor Day Monday, routinely attracting over a million onlookers and participants. In 1990 the traditional early Monday parade (Jouvay, from the French *jour ouvert* or "opening of the day") was still relatively undeveloped, but in later years, it became a popular steelband venue.

For Jouvay, the steelband racks are pulled by trucks through the streets from their panyards to join a parade route, surrounded by some of the more traditional (ol' time) mas bands. No amplified music is allowed into Jouvay, and so the steelbands do not have to compete with the stacks of speakers powering commercial calypsos and soca songs.

But the Road March on Monday afternoon is still the main attraction. Somewhere around 1:00 p.m., the first wave of the 1990 Carnival road marchers reach the reviewing stand. A group of marchers carry flags of various Caribbean nations; then comes the West Indian American Carnival Association flatbed truck, sponsored by Angostura Bitters, playing a popular road march from a previous year, "Somebody," by Baron. "I want somebody to hug up, somebody to squeeze up, somebody to jump up . . ." It is still early, but behind the blue police barricades and the rows of Port-O-Pottys, the crowds are already filling up the sidewalks of Eastern Parkway. Sailor mas bands with colorful sails unfurled, butterflies, devil bands, and other more traditional mas groups turn the Parkway's asphalt into a sea of dancers winin' their hips and taking small, shuffling steps along the parade route, a style of walking called *chipping*. The steelband Pan Rebels, outfitted in green, is pulled along by friends and volunteers through the crowded streets. The band is playing their Panorama entry, "No, No We Ain't Going Home" by Owen Norville. Many of the iron players walking along behind the band seem to be "sitting in" with the band, and some frequently lose the tempo. But this is Road March and there are no judges listening, and the steelbands can hardly be heard over the ambient soca anyway. The increasing difficulty of competing with the amplified sound trucks featuring deejays has diminished pannists' passion for playing in the Road March and has reinforced, year by year, the importance of Panorama and Jouvay as contexts for pan performance.

Having moved through the panyards to the Panorama competition, to Jouvay, and finally to the Road March, I wanted to conclude this chapter with a close-up look at a steelband and at how its leaders and members viewed some of the central issues of this chapter, including Caribbean/Trinidadian identity in New York City, generational divides, and the role of competition. I contacted members of C.A.S.Y.M Steelband to talk with me about their perspectives and their experiences of pan in New York City.

C.A.S.Y.M. STEELBAND, A "FAMILY INSTITUTION"

The Brooklyn-based community organization Caribbean American Sports and Youth Movement (C.A.S.Y.M.) is an organization dedicated to improving the situation of West Indian American children in New York. After a long involvement in sporting activities for youth, the organization started a steelband in 1986, and in 1989 they recruited a young Trinidadian pannist, Arddin Herbert, to move to Brooklyn to become the band's musical director. In a few years, the steelband has become the principal activity of the organization, reflecting the attractiveness of pan to West Indian children and teenagers. The C.A.S.Y.M. Steelband was one of three youth-oriented community-based steelbands in the borough. Almost all of the fifty or so members were of school age and were born in the United States of parents who were themselves from the Caribbean. Perhaps 40 percent were of Trinidadian descent, with girls slightly outnumbering the boys. In addition to the musical director, the group also has captains, vice-captains, and a steelband committee.

The C.A.S.Y.M. Steelband participates in the Saturday night Panorama competition each year in the Labor Day Carnival on Eastern Parkway. The band moves from their church basement rehearsal space onto an open parking lot for the month of August to practice their Panorama calypso arrangement. After they finish practicing each night, the pannists load their instruments—fifteen tenors, seven double tenors, eight double seconds, one four-pan, three cellos, five guitars, three tenor basses, and about seven six-basses plus engine-room percussion instruments—into the back of a moving van for secure storage.

In our many hours of conversation, William Jones [WJ], founder and executive director of C.A.S.Y.M., and Arddin Herbert [AH], musical director of the C.A.S.Y.M. Steelband, repeatedly stressed the role of pan in building a positive identity for West Indian American youths, in developing the discipline and commitment necessary to do well in school, and in building a sense of community. The two community leaders also stressed the involvement of the youths' families as a support network for the band. In the following passages taken from those interviews, we discussed the relationship of Carnival and panorama to the band's goals.

> GA: Tell me a little bit about the early days of C.A.S.Y.M. and what you were trying to do.
>
> WJ: You may be aware that Brooklyn has a large Caribbean population. My experience, as I came here in 1970, was that the children of Caribbean descent . . . experienced what I would call a culture shock. They were having problems in school obviously at that time. There were four schools in the area: Prospect Heights, Wingate, Erasmus, and Tilden. There was a mixed composition of children there. I was involved in soccer in Trinidad, and I was very much involved in community work also, and I met a lot of children. The Five Borough Soccer League was an adult soccer league and we weren't really dealing with the children. I decided to form the Caribbean American Sports and Youth Movement . . . to concentrate on developing the youth in soccer—of course I had a lot of help in that. It was determined that not only should you be playing soccer, but you should be involved in many of the cultural traits of the Caribbean people, and the children love this.

We had dance and drama, but what caught fire is the steelband. It is very visible. When the steelband performs, people want to bring their children into the group . . . I dare say that C.A.S.Y.M. is not an ordinary steelband. The children in this band . . . learn music theory and they have a very big appreciation for the art form. C.A.S.Y.M. is very well developed in a range of music from classic to calypso and we use this as a tool to get the children to understand that education is important. We have a total of about two hundred kids involved both in the schools and outside the schools. The stageside [the performance band] is about fifty. To stay in the stageside, you must be going to school and you must maintain an average. If you have any problems in school, we look for assistance to give to you. I'm very proud to say that in the last three years, 90 percent of our children that graduated from high school went on to college. The band is open to children from five to eighteen, but if you pass eighteen and you are abiding by the rules of the group, we are not going to throw you out. In fact, we have many children who stay in the group and impart the knowledge they have to the younger ones.

GA: When you teach the members music theory, do you use scores and notation or do you do it by rote?

AH: Both. Some of them can read scores and if they can't read scores, I teach them basic note values. When they're in school, we rehearse on Fridays and Saturdays for an average of about two and a half hours. When they're out of school, for the months of July and August, we rehearse from Monday to Saturday, depending on if we have any performances. Most of the players that have left our band—and some were not the best of players—when they went in other bands, they were like really on top there.

WJ: We recruit some children whose parents don't know where to send them. They send them by us and we introduce them to the music . . .

AH: Steel pan daycare!

GA: Do the parents come to you with problems with their kids?

AH: Usually if the parents have a problem, they will come and say, "Well, this child isn't doing too well," and because I have such a good relationship with most of the kids, I can get through to most of them. If it's something that we can't handle, the parents might say, "You are not going to be able to go to rehearsal for one month," and the kids start to straighten up.

WJ: Whenever a child is being disciplined, one of the things they [the parents] take away from them is the steelband, because they know that they are attached to this art form, so it is used as a form of discipline. As a matter of fact, I was just speaking to a parent whose child disappeared [from the group] and on the order of the captain was suspended from the group. The child was crying to the mother, so she called me. I'm trying to show the type of rapport that we have with the parents and the children in the organization.

GA: Tell me about the generational problems. Are the conflicts pretty intense? Are there pressures on West Indian kids to not look like *jeskummers*—like recent immigrants—and to fit in?

WJ: In 1970, when I came here, we may have had that problem. You'd find some of my peers not wanting to identify themselves with Trinidad, but over the years, you will find that a Trinidadian will want you to know he's a Trinidadian. He don't try to change his accent—he'll speak his colloquial language—like I do at times! I don't think we have that type of problem anymore.

AH: Back then, because of the colonial scene, those countries [in the Caribbean] were looked down on as Third World, second-class. But now I think most people see the more industrialized countries as having the same problems that we have back home, so we see that they are not much better that we are, so we are proud to be who we are.

WJ: In 1979 and 1980 we had a problem that we attacked in a group form. A child coming from Trinidad who had received a quality education, they used to start them all over again. Without testing them, they used to put them some grades lower. And I think it was unfair that they had to stay longer in school to graduate. I don't think you have that problem so much now. How we addressed this is that we had the children themselves help others. If you were good in math, you would help the one who was weak in math. We had a kind of common spirit, and I don't ever want that to break from the group, 'cause it helped a lot . . . each one helping one. We look at this group as a family institution. There are children in this group now aged six and seven whose sisters and brothers were in the band, and it continues. Having had the opportunity to watch the players grow, some of them from age ten, to see the development, it's a joy to behold where I'm concerned. Watching these guys trying to do like Arddin . . . and they have really advanced. It's incredible, it's a thrill.

To carry on a steelband with young people throughout the year—we go throughout the year—is a difficulty. That's why you get most of the bands operating only during the summer for Panorama. After that they're nonexistent. But it's a painstaking thing, and you have to have the support of the parents, and we do, I must say. We are blessed with having the support of the parents. The children want to come out and practice on Friday night and Saturday, and it's taxing on the parents to come and pick them up.

GA: Do you go on the road for the Monday Carnival parade?

WJ and AH: Not in the evening [in the main parade], only in the morning for Jouvay.

WJ: It's a very ticklish subject. I am concerned, as are most of the parents—remember we are dealing mostly with teenagers of thirteen or twelve—that to have such a mass of children under control in the "heat" of the festival is difficult. So we much prefer to take part in the Jouvay in early morning.

AH: What I try to maintain is that C.A.S.Y.M. Steelband is *not* a Panorama band. If you want to be part of the Panorama, you have to be here for the entire year doing the same thing these kids have been doing, hard work.

WJ: You can't be coming in and out. You have one set of rules all the time. If you have people coming in, they can corrupt what you have going and it's not a good thing. And while you're competing, you want to win, [still] he [Arddin Herbert] doesn't really like to go to Panorama because you're not benefiting anything by it, and you're not improving very much—you spend a number of hours on one particular tune, whereas you could be expanding the knowledge of the children in other areas with the time. Panorama is very time-consuming and very expensive and not that rewarding. So that, in this aspect, I really agree with him. But it has become such a passionate thing with the children—it's hard when you see their faces to tell them no, you know. Economically, we nearly said no this year, as a matter of fact we aren't sure yet [both laugh]. If this thing [a benefit concert] don't turn out right, it's no!

WJ and AH together: I never liked competing with the art form, because I have my view that the art form should be expressed pure on stage. Competition leaves a lot of hard feelings. The only reason why I do it, as he said, is that the kids look forward to it. And right now there isn't a substitute that could equal or surpass Panorama in terms of the hype and the adrenaline. If I could, I would.

WJ: We have been trying to get schools involved, and I must say that there's a particular school in Queens. The type of interest that the principal shows encourages you to go out there. We make the tutoring of the pupils free of cost and they purchase their own pans. You know, it's a pleasure to go there when

> you have a foreigner [a non–West Indian] showing you that type of interest in the art form, so we feel we should expend our energies there, even though sometimes it's inconvenient. Right here on our doorsteps [in the West Indian community], they like the panyard, but for one day alone.

Jones's closing remark about "one day alone" raises one of the chief laments of pan enthusiasts: that interest in pan is restricted to carnival season (Panorama and Jouvay) only. Steelbands don't find work at parties, weddings, or festivals during the rest of the year, and enthusiasts buy recordings only as audio souvenirs of Carnival. As with calypsos, the steelband has become a seasonal expression with little chance for performers to maintain a living at it year round.

CONCLUSIONS

This chapter has pointed to many paradoxes of steel pan performance in Brooklyn and throughout the diaspora. For the most part, steel pan in Brooklyn is an amateur, ensemble-based musical form, but it is heavily dependent upon individual professionals who serve as tuners and arrangers and who play a central role in the transmission of the tradition. It is not a commercial music per se; the players are not paid, the instruments are notoriously difficult to record, and there is only a very small market for steelband recordings (one almost never hears them on radio, even on West Indian broadcasts). Panorama performances require extraordinary skill and dexterity, but there are only a few weeks each year in which most steelbands have the opportunity to play. Pan is historically a *Trinbagonian* art form (it is the national instrument of Trinidad and Tobago) that now finds itself embraced as a symbol of pan–West Indian identity.

Finally, pan in Brooklyn is a local phenomenon, situated in panyards, on the stage at the Brooklyn Museum Panorama, and on parade along Eastern Parkway; but it is very much a transnational phenomenon, too. Pan performances at Panorama in Brooklyn are linked to the previous winter's Carnival in Trinidad and Tobago by the circulation of calypsos through the diaspora and by the flow of personnel (arrangers, calypsonians, and some pannists) among the various Carnivals. Although the songs are often recycled from last winter's Trinbagonian Carnival, the Brooklyn arrangements must be new and different. As a result, steel pan intimately links the Anglophone West Indies and its diaspora in cultural expression and creativity. Moreover, these paradoxes I have identified—amateur vs. professional, national vs. West Indian, local vs. transnational—are in constant flux precisely because pan is a living, dynamic art form in which so many diasporic West Indians as well as some outsiders invest their time, energy, and passion.

Pan is in no danger of dying out in Brooklyn, although there continues to be spirited debate about the state of the tradition. There are a growing number of pan activists ready and willing to keep existing groups together and to organize new groups. Large numbers of young West Indian Americans appear genuinely excited about steelbands and about performing at Carnival. The Brooklyn steelbands consist predominantly of West Indians; for them, pan remains a chief form of cultural assertion and an outlet for exploring pan–West Indian ethnic identity. Pan is a "we ting" ("we thing"), a cultural expression that symbolizes West Indian cultural creativity and hybridity and maintains an affective link to the Caribbean. This link has been more or less continuous, involving first- and second-generation West Indian Americans, but it cannot be assumed that identity issues are somehow consensual or resolved. To the contrary, steel pan becomes a factor in the negotiation of contrasting visions of Trinidadian, West Indian, and Caribbean American identities. Pan is also a vehicle for the display or performance of identities for the benefit of surrounding communities and ethnic groups. At Panorama, in the Jouvay parade, and in the Carnival Road March, West Indians also make pan a "dey ting" (something for "them"), sharing their art with hundreds of thousands of spectators of varied cultural backgrounds.

LISTENING TO "FIRE COMING DOWN" BY PAN REBELS

The track that accompanies this chapter is an arrangement of a calypso called "Fire Coming Down" from the 1994 Carnival season, written by Robbie Greenidge and calypsonian Austin "Superblue" Lyons. (See Chapter 12, Track 1.) The calypso was intended from the start to serve as the basis for a steelband Panorama arrangement, and was composed specifically with a leading Trinidadian steelband, the WITCO Desperados (aka Despers), in mind. It is, in fact, *about* Despers.

Despers is based in the district of Laventille, a lower-class neighborhood on the hills overlooking the city of Port-of-Spain, and the image of "fire coming down" refers to the fiery sound and the pans of Despers coming down into the city for Carnival. In the first chorus, Greenidge and Lyons describe the setting for the progress of the steelband into the city: "Lord the fire start to approach / In front Mother Taffe church / Is St. Barbs and Picton, Rose Hill and John John . . ."

The second chorus describes the sound of the orchestra and its engine room:

> Fire heat in the place (x4)
> Like the heat from the engine room
> Catch a chord in the tune
> In the key and tempo a bass line explode
> [onomatopoetically] Poo boo doo boo doo boo doo boo doom
> Fire, heat in de place
> Mama yo [Creole for "mothers"] Desperados have them up on their toes
> Fire coming down (x4)
> Heat! (x10) Fire coming down
> Jump (x10) Despers coming down.

Throughout the pan arrangement of "Fire Coming Down" we will hear the double quarter-note articulation of the word "fi-re" on (beats 3 and 4 of certain measures), and we'll hear the half-note repetition that accompanies the words "heat" and "jump" (often with a responsorial echo in the lower pans). This arrangement for Pan Rebels includes only the first 6:11 out of close to 10 minutes, but it captures many typical aspects of Panorama arrangements (in order to secure rights to the performance, we were asked to include less than two-thirds of the original recording). As you listen to the arrangement, try to follow along with the description of its component features, below:

0–0:33 Introduction. This short introduction establishes the starting key (G major) and employs various motives from the verse and chorus along as well as a chromatic run (at 0:25) to delay the start of what will be (for the audience) the well-known first verse.

0:33–0:50 First verse in G. In the first line, try to hear the lyrics of the calypso: "I ya yo, the party end up on the road."

0:50–1:07 Verse repeated in the same key.

1:07–1:34 Chorus, first part. The main motive starts out at 1:07 and it is based on the phrase of the song "Fi-re heat in the place." This section ends with a syncopated riff, typical of sectional markers in Panorama arrangements.

1:34–1:57 Chorus, second part. Now you'll hear the repeated melody associated with the lyrics: "Fire coming down" followed by the stark chords articulating the words "heat" and "jump."

1:57–3:18 Development section, part 1. This part begins with what seems to be a modulation from G on the same rhythmic vamp that we heard at the end of the "chorus, first part." At 2:05, the arranger begins to treat motivic elements of the verse and chorus in an extended development section, and contrary to the sense of modulation earlier, the key of G holds throughout. Try to identify melodies that you have heard in the first renditions of the verse and chorus as the arranger plays with variations on these themes. This section ends with undulating chromaticism.

3:18–6:11 Development section, part 2. By the end of this next section the arranger has modulated through a few different keys. Listen to the way the arranger places the melodic fragments in the lower pans at 3:45 and then adds the higher pans playing a strident and repetitive phrase at 3:53–4:10. At 4:26 the first theme from the verse comes in in the key of B. By 5:55, the melody has landed in the key of D, the dominant of the starting key.

Following the fade-out of the performance, the band plays a section inspired by Latin percussion and eventually modulates back to the original key for a recapitulation of the verse and chorus and a final coda. Despite the truncated nature of the recording, the 6:11 that we have heard helps remind us of how complex Panorama arrangements have become over the past fifty years and of the level of virtuosity needed to play such pieces (learned by rote) at the tempi expected in carnival performances. Listen to contemporary performances of Panorama steelbands (and see if you can locate the calypso they're playing first in its sung version) and try to apply some of these same principles of analysis to the recordings!

Notes

1. I would like to thank Arddin Herbert, William George, Caldera Carabello, and members of Silhouettes Steelband for their assistance with this chapter. Amelia K. Ingram and Giovanna Perot-Averill edited the text and Giovanna revised two figures for this chapter. In addition, I would like to thank this book's editors, Anne K. Rasmussen and Kip Lornell, for their interest in the subject and for their patience, both with the original and with the extensively revised second edition.

2. Although in the United States and Great Britain the term *West Indian* sometimes encompasses the whole of the Caribbean, I am using the term more restrictively to denote the Anglophone Eastern Caribbean islands (including Trinidad and Tobago) plus Bermuda, Grand Cayman, Jamaica, and the Bahamas, i.e. the former—and in some cases, current—colonies of the British Empire. In Cuba, Haiti, the Dominican Republic, Puerto Rico, and the French Antilles, the term *West Indies* is seldom used as a term of self-reference; instead, these islands employ French and Spanish equivalents of *Caribbean* and *Antilles.* See Kasinitz (1992, 54–59) for demographics of New York's West Indian population.

3. Diasporic carnivals have received sustained attention over the years from researchers, starting with Hill and Abrahamson (1980). Analyses have focused on the transnational circulation of aesthetic practices (Nunley 1988; Manning 1990) between Trinidad and the various diasporic sites and on issues of immigrant identity and politics (Kasinitz 1992; Kasinitz and Fridenberg-Herbstein 1987; Cohen 1993). At the time of the publication of this chapter, little had been said of the role of pan and steelbands in the diaspora, other than Manning's (1990) off-key dismissal of pan in the Brooklyn and Toronto carnivals. Shortly after the original publication of this chapter, Ray Allen and Les Slater published their chapter on Trinidadian music in New York, "Steel Pan Grows in Brooklyn: Trinidadian Music and Cultural Identity," alongside an article by Philip Kasinitz, "Community Dramatized, Community Contested: The Politics of Celebration in the Brooklyn Carnival," both of which appeared in *Island Sounds in the Global City: Caribbean Popular Music and Identity in New York*, ed. Ray Allen and Lois Wilcken (1998, New York Folklore Society and the Institute for Studies in American Music). These two articles provide additional historical and sociocultural context regarding Carnival performance in New York.

4. The positive rewards of asserted ethnicity for West Indians contrast with the situation historically faced by Haitians in North America, where they encountered an especially

virulent form of discrimination based on sensationalist stereotypes of Haitian Vodou, political instability, poverty, and disease. Despite two decades of political activism designed to counteract negative attitudes toward Haiti, Haitian youth are far more likely than their West Indian counterparts to internalize the pejorative associations with national heritage. See Averill (1994b); Schiller and Fouron (1989); or Laguerre (1984) for accounts of Haitian life and culture in New York.

5. Cited in Kasinitz (1992, 141).

6. The organization's website can be viewed at http://www.wiadca.com.

7. Ellie Mannette was a member of one of Trinidad's first steelbands, the Woodbrook Invaders, and he is credited with being the first to use a fifty-five-gallon oil drum as the raw material for a pan. He achieved his greatest renown as a pan builder and technological innovator.

8. In the 1980s and 1990s, younger West Indians gravitated toward the music of Jamaica, especially reggae and forms of dancehall deejays and selectors, resulting in various fusions with soca.

9. For a general history of Carnival in Trinidad and Tobago, see Cowley (1996). Guilbault (2007) significantly expands the analysis of the contest over the cultural and political meanings of carnival and its musics. Following an earlier article by Aho (1987), two ethnomusicological works on the history of pan and the steelband movement detail the struggle for a postcolonial identity (Stuempfle 1995; Dudley 2008), with the latter book focusing more on the agency of arrangers and pannists in the development of pan musical aesthetics.

10. Some of the top Trinbagonian (a common adjectival abridgment of Trinidad and Tobago) conventional steelbands may make enough money to cover costs by winning prize purses in Panorama, the Carnival "bomb" competition, or the Steelband Music Festival as well as by attracting generous sponsorship. Many conventional steelbands feature their sponsors' names preceding the band name; for example, Carib (a beer company), Tokyo All-Stars, or Amoco (petroleum company) Renegades.

11. See Birth (2008, 9). Political tensions between Creoles and Indo-Trinidadians were covered earlier and more broadly in Ryan (1972).

12. This diagram is based loosely on a sketch in *Pro Sound News*, December 1995.

13. See Kronman (1991) for a detailed account of steel pan building and tuning.

14. Trinidadian steelbands were first recorded in the early 1950s by local entrepreneurs, then by North American audio technician Emory Cook, and eventually by such major transnational companies as Decca, RCA, and Columbia. Few if any of these recordings returned any royalties to the bands. With the rise in popularity of sound systems and of soca bands in the late 1970s, steelbands found themselves relegated to a "carnival ghetto"; popular for a few months of the year but with a declining number of engagements for their smaller, year-round performance bands called stagesides. The situation is bleaker in Brooklyn, where few steelbands even bother to organize stagesides; they form only for Panorama and they rehearse only a single arrangement in their repertory each year. Many pannists lament their lack of access to recording studios and to radio and television airplay—in other words, to commercial opportunities for pan.

Glossary

badjohn. Trinidadian slang for a ruffian or hooligan, used to describe early panmen.

beat pan. A more traditional way to say "play" pan.

blend. As a verb, this means to adjust the note heads of a pan so that all of the overtones are consonant with the fundamental pitches and are of comparable intensity or loudness so that the pan is balanced as an instrument and in relationship to the ensemble.

bomb tune. Among early steelbands, this was a foreign tune worked up secretly before Carnival to impress the other bands when they were unveiled like a "bomb." Bands began using short arrangements of well-known classical and pop tunes set to calypso rhythms for this purpose. Bomb competitions have been, off and on, a part of Carnival.

breakaway. This refers to a sudden increase in the intensity of participation, when audiences get worked up and carried away by a song.

broughtupsy. Good upbringing.

cariso/calypso. A broad category (or family, really) of Trinidadian song types derived from nineteenth-century *lavways* (Afro-Trinidadian songs accompanying stick fights) and French-Trinidadian *romances.* One division of contemporary calypso would be by function: *tent calypsos* (topical, with an emphasis on the lyrics, sung in the calypso tents and in the calypso monarch competition), *road march calypsos* (rhythmic and tuneful for use by marching mas bands), *steelband calypsos* (related to road march but written with eventual pan performance in mind, sometimes *about* pan), and dancehall or party *soca.* Before the 1930s, calypsos were often categorized on the basis of the melodic mode they were written in (for example: mi minor or la minor), but most contemporary calypsos are in a major key. Calypsos may also be distinguished by the number of lines of text covered by the basic repeating melody. Old lavways and some short road marches might comprise two lines (call-and-response), called a half-tone calypso; a single-tone calypso would consist of four lines of text per melodic repeat; and the double-tone calypso, eight. Most tent calypsos are of the double-tone variety.

calypso monarch. Winner of the annual calypso competition at Carnival's Dimanche Gras performance.

chipping. Taking small, shuffling steps along a Carnival parade route. Proper chipping conserves the energy of the masqueraders for the two long days in the Trinidadian sun.

Dimanche Gras (Fat Sunday). A show held on the Sunday night of Carnival that includes the competition for calypso monarch and for king and queen mas costumes.

dingolay. Loose, improvised dance steps of an exuberant nature, executed when sufficiently moved by the music.

engine room. The ancillary percussion section of a steelband, usually comprising a drum set, irons or brake drums, congas, shak shak or shaker, scratcher, cow bells, and so forth.

fete. Party.

iron. A common term for the brake-drum instrument in a steelband engine room, struck with one or two iron rods.

jamet. From French *diametre*, jamet Carnival refers to a set of early Afro-Trinidadian Carnival practices that were considered by the ruling colonial elite and middle classes to be outside of the boundaries of proper behavior.

jouvay. From the French *jour ouvert* (opening of the day). Used for the early Monday morning Carnival parade that opens the two days of road march. This event tends to have more traditional mas costumes and to be more informal.

jump up. To join in with a mas band and participate enthusiastically.

konpa. A popular Haitian dance genre and rhythm, originally called *compas-direct.*

lime. Trinidadian slang for hanging out, usually with copious laughter and the consumption of rum.

Mardi Gras. Literally, Fat Tuesday, the Tuesday portion of the pre-Lenten Carnival. Prior to Mardi Gras are Dimanche Gras and Lundi Gras (Fat Sunday and Monday).

mas. From "masquerade," this refers to the costuming component of Carnival. Mas bands parade and compete in the Carnival road march. Participants are said to "play mas."

mas camp. A space used to build and sew the costumes for a mas band.

Pan / steel pan. A melodic percussion instrument made from metal containers (usually fifty-five-gallon oil drums). It has been expanded to include a number of instruments of different ranges, for example, tenor/lead, double tenor, double second, guitar, quadrophonic, three-cello, four-pan/four-cello, tenor bass, six-bass, nine-bass, twelve-bass.

pannist. A player of a steel pan. Formerly *panman.*

panyard. The rehearsal space for a steelband, usually a vacant lot out-of-doors.

Panorama. A competition for conventional steelbands at Carnival (in Trinidad and in Brooklyn).

soca. A dance-band ("party") form of calypso, with disco and other international influences pioneered in the 1970s and popular into the contemporary period.

strum. A rhythmic striking of two notes on the pan to fill in chords of a composition.

road march. The parade component of Carnival and the form of calypso designed to accompany it.

Savannah. The area of Queen's Park in downtown Port-of-Spain where the Carnival (and Panorama) reviewing stands are located.

scratcher. A scraped percussion instrument used in the steelband engine room.

shak-shak. A shaken percussion instrument with internal rattles used in the steelband engine room. Often simply called a shaker.

steelband. An ensemble made entirely of pans and ancillary percussion instruments.

conventional steelband. Panorama-sized steelband, usually close to one hundred or more players.

stageside. A smaller performance steelband (perhaps twenty-five to fifty players), often a subset of a conventional band.

pan around the neck. An historical form of steelband, with pans carried on straps (one or at most two pans per player) so that the ensemble can play while marching, revived in the last few decades or so.

tamboo bamboo. A Carnival music ensemble (predecessor to the steelband) using various lengths of bamboo tubes as percussion and concussion instruments. Largely obsolete except for folkloric performances.
tent. The commercial venues for calypso performances in the months prior to Carnival.
tune. As a verb, this means to build a pan and get it into rough tune. The final stage of working the noteheads, to obtain the proper loudness and alignment of overtones, is typically called "blending."
wine, winin'. A dance move involving a rolling of the hips, often while pressed close to a dance partner.

Selected New York-Area Steelbands

Ad-Lib
C.A.S.Y.M.
Despers USA
Harlem All-Stars
Harmony
Metro
Moods Pan Groove
New Generation
Pan Rebels
Pan Sonatas
Sesame Flyers
Silhouettes
Sonatas

Chapter 12: Musical Example (access through companion website)

Track 1. Pan Rebels, "Fire Coming Down." Basement Records.

References Cited

Aho, William R. 1987. "Steel Band Music in Trinidad and Tobago: The Creation of a People's Music." *Latin American Music Review* 8, no. 1: 26–55.
Allen, Ray and Les Slater. 1998. "Steel Pan Grows in Brooklyn: Trinidadian Music and Cultural Identity." In *Island Sounds in the Global City: Caribbean Popular Music and Identity in New York*, ed. Ray Allen and Lois Wilcken. New York: New York Folklore Society and the Institute for Studies in American Music. 114–37.
Averill, Gage. 1994a. "Anraje to *Angaje:* Carnival Politics and Music in Haiti." *Ethnomusicology* 38, no. 2: 217–47.
———. 1994b. "'*Mezanmi, Kouman Nou Ye?* My Friends, How Are You?' Musical Constructions of the Haitian Transnation." *Diaspora: A Journal of Transnational Studies* 3, no. 3: 253–72.

Birth, Kevin K. 2008. *Bacchanalian Sentiments: Musical Experiences and Political Counterpoints in Trinidad.* Durham, NC: Duke University Press.

Cohen, Abner. 1993. *Masquerade Politics: Explorations in the Structure of Urban Culture Movements.* Berkeley and Los Angeles: University of California Press.

Cowley, John. 1996. *Carnival, Canboulay and Calypso: Traditions in the Making.* Cambridge: Cambridge University Press.

Dudley, Shannon. 2008. *Music from Behind the Bridge: Steelband Spirit and Politics in Trinidad and Tobago.* New York: Oxford University Press.

Greenidge, Robert. 1994. "Fire Coming Down." Panorama arrangement. Transcribed by Steve Popernack, ed. Steve Popernack and Shelly Irvine. Akron, OH: Panyard.

Hill, Donald, and Roger Abrahamson. 1980. "West Indian Carnival in Brooklyn." *Natural History* 88: 72–84.

Kasinitz, Philip. 1992. *Caribbean New York: Black Immigrants and the Politics of Race.* Ithaca, NY: Cornell University Press.

———. 1998. "Community Dramatized, Community Contested: The Politics of Celebration in the Brooklyn Carnival." In *Island Sounds in the Global City: Caribbean Popular Music and Identity in New York*, ed. Ray Allen and Lois Wilcken. New York: New York Folklore Society and the Institute for Studies in American Music. 93–113.

Kasinitz, Philip, and Judith Fridenberg-Herbstein. 1987. "Caribbean Celebrations in New York City: The Puerto Rican Parade and the West Indian Carnival." In *Caribbean Life in New York City: Social and Cultural Dimensions*, ed. Constance Sutton and Elsa Chaney. New York: CMS. 327–49.

Kronman, Ulf. 1991. *Steel Pan Tuning: A Handbook for Steel Pan Making and Tuning.* Stockholm: Musikmuseet.

Laguerre, Michel S. 1984. *American Odyssey: Haitians in New York City.* Ithaca, NY: Cornell University Press.

Manning, Frank. 1990. "Overseas Caribbean Carnivals: The Art of a Transnational Celebration." *Plantation Society in the Americas: Carnival in Perspective*, ed. Thomas M. Fiehrer and Michael W. Loderick. New Orleans: University of New Orleans. 47–62.

Nunley, John W. 1988. "Festival Diffusion into the Metropole." In *Caribbean Festival Arts*, ed. John W. Nunley and Judith Bethelheim. Seattle: University of Washington Press.

Ryan, Selwyn. 1972. *Race and Nationalism in Trinidad and Tobago.* Toronto: University of Toronto Press.

Schiller, Nina Glick, and Georges Fouron. 1990. "'Everywhere We Go, We Are in Danger': Ti-Manno and the Emergence of a Haitian Transnational Identity." *American Ethnologist* 17, no. 2: 329–47.

Stuempfle, Stephen. 1995. *The Steelband Movement: The Forging of a National Art in Trinidad and Tobago.* Philadelphia: University of Pennsylvania Press.

"Techniques for Recording Steel Drums Live." 1995. *Pro Sound News* (December): 54, 56.

Recordings Cited

Lord Invader. *Labor Day.* Folkways Records.
Lord Kitchener (Aldwin Roberts). "Pan Dingolay." 1991. Soca Hits.
Mighty Sparrow (Slinger Francisco). 1969. "Mas' In Brooklyn." On *More Sparrow More,* Ra2020 (Barbados).
Recording Artists Productions. Grant, Rupert. 1956.
Rudder, David. 1987. "Calypso Music." On *This Is Soca with David Rudder and Charlie's Roots.* New York: Sire Records.
Williams, Dennis. "Pan in Yuh Pan." 1993. Merchant.

Additional Sources

Suggested Bibliography

Hill, Donald. 1993. *Calypso Callaloo: Early Carnival Music in Trinidad.* Gainesville: University Presses of Florida. The accompanying CD contains the first steelband recording ever made.
Hill, Errol. 1972. *The Trinidad Carnival: Mandate for a National Theatre.* Austin: University of Texas Press.
Liverpool, Hollis. 1990. *Kaiso and Society.* Diego Martin (Trinidad): Juba.
Mason, Peter. 1998. *Bacchanal! The Carnival Culture of Trinidad.* Philadelphia: Temple University Press.

Suggested Audiography

Note: There are many early recordings of steelbands in existence, but they are generally difficult to find and of only tangential relevance to this chapter. What follows are a few examples of reasonably contemporary recordings that should be relatively easy to locate and that contain compositions similar to those played by contemporary Brooklyn steelbands. Much easier to locate, though, would be the many recordings of Panorama competitions (in Trinidad and in Brooklyn) hosted on YouTube.

Various. *Panorama: Steel Bands of Trinidad.* Delos 13491 40154.
———. *Pan All Night: Steelbands of Trinidad and Tobago.* Delos DE 4022.
———. *Calypso Season.* Mango Records 539.861-2.
———. *Pan Champs, vols. 1 and 2.* Blue Rhythm Records LP 2430.
Amoco Renegades Steel Orchestra. *Panorama Classics.* Sanch 9203.
Desperadoes Steel Orchestra. *The Jammer.* Delos DE 4023.
Our Boys Steel Band. *Pan Progress.* Mango Records 162 539 916-2.
———. *Pan Night and Day.* Mango Records CCD 9822.
Of special interest are the annual Panorama compilations recorded by Sanch Electronix in Port-of-Spain, Trinidad, (809) 663-1384.

Suggested Videography and Web Resources

Note: Many of the documentaries that have filmic or academic content are now quite dated (see below). There are, however, innumerable videos posted on YouTube or Vimeo from Carnival competitions and other contexts. There area also a few web resources that aggregate pan resources, including videos, such as: http://whensteeltalks.ning.com or http://www.panonthenet.com.

Celebration! 1988. Produced and directed by Karen Kramer. Dr. Morton Marks and Dr. Donald Hill, consultants. Ho-ho-kus, NJ: Film Library. 30 minutes.

Mas Fever: Inside Trinidad Carnival. 1987. Produced and directed by Glenn Micalleff. Photographed and ed. Larry Johnson. Portland, OR: Filmsound. 55 minutes.

Moko Jumbie. 1990. Directed by Karen Kramer. Produced by Karen Kramer and James Callahan. Ho-ho-kus, NJ: Film Library. 15 minutes.

One Hand Don't Clap. 1988. Produced and directed by Kavery Dutta. New York: Rhapsody Films. 92 minutes.

Steelband Music in Trinidad and Tobago: The Creation of a People's Music. 1994. Produced by William R. Aho. Akron, OH: Panyard. 32 minutes. Available at www.youtube.com/watch?v=8nSUO9aEtR8

Steelbands of Trinidad (Pan in A-Minor). 1987. Daniel Verba and Jean-Jacques Mrejean. Hurleyville, NY: Villon Films. 49 minutes.

\- 13 -

FROM THE BAYOU TO THE BAY

Louisiana French Dance Music in Northern California

Mark F. DeWitt

Although ethnomusicologist Mark F. DeWitt now works and teaches in Lafayette, Louisiana, in the region that gave birth to Cajun and zydeco music, he arrived at this research area by way of his graduate student experience in the San Francisco Bay Area of California. There he found a small but loyal cadre of musicians and dancers who provide a fascinating window to a diverse set of musical processes and practices involving ethnic identity, heritage, folk revivals, tourism, migration, and cultural sustainability. Most of these themes flow through the folk dance club Ashkenaz, which is the first musical context introduced in this chapter. DeWitt then guides the reader through the twists and turns of Cajun and Creole ethnic identity and the origins of Cajun and zydeco music in Louisiana and east Texas, comparing and contrasting these two related musical styles. He goes on to describe the movement of significant numbers of Creoles from Louisiana and Texas to California starting in the 1940s, as part of a larger black migration out of the South during that time. For Creoles on the West Coast, music became a symbolically important leisure activity for maintaining their distinct identity in a highly diverse urban milieu. Some musicians who emerged from this community of expatriate Louisianans in California are profiled, including John Semien, Queen Ida (Guillory), and Danny Poullard.

From there, the chapter illustrates how bridges to other social networks were built. At the national level, Cajun and zydeco music were included in the folk and blues revivals of the 1950s and 1960s; Cajun and zydeco also were described as "world music," a category that emerged in the 1980s. At the local level, it meant that the Creoles in California came into contact with musicians and dancers who were involved in the folk revival, such as Eric and Suzy Thompson, as well nationally prominent figures such as record producer Chris Strachwitz and filmmaker Les Blank, who were based in the Bay Area. Two noteworthy intersections for these social and musical worlds were the California Cajun Orchestra and Danny Poullard's garage, where Poullard's mentorship played a crucial role. DeWitt ends the chapter by asking readers to reflect on the sustainability of musical communities in the face of musical and generational change, issues that all styles of music face at one time or another.

13.1. California Cajun Orchestra, circa 1995 (from left): Suzy Thompson, fiddle; Kevin Wimmer, fiddle; Danny Poullard, accordion; Charlie St. Mary, rubboard; Eric Thompson, electric guitar. Kneeling: Sam Siggins, electric bass. Drummer not shown. Photo by Irene Young.

INTRODUCTION

When I was a third-year graduate student in ethnomusicology at the University of California, Berkeley (1992–93), I allowed myself an occasional evening off from studying to explore the San Francisco Bay Area's vibrant musical life. Ashkenaz Music and Dance Café, a folk dance club not far from where I lived in Berkeley, featured a variety of live dance music from around the world (e.g., reggae, calypso, Brazilian samba, West African highlife, Balkan, Greek, Israeli, Cajun and zydeco), a spacious dance floor, low cover charges, and free dance lessons on weeknights. Prior to graduate school, I had attended a couple of zydeco shows, and so I picked one of the zydeco nights on the Ashkenaz calendar and arrived early enough to get the free dance instruction before the live music started.

Walking into the club for the first time, I found a feast for the eyes as I waited for the dance lesson to start. The first thing I noticed was the building's façade and interior design. A photo scrapbook several inches thick, sitting on a stand behind the doorman, showed photos of the 1970s renovation of the building and the basis for its design in pre-Holocaust Ashkenazi Jewish synagogues of eastern Europe. Other photos showed musicians who had played at the club over the years. I recognized some about whom I had read, like zydeco musician Clifton Chenier, and I saw photos of Queen Ida, whom I had seen on the East Coast in the first zydeco show I ever attended. On the wall behind the stage hung dozens of protest signs, many of them lettered in the same hand that appeared on the monthly event calendars photocopied and stacked for dancers to take home. Everything in the club seemed to be made of wood, and the place had a warm, well-broken-in feeling to it.

For the dance lesson, we were separated into groups of leaders (mostly men) and followers (all women) of about ten each to learn the basic steps while facing each other, and then paired up to practice to recorded music and instructed to change partners frequently. In less than an hour, we learned the basics of the waltz and the two-step. By the time the dance started with a locally based live band, several more experienced dancers had arrived to fill the dance floor and show us beginners some smooth moves.

As did many who came before and after me, I found this routine habit-forming. As I returned repeatedly for these dance evenings over a period of months, I started to take an ethnomusicological interest in this context for music and dance. Who were these people who were such good dancers? How did the musicians come to play this kind of music here? How is it that this dance hall designed to look like a synagogue hosts music from all over the world in a lively dance celebration?

Answers to these questions came to me over time, as I returned repeatedly to Ashkenaz and other Bay Area dance venues and as events unfolded over the following twenty years. David Nadel, the founding proprietor of Ashkenaz, was a secular Jew from Los Angeles, a social activist, and an avid folk dancer born in 1946. Living in Berkeley in the 1960s through an era of Vietnam War protests and the Free Speech Movement, he formed his strong political beliefs and also his love for dancing. While he enjoyed dancing at a Greek taverna in Berkeley named Aïtos and in a group called the Westwind International Folk Ensemble, he also wanted to start his own club, so he opened Ashkenaz in 1973. In the early days, the programming employed various kinds of European folk dancing to recordings: Balkan dance, Greek dance, and what was known as "international folk dancing." David's twinned interests of leftist politics and folk music were in keeping with the protest music and singers of the 1960s such as Pete Seeger, Joan Baez, and others.

His decision to fashion the club after a Jewish synagogue, but not to dedicate its use to Jewish music, can be seen as a tribute to his ancestors and as an expression of nostalgia. This positive expression of Jewish identity was one of many indications of a wider "new ethnicity" movement that appeared across the United States in conjunction with the civil rights movement in the 1960s and 1970s, in which groups that had formerly felt great pressure to assimilate into the American "melting pot" were now empowered to express pride in their differences from mainstream society. The expression of nostalgia for prewar Jewish communities echoes the longing of folk revival movements in general for simpler times and lifestyles, and this sentiment has found myriad expressions in revivals of many kinds from klezmer to Cajun music to polka.

A few years after he started Ashkenaz, Nadel began experimenting with hosting different kinds of music and dancing at his club in an effort to reach a broader audience. He found Cajun music and zydeco to be successful in attracting crowds. Looking back at calendars from when I first started attending, there were twenty-one evenings of Cajun music or zydeco at this one club for the first three months of 1993—more than a quarter of the club's programming. While some who played these shows were from Louisiana (John Delafose, Sheryl Cormier), most bands were comprised of musicians who lived in the area: Motor Dude Zydeco, Bayou Pon Pon, Tee Fee, the Cajun Coyotes, Zydeco Magic, Bad Boy Zydeco, the Zydeco Flames, and so on. This brings us to a central question of the chapter: why is music from rural southern Louisiana so popular in urban northern California?

One band name that appeared on the calendar on a Saturday night each month caught my attention: California Cajun Orchestra (with Danny Poullard). When I finally made it to one of their shows, I found that the band was not really an orchestra but only slightly larger than normal, with seven players: accordion, two fiddles, electric bass, electric guitar, drums, and rubboard. Poullard, the accordion player, did not do all the singing but he was definitely in charge, sitting in the center of things wearing his French beret, kicking off the songs with an understated assurance and looking out with approval onto the sea of dancers. When he did sing, it was in French. Suzy Thompson and Kevin Wimmer, the two fiddlers, expertly traded off soloing and accompanying each other, and Suzy did a good bit of the singing as well. Her husband, Eric Thompson, contributed guitar solos, and Charlie St. Mary, the rubboard player, sang a couple of numbers and hollered into his microphone whenever he felt like it, egging on the dancers and other musicians. (An aural snapshot of the California Cajun Orchestra's classic dance hall sound is available on the recording of "Lafayette Two-Step" from the group's second album, with Poullard on vocals, which accompanies this volume.) I would come to find out that the music on the bandstand was the collaboration of Louisiana natives (Poullard and St. Mary) and folk revivalists who had come to the music just as David Nadel had come to folk dancing. Likewise were the people on the dance floor a mixture of these backgrounds and more. The rest of this chapter is dedicated to explaining how things came to this juncture with the California Cajun Orchestra, and where they have gone since.[1]

CAJUNS AND CREOLES, CAJUN MUSIC AND ZYDECO

Anthropologist James Clifford once suggested the word "travel" as a cover term for all of the various ways humans move across the globe and take culture with them (Clifford 1997, 17–91). The case of Cajun and zydeco dance music in Louisiana encompasses a wide range of travel from the 1600s to the present, from the Middle Passage of the slave trade to deportation, voluntary migration, and tourist vacations. The resulting musical styles exhibit traces of their travels from or through France, Africa, the West Indies, maritime Canada, and other parts of the United States. These influences have not just flowed one direction into Louisiana but also back out, as Louisiana natives in the twentieth century left their home state in search of better economic opportunities and as those in Louisiana strove to participate in increasingly globalized cultural tourism and popular music industries. This chapter focuses on one region where Louisiana French culture has traveled intensively since the 1940s: to northern California, settling in the San Francisco Bay Area. Before we consider Louisiana French dance music in Northern California, however, it is necessary to know a few important facts about Cajun and Creole culture in Louisiana.

While Cajun and Creole food and music have been popular topics in the national and international media since the 1980s, the details of their origins in Louisiana are widely and persistently misunderstood. One common misperception is that everyone from Louisiana is a Cajun, which is very far from the truth. As an ethnic group, the Cajuns have a specific history that begins with the Acadians, a group of French settlers who made their home in parts of what are now Nova Scotia and New Brunswick in Canada and who were deported from their settlements by the British beginning in 1755. When the Acadians began settling in rural southern Louisiana some ten years later, they were by no means the only French-speaking group in Louisiana, and as they established themselves in their new home over the generations their identity changed from *acadien* to *'cadien* to Cajun.

Meanwhile, descendants of French people who had come to Louisiana by other routes (directly from France or by way of the West Indies) began to refer to themselves as *créole*. This word was also applied to slaves born in the New World and to free people of color, the offspring of female slaves and their masters who were given their freedom according to the French laws of eighteenth-century Louisiana. After well over two hundred years of Creole history in Louisiana, it is still challenging to obtain a clear perspective on Creole identity. Writer Ben Sandmel says, "'Creole' is a highly controversial word in south Louisiana, involving a complex, biased web of racial and socioeconomic identities . . . Many people who call themselves 'Creole,' by whatever definition, become livid when the name is used by others whom they consider inferior, unworthy usurpers" (Olivier and Sandmel 1999, 15).

When we talk about the people who created zydeco music, we are talking about Louisiana Creoles descended from slaves and free people of color who spoke French and who lived in the same areas where the Cajuns settled, in the bayous and prairies south and west of New Orleans, where they lived by hunting, trapping, fishing, farming, and ranching. Due in large part to the presence of the Cajuns and Creoles, French and Catholic cultural influence has been strongest in the southern part of Louisiana, whereas the northern half of the state more resembles the rest of the Anglophone, Protestant American South.

Cajun and Creole musics as we know them today did not come from somewhere else and arrive in Louisiana; rather they represent a confluence of traveling cultures that coalesced in Louisiana to produce something new and unique. Dance musics from Europe (e.g., contredanse, quadrille, waltz), as well as from West Africa and the Caribbean (e.g., *calinda* or *kalenda*, *bamboula*), were brought into proximity of one another,[2] and by the mid-to-late nineteenth century the accordion (which had been invented in 1829) had been introduced, with the help of German Jewish merchants in the region. By 1928, when the first commercial recordings of Cajun and Creole music were made, the accordion had risen to a level of preeminence in dance bands due to its loudness and ability to be heard over a roomful of dancers. While Cajuns and Creoles were officially separated by strict segregation laws of the time, the dance music played by musicians of both groups was largely a shared tradition. One well-known duo, white (Cajun) fiddler Dennis McGee and Creole accordionist Amédé Ardoin, made several seminal recordings during the first few years of the commercial recording era.[3]

The shared tradition of Cajun and Creole dance music centers around the diatonic button accordion, fiddle (or twin fiddles), and French vocals sung (usually by men) in a high, piercing voice. As early as the beginning of the recorded era, the guitar has been a common addition to provide rhythmic and basic chordal accompaniment. A handmade triangle or corrugated metal washboard might be used for percussion. Earliest contexts for the music were house dances (*bals de maison*) and dance halls where couples would enjoy a variety of dances including quadrilles, mazurkas, polkas, contredanses, waltzes, and *valses à deux temps*. Over time, the popularity of the waltz and the two-step (similar in tempo to the polka, but with different dance steps) crowded out the other dance genres, and influences from American popular music began to be felt in the 1930s from commercial recordings of blues, swing, and country music. It was also during this decade that amplification and a drum kit were first added to the music.[4]

The sound of the diatonic button accordion helps set apart Cajun music from other musical styles, although the instrument is also used in many other styles. The most typical instrument configuration is a single row of ten buttons for the right hand to play melody and, for the left hand, one bass button and one chord button. Each button plays different notes depending on whether the player is pushing or pulling on the bellows of the instrument, analogous to a harmonica, and the notes that can be played are limited to the diatonic collection of the major scale: *do re mi fa sol la ti do*. Most Cajun accordions are tuned to the C major or D major scale. The tuning of the bass and chord buttons encourages the use of major keys, which predominate in Cajun music.[5]

Old-time Creole music, which is sometimes known as *la-la*, also employed the fiddle and the diatonic accordion in duos such as Carrière brothers Dolon and Bébé, and Bois Sec Ardoin and Canray Fontenot. But some Creole accordionists desired the additional note possibilities afforded by diatonic accordions with two or three rows of buttons, which allowed them to play in a bluesier vein. The apex of this movement after World War II was Clifton Chenier's adoption and mastery of the piano accordion, a fully chromatic instrument that can play in any key. With this instrument and with his ear and knack for adapting the rhythm and blues idioms of the 1940s to 1960s to the accordion, Chenier almost single-handedly transformed Creole dance music into a new genre that became known as zydeco. In this new style appearing in the early to mid-1950s, the fiddle fell away, blues influences became more pronounced (including some songs in English), and the old washboard was replaced with a *frottoir* or rubboard, a corrugated metal vest designed specifically as a percussion instrument and worn over the shoulders. The rhythm section came to include drums, bass, *frottoir*, and an electric guitar for rhythm and soloing. In terms of how the music sounds and who created it, "zydeco is not Cajun music," as writer Herman Fuselier likes to remind his readers and radio listeners, thereby addressing another common misconception.[6]

As zydeco music ushered in changes in response to American popular music, so too did Cajun music. Cajun musicians incorporated country music from Texas and Nashville. Western swing saw its day in Louisiana, and even more lasting was the driving honky-tonk sound with fiddle, steel guitar, bass, and drums. The diatonic button accordion made a comeback (after a swing era hiatus) and French vocals stayed, along with the waltzes and two-steps, giving rise to the classic dance hall sound of musicians like Aldus Roger (pronounced RO-zhay) and Walter Mouton (MOO-tõ) that is popular in Louisiana to this day.

These changes to Creole and Cajun music took place from the end of World War II through the 1960s, a period during which the civil rights movement effectively swept away segregationist laws, blacks migrated out of the South, and other ethnic groups (including the Cajuns) began to resist assimilationist pressures in American society and assert pride in their separate identities (the "new ethnicity" movement mentioned earlier). American popular music went through several dramatic changes, including the advent of rock and roll, a widening appreciation of the blues, and a revival of interest in folk music of all kinds. It was also a time that saw migration to Texas and even farther west to California. Creoles and Cajuns who migrated westward intersected with revivalists who came to the music and dance by other routes to form a larger dance community in northern California.

WHEN CALIFORNIA GOT SOUTHERNIZED

Follow the Dust Bowl migration of the 1930s, the 1940s brought a great migration of whites and blacks to California from the South—especially Texas, Arkansas, Oklahoma, and Louisiana—for the World War II wartime industries of building aircraft (in Los Angeles) and naval vessels (in the San Francisco Bay Area). Economic opportunity attracted laborers to the shipbuilding yards, as did the chance for blacks to leave behind the overt racism of Jim Crow laws. Between 1940 and 1949, tens of thousands of migrants to northern California increased the black population of San Francisco by six and half times, Oakland by five and half times, and the East Bay town of Richmond by fifty times. Amongst this large influx of blacks were an indeterminate number of Louisiana Creoles who found themselves under the same new conditions as their fellow migrants, and yet with their French language, Catholicism, and distinctive foodways, they considered themselves a group apart from other southern blacks in the Bay Area after World War II.[7]

Comparisons to Jim Crow aside, the San Francisco Bay Area in the 1940s was hardly a utopia of equal opportunity. Historians support Ray Stevens, a Louisiana native who told me, "Racism is all over America. California, Arizona, Mississippi. It's all the same. One just acted different." Yet very few blacks moved back to the South after their wartime jobs ended, and in the post–World War II period, black migration into California continued despite discriminatory practices by employers, labor unions, and in the housing market. Residential segregation, which was later outlawed, limited blacks to certain neighborhoods in San Francisco, Oakland, and other cities. One effect of this segregation was to make the Catholic parishes in those neighborhoods likely meeting places for Creole migrants, since most other southern blacks were Protestants.

The impact of the influx of southern black culture to the Bay Area was significant. Just as blues music from the South was getting urbanized and electrified in Chicago in the 1940s, so too were smaller blues music scenes developing in Richmond and Oakland, where Bob Geddins and other producers recorded blues men and women who had migrated to the Bay Area, including Lowell Fulson (Oklahoma), Jimmy McCracklin (Missouri), L.C. "Good Rockin'" Robinson (Texas), and Lafayette "Thing" Thomas (Louisiana).[8] The Creole contingent from south Louisiana and east Texas was not as prominent or public, but they formed their own social network based on family and Catholic church connections. A few musicians, like accordionist and Louisiana native John Semien, were invited to play at house dances not unlike those back home. If a musician was not available, recordings might be used. Ray Stevens remembers, ""We'd all get together, make a big gumbo on the weekend, play the music on an old piece of jukebox and dance." Since the food to which they were accustomed—gumbo, jambalaya, red beans and rice, sauce piquante, and other Creole specialties—was not otherwise available on the West Coast at that time, making these recipes for each other and sharing them was as important to the social context as the music.

MUSIC IN A CALIFORNIA CREOLE COMMUNITY

This was the social milieu that greeted many Creoles who moved out to the Los Angeles or San Francisco regions from Louisiana, such as the family of Ida Lewis, who in 1947 was a high school senior. Just as they had done some nine years earlier in moving from Lake Charles, Louisiana, to Beaumont, Texas, Ida's parents Ben and Elvina Lewis moved their family to San Francisco in search of better economic opportunities. Their second oldest daughter Hazel, whose husband was stationed there in the navy, encouraged them to try it. They brought their family and soon found themselves immersed in their new life, a combination of new experiences and continuations of old customs with the help of the fellow Louisiana migrants with whom they worshipped and socialized. Ida's father helped form a social club, whose membership fees were used to rent a social hall for dances. Eventually, someone got the idea to use Catholic church social halls for zydeco dances and to have proceeds from the event benefit the church. Certain churches where Creoles were regular parishioners started having dances with some regularity—All Hallows in San Francisco, St. Francis of Assisi in East Palo Alto, St. Mark's in Richmond, and a few others.

Returning from a trip home to Louisiana, Ida's mother brought back an accordion for her brothers to learn to play. In a memoir she wrote decades later, Ida recalls that although she picked up the accordion and tried it early on, "I had no interest at that time in playing, because girls were not allowed. The accordion was not a very ladylike instrument. And when you were told what was right, what was wrong, you didn't have to make a decision, it was made for you and you just followed through." Her youngest brother Al (who later adopted the stage name Al Rapone) did learn to play the instrument along with other instruments and started his own band, playing a variety of musical styles. Meanwhile, Ida married Ray Guillory, a young Creole man she had first met when she lived in Texas, and settled in San Francisco. When her three children were old enough to go to school, Ida must have changed her mind about the accordion, because she borrowed it from her brother and practiced it when no one else was around.[9]

During the 1960s, while Ida was raising her family and practicing the accordion in semi-seclusion, Danny Poullard also moved to California from Louisiana by way of east Texas, and got interested in the accordion. Danny was born in 1938 near Eunice, Louisiana, into a large family of four brothers and six sisters. As with Ida, French was his first language; he didn't learn English until he started school. His father was a sharecropper who played accordion before Danny was born. John Poullard gave up the accordion after he was mistaken for someone else and shot in the back one night coming home from playing at a dance. Danny rarely saw his father play music while growing up, but he saw relatives around Eunice play music, and he enjoyed going to dances. He expressed interest in learning to play the accordion when he was a pre-teen, but his father forbade it because of the shooting incident. When Danny was thirteen his family moved to Beaumont, Texas, where his father found work and where French language and music were much less prevalent. Danny became more interested in popular music, and he taught himself piano and organ on instruments at his school and church.[10]

Before high school was over, Danny dropped out of school and joined the army. He served for two years, including a tour of duty in Europe, where he found his French to be already rusty and yet useable. After three more years in Texas he was ready to try California, where a sister was living in Los Angeles. He eventually landed a civilian job as a butcher on the Presidio military base in San Francisco. Not long after arriving, he found himself immersed in the network of Creoles living there, including many people that he had known as a child growing up near Eunice.[11]

In his new home, Danny surrounded himself with music. He learned how to play guitar and experimented with the harmonica. He befriended John Semien, who was single and would want to play music whenever anyone came to visit him. This gave Danny a chance to play guitar with other people. In 1969, the same year that he married his wife Ruby, Danny started learning the accordion. Semien had an extra instrument that he let Danny play when he came to visit, and he showed him a couple of tunes. Danny soon got his own instrument, and shortly thereafter Semien cut him loose to learn on his own (Poullard 1985 interview; Tisserand 1998, 207).

In the early 1970s, John Semien acted on an opportunity to record an album in Louisiana. This experience left him dissatisfied with his band back in California, the Opelousas Playboys, which fractured after his return. The other men in the band then approached Poullard to learn more accordion so that they could form a new band. Soon they regrouped as the Louisiana Playboys with Danny on accordion, and started playing house parties and church dances. Semien continued to play dances for a few more years, with decreasing frequency.[12]

As it became apparent to Danny that he had the ability and the opportunity to play the accordion, something he had wanted as a child and had been denied, he redoubled his efforts to learn the instrument as if in an attempt to make up for lost time. His musical point of departure was the prairie Creole style that John Semien played and that developed in the same area of southwestern Louisiana where Poullard was from, near Eunice. Not surprisingly, this was also the style of music that Danny's father had played before Danny was born. Several years after he had forbidden his son to learn the accordion, John Poullard started to play music again and to share what he knew with Danny during brief visits and with Danny's brother Edward. Ed was fourteen years younger than Danny, still lived in Beaumont and so had much greater access to their father. Danny got further instruction from Ed by long-distance telephone, the two brothers playing for each other over the phone. Ed learned to play the fiddle later, after a workplace injury forced him to take a break from the accordion.[13]

Even with these renewed family connections to enhance his music-making, Danny still did most of his learning from recordings. Cajun accordionists Nathan Abshire and Aldus Roger were two of his favorites, and he had videotapes of Roger playing on Louisiana television so that he could watch as well as listen. One day in the garage of his home in Fairfield, California, where a couple of us had come to play music on a weeknight, I found him listening to a recording of Aldus Roger's "Lafayette Two-Step" and playing along with the recording as he had done when he was first learning the song. He stopped playing when the vocalist started singing and explained as the recording continued: "Hear that? That's how I learned, doing that. Repetitive, over and over and over, one song like that. I can play every damn thing on that tape, Aldus Roger, note for note [laughs]. Because I spent many, many nights, boy. Every night, until two or three o'clock in the morning, and I had to go to work, get up at six o'clock, you know?"[14]

He watched visiting accordionists from Louisiana whenever he could, studying what they were doing on the instrument and how they rendered a particular melody. He put recordings on tape and slowed them to half speed (i.e., same key, an octave lower) so that he could learn them, as he says, "note for note," and then play along with them at full speed. He practiced while looking at himself in the mirror, so that he could reinforce the music he was hearing with a visual image of what it looks like to play it. This in turn trained his eye to the point where he became adept at picking up what other players were doing just by watching them. Finally, he took every opportunity to play with other musicians, thereby developing a strong sense of rhythm.

THE WORLD TAKES NOTICE OF CAJUN AND CREOLE CULTURE

In the larger scheme of things, Cajun and Creole music occupied an inconspicuous corner of the postwar folk music revival, but it was there. During World War II, John and Alan Lomax included Cajun songs in their published collection *Our Singing Country* and in a series of recordings, *Folk Music of the United States*, based on field recordings they had collected during trips to Louisiana in the 1930s. In his influential 1952 compilation of commercial recordings from 1927 to 1933, *Anthology of American Folk Music*, Harry Smith included five examples of Cajun music among eighty-four selections. In 1964, fiddler Dewey Balfa and some fellow Cajun musicians were invited to play at the Newport Folk Festival in Rhode Island. The enthusiastic reception they received at this nationally known folk festival was a revelation to Balfa, and he resolved to raise public opinion of Cajun music back home, where it was not highly valued at the time. The New Lost City Ramblers, a popular folk revival group at that time, learned the Cajun song "Parlez Nous à Boire" ("let's talk of drinking") from a field recording that folklorist Ralph Rinzler had made of Balfa and his brothers, and the Ramblers recorded it on a 1966 album, *Remembrance of Things to Come*, a year after the Balfa Brothers had released their own album and version of the song.

In the postwar movement to revive older styles of American folk music, passions ran just as high among those interested in the blues. Record collectors like Harry Smith, who included some blues tracks in his *Anthology*, piqued listeners' interests by finding and reissuing older recordings. Other blues enthusiasts took joy in "rediscovering" old blues men (such as Mississippi John Hurt and Son House) who recorded years ago and were still alive, giving them a chance to have second careers in music at the ends of their lives, and to discover new talent among musicians who played in older styles. One record producer who did all of the above was the San Francisco Bay Area's Chris Strachwitz, founder of Arhoolie Records.[15]

In the same year that the Lewis family arrived in San Francisco to stay (1947), teenager Chris Strachwitz emigrated with his family from lower Silesia (part of Germany through World War II, now in Poland) to the United States. While attending UC Berkeley in the mid-1950s, he became acquainted with record producer Bob Geddins in Oakland and absorbed much about the record business. After graduating from university and going to work as a high school German teacher, Strachwitz bought and sold 78 rpm recordings, made his first field trip to Texas to meet and hear blues guitarist Lightnin' Hopkins, and put out his first records under the Arhoolie label in 1960. Two years later he left his teaching job to pursue his passion for music recording.

Although Arhoolie Records began as a blues label, it was not long before Strachwitz diversified to other folk and popular music that interested him. In 1961 he was making field recordings of Creole musicians in Houston and Lake Charles, Louisiana, and in 1963 he recorded and released an album of Cajun music by the Hackberry Ramblers, making use of a recording studio in Louisiana. In 1964 he first heard and met Clifton Chenier through Lightnin' Hopkins, who was related to Chenier by marriage. Chenier had already had an active career as an R&B artist in the 1950s, touring the South with a full band, but when Strachwitz saw him in a small Houston club, he was singing his blues all in French and playing his accordion with only a drummer backing him up. They found a recording studio in Houston and recorded a few songs, then in 1965 Chenier recorded a whole album of material for Strachwitz in Houston, released as *Louisiana Blues and Zydeco*. Chenier recorded several albums with Arhoolie over the ensuing decade, including a live album at St. Mark's Church in Richmond, California, ending with *Bogalusa Boogie* in 1975. While Chenier had recorded a minor hit record with Los Angeles–based Specialty Records in the 1950s and was extremely popular in Louisiana and east Texas, it was Arhoolie that really secured his international reputation as the "King of Zydeco."

The fact that Strachwitz has been based in Berkeley and El Cerrito, California, for his entire career has had a significant impact on the reception of Louisiana French music in the Bay Area. In addition to the field trips he made to Louisiana and Texas during Arhoolie's early years, he brought musicians to California to play at folk and blues festivals in Berkeley and San Francisco. When Clifton Chenier traveled to California to play for church dances in Los Angeles and San Francisco, Strachwitz helped him book additional shows at folk clubs on his off nights. One time he advertised one of Chenier's church dances in the *San Francisco Chronicle* newspaper, after which he received a call from a church member asking that he please not advertise the dances publicly anymore because the publicity attracted hippies who liked to jump around rather than dance properly. (Still, by all accounts Creole dancers were unfailingly hospitable to outsiders at the church dances.) Strachwitz also helped find gigs for Cajun musicians like Marc Savoy and the Balfa Brothers in California. Savoy, a noted accordion maker and expert player, formed a Cajun trio with his wife Ann and fiddler Michael Doucet called the Savoy-Doucet Band that has recorded several albums for Arhoolie, including a live album recorded partly at Ashkenaz. Marc and Ann hosted musicians from California at their home in Eunice, Louisiana, for extended periods. At Down Home Music, Strachwitz's retail record store in El Cerrito, opened in 1976, local musicians could purchase and learn from the wide variety of Cajun and zydeco recordings (not just those on the Arhoolie label). He had the additional forum of radio at his disposal, through a radio program he hosted twice a month on KPFA-FM in Berkeley from 1965 to 1995.

Another dimension of Chris Strachwitz's contributions to Cajun and Creole music was with his collaborations with documentary filmmaker Les Blank. Growing up in Tampa, Florida, and through his college years at Tulane University in New Orleans, Blank developed a curiosity and keen appreciation for music and food of other cultures. As one film critic put it, "A white Anglo-Saxon Protestant, Blank finds the ethnicity of other peoples more satisfying than the ethnicity he got." After attending film school at the University of Southern California in the mid-1960s, Blank eventually settled in northern California and parlayed his interests into a career as a documentary filmmaker. Although he made his living selling his films to schools for educational use, his lyrical, narrationless work also received critical acclaim and was shown at independent art film venues and festivals. In his filmography of over thirty films made between 1964 and 2007, over half feature music or musicians as the primary subject matter. The overlap in Blank's musical interests with Strachwitz's is notable, from Lightnin' Hopkins and Mance Lipscomb to Clifton Chenier, Marc and Ann Savoy, and Mexican American music. With three films (*Chulas Fronteras*, *Del Mero Corazon*, and *J'ai Été Au Bal*) Strachwitz assumed the role of producer or co-creator. With the help of Strachwitz, Blank made at least six films that feature Cajun and Creole music and culture. Two of his films (*Chulas Fronteras* and *Garlic Is As Good As Ten Mothers*) have been named to the Library of Congress National Film Registry.[16]

Blank's earlier films on Cajun and Creole culture like *Spend It All* and *Hot Pepper* (the latter featuring Clifton Chenier) may have contributed in some way to, and his later films benefited from, a dramatic increase in awareness and appreciation of Cajun and Creole culture on the part of tourists to Louisiana and music consumers everywhere. Well after the folk revival faded from prominence, American popular culture in the 1980s saw a "Cajun craze" that swept through the media, with food and music receiving the most coverage. Part of this was the work of community leaders in Louisiana, whose economy was heavily dependent on the oil industry and who were suffering a severe downturn due to low oil prices. The decision was made to diversify the economy, promote cultural tourism, and create some infrastructure for tourists. This was also the decade when Paul Simon recorded on his landmark album *Graceland* with zydeco artist Rockin' Dopsie, putting Cajun and zydeco on the world music map. During this decade, Louisiana French culture and music also started receiving positive treatment in feature films such as *The Big Easy* and *Belizaire the Cajun.*[17]

THE EMERGENCE OF CALIFORNIA CREOLE MUSICIANS

Ida Guillory got progressively more interested in playing zydeco music as members of the Creole community organized to hire Clifton Chenier to travel to the Bay Area to play church dances and Chris Strachwitz booked him at local festivals. She received encouragement from her husband Ray, who once tricked her into attending a rehearsal of John Semien and the Opelousas Playboys, then asking her to play for them. Thereafter when Ida attended dances where the Opelousas Playboys played, Semien invited her up to the bandstand to play the few songs that she knew. She also started sitting in with her brother Al's band. When local Creole musician George Broussard organized a Mardi Gras masquerade dance in 1975, which he advertised in newspapers, he invited both John's and Al's bands to play and Ida as well. At the dance, Broussard introduced her set by proclaiming her "Queen of the Zydeco Accordion and Queen of Zydeco Music." She played her few songs and thought nothing more of it until two weeks later when her picture appeared with the caption "Queen Ida" in a feature article of the Sunday magazine of the *San Francisco Chronicle*. Journalist Peter Levine had attended the dance, taken photos, and written an article on Louisiana French culture and the immigrants who were continuing its traditions in the Bay Area. Thus did Ida acquire her stage name.[18]

From that point, a musical career unfolded with startling rapidity for the then forty-six-year-old mother of three with five songs in her active repertoire and no band of her own. After the newspaper article, she received numerous calls for bookings that she turned over to brother Al. She began rehearsing with her brother's band and when she had learned enough repertoire to play an entire engagement, he changed the name of the group from the Barbary Coast Band to Queen Ida and the Bon Temps Zydeco Band. In 1976, the year after her unsought initial publicity, she appeared before thousands of people at the Bay Area Blues Festival and cut her first album with GNP/Crescendo Records, a Los Angeles jazz label. She played her first European tour in 1979 and continued to tour there twice a year for several years. Queen Ida and the Bon Temps Zydeco Band received a Grammy Award in 1982 for Best Ethnic/Folk Recording Album for their album *On Tour*, a year before Clifton Chenier received his only Grammy.

Right around the time that Queen Ida acquired her stage name and embarked on her musical career, Danny Poullard was forming the Louisiana Playboys with former members of John Semien's band. As Danny's confidence in his accordion playing grew, the Louisiana Playboys started getting work outside of Creole community events. Danny told me about a Thanksgiving Day in the early to mid 1970s as the beginning of the transition of the music from the Catholic church to venues for the general public. Chris Strachwitz had heard of the Louisiana Playboys and invited them to play on his KPFA radio program on Thanksgiving. Les Blank was at the station watching them, and subsequently got them invited to play for parties, weddings, and art events from Sonoma County to the Monterey peninsula. In 1977 Blank arranged for chef Alice Waters to invite the Louisiana Playboys to play in Berkeley on Bastille Day, in the middle of a "garlic festival" she was having at her famed Chez Panisse restaurant. Blank recorded this event for posterity in *Garlic Is As Good As Ten Mothers*, showing the band (Poullard, Junior Felton, Ben Guillory, and Charlie St. Mary) playing in the middle of the dining room. At another moment in this film, Danny is shown playing Cajun music with Dewey and Rodney Balfa. These gigs represent the beginnings of a bridging between the ethnic community and others in the region who were showing an interest in Louisiana French culture. In 1976 the Louisiana Playboys played the first Cajun or zydeco music heard at Ashkenaz. Queen Ida also played at Ashkenaz several times thereafter, although as she toured more nationally and internationally she played at home less and less. Especially after John Semien's death in the early 1980s, the Creole community began to rely on Danny to play for their dances, as did dancers at Ashkenaz and elsewhere who had become fans of the music. Just as this began to happen, however, the Louisiana Playboys were in the process of breaking up.[19]

THE CALIFORNIA CAJUN ORCHESTRA

While the Louisiana Playboys were still together, Poullard found another performance outlet through his connections with folk revival musicians in the Bay Area. Around 1982 he began sitting in with the Bay Area–based Blue Flame String Band, including Eric and Suzy Thompson. The band's repertoire included old-time, bluegrass, blues, jug band, and Cajun music. Poullard appeared with Blue Flame at sit-down folk music venues such as the Freight and Salvage Coffeehouse in Berkeley, and they also played a few dances at Ashkenaz.[20]

The appearance of the Thompsons signals a shift in the narrative of Cajun and Creole music in California. While the California Cajun Orchestra would have been unthinkable without Danny Poullard, Eric and Suzy were likewise indispensable. They brought decades of musical experience and Bay Area music business connections that helped make the band successful over a fifteen-year period. Their presence was also indicative of a growing interest in the music among the general population (both musicians and dancers) that had begun during the folk revival period and blossomed even more in the 1980s and 1990s, a change that the Thompsons witnessed. Therefore, a closer look at their story is warranted.

Eric Thompson was born in 1946 in Stockton, California, and raised in the San Francisco Bay Area (Oakland and Palo Alto). Music got his attention while he was a high school student in Palo Alto, when he heard the Kingston Trio, whose 1957 hit "Tom Dooley" is credited by some as signaling the beginning of the folk revival's boom period. By his senior year, he was learning rhythm guitar from New Lost City Ramblers records, whose discographical liner notes fascinated him. As he built his record collection, he listened to Pete Seeger, bluegrass, and more. He first learned about Cajun music in the early sixties from Chris Strachwitz and fellow record collector Bob Pinson.[21]

Eric finished high school early, at age sixteen, and concentrated intensely on music for the next four years. He bounced around some after trying college briefly. He met and played music with Jerry Garcia and other future members of the Grateful Dead. He moved to New York for a short time, met mandolinist David Grisman, and put together a contest-winning bluegrass band. Eventually, he went back to school at the University of California, Berkeley, where he earned a B.A. in art history "because there wasn't anything in the Music Department that pertained to what I was interested in." Eric started playing Cajun music while still at Berkeley in the late sixties. In the early 1970s, Eric moved to live on the Preston Ranch property near the town of Cloverdale, in rural northern Sonoma County, California, where a few years later he met Suzy Rothfield.[22]

Suzy Rothfield Thompson was born and raised in Mount Vernon, New York, in a highly educated family where all of the children took lessons on violin, viola, or cello. Although her early violin training was in classical music, her mother also showed her folk guitar basics. Suzy's folk music education continued at a wilderness summer camp in Vermont run by Mike Cohen, brother of John Cohen of the New Lost City Ramblers. It was there that she first played folk tunes on her violin and heard Cajun music, the New Lost City Ramblers' recording of "Parlez Nous à Boire."

After high school, she visited California and fell in love with it. She canceled her East Coast college plans, moved to Berkeley, and attended the university there for a few semesters. Then she moved to Preston Ranch, where she learned her first Cajun music on the fiddle from Will Spires, a folk revival musician who had been playing it for ten years. She had neither a phonograph nor a tape recorder, so she learned entirely from face-to-face sessions with Will, playing along and learning the tunes. Suzy, Eric, Will, and their friends first learned of Louisiana French music via sources such as folk festivals, New Lost City Ramblers recordings, and each other, and therefore the folk revival became their initial frame of reference for Cajun and Creole music and the conduit through which they were able to make contact with musicians from Louisiana. The next formative experience was at a San Diego folk festival in 1976, which Suzy attended:

> When I heard the Balfa Brothers, I just completely flipped out. At that time, we didn't know about the existence of the Creoles here at all, we didn't know about Danny, Queen Ida. . . . And we certainly weren't aware that it was a

dance music. So we just sat there, and I just cried through their whole set. I was really just emotionally overwhelmed by their music, for some reason that I never will understand.

Soon thereafter, Eric and Suzy made their first trip to Louisiana. Just as Eric had done on a trip to Ireland, they visited older traditional musicians to play in their homes and learn some of their music, a pattern that would repeat on several return trips over the years in which they would visit many musicians including Dennis McGee, Dewey Balfa, Wade Frugé, Cheese Read, and D. L. Menard.

For the next two years, Suzy played in an all-woman string band called Any Old Time. They played a variety of acoustic music, including Cajun tunes, old-time string band music, and jug band blues. During this time, Suzy also played and recorded one album with Klezmorim, an influential Berkeley-based klezmer revival band. The next year, Suzy and Eric moved to Ithaca, New York, to form the Backwoods Band, a group that toured extensively for the next two years.[23]

The Backwoods Band's touring schedule allowed for short side trips to Louisiana, when Suzy and Eric would stay in the apartment above Marc Savoy's music store in Eunice. Suzy received a folk apprenticeship fellowship from the National Endowment for the Arts to study fiddle with Dewey Balfa. Meanwhile, the Backwoods Band was breaking up. In Ithaca, Suzy and Eric had become friends with guitarist Alan Senauke, who had been an editor for *Sing Out!* (a folk music magazine) in the 1970s. Together with one of Suzy's bandmates from Any Old Time, they formed the Blue Flame String Band and in very short order booked a tour, played their first date (on the *Prairie Home Companion* radio show in Minnesota), and recorded an album for Flying Fish. By some coincidence, Marc and Ann Savoy were recording an album in the same studio in Alameda, California, so Marc played accordion for the Cajun selections on the Blue Flame String Band's album. Blue Flame, in return, played on several cuts of the Savoy-Doucet LP entitled *Les Harias*. The Thompsons moved back to California in 1982. Blue Flame continued to tour for another couple of years, while also performing on their home turf. The band made its Ashkenaz debut in January 1983 with its music billed as "Old Timey, Cajun, Bluegrass, Blues, Jug Band."[24]

Eventually the Blue Flame String Band sought more work close to home. Since the band played some Cajun music and the Thompsons had been introduced to Danny Poullard by Will Spires, they invited him to sit in with them for the Cajun numbers. Once they started playing more with Danny, they expanded their Cajun repertoire so they could play for dances at Ashkenaz and elsewhere. The Ashkenaz calendar billings for the band over the next two years suggest a gradual metamorphosis from the Blue Flame String Band to the Blue Flame Band with Danny Poullard to the California Cajun Orchestra. By 1988 the California Cajun Orchestra had a monthly Saturday night gig at Ashkenaz that would continue for more than a dozen years.

The California Cajun Orchestra constituted a departure for Eric and Suzy from the sorts of eclectic folk groups in which they have performed both before and since. Suzy describes the difference:

> One reason why we ended up just playing Cajun music, it's easy to describe, it's easy to sell, it's easy to market . . . You're providing a service . . . You don't really have to listen to it, you can just dance to it or socialize to it or whatever. Before that, the bands that I played in were listening bands. This was the first time I ever played in a band that was a dance band. We don't play other kinds of music in the California Cajun Orchestra; we don't even play the other kinds of Cajun music that we like to play. It's become a real conscious thing to have it just be a showcase for Danny and to do what Danny wants.

New sets of expectations from Danny and the dancers also meant a shift from the acoustic string band format to an electric Cajun dance band instrumentation: accordion, fiddle, electric guitar (a new departure for Eric), electric bass, and drums. Drummer Sam Siggins, a veteran local country musician, and bassist Bill Wilson, an experienced blues and country musician, provided solid backup. When he was not playing with the Good Ol' Persons, a Bay Area bluegrass band, fiddler Kevin Wimmer added a lush two-fiddle sound and an occasional vocal. Charlie St. Mary provided an additional Creole dimension with his frottoir playing and bluesy vocals.[25]

The California Cajun Orchestra's performance venues were not limited to folk revival settings like Ashkenaz. Because Poullard and St. Mary were in the band, the Creole community hired them to play at church dances. In 1989 producers Les Blank, Chris Strachwitz, and Maureen Gosling finished the film documentary *J'ai Été au Bal*. Suzy appears in that film in footage shot in the Thompsons' home in California, playing music with D. L. Menard, with Jermaine Jack and Danny Poullard, and also in a "bonus track" on the DVD release of the film, playing and singing "Grand Mamou" with Queen Ida, Poullard, and George Broussard.[26]

The California Cajun Orchestra made two recordings. Suzy pursued and procured funding from the California Arts Council for the group to record for Arhoolie, and the album *Not Lonesome Anymore* was released in 1991. The repertoire consisted mostly of electric Cajun dance hall standards, albeit some heard less often than others, for example some tunes that Danny learned from his father and from John Semien. Perhaps surprisingly, the album received radio airplay in Louisiana after Chris Strachwitz sent out the release to his usual mailing list of radio stations. Awareness there led in 1993 to some rare recognition for a Cajun band not based in Louisiana or Texas: the first-ever "Le Cajun" award to an out-of-state band from the Cajun French Music Association, followed by an invitation to play at Festivals Acadiens in Lafayette, Louisiana, the largest festival of the year devoted primarily to Cajun and Creole French music. While in Louisiana for the festival, they also appeared on the *Rendezvous des Cajuns* live radio broadcast from the Liberty Theater in Eunice, near where Poullard was born. Suzy says: "The thing I remember about being at the Liberty Theater is that we were playing 'Not Lonesome Anymore' and we looked out and Aldus Roger was dancing. That was a huge thrill to see him dancing to us playing his tune." The group made a second album with Arhoolie in 1995, after which the band's personnel saw some turnover, but Danny, Eric, and Suzy remained the core of the group and even made some appearances as the California Cajun Trio. The band continued to perform, although less frequently than in its early years, while Poullard appeared more often with Danny and Friends.[27]

With the California Cajun Orchestra, the question arises as to why Danny Poullard, a Creole musician, consciously chose to call most of the music he played "Cajun music" and use the word "Cajun" for the name of his band. While as an ethnic group, Creoles have been primarily associated with zydeco music, Danny was relatively free in California to follow his own preference for Cajun accordion playing, stemming from the older Creole "French" style that his father played and that bears a closer resemblance to Cajun music than to zydeco. Danny subscribed to the historical view that at one time "it was all French music" and believed that the style of music that today is called "Cajun music" was originally not the exclusive domain of ethnic Cajuns, nor should it be so today. He played Creole music and zydeco, too, but he kept coming back to "Cajun music," which he considered to be a designation of musical style only, not a declaration of ethnic cultural ownership. At the same time, he considered all of Louisiana French dance music a tradition worth preserving. This was a complex set of views for Danny to hold together, since he was divorcing arguments for the preservation of musical tradition and the maintenance of ethnic identity that usually go hand in hand. He was aware that others did not think this way, yet he stubbornly stuck to his opinion that considerations of music should be color-blind with respect to race.

MUSICAL MENTORSHIP

In addition to playing countless dances and making some noteworthy recordings, Danny Poullard left a significant legacy as a mentor to other musicians. In a typical month in the northern California Cajun-zydeco dance calendar around the year 2000, there were approximately forty events with live music supplied by some twenty different bands. Over half the events were played either by Danny himself or by musicians who credited Danny as their teacher. His reputation as a transmitter of the musical tradition became another point of pride with Danny. It began with his enthusiasm for informal music-making, which did not stop when he began fronting his own band, nor was it limited to his fellow Louisiana expatriates (when I approached him about studying accordion, he agreed immediately). Just as he learned by playing with others, others began learning by playing with him. His willingness to play with others of varying skill levels at informal gatherings marked the beginning of his master-teacher phase. If someone had an instrument, he would encourage him or her to get it out or bring it next time even if the person had never played Cajun music before. Just as John Semien had done years before, having people over to his house on a regular basis to make music became part of this pattern.[28]

A second recording of "Lafayette Two-Step," recorded at an after-Christmas party at a Cajun friend's home in Sacramento, illustrates Poullard's musical leadership in a jam session setting. Several others are playing along and singing to this repertoire standard, also known as "Allons à Lafayette," which was the first Cajun song ever recorded and is well-known to all who follow Cajun music. Nonetheless, he is playing a diatonic accordion in an unusual key (F) and he ends a false start by telling the guitarists the opening chord to this song (B flat) in this key. Rhythmically, he carries the entire room with his strongly accented playing and his insistent use of the chord button in the left hand throughout.[29]

Significant in Poullard's teaching is the fact that he literally gave it away. He did not charge for lessons, or for taping material, or for anything else, with the exception of the stipends he received from summer camps. Poullard would work with anyone serious about learning and making at least some progress. If he perceived someone not to be serious, he felt free to disinvite him or her at any time (although he seldom did so) since he had not incurred any obligation by accepting payment.

Poullard did not teach a great number of lessons to individuals, although he would arrange times for them upon request. What happened during one-on-one time, as he called it, varied quite a bit. In any given lesson, a student might have done one or more of the following: tape Danny playing solo to take home and learn new repertoire, videotape him so as to be able to study his fingers, listen to recordings together and comment on them, play an accompanying instrument while he played accordion, play accordion while he played guitar or fiddle, or play accordion together. If he heard something he didn't like from the student, he said something, but he never insisted on a single right way to play a particular tune. Rather, following his particular practice of never playing anything quite the same way twice, there seemed to be a range of acceptable variations for each tune. Learning from recordings was encouraged; in fact, he rather expected that most of his students would learn mostly as he did, working alone with a mirror and recordings. Music notation and tablature were never used. Students arriving with instruction method in hand were told to "get rid of that damn book!" It was acceptable, however, for students who sang to refer to written song lyrics.

At the weekly group music-making sessions that I attended between 1995 and 2000, attendance varied widely, from one to ten or more. The types of teacher-student interaction that happened in the one-on-one sessions also took place in the group. When everyone in the circle was playing music together, some accordionist started the tune and led the group. Leadership did not alternate every song; rather, one person played for a while and then ceded leadership to someone else. Danny often played accordion for a while, taking requests for particular tunes. If there were several musicians present, beginners would usually remain the aural background, either listening to or accompanying the more advanced players. During a song, multiple soloists could take a turn, including a second accordionist. Singing was encouraged but not required.

Danny's stature as the acknowledged leader of the session prevented competition for playing time from taking over the proceedings. Danny did not often have to assert his authority, but he would if he perceived the need. For example, if someone tried to lead off a song or supply an accompaniment from outside of the Cajun or Creole traditions, he would stop everything and remind them that this was a Cajun music workshop. Cooperation was more the norm at these weekly sessions. While a song was in progress, for example, some might exchange information about how the chord changes fit into the song. Between numbers, there were generally two or three conversations going on at once, some about music, some not. Not all of the musical knowledge in this context flowed from Poullard directly, but also from the more experienced students to the less experienced, and thus instruction became a group activity. The more experienced students (and Danny himself) also got something from playing with the less experienced, especially the opportunity to switch instruments and play something that they would not normally play in public.

Eventually, Danny rightfully claimed to have taught a great number of musicians who went on to form their own bands, and he became more of a national figure in the 1990s as a result of his teaching appearances at summer workshops like the Festival of American Fiddle Tunes in Port Townsend, Washington, and the Augusta Heritage Center in Elkins, West Virginia. At Augusta, where he first appeared in 1994, teaching the advanced Cajun accordion workshop became his specialty. Students from around the country came to study there, and when those from California who attended the workshop saw the respect that Danny was getting from the other students and teachers, his reputation rose back home in California as well.

These festivals provided rendezvous points for him and his brother Edward, as well as platforms for them to perform together. Eventually, the Poullard brothers found D'Jalma Garnier in Louisiana to complete a performing trio. Garnier, who like Ed Poullard had gotten grants to study Creole fiddling with Canray Fontenot, was a jazz guitarist from a musical Creole family. Poullard, Poullard, and Garnier recorded an eponymous album of acoustic music in the older Creole style of Bois Sec Ardoin and Canray Fontenot. The album was released in 2001, just a few weeks before Danny's death from a heart attack.[30]

THE VIEW AHEAD FOR THIS DANCE COMMUNITY

This chapter provides a glimpse of a small but thriving dance scene in northern California, organized around cultural practices brought from south Louisiana.

The answer to why Cajun and zydeco music are so popular in California is obviously a nuanced one that involves a dynamic history of migration, folk revival, and globalization over more than a half century. So much social and musical change brought us to this point. What's next?

One writer on contra dance, an Anglo-American form of folk dancing, compares the rural context in which contra dances took place with the urban settings in which one often finds them today. In rural communities, people did (and to some extent still do) have strong social ties reinforced by seeing each other at church, at their children's schools, and perhaps working together. By contrast, "in many urban areas the social dance event has been transformed from a *community dance* to a *dance community*, in which the dance provides the major focus for the participants' relationship with one another. . . . For many urban participants, contra dance is not a supplement to their social life, but rather the hub of it."[31]

Much the same could be said of the Cajun and zydeco scene in the San Francisco Bay Area, a large metropolitan area, especially for those like me who did not grow up with the music, had no family connection, and yet attended multiple dances each week. There is a dance community of people who know each other primarily through dancing, and for the Creoles who attend, there is also the element of the community dance, since they come to see others in their Louisiana social network they have known for decades. Some Creoles also participate in the dance community and have made several friends in the Bay Area through dancing. Further complicating the map of social networks is the presence of an Ashkenaz community born out of loyalty to that particular venue—some attend Cajun and zydeco dances only there and nowhere else, but they might also attend reggae nights or Balkan dances there. There is not one dance community but several communities which overlap and meet on a given night when circumstances align, sharing the dance floor and the bandstand: those who grew up dancing with their relatives and those who had to be shown at a dance lesson; those who understand the French being sung and those who do not; those who are expressing a pride in group identity and those who are simply having a good time.

Arguably, what gives the Cajun and zydeco dance community in northern California a unique character is the significant participation both from Louisiana migrants and from folk revivalists and others who have discovered an affinity for the music. How will this community continue to sustain itself? Immigration from Louisiana to California appears to have slowed since the 1970s, and many Creoles, especially in the second generation (born in California), choose not to patronize the dances at all and rather have decided to let their Louisiana roots recede into the distance.

Andre Thierry is one Creole musician born in California who has decided to continue the tradition. Raised in a family where his grandparents and mother organized dances at St. Mark's Church in Richmond and where zydeco musicians like Clifton Chenier and John Delafose stayed when they traveled from Louisiana to play, Andre started playing the accordion as a child. He was already playing dances with his band Zydeco Magic in his early teens. Since Danny Poullard died, Thierry emerged as the go-to musician for dances in the Bay Area. Queen Ida has retired from performing, although she still makes an occasional appearance at a festival with her son, Myrick "Freeze" Guillory. Still, Andre is hardly the only choice: there are nineteen other bands listed on the monthly Bay Area dance calendar that independent volunteer Ellen Papper has been compiling since the mid-1990s. Suzy and Eric Thompson still play Cajun music occasionally with their group the Aux Cajunals (yes, it's a pun), with Suzy on accordion.[32]

Of course, the future of the dance community in northern California is loosely tied to the health of Cajun and zydeco musics in Louisiana, which are in fact going strong but also under changing circumstances: fewer traditional dance halls, fewer fluent French speakers, and an increasing influence of hip hop among young zydeco bands, just to name a few trends. Interestingly, the example that Queen Ida helped set for women accordion players has been followed by relatively few in zydeco. In Cajun music, Louisiana accordionist Sheryl Cormier launched her career around the same time that Ida did (late 1970s), following whom there have likewise been relatively few women.[33]

Another factor in the continuation of the dance community is the survival of its institutions. In late 1996, Ashkenaz club owner David Nadel was shot and killed in his club by a patron he had ejected earlier in the evening. Suzy Thompson became part of a group that formed a non-profit organization to purchase the building from Nadel's family and to operate the club in the spirit that Nadel had started it, as a venue welcoming to all ages and all cultures. The group did succeed in its goal; Suzy served on the initial board of directors, helped raise funds for the down payment on the building, assisted with its applications to become a non-profit, and wrote grant applications for the organization, which was renamed Ashkenaz Music & Dance Community Center.

As of the summer of 2012, the Bay Area dance calendar indicates that the dance community is alive and well, with over fifty dates in one month ranging from mornings at farmer's markets to the Crawdad Festival in Isleton to Tuesday evenings at Ashkenaz, Friday night zydeco dances at the Eagles' Hall in Alameda, and other venues that less frequently feature the music. Still it is not uncommon when talking with members of this community to hear undertones of worry: that Ashkenaz no longer has Cajun or zydeco on Saturday nights with regularity, that there are not many church dances anymore, that it is difficult for bands to find gigs, that all of the regular dancers seem to be getting older, or that a membership club has folded. Some of this can be discounted as a lack of historical perspective (many membership clubs have come and gone, with seemingly little effect), while other trends (fewer church dances) probably portend a significant change of some kind.

Is this dance community sustainable, and why should anyone care? Ethnomusicologist Thomas Turino has argued that participatory performance (one with no passive audience, as is our case here) affects people in ways that other kinds of musical performance do not, that "habits of thought and value developed by regularly taking part in participatory performance can affect the habit trajectories pertaining to other realms of life." In other words, the dance floor serves as more than a place to have fun; as an egalitarian social realm where people watch after one another, it becomes a model for how we would prefer to live the rest of our lives. Whether or not this California dance community will continue to flourish, only time will tell; what its disappearance would mean is something for you, our readers, to contemplate and discuss.[34]

Notes

1. These initial experiences led me to write an ethnomusicological dissertation on the Cajun and zydeco scene in northern California, which I later reworked into a book, *Cajun and Zydeco Dance Music in Northern California: Modern Pleasures in a Postmodern World* (Jackson: University Press of Mississippi, 2008). Material for the present essay was taken from this book, especially from chapters 4–6. The recording of "Lafayette Two-Step" is taken from the California Cajun Orchestra's 1995 album *Nonc Adam Two-Step* (Arhoolie CD 436) and features Danny Poullard on accordion and vocals, Eric Thompson on guitar, Suzy Thompson and Kevin Wimmer on twin fiddles, and Charlie St. Mary on rubboard and spoken exhortations.

2. Bernard and Girouard 1992; Kein 2000; Daigle 1972/2006. It has frequently been remarked that south Louisiana, culturally, can be considered the northernmost edge of the Caribbean. For more on the meeting of European and African dance in the Caribbean, see Daniel 2011 and Manuel 2009.

3. Brasseaux 2009, 83–84; Arhoolie/Folkloric CD 7007.

4. Brasseaux 2009, 36–48.

5. For more information on the Cajun approach to this instrument, see DeWitt 2003; DeWitt 2012.

6. www.zydecoevents.com/history2.html, accessed June 5, 2012.

7. Broussard 1993, 135–36, 206; McBroome 1993, 92; Johnson 1993, 30–59; Gregory 1989; Gregory 2005.

8. Hildebrand and Moore 1998.

9. Guillory 1990, 168; Tisserand 1998, 209–12.

10. Poullard 1985 interview; Ed Poullard 2006 interview; Fusilier and Adams 1994, 26.

11. Poullard 1985 interview; Poullard pers. comm.; Tisserand 1998, 203, 206.

12. Poullard 1985 interview; Fusilier and Adams 1994, 27; Canaparo 2004 interview.

13. Wood 2006, 280–83.

14. Poullard 1995 session tape.

15. Gioia 2008, 347–400; Hamilton 2008.

16. Hollenbach 1984.

17. Ancelet 1992; Bernard 2003, 112–45.

18. Levine 1975.

19. Tisserand 1998, 108–15; Poullard 1985 interview; Spires 1997 interview; Ashkenaz archives.

20. Thompson and Thompson 1997 interview; Senauke pers. comm.; Ashkenaz archives.

21. Weill 1972, 5; Thompson and Thompson 1997 interview.

22. Weill 1972, 5; Thompson interview, 2006. http://julianwinston.com/music/me_and_my_old_banjo2.php, accessed April 25, 2006.

23. *Any Old Time String Band*, Arhoolie LP 4009 (1978), re-released on Arhoolie CD 433 together with the band's 1980 LP on Bay Records (Bay LP 217). The 1980 album was made after Suzy left the band. Klezmorim, *Streets of Gold*, Arhoolie LP 3011 (1978).

24. Flying Fish FF-275; Arhoolie 5029; Calendar archives, Ashkenaz Music and Dance Community Center, Berkeley, CA.

25. Wimmer originally from New York, had previously apprenticed himself to Dewey Balfa. He later moved to Louisiana to play with Balfa Toujours, the Red Stick Ramblers, and several other bands.

26. Arhoolie CD 5041. Musician credits on the Cajun numbers included Danny Poullard, Kevin Wimmer, Charlie St. Mary, and Beth Weil (bass).

27. Arhoolie CD 356 (1991); Fusilier and Adams 1994; Thompson 2006 interview; Arhoolie CD 436 (1995).

28. For another account of Poullard's musical tutelage, see Kilpatrick 2009.

29. "Lafayette Two-Step" by Danny Poullard and friends at a party in the home of Freida Fusilier, Sacramento, California, 26 December 1994. Field recording by Mark F. DeWitt.

30. Willging 1999; Louisiana Radio Records CD5958. I attended the Augusta Heritage Center's Cajun/Creole Week in 1998 as an accordion student (not in Poullard's class) and returned the following year as an audience member and observed Danny teach the advanced accordion class.

31. Dart 1995, 14.

32. http://calendar10.tripod.com/ (monthly dance calendar), accessed June 4, 2012.

33. http://web.lsue.edu/acadgate/music/scormier.htm, accessed June 4, 2012. In zydeco, Ann Goodly recorded two or three albums and Rosie Ledet is still active as of this writing. In Cajun music, Kristi Guillory is a leading accordionist of the younger generation.

34. http://calendar10.tripod.com/calendars/2012jun.pdf, accessed June 6, 2012. Turino 2009, 113; see also DeWitt 2009.

Chapter 13: Musical Examples (access through companion website)

Chapter 13, Track 1. California Cajun Orchestra. 1995. "Lafayette Two-Step," on *Nonc Adam Two-Step*, Arhoolie CD 436. Public domain. Danny Poullard, accordion and vocal; Suzy Thompson, fiddle; Kevin Wimmer, fiddle; Eric Thompson, electric guitar; Sam Siggins, electric bass; Charlie St. Mary, rubboard; Terry O'Dwyer, drums.

Chapter 13, Track 2. Danny Poullard and friends. 1994. "Lafayette Two-Step," field recording of at a party in the home of Freida Fusilier, Sacramento, California, 26 December 1994. Field recording by Mark F. DeWitt.

References Cited

Ancelet, Barry Jean. 1992. "Cultural Tourism in Cajun Country: Shotgun Wedding or Marriage Made in Heaven?" *Southern Folklore* 49, no. 3: 256–66.

Bernard, Shane, and Julia Girouard. 1992. "'Colinda': Mysterious Origins of a Cajun Folksong." *Journal of Folklore Research* 29, no. 1: 37–52.

Bernard, Shane K. 2003. *The Cajuns: Americanization of a People*. Jackson: University Press of Mississippi.

Brasseaux, Ryan André. 2009. *Cajun Breakdown: The Emergence of an American-Made Music*. Oxford: Oxford University Press.

Broussard, Albert S. 1993. *Black San Francisco: The Struggle for Racial Equality in the West, 1900-1954*. Lawrence: University Press of Kansas.

Clifford, James. 1997. *Routes: Travel and Translation in the Late Twentieth Century*. Cambridge, MA: Harvard University Press.

Daigle, Brenda. 1972/2006. "Acadian Fiddler Dennis McGee and Acadian Dances." In *Accordions, Fiddles, Two Step & Swing: A Cajun Music Reader*, ed. Ryan A. Brasseaux and Kevin S. Fontenot. 363–77. Lafayette: Center for Louisiana Studies, University of Louisiana at Lafayette.

Daniel, Yvonne. 2011. *Caribbean and Atlantic Diaspora Dance: Igniting Citizenship*. Urbana: University of Illinois Press.

Dart, Mary McNab. 1995. *Contra Dance Choreography: A Reflection of Social Change*. New York, NY: Garland.

DeWitt, Mark F. 2003. "The Diatonic Button Accordion in Ethnic Context: Idiom and Style in Cajun Dance Music." *Popular Music and Society* 26, no. 3: 305–30.

———. 2008. *Cajun and Zydeco Dance Music in Northern California: Modern Pleasures in a Postmodern World*. Jackson: University Press of Mississippi.

———. 2009. "Louisiana Creole *Bals de Maisons* in California and the Accumulation of Social Capital." *world of music* 51, no. 1: 17–34.

———. 2012. "From Chanky-Chank to Yankee Chanks: The Cajun Accordion as Identity Symbol." *The Accordion in the Americas: Klezmer, Polka, Tango, Zydeco, and More!*, ed. Helena Simonett. 44–65. Urbana: University of Illinois Press.

Fusilier, Freida Marie, and Jolene M. Adams. 1994. *Hé, Là-Bas! A History of Louisiana Cajun and Zydeco Music in California*. Sacramento, CA.

Gioia, Ted. 2008. *Delta Blues: The Life and Times of the Mississippi Masters Who Revolutionized American Music*. New York: W. W. Norton.

Gregory, James N. 1989. *American Exodus: The Dust Bowl Migration and Okie Culture in California*. New York: Oxford University Press.

———. 2005. *The Southern Diaspora: How the Great Migrations of Black and White Southerners Transformed America*. Chapel Hill: University of North Carolina Press.

Guillory, Queen Ida. 1990. *Cookin' with Queen Ida*. Rocklin, CA: Prima Publishing.

Hamilton, Marybeth. 2008. *In Search of the Blues*. New York: Basic Books.

Hildebrand, Lee, and James C. Moore Sr. 1998. "Oakland Blues." In *California Soul: Music of African Americans in the West*, ed. Jacqueline Cogdell DjeDje and Eddie S. Meadows. Berkeley: University of California Press. 104–23.

Hollenbach, Margaret. 1984. "Herzog's Burdens—Blank's Dreams." *Burden of Dreams: Screenplay, Journals, Reviews, Photographs*, ed. Les Blank and James Bogan. Berkeley, CA: North Atlantic Books. 255–59.

Johnson, Marilynn S. 1993. *The Second Gold Rush: Oakland and the East Bay in World War II*. Berkeley: University of California Press.

Kein, Sybil. 2000. "The Use of Louisiana Creole in Southern Literature." In *Creole: The History and Legacy of Louisiana's Free People of Color*, ed. Sybil Kein. Baton Rouge: Louisiana State University Press. 117–54.

Kilpatrick, Blair. 2009. *Accordion Dreams: A Journey into Cajun and Creole Music*. Jackson: University Press of Mississippi.

Levine, Peter. 2 March 1975. "They Call It Zydeco." *San Francisco Chronicle*, sec. California Living, 24–29.

Lomax, John, and Alan Lomax, collectors and compilers. 1941. *Our Singing Country: A Second Volume of American Ballads and Folk Songs*. New York: Macmillan.

Manuel, Peter, ed. 2009. *Creolizing Contradance in the Caribbean*. Philadelphia: Temple University Press.

McBroome, Delores Nason. 1993. *Parallel Communities: African Americans in California's East Bay, 1850-1963*. New York: Garland.

Olivier, Rick, and Ben Sandmel, photographer/author. 1999. *Zydeco!* Jackson: University Press of Mississippi.

Tisserand, Michael. 1998. *The Kingdom of Zydeco*. New York: Arcade.

Turino, Thomas. 2009. "Four Fields of Music Making and Sustainable Living." *world of music* 51, no. 1: 95–117.

Weill, Rita. 1972. Liner notes to *Berkeley Farms: Oldtime and Country Style Music of Berkeley*. Producer Mike Seeger. New York: Folkways Records FA 2436.

Willging, Dan. 1999. "Digging at the Roots of Creole Music: D'Jalma Garnier of Filé." *Dirty Linen* 80.

Wood, Roger. 2006. *Texas Zydeco*. Austin, TX: University of Texas Press.

Recordings Cited

Any Old Time String Band. 1978/1980/1996. *I Bid You Goodnight*. El Cerrito, CA: Arhoolie CD 433.

Amédé Ardoin. 1930/1934/1995. *I'm Never Comin' Back*. El Cerrito, CA: Arhoolie/Folklyric CD-7007.

Blue Flame String Band. 1982. *Blue Flame String Band*. Chicago: Flying Fish FF-275.

California Cajun Orchestra. 1991. *Not Lonesome Anymore*. El Cerrito, CA: Arhoolie CD 356.

California Cajun Orchestra. 1995. *Nonc Adam Two-Step*. El Cerrito, CA: Arhoolie CD 436.

Chenier, Clifton. 1971/1989. *Live at St. Mark's*. El Cerrito, CA: Arhoolie CD 313.

The Klezmorim. 1978. *Streets of Gold*. El Cerrito, CA: Arhoolie 3011.

Library of Congress. 1942. *Folk Music of the United States*, Album V. Washington, DC.

Lomax, John and Alan Lomax, collectors. 1999. *Louisiana Cajun and Creole Music, 1934: The Lomax Recordings*. Cambridge, MA: Rounder CD 1842-1843.

New Lost City Ramblers. 1966. *Remembrance of Things to Come*. New York: Folkways F-31035.

Poullard, Poullard & Garnier. 2001. *Poullard, Poullard & Garnier*. Lafayette, LA: Louisiana Radio Records CD 5958.

Queen Ida and the Bon Temps Band. 1976. *Queen Ida and the Bon Temps Band Play the Zydeco*. Los Angeles: GNP-Crescendo Records GNPS-2101.

Queen Ida and the Bon Temps Zydeco Band. 1982. *On Tour*. Los Angeles: GNP-Crescendo Records GNPS-2147.

Savoy-Doucet Cajun Band. 1983. *Les Harias: Home Music*. El Cerrito, CA: Arhoolie 5029.

Smith, Harry, compiler. 1952. *Anthology of American Folk Music*. New York: Folkways FP 251, 252, 253.

Thompson, Eric and Suzy. 1989. *Adam and Eve Had the Blues*. El Cerrito, CA: Arhoolie CD 5041.

Films Cited

Always For Pleasure. Filmed, edited, produced, and directed by Les Blank. El Cerrito, CA: Flower Films and Video, 1978.

Belizaire the Cajun. Directed by Glen Pitre. 1986.

The Big Easy. Directed by Jim McBride. 1987.

The Blues Accordin' to Lightnin' Hopkins. By Les Blank. El Cerrito, CA: Flower Films and Video, 1969.

Chulas Fronteras. By Les Blank. With Maureen Gosling. El Cerrito, CA: Flower Films and Video, 1976.

Del Mero Corazon. By Les Blank. El Cerrito, CA: Flower Films and Video, 1979.

Dry Wood. By Les Blank. With Maureen Gosling. El Cerrito, CA: Flower Films and Video, 1973.

Garlic Is as Good as Ten Mothers. By Les Blank. With Maureen Gosling. El Cerrito, CA: Flower Films and Video, 1980.

God Respects Us When We Work, But He Loves Us When We Dance. By Les Blank. El Cerrito, CA: Flower Films and Video, 1968.

Hot Pepper. By Les Blank. With Maureen Gosling. El Cerrito, CA: Flower Films and Video, 1973.

J'ai Été Au Bal (I Went to the Dance). By Les Blank, Chris Strachwitz, and Maureen Gosling. El Cerrito, CA: Brazos Films/Arhoolie Productions, 1989.

Marc and Ann. Produced and directed by Les Blank. El Cerrito, CA: Flower Films and Video, 1990.

Spend It All. By Les Blank. With Skip Gerson. El Cerrito, CA: Flower Films and Video, 1971.

Yum! Yum! Yum! Produced and directed by Les Blank and Maureen Gosling. El Cerrito, CA: Flower Films and Video, 1991.

Interviews

Canaparo, Gary, and Mary Ann Canaparo. Interview by Mark DeWitt, 24 August 2004, Sunol, CA. Audio recording.

Poullard, Danny. Interview by Will Spires, 10 March 1985, San Francisco, CA. Audio recording.

Poullard, Danny. Jam session recording by Mark DeWitt, 13 April 1995, Fairfield, CA. Audio recording.

Poullard, Danny. Interview by Mark DeWitt, 8 September 2000, Fairfield, CA. Audio recording.

Poullard, Ed. Interview by Mark DeWitt, 2006. Email.

Spires, Will. Interview by Mark DeWitt, 26 August 1997, Cotati, CA. Audio recording.

Stevens, Ray. Interview by Mark DeWitt, 29 August 2000, Oakland, CA. Audio recording.

Thompson, Eric, and Suzy Thompson. Interview by Mark DeWitt, 4 March 1997, Berkeley, CA. Audio recording.

Thompson, Eric, and Suzy Thompson. Interview by Mark DeWitt and Sue Schleifer, 27 April 2006, Oakland, CA. Audio recording.

Internet Resources

Caine, Julie and Marié Abe, producers. 2011. *Squeezebox Stories*. http://squeezeboxstories.com/. This one-hour public radio documentary portrays four immigrant groups to California through their accordion-based musical traditions, including the Creole community's zydeco music in Richmond, California.

Papper, Ellen. San Francisco Bay Area Cajun Zydeco Dance Calendars. http://calendar10.tripod.com/.

Rubinstein, Andrea. "San Francisco Bayou" www.sfbayou.com/. Author is a music enthusiast who moved from the Bay Area to Louisiana after several years of running this site.

Ziglar, Richard, and Barry Yeoman, producers. 2012. *Zydeco Nation*. http://www.zydeconation.org/. This one-hour public radio documentary focuses its entire hour on the Louisiana French Creole migration to California and the role that zydeco music has played in maintaining community. In addition to the documentary itself, the website contains photos and additional interviews.

- 14 -

"A SUPERIOR RACE OF STRONG WOMEN"

North Indian Classical Dance in the San Francisco Bay Area[1]

Sarah Morelli

Sarah Morelli is an ethnomusicologist who explores a style of North Indian classical dance, called *kathak* as she experienced it in the San Francisco Bay Area. As both an insider to the kathak scene in the Bay Area and an outsider to the Indian immigrant community, Morelli is in a unique position to evaluate the motivating factors for people of Indian ancestry, who pursue the dance as heritage learners, and that of others, such as herself, who are outsiders to the tradition but who are also dedicated to the serious study and performance of the dance. In situating kathak dance and the Hindustani music that goes with it, Morelli describes the love affair that 1960s America had with Asian and more specifically Indian and Asian forms of spirituality and cultural arts and disciplines like yoga, meditation, and performance including music and dance. Her chapter looks at the themes of power, race, and gender as they are encountered, experienced, and explored by her teacher and his American kathak students, to shed light on the experiences of this particular community practicing and performing a "foreign art" in a "new land." Morelli's contribution to the volume also points to some of the flexible and inexact meanings of the category of "whiteness."

INTRODUCTION

After centuries of immigration to North America from various corners of the globe, we find many kinds of music and dance being taught, practiced, and performed in the United States that are primarily associated with another locale. Examples of such immigrant performance communities discussed in this volume include West Indian steelband music and masquerade, Czech polka music and dance, and mariachi music and dance originally from Mexico, to name just a few. In 1993 ethnomusicologist Mark Slobin commented on the widespread accessibility of musical styles in "contemporary global culture," noting that increasing availability of an eclectic menu of styles "allows anyone anywhere to be attracted to musics of choice, many of which can now be heard close to home" (68). Such

14.1. Chitresh Das Dance Company members in an advertisement for the production *Pancha Jati*, October 4 and 5, 2002. Pictured left to right: Charlotte Moraga, Jaiwanti Das Pamnani, Farah Yasmeen Shaikh, Seibi Lee, Leah Brown. Photos by Marty Sohl. Design by Eric Parker. Courtesy Chitresh Das.

availability has led to the development of music and dance communities where practitioners do not necessarily have ethnic ties to the art forms they practice. Within these music and dance scenes, we might distinguish "heritage" practitioners—those whose family roots connect them to the place identified with the artistic practice—from "affinity" practitioners—those who do not share a common ethnic or national affiliation with the music or dance, and whose connection to the art form is primarily an interest or love for the artistic practice, or an "affinity" (Shelemay 2011; Slobin 1993).[2]

Why is it necessary or useful to make a distinction between heritage and affinity practitioners? These days, one would not expect, for example, a string quartet playing the music of Wolfgang Amadeus Mozart to be comprised of musicians with Austrian or even European heritage, or that the musicians' ethnic backgrounds would affect the quality of their performance. However, in some traditions there remains an expectation that practitioners possess a cultural background and set of physical characteristics, or phenotype, congruent with the art form's place of origin. This expectation is often related to the perceived foreignness of an art form; those considered more foreign in the United States are sometimes described as "ethnic" dances or musics. What might you notice if you reflect on your own assumptions and experiences of "foreign" practices? How might your attitudes differ if studying Tibetan Buddhist practices from a Tibetan monk or from a white American layperson? How might your expectations shift if you see taekwondo presented by a Korean-born martial artist or an African American practitioner? How do you anticipate your experience would differ if you took Argentinian tango classes in its birthplace, Buenos Aires, or in a city in the United States?

This chapter focuses on a group of heritage and affinity dancers in the San Francisco Bay Area practicing kathak, a dance form originally from North India, in order to examine how attitudes regarding the foreignness of the dance have affected its performers and the development of kathak in the United States. Before discussing the diverse membership of this particular dance community, it is important to better understand the wide variety of identities, lifeways, languages, and artistic practices found within the Indian community in the United States.

INDIAN CULTURAL DIVERSITY IN THE UNITED STATES

Great diversity characterizes peoples in the country of India, the broader region of South Asia, and the region's diasporic populations in the United States and elsewhere. Subgroups identify by regional ties, religious affiliation, caste distinction, and/or linguistic background. Literally hundreds of major and minor languages are spoken across India; similarly, the country is home to a vast array of music and dance practices. Just within the realm of arts that are considered "classical," one finds two forms of music, South Indian Karnatak music and North Indian Hindustani music, and eight different forms of dance including kathak.[3] Outside what is generally considered the classical realm, there are numerous other kinds of music and dance including folk, tribal, devotional, and popular styles that can be categorized by their national appeal, regional orientation, or affiliation with a particular community. Today, due in large part to artist emigration from India, several of these art forms are being taught and performed around the globe.[4]

In the United States, many types of Indian music and dance are performed and transmitted through various contexts. Lessons are taught in private homes in most major cities and towns. Classes can be found at a number of colleges and universities like Wesleyan University, where Karnatak music has been taught since the early 1960s. College student groups are also often active in practicing and promoting Indian arts. For example, Ghungroo, sponsored by Harvard University's South Asian Association, is an annual arts showcase that began in 1986 and grew to involve over 300 student-performers in 2011 (Jain 2012). College groups also sponsor intercollegiate competitions, such as George Washington University's Bhangra Blowout. At this annual event in Washington, D.C., teams from across the United States and Canada perform tightly choreographed, vibrantly costumed, high-energy dance routines of bhangra, a folk dance that originated in the region of Punjab, which comprises a northwestern state in India and a neighboring province in Pakistan.

Performing arts are also strongly supported by community organizations, sometimes affiliated with a particular Indian region or linguistic group, such as the Minnesota Malayalee Association, the Bengali Association of Dallas–Fort Worth, the Maharashtra *Mandal* ("Organization") of Los Angeles, or the Gujarati *Samaj* ("Society") of Tampa Bay. In general, the Indian community is known for its active and robust patronage of popular and traditional music and dance concerts, and supports training children in one or more performance traditions, in large part as a means of infusing the youth with knowledge of and pride in their Indian heritage. In Colorado, the Colorado Fine Arts Association (CFAA) sponsors concerts by touring artists from India as well as by musicians and dancers who are part of the local community. Additionally, CFAA sponsors music and dance competitions for the community's youth. Many students involved in such events go on to play important roles in South Asian student organizations on college and university campuses around the country.

Other organizations and events cater to particular age groups or to those interested in specific genres of music and dance. For example, once a month at a popular Manhattan nightclub, the influential DJ Rekha Malhotra spins remixed popular musics from South Asia and the diaspora at the event known as "Basement Bhangra." Independent DJs around the United States are hired to play remixed Indian popular and traditional songs for weddings and other social events. Some members of the South Asian diaspora like DJ Rekha actively reinterpret and combine their artistic influences in new ways. Another example of such innovation can be found in the work of dancer/choreographer Parijat Desai, whose Brooklyn-based Parijat Desai Dance Company explores the blending of Indian classical and Western contemporary styles of movement. Indo-jazz fusion (a musical combination that has been explored since at least the 1950s) today involves several South Asian American musicians including saxophonists Rudresh Mahanthappa and Aakash Mittal.

Certain well-known artists have also created independent schools for Indian classical music and dance in the United States. One of the first such schools was the Ali Akbar College of Music, founded in the San Francisco Bay Area in 1967 by Ali Akbar Khan. Khan was a legendary maestro of the twenty-five-stringed sarod, and taught Hindustani music to students in the Bay Area until he passed away in 2009. Kathak dance master Chitresh Das joined the faculty of the Ali Akbar College in the early 1970s and became a key figure in bringing the kathak dance form to North America.

In the San Francisco Bay Area, those I call "affinity learners"—people with no ethnic or national ties to India—were the first to study with Ali Akbar Khan and Chitresh Das and have had a relatively long history of involvement in North Indian classical music and dance. Over more than forty years in the United States, Khan and Das (who are referred to as Khan-*sāhib* and Chitresh-*jī*, respectfully, by their students) each trained generations of students of varying backgrounds, including both heritage and affinity learners. This diversity provided fertile ground for working with issues stemming from cultural difference that manifested in training, performance, and maintenance of community. I lived in the San Francisco Bay Area (hereafter referred to as the Bay Area) from 2000 to 2003 in order to study with Khan and Das as part of the research I undertook for my PhD in ethnomusicology.[5]

Like many ethnomusicologists, my research primarily involved "participant-observation." In this process, I became part of a community of students and teachers, learning about the community from the inside; as I gained skill in performing Hindustani music and kathak dance, I also learned about how the music and dance were taught. Through both formal interviews and the more informal process of just being there for day-to-day experiences, I gained insight into important issues for members of the community. I was interested in studying these forms of music and dance in their own right—for the pleasure and challenge I derived from their aesthetic beauty and technical complexity. However, being a good student or becoming a proficient performer was not my sole motivation; like other scholars in the humanities and social sciences, I was interested in understanding other aspects of that world, including community dynamics, interpersonal communication, and artistic choices. My means of accessing those understandings was through my insider position as a student and community member. Participant-observation thus meant constantly shifting between insider and outsider points of view: from learning various aspects of the art itself (such as technique, aesthetics, or specific compositions) and taking on the social expectations of an insider, to using my vantage point as an outsider to contemplate and interpret the broader social and cultural ramifications of those experiences.

For Das and his kathak students, I found that issues of race and gender were especially salient, in part because as dancers, their bodies are their medium of artistic expression. Presenting kathak with performers who did not necessarily look "authentic"—and to audiences who often had little understanding of the dance from which to judge artistic merit—proved to be a significant and recurring challenge to Das and his students and was an impetus for various experiments in training and performance. Weaving throughout their experiences, there was a notable subtext of intense negotiations taking place between teacher and students, both on and off the dance floor, through conversation, and by way of artistic choices. In this chapter I look particularly at the themes of power, race, and gender as they are encountered, experienced, and explored by Das and his American kathak students, to shed light on the experiences of this particular community practicing and performing a "foreign art" in a "new land."

WHAT IS KATHAK?

While there are more complete descriptions of kathak elsewhere, here it is useful to provide a quick summary of the dance.[6] Kathak is a multifaceted dance form. In what is considered its most traditional format, it is performed by one solo dancer accompanied by musicians, although choreographed group presentations are also common. The dance shares the same musical framework and terminology as Hindustani music; many dancers train in one or more aspects of the music and accompanying musicians are trained in the Hindustani tradition (also known as North Indian classical music). One of the dance's most notable characteristics is its fast, percussive footwork, performed by slapping bare feet on the floor. Bells, called *ghuṅghrū*, are wrapped around the ankles to emphasize the rhythms of the dancers' footwork.[7] Footwork patterns often correspond to the patterns played by accompanying tabla drummers, and can also be communicated by reciting *bols*, onomatopoeic syllables that imitate the tones and timbres of specific drum strokes on the tabla. In video example 1 on the companion website, a performance by the Chitresh Das Dance Company, the dancers and tabla player are performing pre-composed material in unison; in this case, the compositions are reinforced through simultaneous recitation of the corresponding bols.[8] In solo performances, it is usually the dancer who will determine what patterns or compositions are performed at any given time within a performance—and often spontaneously, without warning; the tabla player's challenge is to jump in and play in synchrony with the dancer. In video example 2, you see an example of *savāl-javāb*, a "question-answer" section in which the dancer (here Chitresh Das) creates impromptu rhythmic phrases that are imitated in the tabla player's response.[9] Fast turns (*chakkars*) on one heel are often executed in a series, each one's completion emphasized by the opposite foot slapping the floor in rhythmic precision (see video example 1, 1:04–1:13 and particularly 1:25).

Kathak dancers keep their hips relatively still, providing stability both for footwork and for movements of the upper body. The dynamics of upper and lower parts of the body are usually quite distinct, though complementing one another. In contrast to the rhythmic sophistication of kathak footwork, movements of the upper body are often graceful and delicate. Facial expression is combined with other upper-body movements, footwork, and turns to portray different characters in telling a story. This storytelling aspect of kathak is called *nritya*. Other portions of kathak repertoire categorized as *nritt*, or "pure" dance, involve compositions with no explicit narrative that are performed solely for the beauty of movement and composition (as seen in video example 1).

For both nritya and nritt—dance with and without storytelling—movement quality may be gendered as *tāṇḍava* (masculine) or *lāsya* (feminine). Tāṇḍava style often involves quick and sharp movements of the upper body usually accompanied by percussive accents with the feet. Lāsya style, on the other hand, emphasizes smooth, delicate movements that do not always involve footwork. These styles, while gendered masculine and feminine, are not relegated to only male or female dancers. Dance scholar Mohan Khokar clarifies: "*Tandava* is masculine, robust, expansive, *lasya* tender, graceful, lyrical. Evidently *tandava* is nearer to men and *lasya* women, but this does not mean that men alone may dance *tandava* and women *lasya*. The two aspects refer simply to the style of rendering the dance, not to who is qualified or privileged to do the rendering" (1979, 49–50).

As a soloist, the dancer, whether male or female, must dance in masculine and feminine styles, portray all of a story's male and female characters, and depict a range of emotions and character-types. Characters might be humans, gods, or demons, and are drawn most often from Hindu mythology. Video example 3 is from a performance of a portion of the Hindu epic the *Ramayana*. In this short clip, Chitresh Das (a male dancer) first portrays male villain Ravan in a state of anger and quickly shifts to frightened female character Sita.[10] Dancers justify this flexibility in gender portrayal through pointing to the Hindu image of *ardhanārīśvara*, a deity whose body is half male (Śiva) and half female (Pārvatī/Śakti), symbolizing the complementarity or interdependence of the masculine and feminine (Kinsley 1986, 49–50). For the kathak dancers I worked with, this figure also suggests that masculine and feminine principles reside in each person; it is the dancer's work to attune him or herself to these different energies and bring them out through the dance.[11]

In addition to this breadth of gender portrayal, Chitresh Das's students learned that there are four general skills a dancer must develop to be fully prepared and able to perform kathak. These are (in Hindi): *taiyārī*, *layakārī*, *khūbsūratī*, and *nazākat*. *Taiyārī* literally means "readiness" and refers to physical fitness and the virtuosity of technique acquired through systematic practice. *Layakārī* indicates rhythmic facility, the ability to work inventively within the rhythmic parameters set forth in the Hindustani tradition. The last two refer to elements of grace: *khūbsūratī*, meaning beauty, is used to describe the dancer's overall form and gracefulness of gait and stance; and *nazākat* denotes subtle aspects of the dance such as gentle movements of the eyes, eyebrows, neck, and wrists, and the use of breath.

Because Das's early American students did not have Indian heritage and did not pass as Indian on stage, their knowledge, ability, and authenticity were sometimes called into question. To counter this, Das focused on training them in taiyārī and layakārī—technical and rhythmic abilities. Speed, power, and rhythmic ability served as more objectifiable measures of the dancers' skill than the subtleties of khūbsūratī and nazākat—particularly for American audience members, who did not generally understand kathak aesthetics. In performances of storytelling (nritya), people often were not familiar with the characters and stories presented (so well known by Indian audiences), and they did not know how to interpret movements that would serve as dramatic cues to cultural insiders. Though the group did present dramatic works, focusing on storytelling highlighted facial expression, and reminded audiences that the faces of the dancers did not look

Indian. Perhaps most importantly, a focus on the subtle movements of kathak did not impress like speed and power; American audiences could appreciate fast footwork and athletic turns, even if they did not fully understand the rhythmic complexity of the compositions being presented.

In this instance of cultural exchange, as with others, the aspects of the art that were familiar to both cultures were those that became augmented in its new locale. As with any transplanted tradition, this one was inflected by the historical trajectory that preceded and influenced its movement. For that reason, it is useful to consider the history of Indian cultural figures and their followers in San Francisco prior to Chitresh Das's arrival.

INDIAN CULTURE-BEARERS IN THE BAY AREA

By the early 1970s, when Das first came to California, the route he followed from India to the United States had already been taken by a number of noted teachers of Indian artistic and spiritual practices. Among the first cultural emissaries to the United States were attendees of the Chicago Parliament of Religions in 1893. This watershed event brought several religious figures from South Asia, including Hindu delegate Swami Vivekananda from India (Brekke 2003, 2). Vivekananda's particularly charismatic presence at the parliament won him several American followers and led to the establishment of religious centers around the country. San Francisco was a particularly receptive site for Vivekananda and his teachings. He first spent time in the Bay Area in 1900, where he founded the Vedanta Society of Northern California and sparked a "fevered pace of activity" among his followers (French 1974, 74). In San Francisco, these devotees began a publication named the *Pacific Vedantin* in 1902. In 1906, with the assistance of the resident monk from India, Swami Trigunatitananda, the Vedanta Society completed construction of the first Hindu temple in the United States, still located at the corner of Webster and Filbert streets (Ibid., 121, 120).[12]

Despite the warm welcome for some South Asian culture-bearers, fears of a "Hindu invasion" or "Turban tide" grew in the US Pacific Northwest as South Asians (particularly Sikhs) who were brought to western Canada to work on the Canadian-Pacific railroads moved south into the US states of Washington, Oregon, and California (Campi 2005). In 1917 hostility in the US toward immigrants from South and Southeast Asia culminated in the Congressional passage of the Asiatic Barred Zone Act, a law banning migration from South and Southeast Asia that was not repealed until 1965 (Purkayastha 2005, 1). "All immigrants except merchants, students, and diplomats . . . were barred" (Campi 2005, fn. 4). Some spiritual teachers and artists, however, managed to travel to the United States, including Paramhansa Yogananda. Best known for his *Autobiography of a Yogi* (first published in 1946), Yogananda traveled across America on spiritual campaigns from 1920 until his death in 1952, teaching and advocating a form of yoga called

Kriya yoga. His teachings endure through the international spiritual organization he founded, Self-Realization Fellowship, which operates almost 200 temples, ashrams, retreats, and meditation centers throughout the United States, forty-four in California alone.

Beginning in the 1930s, Indian "modern" dancers Ram Gopal and Uday Shankar also toured North America. In adapting Indian movements and themes to Western theatrical sensibilities, they (particularly Shankar) followed established conventions of portraying exoticized or romanticized versions of the East, now known as "orientalist."[13] Anthropologist and dance scholar Joan Erdman notes that, although Shankar's productions were "like the 'oriental dances' of westerners . . . what distinguishe[d] Shankar from every western interpreter is that he spent his childhood in India, where he learned dance" (1987, 66). Erdman suggests that in the early twentieth century, though Western dancers "chose oriental themes," they did not use "India's own techniques, movements, rhythms, and styles":

> The main reason for this was the difficulty, even when on tour in India, of seeing regional and classical dance styles presented. Only American modern dancer Ted Shawn, touring with Denishawn in 1926, managed to film three or four *nautch* dancers in northern India. . . . In fact, western oriental dancers (with the exception of [Uday] Shankar's students) were not able to learn any Indian dance until the mid or late 1930s when courageous explorers like Russell Meriwether Hughes ("La Meri") studied bharatanatyam and kathakali in newly founded regional schools in India. (Ibid., 64)

With increased tours and teaching in the United States in the mid-twentieth century, Gopal and Shankar influenced and were influenced by Western dancers including La Meri (Russell Meriwether Hughes), Ruth St. Denis, Ted Shawn, Vaslav Nijinsky, Anna Pavlova, and later Martha Graham.

Shortly following the repeal of the Asiatic Barred Zone Act in 1965, cultural effects resulting from a greater South Asian presence in the United States became markedly more apparent, particularly in San Francisco. As with Swami Vivekananda six decades earlier, San Francisco was a chosen destination for Bhaktivedanta Swami Prabhupada, founder of ISKON, the Hare Krishna movement. A retired Bengali businessman formerly named Abhay Charan De, Swami Prabhupada founded the International Society for Krishna Consciousness in New York's East Village in 1966 and in 1967 moved to the Haight-Ashbury district in San Francisco (Hawley 2004; Bromley and Shupe 1981).

Two notable events in 1967 established San Francisco, and Haight-Ashbury in particular, as an epicenter of what became known as the Hippie Revolution: the "Human Be-In" at Golden Gate Park in January and the "Summer of Love," when thousands converged on the Haight-Ashbury district. Those who identified as hippies were generally invested in challenging the status quo, were involved in social experimentation, and protested the Vietnam War and nuclear weapons.

Social experimentation for some included communal living, open sexual relationships, drug use, and/or exploration of Eastern religions and philosophies; as with most social movements, music was a vital component. Members of the hippie counterculture developed an interest in India, fueled in part by the long-standing presence of Hindu spiritual centers, and more immediately by charismatic Hindu leaders such as Swami Prabhupada. Prabhupada earned national notoriety because of his more famous devotees, including Beat poet and counterculture icon Allen Ginsberg, and members of the legendary psychedelic rock band the Grateful Dead. Interest in India soared when in early 1968, members of the Beatles traveled to India with other Western celebrities to study meditation with Maharishi Mahesh Yogi. In the Bay Area, this confluence of factors provided an atmosphere ripe for the emergence of a local Indian classical music and dance scene.

Two of the first Hindustani musicians to regularly perform in North America were Ali Akbar Khan and his "guru-brother" Ravi Shankar, rising star of the distinctive stringed instrument, the sitar.[14] Each significantly influenced the trajectory of Indian classical music in the West. Ravi Shankar met violin virtuoso Yehudi Menuhin while Menuhin was touring India in 1952. They later performed together on three *West Meets East* albums (1966, 1968, and 1976; compiled and remastered by Angel Records, 1999) and their musical association and friendship endured throughout their lives.[15] In 1955 Ali Akbar Khan and tabla player Chatur Lal came to New York City and Washington on a short but significant tour largely orchestrated by Yehudi Menuhin.[16] Their trip included a performance at the Metropolitan Museum of Art (MoMA) in which Menuhin introduced Khan and Lal and briefly described their instruments and music to the audience. The same introductory format was utilized on the surprisingly successful album *Music of India: Morning and Evening Rāgas* (Angel Records, 1965), which Khan and Lal had recorded at MoMA the day before their live performance (Lavezzoli 2007: 58).[17]

Until the 1960s, Americans' exposure to Indian music was limited first to recordings of classical music and later to the recordings of a handful of pop musicians who incorporated elements of Indian music—particularly the sounds of the sitar and tabla—into their songs. Ethnomusicologist Bonnie Wade notes that the trajectory of Indian classical music in the United States from the elite fine arts realm to the popular music scene was largely due to Beatles member George Harrison's widely publicized study with Ravi Shankar, and his subsequent Indian-inspired musical experiments with the Beatles (1978).[18] Exposure to Indian dance was more limited, though the study of Indian classical dance and music traditions was to become increasingly possible in the United States.

In 1962 ethnomusicologist Robert E. Brown brought the renowned South Indian bharatanatyam dancer Tanjore Balasaraswati to the United States for a brief visit. Her students included Louise Scripps, who, with Brown and her husband Samuel Scripps founded the American Society for Eastern Arts (ASEA) the following year in order to bring performing artists from Asia (Cowdery 1995, 51). In the summer of 1965, the group invited Balasaraswati and her ensemble of

Karnatak musicians, as well as Ali Akbar Khan and tabla player Shankar Ghosh to the Bay Area to teach at Oakland's Mills College (Knight 2010, 205–6). ASEA, later renamed the Center for World Music and Related Arts, has continued to sponsor educational programs, to organize concerts and national tours for Asian artists, and even to direct study programs and cultural tours abroad.[19]

The success of Ali Akbar Khan's first classes in 1965 had a profound effect on the future of Hindustani music in the United States, particularly in the Bay Area. Inspired by the enthusiasm of his American students, Khan decided to return again the next two summers. The following year, in 1968, he moved to the Bay Area, where in the city of Berkeley, he established a branch of his then Calcutta-based Ali Akbar College of Music. At the height of the Vietnam War protests during the summer of 1968, a state of emergency was declared in Berkeley, curfews were imposed, and barricades prevented people from moving from one section of town to another. A young tabla student attempting to cross a police barricade when returning home from class was struck by a policeman's baton and his hand was broken; this incident solidified Khan's feeling that the atmosphere in Berkeley was no longer conducive to studying Hindustani music, and he moved his school to the town of San Rafael in quieter Marin County, just north of San Francisco. Over the course of the next several years, other leading Indian artists were invited to teach at the college, including Zakir Hussain, Swapan Chaudhuri, G. S. Sachdev, and Chitresh Das, who became permanent residents of the area.

DANCING KATHAK IN THE BAY AREA

For approximately the first seventeen years he was in California, the kathak dance master Chitresh Das taught in and around San Rafael and in San Francisco.[20] From there, he and his senior students opened branches of the Chhandam School of Kathak throughout the Bay Area (see Table 14.1). In San Rafael the students were almost entirely affinity learners, especially Americans of European descent (a group Das called his "blondes and brunettes"). In the late 1980s, he opened a branch of the school in Fremont in the South Bay. In this area, considered part of Silicon Valley, there was a growing population from India and other South Asian countries, and the students at this branch of Das's school were largely heritage learners of South Asian descent. From 1998 to 2003 the school expanded extensively in the South and East Bay; the geographical division between the branches continued to be an ethnic one as well, with primarily South Asian American students in the south and southeastern cities of San Jose, Mountain View, and Fremont/Union City, and a greater mix of students in Berkeley and San Francisco. By 2010 the Chhandam School included five branches in the Bay Area and others across North America, with more than 500 students enrolled in classes at a given time.[21]

Table 14.1 Overview of the Chhandam School growth in the San Francisco Bay Area	
1970	Das arrived in the US on a fellowship to teach kathak at the University of MD
1971	Began teaching kathak at the Ali Akbar College, San Rafael, CA
ca. 1978	Taught classes at Ashkenaz world music center in Berkeley intermittently until 1996
1979	Established the Chhandam School of Kathak Dance in Marin County (San Rafael/San Anselmo; closed in 2003) and in San Francisco
1980	Incorporated the Chitresh Das Dance Company
ca. 1988	Taught a kathak course at San Francisco State University until 2005
1988	Began teaching classes in Fremont/Union City (later a branch of Chhandam)
1998	Established a branch of Chhandam in Berkeley
1999	Established a branch of Chhandam in Mountain View
2000	Established a branch of Chhandam in San Bruno (closed in 2005)
2003	Established a branch of Chhandam in San Jose

As the South Asian American presence in the Bay Area grew, the demographics of this kathak community shifted from a majority of affinity learners to primarily heritage learners, that is, first- and second-generation South Asian American students. However, during the first decade of the twenty-first century, the Chitresh Das Dance Company—Das's most advanced group of dancers—was more diverse than the student populations found in most branches of the Chhandam School. Many company members had first gained an interest in kathak at San Francisco State University, where Das taught from 1988 to 2005.[22] The company included dancers ethnically identifying as South Asian, East Asian, African American and white—a group Das called his "Rainbow Coalition" (see the image found at the beginning of this chapter).[23]

This contrast in ethnic composition between the student body and the dance company is worth noting because Chitresh Das Dance Company members provided the public face for the organization, teaching many beginning classes at the affiliated Chhandam School of Kathak and performing at prestigious venues in the Bay Area, across the United States, and internationally. As illustrated in the title "In Perfect Harmony: Kathak Gets and American Edge" from an article written for the *Hindustan Times* newspaper while members of the dance company were on tour in India in 2004, the group was often portrayed as a harmonious assimilation of diverse individuals, united by their dedication to the art of kathak. While this was very much the case, to be a dancer in the Chitresh Das Dance Company also involved confronting the complexities of difference and racially encoded dilemmas of performance.

Difference within Das's dance company was often expressed using the binary oppositions "South Asian" and "white," as well as "Indian" and "non-Indian." Additionally, the terms "Indian" and "American" were used to distinguish between dancers' identities, despite the fact that all of the "Indian" dancers were also US citizens. Though I encountered these categories continuously in the course of my fieldwork, they did not adequately represent the diversity of the student population. I found that additional oppositions emerged in my analysis of everyday discourse, including "spirituality" and "physicality," and "colonizer" and "colonized," though these were seldom explicitly articulated. How does dance serve to mediate between these categories? How do these dancers negotiate the challenge of cultural expression in such manifestly intercultural contexts? How do relationships of power come to be reinscribed in ways that are problematic and/or potentially liberating for the participants?

POWER, RACE, AND GENDER IN KATHAK

In working through an idea that he might be trying to convey to his students, Chitresh Das would develop catch phrases to which he often returned during in-class lectures and informal conversations with students. One such phrase Das would assert during the years of my primary field research from 2000 to 2003 was, "I am creating a superior race of strong women!" This and variations on the phrase were invoked so frequently that it became a well-known refrain among his students, almost all of whom were women. Das would return to such refrains day after day, playing with them, reworking and exploring their many facets much in the same way as when performing kathak he might dance to one line of sung poetry over and over, each time depicting some aspect of its many possible interpretations. Just as the dancing portions of class were a place for Das to work out kinesthetic ideas, lectures and conversations acted as discursive sites in which Das worked to make sense of his and his students' unique place in the world of kathak as it was developing in the United States.

The phrase "a superior race of strong women" seemed to undermine mainstream notions of race, redefining it not through color or other aspects of individual phenotype, but through sex/gender identity—a race of women. For this multi-ethnic group, the phrase emphasized their commonality as "strong women" rather than their outward differences. And as strong women, these dancers were portrayed and defined by their strength and power, undermining common gender stereotypes. But while Das worked to define the group as strong women, on-the-ground experience in this dance world revealed, not surprisingly, that gendered hierarchies and racialized divisions endured. Concepts of race, power, and gender invoked through Das's phrase can be pulled apart to some extent, but they overlap and intertwine in complex ways. So although headings below might seem to divide these ideas into neat categories, in the text as in the lived experience of these dancers, "gender" issues influence experiences of "race," which complicate understandings of "power"—each which also changed over time.

TEACHING THE "BLONDES AND BRUNETTES"

During the 1970s and early 1980s, Marin County was an important and somewhat unique enclave for Indian music and dance training in the United States. While greater diversity was found in later decades, at that time mostly white students studied with select Indian master artists. The training methodology was grounded in the *guru-śiṣya paramparā*, or teacher-disciple tradition, which privileges an unquestioning acceptance of the teacher and his ways, and extends far beyond training in the art—which itself was intense. Das's classes were nicknamed "the torture chamber" and often lasted for more than three hours. The students' difficulties involved more than simply long hours of dancing; many struggled with the hierarchical format of the guru-śiṣya system of training. Das exercised his power over his students by purposely creating stressful situations; some women who trained at that time recall being locked out of class for arriving late, being told that they were not going to perform on the day of a performance, or being given the silent treatment for weeks at a time.

That these "blondes and brunettes" did not look Indian was not initially a problem; however, it became more of an issue as Das's students began to perform with him onstage. One senior dancer remembers, "I think that within our little sphere we all felt at home doing it. Largely because Chitresh-jī [Das] was quite clear to us, 'stop worrying, that's ego. Just dance.'" But she continued:

> I do think that because dance is so visual, on a basic level it does look different. You see a Westerner doing it; it does not look the same as Indians doing it. When you get past a certain level of development, somehow it doesn't matter as much. . . . [But] I know he struggled with . . . how to [work with] these Western-looking bodies, [which are] visually so different. But I feel his answer was go to the core—the core of the study does not have to do with whether you are Western or Indian, really. ("Dancer 1," interview January 18, 2003)

Das's goal was to train his students to dance so strongly that whether or not they looked Indian or not would not be an issue. How does a young teacher of a dance from India drive his new American students to reach that "certain level of development" as quickly as possible? What comprises the "core" of the dance that Das wanted to impart to his students? Another dance student from that time recalled: "He didn't care where your elbows were; he didn't care where your eyesight went;

he didn't care how your shoulders were. He just wanted you to get dancing as fast as you could—footwork only. Because he wanted to build you up as fast as possible . . . to stand as a soloist" ("Dancer 2," interview November 14, 2005).

Going to the "core" of kathak meant stressing the technical and rhythmic aspects of the dance. The close, one-to-one format of guru-śiṣya training in India allows for flexibility in which both the kathak dance materials and manner of training can and have been adapted to suit different individuals and groups. Das's guru, Ram Narayan Mishra, for example, emphasized different aspects of kathak for different students, with the primary determinants being individual proclivities, whether the student was male or female, and the class/status of the student's family (Morelli 2010). For the predominantly white, female affinity learners in the 1970s, Das stressed athleticism and rhythmic ability (taiyārī and layakārī, both developed through training in footwork) more than grace and subtleties of facial expression (khūbsūratī and nazākat). Pedagogically, Das considered taiyārī and layakārī to be foundational skills that needed to be developed before focusing on the more subtle aspects of the dance: "Taiyārī and layakārī is first . . . achievement of technical virtuosity. And khūbsūratī and nazākat, the beauty and the subtlety and delicacy of the beauty is like a matured wine. It didn't come to me overnight, [so] how do you expect young Americans to understand that? So first my emphasis is on taiyārī and layakārī" (Das, interview June 25, 2002).

Video Example 1 demonstrates Das's emphasis on taiyārī and layakārī—athleticism and rhythmic ability—as it appeared even in his choreography from the 2000s.[24] The first portion of the video clip from the piece *Pancha Jati* (2002) features five members of the Chitresh Das Dance Company. Unlike this chapter's other two video examples, which feature Chitresh Das as a solo dancer, *Pancha Jati* involves several dancers moving in close precision with one another. Note the dimmed lights and relatively simple costumes of white silk, both which serve to deemphasize the characteristics of any one individual dancer. The observer is encouraged instead to focus on the lines of the dancers' bodies, their shifting spatial relations, and particularly the fast footwork patterns and rhythmically complex compositions performed in unison and highlighted by vocal recitation.

When the Chitresh Das Dance Company was founded in 1980 and Das's company members began performing with him on stage, issues of authenticity became intensified. One dancer recalls: "If I look back at the selling of himself with Westerners, I think it was difficult for him. People did want to see 'authentic Indians'" ("Dancer 1," interview January 18, 2003). From Das's perspective, the rejection of his students reflected poorly on him:

> When I created a company of blondes and brunettes, I thought I was doing something very noble, but to my astonishment, I was really discriminated [against] very subtly, by one group [who] wrote about Indian dance and music. They are the first people I thought would help me and support me—the Americans [earning] PhDs and writing books—but when another

> American was dancing or singing or [playing] the music, it was not kosher. But that was in the early seventies and it changed later. (Das, interview June 17, 2004)

Even though he felt he experienced discrimination because of his students, Das continued to perform with and market his dance company, insisting that his students be accepted as serious dancers, not just as a novelty. But the dance company seemed at times to be a liability. In 1986, one finds this distinctly color-conscious review of the Chitresh Das Dance Company: "Chitresh surrounded himself with a company of six female dancers, all westerners. They offer a seductive, colorful and friendly background. . . . [T]heir performance is distinctly pale alongside the powerful Chitresh" (Tucker 1986, 53). It had even been suggested in the mid-eighties that these dancers wear black wigs in performance in an attempt to pass as Indian onstage. One of Das's earliest dancers recalled: "The Aman dance company in L.A. was helping Julia [Das's then wife and manager] with promoting the Chitresh Das Dance Company, and they suggested we wear wigs—do that look. I remember talking to Julia about it and us both saying 'no way. I am what I am and this is the dance.' . . . Chitresh-jī wouldn't have liked that idea either" ("Dancer 1," interview January 18, 2003).

In Julia's letter responding to this suggestion, she wrote, "I believe deeply that for Chitresh to perform with wigged dancers would be extremely detrimental to his artistic stature, and also to his marketability" (J. Das 1986). Perhaps responding to the above review by Tucker, printed only four months earlier, she proposed separating Das's solo performances from those of his company, suggesting that "this will allow you to market the very best that there is, to sponsors who want the 'real' thing from India. Also it allows you to offer the Chitresh Das Dance Company as Chitresh's extraordinarily unique experiment in the West" (ibid.). Another dancer from that time more recently elaborated on the effort to find a niche for the dance company:

> It was always a struggle in him: how much to perform, how much to teach—he knew he needed to bring the students along, but he needed to move so fast on the stage in order to reach his goal. . . . And so there was no peace anywhere, there was no balance anywhere. And all of the students were just all of the receptors of all of this friction and anger and frustration . . . We weren't really the main product, but we had to come along somewhere. ("Dancer 2," interview November 14, 2005)

Das struggled to find the appropriate contexts for his young white students to perform. In this process, both teacher and students were forced to think and talk about race, and conceptualized their differences in ways that were sometimes surprising.

QUESTIONS OF RACE AND THE INSECURITIES OF WHITENESS

In her contribution to a volume titled *Music and the Racial Imagination*, ethnomusicologist Deborah Wong reminds us that "to be American and to think about Race means engaging with whiteness and all its performances, yet this encompassing racialization is perhaps the most under-theorized embodiment of all—and therein lies its power" (2000, 58). One of the major privileges afforded to those who are identified as white in the United States is the possibility not to think about the implications their racial status might play in their daily lives. While whiteness is a pervasive, yet underacknowledged element in American culture, it (as with other racial designations) remains a social construct—a creation of society, not of biology. Critical race theorists Richard Delgado and Jean Stefancic expand on the "social construction" thesis, which

> holds that race and races are products of social thought and relations. Not objective, inherent, or fixed, they correspond to no biological or genetic reality; rather, races are categories that society invents, manipulates, or retires when convenient. People with common origins share certain physical traits, of course, such as skin color, physique, and hair texture. But these constitute only an extremely small portion of their genetic endowment, are dwarfed by that which we have in common, and have little or nothing to do with distinctly human, higher-order traits, such as personality, intelligence, and moral behavior. (2001, 8–9)

Although the concept of race is not grounded in biological fact, it remains a pervasive way that members of American society perceive difference. The following discussion examines some atypical usages of whiteness in this particular dance community in order to challenge readers' assumptions regarding the truth or immutability of racial categories.

Within this kathak world, dancers often spoke of race in terms of a dialectical relationship between "Indian" and "white." "Indian," which was sometimes rephrased as "Indian-origin," was a category subsuming all students of South Asian descent, including first-, one-and-a-half- and second-generation Indian, Bangladeshi, and Pakistani American students as well as those from the South Asian Caribbean diaspora. "White" was at times used as shorthand for everyone else, including East Asian American and even African American dancers.

In this context, unlike typical understandings of whiteness in the United States, whiteness was constructed as an absence of South Asian culture or ancestry. For example, in a conversation in 2004 soon after a class in which we both had danced, a student of Indian descent brought up a portion of the class in which Das asked us each to do something one by one. When the only dancers who could accomplish the task to Das's satisfaction were non–South Asian, he used racial difference to push his South Asian American students. She recalled, "He said 'The white women are doing it—why can't you *desīs*?'" (literally, people of a particular *deś* or region/country; colloquially, South Asians; field notes August 24, 2004). This might have been unremarkable except that the "white women" in the situation included the author of this chapter (a fairly typical "white woman") and a six-foot-tall African American woman with long dreadlocks. Sometimes the term "white" also was used to indicate a lack of South Asian cultural knowledge. In an informal conversation I had with another Indian American student, for example, she said to me, "I hate when white people try to say—" and then checked herself, saying, "I don't mean you, I mean *real* whites" (field notes, October 9, 2004). In this and similar instances, whiteness indexed not just a lack of Indian cultural knowledge but a particular form of inauthentic knowledge that was, even decades later, associated with the hippie movement of the 1960s and 1970s.

These dancers, including Chitresh Das, also employed the term white as it is more commonly used to reference skin color. For example, in a 1994 interview with a journalist, Das stated: "The prejudices come from Americans, not the Indians. Critics have said: 'They're so white. They don't look ethnic.' When you say that you're not looking at the art, you're looking at the skin. These women have trained with me for 17 years" (Welsh 1994). Having trained white women since his early adulthood, Das often reacted quickly to dismissive attitudes expressed by outsiders toward his kathak dancers. Later in the interview he spoke out about ethnomusicologists explicitly; here Das's use of the term white also works as a potential critique of their level of South Asian cultural experience or authority: "I'm very tired with the ethnomusicologists, who are all white and are making these rules about who can do what. My dancers are not a bunch of fly-by-night hippies studying with a guru and smoking pot. I was in Marin County in the 1970s. I know who those people were" (ibid.).

In the 2000s, a non-Indian member of the Chitresh Das Dance Company echoed these sentiments. In an interview after class she confided: "Actually that's my biggest issue—not being Indian, the ethnicity. Yeah, it's my biggest issue. Because . . ." her voice trailed off and she decided to move into safer terrain, "well, there are a lot of issues: there's family, there's having to make money, age, and all that" ("Dancer 3," interview December 19, 2002). Later in the conversation, she returned to the subject: "Kathak is not just [about] being pretty, it's being Indian. If you're not Indian, there are a lot of assumptions. People assume that if you're older and you're white, you must be some New Age hippie that's into the—I don't know, some kind of escape . . . it's not really within you; it's not really authentic. You're trying to reach out and assume something else because you're unsatisfied" (ibid.). She then contrasted these assumptions with her own reasons for studying kathak: "I never felt that way about kathak. I've never done it because it's Indian. I've never done it because it's spiritually enlightening. I've just done it because it's *physically really cool*. It's really a challenge, and I just love to dance" (ibid.).

Like Das's construction of "a superior race of strong women," power and physicality seemed here to be used as a defense against the negative stereotypes of hippiedom or New Age spirituality.[25] I must admit that I have not been immune from feelings of defensiveness, and I suspect that at some point in their careers many non–South Asian ethnomusicologists who study the region have struggled with similar issues: a perception by outsiders that their studies arose from spiritual interests, a factor that diminishes the legitimacy of their scholarship. For example, ethnomusicologist Stephen Slawek cites an instance of one particular scholar jokingly calling those attracted to the study of Indian music people seeking "instant enlightenment" (1996, 31). Slawek suggests that this dismissive attitude has affected not only scholars' inner dialogues, but also much of the academic writing on Indian artistic traditions by Western scholars who have "felt compelled not only to distance themselves from the spirituality trope, but also to subvert the trope within their own discourse" (ibid.).

TRAINING "INDIANS" AND "NON-INDIANS"

When I conducted my fieldwork in the early 2000s, many dancers in the Chitresh Das Dance Company and community generally felt that students of South Asian origin, in comparison to non–South Asians, were pushed harder in class and more readily called to task for mistakes, both in dance and in etiquette. (It was generally understood, however, that the training was no longer as intense or difficult as it had been in earlier decades.) In my presence, Das had often justified this stance as a means of breaking down any false sense of entitlement South Asian American students might feel for the dance form. Was his response influenced by aspects of my identity?—as one of his kathak students, as a researcher conducting fieldwork in this community, as a "non-Indian"? At both an intuitive level and an intellectual one, I believe these aspects of my identity did affect my experiences in the field. In the words of anthropologist Jane Cowan, "the fieldworker's personality, temperament, and a whole gamut of intangible, contingent factors inevitably affect the fieldwork process and the social relations it entails" (1990, 55–56).

One evening during a 2004 trip to the Bay Area to visit Chitresh Das and his students, I gained a little more insight into how discourse regarding training "Indians" and "non-Indians" might be adapted to suit differing contexts and audiences. After dinner together, a senior student's husband (who is Indian American) began asking why—from the husband's perspective—was Das so hard on the Indian students? This time, Das did not respond as I had usually witnessed; instead, his response focused on why he tended to ignore the "non-Indians":

> HUSBAND: Is it not also true sometimes that non-Indians also are not doing as well, and you say something? Did that—

> DAS: I don't say so much, but I kind of ignore them and they *fade out*.

STUDENT: Who fades out?

DAS: They fade out, non-Indians. . . . They feel very sensitive that they are not Indians, so they cannot do this [or] that. But when they see a lot of Indians don't know to speak in Indian language[s], they find: okay, that is also there. (June 19, 2004, emphasis mine)

Das's reply indicated that he expected non-Indians, then minorities in the kathak dance community, would give up on their studies of dance form more readily and he displayed some sensitivity to those students' lack of cultural knowledge. Since he spent much of his career teaching white women, he came to identify to a certain extent with their struggle to be accepted in kathak, even suggesting that the public discriminated against him because his students did not look "ethnic" (Das, interview June 25, 2002).

NEGOTIATING SOUTH ASIAN EXPERIENCES AND IDENTITIES

In Das's American kathak community, racial and ethnic categorizations played into dancers' experiences in ways that were complex, multi-faceted, and changing depending on context. While non–South Asians contended with others' assumptions regarding their reasons for studying kathak and their level of expertise, South Asian American students—a newer demographic group for Das—experienced a different set of challenges. With non–South Asian affinity learners, Das's role as a representative of Indian culture was rather clear and uncontested; these students often took Das's perspectives on Indian culture at face value. Heritage learners, on the other hand, had stronger relationships with and understandings of South Asian culture. Their families often had ties to various regions of South Asia; they sometimes spoke different languages, and had different religious and cultural practices than Das. They thus came into the study of kathak with their own, often competing beliefs and ideas about Indian culture. One South Asian American member of the kathak community described this complex dynamic:

> Being a South Asian student in his classroom is difficult. I think there's much more that goes on between him and his South Asian students—him telling you to hold on to your cultural heritage, you [asking yourself], "what is my cultural heritage?" What I think my cultural heritage is [is] different than what he thinks my cultural heritage is. . . . It clashes because you have your own versions of what is Indian, and what it means to be Indian. And I think there's much more contention there . . . It's not an open dialogue, but it's definitely more of a conversation that's happening with him and his South Asian students . . . a negotiation. ("Dancer 4," interview June 18, 2003)

This dancer later described the sometimes fraught relationship between South Asian American family expectations and responsibilities as a dancer:

> As immigrants to this country, I think that there's a huge emphasis on making it financially—being successful. And people just don't think of dance as a viable profession. People cannot move past seeing dance as a hobby. In the Indian community dance is fine, [but only] as a hobby. Like, "it's very nice that you're a well-rounded individual," and "oh how sweet, you're talented," but the minute that it starts to interfere with your roles . . . like [being a] mom, family obligations, making money for some people, [then] it's not cool anymore. So I *do* think that Chitresh-jī is creating—I mean, he pushes women, not only physically, but [also] in terms of women negotiating their roles at home. (ibid.)

Was Das indeed creating a superior race of strong women with the power to transcend externally imposed strictures of race and gender? And if so, is such female empowerment legitimate if created and maintained by a man—who has the power to name and bestow power, and also potentially to take it away? The same dancer quoted above reflected on Das's use of an individual's characteristics: "Chitresh-jī will use anything and everything to make you dance. . . . He will use your ethnicity, he will use your gender, he will use your age, he will use your body, your height . . . I'm telling you; ultimately he'll use whatever he can get on you to make you dance better and stronger. Everything is his tool" ("Dancer 4," interview April 6, 2003).

These comments suggest that all of the students, whether affinity or heritage practitioners, were being "othered" in one way or another as they encountered issues of power, race, and gender in their study of kathak in its new American environment. Das dealt with similar issues as a performer and teacher of kathak in the United States. Creating ways to talk about these issues was one strategy to work with his own experiences while also finding ways to motivate his students to meet a higher standard of performance.

CONCLUSION

In cities around the United States, one can find countless classes and performance scenes in music and dance forms that immigrated along with the people that came to this country. From West African dance, to Irish music, to various forms of martial arts, these and other practices were transplanted from elsewhere and have been adapted to some extent in American locales. In addition to learning steps or notes or other technical aspects of an art form, students' experiences often involve other complex underlying and often understated unarticulated cultural negotiations that take place in the practice studio or rehearsal room and are expressed in public performance. This chapter examines some of the complexities and unresolved issues in the lived experience of one community practicing a "foreign" dance in the United States.

In her article on musical communities, ethnomusicologist Kay Kaufman Shelemay notes "a variety of motivations" for the affinity learner of music that are applicable to the kathak community discussed in this chapter: "Musical affinity can be driven by sheer sonic [aesthetic] attraction, whether based in a desire for the familiar or search for the new; it can catalyze a preoccupation with what is perceived as exotic" (2011, 374). She adds that, as in the case of Chitresh Das, "The role of a charismatic musician or performer is often a particularly powerful element added to the musical draw in the case of affinity communities" (ibid.). While kathak is beautiful and compelling to many, for those learning in the United States, whether heritage or affinity oriented, whether primarily motivated by the dance's athletic, aesthetic, or cultural aspects, the experience also involves navigating challenging experiences as the dance form develops roots and grows in this new environment.

Notes

1. I wish to express my appreciation particularly to Pandit Chitresh Das, Celine Schein Das, and all the kathak dancers in this community who have shared the dance space and their experiences with me, including Gretchen Hayden, Michele Zonka, Noelle Barton, Charlotte Moraga, Seibi Lee, Rachna Nivas, Joanna Meinl, and Rina Mehta. Sincere thanks to editors Anne Rasmussen and Kip Lornell, as well as to Parijat Desai, Stephen Scaringe, Patricia Tang, and John Tiedemann for their insights and feedback in the writing of this chapter.

2. Kay Kaufman Shelemay discusses three processes by which individuals become members of musical communities: descent, dissent, and affinity (2011). This chapter deals with the categories of descent and affinity, but not with dissent. See also Mark Slobin's discussion of affinity, which he differentiates from choice and belonging (1993, 55).

3. Dance forms are recognized as classical (*śāstrīya*) by the Sangeet Natak Akademi, the Government of India's national academy for the performing arts, on the basis of their grounding in principles from the Natya Shastra (*nāṭya śāstra*), an approximately two-thousand-year-old treatise on the dramatic arts. Those currently considered classical include kathak, bharatanatyam (*bharatanāṭyam*), odissi (*oḍisī*), kuchipudi (*kuchīpuḍī*), mohiniattam (*mohinīaṭṭam*), kathakali (*kathakalī*), manipuri (*maṇipurī*), and most recently, sattriya (*satrīyā*).

4. See, for example, O'Shea 2007, Srinivasan 2011.

5. Although I generally follow the convention of referring to people by their last names in this chapter, as a student and in other contexts I would refer to my teachers using other terms connoting connection and respect, including "Khan-sāhib" and "Chitresh-jī."

6. Texts on kathak with more thorough descriptions of the form include Khokar 1979; Kothari 1989; Massey 1999; Saxena 1991. See also the films *Circles-Cycles: Kathak Dance* (Gottlieb 1988) and *Upaj: Improvise* (Uchiyama 2013).

7. Ghuṇghrū is a more precise transliteration for "Ghungroo," which is also the name of the Harvard South Asian Association's annual show.

8. www.youtube.com/watch?v=f3CDAs-bWpg "Kathak—Glimpses of Pt Chitresh Das' [*sic*] intricate choreography."

9. www.youtube.com/watch?v=3SxWyvli7es "Kathak—Lightning speed feet of Pt. Chitresh Das."

10. www.youtube.com/watch?v=W50yvRH4EP0 "Incredible Kathak Abhinaya by Pandit Chitresh Das."

11. For a more thorough discussion of the performance of gender in Kathak, see chapter 5 of Morelli forthcoming; Shah 2008.

12. Upon the temple's completion, Swami Trigunatitananda published a pamphlet describing the building's features. Though the building served as the meeting site for a Hindu organization, he wrote, "This temple may be considered as a combination of a Hindu temple, a Christian church, a Mohammedan mosque, a Hindu math or monastery, and an American residence" (http://sfvedanta.org/the-society/history/).

13. There is a long history of portrayals of South, East, and Southeast Asia and the Islamic Middle East in Western arts that are now described as "Orientalist" (Locke 2001, 699). The "mysterious East" appeared in European dance performances as early as 1626, when the *Grand Bal de la Douairière de Billehahaut* premiered at the court of Louis XIII, King of France (Warren 2006, 98). India and Indian characters appeared in several operas and dance productions in the seventeenth, eighteenth, and nineteenth centuries.

14. Ali Akbar Khan and Ravi Shankar both trained under Ali Akbar Khan's father, Allauddin Khan. As "guru brothers," they performed together on a number of occasions early in their music careers. Ravi Shankar was also the younger brother of dancer Uday Shankar; as a boy, Ravi toured with his brother's troupe through India and Europe.

15. Menuhin called his musical collaboration with Shankar "one of the two great adventures in my life" (Fox 1995).

16. As part of this trip, Khan, Lal, and bharatanatyam dancer Shanta Rao were "the first Indian classical artists to appear on television in the United States" by performing on *Omnibus*, a program broadcast live in New York from 1952 to 1961 that featured programming on the arts, humanities, and sciences (Lavezzoli 2007, 59).

17. The album was remastered and rereleased as Disc 1 of *Then and Now* (AMMP Records, 1995).

18. The Beatles' best-known song utilizing Indian sonic materials is "Norwegian Wood." For discussions of Western experiments with Indian musical materials from that era, see Cupchik forthcoming; Reck 1978 and 1985; Silver 1978; Wade 1978. Cupchik 2013 analyzes the collaboration between Ravi Shankar and George Harrison, highlighting the role of Ravi Shankar's senior sitar student, Shambhu Das.

19. The organization relocated from San Francisco to San Diego in 1979.

The *zaffah*, an elaborate procession of the bride and groom, at a Detroit wedding. Musicians flank the couple and animate the event with loud mizmar and drum music. Two videographers capture the affair, while young children scramble to get out of the way. Photo by Anne K. Rasmussen.

"Polka King" Romy Gosz, with trumpet, poses with his band at a wedding dance on a farm in the vicinity of Wisconsin's Manitowoc and Kewaunee Counties, 1950s. Courtesy Jim Eisenmann.

Joe Tomesh, piano accordion, and John Tomesh, button accordion, play a Czech song while their siblings sing along—(L-R) Tony Tomesh, Lilian Tomesh Dvorak, Dorothy Tomesh Schwab, Albert Tomesh—at a house party, Haugen, Wisconsin, 1990. Photo by Jim Leary.

Musicians gather to jam weekly at the Green Briar Restaurant in Brighton, Massachusetts, in the spring of 2014. Photo by Deb Carleton.

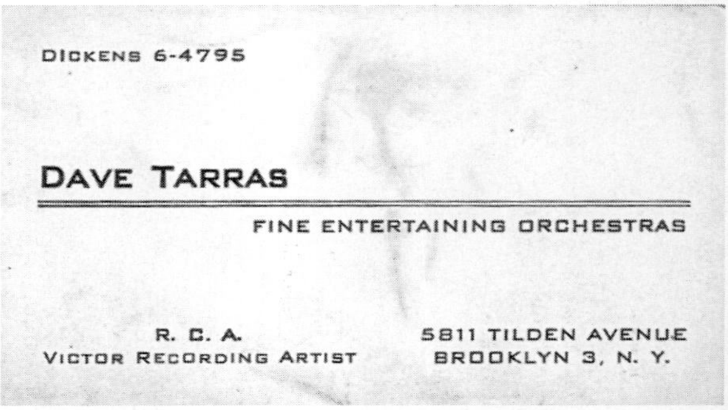

Dave Tarras's business card, ca. 1950. Courtesy Henry Sapoznik.

Linda Ronstadt's 1987 album *Canciones de Mi Padre* brought major public attention to the mariachi and its music, especially in the United States, winning a Grammy for Best Mexican-American Performance and selling more than two million copies.

A judge (on the left, holding a clipboard) looks on while competitors dance for a Men's Grass dance competition at the 2011 Saginaw Chippewa Tribal Powwow. Photo by Christopher Scales.

The powwow drum group Meskwaki Nation, performing at the 2011 Saginaw Chippewa Tribal Powwow. Photo by Christopher Scales.

Tohono O'odham pascola dance, learned from the Yaquis, is performed at some Tohono O'odham village feasts. Here pascola Freddie Segundo dances to music provided by Frank Pedro on violin and Alex Manuel on guitar, in program at Topawa Day School in February 1981. Photo by Jim Griffith.

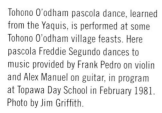

Onk Akmel—The Salt River Band. Photo by Jim Griffith.

Pueblo of Jemez Matachina musicians play in Ponderosa, NM on August 28, 2010, featuring Adelaido Martinez's grandson, Lawrence Trujillo (right) on violin, and Pueblo musicians Jerome Fragua (middle) on guitar and Kathleen Gauchupin (left) on violin. Photo by Brenda M. Romero.

Musicians Andrew Chacón (guitar), David García (violin), Melitón Medina (violin), and Candida Romero (violin) face the Abuelo and Malinche dancers in front of the Chapel for St. Anthony in Alcalde, New Mexico December, 2010. Photo by Larry Lamsa.

Singers in the "hollow square" led by Zachary Davis at the Kentucky State Sacred Harp Singing, 2010. Photo by Ron Pen.

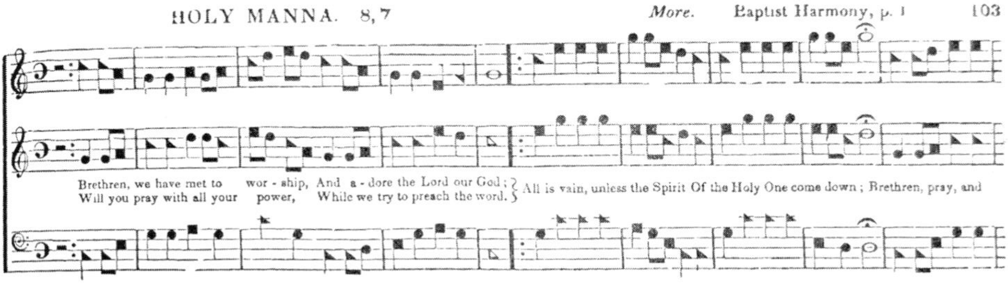
HOLY MANNA. 8,7
More. Baptist Harmony, p. 1
103
Brethren, we have met to wor - ship, And a - dore the Lord our God;
Will you pray with all your power, While we try to preach the word.
All is vain, unless the Spirit Of the Holy One come down; Brethren, pray, and

ho - ly man - na Will be shower'd all around

2 Brethren, see poor sinners round you,
Trembling on the brink of wo;
Death is coming, hell is moving;
Can you bear to let them go?
See our fathers—see our mothers,
And our children sinking down;
Brethren, pray, and holy manna
Will be shower'd all around.

3 Sisters, will you join and help us?
Moses' sisters aided him;
Will you help the trembling mourners,
Who are struggling hard with sin?
Tell them all about the Saviour,
Tell them that he will be found;
Sisters, pray, and holy manna
Will be shower'd all around.

4 Is there here a trembling jailer,
Seeking grace, and fill'd with fears
Is there here a weeping Mary,
Pouring forth a flood of tears?
Brethren, join your cries to help them
Sisters, let your prayers abound;
Pray, O! pray, that holy manna
May be scatter'd all around.

5 Let us love our God supremely,
Let us love each other too;
Let us love and pray for sinners,
Till our God makes all things new
Then he'll call us home to heaven,
At his table we'll sit down.
Christ will gird himself, and serve us
With sweet manna all around.

A favorite of the shape note singers, "Holy Manna," was initially published in William Moore's *Columbian Harmony* (1829). Photo by Ron Pen.

The I.C. Glee Club became the first Memphis quartet to record in the late 1920s. Photo by Kip Lornell.

These singers graced the airwaves and performed at local churches in the late 1940s. Photo by Kip Lornell.

In 1996 the Silhouettes Steel Orchestra, Inc. competed in Panorama, the preeminent steelband competition held annually since the early 1960s. Photo by Gage Averill.

Cliff Alexis, building pans in the United States. Photo by Gage Averill.

Queen Ida at a San Francisco church hall, ca. 1978. Photo by Gary C. Canaparo.

Louisiana Playboys performing at St. Francis of Assisi church, East Palo Alto, California, circa 1977–78. From left to right on stage: unknown fiddler; Junior Felton, guitar; Ulysse Gobert, fiddle; Danny Poullard, accordion; Charlie St. Mary, rubboard. Photo by Gary C. Canaparo.

Chitresh Das performing with Zakir Hussain (then tabla instructor at the Ali Akbar College of Music) and American students of Ali Akbar Khan in 1975 for *Ananda*, a program that aired on the San Francisco–based PBS television affiliate KQED. Photo courtesy of Chitresh Das.

Located in San Francisco, this is the first Hindu temple in the United States. The Vedanta Society of Northern California temple (1908). Courtesy Vedanta Society of Northern California.

Pioneer Asian American music band Hiroshima with Japanese koto performer June Kuramoto. Courtesy Susan Asai.

Bikini Kill headlined this Halloween benefit for ABC No Rio. Courtesy of Elena Humphreys.

An early Riot Grrl New York City zine cover. Courtesy of Elena Humphreys.

20. After moving from Berkeley to Marin County in 1968, the Ali Akbar College of Music changed locations several times in and around San Rafael before settling on its current location in San Rafael.

21. More information about the Chhandam School of Kathak and the Chitresh Das Dance Company can be found on the website www.kathak.org. This chapter focuses on this kathak community's experiences in the Bay Area. However, senior students of Das have also opened kathak schools affiliated with Chhandam in areas outside the Bay Area: Joanna Das in Toronto (opened in 1990); Gretchen Hayden in Boston (1992); Pratibha Patel in Folsom, CA (2007); Rina Mehta in Los Angeles (2008); and Seema Mehta in Mumbai, India (2010).

22. Das's class at San Francisco State University was the first university-accredited kathak course in the United States; www.kathak.org/index.php/pandit-chitresh-das/about-pandit-das.

23. This phrase is borrowed from the name of Rev. Jesse Jackson's non-profit organization, the National Rainbow Coalition, which was founded in 1984 and in 1996 merged with another organization Rev. Jackson founded, Operation PUSH (People United to Save Humanity).

24. www.youtube.com/watch?v=f3CDAs-bWpg "Kathak—Glimpses of Pt Chitresh Das' [*sic*] intricate choreography."

25. Theologian Richard Kyle describes the New Age as a nebulous and diffuse "cultural trend" drawing heavily on Indian and other Eastern religions as well as Western occultism, modern psychology, natural science, and even Christianity (1995, 9, 75). In San Francisco in the 2000s, the "spirituality trope" of the New Age was especially prevalent. Several members of the Chitresh Das Dance Company, particularly those who grew up in the area, had a positive and accepting outlook on beliefs and practices associated with the New Age; but like "hippie," negative connotations associated with the term "New Age" led most in the kathak community to avoid its explicit use.

Glossary

ashram [*āśram*]. A sanctuary or hermitage reserved for spiritual adepts, these are often located in relatively uninhabited areas. The term also has come to be used for centers of yoga, meditation, and other Indian religious or cultural practices.

bhangra. The term for both a genre of music and type of folk dance that originated in and is representative of the Punjab region, comprising a northwestern state in India and a neighboring province in Pakistan. Bhangra dance is today a conglomeration of various Punjabi dances with different names. Since the 1990s, both the dance and music have been fused with elements of popular music and dance from the West and have been performed widely in the South Asian diaspora.

bol(s). Utterance, word(s). A term for the representative language in North Indian music and dance that communicates rhythmic patterns and often the manner of producing those patterns. Kathak makes use of bols derived from various drums (tabla and *pakhāvaj*) and some that are specific to the dance. In Kathak there is not always a direct correspondence between bols and their technical delivery; kathak dancers can thus interpret one bol pattern in a variety of ways.

chakkar. Turn, revolution. Used specifically in Kathak to refer to swift turns executed on the heel of one foot (usually the left).

desī. People of a particular *deś* or region/country; colloquial: South Asians.

ghuṇghrū. Dance bells, which are strung together and tied around dancers' ankles.

guru-śiṣya paramparā. Teacher-student tradition. The cultural framework for training in Hindustani music, kathak, and other systems of knowledge in India.

Hindustani [*Hindustānī*]. The classical music of North India.

Karnatak [*Karṇāṭak*]. The classical music of South India.

kathak. One of eight types of dance currently recognized as classical (*śāstrīya*) by the Sangeet Natak Akademi, the government of India's national academy for the performing arts. Kathak is known for its percussive footwork and fast turns ending in crisp stances, complemented by subtle movements of eyes, eyebrows, wrists, and neck.

khūbsūratī. Beauty/handsomeness of face or form.

lāsya. "Feminine" style dancing, characterized by soft, subtle, and graceful movements.

layakārī. Facility in rhythm and working inventively within rhythmic parameters.

nazākat. Softness, delicacy, elegance. Derived from Persian *nāzuk*.

nritt [*nṛtt*]. "Pure dance." Dance without narrative.

nritya [*nṛtya*]. Dance combining storytelling and rhythmic expression.

sarod. A twenty-five-string fretless lute instrument with a stretched goatskin head and steel fingerboard. The instrument has four main playing strings that are played with a pick (often made out of coconut shell) and by pressing the string against the fingerboard with the musician's fingernail. Some strings are used for rhythmic emphasis and several others are considered "sympathetic." Sympathetic strings are rarely plucked; instead each string, tuned to a specific note, will vibrate when the same note is played on the main strings.

sitar [*sitār*]. A stringed instrument with a long, hollow fretboard, movable frets, and a gourd that serves as a resonating chamber at its base. Like the sarod, the sitar has main playing strings, strings used for rhythmic emphasis and sympathetic strings. The main strings are plucked with a wire plectrum (*mizrāb*) and can be individually pulled along a fret to create microtonal variations and glissandi, called *mīnd*.

tabla [*tablā*]. The most popular drum in North Indian classical music today, the tabla is actually a set of two closed-bottomed drums, called the *bāyāṇ* (typically played by the left hand) and *dāyāṇ* (played by the right). Together, these drums create the complex catalog of sounds used in tabla solos, in accompanying Hindustani vocal and instrumental music and kathak dance, and in increasingly diverse genres of music around the world.

taiyārī. Readiness. The virtuosity of technique acquired through systematic practice.

tāṇḍava. "Masculine" style dancing, characterized by sharp movements, strong footwork, and robust movement.

Chapter 14: Video Examples (access through companion website)

Video Example 1. www.youtube.com/watch?v=f3CDAs-bWpg "Kathak—Glimpses of Pt Chitresh Das' [*sic*] intricate choreography."

Video Example 2. www.youtube.com/watch?v=3SxWyvli7es "Kathak—Lightning speed feet of Pt. Chitresh Das."

Video Example 3. www.youtube.com/watch?v=W50yvRH4EPo "Incredible Kathak Abhinaya by Pandit Chitresh Das."

References Cited

Brekke, Torkel. 2003. *Makers of Modern Indian Religion in the Late Nineteenth Century*. Oxford and New York: Oxford University Press.

Bromley, David G., and Anson D. Shupe Jr. 1981. *Strange Gods: The Great American Cult Scare*. Boston: Beacon Press.

Campi, Alicia J. 2005. "Closed Borders and Mass Deportations: The Lessons of the Barred Zone Act." Published by the American Immigration Law Foundation. www.ailf.org/ipc/policy_reports_2005_barredzone.asp#note4. Accessed February 12, 2007.

Fox, Sue. 1995. Interview with Yehudi Menuhin and Ravi Shankar. "How We Met: Yehudi Menuhin and Ravi Shankar." *Independent* (UK), October 1. www.independent.co.uk/arts-entertainment/how-we-met-yehudi-menuhin-and-ravi-shankar-1575503.html. Accessed August 18, 2013.

Cowdery, James R. 1995. "The American Students of Balasaraswati." *UCLA Journal of Dance Ethnology* 19: 50–57.

Cupchik, Jeffrey W. 2013. "Polyvocality and Forgotten Proverbs (and Persons): Ravi Shankar, George Harrison and Shambhu Das." *Journal of Popular Music History* 8 (1): 68–90.

———. Forthcoming. "George Harrison: South Asian Music, Subjectivity and Bricolage in the Era of Psychedelia." *Journal of Popular Music and Society*.

Das, Julia. 1986. Unpublished letter to Michael Alexander, Alexander Artists Management. November 17.

Delgado, Richard, and Jean Stefancic. 2001. *Critical Race Theory: An Introduction*. New York: New York University Press.

Erdman, Joan L. 1987. "Performance as Translation: Uday Shankar in the West." *TDR: The Drama Review* 31 (1): 64–88.

French, Harold W. 1974. *The Swan's Wide Waters: Ramakrishna and Western Culture*. Port Washington, NY: Kennikar Press.

Gottlieb, Robert S. (producer). 1988. *Circles-Cycles: Kathak Dance* (film). Berkeley: University of California Extension Media Center.

Hawley, John Stratton. 2004. "Global Hinduism in Gotham." In *Asian American Religions: The Making and Remaking of Borders and Boundaries*, ed. Tony Carnes and Fenggang Yang. New York: New York University Press. 112–37.

Jain, Poonam. 2012. "Harvard Ghungroo." *Times of India*, May 11. http://articles.timesofindia.indiatimes.com/2012-05-11/news/31668557_1_culture-mechanical-engineering-students. Accessed December 15, 2012.

Khokar, Mohan. 1979. *Traditions of Indian Classical Dance*. Delhi: Clarion Books.

Kinsley, David R. 1986 [1997]. *Hindu Goddesses: Visions of the Divine Feminine in the Hindu Religious Tradition*. Berkeley: University of California Press.

Knight, Douglas M., Jr. 2010. *Balasaraswati: Her Art & Life*. Middletown, CT: Wesleyan University Press.

Kothari, Sunil. 1989. *Kathak: Indian Classical Dance Art*. New Delhi: Abhinav.

Kyle, Richard G. 1995. *The New Age Movement in American Culture*. Lanham, MD: University Press of America.

Lavezzoli, Peter. 2007. *The Dawn of Indian Music in the West*. New York: Continuum.

Locke, Ralph P. 2001. "Orientalism." In *The New Grove Dictionary of Music and Musicians*, ed. Stanley Sadie, 2nd ed., vol. 18. New York: Grove. 699–701.

Massey, Reginald. 1999. *India's Kathak Dance, Past, Present, Future*. New Delhi: Abhinav.

Morelli, Sarah. 2010. "Intergenerational Adaptation in North Indian Kathak Dance." *Anthropological Notebooks* 16 (3): 77–91.

———. Forthcoming. *Tales of a Modern Guru: Pandit Chitresh Das and Indian Classical Dance in Diaspora*. Champaign: University of Illinois Press.

O'Shea, Janet. 2007. *At Home in the World: Bharata Natyam on the Global Stage*. Middletown, CT: Wesleyan University Press.

Purkayastha, Bandana. 2005. *Negotiating Ethnicity: Second-Generation South Asian Americans Traverse a Transnational World*. New Brunswick, NJ: Rutgers University Press.

Reck, David. 1978. "The Neon Electric Saraswati." *Contributions to Asian Studies* 12: 3–19.

———. 1985. "Beatles Orientalis: Influences from Asia in a Popular Song Tradition." *Asian Music* 16 (1): 83–149.

Saxena, Sushil Kumar. 1991. *Swinging Syllables: Aesthetics of Kathak Dance*. New Delhi: Sangeet Natak Akademi.

Shah, Purnima. 2008. "Negotiating Gender in Contemporary Kathak Dance Choreography." *Samipya: Journal of Indology* 25 (1–2): 1–15.

Shelemay, Kay Kaufman. 2011. "Musical Communities: Rethinking the Collective in Music." *Journal of the American Musicological Society* 64 (2): 349–90.

Silver, Brian. 1978. "Henry Cowell and Alan Hovhaness: Responses to the Music of India." *Contributions to Asian Studies* 12: 54–81.

Slawek, Stephen. 1996. "Engrossed Minds, Embodied Moods and Liberated Spirits in Two Musical Traditions of India." *Bansuri* 13: 31–41.

Slobin, Mark. 1993. *Subcultural Sounds: Micromusics of the West*. Middletown, CT: Wesleyan University Press.

Srinivasan, Priya. 2011. *Sweating Saris: Indian Dance as Transnational Labor*. Philadelphia: Temple University Press.

Uchiyama, Hoku (director, writer). 2013. *Upaj: Improvise*. San Francisco: Hindipendent Films.

Wade, Bonnie. 1978. "Indian Classical Music in North America: Cultural Give and Take." *Contributions to Asian Studies* 12: 29–39.
Warren, Vincent. 2006. "Yearning for the Spiritual Ideal: The Influence of India on Western Dance 1626-2003." *Dance Research Journal* 38 (1 & 2): 97–114.
Welsh, Anne Marie. 1994. "Classic Kathak Dance Transcends Culturalism: Art Matters, Not Artists' Skin Color." *San Diego Union-Tribune*. Thursday, April 21. Entertainment section, 24.
Wong, Deborah. 2000. "The Asian American Body in Performance." In *Music and the Racial Imagination*. Ronald Radano and Philip Bohlman, eds. Chicago: University of Chicago Press. 57–94.
Yogananda, Paramhansa. 1946. *Autobiography of a Yogi*. New York: Philosophical Library.

- 15 -

SANSEI VOICES IN THE COMMUNITY

Japanese American Musicians in California

Susan M. Asai

Susan Asai is an ethnomusicologist with a long-standing interest and firsthand experience in the music cultures of Japan and of people of Asian heritage in the United States. Asai's essay problematizes the entity "Japanese American music" as she investigates the notion and practice of music making among three generations of Japanese Americans, focusing most specifically on sansei, or the third generation. Working from a framework that highlights theories of ethnicity and identity formation, Asai asks what has been inherited, what has been forgotten, what is relearned, and what is invented for each generation of Japanese Americans. The author addresses the role of cultural intrusion and the devastating effects of the internment of Japanese Americans during World War II. She, furthermore, considers the interface of Japanese American musicians with mainstream American artistic and cultural trends, such as jazz, swing, and the civil rights movement. To exemplify some of the forces at work in the creative processes of sansei, a group of which Asai herself is a member, the author provides biographical profiles of three sansei artists who speak for Asian American communities.

INTRODUCTION

The relationship of music and identity is of interest at a time when Americans of color choose to retain aspects of their forebears' cultures as a positive way to reinvent themselves in an effort to counterbalance their marginalization within American society. Such populations have discovered that one's ethnicity is important as both a social identity and a political force. Among the numerous studies of Japanese American identity, a growing number of scholars are using the parameters of music to discuss the construction of identity. The emergence of a substantial body of compositions makes it possible to study identity as expressed in musical forms. Asian American literature written in the past thirty-five years often refers to the notion of "finding a way home" or building a sense of self by returning to one's ethnic heritage (Thornton 1992, 165–74). Many Asian American musicians choose to follow that path and create new work.

15.1. Nobuko Miyamoto and Chris Iijima performing Asian American political commentary songs in the 1970s. Photo by Bob Hsiang.

Very few Americans know anything about the four, and now five, generations of Japanese Americans living in the continental United States. The first generation, or *issei*, perpetuated the musical traditions and practices of their homeland. Many maintained traditions of the culture they had left behind as a source of aesthetic pleasure and pride from which they could draw as they faced discrimination and alienation here in the United States. Musical activities in San Francisco and Los Angeles serve as examples of *issei* music making in urban centers. *The Japanese American Yearbook*, published in 1914, recorded a variety of music instruction offered in San Francisco at that time: *koto* (thirteen-stringed zither), *shamisen* (three-stringed plucked lute), *shakuhachi* (bamboo end-blown flute), piano, choral music at the YWCA, *yōkyoku* (*nō* drama recitation), and Satsuma *biwa* (four-stringed plucked lute). Due to the introduction of Western music to Japan in the Meiji period (1868–1912), many *issei* were familiar with this music and some sang and played piano and other instruments. Singing Christian hymns as members of gospel societies in San Francisco appealed to the pro-Western attitudes of those who wanted to become Americanized as quickly as possible (Asai 1995, 432–33).

Issues of a Japanese newspaper, *Rafu Shimpo*, from 1926 to 1941 provide information about musical performances in and around Los Angeles. Reports of traditional Japanese music mention *sankyoku* (chamber music featuring koto, shamisen, and shakuhachi), *jōruri* (narrative shamisen music for puppet plays), biwa music, *utai* (*nō* theater songs), *shigin* (Chinese poems set to music), *nagauta* (narrative songs for kabuki theater), *hauta* (a genre of short shamisen-accompanied songs), and *naniwabushi* (popular-style narrative shamisen music) (Asai 1995, 430).

Music of the second generation, or *nisei*, reflects the increased assimilation of Japanese Americans in the United States. Many nisei maintained continuity with the past by sustaining musical traditions of their issei parents: the classical repertoire of traditional instruments and song genres, theater music, folk music, and Japanese popular songs. They also, however, looked to American popular music styles, such as swing, in moving beyond the music of the first generation. Nisei also made seminal efforts toward mixing Japanese and American musics that the next generation, following in their footsteps, would further explore and extend (Asai 1995, 432–36).

Music of the third generation, or *sansei*, embraces countless musical styles heard in American mainstream culture, as well as innovative, experimental forms. The spectrum of sansei musical activity includes traditional Japanese, nearly every genre of Western music, and syntheses of Japanese and American music (particularly jazz-based idioms). The joining of Japanese and American musical elements links sansei to a Japanese past while also functioning as a statement of their social and cultural identity as Americans (Asai 1995, 449).

The great concentration of Japanese Americans in California provides a fertile environment for music making. Additionally, a consideration of the social, political, and economic discrimination endured by Japanese Americans on the West Coast provides some background for understanding the retention of ethnicity among sansei. The inhospitable attitude toward first and second generations shaped "Japanese ethnic solidarity," an identity that Japanese Americans shared as "countrymen" holding "common cultural values." Japanese ethnic solidarity in turn provided an economic base that reinforced ethnic cohesiveness (Takaki 1989, 180). The retention of cultural traditions, such as music, became an expression of that ethnic cohesiveness.

The varied backgrounds and musical development of the artists discussed below illustrate the range of music making among sansei. This discussion does not attempt to define sansei music making in all of its stylistic permutations. Rather, it searches for the relationships among music, ethnicity, and community. The distinct musical voices and socialization of the three artists exemplify these relationships. This study is also my personal quest as a sansei musician to explore what my music making expresses about me, and the varying ways in which we sansei perceive ourselves and our music.

IN SEARCH OF AN IDENTITY

Theories of identity formation developed primarily by sociologists provide the framework for investigating the relationship between sansei music and ethnicity. Ethnomusicologist Gerhard Kubik describes ethnicity as a social response of a particular population who have experienced "cultural conflict and aborted transculturation." He discusses the concept of ethnicity and the rise of ethnic movements as an ideologically programmed response to "outside aggression, deprivation, discrimination, and holocaust . . . the traumatic collective experience of a group" (Kubik 1994, 41). The internment of 127,000 Japanese Americans on the West Coast and Hawaii during World War II is an example of cultural conflict turned into complete social, economic, and political isolation. The existential trauma of first- and second-generation Japanese American internees continues to affect the consciousness and identity of the third-generation Japanese Americans, most of whom were born after the internment.

The idea of ethnicity as a process, rather than as a state of being, was originally developed by the historian Oscar Handlin (1951), whose work with European immigrants led him to declare that ethnicity was "shaped as much by processes that occurred in the New World as by the cultural content they brought with them from the Old World" (as cited in Fugita and O'Brien 1991, 20). This idea progressed into the concept of an emergent ethnicity, describing how the "specific cultural content will change as the ethnic group faces different structural exigencies" in an evolving identification (Fugita and O'Brien 1991, 21). Ethnicity is presented as having a built-in flexibility and is sensitive to historical events that have shaped or influenced the development of a particular ethnic group.

Fugita and O'Brien's research in *Japanese American Ethnicity: The Persistence of Community* is significant in proposing how the emergent-ethnicity perspective allows for greater play between being structurally assimilated and retaining ethnicity. The perspective specifies that individuals in varying degrees "transform the nature of their ethnicity" rather than negate it completely. The proportion of assimilation and retention varies and changes according to the exigencies that an individual or community faces in society (1991, 22).

A second theoretical framework for this study is Marcus Hansen's sociological thesis, called "the law of the return of the third generation." He posits that the third generation of any immigrant group, who are in a more secure position in terms of socioeconomic status and identity as Americans, is more inclined to reclaim their ethnic heritage than the second generation, who strove to become part of the dominant culture in their "efforts to overcome discrimination and marginality" (Montero 1981, 829). Sociologist Stanford Lyman further explores Hansen's idea by proposing that the third generation may also experience a certain ambivalence or dilemma. He states that sansei "do exhibit a certain 'Hansen effect'—that is, a desire to recover selected and specific elements of the culture of Old Japan—but in this endeavor itself they discover that their own Americanization has limited the possibility of very effective recovery" (Lyman 1971, 63). Despite the large-scale assimilation of many sansei, it is still useful to consider Hansen's effect as applied to musicians whose work exhibits aspects of the music of "Old Japan." The strong influence that traditional Japanese music has had on some sansei musicians is interpreted by the artists themselves as reclaiming their ethnic heritage.

A SENSE OF COMMUNITY

Cohesive Japanese American communities in California are a manifestation of the marginality and isolation experienced by the first and second generations. Fugita and O'Brien's research explores the sense of community cultivated among Japanese Americans based on traditional Japanese social and kinship relationships. Ronald P. Dore describes local community life in homeland Japan as one of cohesion, of carefully constructed social relationships that preserve order and notions of duty and obligation to the broader community; all are necessary in order for individuals to maintain the honor of their family (1958, 22). Even though Japanese American families live scattered throughout California, quasi-kin social relationships continue to bind individuals to their ethnic community.

The relationship between community and individual identity is explored in Wendy L. Ng's "Collective Memories of Communities." Ng discusses "community memory" as the catalyst that links past and present generations to a particular community in which individuals "derive a sense of belonging, identity, and meaning in their lives" (1991, 104). Community memory encompasses the history and collective memories of individuals and the community as a whole. She suggests that history has played an important role in shaping the Japanese American community, and today, past actions have taken on new and reinterpreted meanings in the context of justice and civil rights (1991, 103). In the 1980s, the call for redress and reparations, addressed to the United States government, prompted Japanese Americans to exercise their civil rights and become more politically active. The political activism of Japanese American communities is important in understanding the basis for the creative work of some sansei musicians.

SANSEI: A BROADENED MUSICAL LANDSCAPE

Sansei form a diverse group. The music they play includes European classical and contemporary styles, traditional Japanese music, Broadway musicals, jazz, soul, pop, assorted rock styles, country, funk, and various fusions of popular music. The story of music making among sansei is not very different from that of the mainstream population of the United States. Nevertheless, there is a growing musical landscape cultivated by sansei who center their creative efforts on music that explores and fulfills their ethnic well-being as Americans of Japanese descent.

A broader Asian American music that served to express the political motivations and aspirations of the Asian American movement in the 1970s preceded Japanese American music. The political origins of Asian American music imbue it with a certain revolutionary character. The movement continues to function as a platform for greater sociopolitical consciousness and empowerment of Asian Americans. The civil rights movement and the ensuing Black Power movement provided the impetus for the political power Asian Americans now feel.

Asian American activists involved in the movement realized the need for cultural forms that would provide a means to express their newly emerging identity. Certain artists within Asian American communities developed work in response to the growing political consciousness raised by the movement. William Wei outlines "two competing but interrelated approaches to Asian American culture: political and aesthetic." (1993, 64). The political approach was shaped by Marxist cultural theory, emphasizing making art responsible to the people and, by extension, Mao Tse-tung's belief that "art must meet first a political requirement and only secondarily aesthetic criteria" (Wei 1993, 64).

In finding a voice, many Asian American artists turned toward their own history and experience (Wei 1993, 54). In the late 1960s and 1970s, folk music, inspired by the socially conscious songs of Woody Guthrie, Pete Seeger, and Bob Dylan, served to express the struggles and prejudices faced by Asians in the United States. Motivated by increasing political and social awareness, music groups comprised of members of various Asian ethnicities emerged. Recordings within this genre include those by Chris Iijima, Joanne Miyamoto, and Charlie Chin (New York City), and Yokohama California led by Peter Horikoshi (San Francisco). Both groups performed in folk song style, expressing their identity as Asian Americans and their move toward effecting positive social change.

The political approach to art has appealed to certain sansei musician-composers for whom music is an artistic expression of sociopolitical and psychological responses to being Japanese American. Music in this context functions as a form of social commentary and ideology, defining who people of Japanese ancestry are and how they can foster positive change. Japanese American music in this vein is an expression of group social and political solidarity within the larger context of Asian America. As an art form, it expresses the values, cultural identity, and political awareness of people of Japanese descent in America.

Not all sansei musicians, however, choose to be explicitly political in their art. In their artistic development, the concerns of many artists are not political and their energies are directed toward achieving a more broadly conceived musical vision. Some may still incorporate themes of identity, cultural conflict, and alienation in their work, but the work itself does not have a political agenda. Reaching wider, more diverse audiences and attaining some commercial success are greater priorities in their quest for "art for art's sake."

THE EMERGENCE OF A TRANSCULTURATED MUSIC

The study of traditional Japanese music is one avenue taken by many Japanese American musician-composers who seek sound referents for their own work. The study and performance of Japanese music directly connects sansei to the "musical memory" of past generations. The exploration of traditional Japanese genres and musical elements appears to be the first stage in many a composer's creative journey. The sonic offerings of traditional music include the timbre and idiomatic playing styles of various Japanese instruments, as well as its indigenous pentatonic melodies, rhythms, forms, or stylistic and aesthetic aspects. An example of an aesthetic concept is *ma*, or "silent beat," employed in classical music styles, whereby the silences between notes are as integral to a composition as the sounding of notes.

Japanese court music, or *gagaku*, is one source of inspiration for sansei traveling the traditional music route. The former Japanese Imperial Household court dancer Suenobu Togi is solely responsible for the dissemination of court music in the United States. From 1960 on, he taught many seminars in Boston; San Francisco; Los Angeles; Austin, Texas; and Boulder, Colorado. In Los Angeles, Togi established gagaku groups at the University of California, Los Angeles, as one of the music ensembles in the ethnomusicology program, and at both the Senshin Buddhist Temple and the Tenrikyo Temple. Under the tutelage of Togi, the San Francisco Gagaku Society, directed by the pianist and koto player Miya Masaoka from 1990–98, continued the court music tradition. Masaoka points out that gagaku's pan-Asian origins—Chinese, Korean, Indian, and Southeast Asian—make it an ideal music for bringing together musicians of various Asian backgrounds. The San Francisco Gagaku Society reflects the spirit of the broader Asian American cultural movement. Pan-Asian thinking grew out of the sociopolitical realization that to become part of mainstream American society and "to interact with others on equal terms, ethnic groups had to first distinguish themselves as a separate and empowered population" (Schulze 1992).

Other forms of traditional music from which musician-composers draw include Japanese folk *taiko* drumming, regional folk songs, and the classical repertories of the koto, shamisen, and shakuhachi. Elements of these musical genres are incorporated into a wide spectrum of contemporary musical styles. The American aspect of the Japanese American music equation may be found in the use of such genres as folk music, rock, jazz-based music, jazz fusion, or pop songs with lyrics that express ideology or personal statements about what it means to be of Japanese descent in the United States. English lyrics offer an outlet for expressing attitudes about working conditions, prejudicial treatment, social alienation, and the political, racial, and economic injustices of the internment camps during World War II.

DISTINCT SANSEI VOICES

This section is a journey into the musical and communal life of three contemporary sansei musicians in urban California. Interviews with the musicians focused on the following questions: "How would you describe your socialization growing up and do you feel connected to a Japanese American or Asian American community?" and "Does your music reflect how you ethnically identify yourself?"

Nobuko Miyamoto: Tale of a Socially and Politically Active Songster

(Joanne) Nobuko Miyamoto's music within Asian American communities spans a period of more than forty years and includes a few musical styles. Among Asian Americans, she pioneered the use of music for raising political and social consciousness and calling to action this population in the 1970s. *A Grain of Sand: Music for the Struggle by Asians in America* (1973), an album Miyamoto created with Chris Iijima and Charlie Chin, features some of the first Asian American songs with social and political commentary. The songs on this seminal album follow in the footsteps of Woody Guthrie's, Pete Seeger's, and Bob Dylan's socially conscious folk music.

Born in Los Angeles in 1939, Miyamoto grew up during the upheaval of the Japanese American internment during World War II. After the war she and her family lived with her aunt and uncle, creating close ties to other Japanese American families for economic survival and moral support. As a youth, Miyamoto lived in three different neighborhoods of Los Angeles—Crenshaw, Boyle Heights, and Pico Union—where substantial numbers of Japanese Americans formed communities.

Several musical styles influenced her development as a musician. She has a strong memory of her uncle singing *utai* (a vocal style used in *nō* theater), which formed an interesting cultural juxtaposition to Miyamoto's European classical piano studies. She felt spiritually attached to European classical music—preferred by her mother and father—because it was music that could take her to another place. She was also influenced by the pop music of the 1950s and 1960s, in particular the singer Frank Sinatra.

Miyamoto's vocal training facilitated her involvement in singing songs of the Asian American political movement. At the age of seven she sang Bach chorales, studying with a teacher who believed that children could sing four-part harmony. Later, a jazz vocal teacher broadened her repertoire with the music of Billie Holiday, Lena Horne, Sarah Vaughan, and other American masters. Her first professional stint as a jazz vocalist lasted for eight months at the Colony Club in Seattle, where Pat Suzuki had performed before heading to New York City. Miyamoto experienced a political awakening when she came under the influence of young people in her audience who were actively involved in protesting the Vietnam War.

She worked with an Italian filmmaker who documented the lives of black people in the United States. The docudrama, *Seize the Time*, recorded the transformation of a man into a revolutionary nationalist as a result of joining the Black Panther Party. From 1967 to 1968 Miyamoto traveled around the country making films. During this time, the civil rights movement was in full swing and the Black Panther Party was at its height of popularity and influence. Miyamoto's exposure to the Black Power movement and others' struggle for equality spawned her political awareness and activism. Her role as a songster of the Asian American movement in the 1970s was significant in her search for an identity: "I had never been around militant Asians before. It was during Vietnam and there were all the news clips of Asians being killed again: World War II to Korea and Vietnam, three wars in which Asians were body counts. So a lot of consciousness was being raised through that, and then there were questions of our own identity" (Noriyuki 1995, 2).

The Vietnam War raised questions about self-identity for Asian American activists as they realized that their heritage as Americans was not acknowledged by other Americans, who instead viewed them as foreigners and, in the context of the war, resented them.

In New York City, Miyamoto came into contact with politically minded Japanese Americans—Yuri Kochiyama and the Iijima family—who were active in Asian Americans for Action (AAA). While working with AAA, Miyamoto and Chris Iijima began to write politically motivated music. During a weeklong conference that brought Asian American political groups together in Chicago, the pair collaborated on their first song, "The People's Beat," which was inspired by a speech made by Fred Hampton, a Black Panther who had recently been killed by FBI agents. Before presenting their song, Miyamoto and Iijima showed two films: one of the atomic bomb exploding on Hiroshima and another about the Vietnam War. The films supported their talk about the similarity of attitudes that Americans held toward people of both African and Asian descent. Afterward, they performed "The People's Beat," calling for stronger ties between Asian and black political agendas.

Continuing their musical partnership, Miyamoto and Iijima wrote five songs that were sung for Asian American community organizations across California such as Yellow Brotherhood in Los Angeles, the Japanese Community Youth Council in San Francisco, and the Yellow Seed youth program in Stockton. In 1970, one year after their first performance, Charlie Chin, whom they had met at New York University, joined the duo. For the next three years, the trio traveled throughout the United States.

Miyamoto, Iijima, and Chin built their reputation as proponents of the political approach to music and served as voices for politically active Asian Americans. Their songs criticized capitalism, racism, and sexism, and propagated socialist views that were intended to liberate and empower people of color in the United States. The trio sang at protest demonstrations on college campuses and community-based events across the country, encouraging the emergence of other Asian American music groups.

The group strove to create a sense of unity among people of color, as promoted in the Third World Strike at San Francisco State that lasted from November 1968 to March 1969. They extended their artistic reach by writing political songs in Spanish for the Puerto Rican and Dominican squatters' movement in New York City during the early 1970s. Their popularity with this segment of the population resulted in a recording of two songs—"Venceremos" and "Somos Asiaticos" (the latter was released in Puerto Rico)—and a year of singing engagements for Puerto Rican organizations and communities. Their summit performance was at the

Puerto Rican Liberation Day celebration at Madison Square Garden in New York City. At The Dot coffeehouse in New York City, they joined *nueva canción* singers and *cancionero* poets, who were accompanied by *cuatro* (four-stringed plucked lute) players. The trio's experience with Latino musicians and poets introduced them to the idea of using the arts as a vehicle for expressing the struggles for freedom and equality in Puerto Rico, Peru, the Dominican Republic, Chile, and Cuba; soon songs of the *Nueva Canción* Movement became part of their repertoire.

As musical ambassadors, Miyamoto, Iijima, and Chin joined forces with people of color in New York City. Yuri Kochiyama, a nisei who was involved with both the black nationalist movement and the Asian Americans for Action, invited the three to perform for black political events. They freely traversed Asian, black, and Latino communities, schools, and colleges, bringing their political messages through song.

Returning to Los Angeles in 1973, Miyamoto continued her musical career without Iijima and Chin. Friends introduced her to Benny Yee, a keyboard player who had just left the band Hiroshima (discussed below). Together, they formed Warriors of the Rainbow, a jazz fusion band, with the Japanese American saxophonist Russel Baba and the drummer E. W. Wainwright. The Warriors went through several transformations over a five-year period. Miyamoto and Yee wrote socially aware though not politically direct songs for Warriors.

Miyamoto's work also reflects her connection to the Japanese American community in Los Angeles. As an artist and activist, she chooses "to create in the community something that reflects the community." Her early involvement with Japanese American groups was through dance, and she performed ballet at Nisei Week talent shows for a number of years. From 1975 to 1978, she taught modern dance at the Senshin Buddhist Temple in Los Angeles, bringing her into close contact with other Japanese Americans. Her large classes of twenty to forty people were evidence of the community's strong desire for cultural activities. Her recognition of the community's hunger for cultural events provided the impetus for Miyamoto to form Great Leap, Inc., so that she might produce original work for the stage. From its inception, Great Leap has played an important role in showcasing the work of many Asian American performers (Fong 1995, 1). Great Leap's Slice of Rice performance series featured solo theater pieces that combine music, dance, and drama.

In 1990, turning fifty years old prompted Miyamoto to create an autobiographical one-woman show, titled *A Grain of Sand*—after her 1973 album—which she performed in venues across the country. It is an ambitious work that outlines the shaping of Miyamoto's experiences, attitudes, and activism as a Japanese American woman. It is a statement of who she is and how she identifies herself. She performed *A Grain of Sand* at numerous theaters throughout New England, the Midwest, and the West Coast, targeting college-age audiences.

Miyamoto's support of the Japanese American community in Los Angeles also includes performances that she did for redress and reparation movement events, some of which address the Japanese American experience. "Gaman," a song on her album *Best of Both Worlds*, describes the internment experience. Produced by Great Leap, the Public Broadcasting System aired a short film of the song, with a series of drawings by Betty Chen. Subsequently, Miyamoto performed "Gaman" with slides or showed the film at various redress and reparation events.

Miyamoto wrote two songs that express her close ties to the Japanese American community. "Yuiyo Bon Odori" and "Tampopo" (heard on the accompanying website: Chapter 15, Track 1) are Japanese-style folk songs with verses sung in English and choruses sung in Japanese. The O-Bon festival—a commemoration of the souls of deceased ancestors—at the Senshin Buddhist Church in July 1995 included a live performance of the two songs by the group Friends of the Yagura. Both songs accompanied Japanese folk dancing for the O-Bon festival. The two songs are based on the musical structure, mode, and rhythms of traditional Japanese folk songs. In the traditional manner, the shamisen (three-string plucked lute) and shakuhachi (bamboo transverse flute) duplicate the main, sung melody and the *taiko* (barrel drum) and *atarigane* (brass gong) accent the rhythm. The American aspect of this music is the text of the verses written in English.

Prompted by Senshin's Reverend Masao Kodani, Miyamoto's use of English is an attempt to form a link between generations.

Miyamoto wrote "Yuiyo Bon Odori" on commission from the Southern District Buddhist Education Committee in California. The song was first performed on August 18, 1994, at the Southern District O-Bon worship service and Bon Odori held at the Japanese American Cultural and Community Center in Little Tokyo, downtown Los Angeles. Continuing to write music for Bon Odori celebrations, Miyamoto composed "Tampopo" in 1994. The traditional context of the O-Bon festival joins Japanese folk music primarily as an accompaniment to folk dancing. Within the Los Angeles Japanese American community, the performance of "Yuiyo" and "Tampopo" for O-Bon festivals represents an American contribution to a traditional Japanese event. The use of Japanese folk music style and instruments serve to authenticate the songs and reaffirm the community's heritage.

Tampopo Ondo (Dandelion Ondo)

Tampopo Tampopo Kiotsuke-yo, Moshi Kaze Fukeba Aaa-
1.) Ah—
The seed of the dandelion, scatters in the sky
    Tampopo Tampopo—Hi-Hi
A windblown weed, a wildflower, watch it fly
    Tampopo Tampopo—Hi-Hi
Dancing on the wind, spinning from a world it leaves behind,
Dancing on wind, new life begins.

Okagesama de Yare Yare Sore
Okagesama de Yare Yare Sore
Okagesama de Through all the forces
Okagesama de Through the shadows and the light
Okagesama de The unknown forces—dandelion
Hi-Hi-Hi-Hi-Hi-Hi-Hi, Hi-Hi

2.) Ah—
The seed of a dandelion, scatters in the sky
Tampopo Tampopo—Hi-Hi
A windblown weed, a wildflower, watch it fly—
Tampopo Tampopo—Hi-Hi
Dancing on the wind, spinning to a world it leaves behind,
Dancing on wind, new life begins.

Yare Yare Sore Yare Yare Sore
Okagesama de Yare Yare Sore
Okagesama de Yare Yare Sore
Okagesama de On this special night
Okagesama de Past and present are one
Okagesama de On this night of O-bon
Okagesama de Dandelions return
Hi-Hi-Hi-Hi-Hi-Hi, Hi-Hi

3.) Ah—
The seed of the dandelion, bursting in the sky
Tampopo Tampopo—Hi-Hi
A windblown weed, a wildflower, watch it fly
Tampopo Tampopo—Hi-Hi
Dancing on the wind, spinning to a world beyond the eye
Dancing on the wind, new life begins—Hey

Okagesama de Yare Yare Sore
Okagesama de Yare Yare Sore
Okagesama de On this night
Okagesama de The old and the young
Okagesama de All the dandelions
Okagesama de Dance as one—Dance, Dance as one

Okagesama de Yare Yare Sore
Okagesama de Yare Yare Sore
Okagesama de Not a rose or an iris

Okagesama de   Not a bird of paradise
Okagesama de   Not an orchid or a lily

Just a simple dandelion,
  Tada no Tampopo
Just a simple dandelion,
  Tada no Tampopo
Just a simple dandelion,
  Tada no Tampopo
Just a simple dandelion,
Tampopo Tampopo
Tampopo Tampopo

Translation of terms:

kiotsuke-yo: careful
moshi kaze fukeba: if the wind blows
okagesama de: with your help
tada no tampopo: a simple dandelion

Miyamoto's songs have a didactic Buddhist message that is intended as an expression of Japanese American Buddhist culture. The song implies learning to hear and receive the Truth through the practice of "just dancing," as interpreted by the Jōdo Buddhist sect. The accompanying notes to the song describing Bon Odori state:

> According to Jōdoshinshū, Truth and Reality are ours for the receiving. We need do nothing but hear and receive the Truth. But to simply hear and receive is as difficult as it is to just dance. To "just do" anything is extremely difficult, for it involves setting aside one's ego for a moment. Bon odori is an exercise in "just dancing," in "just hearing and accepting," in "being a river forever flowing and changing instead of a riverbank forever watching."

"Tampopo" reflects not only Miyamoto's own spiritual beliefs but also the beliefs and practices of Japanese American Buddhists. Many sansei are active members of Buddhist temples in southern California. Buddhism, a religion of their Japanese heritage, plays an important role in reinforcing their ethnic identity.

Nobuko Miyamoto's creative life narrates the arrival of music that expressed a political awareness and a search for identity among Asian Americans in the wake of the Black Power movement and the Vietnam War. Her early work is strongly linked to the broader Asian American movement, while her later work not only connects to the Japanese American community, but also gives voice to a number of cultures reflecting the diversity of Los Angeles. The artist's latest recording, *To*

All Relations—translated from the Lakota expression *"Mitakuye Oyasin"*—is described by Miyamoto as a "gathering of tribes" and features diverse instrumentation and musical elements. The spiritual and cultural breadth of her work is widely felt, and a number of sansei musicians in Los Angeles acknowledge the impact she has had on them as artists.

Miyamoto's ties to the community are both national and local. The songs that she sang on her own and with Iijima and Chin addressed Asian American communities nationwide. Locally, her music, dance, and theater performances, music for O-Bon festivals, and other community events and venues project her identification with Buddhism and the Japanese American community in Los Angeles. The original songs "Yuiyo Bon Odori" and "Tampopo" are a tribute to her Japanese roots; they are intentional in their imitation of Japanese folk music as a way to authenticate and distinguish the Japanese aspect of this Japanese American music.

Mark lzu: Traversing Boundaries

Mark Izu is a central figure in the Asian American music scene in the San Francisco Bay Area. For forty years he has been active in the Asian American contemporary arts scene as a bassist, composer, bandleader, music curator, and arts advocate. Izu's artistic direction of the annual Asian American Jazz Festival is well respected, both nationally and internationally. His music is a creative hybrid that combines his study of traditional Japanese and Chinese music with a strong interest in the music of avant-garde jazzmen Charles Mingus and Albert Ayler. Izu developed his innovative music over decades, and the vocabulary featured in his work is a mature and subtle synthesis of many musical influences. Currently, he composes music collaboratively with his wife Brenda Wong Aoki, a storyteller and dramatist who weaves wonderful narratives based on folk tales, family histories, or other original material. Together they dramatize stories with music, creating pieces that stir an atmosphere of mystery, fantasy, or other worlds.

Izu grew up in Sunnyvale, a white community near San Jose, California. His varied musical training began in the fourth grade with studies in clarinet. His musical interest broadened to include the music of other cultures—Chinese, Japanese, and Korean—to which he had access at the audio library of the San Jose Public Library. Because of his interest in Asian music, Izu's mother encouraged him to study Japanese koto during one summer while he was in junior high school. During his high school years, Izu moved on to playing the guitar and joined various rock bands. Around that time he was exposed to the music of John Coltrane, making jazz an integral force in his music.

Izu talks about early influences that inform his music. He had always been intrigued by the smell of incense and the chanting and sound of gongs he heard at Buddhist funeral services he attended with his family. Izu also listened to his parents' Japanese music recordings and was especially moved by court music.

Japanese court music created an interesting complement to Coltrane's music and European classical music, both of which he learned to play on the string bass.

After only a year and a half of playing bass, he successfully auditioned for the music program at San Francisco State University. For four years, eight hours a day, Izu locked himself in a practice room to practice bass and compose. He also joined the Chinese music group Flowing Stream Ensemble, where he met a master Chinese musician and studied *ehr-hu* (two-stringed bowed lute) and *sheng* (bamboo mouth organ). The Flowing Stream Ensemble was a semiprofessional music group that played Cantonese folk music. By going to informal rehearsals that also functioned as social gatherings, Izu managed to learn the idiomatic style and musical phrasing of the two instruments.

During his four years at the university he also heard about a Japanese gagaku (court music) ensemble led by Suenobu Togi that was part of the Institute of Buddhist Studies in San Francisco. Joining the ensemble, Izu studied the *shō* (bamboo mouth organ) and met innovative Japanese American musicians—Russel Baba, Gordie Watanabe, Robert Kikuchi-Yngojo, Paul Yamazaki, Makoto Horiuchi, and others. Joining the gagaku group proved to be a turning point in Izu's musical development; he remarked, "for the first time, I felt like I belonged someplace." The years 1976 and 1977 stand out as a fertile time because everyone in the group was writing his own music. After gagaku rehearsals, they would go to Chinatown to eat and talk. From that time on, Izu started playing bass with Baba, Horiuchi, and others. In addition, he would go down to the Mission area of San Francisco and learn salsa in workshops given by Carlos Frederico.

This period also marks Izu's collaboration with Lewis Jordan, a poet and musician whom he met at the Blue Dolphin in San Francisco. The Blue Dolphin was a club that featured alternative music, including music set to poetry. In 1977 Izu and Jordan formed Marrón, an African and Asian American ensemble whose members included Ray Collins (saxophone), Yamazaki (clarinet), Kenny Endo (trap drums), Duke Santos (congas), and Watanabe (guitar). The group ended up as an eight- to nine-piece band that became too large to find jobs, and thus disbanded.

Izu maintained his musical partnership with Jordan by joining Jordan's quartet for a performance in West Germany and forming a recording company with the saxophonist. They started RPM Records because there were very few venues for Jordan and Izu to record their style of alternative, new jazz music. The release of their first album, *Path of the Heart*, generated more jobs and the recording of several more albums.

United Front, a quartet formed in 1979, was Izu's next band with saxophonist Jordan, trumpeter George Sams, and percussionist Anthony Brown. The quartet's repertoire included music that expressed political ideas. They went to Europe every year and recorded several albums. The quartet, however, never reached the point where all the musicians were able to make a full-time living through music (Yanow 1994, 30). Izu believes the band's music was ahead of its time.

Following this endeavor, Izu played bass on pianist Jon Jang's first two albums—*Jang* and *Are You Chinese or Charlie Chan?*—which were produced by Izu's RPM Record company. The collaboration led to performances with Jang and saxophonist Francis Wong in the annual Asian American jazz festival. Since that time, Izu has recorded numerous albums as a sideman with key Asian American musicians; written scores for documentaries, theater, and a silent film; and recorded *Circle of Fire*, which was his first session as a leader (Yanow 1994, 33).

Izu's bass playing engages the eclectic influences of Japanese court music, Cantonese folk music, and jazz-based music. When interviewed, he spoke about the difficulty of learning different musical styles and instruments (bass, ehr-hu, sheng, and shō), but, in the course of time, all of these styles intertwined in becoming part of his musical vocabulary. An important concept in Izu's music is the concept of space—*ma*, in Japanese. Izu described ma in the following way: "It's the space around the notes that define what the note is and how the note sounds and feels." He applies this concept to many of his pieces, including "Scattered Scars"—which is about his parents' internment experience—and "The Shadow," on his *Circle of Fire* recording. He learned the concept of ma while learning Japanese court music.

Izu's compositional process varies depending on the piece. For example his collaboration with musician Jin Hin Kim provided the opportunity for him to become familiar with the idiomatic style of the Korean *komungo* (six-stringed plucked lute). He could then use a rhythmic approach for a composition that successfully incorporated that style. When he studied Japanese court music, Izu learned that music was "a matter of shaping the whole performance, not its individual components" (Ahlgren 1992). Instruments from different cultures find their way into many of his compositions. In reference to their use, he said, "My philosophy of fusing different cultural instruments is that you don't just add [them] to music that already exists; you build . . . from the ground up" (Ahlgren 1992).

Izu's music is eclectic and is self-described as "new jazz." He is most interested in experimenting with musical timbres and textures. One direction he has taken is to create pieces that feature taiko drumming and work around the rhythms associated with this instrument. Three of his musical sketches are dedicated to people in the community who have been committed to the arts for many years. The music of the African American pianist Horace Tapscott and conversations with him inspired Izu to write musical vignettes about people. Izu says that he is motivated to write such pieces because he believes that it is important for musicians to acknowledge each other's music.

Much of Izu's current musical output is created in collaboration with his storytelling and dramatist wife, Brenda Wong Aoki. His works are musical settings and accompaniments that enhance the dramatic narrative plays written by Aoki. Izu writes music that he can perform himself on a variety of instruments or for ensembles featuring taiko drums and jazz instrumentation. He has also had an opportunity to write a full score for symphony orchestra. In 1997 Kent Nagano, musical conductor of the Berkeley Symphony Orchestra, commissioned Izu to write and score orchestral music for the piece "Mermaid," based on Aoki's play *Mermaid Meat and Other Japanese Ghost Stories*.

Other media that Izu writes for are films. He has written film scores for Steven Okazaki's Academy Award–winning *Days of Waiting*; Emmy-winning documentary *Return to the Valley*; the DVD release of Sessue Hayakawa's 1909 masterpiece *The Dragon Painter*; *American Sons*; and the documentary about Vietnamese boat people, *Bolinao 52*. For this last film, he received a Northern California Regional Emmy Award for outstanding Musical Composition/Arrangement for his score.

When asked "Who is the audience for your music?" Izu explained that it depended on the concert's venue, location, and where it is advertised. He mentioned that, in general, his audience runs the gamut. He talked about the annual Asian American Jazz Festival—the venue that drew the largest crowds for Asian American jazz-based music—and its twofold goal to build Asian American participation and audiences at large. He stated that it is important to develop audiences from both Asian and non-Asian populations in order to cultivate future support. Illustrating what he considers ideal, Izu cited the audience who came to see the film *The Dragon Painter*, for which he composed and played the musical score at Chicago's Walker Art Museum: a mix of Asian and non-Asian film buffs, jazz aficionados, and people interested in his latest work. He feels satisfaction when he can attract such a group.

Izu's various jobs have put him in touch with the Bay Area's Asian American community. In 1989 he became the director of the Kearny St. Workshop, which started out as an Asian American grassroots organization supporting the tenet that art is a vehicle for bringing about social change (Wei 1991, 87). A division of the workshop, the Isthmus Press, published two photo journals called *Pursuing Wild Bamboo*, containing photographs that narrate episodes in the lives of artists. In the visual arts, the workshop started out as a community resource and service center by making silk-screened posters for community events; then people started doing their own work and exhibiting at San Francisco's Yerba Buena Arts Center. Until 1998 the main performance event of the workshop was the Asian American Jazz Festival. Izu's role as both artistic director and resident bassist of the festival joins his musical world with that of the Asian American community.

The Japanese American population is also a focus of Izu's efforts. He worked as the transportation coordinator at Kimochi, a Japanese American senior citizen center in San Francisco's Japan Town. Izu also served as artistic director and composer for the February 1995 Day of Remembrance concert (commemorative event of Japanese American internment) in San Francisco. The music for this event was intended to convey a portrait of the lives of internees in concentration camps during World War II. It celebrates the resilience of Japanese Americans who survived the humiliation and degradation of the camps. The hope was that the audience would gain more understanding and appreciation of what happened in this dark period of American history. The concert featured guest artist Janice Mirikitani, a poet who was chosen for her ability to "capture the moment" and to express the anger, the spirit, and compassion generated by the camp experience. Her poem about ten children who died while interned at Tule Lake was accompanied by music composed by Izu and modern dance performed by Judy Kajiwara (*ImprovisAsians!* 1995, 4).

Izu's other contributions to the community involved serving as the artistic director and composer for the Concert of a Thousand Cranes, concluding the 1995 Asian American Jazz Festival at the Asian Art Museum in San Francisco's Golden Gate Park. His piece "HIBAKUSHA! Survivors" (heard on the accompanying website: Chapter 15, Track 2), a commemoration of the atomic bomb survivors in Hiroshima and Nagasaki, incorporates chants of the Karok Indians' Healing the Earth ceremony. In the final movement, the Karok chants are performed in tandem with Izu's composition, exemplifying the more integrated approach of some of his later compositions (*ImprovisAsians!* 1995, 5).

Izu composed "HIBAKUSHA! Survivors" for a commission by Asian Improv aRts, an Asian American arts umbrella organization in San Francisco. He decided to write about the atomic survivors after reading about the offspring of radiation victims. He noted, "I realized that the most damage that is done by radiation to the human race is on the genetic level, the altering of our DNA. This literally changes one's past, present, and future." That his father served in the acclaimed all-Japanese American 442nd Battalion during World War II, and that his mother's family is from Hiroshima further reinforced his decision to write on this somber theme. Izu noted that many *hibakusha*, or survivors, were Japanese Americans visiting Japan to connect with relatives or to study at the time the war broke out. He conveyed the moving experience of hearing hibakusha tell how their lives changed and how even now they are trying to be recognized by the United States government for financial compensation.

Izu's idea of incorporating into "HIBAKUSHA!" the chants of the Karok people's Healing the Earth ceremony occurred to him after he was invited to attend the event. Every year the the Californian Karok perform ceremonies to heal the earth; they fast, pray, chant, and dance for two weeks on their sacred grounds. Very few non-Karok people are invited; thus Izu's attendance was an honor. Personally touched by the experience, he asked his Karok friend Julian to perform a healing chant at the end of "HIBAKUSHA!"

"HIBAKUSHA! Survivors," in five movements, is scored for a mixed ensemble of Asian and European instruments. A subtext for the musicians is indicated in the score. The piece is a spiritual, emotional journey. Izu wanted to re-create some of the feelings he had during the Karok ceremony. The subtexts and musical description of the composition are as follows:

I: numbness/shock/self awareness, starts after the bombing
II: confusion/anger/realization (the most dense and atonal)
III: questions/the unborn, past/present/future (begins with strings and evolves into imitative motifs initiated by the trombone; the image is that of a drop of water creating ripples on a still pond)
IV: understanding/coping/telling the story (based on a Japanese *saibara* song, a vocal piece from the court music repertoire about a fleeting moment of the ocean at Ise)
V: healing/ritual (a Karok chant to the accompaniment of the Japanese court instrument shō, and the Chinese equivalent, sheng)

Izu's music and activism depicts his affiliation with the larger Asian American community, rather than the exclusively Japanese American one. A pan-Asian orientation is central to the political, social, and artistic endeavors of many people of Asian descent in the United States today, owing to the powerful influence and legacy of the Third-World Strike at San Francisco State and the Asian American political movement in the 1970s. The broader Asian American sphere better serves musicians, like Izu, who collectively endeavor to form a broader base from which to build opportunities and exposure for themselves. Izu does not limit himself to the influences of his Japanese heritage, but is open to traditions that expand his musical vocabulary. With his musical and arts advocacy activities, Izu has helped cultivate a flourishing landscape for Asian American musicians whose music defies categorization and expresses their individuality. His many leadership roles and experience as a bassist/composer/bandleader place him in a prominent position to broaden the musical landscape further.

June Kuramoto: The Japanese Koto Innovator

June Kuramoto's koto playing heralds a new direction for the traditional instrument that dates back to seventh-century Japan and even earlier in China and Korea. In addition to being an accomplished traditional koto player, Kuramoto is adept at improvising music for the Los Angeles–based band Hiroshima, whom many consider the quintessential Japanese American music group. Hiroshima began as a musical voice for the Asian American political movement in southern California during the 1970s. The group's compositions, particularly their older songs, represent a transculturated form of music. The use of traditional instruments, musical modes, and rhythms projects a Japanese heritage, while a rhythm-and-blues and jazz fusion-based musical style expresses an American identity.

June Kuramoto's background differs from most sansei. She was born in Japan but moved to Los Angeles with her family when she was quite young. Kuramoto is considered a sansei since her father was a nisei. She grew up in the Crenshaw area of west Los Angeles and attended Dorsey High School, which was one-third African American, one-third Japanese American, and one-third European American.

Kuramoto remarked, "Dorsey High School was a multiracial school, so I got exposed to Jewish, black, and Japanese American students. That helped me sense a true community where keeping your identity was very important as to who you are; but we were all a microcosm of something greater, so we all got along. It was ideal." She felt fortunate to have the best of all worlds to draw on, to share with others, and to observe.

When she was a child, Kuramoto considered herself Japanese and not Japanese American because her impression was that she and her family would go back to Japan. Going back to Japan was her assurance that everything would be better, as her family earned a meager living in Los Angeles. As time passed, Kuramoto faced the reality that she would not return and her identity began to alter. People from Japan looked at her differently because she was no longer fluent in Japanese and her mannerisms and appearance had become more Americanized. Because she was born in Japan, however, she always felt a strong connection to her heritage. Kuramoto is an example of an individual caught between two cultures; she commented that there are times when she feels that she is a person without a country because she is marginalized by both Japanese and Americans. This is a sentiment more characteristic of nisei, second-generation Japanese Americans.

For Kuramoto, the experience of playing the koto closely aligns with her perception of being Japanese American. In grammar school she walked ten blocks with her instrument to play at school for Girl's Day, an annual Japanese celebration in March. The koto also bound her to the community, and as a youngster she played regularly at Keiro, the Japanese American retirement home in Gardena and for the "*ken* picnics" sponsored by organizations that represented districts—or prefectures (ken)—in Japan, from which Japanese American families trace their lineage.

She chose to play the koto not only because it was her connection to Japan but because she loved the sound of the instrument. At the age of six she began studies with Kazue Kudo, formerly the leading koto teacher in Los Angeles. She also learned about the history and background of the instrument from Kayoko Wakita at Los Angeles City College. Kuramoto's extensive classical koto training has given her a firm foundation for playing the less demanding structures and techniques required for pop music. After venturing into pop, rock, jazz, and blues styles, she always returns to the classical koto repertoire as her source of inspiration. The alternation between playing Japanese classical music and American popular music illustrates how Kuramoto perceives herself—a mix of both Japanese and American.

Something of a purist, Kuramoto prefers to retain the unique sound of the koto by performing in the various pentatonic modes traditionally used for the instrument. She superimposes this mode onto whatever key the rest of the band plays in, allowing her the wider range that she needs on the instrument for her improvisations. Kuramoto is most comfortable with pentatonic scales as her earliest musical training is Japanese, not Western. The challenge of fitting the idiomatic playing style of the koto into a contemporary music format, by playing over the chord changes, is met well by Kuramoto, who is given free rein in the band.

Kuramoto's past activity in the Japanese American community confirms her identity with this population. Before her active involvement with the band Hiroshima, she helped to organize the first health fair for the Japanese American Community Service (JACS). Kuramoto also served as an adviser for students in the Go for Broke program, helping Asian American high school students with problems related to adolescence. In addition, she worked with the Asian American Drug Abuse Program (AADAP), which was originally affiliated with a halfway house. Her community activism also includes past participation in demonstrations and marches with Asian Americans who advocated for peace during the Vietnam War, as part of the Asian American movement.

The political ferment of the Asian American movement provided the impetus for the founding of Hiroshima. The band embodied an identity for people of Asian descent at that time. Blacks identified with the rhythm and blues, jazz, and soul sound of the band; Chicanos and Latinos had Santana and Malo as their musical emblem of identity; but there was no music to which Asian Americans felt rooted. Kuramoto had always wanted to include the koto in a contemporary musical setting. She approached rock musicians Dan Kuramoto and his brother John because they were performing their own music, separating themselves from Asian American cover bands that were prevalent in the 1970s. The Kuramoto brothers came up with the concept of naming a band Hiroshima, a name that would represent both the atomic age and the phoenix-like image of that city rising from the ashes. June collaborated with the brothers, and the band Hiroshima was born.

The band's political leanings are closely associated with bandleader Dan Kuramoto, who served as the director of the Asian American Studies Program at California State University at Long Beach. As an academic, he also helped form Asian American Studies Central, an umbrella organization that supported the emergence of Asian American groups and activities, such as film and media organization Visual Communications, newspaper *Gidra*, and picnics that brought the community together.

From the start, Hiroshima had a reciprocal relationship with the Japanese American community. The group played for community organizations such as Joint Communications, AADAP, Amerasia Bookstore, Little Tokyo Service Center, JACS, and the annual potlucks of the Asian American Studies Program at California State University, Long Beach. Many of their performances were benefits. The community reciprocated by providing support for the group's first album by calling the radio stations to request the music of Hiroshima and purchasing their albums.

The band officially formed in 1975 and landed their first record deal in 1979. Hiroshima appeared on the Arista label for their first two albums (*Hiroshima* and *Odori*). They were nominated for the Best Instrumental Grammy Award for "Winds of Change," a song from their second album. They recorded their third through seventh albums on Epic/Sony Records. For their eighth and ninth albums they switched to Quest Records/Warner, and the band was voted Best Jazz Group by Soul Train (a predominantly black organization) in the instrumental music category. To date, the group's output includes sixteen albums, with *Departure* their most recent album released in 2011.

Within the community, Hiroshima has won Best Image awards from a Chinese American organization and the Asian American Political Alliance (AAPA). In 1995 the Japanese American Cultural and Community Center in Los Angeles conferred the President's Award on the group and the Pacific American Consortium on Education (PACE) presented them with a recognition award.

In solo concerts, Kuramoto performs mostly her own tunes, which appear on Hiroshima's albums but are never performed live by the group. As a complement, she plays one or two traditional koto pieces to demonstrate the flair of the instrument in that style. Sometimes she will also include the compositions of others—such as Kazu Matsui's "Morning Mist Across the Sea." Kuramoto schedules solo concerts not only to motivate herself to practice but to provide opportunities for musicians who need work. In addition to her solo performances, her creative output includes three albums: *Spirit and Soul* (2002), *The Way of Tea* (2005), and *Under the Stars* (2009).

When asked about who her audience is, Kuramoto—like Izu—replied that the audience varies depending on the venue. For example, when the band went on its first national tour, they played in a concert space in Chicago that attracted a black audience, and when they performed in a different part of the city, the audience was white. They only tour major cities that have diverse audiences, but often the demographics of their audience range widely. In general, Hiroshima's audiences are a mix of Caucasians, blacks, and Asians. Their audiences also tend to be intergenerational; families come because Hiroshima presents a "clean show."

Even though they tour, the band continues its mission to promote music as a communal activity among Japanese Americans, especially in Los Angeles. Audiences respond emotionally, or "tune in," to their music because it embodies a specific social identity for Japanese Americans and Asian Americans in general. When they perform at the Greek Theater in Griffith Park, the concert is a reunion for many members of the Asian American community, particularly Japanese Americans, who come out and have a wonderful time.

Among the three musicians presented here, June Kuramoto stands out as having the greatest musical connection to her Japanese heritage. She has the rare ability to expertly perform classical koto music, as well as improvise in a popular music setting. Her firm identity with Japanese culture is reflected in her koto playing for Hiroshima, in which she retains a traditional koto sound by employing pentatonic modes. Kuramoto's musicianship allows her to traverse between the worlds of Japanese classical and American popular music.

Kuramoto's ties to the Japanese American community in Los Angeles are evident not only in her work with community organizations but also in her activities with Hiroshima. The band, from its early beginnings, has enjoyed a reciprocally supportive relationship with the community. She and members of the band are emblems of a Japanese American identity whose music intends to be a voice for not only Japanese Americans but all Asian Americans. Hiroshima strives to convey to general audiences, in Dan Kuramoto's words, that "Asian Americans want a voice, we have things to say and that we are creative people who have great feelings and great passions" (Kubo 1974). Their music intertwines Japanese music, through the timbre and pentatonic sound of the koto, with pop music elements. They aim to blur boundaries, so that if you were to listen to them with your eyes closed you might think that you were hearing an American mainstream fusion band. This subtle blending of Japanese and American sounds is metaphoric of the bicultural identity many Japanese Americans experience. Today, many active Asian American musicians—especially those of Japanese descent—point to Hiroshima as their source of inspiration; the band's music continues to be a legacy of Asian American pride.

CONCLUSION

The life stories of these artists elucidate the variety of social processes that these individuals underwent in developing their ethnic identity as Japanese Americans. In accordance with Hansen's theory, the sansei musician-composers in this study chose to return to their Asian heritage in their efforts to musically innovate. Each artist strikes a different balance between assimilation and retention of their Japanese ethnicity. As a member of the group Hiroshima, Kuramoto is the most mainstream musician, yet her ties to Japanese culture and the Los Angeles Japanese American community remain strong. Miyamoto draws inspiration and support from the Japanese American community but also embraces other cultures, while Izu exemplifies a broader Asian American identity that he has cultivated in a more avant-garde music sphere.

The sansei's stories also illuminate the political force and influence of the Asian American movement, which initially formed in response to racism and social inequalities. Their sociopolitical activism supports the validity of Kubik's notion of ethnicity as a social response to the aborted transculturation Asian Americans experience in this country. A positive and proactive attitude toward one's Asian heritage as a source of political and social empowerment, rather than embarrassment or shame, is a constructive aspect of the Asian American movement. The transformative power of the movement ushered in a newly discovered pride and interest in the cultural memory of previous generations. The creation of a new identity gives Asian Americans a chance to positively define who they are in countering the stereotypes and views American society has assigned them.

The grassroots level of activities within the Asian American movement in the 1970s created strong connections between individuals and the community. This is certainly true of the artists presented in this study, all of whom have been involved with health, social, or arts organizations and whose music serves as an important communal bond. Miyamoto's "Tampopo Ondo" is an example of music written specifically for the O-Bon festival. The impetus for Kuramoto's music stems from her connection to Japanese American and Asian American audiences, while the eclectic approach of Izu's work mirrors his broader reach to an Asian American and even a new music audience.

Ng's study is pertinent to the association between *sansei* identity and community because of her focus on a collective memory in which "knowledge of the past is transmitted from one generation to another through culture—traditions, rituals, and folklore" (1991, 103). For sansei musicians, the collective memory serves as a critical source of knowledge and traditions from which they can draw. From this connection one may also infer that if music existed as part of a community's past, it could be considered a shared collective memory—a "musical memory." It then follows that musical memory also may be passed down through the generations and thus exist in the minds of subsequent generations. This memory perhaps accounts for the compositions of sansei musician-composers who synthesize elements of traditional Japanese music in their work as a way to develop their own voice. Kuramoto employs the koto and its idiomatic playing style as her Japanese American voice. Miyamoto draws on Japanese folk music as an expression of her heritage, while Izu experiments with aspects of Japanese court music, taiko drumming, and aesthetic concepts. By incorporating some aspect of traditional Japanese music, sansei musician-composers are able to express their feelings and come to terms with an essential part of themselves.

The musical lives presented in this study give voice to a historically silent population. Those who choose to write and perform music that reflects their ethnicity contribute to our understanding of the relationships between music, ethnicity, and community. By preserving bonds with their communities and building identity through music, Japanese American musicians cultivate a sense of place where they feel anchored and empowered.

Chapter 15: Musical Examples (access through companion website)

Track One. Tampopo. Nobuko Miyamoto. Courtesy of the artist.
Track Two. Hibakusha. Mark Izu. Courtesy of the artist.

References Cited

A Conversation with Mark Izu. 1995. *ImprovisAsians* 4, no. 1.

A *Grain of Sand: Music for the Struggle by Asians in America.* 1973. Liner notes by Chris Kando Iijima, Joanne Nobuko Miyamoto, and Charlie Chin. Paredon Records, P-1020.

Ahlgren, Calvin. 1992. "Izu: 'Circle' Ready to Get Off Square One." *San Francisco Chronicle*, 23 February.

Asai, Susan. 1995. "Transformations of Tradition: Three Generations of Japanese American Music Making." *Musical Quarterly* 79, no. 3: 429–53.

Dore, Ronald P. 1958. *City Life in Japan*. Berkeley: University of California Press.

Fong, Giselle L. 1995. "Nobuko Miyamoto—A Grain of Sand Sings to Warriors." *Tozai Times* 11: 128.

Fugita, Stephen S., and David J. O'Brien. 1991. *Japanese American Ethnicity: The Persistence of Community.* Seattle: University of Washington Press.

Jayo, Norman, and Paul Yamazaki. 1986. "Searching for an Asian American Music: Robert Kikuchi-Yngojo." *East Wind* 5, no. 1: 11.

Kitano, Harry H. L. 1969. *Japanese Americans: The Evolution of a Sub-culture*. Englewood Cliffs, NJ: Prentice-Hall.

Kubik, Gerard. 1994. "Ethnicity, Cultural Identity, and the Psychology of Culture Contact." In *Music and Black Ethnicity: The Caribbean and South America.* Ed. Gerard Behague. New Brunswick, NJ: Transaction.

Lyman, Stanford. 1971. "Generation and Character: The Case of Japanese Americans." In *Roots: An Asian American Reader.* Los Angeles: UCLA Asian American Studies Center.

Miyamoto, Nobuko. 1984. Notes to "Yuiyo Bon Odori" (Unpublished).

Montero, Darrel. 1981. "The Japanese Americans: Changing Patterns of Assimilation over Three Generations." *American Sociological Review* 46: 829–39.

Noriyuki, Duane. 1995. "Nobuko Miyamoto, Civil Rights Activist." *Los Angeles Times*, 19 July.

Ng, Wendy. 1991. "The Collective Memories of Communities." In *Asian Americans: Comparative and Global Perspectives.* Ed. Shirley Hune, Stephen S. Fugita, and Amy Ling. Pullman: Washington State University Press.

Schulze, Margaret. 1992. "New Group Devoted to Ancient Japanese Music." *Hokubei Mainichi*, 10 January.

Takaki, Ron. 1989. *Strangers from a Different Shore: A History of Asian Americans.* Boston, Toronto, and London: Little, Brown.

Thornton, Michael C. 1992. "Finding a Way Home." In *Asian Americans: Collages of Identities.* Cornell Asian American Studies Monograph Series, no. 1. Ithaca, NY: Asian American Studies Program, Cornell University.

Trimillos, Ricardo. 1986. "Music and Ethnic Identity: Strategies Among Overseas Filipino Youth." *Yearbook for Traditional Music* 18: 9–20.

Wei, William. 1993. *The Asian American Movement.* Philadelphia: Temple University Press.

Yanow, Scott. 1994. Enthusiasm. *Jazziz* 11, no. 2: 28–34.

Interviews

1987. Telephone interview with Arawana Hayashi, Boston, 28 June. 1987. Telephone interview with Paul Yamazaki, San Francisco, 18 July.

1987. Telephone interview with Brian Auerbach, San Francisco, 18 July.

1987. Telephone interview with Mark Izu, San Francisco, 19 July.
1987. Personal interview with Seizo Oka at the Japanese History Archives, San Francisco, 21 July.
1987. Telephone interview with Suenobu Togi, Los Angeles, 22 October.
1994. Personal interview with Miya Masaoka, San Francisco, 3 August.
1994. Personal interview with Seizo Oka, San Francisco, 15 August.
1994. Personal interview with Mark Izu, San Francisco, 14 August.
1995. Personal interview with June Kuramoto, 18 July.
1995. Personal interview with Nobuko Miyamoto, 25 July.

Selected Discography

Tatsu Aoki. 1994. *Kioto.* Asian Improv Records.
Kenny Endo Taiko Ensemble. 1994. *Eternal Energy.* Asian Improv Records AIR 0021.
Hiroshima. 1979/1980. *Ongaku.* Arista ARCD 8437.
Hiroshima. 1996. *Urban World Music.* Quest Records/Warner.
Hiroshima. 2011. *Departure.* CD Baby.
Glenn Horiuchi. 1989. *Issei Spirit.* Asian Improv Records.
Glenn Horiuchi. 1989. *Manzanar Voices.* Asian Improv Records AIR 006.
Glenn Horiuchi. 1991. *Poston Sonata.* Asian Improv Records AIR 008.
Mark Izu, Lewis Jordan, Anthony Brown, and George Sams. 1981. *United Front.* RPM Records RPM 1.
Mark Izu and Lewis Jordan. 1988. *The Travels of a Zen Baptist.* RPM Records RPM 6.
Mark Izu. 1992. *Circle of Fire.* Asian Improv Records AIR 0009.
Mark Izu. 1998. *Last Dance.* Bindu Records BIN 0205-2.
Mark Izu. 2007. *Mermaid Meat.* Pele Productions/Wazo Music.
Mark Izu. 2007. *Threading Time.* Wazo Music.
Mark Izu and Christopher Yohmei Blasdel. 2009. *Navarasa: Duets for Shakuhachi and Contra Bass.* Wazo Music.
Bob Kenmotsu. 1992. *The Spark.* Asian Improv Records AIR 0010.
June Kuramoto. 2002. *Spirit and Soul.* Junku Music 99236.
June Kuramoto. 2005. *The Way of Tea.* Junku Music.
Miya Masaoka. 1993. *Compositions/Improvisations.* Asian Improv Records AIR 00014.
Nobuko Miyamoto. 1997. *To All Relations.* Bindu Records.
Murasaki Ensemble. 1994. *Niji.* A Murasaki Production. THE 8994.
Noh Buddies. 1984. *Noh Buddies.* Sansei Records SR 442.
Sounds Like 1996: Music by Asian American Artists. 1996. Asian Improv Records IEL 0002.
Visions. 1991/1992. *Time to Discover.* Mina Productions MPCD 75.
Yutaka Yokokura. 1978. *Love Light.* Alfa Records ALR 6009.

Videography

Hiroshima. YouTube. "Hiroshima—One Wish." www.youtube.com/watch?v=sJEzRA_FbFo.

Hiroshima. YouTube. "Thousand Cranes Hiroshima; Live." www.youtube.com/watch?v=DzpqS33lmSI.

Mark Izu. *Don't Lose Your Soul* [Film about Mark Izu and Anthony Brown]. Jim Choi Independent Production. chzamag@gmail.com.

Mark Izu. YouTube. "Dragon Painter—Music by Mark Izu." www.youtube.com/watch?v=fBTqEMcft8E.

Mark Izu and Brenda Wong Aoki. YouTube. "Kuan Yin—Hell—Full Section Runtime 6_49V3.mov." www.youtube.com/watch?v=EopVozbrWdk&feature=plcp. "Mermaid BSO Fisherman4x3.mov". http://www.youtube.com/watch?v=yOuAqrHM9-E&feature=plcp

"Kabuki Cabaret (SJJF)" www.youtube.com/watch?v=B6MYoEr7_sE&feature=plcp

June Kuramoto. YouTube. "June Kuramoto with her band Hiroshima @ The Cherry Blossom Festival, Monterey Park, CA." www.youtube.com/watch?v=jme2ZoHIzQU.

Mabalot, Linda. 1993. *Hiroshima Twenty Years Later.* Los Angeles: Visual Communications.

Nobuko Miyamoto. YouTube. "Nobuko Miyamoto & Charlie Chin—A Song For Ourselves." www.youtube.com/watch?v=XcxmJDn5DLk.

Nobuko Miyamoto. YouTube. "Yellow Pearl—Performed by Nobuko Miyamoto, Charlie Chin, and Taiyo Na." www.youtube.com/watch?v=Z2C9pUhq9lo.

Nobuko Miyamoto. YouTube. "B.Y.O. CHOPSTIX—Get yours at: chopstix.greatleap.org!" www.youtube.com/watch?v=n65SuQKverM.

Zantzinger, Gei. 1990. *Susumu* [about Sumi Tonooka's composition "Out from the Silence" inspired by her mother's World War II internment]. University Park: Continuing and Distance Education, Pennsylvania State University.

- 16 -

CONSTRUCTING COMMUNITIES AND IDENTITIES

Riot Grrrl New York City

Theo Cateforis and Elena Humphreys

In this chapter, Theo Cateforis and Elena Humphreys examine the musical activist movement Riot Grrrl, a largely gender-based underground community that emerged in the early 1990s in various local punk scenes throughout the United States, such as Washington and New York City. Riot Grrrl was significant for the ways in which it encouraged young women to solidify communities and foster creative spaces around female issues within the domain of the traditionally exclusively male punk lifestyle. From the politics of Riot Grrrl fanzine publications to the socially charged musical statements of various Riot Grrrl bands, the movement achieved a place of prominence within the contemporary 1990s alternative rock culture, and garnered national media attention. Focusing on the grass-roots impetus behind this sociomusical phenomenon, the coauthors recount the initial formation and activities of one regional chapter in the larger riot grrrl landscape—that of Riot Grrrl New York City. At the time that Cateforis and Humphreys conducted the research for and wrote this chapter in the mid-1990s, they were both involved with alternative music and Riot Grrrl in different ways. Cateforis was a doctoral student in musicology at Stony Brook University, and had presented numerous papers on post-punk, alternative, and Riot Grrrl. Humphreys, who had recently received her masters of fine arts in the visual arts from Stony Brook University, was one of Riot Grrrl New York City's founding members, and had long been active as a musician and artist in the New York punk scene. Their chapter, which appears here unrevised from this book's first edition, combines the authors' outside and inside ethnographic perspectives, presenting Riot Grrrl New York City through a mixture of personal depiction, interviews, and theoretical interpretation. In particular, they give special attention to the group's negotiations with private and public identity and their confrontations with the media's intrusive gaze. While Riot Grrrl New York City and other chapters would regenerate and appear in different manifestations into the early 2000s, by the new millennium the broader movement had largely faded from public awareness. In recent years, however, Riot Grrrl has thrived as a historical presence, a subject of scholarly interest, and a vital point of inspiration for many current female musicians such as Beth Ditto of the Gossip. Its most significant legacy, though, may be the numerous summer rock camps for girls that have begun to appear in cities across the United States, many of them directly echoing Riot Grrrl's strong messages of female empowerment and musical creativity.

> Like she-devils out of Rush Limbaugh's worst nightmare, a battery of young women with guitars, drums and a generous dose of rage stampeded into popular consciousness earlier this year [1993]. They do things like scrawl SLUT and RAPE across their torsos before gigs, produce fanzines with names like *Girl Germs* and hate the media's guts. They're called Riot Grrrls and they've come for your daughters.
>
> (FRANCE 1993, 23)

Throughout 1992 and 1993, numerous sensationalized accounts, like the above passage from *Rolling Stone*, appeared in such newsstand publications as *Spin* (Nasrallah 1992), *Newsweek* (Chideya 1992), *Seventeen* (Malkin 1993), and *Glamour* (Borchers 1993), describing a new youth subculture that had emerged out of the American underground punk movement. Riot Grrrl, as the confrontational name suggests, consisted of teenage girls and women who had claimed the innocent freedom of girlhood and adolescence and transformed it into a riotous, raging growl. Riot Grrrl's aggressive stance was evident most visibly in the music of punk bands, as, for example, Bikini Kill and its lead singer, Kathleen Hanna, whose lyrics in such songs as "Suck My Left One" stood as a defiant blast against the dominance of patriarchy in American society.[1]

On a more private level, Riot Grrrls organized meetings where they could question gender roles and confront their identities while speaking openly about their experiences with rape, sexuality, racism, oppression, and domestic violence. Most observers considered Riot Grrrl to be a new wave of feminism, supposedly drawing inspiration from such feminist bestsellers as Susan Faludi's *Backlash* and Naomi Wolf's *Beauty Myth* and from empowering, autonomous performers like Madonna.[2] The media characterized Riot Grrrl as a national phenomenon dispersed throughout various American cities and towns: "a support network of activist 'girls' who are loosely linked together by a few punk bands, weekly discussion groups, pen-pal friendships and more than fifty homemade fanzines" (Chideya 1992, 84). Descriptions like these, though, fail to distinguish how different regional Riot Grrrl groups reflect the very real cultural separations that mark America's diverse urban and rural landscape.

This ethnographic essay traces the formation of one specific Riot Grrrl group in the geographic region of New York City, detailing their activities in that city's small, independent punk community from the autumn and winter of 1992 through the spring of 1993.[3] As with any ethnographic research, this essay reveals as much about its authors as it does its subjects. Theo Cateforis is a musicologist with strong interests in American music, who often studies various alternative rock and punk music styles. Elena Humphreys is an artist and musician who has spent many years in the New York City punk scene and was an active member of Riot Grrrl New York City (hereafter referred to as Riot Grrrl NYC). Together, our study, which joins Elena's voice with the voices of other women involved in Riot Grrrl NYC, reveals the combined perspectives of an "outside" ethnographer and an "inside" ethnographer. Above all, in this essay we will focus on Riot Grrrl as an empowering

16.1. The cover of *Riot Grrrl NYC* 4. Courtesy Elena Humphreys.

idea central to the women and girls involved in Riot Grrrl NYC's social collective. Our ethnographic narrative is framed by some basic questions: How were girls and women introduced to Riot Grrrl, and what purpose did it serve in their lives? How, through such activities as music making, did Riot Grrrl NYC relate to the city's established punk community? In what ways did the members of Riot Grrrl NYC build an internal group identity? Lastly, how did Riot Grrrl NYC negotiate its external, or public, identity and reconcile the gaze of the media?

NEW YORK PUNK AND RIOT GRRRL NYC

The New York City punk scene out of which Riot Grrrl NYC evolved has a long history that dates back to the late 1960s and early 1970s.[4] This scene coalesced in 1974 and 1975 when such artists as Patti Smith and bands like Blondie, the

Ramones, Talking Heads, and Television began playing and socializing at a Lower East Side club, CBGB.[5] Of these groups, the Ramones most typified an angry, edgy, unrefined sound, which would prove influential among the numerous British punk bands who followed in the wake of the Sex Pistols' success in England. The Ramones played short, clipped songs that featured distorted guitars, minimal, repetitive chord progressions, sharp, declamatory vocals, and a propulsive rhythm section. In the mid to late 1970s their simple, direct music stood as an antithesis to the excessive technology and indulgent instrumental virtuosity associated with the majority of large stadium and arena bands dominating the record industry. Punk bands challenged this hierarchy, proving that music making was not an exclusive domain but rather that it could and should be open to anyone.

In the late 1970s and early 1980s American punk became known by a new prefix—hardcore—and its sound was characterized by tempos much faster than that of earlier punk bands. Where the early New York punk scene had been unified by a sense of musical experimentation and a fairly ragged, intense sound, the new hardcore punk scene became codified around distinct musical traits. In particular, bands started displaying the increased instrumental technical proficiency necessary for the blistering speeds that the hardcore style dictated. Audiences began more and more to expect and demand that punk bands have a certain level of competency both on their instruments and in their songcraft. Punk rock had become competitive, and within this arena fans were less accepting of bands who sounded relatively amateurish. During this same period, hardcore punk began to take the shape of an especially male-dominated subculture. Women found themselves on the periphery of punk's musical endeavors, excluded from predominantly male bands. At live shows they felt marginalized, often forced to the back of the venue, away from those male audience members who were slamming into one another and participating in a form of hardcore punk dancing known as slamdancing or thrashing. Gavin van Vlack, a member of the 1980s New York hardcore band Absolution, describes how the area reserved for thrashing, referred to as "the pit," encouraged ritualistic male bonding: "If you don't want to get hurt, you don't step into the pit. It's all a part of it. Also you get your aggressions out and they're letting their aggressions out. You're bound to get hurt. The big macho guys showing how much they can take. Showing their physical prowess. Yeah, it's a rite of passage thing" (Hurley 1989).[6]

Punk scenes in other cities in the United States during the 1980s suffered as well from similar stifling environments. In 1990 three women in Olympia, Washington—Molly Neuman and Alison Wolfe, who together eventually would form the band Bratmobile, and Tobi Vail, one of the members of Bikini Kill—decided to react against that city's stagnant male-dominated punk scene. They wanted to create an environment where other women would feel more encouraged to learn how to play instruments, form bands, participate in shows, and ultimately voice their political awareness. Through a series of meetings, they attracted other interested women, and soon they adopted the name "Riot Grrrl" as a descriptive phrase for the group's feminist-based ideas. During 1991 various people from Riot Grrrl Olympia either visited or relocated to the Washington, D.C., area, and by 1992 Riot Grrrl DC had developed as a large and active contingent. During the spring and summer of that year, two events in Washington, D.C., finally led to Riot Grrrl's explosive dissemination. First, in early April many women interested in Riot Grrrl met in Washington at the pro-choice rally, March for Women's Lives. Then, almost four months later, Riot Grrrl DC was host to the first national Riot Grrrl Convention. The event, which met for three days, drew a wide range of participants who attended workshops on such topics as "Rape," "Unlearning Racism," "Fat Oppression," and "Domestic Violence." The convention also featured presentations by poets and spoken-word artists but was focused primarily around performances by numerous all-female bands. Afterwards, many girls and women who had attended the convention returned to their cities, colleges, or hometowns determined to begin their own Riot Grrrl chapters. In New York City, the women who began recruiting for a Riot Grrrl group received their first responses from women and girls already in fledgling local punk-rock groups, or from those female members of the local punk community interested in joining a band. Elena Humphreys recalls this early social dynamic:

> I was at a house party of a friend of mine, Tina [Lagen], who I worked with. There were ten or twenty people there all hanging out, just women. It was about fifty percent gay, fifty percent straight women who all knew each other from work, or from the punk scene in New York. Tina was starting a band with Jill [Reiter] and this girl Glynis and they needed a bass player. I mentioned I had a bass but I didn't know how to play it. They said I should be in the band anyway and to come to the first practice. At this party Tina was handing out fliers and wanted to start a Riot Grrrl New York City. A couple days after our first band practice, the first Riot Grrrl NYC meeting occurred which I had learned about from the flier. Tina had another band, Delta Dawn, and the two bands and four other girls made up the first meeting. (Humphreys 1995)

Riot Grrrl NYC also brought together a variety of women whose backgrounds were not necessarily in music but rather reflected New York City's specific position as a thriving underground media and arts capital. Situated near such institutions as New York University and the Parsons School of Design, various liberal presses—for example, the *Village Voice*—and numerous art galleries and shops, the Riot Grrrl NYC meetings became a haven for many high school girls and college-educated women who were interested in activist politics. Many of the women drawn to the meetings were already familiar with the alternative scene and had received Riot Grrrl fliers at local events, such as Wigstock, a large annual New York City festival celebrating gay cultural diversity. Others, however, had relatively little experience with music or the New York punk community. Two members of Riot Grrrl NYC, Sarah Valentine and Diana Morrow, describe how, at first, they saw the group as a positive avenue to the New York punk scene and feminist politics:

> Initially my involvement with Riot Grrrl was supposed to be as a journalist. I was an intern at an underground anarchist newspaper, and my editor wanted me to do a story on Riot Grrrl. At the time, I was very interested in discovering more about music and wishing to hang out with people who I could do that with. Going in there, I didn't expect to be involved with it, I expected just to be a journalist . . . [but, eventually] I felt compelled to stay. (Valentine 1995)
>
> The first time I heard about Riot Grrrl was at a Take Back the Night march. Someone gave me a flier, and then later I saw a girl [in one of my classes at the Parsons School of Design] who had a necklace or something that had Riot Grrrl on it, and I asked her about it and she told me to come to the meeting . . . [I got involved] because I was looking for some sort of activist outlet and there wasn't really one that I could relate to. I had gone to a couple of WAC [Women's Action Coalition] meetings and they were horrible. (Morrow 1995)

As one of Riot Grrrl NYC's fliers declared, the group "comprises individuals who determine our mood and direction."[7] But the group also set certain borders around their collective ideological identity. In the same flier, Riot Grrrl NYC defined their constituency: "Girls/women 16 to ? primarily involved in alternative music scenes. we are bisexual, gay and straight. multicultural. multifaceted. we are diverse in beliefs but concur on this: sexism, homophobia and racism run rampant in our 'scenes.' we want to do something about it. now" ("Is She a Riot Grrrl?" flier).

Most noticeably, this statement excludes, through its gender-based terms, the presence of boys and men. And it is clear that such definitions often had a ruinous effect on the tenuous relationship that Riot Grrrl as a whole enjoyed with various existent underground scenes. Editorials began to appear within the alternative presses, for example, characterizing Riot Grrrl as a group that believes "males are responsible for all the world's problems" (Goad 1994). Many people accordingly perceived that Riot Grrrl was a group exclusionary, and thus hostile, to men. Yet, in truth, most Riot Grrrl groups did not present themselves as such. Rather, as Riot Grrrl NYC's members explained, the male-dominated punk scene had excluded women's voices for so long that unless a group like Riot Grrrl carved out its own space, women would never have the opportunity to work within the punk scene. Thus in promoting a "constructive solidarity between women," Riot Grrrl ultimately sought to break down gender barriers and secure "mutual respect and appreciation between women and men in [their] creative efforts" ("Is She a Riot Grrrl?" flier).

The community that Riot Grrrl NYC fostered in their first meetings during the waning months of 1992 began in relative isolation. The women normally would gather in one of the members' kitchen or living room areas, nestled away in an apartment in downtown Manhattan. Spaces such as these provided a safe atmosphere conducive to the sense of support the women and girls were seeking. Even more so, these spaces reflected the reality of the members' living circumstances. For in New York City there are virtually no houses; many residents involved in the alternative scene, therefore, live in the most convenient, economical apartment space available. As a result, the alternative community is widely dispersed. Unless the members of Riot Grrrl NYC chose to live as "squatters," holding their meetings illicitly in abandoned buildings, they would not have access to any large personal or communal spaces.[8]

These factors differed considerably from the social dynamics of Riot Grrrl groups in other regions. In D.C., for example, Riot Grrrl grew out of a punk community that, for many years, had been gravitating around small neighborhoods and housing complexes. Since the early 1980s the Washington hardcore punk scene has revolved around Dischord House, a home out of which Ian MacKaye, of the band Fugazi, operated the local record label Dischord Records. Likewise, many members of the D.C. punk scene often meet at the Embassy, a sizable house capable of accommodating numerous people. The members of Riot Grrrl NYC debated whether or not they too should try to locate a public meeting space. On the one hand, some of the members were concerned that in its first few months Riot Grrrl NYC had not expanded far beyond a handful of friends and acquaintances. Even though the group had been announcing its meetings via fliers and posters, these were often lost amidst the dozens of other fliers and posters plastered around the city each week advertising a dizzying array of new alternative cultural events. Furthermore, since most women or girls in the city were understandably hesitant to attend an event listed at the private residence of someone they did not know, Riot Grrrl NYC was not attracting many new members. On the other hand, if the group moved to a public space they would risk possible intrusions upon their private meetings. Eventually Riot Grrrl NYC did arrange with a local co-optive punk record store, Reconstruction Records, to hold their publicized meetings in the store's space after it had closed for the night. Located on East Sixth Street in the heart of New York's East Village, the store provided a meeting space much less threatening to newcomers and interested outsiders.

On one occasion, some of the male members from the Reconstruction Records collective, who had not been informed of Riot Grrrl NYC's special arrangement, accidentally walked in on a meeting and were asked by the group to leave. The store members contested the group's private claim to the store's public space, however, insisting that Riot Grrrl NYC had unrightfully commandeered a collective punk domain. Uncomfortable incidents such as these typified Riot Grrrl NYC's difficult transitions between private and public meeting spaces. These negotiations of space are especially striking because they seem to reinscribe the underlying gender divisions that govern private and public spaces in many traditional patriarchal societies—divisions where the house is intimate and secretive and the private domain of women, while the outside world is an open meeting place and the public domain of men.[9] That Riot Grrrl NYC favored the sanctity offered by a private space reflects the gendered nature of the sensitive personal experiences that women were recounting and confronting during group meetings. Should the members of the group know in advance that males might be involved in a meeting, they could allow for the men's participation in the discussions. Once, male musicians in the local band Vitapup, who were sympathetic to Riot Grrrl's cause and wanted to participate by playing in a benefit for the group, were allowed to attend a special meeting on the condition that they wore dresses. By complying with these gestures, the men openly compromised their gender roles and, accordingly, neutered their positions of male power. Such occurrences were exceptional, however. Although Riot Grrrl NYC advertised open meetings for the last Wednesday of every month, inviting men to attend, none ever appeared. As one Riot Grrrl observed, "[the men] weren't really interested in coming, they just wanted to assert their power by having the opportunity to come" (Humphreys 1995).

SUBVERSIVE POWER: RIOT GRRRL NYC AND FANZINES

Of all the projects the members of Riot Grrrl NYC discussed at their meetings, the most consistently realized took shape in the group's published fanzines. Fanzines have long enjoyed a tradition in punk scenes as alternatives to the mainstream music press. Their contents range from contentious editorials, music reviews, interviews, and media clippings to poetry, artwork, and politically pointed anecdotes. Fanzines are easy to construct and reproduce. Beyond the material cut and pasted on the fanzine's pages, all one requires to manufacture the final product is access to a xerox machine. Even before Riot Grrrl had been widely adopted as a revolutionary moniker, Olympia-based fanzines, such as *Jigsaw*, *Girl Germs* (written by members of Bratmobile), and *Bikini Kill*, had served as effective means for communicating immediate and unmitigated feminist viewpoints to other regional areas, in ways that helped spark activism and awareness among women in various local punk scenes.

The majority of Riot Grrrl fanzines represented the efforts of either individuals or perhaps two or three collaborators. When Riot Grrrl NYC planned their chapter's fanzines, however, they wanted to capture the pluralistic composition of their collective. Therefore, they conceived their fanzine as a group project. Diana Morrow describes how Riot Grrrl NYC organized their fanzine production through special meetings:

> There were maybe ten girls squished into this tiny New York apartment living room/bedroom. Everybody brought a little thing that they did, whether it be a poem or a drawing or whatever. And we sat there and actually cut and pasted and put things together in some kind of order. Everybody brought something, and everybody contributed to the making and the laying out of the pages, and eventually we would go down together to Kinko's [a copy/print center] and xerox it. (Morrow 1995)

Because the fanzines originated in this manner, they normally displayed a fragmentary character. Looking through the collage of material that populates each issue, however, one notices that the contributors address some basic themes:

1. Raising awareness and encouraging critical thought: In the fanzines, one might find a newspaper article reporting or detailing acts of sexual abuse, or homophobic or racist hatred. The third issue of *Riot Grrrl NYC*, for example, carries a newspaper clipping—"Stalked By Neo-Nazi Terrorists, Lesbians Flee Underground"—about seven lesbian women who had been chased out of Oregon and were seeking refuge in San Francisco. Scrawled in at the end of the article are added comments encouraging readers to send relief aid to the women. Dotting the pages of fanzines, as well, one finds short essays or pieces asking readers to consider the issues surrounding such topics as pornography, the dangers of smoking, or the horrific realities of incest. Or a contributor might simply include references to provocative literature, ranging from samples of ecofeminist poetry to the critical writings of bell hooks.[10]

2. Personalizing issues of sexual identity and experience: Within the fanzines' pages some Riot Grrrls share their poetry, fiction, or artwork. Authors might depict, from a woman's perspective, the muted horror of sexual abuse or rape. Other submissions describe intimate lesbian encounters and awakenings. Some entries confront the reality of such eating disorders as bulimia and anorexia. Above all, most of the authors draw attention to women's bodies, exposing how they are often violated through the force of male possession, judged and demeaned through societal definitions of femininity, and ultimately imprisoned by the machinations of capitalist culture.

3. Subverting Images of Women: Perhaps the most striking aspects of the fanzines resonate in their visual content. In each issue, Riot Grrrls freely plunder images of women, from photographs to cartoons and drawings, and recast them in a jumbled, decontextualized fashion, around the fanzine's prose and clippings. Judith Butler has commented how such disruptive actions potentially "make gender trouble" (Butler 1990, 34). That is, by mobilizing stereotyped images of women in a subversive manner, one can demonstrate that these images are not "natural" but rather constructed versions of a feminine gender that is molded, shaped, and perpetuated by society and the mass media. The cover of issue number 4, from January 1993, serves as an excellent example (see Fig. 16.1). Here, three contrasting images compete for the reader's attention. The image in the lower left-hand

corner, a seated woman, legs crossed and surrounded by brick, intently loading a rifle, emphasizes Riot Grrrl's determined feminist, activist stance.

In the lower right-hand corner, a drawing shows a Girl Scout troop and its two leaders. Most likely lifted from a Girl Scout manual, the image and an accompanying text that describes in detail a Girl Scout induction ritual, are reclaimed by Riot Grrrl to symbolize their own group's solidarity. The act, however, is brazenly ironic, creating a paradox between the combined Girl Scouts and riot grrrls imagery. A swirl of conflicting meanings comes to the surface: in one sense, the image of the young Girl Scouts is positive and empowering; it emphasizes the pre-adolescent freedom that Riot Grrrl, by its very namesake, in some ways hopes to recapture and celebrate. At the same time, though, the Girl Scout troop members, dressed in uniform and standing at attention before the two women, present a negative image of conformity and subservience. The drawing foregrounds the power structure and socialization process inherent in becoming a Girl Scout. Ultimately this is a process that Riot Grrrl, as a leaderless group composed of individual voices, insistently denies.

Lastly, in the upper right-hand corner, two cartoon women apparently are modeling the issue's cover-price placard. Their exaggerated features, dominated by glowing smiles, are entrenched stereotypes of American beauty and femininity. Inside the fanzine, though, one finds an article exposing the realities behind these ideals: "An ineluctable part of modeling is the pressure to retain your ethereal look against the ravages of time. Low-calorie is your god; zits are your devil. Most models starve themselves. They smoke heavily and drink gallons of coffee to throttle their appetites" (*Riot Grrrl NYC* 4 [1993]: 13). In this light, the cartoon images appear doubly, and sadly, unreal. And it is in such instances as these that the texts of the fanzines seem most powerful; for, rather than criticizing the women in the images, the reader is instead led to question the patriarchal forces in our society that drive women to aspire to such mentally and physically damaging standards. Early Riot Grrrl fanzines are overflowing with similar prose and imagery that seek not only to strip away the veneer suffocating women in society but also to deploy strategies and advice by which women can reclaim their power as individuals.

RIOT GRRRL AND MUSIC

From Riot Grrrl's earliest stages, the movement enjoyed its greatest exposure via its musical manifestations and associations. In 1992 and 1993, various Olympia and D.C. bands, such as Bikini Kill, Heavens to Betsy, and Bratmobile, and England's Huggy Bear produced and distributed their music through small independent record labels like Kill Rock Stars, securing Riot Grrrl's visibility throughout America and the United Kingdom. On a more local level, we want to examine how and why the act of musical performance was integrated as part of Riot Grrrl

NYC's social configuration. Many members of Riot Grrrl NYC had little or no musical experience and joined the group because they were seeking a safe environment where they could learn various instruments and create music expressing their uninhibited viewpoints. It was for this reason, among others, that Jill Reiter first decided to join Riot Grrrl NYC. Jill had been involved with the punk scene in New York and was struggling to learn guitar. Like other aspiring New York women musicians, however, she found herself disenfranchised. The New York punk scene was largely monopolized by all-male bands, and because punk musicians rarely were willing to give women lessons on their instruments, this network seemed resistant to most women's musical endeavors. In Riot Grrrl NYC, though, Jill found a supportive forum where musicians could practice, make mistakes, grow, and experiment. In this environment, she was able to form the band Double Zero. If Jill's band, in their early developmental stages, had performed at a club for a predominantly male audience, they would have faced a group of adversarial spectators, predisposed to dismiss their music. But playing their initial shows for Riot Grrrl NYC members, they were assured of an audience they knew would offer not only encouragement but also advice and constructive criticism. In this sense, Riot Grrrl NYC meetings sometimes functioned as musical workshops. Those women who were accomplished musicians offered to share their experience and to work with women who were beginning on their instruments. The members of Riot Grrrl NYC thus forged in the male-dominated punk scene a new female-gendered oral musical culture. Within Riot Grrrl's safe space, they essentially initiated a closed musical transmission that was capable of surviving across generations of women and girls.

Riot Grrrl was especially important for lesbian women like Jill, because for the first time they had an opportunity within their own musical scene to express their desires and explore their identities. Before Riot Grrrl NYC's formation, the New York hardcore punk scene of the 1980s had been tainted by severe homophobic outbursts, effectively alienating many of the community's gay and lesbian members. Historically, however, punk had never been an avenue frequently traveled by lesbian musicians. Feminist and lesbian music more often was the exclusive province of folk performers involved in independent women's music labels like Olivia Records, or was more known through such prominent artists as Tracy Chapman and Michelle Shocked. In New York City, many gays and lesbians also clustered around the club culture of techno, rave, and house music. As various writers have discussed, within these gay and lesbian communities, the prominence of role playing, "camping" or "masquerading" gendered identities, has long distinguished the interaction between the scene's participants (Case 1989; Butler 1990; Peraino 1992; Currid 1995; Robertson 1996). Male members of the house music communities who dress as drag-queen disco divas, women who assume roles of the masculine "butch" and feminine "femme dykes"—these are both measures of camp. Their deliberate posturing makes conspicuous their adopted gender roles. And, ultimately, their actions expose gender as a mask, part of a costume we all wear throughout our daily interactions. Camp thus acts as "a performative strategy, as well as a mode of reception, [which] commonly foregrounds the artifice of gender and sexual roles" (Robertson 1996, 14). Riot Grrrl NYC attracted many lesbian and bisexual women, and resultantly the ironic, and often humorous, gender manipulations associated with camp's discursive maneuvers began permeating the music of many Riot Grrrl bands.

Double Zero's "Gas, Food, Satan" revels in this practice of masquerade (Chapter 16, Track 1). On the surface, the song is couched in typical raucous punk anger, characterized by its distorted guitars, raspy, shouted vocals, and rough, direct production values. But from the moment the lead singer interrupts the introductory stuttering drum cadence with a stream of random phrases, "big wheels walking, 'n I feel shocking, eyeballs whopping," she sets an uproarious, satiric tone. She adopts the role of the macho hard-rock male lead singer, creating a composite persona constructed out of stock conventions. The opening section's chugging, syncopated, two-bar riff provides a backdrop for her first litany of loose shouted signifiers: "four-wheel, ten-gauge . . . you are my gas station . . ." In the chorus that follows, she wraps herself more clearly in the guise of the male outlaw, on the run stealing and killing at will:

> Everything I own, I've stolen
> Everyone I know is no one
> Every time I kill in your world,
> An angel gets her wings

This is a more powerful and purposeful section, underscored by repetitive guitar riffing and a driving backbeat in the drums.

The next section of the song is more restrained and effectively serves as a foil, offsetting the momentum built up through the chorus. The singer recedes into a spoken narrative that relates the hardships of outlaw life. Her voice sounds desolate, tinged with a regret mirrored in the accompaniment of the sighing, melodic bass chords. In a normal rock song setting, such direct vocal expression and somber musical shading would invite the listener to join the singer in reflecting upon the harsh realities of his chosen lifestyle. But "Gas, Food, Satan" parodies these sentiments. The barren wasteland that the singer conjures forth is a cartoonish terrain littered with incongruous symbols of masculinity: "Out here it's all about dope and drugs, and four wheel drive, and meat." Combined with the band's convincing musical stylistic appropriations, the vocalist's delivery sounds all the more amusing. Near the end of "Gas, Food, Satan," the song's rock groove momentarily dissolves into a menacing, rumbling bass glissando over which the singer slowly builds to a frenzied climax: "In my dreams, I'm running across that open field, out to the highway." This neatly outlines the song's overriding trope—the liberating "open road" that is mythologized in countless male rock anthems, stretching from Steppenwolf's "Born to Be Wild" through Van Halen's "Runnin' with the Devil."[11]

When Double Zero engaged such masquerades at their live shows, they were entertaining an audience fully aware of the camp display unfolding before them. As they simultaneously played upon—and claimed for their own—these well-worn tokens of male empowerment, they reinforced a sense of community between performers and spectators. Where women musicians in punk traditionally had found themselves objectified under the gaze of a primarily male audience, Riot Grrrl performances subverted such situations. During Double Zero's performances, band and audience were equal participants in the masquerade. The women in the audience gazed at the band, and the group returned the spectators' gazes, enacting a sexually charged atmosphere between the bodies on stage and the bodies in the pit. Such performances were instrumental in the formation of a strong New York City queercore movement, signaling the insurgence of gay and lesbian voices in the punk community.

Queercore was already in its nascent stages on the West Coast when Selena Wahng, an accomplished bassist and singer, moved from San Francisco to New York in the late summer of 1992. Her punk band, Lucy Stoners, had appeared with three other bands earlier in the year on a groundbreaking underground seven-inch single, *There's a Dyke in the Pit*, a record whose jolting title deftly captures the male sexual paranoia and insecurity that dominated the hardcore punk scene of the 1980s. Almost immediately upon her arrival in New York, Selena attended a Riot Grrrl NYC meeting. She was already familiar with the Riot Grrrl movement and hoped the group would provide for her an outlet where she could continue her musical efforts. While Selena had been using her music to politicize her gendered position as a woman, an Other in society's eyes, at the same time she also saw Riot Grrrl as a place where she could explore her ethnic background and her experiences as a different type of Other: a Korean American woman involved in the punk scene. Traditionally, punk communities throughout the United States have always held limited appeal for groups outside the white middle-class social strata. In the 1980s, white racist, patriotic skinhead groups, though sometimes not directly related with the punk community, had especially damaged much of the scene's reputation through their rhetoric and violent demonstrations at punk shows.[12] Only with the appearance of groups such as Riot Grrrl were these social and political values contested.

Selena Wahng's "Killing for Pleasure" (Chapter 16, Track 2 on accompanying website) is a composition that relates experiences from a vantage point firmly outside of punk's normal young, white male constituency. As she describes, the song, on which she sings and plays bass, drum beats, and samples, represents "the sound of rape repeating over and over again" (Wahng 1995).[13] These sounds show the influences of two divergent musical styles. On the one hand, she draws upon the musical tradition of the shaman—in Korean society, a powerful female authority figure who communicates with spirits through ritual practices. Together with the song's constant, pounding percussive attacks, Selena's oscillating background voices, droning and chanting throughout, imitate the shaman's ceremonial incantations and musical accompaniment. On the other hand, the song derives its chaotic energy from punk rock. In particular, the two foreground elements, Selena's distorted, detuned electric-bass melody, and her screaming vocal projections, vibrate with punk's buzzsaw rage. Of these two, it is Selena's wailing voice that most of all enwraps the listener. Her screams are controlled yet unpredictable, sometimes repeatedly mimicking the melodic material of the bass and the background vocals, and other times twisting into irregular garbled, guttural, reverbed shapes. In the context of the song, their meaning seems double-edged. In one respect the screams are stimulating. We identify emotionally with their visceral timbre, their release of rage and frustration, their rousing display of power. But the screams are also horrific. They all too easily resonate with the tortured pain and experience of rape. That "Killing for Pleasure" exudes such intensity is a testimony to the identification and intersubjectivity of the performer's voice with those voices of the listening audience. In Riot Grrrl NYC, such musical performances served to strengthen the group's communal foundation.

PUSSYSTOCK, RIOT GRRRL, AND THE MEDIA

The members of Riot Grrrl NYC realized early on that if they were to fund any musical activities or other projects the group was interested in, they would need to raise money. Since music was the most visible component and certain to draw the most interest, they decided to organize and sponsor a benefit concert, an event which they chose to name Pussystock, an amusing twist on the American pop-culture icon. Riot Grrrl NYC could only hold this benefit, however, if they secured the proper public space. ABC No Rio, a well-known local punk rock collective and club, made their performing area provisionally available for the event, allowing Riot Grrrl control of the concert's arrangement, promotion, and contents. At the initial Pussystock meetings, each Riot Grrrl member volunteered the name of a local or East Coast band that they thought would be appropriate for the benefit. The bands that eventually agreed to play the benefit included the Riot Grrrl NYC band Delta Dawn; two groups from New York City, Wives and Vitapup; the Maul Girls (New Jersey); Bimbo Shrineheads (Connecticut); Slant 6 (Washington, D.C.); and a local performance artist, Penny Arcade, who would act as emcee.

In most alternative or punk scenes, small bands and artists such as these release their music through independent labels and neither can afford nor desire any outside management. They generally operate in a fairly autonomous fashion, handling their own correspondence and arranging their own tour schedules. One can find the band's mailing address or phone number on their cassette or seven-inch vinyl releases, or attached to the end of some fanzine review. Riot Grrrl NYC simply sent out invitations to each of the bands, offering not only to pay the expenses for their travel into the city but also to provide for them free lodging and a home-cooked dinner. After enough bands had been contacted and had confirmed that they would participate, members committed to different promotional activities. For the benefit, which was to occur in January 1993, they made fliers, contacted various local underground radio stations, and advertised on bulletin boards throughout the city's village area.

At the show, the predominantly female performers voiced a noise, anger, and celebration that set in motion an exciting set of parameters:

> It was exhilarating and thrilling and really wonderful, because it was a world that we had created and which we were participating in and leading and experiencing our own power that we had as women. And it was alternative, queer, punk women at that, not just upper middle class [activist women] . . . real grass rootsy, strong individuals, experiencing something that they had created. (Valentine 1995)

The members of Riot Grrrl NYC set no age restrictions on the Pussystock show and, as was customary in the punk scene, only charged five dollars admission.[14] Since Riot Grrrl NYC had asked only obscure punk bands to play, they expected a small audience typical for the New York punk community and ABC No Rio. The event, however, drew a larger crowd than anticipated and unfortunately ushered in a more pernicious element as well. ABC No Rio's small performance space was overrun by interested media parties who had no connection with the punk community. Their curiosity added a new dimension to Pussystock, one that trampled the benefit's underlying principles. Another member of Riot Grrrl describes how the media ultimately disrupted the benefit's atmosphere:

> Somebody got hold of the fliers and we had camera crews from Germany, Canada, Australia, Japan coming in and trying to get in free, annoying people with their lights and cameras. People were interviewing girls who weren't even involved with Riot Grrrl, and asking them about Riot Grrrl and making their words some quintessential statement on Riot Grrrl. Media crews were saying [to the members of Riot Grrrl] "We're doing you a favor, so we should get in free." But this was a benefit and these people were bringing in like thirty people to shoot film . . . and people couldn't dance at the show because the camera crews were right up front documenting stuff. They were interviewing people in the bathroom, it was just a mess. It got to the point where we had to start throwing people out. (Humphreys 1995)

Through Pussystock, Riot Grrrl NYC had witnessed firsthand the havoc that an intrusive media could wreak on their endeavors. While this was the first manifestation of a truly ravenous press corps that they had seen, the other major regional Riot Grrrl groups had held antagonistic relationships with the mainstream media for practically an entire year. Because Riot Grrrl NYC encountered, and was affected by, problems similar to those that other Riot Grrrl groups faced, it is worth examining in depth the terms of Riot Grrrl's relationship with the national media.

On a basic level, the members of Riot Grrrl NYC voiced their dissatisfaction with the press's activities in a manner that echoed the timeworn complaints of any person or group subject to the interpretation of the printed word. That is, they felt that the media, by either decontextualizing the words of Riot Grrrl members, fabricating their own Riot Grrrl quotes, or misconstruing the group's purpose, were in some way misrepresenting Riot Grrrl. While even the most distorted accounts of Riot Grrrl generally professed their sensitivity or sympathy toward Riot Grrrl's feminist activist concerns, these same media reports refused to accept that Riot Grrrl was not a stable entity, but rather a diffuse collective of individuals each seeking their own form of empowerment. Ultimately, the press devised tactics by which they could consolidate a packaged image of Riot Grrrl and sell it to the public. Some of these means were blunt, others more insidious.

The article that Riot Grrrls across the country most unanimously decried appeared in the national music magazine *Spin*. In this article, the journalist describes a scenario from the 1992 DC Riot Grrrl Convention: A teenage girl, Erika Reinstein, walks past a group of onlookers "startled by her appearance": "Reinstein's jeans were slung low, and her midriff exposed . . . a message written in thick black marker on her stomach: RAPE . . . Reinstein wrote RAPE on her belly to break the silence surrounding the crime" (Nasrallah 1992, 78–80). Any injustices Reinstein had unmasked, however, were silenced by *Spin* in favor of a fashion statement. On the page facing the above text, the reader sees an airbrushed photograph of a pouting lipsticked woman with the words *Riot Grrrls* stenciled across her arm. While the conjunction of text and imagery would lead readers to assume the photograph was of Reinstein, in fact *Spin* had substituted in her stead a photograph of a glamorized—and unidentified—model.

An even more troubling, though less cited, article appeared in the major British weekly music newspaper *Melody Maker* (Joy 1992). The newspaper featured as its cover story a report on Riot Grrrls and "the new girl revolution." Adorning the cover was a photograph from the Re/search archives, a picture of two scantly clad women mudwrestling, one standing triumphantly over the other, arms akimbo and smiling confidently at the camera.[15] While these women obviously had no relation to Riot Grrrl, the newspaper completed the travesty by inscribing over the picture an invitation to the reader to join the women frolicking in the mud: "Riot Grrrls! You wanna play . . . ?" What were the chances that for most of the paper's readers the cover page provided any effect other than mere titillation? How many of these readers would look beyond such images and read about the issues that were confronted by a Riot Grrrl fanzine?

Not all articles resorted to such extreme measures. Instead, more commonly, the authors would tacitly acknowledge that Riot Grrrls were "diverse" or "atypical," but then proceed to sketch out their own reductive, homogenous description of Riot Grrrl:

> While no Riot Grrrl could be considered typical, Tiffany, a student at a small, Catholic, New England college, displays a few common traits: "People here think I am weird because I am political and I go to the dean's dinner in a little black dress with big boots and a shaved head and I study a lot." Smart, literate, and mad as hell, Grrrls began with young women like Tiffany. (Nasrallah 1992, 80)

> Meetings, which now go on in enclaves on the East Coast and in Toronto, draw women as young as fourteen and as "old" as twenty-five, mostly with cropped and/or dyed hair, bright red lips, and body paint. (Bernikow 1993, 165)

> The [fan]zines reflect the style of the Riot Grrrls themselves, who mix babydoll dresses and bright red lipstick with combat boots and tattoos. (Borchers 1993, 134)

> The Riot Grrrl refusal to conform to fashion dictates, however, has created a "look" of its own . . . So you'll see Riot Grrrls in fishnet stockings and army shorts, cinch-waisted dresses with combat boots, or miniskirts with long underwear. (Malkin 1993, 81)

While such descriptions as these diminished and damaged Riot Grrrl's stance as a collective group of individuals, they also provided the movement with wide public exposure. Many of Riot Grrrl NYC's members thus reacted ambivalently toward the media:

> If Riot Grrrl had stayed out of the media, we would have reached other people in other cities through [fan]zines, but we wouldn't have reached people outside of the underground network. It was like hot and cold with those things. Part of me was like "I don't want an article in *Seventeen* magazine because they're gonna say really dumb things." Yet, how do you reach the kid in Oklahoma if the only records they have [available to them] are *Steely Dan*? (Humphreys 1995)

The members of Riot Grrrl NYC had learned from Pussystock that they somehow had to protect themselves from the media's probing gaze. After the benefit, the group met and decided they would follow the example set by the Riot Grrrl chapters in Olympia and Washington, D.C., and institute a media blackout. They no longer welcomed any members of the press to the meetings, and would only grant interviews under the stipulation that the journalist talk with *all* the women and girls involved in the group. Though inquiries from the press would never fully subside, they did begin gradually to abate.

Despite Riot Grrrl NYC's souring experience with the media, Pussystock had been an overwhelming success, and the group agreed they should start planning another benefit immediately, an event reasonably enough entitled Pussystock II. At the same time that Riot Grrrl NYC was attracting more women from the alternative scene, the group was also encountering some growing pains. Specifically, Riot Grrrl NYC recognized that their group, which was predominantly white, middle-class women and girls, was not significantly diversified. The privileged socioeconomic stature enjoyed by some Riot Grrrls in various regional groups had led many critics to join in a wholesale dismissal of Riot Grrrl's activities. In Riot Grrrl NYC, one of the group's more outspoken members, Claudia von Vacano, had attempted to rectify the situation, soliciting contributions from Latino, African, and Asian women to feature in her fanzine *Lost ID.* And for Pussystock II, Riot Grrrl even placed on the opening-night show a well-known local gospel group, Faith. But such ventures did not dramatically alter the group's predominant cultural composition. From its very origins the Riot Grrrl movement had been embedded in punk communities, and thus Riot Grrrl NYC's limited social makeup continued to reflect the white middle-class complexion of the larger punk subculture itself. At best, with Pussystock II, which took place in early May 1993, the members of Riot Grrrl NYC found themselves a much more known quantity in the public's eye, and thus capable of drawing a more varied crowd than the previous benefit's audience. Sarah Valentine had written a full-page article describing the benefit for a local community newspaper, *Downtown*, and consequently a larger number of men and older women from outside the New York punk community attended the shows.

Pussystock II extended across five nights at five different venues and featured numerous local female and mixed-gender bands who, for one reason or another, had not been able to play for the first benefit. The range of bands was diverse: some bands—for example, Chickenmilk and Sexpod—played a melodic "pop" style of punk. Another band, No Commercial Value, veered more toward ska-influenced punk.[16] God Is My Co-Pilot mixed eclectic styles from funk to polka in a noisy experimental post-punk collage. Riot Grrrl NYC, as a whole, prepared more fully for the event. Two members, Elena Humphreys and Tina Lagen, had contacted each of the bands before the benefit, and received tracks that they included on a cassette compilation entitled *Mudflower*, produced through their own independent label, Flytrap Records. Most importantly, Riot Grrrl NYC briefed the audiences at the shows—the press were allowed no pictures or interviews. The group had prepared a press release containing brief quotes from a large number of Riot Grrrl's members. These were the only statements to which they allowed the media access.

Pussystock II was an enormous success and established Riot Grrrl NYC as one of the most active group chapters in the country. For many of the women involved in the group, this proved to be a culminating point in their activities. In the strenuous months throughout the winter of 1992 and spring of 1993, they had gone through various rites of passage. The majority of Riot Grrrl NYC members from this period soon drifted away from the group. Speaking with the members of Riot Grrrl NYC three years after these events, we find the movement's loose revolutionary slogans realized in a manner quite unlike the press's distorted vision of a "female utopia" (Malkin 1993, 81).

More realistically, Riot Grrrl NYC served as a supportive workshop that fostered, among its members, practical communicative and artistic skills applicable far beyond the group's small social domain. Sarah Valentine now works as a promoter and specializes in shows featuring female punk-rock bands that highlight women musicians and artists. Diana Morrow, who edited issues of the *Riot Grrrl NYC* fanzine, published in the spring of 1995 her premiere issue of *Princess* magazine, a glossy fanzine combining theoretical analysis and personal writings on feminist, queer, racial, and class issues. Another member of the group, Abby Moser, realized her creative goal and completed a documentary film project about Riot Grrrl NYC entitled *Riot Grrrl NYC.* As Selena Wahng describes, the time these women spent in Riot Grrrl NYC ultimately proved most important, both as a point of initiation and as a momentary cathartic release:

> Riot Grrrl is really good for very young girls, their first contact with feminism and organization. It really can't serve as anything more elaborate . . . I think to get up there on stage and scream and yell and play loud music is a healthy outlet . . . The act of doing that is important. Riot Grrrl is all about speaking out and inhabiting your anger and your pain in that way. But I also feel that after you do that for whatever amount of time, you have to start exploring other things deeper than that. You can't just be stultified in this moment of anger that you felt at some past time. (Wahng 1995)

RIOT GRRRL: A POSTSCRIPT

While most of those members who had been involved with Riot Grrrl NYC during 1992 and 1993 eventually left the group, Riot Grrrl groups still meet in New York City and across the country. Many of the young girls and women in Riot Grrrl NYC today have no tangible connection with the women from the beginning New York chapter. Such a rapid decay and growth rate between generations would indicate that Riot Grrrl's communities are not modeled upon stable lineages. Rather, Riot Grrrl is wrested from history, perpetually reinventing its identity in accordance with the goals and concerns of new Grrrls. Precisely because Riot Grrrl does not adhere to one agenda, the movement has succeeded beyond its formative generations. For the moment, the media no longer considers Riot Grrrl a shocking proposition, and thus it seems unlikely that the generation of girls and women currently involved with Riot Grrrl will soon suffer again the degree of lavish mainstream attention that Riot Grrrls previously attracted.

What is more interesting for the cultural analyst, though, is to trace the ways that the word *Grrrl* has loosed itself from the movement and achieved a strong presence elsewhere in popular culture. On the one hand, *Grrrl* has accrued its own significance to the extent that one finds it linked to various popular trends. Articles in *Seventeen* (Solin 1995) and *Wired* (Cross 1995), for example, have contained profiles on a "Biker Grrrl" and a "Modem Grrrl" respectively. A recent anthology collecting interviews with such women rock musicians as Courtney Love, Kim Gordon, and Liz Phair cobbles together artists under one uniform title: *Grrrls* (Raphael 1996).[17] In each of these cases the author uses *grrrl* as a descriptive means of filling out a gendered character profile—a rebellious, daring sensibility that breaches convention in some fashion. In this sense, Riot Grrrl has remained in the public sphere as a positive and powerful signifying idea. On the other hand, as the word *Grrrl* gains more familiarity through commercialization, Riot Grrrl is trivialized and its potential as a liberating signifier reduced. In its wake, though, Riot Grrrl has affected most powerfully the complexion of the American underground rock scene. As we write this essay, the number of mixed-gender and all-female rock and punk bands in the mid-1990s has escalated beyond a point that any people in the alternative music scene in 1990 or 1991 could have realistically imagined or foreseen. This remains Riot Grrrl's most visible and audible legacy.

Notes

1. Kathleen Hanna's lyrics from the second verse of "Suck My Left One" (Bikini Kill KRS204, 1992) are typical in their directed outrage:

> Daddy comes into her room at night
> He's got more than talking on his mind
> My sister pulls the covers down
> She reaches over, flicks on the light
> She says to him: "Suck My Left One, Suck My left One."

2. During the late 1980s and early 1990s, academics were fascinated with Madonna's position as a potentially subversive political force in popular culture. The culminating point was perhaps Cathy Schwichtenberg's 1993 collection of essays, *The Madonna Connection.*

3. Throughout this essay we will differentiate in a general sense between communities and scenes. Communities consist of a stable population, who are united by some sense of common history and tradition. Scenes, on the other hand, are more diverse and represent what Will Straw refers to as a "cultural space in which a range of musical practices coexist" (1991, 373). For a detailed discussion of communities and scenes, see Straw's article as well as that of Holly Kruse (1993), who argues the importance of translocal scenes in alternative music.

4. For the most thorough descriptions of the New York punk scene's formative years, see Roman Kozak (1988) and Clinton Heylin (1993).

5. CBGB did not begin as a punk club. The club's moniker is shortened from its proper title: CBGB and OMFUG. This stands for Country, Bluegrass, Blues and Other Music For Uplifting Gourmandizers.

6. Hurley (1989). This book has no page numbers; the quote is taken from the section entitled "The Clubs."

7. Quoted from a Riot Grrrl NYC flier, the header of which contains a drawing of a winged angel accompanied by two questions: "Is She a Riot Grrrl?" "Are you [a Riot Grrrl]?"

8. Squatting is common in the New York City punk community. Groups of punks will move into vacant public buildings, connect electrical, gas, and water services, and renovate the building for living accommodations. They are always in danger, however, of being evicted by the city.

9. For classic discussions of the dialectical conception of private and public space, see Pierre Bourdieu's extensive anthropological writings on the Kabyle tribal members of Algeria. In recent years, ethnomusicologists have both elaborated on and problematized these gendered divisions of space. Jennifer C. Post (1994) provides a summary of the relation between public/private gendered space as it specifically relates to musical performance.

10. bell hooks has dealt with numerous feminist topics in her writings and in particular has addressed issues concerning African American women in today's society.

11. For a detailed analytical discussion of Van Halen's "Runnin' with the Devil" and the signification of freedom and power in heavy metal, see Walser (1993, 41–54).

12. For a concise discussion of the relationship between skinhead and punk subcultures, see O'Hara (1995, 33–43).

13. From notes on the recording provided by the composer/performer.

14. Many clubs in New York City cater only to crowds of ages twenty-one and over or set an age limit at eighteen. Occasionally bands and management will allow special "all ages" shows, admitting audience members under the age of eighteen. Most punk bands who play smaller clubs, such as ABC No Rio, refuse to charge over five dollars at their shows. This tradition has its noticeable roots in the Washington, D.C. punk scene and is still upheld by such successful bands as Fugazi, who consistently sell out large clubs and small theater venues across the country.

15. Re/search is a publication series that includes volumes on various unusual pop-cultural styles and genres, bizarre subcultural phenomena, and controversial performance artists.

16. Ska is fast-tempo, rhythmically jerky Jamaican dance music that gained notoriety among punk crowds in England in the late 1970s.

17. Of the artists Raphael interviews, only one group, Huggy Bear, is directly aligned with Riot Grrrl. The others fall more loosely under the amalgam "women in rock."

Chapter 16: Musical Examples (access through companion website)

Track 1. Double Zero, "Gas, Food, Satan."

Track 2. Selena Wahng, "Killing for Pleasure."

References Cited

Bernikow, Louise. 1993. "The New Activists: Fearless, Funny, Fighting Mad." *Cosmopolitan* (April): 162–65, 212.

Borchers, Karen R. 1993. "Grrrl Talk." *Glamour* (May): 134.

Bourdieu, Pierre. 1977. "The Dialectic of Objectification and Embodiment." In *Outline of a Theory of Practice*, translated by Richard Nice. Cambridge: Cambridge University Press. 87–95.

———. 1979. "The Kabyle House or the World Reversed." In *Algeria 1960*, translated by Richard Nice. Cambridge: Cambridge University Press. 133–53.

Butler, Judith. 1990. *Gender Trouble: Feminism and the Subversion of Identity.* New York: Routledge.

Case, Sue-Ellen. 1989. "Toward a Butch-Femme Aesthetic." In *Making a Spectacle: Feminist Essays on Contemporary Women's Theatre*, ed. Lynda Hart. Ann Arbor: University of Michigan Press.

Chideya, Farai. 1992. "Revolution, Girl Style." *Newsweek*, 23 November: 84–86.

Cross, Rosie. 1995. "Modem Grrrl." *Wired* 3, no. 2: 118–19.

Currid, Brian. 1995. "'We Are Family': House Music and Queer Performativity." In *Cruising the Performative: Interventions into the Representation of Ethnicity, Nationality, and Sexuality*, ed. Sue-Ellen Case, Philip Brett, and Susan Leigh Foster. Bloomington and Indianapolis: Indiana University Press. 165–96.

France, Kim. 1993. "Grrrls At War." *Rolling Stone* 8–22 July: 23–24.

Goad, Debbie. 1994. "Riot Grrrls Rrreally Borrring." *Your Flesh* 29: 22.

Heylin, Clinton. 1993. *From the Velvets to the Voidoids: A Pre-Punk History for a Post-Punk World.* New York: Penguin.

Humphreys, Elena. 1995. Interview.

Hurley, Bri. 1989. *Making a Scene: New York Hardcore in Photos, Lyrics and Commentary.* Boston: Faber and Faber.

Joy, Sally Margaret. 1992. "Revolution Grrrl Style Now!" *Melody Maker* 10 October: 30–32.

Kozak, Roman. 1988. *This Ain't No Disco.* Boston: Faber and Faber.

Kruse, Holly. 1993. "Subcultural Identity in Alternative Music Culture." *Popular Music* 12, no. 1: 33–41.

Malkin, Nina. 1993. "It's A Grrrl Thing." *Seventeen* (May): 80-82.

Morrow, Diana. 1995. Interview.

Nasrallah, Dana. 1992. "Teenage Riot." *Spin* (November): 78–81.

O'Hara, Craig. 1995. *The Philosophy of Punk.* San Francisco: AK Press.

Peraino, Judith. 1992. "'Rip Her to Shreds': Women's Music According to a Butch-Femme Aesthetic." *Repercussions* 1, no. 1: 19–47.

Post, Jennifer C. 1994. "Erasing the Boundaries between Public and Private in Women's Performance Traditions." In *Cecilia Reclaimed: Feminist Perspectives on Gender and Music*, ed. Susan C. Cook and Judy S. Tsou. Urbana: University of Illinois Press. 35–51.

Raphael, Amy. 1996. *Grrrls: Viva Rock Divas.* New York: St. Martin's Griffin.

Riot Grrrl NYC. 1992–93. "Is She a Riot Grrrl?" Flier.

———. 1992. *Riot Grrrl NYC* 3. Fanzine.

———. 1993. *Riot Grrrl NYC* 4. Fanzine.

Robertson, Pamela. 1996. *Guilty Pleasures: Feminist Camp from Mae West to Madonna.* Durham, NC: Duke University Press.

Schwichtenberg, Cathy, ed. 1993. *The Madonna Connection: Representational Politics, Subcultural Identities, and Cultural Theory.* Boulder, San Francisco, and Oxford: Westview Press.

Solin, Sabrina. 1995. "Biker Grrrl." *Seventeen* (June): 54–56.

Straw, Will. 1991. "Systems of Articulation, Logics of Change: Communities and Scenes in Popular Music." *Cultural Studies* 5, no. 3: 368–88.

Valentine, Sarah. 1995. Interview.

Wahng, Selena. 1995. Interview.

———. 1995. Notes to "Killing for Pleasure."

Walser, Robert. 1993. *Running with the Devil: Power, Gender, and Madness in Heavy Metal Music.* Hanover, NH: Wesleyan University Press.

Additional Sources

The study of the 1990s Riot Grrrl movement and its music poses certain problems for research. While one can easily obtain the recordings of well-known Riot Grrrl groups such as Bikini Kill or Bratmobile, released on the still vital indie label Kill Rock Stars (http://www.killrockstars.com/), tracking down the music of local bands on small, and long defunct, record and cassette labels is much more difficult. Many records and fanzines were created and distributed by individuals; they were 'of the moment' and not intended to live on as part of some company's back catalogue. In recent years, however, some research institutions, most notably New York University's Fales Library, have acquired special collections of Riot Grrrl zines and various materials. Beyond these primary source collections, there is a wealth of secondary literature, as well as documentary videos, devoted to the history and analysis of riot grrrl. In general, these studies tend to focus on Riot Grrrl's relationship to punk, feminism, visual culture and the print media of its zines. The list of scholarly articles and essays devoted to Riot Grrrl is too lengthy to include here. What follows are those books and DVDs that contain substantial and/or especially insightful material on Riot Grrrl.

Books

Kearney, Mary Celeste. 2006. *Girls Make Media.* New York: Routledge. Kearney, a media studies scholar, provides both an overview of Riot Grrrl's connections to feminism and youth culture and a detailed reading of grrrl zines.

Leonard, Marion. 2007. *Gender in the Music Industry: Rock, Discourse and Girl Power.* Aldershot, UK and Burlington, VT: Ashgate. Working from the observation that rock music has traditionally been coded masculine, this study examines the significance of women rock musicians in the 1990s, with two chapters focusing specifically on Riot Grrrl.

Marcus, Sara. 2010. *Girls to the Front: The True Story of the Riot Grrrl Revolution*. New York, London: Harper Perennial. Marcus's vividly detailed book, which is drawn from numerous interviews and print sources, concentrates on Riot Grrrl's formation and its most active period of the early 1990s.

Meltzer, Marisa. 2010. *Girl Power: The Nineties Revolution in Music*. New York: Faber and Faber. This popular press title lacks the journalistic depth and academic rigor of the other titles on this list, but is one of the few attempts to explore not only Riot Grrrl's origins, but its wide ranging musical and cultural legacies across the latter half of the 1990s.

Monem, Nadine, ed. 2007. *Riot Grrrl: Revolution Girl Style Now!* London, UK: Black Dog Publishing. This UK-based collection of historical and analytical essays focuses equally on Riot Grrrl in the United States and Britain.

Piepmeier, Alison. 2009. *Girl Zines: Making Media, Doing Feminism*. New York and London: New York University Press. While Riot Grrrl provides the historical backdrop for this study, its focus is specifically on the feminist ideologies and issues of girl and grrrl zines.

Videos

Koch, Kerri. 2006. *Don't Need You: The Herstory of Riot Grrrl*. New York: Urban Cowgirl Productions. This documentary presents a narrative of the Riot Grrrl movement, primarily through interviews with notable figures like Kathleen Hanna of Bikini Kill and Alison Wolfe of Bratmobile.

Moser, Abby. 2011. *Grrrl Love and Revolution: Riot Grrrl NYC*. New York: Women Make Movies. Abby Moser's compelling documentary, filmed between 1993 and 1996, expands upon, in visual and aural terms, many of the issues relating to Riot Grrrl NYC that are discussed in our essay.

INDEX

INDEX

INDEX